I0517039

INVADED ON ALL SIDES

The River Raisin Region
and General Winchester's Campaign, 1813

by Ralph James Naveaux
Updated, Annotated, & Revised 2022

Photo: Michigan Militia & U.S. Regulars Priming & Loading Muskets
Annual River Raisin Battlefield Commemoration
(Kenneth Howard in foreground)
Photo Courtesy of Dave & Sue Grassley
Floral City Images, Monroe, Michigan

Invaded On All Sides
The River Raisin Region
and General Winchester's Campaign, 1813
by Ralph James Naveaux
Updated, Annotated, & Revised 2022

MISSION POINT PRESS

Published by Mission Point Press
2554 Chandler Rd.
Traverse City, MI 49696
(231) 421-9513
www.MissionPointPress.com

Cover and interior design by Sarah Meiers

ISBN 978-1-958363-23-2
Library of Congress Control Number upon request

Printed in the United States of America

Forward / *Avant-Propos*

THE BATTLES OF THE RIVER RAISIN
Collision of Empires / Clash of Cultures

**Reproduction of a Voyageur Trade Canoe on the River Raisin
during the Old French Town Days Festival**
Photo by Author

The mud-brown waters of the River Raisin flow sometimes peacefully, sometimes violently through downtown Monroe, Michigan, until they mix with the reflecting waves of Lake Erie. Looking at the homes, businesses, and industries crowded along the river's banks, there is little to suggest that this place was once an oasis in a vast wilderness and a flash point in a terrible struggle between rival nations.

From January 18th to January 23rd, 1813, the banks of the River Raisin, just a couple miles from its mouth on Lake Erie, became a battleground where the forces of the United States and Great Britain fought each other for the control of the Lower Great Lakes. At stake was the destiny of Michigan, Upper Canada, and the Native-American alliance spearheaded by Tecumseh.

French Town on the River Raisin, now the city of Monroe, was the scene of what may arguably be called the largest field battle ever fought within the present confines of the State of Michigan.[1]

The Battle of the River Raisin was not the most decisive action of the War of 1812, for the British and Native people who won it lacked the resources to fully exploit the advantages gained by their victory. Nonetheless, it represented a major disaster for American arms.

By the end of the fighting on January 22, 1813, an entire army had been destroyed. For the next eight months the upper Great Lakes were controlled by the British, and the neighboring American states and territories lay open to invasion. Moreover, Tecumseh's coalition of warriors was given renewed hope that by this triumph and their continued resistance, they might yet secure their native lands from the advancing tide of white settlers.

For the losers, this battle caused the largest total American casualties of any single day's battle during the entire war. Most of those killed, wounded, missing, or captured were from the state of Kentucky.

For years afterward, wives and children gathered with parents and grandparents in village after village throughout that state. They continued to mourn and patiently wait, often in vain, for their missing loved ones to return.

The debacle at the River Raisin and the subsequent murder of some wounded Americans served to galvanize U.S. forces on the western frontier. "Remember the Raisin" became the battle cry by which a newly-reformed army sought to avenge their countrymen and turn defeat into victory in the Old Northwest.

---

1   Actually, the name French Town was a misnomer. There was no central downtown, but rather an elongated settlement area that stretched for a dozen miles on either side of the River Raisin. Prior to the War of 1812, the community was known, in one form or another, as Rivière au Raisin. Americans designated the area as Frenchtown due to the ethnicity of the overwhelming number of its inhabitants. Note the variety of Frenchtowns, Chinatowns, Germantowns, and Little Canadas, across the United States.

Ralph Naveaux, Kevin Lindsey, Chris Momany, & Dick Micka
Members of the reconstituted Company of Captain Hubert Lacroix
Michigan Legionary Corps & 2nd Michigan Territorial Militia Regiment
Photo by Bill Saul

DEDICATION

This book is dedicated to all the families whose ancestors were affected by the Battle of the River Raisin, regardless of their race, ethnicity, nationality, or religion. Their stories form an important part of our local and historical heritage.

As a dedicated reenactor with 50 years of Living History under my belt, I can assure the reader that the vast majority of us approach our roles with curiosity, respect, and a desire for authenticity. I hope that those unpaid and unsung reenactors whose photos appear in this work can continue use their knowledge to educate the public and honor those who came before us. Hence, a big thank-you to them and their comrades.

—Ralph Naveaux

FORMAT & ACKNOWLEDGEMENTS

I would like to express my gratitude to the management and staff of the Monroe County Historical Museum and the River Raisin National Battlefield for their kind assistance and cooperation.

Thanks also goes to a number of individuals, including Dr. James DeVries, Gerry Welch, Pat Tucker, Gary Allward, and Marc Meyer for their help, suggestions, and corrections in reviewing portions of this book. Dennis Au gave me many pointers on research documents. Lynn Reaume and Jim Ryland scanned maps for me, while Lynn also helped with indexing and proofreading. Thanks also to Dr. Laboe, Chris Momany, Bill Saul, the Grassleys, and others who shared their family stories with me or provided photos.

In researching and writing this book, I attempted to put the narrative into chronological order, as though we were reading about these events as they occurred, day by day. Actually, many of the facts, or alleged facts, were taken directly from depositions, diaries, family stories, and letters recorded by various participants. Where possible, I tried to cross check their entries with official records and with accounts written by other participants or by later historians.

The obvious problem with this approach came whenever the accounts disagreed, which was quite often. In such cases, I still had to assign the event to a specific date and location, relegating any conflicting evidence to the extensive footnotes.

Many people assume history is just a dry recitation of facts, but historical research is actually very dynamic, forever changing with new discoveries and new interpretations of the old evidence; hence the need for revisions and updates. This is the creative process that makes the study of history so fascinating for both amateurs and professionals.

The Monroe County Historical Museum Archives collects items about the Battle of the River Raisin. If you have access to information regarding participants, especially if it is a personal account of their experiences, please contact the Monroe County Historical Museum Systems, 126 S. Monroe St., Monroe, Michigan 48161.[2]

---

2   When the first edition of this book was written, the River Raisin National Battlefield Park had

The reader will note my use of some very long footnotes. Besides giving sources of information, footnotes allow the reader to get deeper into the details. They are there if the reader wishes to consult them, but are not necessary for a quick read. The previous edition used endnotes for the same purpose, but readers found it too disruptive to keep referring to the back of the book. However, I have retained some of the endnotes, along with sections deleted from my original text, in the form of appendices.

---

not yet come into existence. As this revised edition comes to print, the National Park Service has taken over the responsibility of interpreting the battlefield for the general public. While the county museum still collects items related to the War of 1812, so too, does the battlefield park, its affiliated groups, the River Raisin National Battlefield Park Foundation and the Friends of the River Raisin Battlefield.

TABLE OF CONTENTS

MAPS, IMAGES & ILLUSTRATIONS
IN ORDER OF APPEARANCE

143	FAMILIES ON BATTLEFIELD	308	WIDOW'S AFFIDAVIT
146	REENACTORS IN FARM FIELD	317	COMPOSITE POST WAR MAPS
148	HULL'S ROAD TO DETROIT	321	US BATTLE ORDER JAN. 18
150	PAINTING OF COUTURE HOME	322	UK BATTLE ORDER JAN. 18
152	PHOTO OF MILITIA ASSEMBLING	322	CAP BADGE
154	BRITISH ATTACK JANUARY 22	323	US CASUALTIES CHART JAN. 18
155	PHOTO OF MASON RUN TODAY	331	KENTUCKY HORSEMEN
156	SKETCH OF WINCHESTER'S HQ	335	FIREARMS DISPLAY
158	CEREMONIAL MUSKET VOLLEY		
161	EARLY SKETCH MAP		
164	BRITISH ARTILLERY & INFANTRY		
166	MAP OF U.S. RETREAT JANUARY 22		
167	MILITIA FIRING IN OPEN FIELD		
170	NPS BATTLE MAP FOR JANUARY 22		
171	PAINTED PANORAMA OF BATTLE		
175	MAP OF POSSIBLE AMBUSH SITES		
176	NATIVE WARRIOR IN PURSUIT		
180	DOCUMENTARY AMBUSH SCENE		
185	NPS MAP OF BATTLE'S LAST MOVES		
190	SKETCH OF WINCHESTER'S CAPTURE		

DRAMATIS PERSONNAE

You are going to meet a lot of people in this book, some of whom you will have read about in history texts, as they played a major role in the War of 1812. Most, however, have been forgotten. These minor characters are nonetheless very real. None have been invented. They all had hopes and fears, just like the rest of us. Moreover, they actually trod these very grounds which gave rise, two centuries later, to River Raisin National Battlefield Park.

Some of these people appear once or twice, while others weave their way in and out of the narrative, depending on the extent of information about them. All had lives before the climactic Battle of the River Raisin. Most also had lives to live after the battle. Women and Native-Americans are perhaps somewhat under-represented because of the comparative lack of written documents relating to them as individuals.

Family stories are notoriously difficult to corroborate, and personal reminiscences are sometimes contradictory. Still, the local stories are extremely important. They give us a realistic sense of time and place.

This book is not meant to be just a military history, although Winchester's Campaign and the battles at the River Raisin form the centerpiece of our tale. This is really the story of an entire community — actually, several communities — that worked, ate, played, and struggled through a very difficult time in the history of the Western Lake Erie Basin.

Tecumseh managed to miss the battle, so less-famous warriors led the way; men like Roundhead, Walk-in-the-Water, Waugon, and others.

Colonel Henry Procter earned a promotion to General for his role in opposing Winchester at the River Raisin. In this, he was ably assisted by Lt. Colonels Elliott and St. George, as well as Majors Muir and Reynolds.[3]

There were various factions among the local inhabitants. Among the English-speaking minority, there were so-called collaborators (Woodward) Indian fighters (Knaggs) merchants willing to sell to either side (McDougall) and opportunists (Bond). Some men even ended up with a price on their heads (James Bentley, Medard Labadie, & James Knaggs).

The French-speaking majority made up about 90% of the settlers living

---

3   Although his ranks are frequently confused, Procter was promoted to lieutenant colonel in 1800; colonel in 1810; and brigadier general in February of 1813, after the Battle of the River Raisin. A few months later, he was made a major general.

1

along the River Raisin and was itself divided into two major camps. On the one hand were the Navarres and their pro-American friends and relatives. They were opposed by the fur trading Lasselles, who were perhaps more pro-Native American than pro-British.[4]

---

4   For further information on the Kentuckians, British military, Canadians, Native Americans, and local inhabitants who took part in the Battle of the River Raisin, the reader should refer to Appendix A towards the end of this book.

SETTING THE STAGE FOR THE WAR OF 1812

The Battle(s) of the River Raisin may be seen as a single incident in the larger context of the War of 1812. Going even further, in *The Sixty-Years' War for the Great Lakes*, David Curtis Skaggs and Larry Nelson compellingly put forth the idea that the War of 1812 was just one war, among several, in a series that would determine the destiny of this part of the world.

Native pictographs excepted, the written history of the Great Lakes goes back to the 17th century when French explorers, traders, and missionaries began recording their journeys into the upper Great Lakes.

Native Peoples often welcomed these contacts, but the newcomers brought changes, for better or worse. European economic, cultural, and technological benefits habitually came with a price; disease, cultural dislocation, destruction of resources, loss of independence, and even war.

The so-called Beaver Wars engulfed the Great Lakes region when the Iroquois (*Haudenosaunee*) Confederacy, armed with guns from their Dutch and British trading partners, drove the Hurons and other French-allied tribes from their homelands. The lower Great Lakes remained an Iroquoian hunting and raiding preserve until the displaced Odawas, Potawatomies, and others fought their way back in the 1600s.

Antoine de la Mothe-Cadillac founded a settlement at Detroit in 1701 in order to preserve French interests in the area and provide a stable environment to conduct trade with the various Indian nations. A bit of a rogue, he nevertheless clearly understood the strategic importance of the Strait, or *le Détroit*, in controlling access to the upper lakes.

French efforts to keep British traders and land speculators out of the Great Lakes and the Ohio Valley provided the sparks which ignited the French and Indian War in 1754. This proved to be the last in a century of wars between the kings of France and England over who would dominate North America.

After the conquest of Canada in 1760, British rangers under Major Robert Rogers peacefully occupied *le Détroit*. In 1763, nearly bankrupt, and weary of what had turned into a world-wide struggle, Louis XV ceded his claim to North American lands east of the Mississippi, along with their inhabitants, to King George of England. French territory west of the Mississippi was secretly ceded to Louis' cousin, Charles III, the Bourbon king of Spain.

At Détroit, the French settlers, or *habitants*, accepted their fate with

3

some resignation. Many of them left for France or other French or Spanish colonies, but most remained to become British subjects. They were thankful that, by the Grace of God, certain political, economic, and religious rights had been guaranteed to them by the British Crown, and they longed for the security and stability that peace would provide.[5]

Michigan's Native Peoples, on the other hand, had greater difficulty adjusting to their new overlords. As far as they were concerned, they had not been defeated. They were King Louis' allies, not his subjects, and the French Crown had no right to turn either their lands or themselves over to the British Empire.

The British aggravated the situation by ignoring the complex kinship and trading networks which had united the French and Indians, and they attempted to dispense with the expensive gift-giving tradition which normally cemented Native American alliances. Proud chieftains were insulted and dismissed by their British counterparts, who believed it was no longer necessary to court the favor of the "savages." The simmering pot quickly boiled over into a rebellion of tribes led by Pontiac of the Odawas.

The British posts north and west of the Ohio River soon fell to this warrior alliance, with the exception of Detroit, Niagara, and Fort Pitt. Profiting from Pontiac's inability to supply or maintain a united force of Native tribesmen, however, the British gradually regained control. Still, "Pontiac's Conspiracy" had delivered quite a shock to the empire, and the British authorities began to think seriously of designating the Northwest as a kind of Native trading and hunting reserve, in which white settlement would be heavily restricted.

Here, the English Crown fell afoul of the desires of their own land-hungry colonists. The Québec Act cut this region off from general settlement and became one more grievance, added to taxation and other issues of political and economic control, which fanned the flames of revolution in 1776.

After 7 years of war and thanks to the intervention of France, the United States of America gained its independence by the 1783 Treaty of Versailles.

---

5   The French word *habitant* has the same meaning as *inhabitant* in English. However, over time, it has taken on more specific meanings. In this book, *habitant* is used to refer to inhabitants of French-Canadian extraction, particularly those residing and owning lands along the River Raisin. In period documents, they are generally called *French* by the Americans and *Canadians* (*Canadiens*) by British officials and English-speaking settlers in Canada. Modern authors sometimes refer to them as Creoles (being native to America) or even Métis (due to their frequent association with Native Americans).

One of the first challenges faced by the new republic was asserting control over the Northwest Territory, which included most of the Great Lakes.

Standing in the way were the Native tribes living north and west of the Ohio River who felt, for a second time, that they had been abandoned, but not defeated. British agents encouraged Native people to continue their resistance to American encroachment, and the British maintained garrisons at Detroit and other locations in what was now nominally a U.S. territory.

At the end of the American Revolution, the U.S. Army was reduced to almost nothing. A regular standing professional army was not only expensive to maintain, it was considered a general threat to world peace and to individual liberty. Reliance was placed on the defensive qualities of a relatively untrained militia to handle emergencies such as civil unrest and Indian raids, or to oppose an invasion.

It was recognized that this system lacked the capability for carrying out a sustained offensive on foreign or enemy soil. Yet this is precisely what was going to be needed to bring the Northwest Territory securely under American jurisdiction.

In the last decades of the 18th century, American Generals Harmar and St. Clair successively led rag-tag armies composed largely of militia volunteers north into the Ohio wilderness, only to see their forces routed and destroyed by a coalition of tribesmen led by Little Turtle of the Miamies.

Although frustrated, the Americans would not give up. General "Mad Anthony" Wayne spent months training and supplying his well-disciplined Legionary Corps. In 1794, he attacked the Indians along the Maumee River and defeated them in the Battle of Fallen Timbers.

The discouraged warriors looked for help from the British garrison at nearby Fort Miamis, only to find that the post commandant, Major Campbell, was under orders not to create an international incident by firing on American troops. The following year, feeling abandoned once again by the British, most of the tribes signed the Treaty of Greenville.

In 1796, the British finally evacuated Detroit and their other posts in the Northwest Territory in compliance with the terms of Jay's Treaty, which temporarily settled the differences between the United States and Great Britain and ushered in a period of increasing prosperity and trade between them. The encroaching tide of new American settlers could no longer be stopped.

Tensions grew with Revolutionary France, however, which considered

**Map Segment based on "The Army Medical Department, 1775-1818"
by Mary C. Gillet
Army Historical Series, U.S. Government Printing Office,
Washington, D.C., 1981**
This map is a work of a U.S. Army soldier or employee, taken or made as part of
that person's official duties. As a work of the U.S. federal government, the text is
in the public domain.

the 1795 Jay Treaty a betrayal of the alliance forged with America during
the Revolutionary War. At this time, the newly-created French Republic was
in a struggle for political survival against almost all the kings of Europe.

The result was international political intrigue and the release of French
privateers to prey on American shipping. Although the fledgling U.S. Navy
was able to capture over a hundred privateers, U.S. maritime losses amounted
to $20,000,000 between 1798 and 1801.

The quasi-naval war in the Caribbean was quietly ended with a treaty
between the United States and France in 1800, in which the U.S. gave up
some claims for damages, while the French dropped efforts to hold the
United States to the terms of their old alliance.

President John Adams lost the next election to Thomas Jefferson. The
1801 Peace of Amiens was concluded between Britain and France, leading

Jefferson's Democratic-Republican Party to cut expenses and dismantle the military system which had been built up by the Federalists. But peace in Europe was not good for American business. The U.S. export trade fell almost 50% between 1801 and 1803.[6]

At least by now it appeared that the question of who would control the Great Lakes had been answered. With the Louisiana Purchase, it seemed obvious the French would not be coming back to re-establish their former colony. American settlers poured into the Northwest Territory. In 1803, Ohio became the 17th state to enter the union. Michigan was organized as a separate territory in 1805. In 1809, James Madison assumed the presidency.

From 1795 to 1811, the frontier was at peace, if sometimes tenuously, as the U.S. Army tried to keep squatters from occupying land reserved for Native Americans, while, at the same time, the government continued to negotiate land concessions from them.

In 1807, William Hull, the governor of Michigan Territory, signed a treaty with the Potawatomies, Ojibwas, Odawas, and Wyandots. The treaty reserved 4 square miles on Maumee Bay for the Odawas, including the villages of Meshkemau, Wassonquet, and Waugau; and 3 square miles on the River Raisin, where it was joined by the Macon, for Chief Moran and the Potawatomies.[7]

The Ojibwas received 2 separate square-mile sections on the River Rouge, including Seganchewan's village; 2 more square-mile sections at Tonquish's village near the River Rouge; and 3 square miles on Lake St. Clair, at Macaunse's village.

The Treaty of 1785 had reserved two towns, Brownstown and Monguagon, for the Wyandots. The Wyandots failed to gain a guarantee for their two villages in the 1807 treaty, but this was rectified by a bill passed through Congress in 1809. Both Brownstown and Walk-in-the-Water's village

---

6   Hickey, Donald R. The War of 1812. Urbana & Chicago: University of Illinois Press, 1989, p. 6-7: The Federalists had alienated Americans with high taxes and an elitist attitude. Once in power, the Democratic-Republicans began reducing taxes, while still paying off the national debt. They cut both the army and navy, saying *"Show me a nation possessed of a large navy, and I will show you a nation always at war."* Instead of the regular armed forces, the Democratic-Republicans planned to rely on a cheap, democratic alternative — local militias and privateers.

7   Other Odawa villages were located along the Maumee River, including those of Nawash and Tontoganie near Roche de Boeuf and Kinjoino at Wolf Rapids. McCarty's village was located south of the Maumee, near Presque Isle. The Lower and Upper Tawa Towns were near Blanchard's Fork.

at Monguagon were included. Unfortunately, the Wyandot occupation of their villages was only guaranteed for 50 years.[8]

During this time, many Native tribesmen sought to preserve their families and some of their lands by integrating themselves more thoroughly into the European way of life. They invited missionaries to come to their villages as teachers, built substantial log homes, and learned to farm like White men.

Some, however, longed for the independence and traditions of the old ways. They listened to the Shawnee Prophet, who preached self-reliance and rejection of White culture. They listened to the Prophet's brother, Tecumseh, who called for unity and even armed resistance to preserve their hunting grounds and their way of life. They listened, and waited, for one more chance.

An initial clash occurred in 1811 at the Prophet's village at Tippecanoe, where William Henry Harrison, the governor of Indiana Territory, put the lie to the Prophet's assurances of invincibility against the white men's bullets.

Tecumseh, who had been absent, returned to find Harrison's army in control and the Prophet's warriors scattered and dispirited.

After the Battle of Tippecanoe, the disgruntled Indians regrouped and armed themselves with homemade bows and arrows. They looked increasingly toward the British for support. The chance they were all waiting for would not come till the following year, when the United States would be embroiled in another war against the mighty British Empire.[9]

The United States had a long list of grievances for declaring war against Great Britain, its former mother country and colonial overlord. Once more at war with Napoleonic France, the British government established a blockade of Europe and restricted the rights of neutral countries to trade with the enemies of King George.

This policy hurt Britain's enemies, while strengthening its worldwide domination of trade and navigation. In 1807, the British issued the Orders in

---

8 See: "Michigan's Indian Reservations, 1807–1855," by Larry M. Wykoff, 2019.
9 William Henry Harrison was born in Virginia in 1773. In the 1790s, he served as aide-de-camp to General Anthony Wayne, Secretary of the Northwest Territory, and territorial delegate to Congress. From 1801 to 1813, he was governor of Indiana. After the War of 1812, he became a U.S. senator and U.S. minister to Columbia. In 1840, "Tippecanoe" Harrison was elected the 9th President of the United States. Unfortunately, a month after his inaugural speech, he died from the effects of pneumonia.

Council, which required neutral vessels sailing to enemy-controlled European ports to stop in England for inspection and payment of transit duties.[10]

The British, feeling Napoleon was a menace to peace and the old-world order, believed they were fighting to preserve not only the "rights of Englishmen," but freedom around the world, as well. In so doing, however, they gradually suppressed civil liberties at home, alienated neutral nations, and increased the burden on the subjects of their empire.[11]

The United States was embarrassed and economically injured as the British boarded American ships, seized contraband, and impressed American seamen into their navy.

By the doctrine of "inalienable allegiance," all persons born under the rule of King George, which was the case for many Americans, remained his subjects for life, regardless of their current citizenship. It was also easy for the British to suspect that many American sailors were British deserters. About a quarter of U.S. seamen actually did fall into that category.

In 1807, a serious incident occurred off Norfolk, Virginia, when an American naval ship, the *USS Chesapeake,* was fired on by *HMS Leopard* and boarded by a British press gang. Three American seamen were killed, 18 wounded, and 4 more seized as deserters.[12] By 1809, the British were forcibly impressing a thousand American sailors into their navy each year. Self-respect demanded the United States react in some fashion to maintain its sovereignty and defend neutral trading rights for non-belligerents.[13]

Methods short of war, such as the Non-Importation Act of 1806, the 1807 Embargo Act and the 1809 Non-Intercourse Act were adopted to pressure the British into concessions, but these were unpopular and even

---

10 Hickey, Donald R. The War of 1812. Urbana & Chicago: University of Illinois Press, 1989, p. 18-20: The French also seized ships and cargoes by virtue of Napoleon's Berlin Decree of 1806 and his Milan Decree of 1807; however, such rules were mainly enforced in French-controlled ports, rather than on the high seas. In all, some 900 American ships were confiscated by French authorities in the years 1807-1812.

11 Coles, Harry. War of 1812.

12 Horseman, Reginald. The War of 1812. New York: Alfred A. Knopf, 1969.

13 Hickey, Donald R. The War of 1812. Urbana & Chicago: University of Illinois Press, 1989, p. 11: Between 1803 and 1812, the British forcibly impressed about 6,000 American citizens into their navy, where they were subjected to harsh discipline and much lower pay. This amounted to between 5 and 10% of America's merchant sailors.

counterproductive, especially in New England where sea-borne trade was vital to the economy.[14]

Meanwhile, another serious incident occurred on May 16, 1812, when the American frigate *President*, charged with protecting American commerce, engaged in a 45-minute firefight with a British corvette, *Little Belt*, which was patrolling off New York. It was not clear who fired first, but the British lost 9 dead and 23 wounded, leading British newspapers to call for retribution.

Most Federalists in the Northeast opposed the war, but representatives from the West and South were generally in favor. Western and southern farmers blamed British trade restrictions for loss of export markets.

In the region of the Great Lakes, American officials and fur traders complained that British agents were doing business in U.S. territory, stirring up Native American resentment, and supporting war-prone activists like Tecumseh and the Prophet.

Henry Clay and the War Hawks felt war was necessary to protect American interests and honor. To gain popular support, they were able to tap into a growing nationalistic pride in their young country.[15]

They recognized that war would help unify the country and solidify their hold on government power. They could silence their Federalist critics with accusations of disloyalty and defeatism.[16]

---

14 The Embargo Act was aimed against both Britain and France by eliminating trade from American ports. It failed when Napoleon's invasion of Spain and Portugal caused those countries to open their colonial ports to British trade. It also harmed American coastal ports which depended on ocean commerce.
   The Non-Intercourse Act allowed only indirect trade with both England and France via third countries. Macon's 1810 bill ended these trade restrictions, but threatened to reinstate the Non-Intercourse Act against either belligerent, if the other rescinded their own trade restrictions. Napoleon beat the British to the punch by offering to drop his Berlin and Milan Decrees if either Britain rescinded its Orders in Council or the United States enforced the Macon Bill against England. The British followed suit on June 23, 1812, repealing the Orders in Council, but it was too late to avoid war with the United States.

15 Beyond that, American expansionists had a lust for land that seemed to know no bounds. Even the purchase of the vast Territory of Louisiana from Napoleon did not divert American settlers from moving northward into British Canada, or from looking southward to Spanish Florida. Americans came to believe that it was their "manifest destiny" to dominate the entire continent.

16 Hickey, Donald R. The War of 1812. Urbana & Chicago: University of Illinois Press, 1989, pp. 27-105: The Federalists criticized Democratic-Republican mismanagement and were particularly against invading Canada, which had essentially done nothing to provoke it. They preferred instead to conduct a naval war against England. After war broke out, mobs rioted and beat up Federalists in Baltimore and elsewhere. The Democratic-Republicans retained control of Congress and the

President Madison delivered his war message to Congress on June 1, 1812, citing as reasons the British practices of impressment, harassment of American shipping, blockades, Orders in Council, and support of Native-American resistance movements in the west. The declaration of war passed the House on June 4, was ratified by the Senate on June 17, and was signed into law June 18, 1812.[17]

The military strategies leading up to the Battle of the River Raisin will be discussed in another chapter. Here, it may be worthwhile to point out that the fight was symptomatic not only of a political and military struggle between the United States and the Kingdom of Great Britain, but also of a clash between cultures.

Kentuckians, Yankees, British Loyalists, *Canadiens*, Native Americans, and French *habitants* represented a variety of customs, languages, and economic practices, many of which were in opposition to each other.[18]

Presidency in the 1812 elections, but the Federalists did make some gains as the realities of the war made it more unpopular. The beginning of 1812 saw the American government dealing with a badly needed expansion of the U.S. military. The constitutional question as to whether or not the American militia could be compelled to fight outside the boundaries of the United States immediately arose, but was never adequately answered. The Department of War was miniscule, consisting of the Secretary of War and a few clerks who handled routine military paperwork. Congress resisted raising taxes and spending money to build up the army and navy, but they did establish a Quartermaster Department and an Ordnance Department.

17 Lewis, Virgil A., Third Biennial Report of the Department of Archives and History of the State of West Virginia. Charleston: The News-Mail Company, 1911, p. 144: On the 18th of June, 1812, Congress passed an Act declaring "that War ... is hereby declared to exist between the United Kingdoms of Great Britain and Ireland and the dependencies thereof, and the United States of America and their Territories. Of this, the President, James Madison, on the next day made proclamation thereof."

18 Dr. James DeVries, an instructor of history at Monroe County Community College and author of several works on local history, often insisted that the actions and motivations of participants in the River Raisin campaign can best be understood if the reader is aware of the background of the separate national or cultural groups that were involved. He delineated four major categories; the Americans (mainly Kentuckians), the Native Americans, the British (and their Canadian subjects), and the local "Mushrat" French. Each of them had their own characteristics, and their own, often conflicting, motivations. See Appendix A for more information on the various groups involved.

THE DETROIT CAMPAIGN
LA CONQUÊTE DU DÉTROIT

Building Hull's Road to Detroit, June and July, 1812:

In the beginning, the American strategy for winning the War of 1812 seemed to promise every chance for success. The main blow would be aimed at the closest and most vulnerable British possession, Canada. Even with British help, the 500,000 inhabitants of Britain's North American colonies would have a hard time defending their long border against multiple invasion forces from the United States, whose population numbered an overwhelming 7,250,000.

To defend Montréal and Lower Canada (today's Province of Québec) the British had 4,450 regular infantrymen and 2,000 militiamen stretched along a 1,700-mile border from Kingston to Québec City. To protect Upper Canada's 1,300 miles of watery borders (present-day Ontario) there were only 1,450 regulars and 1,800 militiamen. The Americans could attack almost anywhere.[19]

The American plan was to stretch the British and Canadian defense forces to the breaking point by attacking on 3 fronts, aiming at Detroit, the Niagara Peninsula, and Montréal. As it turned out, however, poor planning, coordination, and troop quality turned all three invasion plans into failures.

The first attempt was led by Michigan Territorial Governor William Hull. In the months prior to the war, this respected Revolutionary War veteran had visited Washington, D.C., to urge the President to build a fleet of warships on Lake Erie and to send an army to defend Detroit.[20]

---

19 Reynolds Narrative in Coffin, William F. 1812: The War and its Moral; a Canadian Chronicle. Montréal: John Lovell, 1864. To these could be added the Native-American alliance and a small naval establishment on the Great Lakes, which was unopposed at the beginning of the war. Wikipedia's online encyclopedia gives the total manpower figures for the War of 1812 as the following: 99,000 US regulars, 10,000 US volunteers, 3,000 rangers, 458,000 militiamen and 600 US-allied Indians vs. 10,000 British regulars, 86,000 Canadian militiamen, and 3,500 British allied Indians.

20 William Hull came from an illustrious New England family and could trace his lineage back for five generations in America. Born in 1753, he was a graduate of Yale and joined the legal profession in 1775. After the opening shots of the Revolutionary War were fired at Lexington that year, he raised a company of volunteers and served as their captain in Colonel Webb's Connecticut Regiment. His advance through the ranks was steady, becoming lt. colonel of the 8th Massachusetts Regiment in 1779 and then inspector of the army under Baron von Steuben. His battle credits included Trenton, Princeton, Saratoga, Fort Stanwix, Monmouth, and Stony

12

Located 300 miles from the nearest American supply depot, Detroit, as well as the rest of Michigan Territory, seemed isolated and exposed to British or Indian attacks. Without a fleet controlling Lake Erie, Hull feared that an army at Detroit could not be maintained. The small, far-flung American outposts at Fort Mackinac and Fort Dearborn (Chicago) were in even more danger.

Governor Hull did not get his fleet, but he did get his army, which he somewhat reluctantly agreed to command with the rank of brigadier-general.

Hull's combat force included a regiment of regular U.S. infantry and three regiments of Ohio Militia. With these, he cut a supply road from Urbana through the dreaded Black Swamp of northwestern Ohio.[21]

By the first of July, Hull and his men had reached the Maumee River, where they made contact with elements of the Michigan Militia. It was here that General Hull made his first serious mistake. To spare his tired horses, the General had some of the army's baggage unloaded and put aboard a chartered schooner, the *Cuyahoga Packet*. Included were hospital stores, entrenching tools, and a trunk containing muster rolls for his army.

To reach Detroit, the ship had to pass near the British base of Fort Amherstburg at Malden, situated close to mouth of Lake Erie. As the *Cuyahoga* passed Malden, the British seized the vessel.

It was not until 2 a.m. the next morning that Hull received official word that war had been declared.[22] Undaunted, Hull forged ahead, assisted

---

Point. After his illustrious service in the Revolution, Hull was appointed governor of Michigan upon its formation as a territory in 1805. With war imminent in 1812, he reluctantly accepted a brigadier general's commission and took command of the Northwestern Army.

21 The Black Swamp was a foggy, gummy mass of mud and water bigger than the State of Rhode Island. Hull traced his route through open prairies of eight-foot-tall grass intermixed with forests of poplar, oak, beech, ash, and linden, all covered with a foot, or several feet, of water.
    To increase the discomfort while navigating the oozing mass, there were a lot of rattlesnakes, wolves, ticks, mosquitoes, and biting flies. Not only that, but there was the ever-present danger of contracting a debilitating disease known as the aigue. The swamp was considered to be passable for wagons or even pack horses only in the hot dryness of summer or the frozen dead of winter.

22 Although war was declared on June 18, the understaffed War Department neglected to immediately send a courier to notify Hull and his army. Instead, a letter was simply placed in the regular mail. An alert postmaster in Cleveland fortunately noticed the letter, recognized its importance, and rushed it forward to Hull by an express rider. Unfortunately, he arrived too late to prevent the ship from sailing. Nonetheless, Hull should have been more careful, since he fully expected war to be declared. Thanks to their fur trade contacts, the British at Malden had already received the news when the *Cuyahoga* came sailing by.

by the men of Lacroix's company, who cleared Hull's road through their home District of Erie and across the marshlands north of the River Raisin.

Hull's army spent several days in the River Raisin country, before crossing the River Huron on the 4th of July. By the 6th, Hull was in Detroit, and on the 12th, he began the westernmost thrust of the invasion of Canada.

The Invasion of Canada, Detroit, July 12, 1812:

After feinting a crossing further downriver towards Malden, General Hull launched his troops against the town of Sandwich, slightly upriver from Detroit. The British evacuated the town and mustered their forces at Fort Amherstburg.

Hull issued a proclamation offering the inhabitants protection, but warning them not to resist the invasion. Anyone found fighting alongside the Indians would be dealt with harshly and their homes subject to destruction.

The general moved his army to threaten Fort Amherstburg, but was checked after a sharp skirmish at the River Canard on July 16. He also sent raiding parties out to seize supplies and intimidate the local population.

Certain he could not take Fort Amherstburg at Malden without the proper siege artillery, and doubting the reliability of his over-eager militiamen, Hull withdrew back towards Sandwich, content that he had fulfilled at least part of the overall strategic mission for the invasion of Canada.

In the interim, with no American opposition on Lake Erie, the British were able to reinforce Fort Amherstburg by water, while Tecumseh's warriors moved to block Hull's only supply route, Hull's Road, which ambled southwestward from Detroit towards French Town on the River Raisin.[23]

On July 17, a force of British soldiers, Canadian voyageurs, and warriors from the Odawa, Ojibwa, Dakota, Menominee, and Winnebago Nations captured the American fort on Mackinac Island without firing a shot. When the news reached General Hull over a week later, it caused him to adopt a completely defensive attitude. The fall of Mackinac would expose both Detroit and Chicago to attacks by the northern tribes.[24]

---

23 Period accounts tend to use Amherstburg and Malden interchangeably. Technically, the name of the British fort at this time was Amherstburg, but the nearby town and surrounding area were called Malden. When the American army took over the area in the fall of 1813, they repaired the fort and called it Malden, which is the name it bears today, while the town is now known as Amherstburg.

24 The British force was led by Captain Charles Roberts and was composed of 46 regular troops,

Original logs forming a corduroy road
Preserved at Hull's Trace Unit, River Raisin National Battlefield Park
Photo by Jim Ryland

On July 26, Colonel Henry Procter of the 41st Regiment arrived with reinforcements to take command of Fort Amherstburg. By then, General Hull was convinced his worst predictions were coming true. On July 29, he sent Winnemac, a trusted Potawatomi, with a message to Captain Nathan Heald to evacuate Fort Dearborn (Chicago) if he could do so safely.[25]

---

260 Canadian militia and voyageurs, and several hundred Native warriors. Total British strength may have amounted to over a thousand men in all. The British agent in charge of the Indians was Robert Dickson, called Mascotaph, or Red-Haired Man, by the Sioux. He was born in Scotland, but married Totowin, sister of Red Thunder, and the Sioux were devoted to him. The 6-foot-tall, highly literate fur trader, dressed in the Indian fashion, led a colorful array of western warriors in support of the British and Canadian attack force. In addition to over 50 Sioux and a couple hundred Ojibwas, there were several dozen Winnebagoes under one-eyed Big Canoe, 40 Menominees or Folles Avoines under Tomah, 30 Odawas led by the mixed-race Amable Chevalier, and hundreds more Ojibwas and Odawas on the way. Having received only unofficial warnings of the commencement of hostilities, the American commander, Lt. Porter Hanks, quickly surrendered his 61-man garrison, once he saw the British had established an artillery position on the heights overlooking the fort.

25 Quimby, Robert S., The U.S. Army in the War of 1812: An Operational and Command Study, Vol. I, East Lansing: MSU Press, 1997, p. 49. There were actually two Potawatomies named Winemac in 1812. The one referred to here was pro-American and supported the United States during the war.

American Militiamen at the Bicentennial of the Battle of the River Raisin
Photo Courtesy of Dave & Sue Grassley, Floral City Images

The fight for Hull's Road and the Fall of Detroit, August, 1812:

General Hull was facing increasing unrest on the part of his Ohio militia officers, who thought they could overrun Fort Amherstburg. Hull almost gave them the chance, but learning of the arrival of British reinforcements, he decided to concentrate on defending Detroit and his supply line to French Town.

On August 5, Major Van Horne re-crossed the Detroit River with orders to open the road to French Town. His 200 men were ambushed and routed by a small band of Tecumseh's warriors at Brownstown. Only the speed of their flight kept losses as light as 17 killed. On August 8, General Hull pulled the bulk of his army back across the river to Detroit.

On August 9, Lt. Colonel Miller made a second attempt to open Hull's Road, with a force of 600 men. A force of British and Indians led by Muir and Tecumseh were waiting for him. However, this time the American army swept the field. Despite his victory, Miller did not advance to French Town. His 18 dead and 60 wounded required attention. He had not brought enough supplies for his tired and hungry men, and he, himself, was ill.

Major-General Isaac Brock arrived at Malden with reinforcements on the night of August 13. Two days later, on August 15, Brock sent Hull a demand to surrender or risk subjecting the city of Detroit to the vengeance of his Majesty's Indian allies. Upon Hull's refusal, the British opened an artillery bombardment from batteries across the River in Sandwich and from the gunboats *Queen Charlotte* and *General Hunter*.[26]

Prior to this time, Captain Brush had arrived at the River Raisin with a large escort and 300 head of cattle. Unable to continue without reinforcements, Brush holed up at the Wayne Stockade.[27]

Couriers rode to Detroit to arrange for Colonels McArthur and Cass[28] to lead a column by a circuitous route to avoid the Indians and link up with Brush's convoy at Godfroy's trading post on the River Huron. The link-up failed.[29]

McArthur's men returned to Detroit on August 16, only to find out that, in their absence, the British and Indians had crossed the river from Malden and were now between them and the rest of the American army. His scouts also reported that they had seen a white flag flying over Detroit.[30]

After a brief bombardment that morning, General Hull surrendered the city and 60,000 square miles of Michigan Territory to the British. McArthur's men were included in the surrender, as were the troops at French Town.[31]

Meanwhile, at Georgetown, Kentucky, another American army was

---

26 That same day, troops evacuating Fort Dearborn, at Chicago, were ambushed and wiped out by the Potawatomies.

27 The Wayne Stockade was built by the 2nd Michigan Territorial Militia Regiment in 1806 or 1807 on private claim 124 on the north side of the River Raisin.

28 Lewis Cass was born in New Hampshire in 1782. Son of an army officer, Cass taught school in Wilmington, Delaware, and then took up law when his family moved to the Northwest Territory. He was on the committee to investigate Aaron Burr's activities and became Marshal of the State of Ohio in 1807. In 1812, he commanded one of Hull's Ohio regiments and drove in the British outposts at the River Canard. A vocal critic of his general, Cass ended the War of 1812 as a brigadier-general and became governor of Michigan Territory. In later years, he served as Secretary of War, Minister to France, U.S. Senator, and Secretary of State. He was also a major supporter of Indian removal.

29 The site of Godfroy's Trading Post is in present-day Ypsilanti.

30 Duncan McArthur was a lieutenant colonel commanding one of Hull's volunteer regiments. He and the other militia colonels were jealous of each other and highly critical of General Hull. He would later serve with General Harrison, whom he also criticized. After the war, he amassed a fortune and became governor of Ohio.

31 Hull's main reasons for surrendering were a lack of supplies, unreliable troops, a disparity in numbers, and fears of an Indian massacre of the civilian population if they encountered heavy resistance. Hull was court-martialed and condemned to death for cowardice and neglect of duty, but President Madison commuted the penalty out of regard for his past services during the Revolutionary War. Hull's papers and Brock's final report, which may have helped exonerate him, were lost when the British ship, *Detroit*, was burned near Fort Erie in October.

being assembled to reinforce General Hull at Detroit. It was expected that Colonel Wells would command the expedition on its march northward.[32]

When word reached them at Newport of the fall of Detroit, their aim shifted to the defense of the exposed communities on the Ohio frontier, and if possible, the recapture of Detroit. General James Winchester, who up to now was charged with equipping and expediting this force, felt the time had come for him to assume field command.[33]

The Surrender of the Wayne Stockade, August 17, 1812:

At the Wayne Stockade on the River Raisin, Captain Brush and his Ohio militiamen refused to abide by Hull's surrender terms and fled home to Ohio, followed by Isaac Lee's mounted detachment of local Michigan Militia. The Ohioans left behind their invalids and the remaining Michigan militiamen, who handed over what government-issued weapons they had, including a small brass cannon, and were placed on parole. The British and Indians quickly occupied the River Raisin settlement.[34]

After an initial flurry of pillaging and horse stealing, they began requisitioning supplies in a more controlled and orderly manner. For the next

---

32   The army consisted of the First Kentucky Volunteer Regiment, commanded by Colonel John M. Scott; the 5th Kentucky, under Colonel William Lewis; the First Rifle Regiment, led by Colonel John Allen; and the 17th U.S. Infantry Regiment, headed by Colonel Samuel Wells. The troops were mustered on August 15th and 16th, and listened to speeches by Reverend James Blythe and Henry Clay, who charged these citizen volunteers with sustaining their dual character as both Kentuckians and Americans. On the 19th, the troops started off on a 6-day, 80-mile march along the Dry Ridge Road to Newport and Cincinnati, on the Ohio River.

33   Winchester, James, Historic Details Having Relation to the Campaign of the North-Western Army under Generals Harrison and Winchester, Lexington: Worsley & Smith, 1818, p. 9. Harrison was later appointed commander in spite of Winchester's objections.

34   The cannon was identified as a 2 ¾-inch brass howitzer, however, it is thought that the 19 shells taken with it were probably 2¾ inches in diameter, making the howitzer actually a 2.91-inch (3-pdr.) identified as a series A or C, King Howitzer. See: Davidson, William E. "Summary Remarks on the Evolution of the Sea Service 3-pounder Swivel Howitzer into the U.S. Army's 2 ¾ inch King Howitzer: 1775-1820, Myths and Facts," Military Collector & Historian, Vol. 67, No. 1, spring, 2015, pp. 48-75.
     Although I refer to these cannons as brass, they are actually bronze. Historic documents often confuse the two, because each is an alloy of copper. Bronze is harder and stronger (10% to 15% tin) while brass is softer (15% to 40% zinc). So bronze was used for statues, bells, and cannons, while brass was used for pots, kettles, utensils, and a variety of small articles and parts. Church bells could thus be melted down for making cannons, but brass kettles could not. See: B. A. R. Shot, Spring Issue, 2021, of the Quarterly Newsletter of the Northwest Department of the Brigade of the American Revolution, edited by Karen Kashary.

five months, the population of the River Raisin country would be at their mercy. Many of the English-speaking settlers left their farmsteads in the care of their French *habitant* neighbors and headed for Cleveland or other towns deep in American controlled territory.

At Cleveland, the River Raisin refugees found the people there were in a panic. Numbers of farmers had fled the area, leaving behind their crops and barns. Here, however, the abandoned property was appraised, and the owners credited with the value. The crops were then harvested by the army.

The farmers who had fled Cleveland and the Cuyahoga Valley moved 20 or more miles further to the east, until they felt safe. Even there, they found many abandoned farms, some of which they occupied.

The situation was soon stabilized, however, when military detachments from the east arrived to garrison the area.[35]

With the collapse of the Michigan front, General Brock was able to re-concentrate his forces to repel the second American invasion force, which had finally gotten underway on the Niagara Peninsula.[36]

---

35 History of Cuyahoga County, Ohio; Part Second, The City of Cleveland, Odd Fellows and Knights of Pythias, compiled by Crisfield Johnson, Published by D. W. Ensign & Co., 1879, Chapter X, "The War of 1812," Transcribed by Helen Rosenstein Wolf: *"On the 26th of August Brigadier General Simon Perkins arrived at Cleveland with a large body of militia. General Wadsworth sent him forward to Huron with a thousand men, to build block-houses and protect the inhabitants. General Reazin Beall was soon after sent westward with another body of troops on a similar errand."*

36 Quimby, Robert S., The U.S. Army in the War of 1812: An Operational and Command Study, Vol. I, East Lansing: MSU Press, 1997, p. 59: Henry Dearborn was a Revolutionary War veteran and served as Secretary of War from 1801 to 1809. In 1812, he was the Commanding General of the United States Army. Despite receiving letters from Secretary of War Eustis to launch diversionary attacks at Niagara and Kingston in support of Hull's campaign at Detroit, General Dearborn had negotiated a temporary truce on his own initiative. He invited General Hull to participate, but his letter did not reach Detroit until after Hull's surrender. The truce officially went into effect on August 9, halting all offensive operations in the Niagara Theater for about a month. General Brock probably did not know about the truce until after his return from Detroit. The city of Dearborn, Michigan, was named in honor of General Henry Dearborn.

THE RELIEF OF FORT WAYNE
AU SECOURS DU FORT WAYNE

Newport, Kentucky, to Piqua, Ohio, Aug. 27 to Sept. 1, 1812:

The three Kentucky volunteer regiments rendezvoused at Georgetown, Kentucky on August 15, 1812, and were reviewed the next day by Governor Scott and Generals Winchester and Payne. Leaving on the 19th, they traveled through incessant rain and finally arrived at Newport. They began crossing the Ohio River on August 27th and were concentrated at Cincinnati by the 29th. They reached Dayton the evening of the 30th and were camped at Piqua by Tuesday, Sept. 1st.

Most of the men had been recruited in their home communities by district officers authorized to offer bounties and clothing to men between 18 and 45 years of age. However, boys as young as 14 could be accepted with the written consent of their parents. Size was of no great concern, but the recruit had to be healthy, free from leg sores, scurvy, ruptures, and other infirmities.[37]

By this time, the men were beginning to feel part of a well-trained military unit. They had been practicing battle maneuvers during the long march north, and had learned such things as how to change direction by swinging each battalion on its center.[38]

As they swaggered into Dayton during the evening of August 31st, they were greeted by the firing of a cannon. Unfortunately, the reception was marred by an accident. One of the men firing the welcoming shot lost his hand, while another was badly wounded.[39]

---

37 Knopf, Richard C., Document Transcriptions of the War of 1812 in the Northwest, Vol. X, pt 1, Columbus: Ohio Historical Society, 1962, pp. 55-57: Recruiting Instructions issued by Brigadier General J. Winchester. Regulars were signed up for 5 years' service in exchange for a bounty of $16, and a promised bonus of 3 months' pay and 160 acres of land at the end of their enlistment. Having sore legs may refer to having visible sores on the leg.

38 This was not done by the old parade ground method of wheeling the entire line, which was impractical in wooded terrain. Instead, they were taught to march in a single file, divided in the center into two divisions. On command, the man in the rear of the front division steps 2 paces to the right, while the man in the front of the rear division steps 4 paces to the left. At the same time, the rest of the front division faces about. At the word "March!" the front division files off, forming to the right of their rear man, while the rear division files forward to the left of their front man, thus forming a line at right angles to where they had been.

39 Darnell, Elias, Journal. Philadelphia: Lippincott, Grambo, and Co., 1854, p. 10. The arrival in Dayton was marred as *"One of the men who were firing the cannon got one of his hands shot off, and the other badly wounded."* We are left to imagine how this accident might have happened when

20

By Tuesday, September 1st, elements of the army had established their forward base camp at Piqua.[40] Allen's regiment arrived on the 3rd.

Until now, General Winchester had exercised the responsibility for raising this army to reinforce both Detroit and Fort Wayne. At the same time, however, Kentucky's governor, Charles Scott, placed his state militia under the command of Governor William Henry Harrison of Indiana.[41] General Harrison joined the army on the march to Piqua, to three cheers from the troops.[42]

Sixty-year-old Brigadier General James Winchester was a Revolutionary War veteran who had moved to Tennessee from Maryland. He was a logical choice to lead the army, but he seemed foreign to the homespun militiamen who made up the bulk of the Northwestern army. Winchester also lacked experience in frontier warfare.[43] Not only that, but he had not seen active

---

firing a blank charge, but a premature explosion of a bag of gunpowder while being rammed down the barrel could result in the loss of the rammer's hand.

40 In 1793, Anthony Wayne had Fort Piqua built on the site of an old Indian village about 27 miles north of Dayton, Ohio. Early in 1812, this was made a government agency, and at the outbreak of the war, several Native tribes or villages that wanted to remain neutral were removed to this point and placed under the supervision of Indian Agent John Johnston.

41 Charles Scott was born in Virginia in 1739, making him about 72 years old at the start of the War of 1812. As a Jeffersonian Republican, he was elected Governor of Kentucky and served from 1808 to 1812. A hard drinker, accustomed to swearing, Scott died on October 22, 1813.
Replacing Governor Scott was another Jeffersonian Democratic-Republican, 62-year-old Isaac Shelby. A Revolutionary War veteran who had fought at the Battle of Cowpens in 1781, Shelby had already served as the very first governor of Kentucky from 1792-1796. In 1813, Governor Shelby would actually take the field, personally leading his state troops in Harrison's campaign up the River Thames. Born in Maryland in 1750, he moved to Kentucky in 1776. He died there on July 18, 1826.

42 Quimby, Robert S., The U.S. Army in the War of 1812: An Operational and Command Study, Vol. I, East Lansing: MSU Press, 1997, p. 95.

43 "Fort Winchester," by Charles Slocum. Ohio Archaeological and Historical Publications, Vol. IX. Columbus: Heer Publishing Co., Ohio State Archaeological Society, 1901, pp. 253-277: *"James Winchester was born at White Level (now Westminster), Maryland, Feb. 6, 1752. He was appointed Lieutenant in the 3rd Maryland Regiment, May 27, 1778, and served in the Continental Army until captured by the British sometime later. He was exchanged December 22, 1780. Soon thereafter he removed to Summer County, Tennessee, where he was married. He there attained to…a large estate. He was commissioned Brigadier General in the United States Army March 27, 1812. After the surrender of General Hull, General Winchester was directed by the Secretary of War to take charge of the Army of the Northwest…"*
General Harrison had been an aide to General Wayne in his 1794 campaign and later served as Secretary of the Northwest Territory until becoming the first governor of Indiana Territory. He also was Superintendent of Indian Affairs and had made 13 treaties with them by the time of the 1811 Battle of Tippecanoe, where he defeated the Indians led by Tecumseh's brother, the

duty for 30 years, and his lifestyle had made him less suited for an arduous campaign.

On the other hand, the younger and more energetic William Henry Harrison was popular among the frontiersmen, especially for his victory at Tippecanoe in 1811. He understood the militia and had been involved in western military campaigns since his days as a young subaltern serving in the Legion of the United States under Mad Anthony Wayne. As governor of Indiana, Harrison also had the political clout to get his way, despite Winchester's seniority as a general.

Harrison had won the first round on August 27, when Winchester's force was transferred to his command. Winchester had declined Harrison's offer to accept a subordinate position, but he would wait in the wings until he could resume his role as commander of the Northwestern Army.[44]

Maumee Rapids, September 1, 1812:

As the sun rose high over the Maumee Rapids on September 1st, 1812, a small crowd of local inhabitants watched the arrival of a côterie of British and Canadian officers who had come to check on the situation there.[45]

Prophet. At the start of the War of 1812, Governor Scott appointed him to Major General of the Kentucky troops.

44 Dissertation of Rex LeRoy Spencer, Ph.D. "The Gibraltar of the Maumee: Fort Meigs in the War of 1812." Muncie, Indiana: Ball State University, 1989. Harrison was commissioned a brevet major general of the Kentucky Militia, but this did not entitle him to outrank Winchester, whose brigadier general's commission was from the War Department. Winchester would soon receive orders from Secretary of War William Eustis to take command of the army, which he would do after it arrived at Fort Wayne. Harrison would then return to Piqua to take charge of gathering reinforcements, while his political friends lobbied on his behalf. Within days, President James Madison appointed Harrison commander-in-chief of the Northwestern Army, and Winchester became his subordinate. It was not until December 2nd, however, that the president confirmed Harrison's rank of Major General.

    All was not perfect among the rank and file, either, as friction occurred between the regulars and volunteers. Officers of the regular army attempted to camp their men away from the influence of the undisciplined militia volunteers. For their part, the volunteers regarded the regular officers as martinets, who had to resort to physical punishment in order to control their men.

45 Known as Port Miami, the settlement at the rapids stretched for several miles on both sides of the Maumee River. At the beginning of the War of 1812, the population numbered about 400 people, with the French *habitants* and old-time British settlers on the north bank, and the newer Yankee families on the south side. Shortly after the American army surrendered Detroit, the majority of Yankees fled, their property was plundered, and their farms were destroyed. See: Tucker, Patrick M., "The Mysterious Ruins: Rescuing the Spafford farmstead from the forgotten war of 1812," North American Archaeologist, Vol. 39 (2) 2018, pp. 87-130.

Colonels Procter, St. George, Nichol, and Elliott made an impressive sight, accompanied by Engineer Captain Dixon, some other officers, an interpreter, and quite a large retinue of Native warriors.[46]

Colonel Procter had considered sending Colonel Matthew Elliott on to Fort Wayne to restrain the Indians there, since a temporary truce signed at Niagara was supposedly in effect, but Elliott was too ill to ride a horse. Anyway, the Indians were not in a mood to be held back from attacking the fort.[47]

Lewis Bond was one of the few remaining "Yankees" at the Rapids at this time, so he tried to keep at least one of the French *habitants* between him and the Indians. But the warriors soon began to search through the crowd for him.

They were stopped by Colonel Elliott who told his interpreter to lead them away. Colonel Nichol then came forward and called for Bond to show himself.

When Bond hesitantly stepped out of the crowd, Colonel Nichol told him there was no guarantee the Indians wouldn't kill him when the British officers departed. Since the American forces had retreated beyond Sandusky, he suggested that Bond should seek British protection at Detroit or Malden.[48]

---

46 Born in Scotland around 1780, Robert Nichol worked on the Great Lakes as a seaman and as a clerk for John Askin before going into business for himself. In 1812, he served as lieutenant-colonel of the 2nd Regiment of Norfolk Militia and was appointed quartermaster general of Upper Canada. After the war, he engaged in politics. Nichol was killed in 1824, when, not long after being appointed a judge in the Niagara District, his horse and buggy fell over a cliff at Queenston Heights.

47 Cruikshank, Lt. Col. E. A. Harrison & Procter. Ottawa: The Royal Society of Canada, 1911: Procter received word of the armistice in a letter from General Brock on August 25. The British dismissed 800 warriors gathered at Malden, who departed with some dissatisfaction. The Prophet returned to the Wabash, while Tecumseh made plans for a long journey southward to recruit warriors among the Cherokees and Creeks. (Hull's force could have participated in Dearborn's armistice, but this information did not reach Detroit until sometime in September.)

48 Bond agreed that was a good idea. To transport his family, he would need some kind of craft. As none were available at the Maumee, he decided to send to the River Raisin for a boat. An hour later, Bond was horrified to see the Indians returning, but to his relief, they offered their hands in farewell.

Two days later, Lewis Bond was still at the Maumee when another band of Indians passed through. Bond kept safely out of sight, while the French *habitants* greeted them and learned that these warriors had been involved in the ambush and destruction of the American garrison at Fort Dearborn, Chicago.

On September 4th, a large canoe manned by two *Canadiens* finally arrived from the River Raisin. After loading as much of the family belongings as possible, they soon departed, but were

Tecumseh's Coalition, September, 1812:

At the Maumee Rapids,[49] Native raiders had set fire to several cabins and slaughtered the hogs and chickens of the remaining *habitants* with great abandon, but that was not the worst of it. The effect of Tecumseh and the British-Native alliance was being felt all across the Northwest Frontier.

Led by Missilimetaw, a close advisor to Tecumseh, a band of Shawnees killed two bee hunters out searching for honey in the woods and then went on to raid and burn the village of Pigeon Roost on September 3rd. Twenty-Four men, women, and children were killed.[50]

On September 4th, 600 Indians began an 8-day siege of Fort Harrison, but

---

hampered by strong head winds.

On the 7th, the breeze turned fair and changed direction. They made good progress and kept a good distance out into the lake. Approaching the Raisin, they spied two boatloads of Indians close in to shore. One of the boats turned to chase them, but a contrary breeze prevented it from catching up.

All were happy to reach the River Raisin, until they discovered the Indians were causing trouble there, too. Early the next morning, they joined two other refugee families on board a boat belonging to Captain Elliott. By midnight, they found themselves on the Canadian shore, about 3 miles below Fort Amherstburg.

There, a Mr. Hartley took them in, along with the two River Raisin families, one of which consisted only of a mother and her children, the father having been killed by the Indians. Bond stayed about a week before going up to Malden to arrange for passage on a cartel vessel bound from Detroit to Erie.

See: "Lewis Bond's Journal," in Knopf, Richard C. Document Transcriptions of the War of 1812 in the Northwest, Vol. X, Pt. 1, Columbus: Ohio Historical Society, 1962, p. 189: *"I remained one week at the house of Mr. Hartley, when hearing of a Cartel vessel expected down from Detroit bound to Erie, I went up to Malden and was kindly received in the house of Mr. Innis, a merchant of that place, where I remained 3 days.*

The vessel came, but was so crowded with passengers that a passage could not be had. Being told that I could not be allowed to stay on the Canada side; Mr. Innis procured me a passage on board a king's boat to Detroit.

…at Detroit…I was obliged to reside for some time in the same house with a violent British family and hear their boastings and national insulting language, otherwise their people behaved well enough, and sometimes with kindness, for although many families had left Detroit, yet house room was extremely hard to be had by reason of so many people being obliged to move in from the out settlements; 2, 3, 4, and in some instances five families living in one house."

49 Butler, Stuart L., Real Patriots and Heroic Soldiers; General Joel Leftwich and the Virginia Brigade in the War of 1812, Westminster, Md: Heritage Books, 2008, p. 79. The land along the Maumee River was home to perhaps 400 *habitant* and Yankee settlers, and as many as 3,000 Native Americans.

50 A posse of 150 militiamen was sent after them, but failed to overtake them. See: Gilpin, Alec R., The War of 1812 in the Old Northwest, East Lansing: MSU Press, 1958, (Bicentennial Edition introduced by Brian Leigh Dunnigan, 2012) p. 137. For a fascinating, fictional tale about a bee hunter's escape from the Indians in Michigan, see one of James Fennimore Cooper's lesser-known novels, The Oak Openings; The Bee Hunter, originally published in 1848.

failed to overcome the 50-man garrison. They burned the fort's blockhouse and killed a couple of the local settlers, but retreated shortly before Colonel Russell arrived from Vincennes with a thousand regulars and militiamen.[51]

The march to the St Marys, September, 1812:

On the 5th of September, a couple hundred Winnebagoes and Sauks attacked Fort Madison in Missouri, but success eluded the Indians once again. The tribesmen departed after using up most of their ammunition.[52]

Meanwhile, at Piqua, the men of the Northwestern army learned that Native American warriors were laying siege to Fort Wayne. Lt. Col. John Allen was ordered to abandon his heavy baggage, draw extra ammunition, and take his regiment on a forced march to relieve the garrison there.

Allen's men were proceeding at a fast pace towards Fort Wayne, when they received an order to detour to the St. Marys River and wait to be reinforced by 3 companies detached from the regiments of Scott and Lewis.

Having received word of a large British force advancing up the Maumee River, equipped with artillery to batter down the walls of the fort. General Harrison decided to concentrate all his troops to counteract this threat.

Harrison drew his troops up into a circle around him and announced he would lead them on a forced march to save the fort. Harrison also read aloud the Articles of War.

Only one man, from Scott's 1st Kentucky Regiment, refused to abide by those articles and chose to return home. A couple of his comrades asked permission to escort him out of camp. Placing him upon a fence rail, they carried him down to the Miami River and baptized him in the name of "*King George, Aaron Burr, and the Devil. ...they ducked him several times in the water, and washed away all his patriotism.*"[53]

---

51 Even then, the area was not safe. On September 13, the Potawatomies captured a supply wagon following the army's trail to Fort Harrison. Two more were captured on the 15th. On the 16th, a family was killed at Lamotte Prairie.

52 The Winnebagoes, or Ho-Chunks (Hoocąągra), were committed to Tecumseh. Many Sauk (Thâkîwaa) chiefs preferred a neutral policy, but their young men, and some of their leaders, like Black Hawk, joined in the 4-day siege of Fort Madison. The fort's defenders survived a hail of bullets and fire arrows with the loss of only one man killed. One of the Winnebagoes was also killed. The garrison would be forced to evacuate and burn the fort in the fall of 1813.

53 Lossing, Benson J. The Pictorial Field Book of the War of 1812, Glendale, New York: Benchmark Publishing Corp., 1970, Reprint. pp. 314-16. See also: "Fort Winchester," by Charles Slocum, Ohio Archaeological and Historical Publications, Vol. IX, Columbus: Heer Publishing Co., Ohio State

A supply of gun flints had arrived, and the general ordered more, plus 300,000 rations to be transported on the backs of 300 pack horses.[54]

Short on supplies, the army would have to go on half rations of flour, but each man would get an extra half ration of beer to make up for it.

At noon on September 6th, the main army departed Piqua, leaving their sick and extra baggage behind.[55]

After two days and 32 miles of trudging through prime forest and across a wide, dry prairie, they finally overtook Allen's party on the afternoon of

Archaeological Society, 1901, pp. 253-277. Indians began firing on Fort Wayne on Sept. 5. A friendly Frenchman had also arrived at Fort Wayne with word of Detroit's capture. He freely offered details of what he had seen of the organization and intentions of the British forces that were being sent to support the Indians. Warnings were transmitted to Harrison at Piqua on Sept. 5 and 6.

54 Letter Harrison to Col. Buford, Sept. 9, 1812, in Harrison Papers, Indiana Historical Society.

55 Knopf, Richard C. A Short Chronology of the War of 1812 in the Northwest. Columbus: Anthony Wayne Parkway Board, Ohio State Museum, 1980: At their first campsite, the expedition suffered its first casualty when a soldier was accidently shot by a sentry. The poor man was left behind at a blockhouse along the St. Marys River. They would overtake Allen's regiment early on the 8th at Girty's Town on the St. Mary's River. Major Richard M. Johnson would join them there, bringing Harrison's total force to 2,200 men. Most of the mounted troops remained at Girty's Town to select Richard M. Johnson as their commander. That evening, they rejoined the army at Shane's Crossing, camping a half mile above the army's main camp.

See also: Quimby, Robert S., The U.S. Army in the War of 1812: An Operational and Command Study, Vol. I, East Lansing: MSU Press, 1997, p. 98, and Darnell, Elias, Journal. Philadelphia: Lippincott, Grambo, and Co., 1854, pp. 10-11. A standard daily ration for an American soldier in the War of 1812 consisted of 18 ounces of flour, biscuit, or bread; 20 ounces of beef; 12 ounces of pork and 4 fluid ounces (1 gill) of whiskey. The soldier had to procure vegetables and other items on his own. See: The Old North West Notebook, blog by Dan Wilkins, Oct. 1, 2016.

Girty's Town had been established as a trading post by James Girty in 1783. Girty was gone by 1790, but Anthony Wayne had Fort St. Marys built there in 1795. The fort was abandoned the following year, but rebuilt nearby in 1813. At that time, it was often called Fort Barbee. The Treaty of St. Marys was signed there in 1818. The 99-mile-long St. Marys River was called the *Kokothikithiipi* by the Shawnees and the *Nameewa siipiiwi* (Sturgeon River) by the Miami-Illinois. Usually the name is spelled *Marys*, not *Mary's*. Fort Barbee, along with Fort Amanda on the Auglaize and Fort Jennings on the Ottawa River guarded the western supply route between Piqua and the Maumee Rapids.

Fort Amanda was built by Lt. Col. Robert Pogue, who named it after his 12-year-old daughter. The 160-foot square stockade never saw any fighting, but proved an important supply post and hospital. About 75 pirogues were built there to carry supplies during the winter of 1812-1813. The post was abandoned at the end of the war, but a nearby cemetery contains the remains of soldiers who died from sickness or wounds. The fort is no longer standing but a granite monument was built in 1915 at the site of the original fort. Today, the site contains a memorial monument and is partly owned by the Ohio History Connection and maintained by the Johnny Appleseed Metropolitan Park District.

September 8 at the First Crossing of the St. Marys, also known as Girty's Town.[56]

Continuing under dark and threatening skies, the army reached the second crossing of the St. Marys, called Shane's Crossing, on September 9th. There, they found Colonel Adams and some Ohio militiamen, most of whom joined them.[57]

While at St. Marys, the volunteers found an African-American man living with a white woman. Several Kentuckians recognized him as an escaped slave. They decided to send the young black man back to his owner, and they put the white woman to work as an army cook.[58]

Orders that night were for two or more guns to be fired in quick succession to signal an "alarm," at which the entire army would form a hollow square.

If just one shot was heard, the officer of the guard would investigate and either order two more shots, or call out "*All is well*," to be repeated throughout the camp.[59]

On the 10th, Harrison's army marched 12 miles in two columns through prime forest and a wide prairie that stretched for over 6 miles.[60] The grass

---

56 Lt. Col. Allen's 1st Rifle Regiment spent several days in this camp, where Capt. Bland Ballard reported his company baggage consisted of 1 wall tent, 14 common tents, 14 commissary kettles, 10 tin kettles, 14 tin pans, 87 canteens, 4 axes, 1 spade, 19 muskets, 19 cartridge boxes, 100 flints, 8 gun worms, 17 picks and brushes, 114 cartridges, 4 screwdrivers, 31 pounds of powder, 60 pounds of lead, 1 orderly book, paper, and 4 quills. See: Orderly book of Captain Bland Ballard, Winchester Papers, Burton Historical Collection, Detroit Public Library.

57 Quimby, Robert S., The U.S. Army in the War of 1812: An Operational and Command Study, Vol. I, East Lansing: MSU Press, 1997, p. 98. Multi-lingual Antoine Shane (Chêne), a French-Odawa métis, supported the Native American coalition of tribes and fought for them at St. Clair's Defeat. In 1795, he became an interpreter for Anthony Wayne and served as a scout for the Americans during the War of 1812. For his service, he received a land grant at the Second Crossing of the St. Marys, or Half Way Cross, site of Shanesville from 1820 until 1866, when the village was incorporated as Shane's Crossing. In 1890 the postal service required a name change. The inhabitants chose Lachine, but the post office redesignated it as Rockford, Ohio.

58 The Kentuckians called the woman the "Negro's Mammy." CLIFT, G. GLENN. "WAR OF 1812 DIARY OF WILLIAM B. NORTHCUTT." *The Register of the Kentucky Historical Society* 56, no. 2 (1958): 165-80. Accessed April 19, 2021. http://www.jstor.org/stable/23374326.

59 Darnell, Elias, Journal, Philadelphia: Lippincott, Grambo, and Co., 1854, p. 13. The troops also feared a rear attack while on the march, in which case the rear battalions of Lewis' and Allen's regiments would turn about on their center, while the forward battalions would face right or left and march outward to each flank to form the sides of the square, in concert with the troops forming the front line. Darnell was a private in Williams' company of the 5th Kentucky.

60 Clift, G. Glenn, Remember the Raisin, Frankfort: Kentucky Historical Society, 1961, p. 27: Clift mentions the troops were drinking water from the wagon ruts. As they approached the St. Marys

was as high as a man's head. Only an occasional clump of trees rose above the otherwise flat surface of the land.

The extra rations of beer promised to the men were not adequate to sustain them during the hot march northward. There were few potable water sources, so the men had to scoop water from ruts made by the wagons.

Blythe, Parker, and Huston, from Hart's company of the 5th Kentucky collapsed from exhaustion. Captain McCalla loaned Blythe his horse and marched on foot with the privates, carrying his musket and cartridge box.[61]

Thirsty and on half rations, they halted about 17 miles from Fort Wayne and pitched their tents in a hollow square behind a breastwork, which they dubbed "Camp Union."

Too tired to make supper, the men dropped to the ground, and fell asleep, with their knapsacks on their backs and their guns in their arms.[62]

River, they marched ready for battle, with Scott's 1st and Lewis' 5th regiments in single file 200 yards to the left of the road, Wells' 17th U.S. and Allen's 1st Rifle regiments to the right, and the baggage in the road. Colonel Adams' Ohio volunteers formed the advance guard a half mile to the front, and also covered the right flank. The Kentucky mounted riflemen covered the left, while Garrard's dragoons protected the rear.

Bland Ballard recorded in his orderly book that the advanced guard was mounted and spread across the front of the advancing army, 400 yards in front, with scouts ranging another 400 yards in front of them. If attacked, the advanced guard would hold their position as long as possible to allow the infantry to form their battle lines, and then retreat through gaps left in the lines. The flanking guards would attempt to outflank any advancing enemy. General Payne was in overall command of the infantry, with Scott leading the left-hand column of his own 1st KVM and Lewis' 5th KVM, and Wells leading his own 17th U.S. Infantry and Allen's 1st Rifle Regiment on the right.

If attacked in front or rear, each regiment would pivot on its center to form a double battle line facing the enemy. If surrounded, the second battalion of the rear regiments would file to the center and turn to face the enemy, thus forming a square. To confront an overlapping frontal attack, the rear regiments, after forming the 2nd battle line, could break off by files from the right of companies and move up alongside the regiments in the front line. See: Orderly book of Captain Bland Ballard, Winchester Papers, Burton Historical Collection, Detroit Public Library.

61 Blythe would survive, only to die at the River Raisin in January.

62 A typical day began an hour before daybreak with the first tap of the drum at the deputy adjutant general's quarters, which was repeated throughout the army as the signal to rise and begin making breakfast. The second tap was given ten minutes before reveille. At "reveille," the army assembled in the square formation of camp or in battle order, where the troops would remain until orders were given. Scouting patrols were usually sent out at daylight. To prepare for the march, the "general" was beaten to signal the striking of the tents and packing of baggage. Upon hearing the "assembly," the troops would form the line of march, with the baggage wagons placed on the road or trail. "Yankee Doodle" required field officers to report to general headquarters. See: Orderly book of Captain Bland Ballard, Winchester Papers, Burton Historical Collection, Detroit Public Library.

Camp "Fight On," 10 miles from Fort Wayne, Friday, Sept. 11, 1812:

On September 11, Harrison's army had its first real contact with the enemy when 20 scouts led by Lieutenant Suggette spotted fires still burning in a hastily abandoned camp. A short skirmish then ensued, in which the Kentuckians claimed to have recovered a rifle dropped by a wounded warrior.

The army halted early that day, at a spot convenient to water. Sentinels were posted to keep the horses from drinking too much (and the men from washing their tired and blistered feet) until the quartermaster designated a suitable spot for the men to set up the tents.[63]

Captain McCalla had to keep his mind busy so as not to notice the fatigue. They had made 25 miles in the last two days. This morning, they had marched almost 13 miles, and then stopped to build a fortified camp. The ringing of axes could be heard in every direction, with trees falling like thunder. It was starting to rain lightly, the first they had experienced since leaving Cincinnati.

In the evening, John McCalla would find the time to write a friend at home, giving his regards to his parents and telling them that his cousins and the Todds, who were with the expedition, were all well.

His thoughts also turned to a certain letter he had received from a hometown girl named Nellie. It was full of gossip about all the local belles, including one he thought very highly of. Her name was Annie. At the mention of her name, his heart had suddenly turned amorous. No doubt about it. He was determined to get married as soon as he returned. Maybe Annie would be the one.

During the night, the army horses knocked down McCalla's tent while he was fast asleep inside. He was so dead to the world that he hadn't even noticed it until he was finally awakened by an alarm gun. Groping for his musket, he found himself trapped under the canvas, and had to struggle to crawl out.

The troops were called out in battle formation and stood for 15 minutes, but no attack came. Sentries remained at their posts for an hour after their duty had expired. The weather turned dark and stormy, and alarms occurred

---

63   Orderly book of Captain Bland Ballard, Winchester Papers, Burton Historical Collection, Detroit Library. The encampment was arranged with company wagons facing to the rear in a line some 30 feet behind the field officers' tents, while the Quartermaster, baggage, and commissary wagons were placed behind the commandant and regimental officers' marquees.

all through the night.[64] The nervous camp sentries sounded alarms at 11 p.m. and 3 a.m. Every hour, half the men stood to arms in the mist, while the other half returned to their tents to rest. The watch word for the night was "Fight on."[65]

Fort Wayne, August 28, September 12, 1812:

Bondi was well-known at Kekionga, where he had lived since the age of 12. The 50-year-old fur trader had married a Miami woman and was considered a member of the Miami tribe.

One day, Potawatomi chief Metea paid him a friendly visit, but, before leaving, he warned Antoine that his people were planning an attack.[66]

In turn, Bondi alerted Indian Agent Benjamin Franklin Stickney, who passed the word on to Fort Wayne's commandant, Captain James Rhea.[67]

Rhea sent couriers to General Harrison for help and prepared to defend his post with his garrison of 70 soldiers and 4 small cannons. Unfortunately, one of the messengers, Agency Clerk Stephen Johnston, was intercepted less than a mile from the fort by the Potawatomies on August 28th. He was shot, tomahawked, scalped, and stabbed 23 times.[68]

The Indians had been gathering around Fort Wayne since late August,

---

64 Letter of John McCalla, Sept. 11, 1812, original in Monroe County Historical Museum Archives. See also: Atherton, William. Narrative of the Suffering and Defeat of the North-western Army, under General Winchester. Frankfort: A.G. Hodges, 1842, p. 6. Atherton was a private in Simpson's company of the 1st Rifle Regiment.

65 "Darnell's Journal," Bulkley, John McClelland, History of Monroe County, Michigan, Vol. I, Chicago: Lewis Publishing Co., 1913, p. 74. Also: Darnell, Elias, Journal, Philadelphia: Lippincott, Grambo, and Co., 1854, pp. 16-17: "*We were alarmed by the report of some guns which were fired by the sentinels; we formed in order of battle for half an hour, during which time it rained very hard, and rendered many of our guns unfit to do execution, except by bayonets. The alarm must have proceeded from the timidity of the sentinels.*"

66 Six feet tall and scar-faced, Metea was a prominent orator who had led warriors in the attack on Fort Dearborn. While scouting Harrison's army, his arm was shattered by a bullet fired by a sentry. His name was a play on words that could mean "kiss me" or "the sullen one." After the war, he was a skillful, if unsuccessful, negotiator of treaties to preserve Native lands with Lewis Cass and others. He died after one such treaty negotiation at Fort Wayne in 1827, having poisoned himself by mistaking a bottle of nitric acid for a bottle of alcohol. Some claimed he was murdered. Metea Park in Allen County, Indiana, is named for him.

67 Haffner, Brenda K., The Godfroy's Wea and Miami Indians and their French Relatives, Vol. II, Lafayette: 2014, pp. 270-271.

68 Letter Lt. Daniel Curtis, Oct. 4, 1812, as quoted in Haffner, Brenda K., The Godfroy's Wea and Miami Indians and their French Relatives, Vol. II, Lafayette: 2014, pp. 270-273.

under the leadership of Winnemac (*Catfish*), Five Medals of the Potawatomies, and Chapine, a Miami war chief from the Wabash.

The local Miami Indians had so far shown no sign of hostility, and had even sent volunteers with Captain Wells to aid the Americans in what turned out to be the unsuccessful evacuation of Fort Dearborn in July, but the captain feared they would join the Potawatomies once the shooting started.[69]

To clear a field of fire around the fort, Captain Rhea employed an Indian boy to burn some of the nearby houses. Over the ensuing days, hostile warriors would burn much of what remained outside the walls.

On September 4th, Rhea invited Winnemac to meet with him inside the fort, where he plied the chief with wine in an effort to defuse the situation. The captain, however, got drunk, and Winnemac left thinking Rhea was a weakling. While Captain Rhea remained drunk and indisposed, Agent Stickney, assisted by Lieutenants Curtis and Ostrander, took effective command of the garrison.

Well before dawn on the following day, five young warriors crept behind a root house near the fort while it was still dark. At about sunrise, they spotted two soldiers returning from an outhouse and shot them dead.[70]

Indians continued to fire at the fort's sentinels throughout the day on Sept. 5th. The defenders tried to conserve their ammunition, determined to fire back only when they felt they had a sure shot, or to repel assaults.

The garrison learned help was coming, however, when Major William Oliver arrived with news from General Harrison. Dressed in Native American fashion, and guided by four Shawnees, he had managed to sneak through the Indian lines without being discovered.[71]

At 8 o'clock Winnemac's warriors launched a barrage of fire arrows at the fort, but the inhabitants managed to wet the walls and roofs with water

---

69 Little Turtle, their great leader, had been a major proponent of peace, but he was no longer among them. Only a month before, the venerable chieftain had been camped at his son-in-law's cabin before Fort Wayne to have his gout treated by the garrison surgeon. Unfortunately, he had died there on July 14, at the age of sixty-five, while resting under the shade of a tree.

70 Fort Wayne consisted of 4 long buildings made of squared logs facing each other across a central parade ground. The rear of each building formed a section of each of the outer walls that enclosed the parade ground. The perimeter of the fort was completed with picketing, gates, and a couple of corner block houses. Hosmer, Hezekiah Lord. Early History of the Maumee Valley. Toledo: Hosmer & Harris, 1858, p. 31. Hosmer estimates less than 100 defenders against 600-800 attackers.

71 Hosmer, Hezekiah Lord, Early History of the Maumee Valley, Toledo: Hosmer & Harris, 1858, p. 32.

from the garrison's well. Intermittent firing continued through the night until 3 in the afternoon of September 6.

Overnight, Native warriors had set up some logs in the distance to look like artillery pieces, and they now summoned the fort to surrender. The "Quaker" guns did not fool the garrison, however, and the standoff continued.[72]

The warriors retired to their camp to rest and resupply, but resumed the firing about 9 o'clock that night. Five or six hundred Indians attacked the fort under the cover of darkness, but did not succeeded in scaling the fort's walls.

The Indians also employed diplomacy, asking for a meeting to end the hostilities. Thirteen Native leaders, selected by Stickney, were allowed to enter the fort for a parley, with Bondi in attendance as a witness and interpreter.

After receiving his gift of tobacco, Winnemac apologized for the killing of Stephen Johnston and the two soldiers, along with other depredations, all of which he blamed on his young, uncontrollable warriors.[73]

At one point, the conversation became a bit heated, however, and Winnemac declared, "...*If my Father wishes war, I am a man!*"

Seeing the chief place his hand under his blanket as if reaching for a hidden weapon, Bondi jumped up and tapped on the handle of his knife. At this, the parley broke up.

A few days later, the assailants subjected the fort to a fusillade of small arms fire that lasted 12 hours. On the morning of September 10th, the warriors attacked again, yelling to frighten the garrison, but they were driven back.[74]

When their scouts reported the approach of Harrison's army the Indians lifted their siege and began to disperse. Before leaving, they devastated the surrounding farmsteads and burned the local grist mill.[75]

---

72 They made a great show, going so far as to fill the logs with gunpowder and touch them off. The warriors made a cannon out of a conveniently sized log, which they split, hollowed out, and charred black. They secured the pieces with metal bands from wagon wheel hubs, and mounted the log on the hind wheels taken from a wagon. CLIFT, G. GLENN. "WAR OF 1812 DIARY OF WILLIAM B. NORTHCUTT." *The Register of the Kentucky Historical Society* 56, no. 2 (1958): 165-80. Accessed April 19, 2021. http://www.jstor.org/stable/23374326.

73 Thirty-five-year-old Stephen Johnston was an assistant to agent Stickney. He is buried in the Johnston family cemetery in Piqua.

74 See: Brown, Samuel, Views of the Campaigns of the North-Western Army, Troy, NY: Francis Adancourt, 1814, p. 29: Brown states 2 soldiers and the brother of Governor Meigs of Kentucky were killed.

75 Lossing, Benson J. The Pictorial Field Book of the War of 1812, Glendale, New York: Benchmark

Meanwhile, screened by mounted troops, the American relief army trudged through the swamps in a loose, hollow-square formation, ready to defend themselves against a surprise attack from any direction.

On September 12th, they marched past the smoking remains of farm houses and outbuildings. Tired and thirsty, the first of Harrison's mounted troops arrived at the fort at 3 p.m., where they received a hero's welcome from the 125 beleaguered soldiers and civilians (of whom 25 were women and children).[76]

Elias Darnell was impressed with Fort Wayne, situated as it was in rich, well-timbered land, suitable for farming. He guessed about 400 acres had been placed under cultivation, but the once-neat farm houses had been reduced to ashes by the Potawatomies, who also destroyed the livestock, grain, and hay.[77]

Captain John McCalla was equally impressed, although he was more concerned with the destruction caused by the war, the military burial of the

---

Publishing Corp., 1970, Reprint, pp. 314-315.

76 Based on Samuel Lewis' 1812 "A Correct Map of the Seat of War," the expedition took a good two days to cover 32 miles between Piqua and Girty's Town (Sept 6-8), another day to cover 6 miles to Union Camp (Sept. 9), a day to cover 12 miles to Shane's Crossing (Sept. 10), covered twelve miles the next day (Sept. 11), 13 miles the next (Sept. 12), leaving just 7 miles to cover before reaching Fort Wayne on the final day (Sept. 13). Calculations - Courtesy of Marc Meyer. My narrative, in line with various accounts, puts the arrival at Fort Wayne on the 12th, and Camp Union after, rather than before, Shane's Crossing. My total mileage does fall a little short, but may be explained by variations in the estimates made by the participants on the march.

"Fort Winchester," by Charles Slocum. Ohio Archaeological and Historical Publications, Vol. IX, Columbus: Heer Publishing Co., Ohio State Archaeological Society, 1901, pp. 253-277. Slocum says *"They arrived at Fort Wayne Saturday morning, September 10th, having advanced with great caution and with but little advance-line skirmishing with the enemy, to the great joy of the garrison, which had lost three men during the siege."* It would seem Slocum's date was in error; most sources give the arrival as September 12, which was a Saturday. In 1812, September 10th fell on a Thursday. However, William Northcutt listed their arrival in his diary as 3 o'clock in the evening of September 9th. See: CLIFT, G. GLENN. "WAR OF 1812 DIARY OF WILLIAM B. NORTHCUTT." *The Register of the Kentucky Historical Society* 56, no. 2 (1958): 165-80. Accessed April 19, 2021. J-Stor.

77 Darnell, Elias, Journal. Philadelphia: Lippincott, Grambo, and Co., 1854, pp. 16-17. *"Fort Wayne is situated on the south side of the River Maumee, opposite the junction of the River St. Mary's and St. Joseph, which are considerable navigable streams ..."* The government factory (Indian trading post), Indian Council House, and the Indian agent's house were all destroyed, as well as the blacksmith and sutler buildings. So, too, were the homes in the French village that surrounded the fort. Not all the destruction was done by the Native warriors, since the fort's garrison also took down some of the buildings to create a clear field of fire for the defenders.

two dead soldiers, and the arrest of Captain Rhea, the fort's commander, on charges that he had schemed to surrender the fort in a cowardly manner.[78]

That night, the army's camp was subjected to sniper fire. The Indian fired shots into the exposed tents, but nobody was actually hurt. After stealing several horses, the attackers faded away with the coming of daylight.[79]

With Fort Wayne secured, General Harrison sent out several detachments to raid nearby enemy villages. Colonel Wells was ordered to lead the Ohio and Kentucky volunteers to destroy Five Medals' Potawatomi village at Elkhart, but a large portion of his men objected to making the trek of almost 60 miles.

Taking only the willing, Wells left with on September 14th, captured and destroyed the abandoned village on the 16th, and returned on the 17th or 18th.[80]

---

78 Holliday, Murray. <u>The Battle of the Mississinewa, 1812</u>. Marion, Indiana: Grant County Historical Society, 1964, footnote p. 7: James Rhea was a native of New Jersey. He assumed command of Fort Wayne when Nathaniel Heald was transferred to fort Dearborn. Rhea appeared intoxicated throughout the siege and was arrested by Harrison, but allowed to resign quietly from the service.

   See also: Letter John McCalla to Capt. B. Gaines, Sept. 13, 1812, original in Monroe County Historical Museum Archives. McCalla and the men were in good spirits, although rumors abounded about where they would go from here. Somewhat disappointed that the enemy had retreated without a fight, McCalla consoled himself with a tour of Fort Wayne. He enjoyed seeing the 4 puny cannons that General Wayne had used at Fallen Timbers in 1794. Everyone was in good health as well, except for a few unfortunates who had fallen victim to various accidents. One man in Johnson's regiment had been shot through both thighs by a discharge from a fallen musket. It was feared he might die. McCalla, himself, had stepped on a nail and run it through his foot. The wound looked even worse than it felt, and he hoped it wasn't dangerous.

79 CLIFT, G. GLENN. "WAR OF 1812 DIARY OF WILLIAM B. NORTHCUTT." *The Register of the Kentucky Historical Society* 56, no. 2 (1958): 165-80. Accessed April 19, 2021. http://www.jstor.org/stable/23374326.

80 The units participating were the 17th U.S. Infantry, Scott's Kentucky Regiment, 3 companies of Johnson's mounted riflemen, and about 100 of the Ohio volunteers led by Col. James Dunlap.

   See: "We Lay There Doing Nothing: John Jackson's Recollection of the War of 1812," edited by Jeff L. Patrick, appearing in the <u>Indiana Magazine of History</u>, LXXXVIII, June, 1992, published by the Trustees of Indiana University: John Jackson served in several Ohio militia units. Of the expedition against Five Medals' village, participant Jackson reported that, *"...being within 2 miles of the Indian town known as Obbenobbe or Five Medals Town, we were formed into 2 lines, the right wing led by Col. Wells with the Regulars, the left by Audrain, a Frenchman, who had been our guide from Fort Wayne...we marched on and surrounded the town, but found nobody at home. All had fled that morning. The fires still burned in their wigwams, in one of which was a kettle of pumpkin or squashes, boiled soft, which we supposed to be poisoned, and no one dared eat of it. They had a quantity of corn, some of which was found buried, some hung up to dry, and a quantity on the stalk. They had also a quantity of potatoes, pumpkins, and squashes. Most of their valuable property had been taken away. Col. Wells ordered the wigwams to be set on fire, and in a few minutes, they were*

On September 15, General Payne, accompanied by Harrison, advanced 30 miles to attack four flourishing Miami villages near the forks of the Wabash.

The force, consisting of Lt. Col. Allen's regiment, some of Lt. Col. Lewis' riflemen, and Capt. Garrard's dragoons, struggled across rough terrain and almost impenetrable thickets. The men's clothing was ripped, and the horses became jaded from floundering through deep holes in the swamps.[81]

On the second day, they struck a village occupied only by chickens, which the Kentuckians chased in a flurry of activity that totally exhausted both predator and prey. Nonetheless, the chickens were soon killed, dipped in a nearby stream, plucked, and cooked over fires made from wood stripped from Native lodges and cabins.

Before destroying the village, the volunteers recovered a number of blacksmith tools and opened up a freshly-built grave mound. The grave contained the body of an old man wrapped in a blanket. A tin pan filled with silver brooches had been placed on his chest and a rifle at his side. The top of the raised structure of logs and mud having been removed, one of the militiamen was pushed and fell down onto the cadaver, much to the merriment of his mates.

Pushing on downriver for 15 miles, the Kentuckians razed White Loon's town, which had also been abandoned. Altogether, the troops succeeded in burning numbers of deserted bark and log cabins. They also devastated many acres of corn, potatoes, pumpkins, watermelons, cucumbers and a variety of beans. They, too, were back at Fort Wayne by September 17th or 18th.[82]

---

all in flames...as we had nothing along except what was in our knapsacks, which had become very light, the men were ordered to take as much potatoes and corn as they could carry. We then marched back to Elkhart Prairie and encamped...Some sport was made that night trying to roast potatoes. Every person knows that it requires hot ashes and coals, which we had not, and the method that some undertook was to put down leaves and dirt, and then build a fire over them. When it was thought they were roasted, they were taken out, and the skin found burnt as black as a coal and the inside as raw as it ever was, and after having a good laugh over it, we went to parching corn for our supper. The next morning, we could roast our potatoes right. We started in the morning and made a hard day's march to Blue River, and that night one of the men died with cholic, having eaten too much corn. In the morning he was wrapped in his blanket and laid beside a log and covered with chunks and poles, after which we continued our march to Fort Wayne and arrived there in the afternoon, pretty well fatigued." A rock historical marker for Five Medal's village can be found in Baintertown Park at the intersection of CR 42 and CR 29, near New Paris, Indiana.

81 Wesley, Edgar, "A Letter from Colonel John Allen," Ohio History Journal, Vol. 336, No. 3, July, 1927, pp. 332-339. Letter dated Oct. 2, 1812.

82 White Loon (*Wapamangwa*) was a Miami leader who signed the 1795 Treaty of Greenville. He

A lack of provisions and the desire of his Ohio militiamen to return home had prevented Col. Wells from attempting to destroy Little Turtle's old village on Eel Run, but Colonel Simrall and his 320 dragoons had arrived at Fort Wayne on the 17th and were sent out to complete that mission the next day.

They incinerated most of Little Turtle's village, sparing only the buildings erected by the U.S. government in recognition of the late chief's efforts to promote peace. A second Miami settlement was obliterated on the Wabash. None of the expeditions encountered any resistance.[83]

The destruction undermined the efforts of the Owl and other peaceful Miami chiefs who were trying to maintain some semblance of neutrality. A peace delegation to Harrison also suffered a discouraging setback when the general demanded they send 5 chiefs to Piqua to be kept as hostages.[84]

The British on the march from Amherstburg, September 16, 1812:

Brevet Major Muir, a brave, 46-year-old Scotsman with 17 years' service in the British 41st Regiment of Foot, was leading an expedition to reinforce the Indians besieging Fort Wayne, Indiana. He had left Malden at the head of 150 regulars of the 41st regiment, 150 militiamen from Caldwell's and

---

was a veteran of several battles in the 1790s and during the War of 1812. He accompanied the Miamies on their forced relocation to Kansas, but was granted an exemption and returned to Indiana where he died November 22, 1876 at the age of 107. CLIFT, G. GLENN. "WAR OF 1812 DIARY OF WILLIAM B. NORTHCUTT." *The Register of the Kentucky Historical Society* 56, no. 2 (1958): 165-80. Accessed April 19, 2021. http://www.jstor.org/stable/23374326. See also: Darnell, Elias, *Journal*, Philadelphia: Lippincott, Grambo, and Co., 1854, pp. 18-19. According to Darnell, *"...we proceeded on to the waters of the Wabash; five miles from Fort Wayne we encamped. Next morning, we came to an Indian hut and a small cornfield, two miles from our encampment; here all the wagons and baggage were left, and Captain Langhorne's company as a guard; from this place we marched 23 miles to an Indian town at the forks of the Wabash; we found the town evacuated; we pulled down some of their houses and built up fires and encamped; we had plenty of roasting ears of the best kind. It is a small kind of corn, shallow grain, and very suitable for roasting ears, which answered us a very good purpose, as we had only a little provision with us. We marched through their towns, four in number...We cut up their corn and put it in piles, 60 or 70 acres, so that it might rot. ...Their houses were all burnt by the orders of General Harrison; some of them were built of bark and some of logs."*

83 There is a historical marker for Little Turtle's village on E. Old Trail Road, CR 450 E, 5 miles east of Columbia City, Indiana.

84 Holliday, Murray, The Battle of the Mississinewa, 1812, Marion, Indiana: Grant County Historical Society, 1964, p. 9. Helen Hornbeck Tanner gives the timeline for some of these Indian fights in her Atlas of Great Lakes Indian History. Col. Russell relieved Fort Harrison on Sept. 16, after a 2-week siege; Miami villages on the Wabash were burned Sept. 16; 2 Odawa towns destroyed Sept. 16; Little Turtle's hit Sept. 17; and Five Medals' Sept. 18. Little Turtle died of gout and Bright's Disease on July 14th at Fort Wayne.

Elliott's companies of the 1st Essex and Jacob's company of the Kent County Militia, and some 600 Indians under Colonel Matthew Elliott. To batter, bombard the fort's walls and intimidate the garrison, he had a light howitzer and two light 3-pounder field guns manned by 20 Royal Artillerymen directed by Lt. Felix Troughten.[85]

The artillery and infantry moved by boat along the Lake Erie shore line, past the mouth of the River Raisin, and then up the Maumee to the Rapids. Meanwhile, most of the Indians, led by the aged Colonel Elliott and Captain Caldwell of the British Indian Department, came on horseback through the River Raisin settlement, escorting a train of packhorses. At the Raisin, they were joined by 47 well-armed and mounted French Town volunteers who were engaged to help drive a large herd of cattle.[86]

Colonel Procter had dispatched Muir's force despite General Brock's armistice letter of August 25. He knew the Indians were not giving up. A defeat at Fort Wayne would dispirit them and open the way for an American advance down the Maumee, perhaps endangering his own base at Malden. He might be forced to concentrate all his available forces there, abandoning Detroit and evacuating all of Michigan Territory.

On the other hand, if the Indians did produce a victory against the Americans, Procter wanted British troops to be on hand to show Britain's support, and also to keep them from committing any "uncivilized" barbarities.[87]

A prolonged spell of dry weather made navigation difficult, but the real

---

85   The light howitzer may well have been the brass howitzer taken from the Wayne Stockade at the River Raisin on August 20, after the surrender of Detroit. It was marked with a molded "D. KING-PHILADa-1793" on the base ring. Although originally designed to be carried on a pack horse, it may have been mounted on a modified British 3-pdr carriage. Two other King Howitzers had been captured at Detroit. See: Davidson, William E. "Summary Remarks on the Evolution of the Sea Service 3-pounder Swivel Howitzer into the U.S. Army's 2 ¾ inch King Howitzer: 1775-1820, Myths and Facts," Military Collector & Historian, Vol. 67, No. 1, spring, 2015, pp. 48-75.

86   Cruikshank, Lt. Col. E. A. Harrison & Proctor; the River Raisin, from the Transactions of the Royal Society of Canada, Vol. IV, Section II. Ottawa: Royal Society of Canada, 1911, p.123. John Richardson described the small field guns as light 3-pdrs, but couldn't recall the caliber of the small howitzer. See: Casselman, Alexander Clark. Richardson's War of 1812. Toronto: Coles Publishing Company Ltd. (The artillery crews may have included militia volunteers.)

87   Letter Brock to Prevost, MPHC, Vol. XV, 147-8. Cited in Buckman, Randall OL. The Confluence; the Site of Fort Defiance. Defiance: Defiance College Press, 1994, p. 260-271: Brock added that the Indians expected British help, and he had assured them the British would never negotiate a peace without consulting them. Procter probably did not yet know that the time limit for Dearborn's armistice with Brock had already expired.

work began at the Maumee Rapids where the artillery and provisions had to be hauled across a ten-mile portage. The empty boats were towed over the rapids by the troops and by men drafted from the local French *habitants*.

The first to arrive at the rapids were not the British, however, but Sac-a-manc and a score of Delaware warriors.

Perish Manor and a group of *habitants* were waiting apprehensively in front of Beaugrand's store, when they saw the warriors come out of the woods and draw up in line, as if preparing to fire their weapons.[88]

Just then, Jean-Baptiste Beaugrand, a prominent Indian trader, came running out, waiving a white handkerchief. The Delawares lowered their guns, and came in at a run.

Fortunately, all they desired was to do a bit of bragging about their role in forcing Governor Hull to surrender at Detroit.

The Delawares stayed only a short time, but within an hour a larger party of about 100 soldiers and as many Wyandots and Potawatomies appeared. They were looking for local guides.

Although he tried to feign lameness, Manor was one of those pressed into service. As they approached the head of the Rapids, Manor's acting finally convinced his captors that he was useless, and they released him.

About half way back to the rapids, the now limber Manor was stopped by a band of Potawatomies who demanded to know what he was up to. He told them he had been ordered back to procure forage for the cattle and horses. Once again, he appeared legitimate and was let go.

Manor's lameness suddenly returned, however, when he encountered the main British force. He was taken to Colonel Elliott, who interrogated him closely. Elliott was a bit lame himself, suffering from a bout of lumbago. Manor managed to convince Elliott that he was both lame and incompetent, whereupon the old colonel dismissed him with no more than a curse.

Finally, back at Beaugrand's, Manor decided the area was getting too hot for him, and he left for the mouth of the river. There he planned to join his wife and daughter, who were staying at the home of Robert Navarre.

As luck (or the lack thereof) would have it, on his way downstream he

---

88 Hosmer, Hezekiah Lord. Early History of the Maumee Valley. Toledo: Hosmer & Harris, 1858, pp. 32-34. Some of this and the following details may be a mixture of memories from Manor's experiences in July and August, as well as in September.

encountered some British gunboats at the mouth of Swan Creek, a tributary of the Maumee.

Lieutenant Mills of the Canadian 1st Essex Militia Regiment was not impressed with Manor's account of himself and therefore took him into custody, confining him below deck. There he remained for 3 days until Jean-Baptiste Beaugrand found out and was able to use his personal influence to secure Manor's release.[89]

Forks of the River, ½ mile from Fort Wayne, September 19, 1812:

It was a sad day for the Army of the Northwest when General Harrison relinquished his command to General Winchester, who had just rejoined this force the day before. The men didn't understand the politics involved, but they respected and admired Harrison for his victory at Tippecanoe and his frontier-style familiarity. Their feelings towards General Winchester were not the same, even though he had initially raised this army. The troops nearly rioted when they heard Winchester was assuming field command.[90]

The orders, however, were clear. They came directly from William Eustis at the War Department. General Winchester was to take personal command of the troops and reinforcements of the Northwestern Army and march them directly to Detroit.[91] Harrison retained control of troops in his

---

89 Toledo Pioneer Biographies + Early History of the Maumee Valley.

90 Darnell, Elias, Journal. Philadelphia: Lippincott, Grambo, and Co., 1854, p. 20. See also Clift, G. Glenn. Remember the Raisin. Frankfort: Kentucky Historical Society, 1961, p. 31: Citing the diary of William B. Northcutt, a private in Capt. Garrard's horse troop, Clift reports some of the pranks the unruly militiamen claimed to have played on their despised general. Sitting down across a pole to relieve himself one dark night, Winchester practically stabbed himself on a porcupine skin that had been planted there. On another occasion, the troops sawed his pole almost in two, which collapsed when he sat on it, dumping him into the mess.

91 Dissertation of Rex LeRoy Spencer, Ph.D. "The Gibraltar of the Maumee: Fort Meigs in the War of 1812." Muncie, Indiana: Ball State University, 1989. Winchester had received the orders on September 9, and had hurried forward to join the army at Fort Wayne. Of course, they had been written much earlier, before the War Department was even aware that Detroit had fallen into the hands of the enemy. On Sept. 17, Harrison would be appointed commander-in-chief of the entire Northwestern Army. Winchester was then given the choice of remaining as Harrison's subordinate or transferring to the army on the Niagara frontier. Winchester chose to stay, and Harrison placed him in command of what he re-designated the left wing of the Northwestern Army, essentially the same force Winchester currently commanded at Fort Wayne. Harrison then turned his attention to mobilizing a large enough force to both defend the Ohio frontier and to retake Detroit.

home territory of Indiana, as well as all Kentucky troops north of the Ohio, except for Winchester's men.[92]

Riding off to St. Marys, Harrison fired up the men there with a patriotic speech. It was there that he received a War Department notice of September 1, that he and Winchester should coordinate their efforts to recover Detroit and that the necessary artillery, supplies, and reinforcements would be forthcoming.[93]

At Piqua, on the 24th, Harrison received notice of his assignment to command the entire Northwestern Army, including the force then under General Winchester.[94] Harrison decided to designate Winchester's force as the left wing of the Northwestern Army. This force nominally was counted at well over 2,000 men, but when it left Fort Wayne, it was now down to just under that number.[95]

---

92 Letter Adams to Eustis, Sept. 19, 1812, Knopf, Richard C. Document Transcriptions of the War of 1812 in the Northwest, Vol.VI, pt 3. Columbus: Ohio Historical Society, 1962, p. 164.

93 Quimby, Robert S., The U.S. Army in the War of 1812: An Operational and Command Study, Vol. I, East Lansing: MSU Press, 1997, p. 101, 105: A mounted force, including Johnson's mounted infantry, could be quickly concentrated at St. Marys, while Colonel Findlay's mounted riflemen could serve as a reserve, even though Findlay, himself, was still on parole from his capture at Detroit. This force could sweep the back country by going up the St. Joseph from Fort Wayne, crossing the headwaters of the River Raisin, and swinging east to Brownstown. Johnson's mounted troops could also be used on their own for a *coup de main* against Detroit, but Harrison feared his forces might get cut off and stumble into the same trap as General Hull if he pushed them forward too soon.

   The weakness of the plan to launch a swift attack on Detroit was that such a mounted force could not hold Detroit without reinforcements and supplies. It would also expose American supporters at Detroit to retaliation from the Indians. It might be better to use them to harass Native-American villages and prevent the villagers from interfering with the movements of his three main columns. A major offensive could not begin until the ground was sufficiently frozen to permit the passage of artillery, and the British ships on Lake Erie were bottled up by the ice. See also: Winchester, James. Historic Details Having Relation to the Campaign of the North-Western Army under Generals Harrison and Winchester. Lexington: Worsley & Smith, 1818, p. 85: Capt. Thomas Eastland wrote General Winchester in a July, 1817, letter that Harrison attempted to get the officers at St. Marys to sign a petition preferring him to command the army over Winchester, but Colonel Barbee objected. This location was probably at Girty's Town, also known as Fort Barbee and St. Marys, at the present-day city of St. Marys, Ohio. Harrison also stopped Colonel Jennings' advance on September 25, ordering him to build blockhouses and wait. To Eastland, it seemed Harrison intended to curb Winchester's ability to operate independently by starving Winchester's force of supplies.

94 Secretary of War William Eustis had decided two days earlier to promote Harrison above Winchester.

95 Under good conditions, supplies could be brought up to the Maumee Rapids by way of Hull's Road from Urbana or brought westward from Cleveland and Sandusky along the 115 miles of trails that led to the Rapids. Winchester was greatly in need of artillery, of which he had none.

Harrison was also assembling a right wing, to be made up of 3,000 Pennsylvania and Virginia militiamen. Once organized in eastern Ohio, this wing was intended to march to the Maumee by way of Upper Sandusky.[96]

A central column of a thousand Ohio militiamen was being gathered under the command of General Edward Tupper at Urbana. They would follow Hull's Road to meet Winchester on the Maumee.

They would be backed up by an army of 1,500 Ohio volunteers led by Brigadier General Simon Perkins via Lower Sandusky.

Located 40 miles north of Dayton and 40 miles west of Columbus, the town of Urbana was laid out in 1805 and was used as an assembly and training area for General Hull's army in 1812. For a time, it served as headquarters for the Northwestern Army.

General Winchester was also formulating his own plans for an advance down the Maumee River in order to establish a supply base at Anthony Wayne's old Fort Defiance at the junction of the Maumee and Au Glaize rivers. After being resupplied, a second bound could take him as far as Roche de Bout at the end of the Maumee Rapids. Fort Deposit, General Wayne's temporary supply base, had been located there in 1794, and it was also near where General Hull's Road crossed the Maumee. Once astride Hull's trace, an American force would become a direct threat to the British at both the River Raisin settlement and ultimately Detroit or Fort Amherstburg.

See also: Quimby, Robert S., The U.S. Army in the War of 1812: An Operational and Command Study, Vol. I, East Lansing: MSU Press, 1997, pp. 101-105: Harrison built a chain of forts northward from Franklinton, along the Sandusky-Scioto Trail, which followed the Sandusky River and came to be known as the Harrison Military Trail. This trail connected Upper and Lower Sandusky and was eventually protected by 4 forts: Fort Ferree (Upper Sandusky, Ohio) Fort Ball (Tiffin, Ohio) Fort Seneca (Old Fort, Ohio) and Fort Stephenson (Lower Sandusky - Fremont, Ohio). General Harrison was amassing an overwhelming force, but it would require the support of some heavy artillery and the transport of a million rations, in stages, to the neighborhood of its intended assembly point at the Maumee Rapids.

96 General Leftwich's 700-man Virginia Brigade would arrive at Delaware, Ohio, on November 5th. Lt. Col. Ferree's 511-man Pennsylvania Regiment, part of General Crook's Brigade, would arrive at Mansfield on November 13 and join Major Nelson's 5th Pennsylvania Battalion at Upper Sandusky by December 15, all in support of General Simon Perkins' brigade at Lower Sandusky. Their first assignments involved the building of roads and depots for the transport and stockpiling of supplies, including cannons, ammunition, and a million rations. See: Butler, Stuart L., Real Patriots and Heroic Soldiers; General Joel Leftwich and the Virginia Brigade in the War of 1812, Westminster, Md.: Heritage Books, 2008, pp. 66-69.

MANOEUVERS ALONG THE MAUMEE
OF THE LAKE
JEU D'ÉCHECS SUR LA RIVIÈRE DES MIAMIS DU LAC

Camp Maumee, 3 miles east of Fort Wayne, September 23-25, 1812:

On the evening of September 22nd, General Winchester wrote to Governor Return J. Meigs of Ohio, expressing his joy at the *"prospect of regaining lost territory"* and of his hope *"to winter in Detroit or its vicinity the ensuing season..."* where he would *"...wipe away the stain on the American character at Detroit..."*

Privately, the general was concerned about the state of the army's ammunition. His men had been wasteful, even on the march, so he ordered the officers to inspect them each morning, and account for any missing cartridges.

For the sake of safety, loaded weapons were not to be stored in the wagons.[97] However, that did not save Private Hume from being killed when he carelessly tried to shoot a large fish by poking the muzzle of his musket into the water. When he pulled the trigger, the barrel burst and tore off half his face.[98]

The men's health was also an issue. The volunteers were still dressed in hunting shirts of cotton and linen, already worn by marching through the brush. Even the regulars were still in summer clothing, many of their shoes were worn out, and their undersized blankets were inadequate for the coming winter season.

The whole army needed more woolen blankets, capotes, stockings, and shoes. The general had already written the War Department, suggesting they send such goods to the militia in lieu of pay.[99]

---

97 Winchester's General Orders, Sept. 22, 1812, in O A&HQy Vol. IX.

98 CLIFT, G. GLENN. "WAR OF 1812 DIARY OF WILLIAM B. NORTHCUTT." *The Register of the Kentucky Historical Society* 56, no. 2 (1958): 165-80. Accessed April 19, 2021. http://www.jstor.org/stable/23374326.

99 Letter Winchester to Eustis, Knopf, Richard C. Document Transcriptions of the War of 1812 in the Northwest, Vol. VI, pt 3. Columbus: Ohio Historical Society, 1962, p. 184. Due to high demand, blue wool was scarce and expensive. As a matter of expediency, the military began ordering uniform coats and pantaloons of drab (brown), black, green, or gray. Black was chosen for the 17th U.S. Infantry. New recruits were usually issued white linen or cotton uniforms. Unfortunately, the 17th would not receive their wool coats in time for the Battle of the River Raisin. See: Barbuto, Richard, Staff Ride Handbook for the Niagara Campaigns, 1812-1814, Fort Leavenworth: U.S. Combat Studies Institute Press, U.S. Army Combined Arms Center, 2014, p. 10.

With 6-days' worth of rations, Winchester put his army into motion at 9 a.m., following Anthony Wayne's old trail down the Maumee towards Defiance.[100]

From Defiance, Winchester planned to move to the Maumee Rapids, where he expected to be joined by militia units from Pennsylvania and Virginia.[101]

Setting a cautious pace along the left (north) bank of the Maumee, they would halt each day at 3 in the afternoon. The need to cut a road for the wagons and fortify their camp each night restricted their progress to 6 miles a day.[102]

To support Winchester's advance, Lt. Col. William Jennings' 2nd

---

100 "Fort Winchester," by Charles Slocum. Ohio Archaeological and Historical Publications, Vol. IX. Columbus: Heer Publishing Co., Ohio State Archaeological Society, 1901, pp. 253-277. He also asked for two infantry regiments, fully clothed and armed, to join him at the Maumee Rapids by October 15th, and for a third regiment to proceed from Piqua and open a supply road to Defiance, so he could re-supply his army on its way downstream. In his order of march, dated September 22, 1812, Winchester placed the "...front guard in 3 lines, two-deep in the road, and in Indian files on the flanks at distances of 50 and 100 yards, as the ground will admit..." Capt. Garrard and 20 of his men moved out ahead of the advance guard as it marched. They were followed by a fatigue party of a captain, ensign, 2 sergeants, 2 corporals, and 50 men who worked feverishly on improving the trail for the passage of the army's baggage. On the road behind them came the General, his staff, and the baggage train. Half the fatigue party would work, while the other half carried their arms and kept watch. Cavalry and infantry were posted on each flank and in the rear. The 3 regiments of Kentucky militia, Colonel Wells' corps of regulars, and Garrard's troop of volunteers originally totaled about 2,200 men. Wells' and Allen's regiments marched in columns on the right, with Scott's and Lewis' on the left.

101 CLIFT, G. GLENN. "WAR OF 1812 DIARY OF WILLIAM B. NORTHCUTT." The Register of the Kentucky Historical Society 56, no. 2 (1958): 165-80. Accessed April 19, 2021. http://www.jstor.org/stable/23374326. This was in accord with General Harrison's plan to assemble an army of 10,000 men to attack Detroit. The Right Division of the Northwestern Army, consisting of 250 mounted men, 28 field pieces, and 2 brigades of Pennsylvania and Virginia militia, was to join a brigade of Ohio Militia at Upper Sandusky. The whole would amount to about 5,000 men. Some 12 hundred more Ohio militiamen would march up Hull's Road from Urbana, while Kentucky troops posted along the Au Glaize River would reinforce Winchester.

102 Orderly book of Captain Bland Ballard, Winchester Papers, Burton Historical Collection, Detroit Public Library: On Sept. 24, they made only 3 miles, camping 17 miles from Fort Wayne. On Sept. 24, they were 18 miles; Sept. 26, 33 miles; Sept. 27, 38 miles. Part of the reason for the slow progress was the time consumed in building fortified camps. A fence at least 4 feet high was constructed between 15 and 75 feet from the tent lines, and brush was cleared for at least 30 feet beyond that. A narrow opening was left in the fence in front of each company. The Brigade Quarter Master would go ahead of the army and lay out the camp, and the regimental quarter-masters would conduct their regiment to its assigned place. Winchester complimented his troops on their efficiency in forming for battle and their excellence in fortifying their camps.

Kentucky Volunteer Regiment was ordered to reconnoiter Defiance, open a road to that place, and build blockhouses on the Auglaize, while Colonel James Findlay's mounted regiments were to destroy the Odawa towns on Blanchard's Fork.

Colonel Jennings' regiment proceeded along the St. Marys and Auglaize Rivers. Unfortunately, they only put about 30 miles behind him before receiving reports from their scouts that a body of Indians was occupying their destination.

Jennings therefore halted and began building blockhouses on the Auglaize, about 35 miles from St. Marys. This halt would result in Winchester running out of flour and having to place his men on half rations of beef.[103]

Although still not popular among his militia volunteers, due to his status as a regular officer, Winchester's conduct on this march to Defiance was earning him some points. Major Davenport of the 17th Infantry noted a definite change in sentiment, at least for the moment.[104]

Tensions rose, however, when a small patrol failed to return from a scouting mission on September 25th.[105]

The Death of Ensign Liggett, September 25, 1812:

On September 25, Ensign Liggett took 4 men of McCracken's Woodford County militia company on a scout towards Defiance. At about sunset, they made camp in a glen and began cooking their meal around a large, roaring fire. Being neighbors back home, they settled in for some pleasant conversation while enjoying the fresh taste of some plums they had picked along the trail.

The group was suddenly surprised by a French interpreter and half a

---

103 "Fort Winchester," by Charles Slocum. Ohio Archaeological and Historical Publications, Vol. IX. Columbus: Heer Publishing Co., Ohio State Archaeological Society, 1901, pp. 253-277. By late October, Fort Jennings would consist of a breastwork of logs that enclosed a blockhouse and an acre of ground. Of the 2nd regiment's 8 companies under Jenning's command, one would be detached to fight at the River Raisin. This was the company of scouts and spies led by Captain Henry James. See: Knopf, Richard C., A Short Chronology of the War of 1812 in the Northwest, Columbus: Anthony Wayne Parkway Board and Ohio State Museum, 1960.

104 Winchester, James. Historic Details Having Relation to the Campaign of the North-Western Army under Generals Harrison and Winchester. Lexington: Worsley & Smith, 1818, p. 82.

105 Captain Bland Ballard of LTC Allen's First Kentucky Rifle Regiment was placed in charge of a 60-man detachment of spies to scout ahead of the army. He was assisted by Lieutenant Harrison Munday from Kerley's company of the First Kentucky Rifles and Ensign James Liggett of the 17th U.S. Infantry.

Elite British troops from the 41st Foot are shown advancing through woods portrayed by reenactors during the War of 1812 Bicentennial
Photo by Bill Saul

dozen Indians who had spotted their fire in the darkness. The scouts instantly rushed for their weapons, but held their fire when they saw the new arrivals extending their hands as a sign of peace and proclaiming that they were merely hunters on their way home. They asked what Liggett and his men were doing there.

Warily, Liggett responded with a lie, saying that he and his men were scouts for a 5,000-man expedition led by General Winchester, and that this enormous army was camped only 4 miles behind them. To further intimidate the Indians, Liggett added that they were awaiting the arrival of a second army bringing 3,000 reinforcements.

The ensign then asked if British soldiers were in the Indian camp. When the Natives said there weren't any, Liggett informed them he would escort them to the American army's camp. At that, the Indians gave up their subterfuge and called on the soldiers to surrender. Liggett saw he was surrounded, but refused to surrender until assured they would not be murdered.

A deal was struck. The prisoners could keep their weapons until they reached the British camp, where they would be under the protection of

British officers. As they walked, the prisoners talked freely in English, making exaggerated claims about the numbers of American troops in the area.

Before they reached the British camp, it began to get really dark, and the Indians became nervous about the situation. They thought they overheard the Americans conspiring to take them by surprise and kill them. Fearing their detainees might actually make a break for it, they hatched a plot to strike first.

Speaking in their own language, so as not to alarm the Americans, the Indians carried out their plan in perfect coordination. Five of the warriors walked up behind and to the side of the prisoners and, at a given signal, raised their war clubs. Four soldiers fell dead, but Liggett jumped for cover behind a tree. As he ran, he raised his rifle to fire, but the interpreter shot him.

Staggering off, Liggett tried to make his way through the brush, but he could not evade the Indians. Two of them pursued him closely and finished him off. The warriors scalped all the dead men. One warrior used a silver-handled dagger to cut off the ensign's ears as further proof of their encounter.[106]

British troops on the Maumee, 12 miles above Defiance, Sept. 24-27, 1812:

Shadrack Byfield of the 41st Foot was feeling tired and hungry as Brevet Major Muir's infantrymen trudged steadily through the woods on the north bank of the Maumee River. Light filtered dizzily through the overarching canopy of leaves. There were no signs of human habitation, not even a native wigwam to break the monotony of the forest.

Although the boats were now lighter without the troops, they still contained the ammunition and provisions, and their crews struggled to snake them up the increasingly shallow stream.[107]

On the morning of September 25, the white-haired Muir and his men

---

106 See: Casselman, Alexander Clark. Richardson's War of 1812. Toronto: Coles Publishing Company Ltd.; Cruikshank, Lt. Col. E. A. Harrison & Proctor; the River Raisin, from the Transactions of the Royal Society of Canada, Vol. IV, Section II. Ottawa: Royal Society of Canada, 1911, pp. 123-4; McAfee, Robert. History of the Late War in the Western Country. Bowling Green, Ohio: Historical Publications Company, 1919 (reprint of 1816 original edition.) p. 151-2; and Byfield, Shadrack, "A Common Soldiers Account," Recollections of the War of 1812, Toronto: Baxter Publishing Company, 1964 reprint of 1828 edition. Historical marker is located at the entrance to the Bend Access to the Maumee River, NE corner of the Bend Rd bridge, near Sherwood, OH.

107 Byfield, Shadrack, "A Common Soldiers Account," Recollections of the War of 1812. Toronto: Baxter Publishing Company, 1964 reprint of 1828 edition. Also: Casselman, Alexander Clark. Richardson's War of 1812. Toronto: Coles Publishing Company Ltd., p. 93.

broke camp and crossed to the south bank, marching the entire day until they reached a point about 12 miles upstream from the ruins of old Fort Defiance.[108]

By now, rations were becoming a problem. For the past 4 days, Byfield and the other troops had been subsisting on short rations, and there was only enough left for maybe 2 more days. Muir had sent Captain Elliott back to the Rapids for more cattle and flour that had been deposited there. The cattle could be driven, but the flour would have to be carried on the men's backs, as the water was too low and there were few pack horses available.[109]

While they rested that evening, 9 or 10 Indians scouted ahead for five or six miles. After dark, Muir and his men were alarmed to hear firing fairly close at hand. The men stood to their arms, tense and wary, while they waited for an attack to come. A half hour later, about 9 p.m., an interpreter and six Indian scouts came bounding out of the woods, waving several scalps.

Leaping and splashing, they crossed the Maumee and reported that they had captured and killed Ensign Liggett of the 17th U.S. Infantry and 4 American scouts. Unfortunately, the news extracted from them was less comforting. Two American armies were coming towards them.

Both of these forces sounded too big to handle, so Muir quickly sent a runner to summon his allies to his support. The largest body of Native Americans was a dozen miles away on the other side of the Maumee River, where Col. Elliott and some 600 warriors were camped opposite the ruins of old Fort Defiance.[110]

The advance to Fort Wayne was now forgotten, as Major Muir ordered his supply boats to head back downstream. The British troops lay that night under arms, and, on the morning of Sept. 26, Muir took up a position on high ground overlooking the ford at which the Americans might cross to the south bank.

---

108 They were about 40 miles from their objective at Fort Wayne.

109 Byfield, Shadrack, "A Common Soldiers Account," Recollections of the War of 1812. Toronto: Baxter Publishing Company, 1964 reprint of the 1828 edition. Some of the men were already running out of food. Even Lieutenant Barnett had been seen begging provisions from his men, saying he had eaten nothing all day. Byfield and his comrades took pity on him and shared what they had.

110 Letter Muir to Proctor, Sept. 26, 1812, Michigan Pioneer and Historical Society Collections. Lansing: Wynkoop, Hallenbeck, Crawford Co., 1909, Vol. XV, pp. 148-9. See also: Cruikshank, Lt. Col. E. A. Harrison & Proctor; the River Raisin, from the Transactions of the Royal Society of Canada, Vol. IV, Section II. Ottawa: Royal Society of Canada, 1911: Cruikshank says that Muir moved his force to high ground, commanding a nearby ford in the river.

Colonel Elliott and the Native warriors joined them about midday, and more scouts were sent out. When no enemy appeared, Muir became uneasy that Winchester's force might continue along the north bank of the Maumee, thus bypassing his position and cutting off his retreat. He therefore ordered his troops to fall back to Defiance. From there, the British crossed the river to the north bank, and made camp near their Native American allies.

As they did so, several scouts returned with unconvincing reports, but finally at nightfall, Split Log, a Wyandot chief from the Amherstburg area, came in to say he had scouted around the entire American army, which was camped only 8 miles away. He estimated the enemy outnumbered them by 2 to 1.

Taking stock of the situation, Muir couldn't decide if his artillery would be an advantage or a liability. The guns were ready to deploy if suitable ground could be found with a wide range of fire.

Unfortunately, even light artillery was hard to transport. It had taken 3 days to move the cannons just 8 miles, since the water was so low and they couldn't be shipped any further by boat. If the army had to retreat quickly in the face of superior numbers, it was likely they would have to abandon the artillery.

The situation was not promising, so Major Muir sat down and began a letter to Colonel Procter back at Malden, warning him to ready the defenses of Detroit and Fort Amherstburg.[111]

Although 149 more Indians joined up the next morning, Muir doubted their numbers would be sufficient to handle the approaching Americans. Still, he hoped they could ambush Winchester's men while they were still on the march. He therefore sent Capt. Caldwell and Lt. Askin out with 60 warriors to reconnoiter the enemy and see if they were advancing. For an hour, Muir waited tensely, hearing gunshots off in the distance.[112]

Caldwell's party finally returned, minus one of the scouts, who had

---

111 Letter Muir to Proctor, Sept. 26, 1812, <u>Michigan Pioneer and Historical Society Collections.</u> Lansing: Wynkoop, Hallenbeck, Crawford Co., 1909, Vol. XV, pp. 148-9. T

112 Lossing, Benson J. <u>The Pictorial Field Book of the War of 1812.</u> Glendale, New York: Benchmark Publishing Corp., 1970, Reprint. p. 327. The American force they had encountered consisted of American scouts and about 40 of Garrard's dragoons, led by Captain Bland Ballard. Ballard's mission was to recover the bodies of Ensign Liggett and his men. On their way, they discovered the Indians in ambush positions and charged them on horseback. The Indians melted away into the swamps, where the dragoons couldn't follow.

been killed in the skirmishing. Soon after, more Indians came in to report that a second warrior had been killed. The enemy was only 2 miles away, and coming on fast.

Major Muir was surprised that the assembled warriors were apparently not reacting to this news and asked Colonel Elliott what they were up to. Elliott went off to see the Wyandot chief Roundhead, and soon returned with his answer.

Roundhead had indicated that Muir should choose a good spot on the open plain to site in his guns, and the Indians would support him by out-flanking any force that the enemy sent against him. The major then deployed his artillery along a road skirting the woods. He positioned his infantry to protect them.[113]

No sooner were the cannons in place, than Colonel Elliott came galloping back to inform Muir that the Indians would not be coming that way after all, and that he should fall back through the woods and stop at the first suitable place.

So, Muir's men hauled the guns back 4 miles through the trees to a clearing which the Indians had reported would give them a clear field of fire. Muir was not satisfied, however, since there was less than a hundred yards of open field in any direction.

He told the Indians he had brought the artillery along to batter down the walls of Fort Wayne, and he was not about to risk losing them in a close-quarters fight in the woods. The major then ordered Lt. Felix Troughten of the Royal Artillery to withdraw the cannons to old Fort Defiance. From there they could be loaded on boats and taken back to Fort Amherstburg.

That night, Major Muir attended the Indian council along with Colonel Elliott. He left with the impression that the warriors would attack the enemy in the morning. Muir planned to support them with his remaining troops.

What he didn't understand, however, was the negative effect that his withdrawal of the cannons would have on the confidence of his allies.[114]

---

113 Cruikshank, Lt. Col. E. A. Harrison & Proctor; The River Raisin, from the Transactions of the Royal Society of Canada, Vol. IV, Section II. Ottawa: Royal Society of Canada, 1911, p. 125.

114 Letter Muir to Proctor, Sept. 30, 1812. Michigan Pioneer and historical Society Collections. Lansing: Wynkoop, Hallenbeck, Crawford Co., 1909, Vol. XV, pp. 151-5.

THE "BATTLE" FOR DEFIANCE
THE SITE OF FORT DEFIANCE

PRESENT-DAY VIEW OVERLOOKING THE MAUMEE RIVER
Photo by author

American advance guard, north bank of the Maumee, Sept. 25-27, 1812:

On the night of September 25th, one of Ballard's scouts, a man named Hannon, returned to camp in a panic. He had found the mutilated remains of Lt. Liggett and four men along an old deer track 5 miles from camp. The hour being late, Winchester resolved to recover the bodies in the morning.[115]

On September 26th, Winchester broke camp. As his men began clearing the road, his secretary, Captain Woolfolk, went on ahead with Captain Ballard and his mounted "spy" company to bury the remains of Ensign Liggett's party.

They soon noticed mounted Indians dressed in blue watching them. Uncertain of their strength, Ballard withdrew to high ground, 200 yards in his rear.

Instead of chasing directly after Ballard, the Indians filed off to their right, making a wide circle to cut off his retreat. In so doing, however, they

---

115 CLIFT, G. GLENN. "WAR OF 1812 DIARY OF WILLIAM B. NORTHCUTT." *The Register of the Kentucky Historical Society* 56, no. 2 (1958): 165-80. Accessed April 19, 2021. http://www.jstor.org/stable/23374326. Northcutt, a dragoon in William Garrard's company, claimed the bodies were found the same night that Liggett's party had left on their scouting foray, but other accounts seem to indicate the following day. At any rate, there were 2 attempts to retrieve the bodies.

50

went right past Ballard's new position, allowing the Kentuckians to make their escape.

That evening, Lieutenant Harrison Munday and the rest of the company of spies came upon the scene and spotted the warriors. Yelling like Indians, they charged and scattered them.[116]

Believing he was outnumbered, Munday called off the attack and his detachment raced back to the safety of the main army, with the Indians in hot pursuit.[117]

Liggett's demise, coupled with the report of his scouts, caused General Winchester to draw in his flanking columns, fall back to his camp, and prepare to fend off an enemy attack.[118]

On the morning of September 27, General Winchester established a new camp five miles further downstream on the road to Defiance and issued orders not to fire at anything except the enemy.

Captain Ballard was sent out once again, on foot, to take care of the remains of Liggett and his men. They were supported by Garrard's troop of dragoons, which followed some 200 yards in the rear, far enough away so their clattering would not interfere with the careful listening of the scouts.[119]

Unfortunately, the mounted dragoons fell a quarter mile behind when they encountered a deep creek, which was difficult to get their horses across.

---

116 Lieutenant Monday (or Munday) of Capt. Kerley's Co., 1st Rifle Regiment, resigned his commission on October 14, 1812.

117 McAfee, Robert. History of the Late War in the Western Country. Bowling Green, Ohio: Historical Publications Company, 1919 (reprint of 1816 original edition.) p. 153. They were 33 miles from Fort Wayne. See also Col. Allen's Oct. 2, 1812, letter to Judge Logan, quoted on pages 32-33 of G. Glenn Clift's Remember the Raisin! Also in Wesley, Edgar, "A Letter from Colonel John Allen," Ohio History Journal, Vol. 336, No. 3, July, 1927, pp. 332-339. Letter dated Oct. 2, 1812.

118 Cruikshank, Lt. Col. E. A. Harrison & Proctor; the River Raisin, from the Transactions of the Royal Society of Canada, Vol. IV, Section II. Ottawa: Royal Society of Canada, 1911, p. 124; From his maps, the constant alarms in camp, and the reports of his scouts, Winchester believed it likely the enemy intended to make a stand in a strong position behind the Tiffin River, on the north bank of the Maumee. Rather than attack across an obstacle, or possibly fall into an ambush on the march, he preferred to have the enemy come to him. Protected by their fortified camp, his untested army would have a decent chance of holding off an attack by the Native Americans and the British.

119 Garrard's company of light dragoons was an elite unit uniformed in blue coats, red vests, and a leather cap adorned with a black cockade and black plume tipped in red. Originally issued muskets in August, they would exchange them for jaeger or short rifles 3 months later. CLIFT, G. GLENN. "WAR OF 1812 DIARY OF WILLIAM B. NORTHCUTT." The Register of the Kentucky Historical Society 56, no. 2 (1958): 165-80. Accessed April 19, 2021. http://www.jstor.org/stable/23374326.

Temporarily unsupported, Ballard and his 45 Kentuckians suddenly ran into another ambush laid by a hundred warriors. Fortunately, they had forded the creek at an unexpected spot. The ambushers were forced to show themselves as they changed their position. Both sides then raced for the high ground.

Although the Native warriors gained it first, Ballard's men continued their advance, raking the enemy with deadly fire from their rifles.

Hearing Garrard's dragoons galloping to Ballard's assistance, the Indians broke off the action, having wounded only one of the Kentuckians in the ankle, a man from Captain Edmiston's company of the 1st Rifle Regiment.

The Kentuckians pursued the retreating warriors for a short distance, driving them across to the south bank of the Maumee. They then returned to locate and bury the remains of Liggett's party together in a single mass grave.[120]

British camp along the Maumee, September 28, 1812:

Meanwhile, at the British camp, the 28th of September was proving to be a confusing and frustrating day for Major Muir. About an hour before daylight, he received a message from Colonel Elliott that the Indians were packing up.[121]

Thinking this was the signal for a general retreat, the major ordered off his remaining cattle and baggage immediately, but kept the troops assembled for a fight. Had he known what his River Raisin volunteers had been up to, he might have been even more worried.

Taking advantage of the confusion, the *habitants* managed to disappear

---

120 Letter John Allen to Judge Logan, Defiance, Oct. 2, 1812, in Clift, G. Glenn. Remember the Raisin. Frankfort: Kentucky Historical Society, 1961, pp. 32-4. Wyatt Step, Guy Hinton, Wm. Bevis, Wm. Mitchell, all of Woodford — Volunteers in Capt. Virgil M'Cracken's Company. Missing, and assumed to have been killed, was Alexander M'Coy, of Georgetown from Scott's Regiment. See also: Wesley, Edgar, "A Letter from Colonel John Allen," Ohio History Journal, Vol. 336, No. 3, July, 1927, pp. 332-339. Letter dated Oct. 2, 1812. A military headstone for Ensign Liggett is located at the base of the "Liggett/Muir" historical marker on Delaware Bend Road, along the Maumee River in Defiance County. 41° 16.679' N, 84° 30.926' W

121 Cruikshank, Lt. Col. E. A. Harrison & Proctor; the River Raisin, from the Transactions of the Royal Society of Canada, Vol. IV, Section II. Ottawa: Royal Society of Canada, 1911, p. 125: "*An hour before daylight, to his great surprise, he received a message from Colonel Elliott stating that their soothsayers had been busy conjuring all night, and in consequence, the Mackinac and Saginaw Indians were preparing to return home at once.*"

with most of the cattle herd, thus reducing Muir's reserve supply of food. Some of the *habitants* had actually been spies, sending information to Winchester of the approach of the British and Indians.[122]

Half an hour after Elliott's first message, a second note informed Muir that the Indians were determined to attack the Americans, and were asking for British support. The major gave the order to march, and the troops reached the Indian camp in a few minutes.

Upon their arrival, however, the Indians still did not look anything like they were preparing for combat. Colonel Elliott came up and begged Muir to hold his men in place, as the Indians were not yet ready.

As they stood there, Major Muir could not help noticing that the Indians seemed to be collecting their belongings and heading off in different directions in small groups of 6 or 7. When asked what was going on, Elliott replied they were just hiding their property before the battle.

Muir turned to a small group of 3 or 4 interpreters and said, *"I think the camp begins to be very thin."* At that moment, a young Huron passed by and told them that by the time they got into the fight, they would not have even the current numbers present.

A chief from Mackinac also came up to say good-bye. He was taking home 200 of his young men because the Indians were divided in their counsels. Those with horses were going to stay, since they could easily escape if the battle turned against them.

Although his confidence in his allies was now thoroughly shaken, Muir gave the order for his men to resume their march in the direction of where the Indians had indicated they were planning to fight.

They arrived on the east bank of the Tiffin River where it flows into the Maumee, about 3 miles above Fort Defiance. Here they could form in a fairly strong position, with their flanks protected by the fork in the river.[123]

---

122 It seems likely the River Raisin men had volunteered to accompany the expedition in order to repossess some of the cattle that had been requisitioned by the British at French Town. As for one of the spies, Peter Navarre had been hired as a guide. At Turkey Foot, he slipped away to inform Winchester and Fort Wayne of Muir's approach. He then returned to the British. See: History of the Maumee Valley, p. 34.

123 In his letter of September 30, 1812, Major Muir referred to the location for their intended stand as *"the East bank of the North or Little Miami River, branching off...about three miles above Fort Defiance."* This corresponds roughly with the Tiffin River, which flows from Devil's Lake in Michigan's Irish Hills and joins the Maumee about 2 miles west of Defiance, Ohio. Early French traders called it the *Crique au Fève*, (Bean Creek) due to the natural growth of bean plants along its banks. The

Current Vegetation along the Tiffin River in NW Ohio
Photo by author

It was here that the Indians brought in a prisoner, Sergeant McCoy of Scott's Regiment.[124] He told them he was a quartermaster sergeant and had been out looking for honey when he got lost.[125] He had wandered around for 4 days without food before being captured.[126]

Major Muir estimated that his Indian allies had by now been reduced to 330 warriors. Against such odds, he could think only of retreat, and he told Colonel Elliott to so inform Roundhead.

Elliott replied he would still rather try to ambush the Americans, but

stream was renamed the Tiffin River in 1822 after Edward Tiffin, the first governor of the state of Ohio. The river's upper section north of the Ohio Turnpike is still known as Bean Creek.

124 Lossing, Benson J. The Pictorial Field Book of the War of 1812, Glendale, New York: Benchmark Publishing Corp., 1970, Reprint. p. 327.

125 Byfield, Shadrack, "A Common Soldiers Account," Recollections of the War of 1812. Toronto: Baxter Publishing Company, 1964 reprint of the 1828 edition: Cleverly exaggerating the size of Winchester's army, Sgt. McCoy told his captors that the Americans had 3,000 troops in several regiments, including Wells' regulars, Lewis', Scott's, and Allen's Kentucky volunteers, Simmerol's 250-man cavalry regiment, 150 mounted riflemen, a 6-pounder cannon, and 70 supply wagons. They were low on provisions, but expected to be joined shortly at Fort Defiance by another American army bringing extra supplies and 4 cannons. McCoy added that a force under Colonel Jennings was descending the Auglaize to cut off the British retreat. (Byfield reported the prisoner said the Americans had 9,000 troops.)

126 Cruikshank, Lt. Col. E. A. Harrison & Proctor; the River Raisin, from the Transactions of the Royal Society of Canada, Vol. IV, Section II. Ottawa: Royal Society of Canada, 1911, p. 126.

Muir said, *"If we are exposed to one volley, I shall lose all my men, therefore, I think it is advisable to retreat."*[127]

Still, Elliott objected that the Indians were determined to fight. To further his case, he went off to find Roundhead, who agreed to meet Muir.

Upon their return, Muir offered to fall back to the morning campground and wait for Roundhead to gather his people there. Together they would retreat in a solid body, down the Maumee, keeping scouts out far and wide to spy on the advancing Americans.

By means of an interpreter, the Wyandot chief explained that two native conjurers had predicted a victory. They should take advantage of this omen and attack the enemy's advance guard.

The major was sympathetic, but refused to risk being overwhelmed and cut off by superior numbers on the basis of a dream.

Roundhead replied that if the enemy beat them off and attempted to surround them, they could just scatter into small groups and escape off into the woods.

Muir countered that it might work for his warriors, but not for British troops. They needed to stay together and have access to their supplies.

Roundhead reluctantly agreed, and the retreat was set in motion. The next day they caught up to Lt. Troughten and the slow-moving artillery and supplies. Some supplies were destroyed to lighten the load, and the heavy round shot was thrown into the river, but the guns themselves were safe.[128]

Both Roundhead and Major Muir now began to doubt the strength and commitment of their allies.[129]

Winchester's army on the way to Fort Defiance, Sept. 27-30, 1812:

For some time now, Winchester's men had been out of flour and their beef rations had been cut in half, which caused depression, fights and even some thefts. Faced with dwindling supplies, General Winchester sent an express to Harrison, informing him of the weakened condition of his force.

---

127 Byfield, Shadrack, "A Common Soldiers Account," Recollections of the War of 1812. Toronto: Baxter Publishing Company, 1964 reprint of 1828 edition.

128 In fact, Shadrack Byfield reported they had thrown the shot overboard to make the boats draw less water in the shallow river.

129 Letter Muir to Proctor, Sept. 30, 1812. Michigan Pioneer and Historical Society Collections. Lansing: Wynkoop, Hallenbeck, Crawford Co., 1909, Vol. XV, pp. 151-5.

Of the 305 non-commissioned officers and privates in Wells' regiment, not one had a winter coat, a waistcoat, or wool pantaloons, and 47 had no shoes.[130]

On September 27, Captain Hickman arrived in camp with a spy named Riddle. On their return from a scouting mission, they had spotted a small Native American camp and noticed that the Indians seemed negligent in their security as they sat talking and laughing. A detachment was sent after dark to surprise them, but Riddle got lost and the troops were unable to locate their objective.

Moreover, the patches of thick brush they had encountered convinced them it was dangerous to send out such small scouting parties due to the ease with which they could be cut off. Nonetheless, Winchester and his officers felt it necessary to send spies out ahead of the advancing troops, even if it resulted in an ambush.[131]

On the morning of Sept. 28, the army had advanced about a mile when they received word that their scouts had found signs the British and Indians were preparing for a fight. Immediately Winchester formed a battle line and waited.

The forward scouts fired at some Indians they saw to their front, but no attack materialized. The ever-cautious Winchester then pulled his men back to their fortified camp and waited some more, while spies and a cavalry troop set out to discover what the enemy was up to.[132]

The scouts crossed the Maumee River and discovered some wagon ruts, which they hoped had been made by a badly-needed supply train sent by Col. Jennings. However, they eventually concluded that this trail must

---

130 Knopf, Richard C. "A Short Chronology of the War of 1812" in the Northwest. Columbus: Anthony Wayne Parkway Board and Ohio State Museum, 1960. See also: Letter Wells to Eustis, Oct. 3, 1812, Knopf, Richard C. Document Transcriptions of the War of 1812 in the Northwest, Vol.VI, pt 4. Columbus: Ohio Historical Society, 1962, p. 9. This may be a bit of an exaggeration. Perhaps the shoe-less soldiers would have made moccasins. See also: CLIFT, G. GLENN. "WAR OF 1812 DIARY OF WILLIAM B. NORTHCUTT." *The Register of the Kentucky Historical Society* 56, no. 2 (1958): 165-80. Accessed April 19, 2021. http://www.jstor.org/stable/23374326.

131 See: Orderly book of Captain Bland Ballard, Winchester Papers, Burton Historical Collection, Detroit Public Library: On October 25, General Winchester would appoint Abraham Riddle of Langhorne's Company and 5 other volunteers as official spies for the army, entitling them to an additional 75 cents per day, plus 1½ rations of fresh provisions, or some salt, 18 oz. of bacon, and 1½ pounds of biscuit. See also: Darnell, Elias. Journal. Philadelphia: Lippincott, Grambo, and Co., 1854, p. 23. Darnell says the scout's name was Ruddle.

132 Darnell's Journal for Sept. 28-30. Winchester's camp was situated about 5 miles from Fort Defiance, and some 45 miles from Fort Wayne.

have been left by enemy artillery as it advanced towards Fort Wayne, halted, and retreated.

The scouts also found a deserted camp in the woods, with fires still blazing and a strange Native "liberty pole" topped with owl feathers and an offering of tobacco. They used their tomahawks to chop it down.[133]

Thinking his enemy might be on the run, Winchester decided to follow the British trail. Sensing that the British and Indians could make a stand in a strong position behind the Tiffin River, where it joined the Maumee, the General deftly outflanked that potential obstacle by crossing his entire army to the Maumee's south bank and erecting another fortified camp just opposite the mouth of the Tiffin. This put the two armies once again on opposite sides of the Maumee.[134]

On the morning of September 29th, the left wing of the Army of the Northwest left its fortified camp and proceeded on to the ruins of Fort Defiance, with Garrard's musket-armed dragoons leading the way.[135]

Upon arrival they found that the clearing originally made by General Wayne some 18 years before was now overgrown with brush so thick and tall that it had to be laboriously cleared once again. After completing a breast works around their camp, the men slept with their guns in their arms. Assembly was beaten about an hour before dawn, and the men stood to arms, waiting for daylight.

At sunrise, Brigadier General Winchester sent Lt. Colonel Lewis out

---

133 CLIFT, G. GLENN. "WAR OF 1812 DIARY OF WILLIAM B. NORTHCUTT." *The Register of the Kentucky Historical Society* 56, no. 2 (1958): 165-80. Accessed April 19, 2021. http://www.jstor.org/stable/23374326.

134 The army fell back a couple miles on September 28th, and then crossed at a point 4 ½ miles above the juncture of the two streams and some 6 miles above the mouth of the Auglaize. "Fort Winchester," by Charles Slocum. Ohio Archaeological and Historical Publications, Vol. IX. Columbus: Heer Publishing Co., Ohio State Archaeological Society, 1901, pp. 253-277. Winchester, James. Historic Details Having Relation to the Campaign of the North-Western Army under Generals Harrison and Winchester. Lexington: Worsley & Smith, 1818, p. 12. Winchester reported that on September 28, in the face of allied opposition, he ordered a retrograde movement of 2 miles and crossed the river at a ford, without enemy knowledge or opposition.

135 As they neared the fort, Garrard's men were suddenly confronted by a group of armed horsemen, who turned and fled when Garrard ordered a charge. It was soon discovered that they were chasing their fellow countrymen. The dragoons had mistaken the horsemen for mounted Indians, while the horsemen thought the dragoons were British Light Cavalry. CLIFT, G. GLENN. "WAR OF 1812 DIARY OF WILLIAM B. NORTHCUTT." *The Register of the Kentucky Historical Society* 56, no. 2 (1958): 165-80. Accessed April 19, 2021. http://www.jstor.org/stable/23374326.

with a 380-man detachment. They would track the retreating enemy across the Auglaize River and down the Maumee for several miles, without seeing any sign of them.

Meanwhile, the rest of the men begin preparations to construct a new fortification to serve as a hospital and supply depot.[136]

Colonel Wells, the commander of the 17th U.S. Infantry Regiment, was not particularly impressed with the performance of the army thus far. He *"...began to think our men do not shoot as well as men did in our former Indian wars. ...The Indians have 7 scalps from us, and we have not had the good fortune to get one from them."*

---

136 Darnell, Elias, <u>Journal</u>. Philadelphia: Lippincott, Grambo, and Co., 1854, pp. 24-25. See also: Letter Wells to Eustis, Oct. 3, 1812, Knopf, Richard C. <u>Document Transcriptions of the War of 1812 in the Northwest, Vol.VI, pt 4</u>. Columbus: Ohio Historical Society, 1962, p. 9, and Letter Winchester to Eustis, Ft. Defiance, Oct. 7, 1812, Knopf, Richard C. <u>Document Transcriptions of the War of 1812 in the Northwest, Vol.VI, pt 4</u>. Columbus: Ohio Historical Society, 1962, p. 18: *"The army under my command marched from Fort Wayne on the 22 of last month, and arrived at this place on the 29th. Our progress was considerably retarded by small parties of Indians annoying us on our front and flanks. On the 25th, Ensign Leggett of Colonel Wells' regiment was killed and scalped, together with four Kentucky volunteers, about five miles in advance of the line of march. They were sent out as spies, and appeared to have been shot down in the order they were walking. ...We are building 4 blockhouses and bastions, and shall picket the flanks or curtains, within which, a store house and hospital are to be built...."*

THE WAITING PERIOD

LA PÉRIODE D'ATTENTE

Malden, October 2, 1812:

General Harrison continued to extend his network of supply and assembly points throughout Ohio during the fall season. On September 29th, a skirmish on Bull Island in Sandusky Bay finally secured the area around Lower Sandusky for the Americans.

But the British were also busy. By September 30th, Brevet Major Muir and his men had reached the Maumee Rapids on their return from their expedition against Fort Wayne. After skirmishing with a superior American relief force under General James Winchester, Muir's Indians had begun to disappear. Winchester's fortified camps and cautious advance had foiled Muir's hopes of ambushing the American army or cutting off and defeating even a portion of it.

Given diminishing support from his Native allies and the difficulty of bringing up supplies, Muir had decided to retreat. At least, it could be said that he had delayed the advance of the American forces.

On October 2, Muir arrived at Malden, where Colonel Procter was already making plans to strip the River Raisin and Maumee Valley of all the cattle, crops, and other provisions he could. Procter's intention was to leave nothing which could sustain an American advance towards Detroit. He might even induce the Indians to forcibly remove the French *habitants* from their homes along the River Raisin.[137]

The British considered abandoning Detroit and concentrating their strength on the Niagara Peninsula. This, however, would result in the defection of their Native allies, and release the American troops that were defending the Ohio frontier for service elsewhere.

It was therefore decided to hold Detroit and Malden. Spoiling attacks would be launched on American forces gathering along the Maumee or the northern coast of Ohio to forestall any advance into Michigan. Fortunately, land transportation was difficult. The Black Swamp was almost impossible

---

137 Cruikshank, Lt. Col. E. A. Harrison & Proctor; the River Raisin, from the Transactions of the Royal Society of Canada, Vol. IV, Section II. Ottawa: Royal Society of Canada, 1911, p. 127.

to traverse in the rainy season. Even if the enemy reached the Raisin, the road to Detroit had deteriorated to the point where it would be impassable for heavy artillery and wagons, except in winter.

Procter's main fighting force was composed of British regulars and Indians. Canadian militia would be used only as necessary, to augment the main force or provide rear area security. As for the waters of Lake Erie, they remained under British control. To prove the point, the 16-gun square-rigger, *Queen Charlotte,* began to cruise the south shore of the lake between Cleveland and Sandusky.[138]

Winchester's Camp near Fort Defiance, October 3, 1812:

On October 1st, Colonel William Lewis had departed Winchester's camp with 380 men. His mission to locate the enemy took him across the Auglaize, down the south side of the Maumee for 8 miles, then back along the north bank of the Maumee. Plainly, Muir's British force was no longer in the vicinity.

The next day, October 2nd, Harrison arrived with a hundred mounted troops and two days' rations of flour. Upon learning of Harrison's promotion to the rank of Major General, Winchester considered resigning, but decided to stay until Malden could be taken.[139] Harrison was now definitely in command of the entire Northwest Army, but Winchester would retain command of the left wing.[140]

---

138 The British logistical system depended heavily on the St-Lawrence River system. Fort Mackinac and the upper Great Lakes could still be reached through the old fur trade route that left the St. Lawrence at Montréal and followed the Ottawa and Matawa Rivers to Lake Nippissing, then down the French River to Lake Huron. Another route went up the St. Lawrence and across Lake Ontario to the town of York, from where it could be portaged to another old fur route via the Holland River, Lake Simcoe, the Severn, and into Georgian Bay. The more direct water route to Detroit by portaging around Niagara Falls and across Lake Erie took considerably longer to reach the upper lakes and depended on British control of the Niagara Frontier, the Detroit River, and Lake Erie. There was also a rudimentary land route that led from the Niagara Frontier to the Thames River and Lake St. Clair by way of Moravian Town.

139 Winchester, James. Historic Details Having Relation to the Campaign of the North-Western Army under Generals Harrison and Winchester. Lexington: Worsley & Smith, 1818, p. 12: Winchester's description of Harrison's visit was quite terse; he assumed command, inspected the work on the fort, and departed.

140 This force was made up of regulars from the 17th and 19th U.S. Infantry under Colonel Wells and the Kentucky regiments of Scott, Lewis, and Allen. Unfortunately, Colonel John Mitchell Scott's health had finally given out. The 48-year-old doctor and commander of the 1st Kentucky Regiment had not been in good shape for many years. He was sent home in a litter and died

Winchester's soldiers had spent the past several days without bread, and the grumbling had turned to talk of mutiny. That evening Lt. Colonel Allen and several other officers woke Harrison from his sleep and told him they had tried to convince the men not to return home, but had been shouted down.[141]

The following morning, October 3rd, the troops were awakened by the call to arms. Drawn up in a hollow square, they were surprised by news of the approach of Tupper's Brigade, and delighted to see General Harrison once again.

Talking as though he were their father, Harrison shamed them for their mutinous ways and offered to release any of them who missed the comforts and safety of home. By the time the General was finished, their martial pride had been rekindled, and they responded with 3 hearty cheers.[142]

And there was more good news. Harrison announced that 25,000 rations had been assembled at St. Marys, awaiting transport and distribution to this army. Clothing left at Piqua was on the way as well. In addition, reinforcements from Pennsylvania and Virginia would soon be on the march and would swell the size of the Army of the North West to some 10,000 men.[143]

---

on December 20. Meanwhile, other Kentucky regiments were gathering in support at St. Marys under Colonels Jennings, Pogue, and Barbee. An Ohio regiment led by Colonel Findlay, one of Hull's former officers, was also coming on.

141 Brigade Inspector James Garrard wrote: *"We have not drawn a full ration since the 8th of September. Sometimes without beef, at other times without flour, and the worst of all, entirely without salt, which has been much against the health of the men. They bear it with much patience...You would be surprised to see the men appear on the brigade parade. Some without shoes, others without socks, blankets, etc. All the clothes they have are linen..."* See also: Atherton, William. Narrative of the Suffering and Defeat of the North-Western Army under General Winchester. Frankfort, KY.: A. G. Hodges, 1842, pp. 13-15. See also: Letter John McCalla to father, from camp near Ft. Defiance, typescript in 1812 Military Collections, Monroe County Historical Museum Archives: Samuel Campbell wanted a couple pair of shoes and socks, while James Blythe asked for warm socks and overalls, a roundabout jacket, and a woolen cap. Mathew Elder wanted the same, plus a waistcoat, 2 flannel shirts, and a thick blanket. Joseph Bickley needed mittens, pantaloons, a thick pair of shoes, and a box of cigars. John McCalla went for a coat, pantaloons, shoes, shirt, socks, writing paper, 2 boxes of wafers and 2 lbs. of chocolate. See also: Letter Harrison to Platt, Oct. 9, 1812, Harrison Papers, Indiana Historical Society: Back at Piqua, General Harrison issued orders to bring up more food. 5 or 6 thousand rations would be sent via St. Marys, while meat would be sent by way of Urbana.

142 Lossing, Benson J. The Pictorial Field Book of the War of 1812, Glendale, New York: Benchmark Publishing Corp., 1970, Reprint, p. 331. See also: Cruikshank, Lt. Col. E. A. Harrison & Proctor; the River Raisin, from the Transactions of the Royal Society of Canada, Vol. IV, Section II. Ottawa: Royal Society of Canada, 1911.

143 Darnell, Elias, Journal. Philadelphia: Lippincott, Grambo, and Co., 1854, pp. 25-27. Darnell places

In terms of the overall strategic plan, St. Marys would be the main depot for provisions, while Upper Sandusky would be the assembly point for artillery and military stores. Winchester's army would act as a forward corps of observation, while a central column of Ohio militia would advance to Urbana and then up Hull's old road to the Maumee. The right column of Virginia and Pennsylvania troops would proceed to the Maumee via Upper Sandusky.[144]

Supplies were also being brought in from Pittsburgh via the Ohio and Scioto Rivers to Franklinton. From there, they would be hauled over a hundred miles of miserable dirt roads that became impassable for wagons in the fall rains, so that packhorses would have to be substituted.[145]

---

this speech on October 4th, rather than the 3rd. Harrison's orders from the War Department were short, but ambitious. He was to protect the entire northwestern frontier, retake Detroit, and invade Upper Canada, as far as he was able with the forces under his command. On October 4th, the army received a new deputy inspector in the person of Captain Nathaniel Hart, who would die at the Raisin.

144 Upper Sandusky had its beginnings as a Wyandot village. During the American Revolution, Duquat, the Wyandot "Half-King" had his village there. By the early 1800s, the area remained under the control of the Wyandots, and a settlement of free African Americans was also located there. In 1783, the Western Confederacy of Native Nations was formed there to oppose U.S. expansion into the Northwest Territory. In late 1812, Pennsylvania militiamen built Fort Ferree there by order of General Harrison. It sat astride the Harrison Trail, a military road that would soon connect Franklinton (now part of Columbus, Ohio) to Fort Stephenson at Lower Sandusky (modern-day Fremont, Ohio) near the mouth of the Sandusky River. Fort Ferree served as a supply depot and as a temporary headquarters for General Harrison.

145 Franklinton was founded by Lucas Sullivant in 1797 and was the county seat of Franklin County from 1803 to 1824. It was the first settlement in the Scioto Valley north of Ohio's capital at Chillicothe, and had grown to contain 80 buildings, including a handsome brick courthouse. (It was annexed to the growing city of Columbus in 1870.) On October 25, 1812, Harrison established his headquarters at Franklinton, where 700 militiamen had already assembled, greatly outnumbering the local inhabitants. From this strategic central position, he could direct the movements of his converging columns of reinforcements and supplies via Franklinton and Upper Sandusky. (Between September and November, he would spend about 30 days in the town.) In particular, he hoped to assemble a hundred ox teams to transport the heavy artillery he considered vital for taking Detroit. Unfortunately, heavy fall rains made transport difficult, and the breakup of the farms along the River Raisin meant he would have to bring along two wagons of animal fodder for every wagon load of military supplies. But in the meantime, from Fort Wayne and the Maumee Rapids, advanced units could raid Native-American settlements as far west as Lake Michigan. A primary target was Peoria. See: Cruikshank, Lt. Col. E. A., Harrison and Proctor. Ottawa: The Royal Society of Canada, 1911, p. 142. See also: "Journal of Joseph Larwell," Detroit Historical Collections, Detroit Public Library, p. 9. See: Butler, Stuart L., Real Patriots and Heroic Soldiers, Westminster, Md: Heritage Books, 2008, p xxii. See also: Dissertation of Rex LeRoy Spencer, Ph.D. "The Gibraltar of the Maumee: Fort Meigs in the War of 1812." Muncie, Indiana: Ball State University, 1989.

Unfortunately, banks and businesses often refused credit for government purchases, insisting on payment in advance or in gold before shipping supplies. The army's provisions and reinforcements often traveled by difficult routes.[146]

On the 5th, a fatigue party of 240 of Winchester's men started construction on new fortifications 80 yards upriver from the ruins of old Fort Defiance. The new fort would be christened "Fort Winchester," and would consist of four 2-story blockhouses, a hospital, and a storehouse enclosed by sharpened pickets, 15 feet high. Each wall had a large gate in the middle, topped by a sentry house. Enclosing 3 acres of ground, it was much larger than the old fort, which had covered barely a quarter acre.[147]

General Harrison ordered Winchester to leave a small garrison at the completed fort, before continuing down the Maumee as fast as was practical.

There were stocks of corn at the Maumee Rapids, which could help make it a great staging area in which to assemble an overwhelming force for the conquest of Detroit.

General Tupper was ordered to head for the Maumee Rapids to secure it in advance of General Winchester. After Harrison departed on October 4th,

---

146 Frontier armies usually found themselves far from their main source of supply, in this case, at Pittsburgh. From Cincinnati, supplies would be brought up the Miami River, portaged over to the Auglaize, or even to the St. Marys River and then go on to Fort Wayne and down the Maumee to Winchester's camp, which was relocated to a point on the Auglaize, half a mile above the old fort. The poor road system, combined with the reluctance of civilian drovers to hazard their animals in a war zone, made it over ten times more expensive to deliver freight by wagon than by boat. See: Barbuto, Richard, Staff Ride Handbook for the Niagara Campaigns, 1812-1814, Fort Leavenworth: U.S. Combat Studies Institute Press, U.S. Army Combined Arms Center, 2014, p. 12.

147 Trees were felled to wall off the entire peninsula between Winchester's previous camp and this new one and between the Maumee and Auglaize Rivers. The new installation would cover several acres of ground near an old French apple orchard high above the west bank of the River Auglaize. See: Darnell, Elias, Journal. Philadelphia: Lippincott, Grambo, and Co., 1854, pp. 28-29. Darnell adds on October 20, "The General issued an order for the troops to be assembled every morning at 9 o'clock, at such places near the encampment as the commanding officers might deem convenient, and cause the rolls to be called, and mark all delinquents; and there, until 12 o'clock, practice the manual exercise, and maneuver according to Smith's instructions for infantry." See also: Clift, G. Glenn. Remember the Raisin. Frankfort: Kentucky Historical Society, 1961, p. 37: The fort covered 3 acres and was located between First and Third Streets in what is now Defiance, Ohio. A tunnel led down to a timbered shelter at the bottom of the cliff to provide access to the river for water. More details can be found in "Fort Winchester," by Charles Slocum. Ohio Archaeological and Historical Publications, Vol. IX. Columbus: Heer Publishing Co., Ohio State Archaeological Society, 1901, pp. 253-277.

however, taking Johnson's regiment with him, General Edward W. Tupper's brigade of 800 mounted Ohio volunteers showed no sign of moving.

On October 5, some of Tupper's men were on the other side of the river when they noticed 20 or 30 Indians. Thinking they were allies, they allowed them to get too close. The warriors opened fire, killing one of Tupper's volunteers within 300 yards of his camp. A number of Tupper's men initiated a disorganized pursuit, but retreated before falling into a suspected ambush.

Upon their return, Tupper refused to budge from his camp, citing the threat of Indian ambush and arguing that it would distract him from his main mission of proceeding to the Maumee.[148] He also complained of damaged powder and a lack of supplies, even though his men were issued 8 days rations, including all the flour left in Winchester's camp. With no reserve of pre-rolled cartridges, Winchester resorted to taking fixed rounds from his own men under the pretense of conserving ammunition and discretely handed them over to Tupper's men.[149]

On October 7, an exasperated Winchester relieved Tupper and assigned Lt. Colonel Allen to replace him.[150] The Ohioans, however, refused to serve under a Kentuckian. Their enlistments up, 300 of Tupper's men left for home.[151]

---

148 Hearing gunfire, 200 of Tupper's men rushed to collect their grazing horses. Rounding them up, they mounted and chased off in groups of eight or ten in hot pursuit. They were mostly from Simrall's regiment, including Colonel Simrall, himself. Although one of the pursuing parties actually caught up with the Indians, they found themselves outnumbered and retreated five miles back to camp. Fearing more Indians might be lying in wait, Tupper forbid any more troops to cross the river. Five men out hunting wild plums had been killed and scalped, and he declined to risk another unruly pursuit.

149 Winchester, James. Historic Details Having Relation to the Campaign of the North-Western Army under Generals Harrison and Winchester. Lexington: Worsley & Smith, 1818, pp. 15-18. On the 6th, Tupper sent Logan and 6 other Indian scouts out, and they located a band of about 40 or 50 enemy warriors, but Tupper still refused to advance.

150 *Camp Defiance, Oct. 7, 1812, Brig. Gen'l Tupper — Delay, inconsistent with military operations, cannot longer be indulged. You will therefore immediately proceed on the duty ordered yesterday morning, with the troops under your command, exclusive of Colonel Simrall's corps, which shall return without delay to the settlements, for the purpose of recruiting their horses, agreeably to the orders of General Harrison. - J. Winchester, Brig. Gen. U.S. Army.* See also: Knopf, Richard C. "A Short Chronology of the War of 1812 in the Northwest." Columbus: Anthony Wayne Parkway Board and Ohio State Museum, 1960.

151 "We Lay There Doing Nothing: John Jackson's Recollection of the War of 1812," edited by Jeff L. Patrick, appearing in the Indiana Magazine of History, LXXXVIII, June, 1992, published by the Trustees of Indiana University: Around this time, Jackson's company went home on furlough. They would not return until after the Battle of the River Raisin the following January. *"We left our arms*

More Indians were spotted on the 9th, and Col. Wells led 500 men on a 12-mile pursuit on the 10th, which failed to locate any warriors. Reinstated to his command, Tupper broke camp "in a tumultuous manner," proposing to go to the rapids by way of the Odawa towns on Blanchard's Fork, but from there, he led his remaining 200 men to Urbana, where he arrived on October 11.

Tupper complained publicly that Winchester had wanted to send him on a dangerous fool's errand. Winchester demanded Tupper be arrested and an inquiry held, but Harrison refused to take any immediate action.[152]

British foray at the River Raisin, October 8-30, 1812:

Lt. Edward Dewar, of the British Quartermaster General's Department arrived at the Raisin with 25 militiamen accompanied by Roundhead and 14 Wyandots to support the British commissary officer there.[153]

No field estimates were available for the River Raisin, Swan Creek, or Otter Creek, as the settlers had been unable to take a quick survey since so many of their horses had been stolen by the Potawatomies and Delawares.[154]

---

and accoutrements with the Quartermaster and took our clothes in our knapsacks in order to have them washed at home, and started for our homes. Towards evening, we agreed to scatter in groups and not too many stop at one house. We were received very kindly by the inhabitants, and treated as well as it was in their power to do. We all arrived safely at our homes. The men that had families to enjoy the privilege of being with them, and the young men with their sweethearts, and all enjoyed themselves well, until it was time for us to start back. We did not go back in a body, a number being conveyed a considerable part of the way by their friends, in buggies and on horseback. Several of the men hired substitutes; they could readily be had for from 40 to 60 dollars. When we got to Urbana, General Tupper's Brigade had been ordered to march out to the frontier, and to take a stand at some suitable point and to act as frontier guard."

152 Winchester, James. Historic Details Having Relation to the Campaign of the North-Western Army under Generals Harrison and Winchester. Lexington: Worsley & Smith, 1818, pp. 16-18: An inquiry into Tupper's behavior was eventually held, but not until after Winchester had been captured by the enemy and couldn't testify. Winchester suspected Tupper's obstructionism was due to his loyalty to Harrison, adding to his belief that Harrison was deliberately starving the left wing of supplies because of their rivalry. See also: "Journal of Mathew Newsom," as transcribed by James Ohde, Ohio State Museum, Columbus: Anthony Wayne Parkway Board, 1957, p. 3: "Tupper accused Winchester of cowardice, bad management, etc." See also: Gilpin, Alec R., The War of 1812 in the Old Northwest, East Lansing: MSU Press, Bicentennial reprint, 2012, pp. 150-151.

153 Arriving in 1805 with the 100th Regiment from Dublin, Dewar participated in the capture of Detroit in August, 1812. He would die on December 12, due to a burst blood vessel. See: Irving, L. Humfray, Officers of the British Forces in Canada During the War of 1812, Welland Tribute Print., 1908.

154 These small streams (ruisseaux) varied in their spellings and could be referred to as petites rivières

Rivière au Cygne / Swan Creek

About 3,000 bushels of wheat had been harvested so far, but not yet threshed out. This seemed a small amount for such a large settlement. Much had been taken by the Indians, all of whom, except the Wyandots, having lost their corn crops to American marauders. The loss to French Town was not only in grain, but many cattle and hogs had also been destroyed.[155]

Dewar also learned that the local *habitants* had fomented an alarm as a ruse so they could steal back the cattle being collected there. Dewar and his men were able to round up only about 22 of the 50 head of cattle originally purchased by the British.[156]

To make up for the rustling, some armed and mounted River Raisin men offered to escort Dewar and the Wyandots on a reconnaissance to the rapids.

Dewar led them off towards the Maumee, proceeding cautiously along

---

or *criques*, but they broadened out as they flowed through the marshes and into Lake Erie. Their names could be rendered into singular or plural forms, as well.

155 Letter Dewar to M'Donnal, 10-19-1812, Michigan Pioneer & Historical Collections, Vol. XV, 160-71. (See also: Cruikshank's Harrison & Proctor, Draper manuscripts.)

156 Au, Dennis. War on the Raisin. Monroe, Monroe County Historical Commission, 1981, p. 20-21. The Raisin was looked on as a bread basket for the British forces. The first habitations began 2 or 3 miles up the meandering stream from its mouth on the shores of Lake Erie. From there, the farmsteads extended along both sides of the river for about 12 miles. Beyond them were several Native-American villages and a Potawatomi reservation established in 1807. Extensive trade was carried on with these Indians and with those along the St. Joseph River and Lake Michigan. Unfortunately, the war had disrupted the southern trade routes along the Lake Erie Coast and down the Maumee to Fort Wayne and beyond.

Rivière aux Loutres / Otter Creek

sandy trails through savannahs and open oak plains, and across several streams, including Otter Creek.

Stony Creek, Sandy Creek, and Swan Creek were fordable all year, with good, firm bottoms. At *La Loutre* (Otter Creek) many farms had been destroyed after the fall of Detroit, but there were still people living there and a good anchorage for boats.[157]

They reached the rapids that evening, without seeing the tracks of a single enemy. Here, they encountered a couple *Canadiens* who told them no Americans had been seen since Muir's retreat from Fort Wayne. Fearing the area would be occupied by the enemy, it was decided to destroy any homes and supplies which remained there.

The Indians were pretty thorough, but they left one particular building standing, a house belonging to Jean-Baptiste Beaugrand. They had planned to destroy that house as well, but Beaugrand was granted time to remove his personal belongings.

There was a lot of corn in the fields, plus potatoes, oats, and wheat in stock. Cattle and hogs were running loose. The Indians went to work with great abandon, shooting so many hogs that the stench of rotting meat became almost intolerable.[158]

---

157 Brown, Samuel, Views of the Campaigns of the North-Western Army, Troy, NY: Francis Adancourt, 1814.

158 "Lewis Bond's Journal," in Knopf, Richard C. Document Transcriptions of the War of 1812 in the Northwest, Vol. X, Pt. 1. Columbus: Ohio Historical Society, 1962, p. 190.

Dewar sent a couple men across the river to scout Hull's Road, while he took Roundhead and two of his braves to explore upriver.

The rest of the men were left to drive in cattle which had been abandoned in great numbers. They were only able to catch about 20 of the 200 they saw. The animals were just too skittish after being shot at so many times by roving bands of Indians.

Roundhead cut an imposing figure as he rode alongside Dewar. Six-feet-tall and broad-chested, he carried himself as straight as an arrow. His forehead was finely formed, and his cheek bones were just prominent enough to give him an air of intelligence and dignity. His skin was dark, and his head was shaved, except for a scalp lock, which bobbed as he spoke to Dewar with the help of an interpreter. A Wyandot of the Porcupine Clan, his Indian name, *Sti-yeh-tuok*, meant Bark Carrier.

At the upper rapids, Dewar ran into a scouting party of Mascons and Creeks. The Creeks, originally from Florida, were part of a camp that had fallen behind as Muir's force retreated and were now undecided about whether to continue. Dewar talked them into heading back with him to Fort Amherstburg.

In the morning, they were joined by some Kickapoos who said they had taken a scalp while scouting a force of 800 ill-supplied American troops building a blockhouse about 3 miles above Fort Defiance.

Returning to the River Raisin on September 16, Dewar took stock of the situation. The *Canadiens* at the Maumee had estimated there were still some 8,000 bushels of unharvested corn standing in the fields. He would recommend to Colonel Henry Procter that Colonel Elliott and his 800 Indians be sent from Amherstburg to the Rapids to bring in all the grain and supplies they could find.

So, on October 30, 1812, Col. Matthew Elliott embarked for the Maumee with 250 Potawatomies and Delawares in 2 small gunboats, the schooner *Queen Charlotte*, and a number of bateaux.

Meanwhile, at Brownstown, Roundhead was preparing to lead a mounted band of Wyandots south along Hull's Road to French Town. From there, he was to go on to join Mathew Elliott's force at the Maumee Rapids.

To cover the Indian advance to the Rapids, Procter dispatched the 13-gun schooner, *Lady Prevost,* to cruise off Sandusky. She would create a general alarm and distract American forces as far as the Huron River of Lake Erie.[159]

The Americans at Fort Defiance, October 17-29, 1812:

Elias Darnell reported that his company moved into unfinished Fort Winchester, where they received salt, flour, and whisky. On the morning of the 16th, 100 men were detailed to find a suitable location to build pirogues. They settled on a site some 6 miles downriver.

At daybreak on October 17th, a large party of mounted volunteers left Defiance at a brisk trot, bound for Jenning's blockhouse on the Auglaize. Their mission was to fetch the valuable supplies stored there.

They made 35 miles that day and made camp for the night. The men built fires to keep the mosquitoes at bay, but had nothing to cook for their supper. The howling of wolves kept them awake until all the fires had died or been put out.

The next day they traveled the remaining 5 miles and found the blockhouse loaded with plenty of provisions. The next morning, with the help of Captain Daniel Garrard's infantry company, they loaded a string of pack horses with bacon, flour, and other items. That night, they made camp in the rain.

The following morning, the troops were assembled and ordered to fire off their weapons to empty them. Not a single flintlock went off, and the men had to pull their wet charges with ball pullers attached to their ramrods. They arrived at Winchester's camp after dark.[160]

During this time, Winchester's troops had finished work on the

---

159 Cruikshank, Lt. Col. E. A., Harrison & Proctor; The River Raisin, from the Transactions of the Royal Society of Canada, Vol. IV, Section II, Ottawa: Royal Society of Canada, 1911, p. 137. Procter's hold over his Indian allies seemed based largely on his control of British supplies and troops - and that was limited. Pouring over his latest troop returns, Procter noted he had 30 Royal Artillerymen, 256 regulars of the 41st Regiment of Foot, and 117 fencibles of the Royal Newfoundland Regiment available for duty. With Captain Muir on the sick list, he was down to 6 company-level officers. Procter had some serious doubts about the quality of leadership the British Indian Department could provide. Elliott was highly capable, but over 70 years old and in declining health. Colonel McKee was next in seniority. He was brave and influential, but his fondness for liquor had undermined his health and judgement.

160 Major James Garrard and Captains William and Daniel Garrard were the sons of former Governor James Garrard of Kentucky. See: CLIFT, G. GLENN. "WAR OF 1812 DIARY OF WILLIAM B. NORTHCUTT." *The Register of the Kentucky Historical Society* 56, no. 2 (1958): 165-80. Accessed April 19, 2021. http://www.jstor.org/stable/23374326.

fortifications and had started building boats to transport their supplies down the Maumee to the Rapids. The fort was christened "Fort Winchester" on October 19th. On the 20th, Winchester sent a message to Quartermaster Bodley to speed up the supplies. The storerooms were ready, but empty, and there were enough boats to carry 200 barrels of flour.

Several days later, Captain William Garrard's dragoons were detached for service with Major Ball's squadron. The Maumee River was rising and morale was high in expectation that the whole army would soon be on the move. While they waited, the troops held roll call every morning at 9 o'clock, followed by a 3-hour practice according to Smyth's Instructions for Infantry.[161]

By October 23, Winchester was chomping at the bit. He wrote Bodley again, saying the army was about to advance and needed more salt. He also wanted a few thousand hogs to be driven in, to be slaughtered and salted down. Beef on the hoof was no longer adequate. They were getting too lean, and it would be too expensive to pack their meat in barrels.[162]

---

161 *"I have had the honor to receive your dispatch of the 21st Inst., which has been read with attention and concern, to learn that reasons exist to delay the advance of this army, which is in high spirits and anxious to approach the lines of the enemy...The Kentucky Volunteers are now pretty well disciplined, and I am satisfied that I hazard nothing as an officer in saying there is not in the United States a more efficient Militia than the three Kentucky Regiments now at this place; and I feel reluctant in communicating to the ardent spirits which compose this army the idea of a moment's delay in the great work of retaliation..."* - Letter dated Oct. 26, 1812, in the William Henry Harrison Papers: Winchester reported that his spies had returned the day before with news that the settlement at the Maumee Rapids was being abandoned and burned, hundreds of acres of corn were left in the fields, and livestock was running loose. He was planning to leave Defiance before the river was blocked by the ice, move his army down to the Rapids, and build a strong camp there. He had 16 pirogues and some packhorses to carry 73,000 rations of flour and 25,000 rations of whisky, plus 48 wagons to transport all their baggage, 70,000 rations of beef, and 200,000 rations of salt. More pirogues could be built. Beef and pork could be driven on the hoof.

162 Winchester, James. Historic Details Having Relation to the Campaign of the North-Western Army under Generals Harrison and Winchester. Lexington: Worsley & Smith, 1818, pp. 18-19: In the West, a disheartened Brigadier-General Samuel Hopkins was discharging his troops at Vincennes on October 25. They had caused him nothing but trouble since Kentucky Governor Shelby sent them to relieve the settlers of Indiana Territory. Hopkins had marched these men across the Wabash to attack a Kickapoo village on the Illinois River, but he became so disgusted with their behavior that he had felt compelled to retreat to Vincennes. The territory they traversed was so unknown that even his experienced guides, Toussaint Dubois and Joseph Baron, had to admit they were lost. Their 10-days rations were running low and they had found no Indians to attack. After a prairie fire almost destroyed their camp, the men decided to retreat on their own, leaving Hopkins to follow along with a rear guard.
Meanwhile, Colonel Russell, accompanied by Indiana Governor Edwards, was leading over 300 men to rendezvous with Hopkins near Peoria. Failing to find him, Russell bypassed Peoria and

Although hampered by rainy weather, training continued apace.[163] Sloppiness on guard duty was no longer tolerated. Sentries were no longer permitted to sit down near a fire, where the warmth could put them to sleep.[164]

The men's health was a major concern. Each day, a subaltern from each regiment was detailed as camp police to preserve cleanliness. All putrid matter was removed and the tents were swept out. Blankets, bedding, and clothes were aired out in fair weather. Racks were built inside each tent to keep firearms out of the elements and away from the moist ground. Quartermasters were to see that fresh dirt was thrown into the privies and fresh brush cut and placed around them. One or two pit toilets were dug near the fort.[165]

Winter clothing supplies were supposedly on the way. On the 27th, Harrison announced that shipments had been sent from Philadelphia on the 9th of September. Unfortunately, most of the supplies would never arrive.[166]

---

attacked and burned a Kickapoo village some 20 miles further north.

163 Several different training manuals were used by the Americans during the War of 1812. VonSteuben's drill from the Revolutionary War remained in use by many militia units, but Smyth's and Duane's regulations were adopted by the regular military. General Winchester's army used Smyth's, which was based on the French regulations of 1791, but contained elements of Von Steuben and was adapted to fit the conditions in North America. The British army followed Col. David Dundas' 1792 manual, with some variations for the militia.

164 Adjutant Logan's Orderly Book, Winchester Papers, Burton Historical Collection, Detroit Public Library: On Oct. 28, Private Thomas Smith of Captain Mead's Company was recorded as guilty of falling asleep at his post and sentenced to 15 cobs on the bare posterior with a paddle 4" wide and ½" thick, bored full of holes. In another case, however, General Winchester remitted the 10-cob sentence of James Givins from Groghan's Company, who had been caught sitting down on guard duty, apparently asleep, gun out of his hands, on October 25.

Atherton mentions another punishment meted out to a deserter who was made to ride the "wooden horse," which in this case was a sapling bent over with its top fixed to the ground.

A man from Langhorne's company was caught sleeping on sentry duty. His excuse was that if he felt comfortable falling asleep, the rest of the camp should not worry about it either. He was sentenced to stand atop the breastwork for 2 hours and be jeered by the rest of the men. See: CLIFT, G. GLENN. "WAR OF 1812 DIARY OF WILLIAM B. NORTHCUTT." *The Register of the Kentucky Historical Society* 56, no. 2 (1958): 165-80. Accessed April 19, 2021. http://www.jstor.org/stable/23374326.

165 General Orders, Oct. 25, 1812, Winchester Papers, Mich. Pioneer & Historical Collections, Vol.35, p. 278. News also had come in of the disintegration of General Hopkins' volunteer army at Vincennes, which endangered Winchester's supply lines. Morale remained high in Winchester's camp, however, despite sickness, shortages of supplies, and Harrison's cancellation of their advance to the Rapids.

166 Darnell, Elias, Journal, Philadelphia: Lippincott, Grambo, and Co., 1854, pp. 28-29: *"Yet a few days, and the General consoles himself with the idea of seeing those whom he has the honor to command clad in warm woolen, capable of resisting the northern blasts of Canada."* These included 10,000 pairs of shoes, woolen hose, and socks, 5,000 wool pantaloons, 5,000 round jackets, and 5,000

Winchester's men were also getting news from the papers, which often did not improve their morale. It made McCalla rather "down in the mouth" to read articles criticizing Madison, the administration, and the prosecution of the war. His anger turned to depression at comments favoring peace.

John McCalla had just received a letter from his parents and another from Captain Gaines, so he immediately sat down to write his replies. He was proud of the patriotism expressed by his father, and contrasted it with the news they had received of the attitude of the people of the New England states.

McCalla's pen scratched out the sentiments of many of his comrades: *"I have just received your letter by P. Bain. I never so much admired your patriotism as I did when perusing your letter. What a pity that a great many of the New England Folks... are idly and ignobly hanging back and suffering others to step forward...And now Ohio and K. Y. are far before theirs. They are discussing who shall be our next President; we are contending who shall have Canada."*[167]

The captain also testified to his relationship with the slaves and servants who accompanied some of the Kentucky officers, and to the familiar African Americans he had left behind at home: *"We have just joined in a mess with Lt. Caldwell and Ensign Bourne of Price's Company. They have two of the*

---

blankets. A thousand warm watch-coats had been ordered, as well as complete sets of uniform clothing for Colonel Wells' regiment. See also: Reynolds Narrative in Coffin, William F., 1812: The War and its Moral; A Canadian Chronicle, Montreal: John Lovell, 1864: Harrison had consolidated the Ohio troops under Generals Beall and Wadsworth, placed them under the command of General Perkins and ordered them to proceed to Lower Sandusky. From there they were supposed to build a road to the Maumee Rapids, through the Great Black Swamp, which would require no less than 15 miles of causeway. By now, General Harrison had fully realized the difficulty of moving materiel through the Black Swamp and was considering the use of sleds to transport supplies between Sandusky and the River Raisin along the margin of Lake Erie, once ice had formed for the winter. Harrison had redesigned his logistical system by constructing it along several routes, rather than concentrating on improving Hull's road. See also: Gilpin, Alec R., The War of 1812 in the Old Northwest, East Lansing, MSU Press, 2012 edition, p. 157.

167 Letter John McClellan (or McCalla) to parents, Ft. Winchester, Oct. 29, 1812, typescript copy in 1812 Military Collections, Monroe County Historical Museum Archives. McCalla also tried to reassure his parents, commenting in a letter home that *"Our situation here is rather enviable...Scarcely a day passes, in which we do not catch some fine fish. I have caught 40 or 50 fine fellows since I arrived at this camp that would average 2 pounds. They are pike, salmon, and bass, or black perch. We have generally 8 or 10 lying by us in our fish barrel. Our principal want is bacon to cook with them...Mr. Clark says he wants nothing except chocolate, which he will get when the clothing arrives...Our sugar is also just out. Would you believe it? I drink coffee in an equal if not greater quantity than Mr. Clark..."*

finest servants I know of... Remember me also to Jeffery, Jerry, Henry, James, and all the other black friends... "[168]

American Militiamen at the 200th Anniversary of the River Raisin Battle
Photo by Bill Saul

The William Walker Incident, Winchester's Camp, October 27, 1812:

On October 29, a prisoner by the name of William Walker was brought in. Walker was married to a Wyandot woman, and had lived among them for 3 decades. When William Walker arrived at Winchester's camp, he was immediately recognized and seized as a spy.

Nonetheless, Walker protested his arrest, claiming that he had served the American cause as an Indian Agent for William Hull. After the fall of Detroit, he had escaped the British authorities and fled to the American army at Defiance.

Ironically, some of his family members were now in British custody, while he was a prisoner of the Americans.[169]

---

168 Letter John McClellan (or McCalla) to parents, Ft. Winchester, Oct. 29, 1812, typescript copy in 1812 Military Collections, Monroe County Historical Museum Archives. It was not uncommon for the officers to come from slave-holding families. Capt. Richard Hightower, for example, owned eight slaves. The army's commander, General James Winchester, owned dozens of slaves who worked on his plantation at Cragfont in Tennessee.

169 Cruikshank's Harrison & Proctor, p. 139. See also: "Notes on Wyandot and Gen. William Walker," 11-U,13–14(1–2), Draper MS., Joseph Regenstein Library, University of Chicago. William Walker

Although he was unaware of all the details about Walker's evasion, Captain McCalla was glad to hear his report that Sergeant McCoy had not been killed as assumed on September 24, but was being held prisoner at Malden.

Walker also reported that 8 or 10 Indians had been killed during the recent skirmishing, but the warriors were too quick and always retrieved the bodies before the Kentuckians could take their scalps.

For his part, Captain John McCalla thought Walker was French-Canadian, and noted that he was armed indifferently and carried a knapsack.

Several men in camp swore they had been in Detroit at Hull's surrender, and that they had seen him outside the fort, dressed and painted as an Indian.

On the other hand, nobody could actually recall any hostile actions on Walker's part, nor could they disprove his statement that he had been arrested by the redcoats for his efforts to warn the Wyandots that they should drop their alliance with the British or face ruin from the American army.

He claimed to have been confined in a guardhouse at Detroit, pending transfer to a more secure prison. Walker's guards routinely let him out of his cell to warm himself by the fire until the beating of Tattoo.

While sitting there one evening, Walker made a break for it while the guards were preoccupied with a bucket of cider. Slipping out the door, he ran to the ramparts and sneaked between two sentries who had just turned their backs to walk away from each other.

He wasn't hailed till he had already scaled two rows of pickets. Walker did not stop, and the guards did not fire at him as he scrambled out of the ditch and made a ¾-mile dash for the shelter of the woods.

After obtaining a horse from his friend, Jacob Visger, and sending word to his family, Walker headed for Defiance, crossing a hundred miles of swamps, tangled thickets, and brushy ponds.

Major Chambers, commanding the British garrison, and Colonel Elliott, head of the British Indian Department, got in a row over the incident. They put a price on his head, dead or alive, but search parties failed to find the

---

had been adopted by the Indians and settled at Gros Roche (Big Rock, now Gibraltar) about 1790. He married Catherine Rankin and had 7 children. At the beginning of the war, he helped repulse a British raid, but was forced to flee when pro-British Wyandots took over. His oldest son, John R., was wounded at Brownstown and taken prisoner by the British at Detroit. After much pleading, Mrs. Walker got Roundhead to obtain the release of their son. On this current occasion, William Walker was taken prisoner by the Americans, but General Harrison intervened to set him free, on condition that he join his expedition against Canada.

fugitive. Assistance was requested from the Wyandots, but they refused to track down one of their own.

While taking a break in his flight to rest his horse and eat lunch, Walker was surprised by two Potawatomies. One was middle-aged; the other a 19-year-old. Fearing to give himself away by speaking Wyandot, Delaware, or even English, Walker asked in Shawnee if they were on their way to fight the Long Knives.

The older man answered in the negative, saying they were returning to Malden. Walker then asked if they would accompany him to Defiance, instead, and help him capture some prisoners. When they declined, Walker jumped on his horse and sped away, calling them to *"Come on!"*

Looking back, he saw the Potawatomies were not following, so he eased his horse's pace and headed for Winchester's army.

Walker's encounter with Winchester's patrols was less successful. They immediately disarmed him and arrested him as a British spy.

Eventually, he got a letter to General Harrison, who ordered his release. Afterwards, General Winchester offered to take him on as a scout, but Walker refused, saying, *"What do you want with a British Spy? No, sir, no. I will not connect my fate with such an army."*[170]

Winchester's Camp, November 1 — December 1, 1812:

Twenty-one-year-old William Atherton looked on with disgust at the disarray in the American army. The promised winter uniforms had not arrived, and the weather was turning cold. Some militiamen, their enlistments up, had left for home. Others were being struck down left and right by a sudden outbreak of typhus. About 300 became sick, with 3 or 4 dying every day.[171]

---

170 Lyman Draper manuscript, Joseph Regenstein Library, University of Chicago. Back in Detroit, Walker's second son, Isaac, was seized by the British, in lieu of his father. Mrs. Walker appealed to Roundhead, who went to Colonel Procter and obtained his release, over the objections of Colonel Elliott.

171 Darnell, p. 129. See also: Atherton, William. Narrative of the Suffering and Defeat of the North-Western Army under General Winchester. Frankfort, KY.: A. G. Hodges, 1842, p. 17.

    Men were continually wandering out of camp to hunt or scavenge. No Indians had been seen for days, so the troops had become quite careless. Sometimes they left without taking any weapons. The army had run out of bread and was subsisting on poor beef and hickory roots.

    Discipline was becoming lax, although punishments continued. The troops were formed into a hollow square to observe the execution of Frederick Jacoby, who had been sentenced to death for falling asleep at his post. The men watched nervously as the provost guard marched

The troops had been in camp since September, and it looked like they might be there for several months more. The army was wasting away. Many of the men were so destitute of shoes, they couldn't have gone anywhere.[172]

The beef cattle were in such a weak state that it became a running joke for their Dutch butcher to call for help to hold up the selected animal so it could be shot.[173] Because of the constant need to supplement the rations by hunting, there was not a solitary squirrel left alive anywhere near the camp.[174]

Fortunately, the Maumee River abounded with fish. Great quantities were caught with nets and also by hook and line.[175] A few luxuries could be obtained from sutlers at prices set by the commanding general.[176]

The men were waiting for word from General Harrison for an advance on Detroit. Harrison, however, was still gathering supplies and troops. Not much could be done, anyway, until the icy winds of winter transformed the streams and the great lake into frozen highways.[177]

---

the condemned member of the 17th U.S. Infantry in front of them to a mournful tune. An ensign, sergeant and corporal led the 20-man firing squad, which halted and formed, ready to fire. The prisoner was led out a few paces, blindfolded and made to kneel on the ground. Minutes seemed like hours, but a few seconds before the fatal moment, a reprieve arrived. Winchester had judged him to be not of sound mind.

172 Hosmer, Hezekiah Lord. Early History of the Maumee Valley. Toledo: Hosmer and Harris, 1858, p. 34: *The other wing of the army was encamped at Upper Sandusky, more than one hundred miles distant and only accessible by a march through the pathless wilderness.*

173 Speech of General Leslie Combs at the 1872 Veterans Reunion in Monroe. Forage being limited, beef cattle were driven to Fort Winchester to be slaughtered, butchered, salted, and put up in barrels. See: Gilpin, Alec R., The War of 1812 in the Old Northwest, East Lansing, MSU Press, 2012 edition, p. 157.

174 Atherton, William, Narrative of the Suffering & Defeat of the North-Western Army under General Winchester. Frankfort, KY, A. G. Hodges, 1842, pp. 16-19.

175 Darnell, Elias, Journal. Philadelphia: Lippincott, Grambo, and Co., 1854, p. 32.

176 General Orders, Winchester Papers, Michigan Pioneer & Historical Collections, Vol. 35, p. 284. Tobacco was available for 50 cents a pound; whisky, for 50 cents a quart. Tea ran $3 a pound; chocolate, 75 cents a pound; and coffee, 62 ½ cents a pound.

177 Letter Harrison to Sec. of War, Franklinton, Oct. 22, 1812: *"I am not able to fix any period for the advance of the troops to Detroit. It is pretty evident that it cannot be done upon proper principles until the frost shall become so severe as to enable us to use the river and margin of the lake for the transportation of the baggage and provisions upon the ice. To get them forward through a swampy wilderness of nearly 200 miles in wagons or on pack-horses which are to carry their own provender, is absolutely impossible...It is certain, however, that no species of supplies are to be calculated upon being found in the Michigan Territory. The farms upon the River Raisin which might have afforded a quantity of forage are nearly all broken up, and the grain destroyed. This article then, as well as the provisions for the men, is to be taken from this state — a circumstance which...would require at least two wagons with forage for each one that is loaded with provisions...My present plan is to occupy Sandusky and to accumulate as much provision and forage as possible at that place to be taken*

The army, however, could not remain forever in place. On November 2, the corps crossed to the north bank of the Maumee River and established Camp Number 2, where there was a more abundant wood supply. Although sheltered from northerly and westerly winds, the spot was too wet, and Winchester soon began looking for dryer ground a few miles further down the river.[178]

Winchester planned to proceed gradually downstream, building new fortified camps along the way. He knew the movement would have to be slow, as there were only enough wagons to transport the baggage of one regiment at a time. His men were weak with fevers due to the cold, wet weather and swampy ground.

On November 9th, the general ordered each regiment to build 4 pirogues to transport the heavy baggage. On the 10th, Winchester advanced 6 miles forward and built Camp Number 3, where there was plenty of timber for constructing boats or sleds.[179]

At the beating of reveille on the 15th, Winchester sent Colonel Lewis out towards the Maumee Rapids on a reconnaissance in response to a call for support from General Tupper.[180]

On the 16th, General Winchester sent a party of 50 men to Jenning's blockhouse to acquire more supplies for his army.[181]

Contrary to the expectations of the men, the bulk of the army would

---

upon sleds from thence to the River Raisin...The troops at Fort Defiance might advance to the Miami Rapids in a few days. I do not believe, however, that any great advantage would arise from it until the other columns are ready to support them, and it would be productive of the certain disadvantage of consuming provisions forwarded with immense labor and expense, without essentially contributing to the main design..."

178 A marker for the site can be found on E. River Drive in Defiance.

179 The second week in November, Captain Ballard noted deterioration in the condition of their firearms. Officers were ordered to inspect them and have loaded weapons with bad powder delivered to the artificers to be breached and the loads removed. Afterwards, the owners were required to clean them but not reload them until formed for the march or assembled for guard duty.

180 The detachment was composed of 6 captains, 6 subalterns, 6 sergeants, 6 corporals, and 386 privates, carrying 6 days' rations. See the Orderly Book of Captain Bland Ballard, Winchester Papers, Burton Historical Collection, Detroit Public Library. See page 74 for details of this event.

181 The movement, however, was reported to the British and Indians under Colonel Elliott at the Rapids, who became alarmed and requested Colonel Procter to reinforce his foraging party with troops and artillery.

remain stationary for the next 7 or 8 weeks, and Camp Number 3 would come to be known as "Fort Starvation."

Captain John McCalla remained stationed at Camp Number 3, still waiting for orders to join the advance on Detroit, orders that seemed never to come. The days had turned to weeks that blended into one another, so that the young captain had difficulty recalling when, and to whom, he had last written.

There really wasn't much to report, except for the lack of supplies and the sickness among the troops. Forty-nine men were listed as unfit for duty, and that was probably 10 short of those who were actually too ill to work. Three or four officers were down as well.[182]

Many were too weak to even think of their loved ones so far away. They just lay on the cold ground, listening to the noise of the camp. Some of them died in this sad state, including Captain McCalla's friend, Will Barkley.[183]

To make the best use of their limited clothing supply, 75 pairs of mittens and all the watch coats in the army were set aside for the exclusive use of the sentinels on duty. When relieved, the sentries would turn their coats over to their replacements, or hand them in to the officer of the guard to be returned to the supply officer. The rest of the mittens, socks, and shoes, were divided among Winchester's 4 regiments, with any remaining clothing to be shared by the 3 militia regiments.

There was also support from home. Letters were still arriving, and one in particular had caught McCalla's attention as he sat listening to his comrades singing near the end of the day. The letter concerned a certain Annie. His face still flushed when he thought of her.[184]

---

182 Winchester's troops occupied Camp No. 3 through the months of November and December. Located on the north bank of the Maumee, about 6 miles below Fort Winchester, the camp covered 40 acres and was protected by picketing and earthen corner bastions. Independence Dam State Park contains a marker and a monument for soldiers from Ohio and Kentucky.

183 Accidents were one of the hazards of the daily routine. Perry Hawkins, for example, was seriously injured when a tree limb fell on his head. Discipline or the lack thereof, was also a potential problem. Not noted for military courtesy to begin with, McCalla's fellow militiamen had been pushed hard by forced marches, poor food and clothing, and waiting around for action which never came. Yet, it wasn't as bad as one might think. The men usually performed their duties cheerfully, and they still had their amusements. Music lifted morale, so singing and instrumentals were often heard along the line.

184 Letter of John McCalla, Nov. 25, 1812, original in Monroe County Historical Archives. He was relieved to learn that his previous letter to her had not been summarily rejected by her father. Not that there was much in his original letter to alarm anyone. He had not dared to express any

By December 1st, the men were making huts that could keep out the elements much better than simple army tents. Even musicians were detailed for construction duty and given double rations of pork and salt in lieu of flour.[185]

Detail from Ken Osen's Diorama of Mounted Kentucky Riflemen at the former River Raisin Battlefield National Park Visitor Center
Photo by Author, Courtesy National Park Service

---

intimacies or suggest in any way the special feelings he had for her. In fact, he had spent most of his letter making excuses for writing her. He had, however, summoned up enough courage to ask her to write him back. True, he knew her mostly by appearance. After all, he hadn't had much chance to really explore her character. Nonetheless, he found her image intruding more and more into his daily thoughts. McCalla was so flattered by the compliments he had received from his superiors and comrades that he would endure any danger or hardship to retain their approval.

185 Darnell, Elias, Journal. Philadelphia: Lippincott, Grambo, and Co., 1854, p. 37. Orders for December 2 were to cut and sharpen 9-foot pickets, and sink them into a trench 18 inches deep to form a ¾-mile rectangle pierced by two gates and enfiladed by 12-foot square bastions at each corner. The men worked hard and almost completed the entire project in a single day, reducing the number of guards needed to protect the camp. Wells' regiment occupied the right in the traditional position of honor reserved for the regulars. Scott's, Lewis' and part of Allen's regiments covered the front, while the remainder of Allen's regiment held the left. They were on the north bank of the Maumee River, which protected the rear of their camp. See also: General Orders, Nov. 28, 1812, Winchester Papers, Michigan Pioneer & Historical Collections, Vol. 35, p. 297. The orders included the drum and fife majors.

STRUGGLE FOR THE RAPIDS
OF THE MAUMEE RIVER

Maumee Rapids, a little before sunset, November 7, 1812:

Captain Thomas Clark, a British Indian Department interpreter, was out for a late afternoon of hunting, while the Indians were still busy killing hogs and harvesting the corn. Little did he suspect he would soon become a target.[186]

As the light began to fade, Capt. Clark moved off into a cornfield, stalking a flock of wild turkeys. Concentrating on his quarry, Clark never noticed Captain Hinkston and his scouts stalking him.

Suddenly, they were on him. Before he could think of calling for help, or discharging his musket, he felt a knife pricking at his throat. Without a sound, he was bundled off down Hull's Road to Fort McArthur, 75 miles away.[187]

Interpreter Clark talked freely. Besides women and children, the Native Americans at the Maumee Rapids did not exceed 250 Chippewa, Odawa, and Potawatomi warriors, who had come in canoes or on British boats, along with 50 British regulars. In addition, they were expecting 60 Wyandots to ride in from Brownstown. The foraging expedition was expected to last from 10 to 15 days.

Given this information, General Edward White Tupper decided to mount a raid against the rapids. With luck, he could rout the enemy and save the greater part of the valuable corn for his own men.[188]

---

186 Interpreter Clark was from Colonel Elliott's force of several hundred Native people, 50 whites, 2 gunboats, 6 bateaux, and a small schooner which was being assembled near the Rapids to forage for supplies along the Maumee. Some of the Indians had commenced their work, just as the boats were moving in to tie up along the riverbank.

187 Cruikshank, Lt. Col. E. A., Harrison & Proctor; The River Raisin, from the Transactions of the Royal Society of Canada, Vol. IV, Section II, Ottawa: Royal Society of Canada, 1911, pp. 138-9.

188 Letter Harrison to Secretary of War Eustis, Oct. 13, 1812: Back in October, General Harrison had directed "...General Tupper to proceed with the mounted men to the Rapids, and if he should think proper, from the information he should there receive, as far as the River Raisin..."
See also: Knopf, Richard, Document Transcriptions of the War of 1812 in the Northwest, Vol. X, pt. 1. Columbus: Ohio Historical Society, 1962, pp. 1-3: Biographical sketch by A. T. Nye, Dec., 1870: 41-year-old General Edward White Tupper was born in Massachusetts, but had moved to Marietta, Ohio, with his parents as a teenager. His father was a Revolutionary War veteran, and his brother, a major in command of the Marietta garrison at Campus Martius. He had made his living as a merchant, a court clerk for Washington County, and a surveyor of the lands ceded by the Indians. He had been appointed a Brigadier General of the Ohio Militia in 1807. Shortly

Sending a courier to inform Winchester and request his support, Tupper set off from Fort McArthur on November 10th with more than 600 enthusiastic volunteers (two-thirds of his available troops) and a light 6-pounder field gun drawn by 6 horses to deal with the reported enemy gunboats.[189]

With each man carrying his blanket and a knapsack containing 5-days' worth of pre-cooked provisions, he expected to travel 30 miles a day and reach the rapids in a couple days, beating Winchester by at least a day.[190]

Peoria, November 9, 1812:

The village of Peoria and its environs had been inhabited by the French and Indians since the 17th century. Due to their close association with the Potawatomies, the American authorities believed the French inhabitants were secretly aiding and abetting Native raids against American settlements.

In October, Illinois Governor Tinian Edwards led a mounted expedition that burned Black Partridge's abandoned village near the upper shore of Lake Peoria. They skirmished with the Potawatomies in the surrounding area.

In November, an American force under Captain Thomas E. Craig arrived by boat and anchored in the river across from Peoria village, which contained less than 100 inhabitants at that time.

During the course of the evening, some random shots were fired at the boats. There were no casualties, but Captain Craig angrily demanded that the villagers hand over the culprits. The local residents vehemently denied that their people had any involvement in the affair.

Craig backed off, but cunningly waited until the inhabitants were attending Sunday Mass. He and his men then stormed the village, seizing and pillaging the inhabitants' homes, along with the trading house of Thomas Forsyth, the local U.S. Government Indian agent.

Forsyth and the village priest were able to halt the looting, but not before a number of cattle were killed, several wine cellars were emptied, and half the town was in flames.

The troops arrested 41 men, women, and children and took them away

---

thereafter, he had moved to Gallipolis, where he was living when the war broke out in 1812.

189 "Journal of Mathew Newsom," as transcribed by James Ohde, Ohio State Museum, Columbus: Anthony Wayne Parkway Board, 1957, p. 8. Fort McArthur was located north of Urbana near present-day Kenton, Ohio.

190 Letter Tupper to Harrison, Nov.9, 1812. Tupper felt he had sufficient force to win on his own, and speed was of the essence. Tupper would strike the Maumee on November 15, 1812.

on their boats. The prisoners were released 4 days later by order of Governor Edwards and abandoned in bad weather with little food or clothing.

Unrepentant, Captain Craig would later boast of burning the town and evicting the residents. To him, they were a bunch of rascals, and they were lucky he didn't have them all killed and scalped. The destruction of Peoria was followed by the erection of Fort Clark the following year and a subsequent postwar invasion of Anglo-American settlers.

Among the so-called "rascals," however, were the likes of Antoine LeClaire, who went on to found the city of Davenport, Iowa, and Marguerite LaCroix, who would marry John Reynolds, the future governor of Illinois.

Some of the French traders would return to the site, but this was the beginning of the end for French Peoria. It was also the beginning of a legal struggle for compensation on the part of the dispossessed and their descendants, based on deeds dating back as far as the old French Régime.[191]

Detroit, under the occupation, November 14, 1812:

Back on August 21, Colonel Procter had issued a proclamation to regulate the government of Michigan under British occupation. Territorial officials who still remained at Detroit were allowed to retain their positions.

In an effort to maintain an orderly transition to British rule within the ceded territory, Woodward had accepted the position of Secretary of the Territory, which effectively made him the acting civil governor. He had done this to protect the inhabitants of Michigan and see to their welfare, but many were now calling him a traitor for collaborating with the occupying power.[192]

---

191 Even Abraham Lincoln would be involved as a lawyer in handling some of the litigation dating into the 1850s. The suits would hinder the development of the city of Peoria and result in the payment of thousands of dollars to the claimants. The last claim would be settled in 1867. See: "Fort Clark Constructed at Peoria in 1813" by Mark Johnson, Peoria Historical Society, Peoria Magazine, January, 2011. See also: French Peoria and the Illinois Country, 1673-1846 by Judith A. Franke, *Illinois State Museum Popular Science Series*, Vol. XII, Springfield: Illinois State Museum, 1995, p. 95. The city of Davenport, Iowa, was founded in 1836 by Antoine LeClaire, one of the refugees from Peoria. See: Foxcurran, Bouchard, and Malette, Songs Upon the Rivers, Montréal: Baraka Books, 2016, p. 252, and Gitlin, Jay, The Bourgeois Frontier, New Haven: Yale University Press, 2010, p. 66.

192 "Lewis Bond's Journal," in Knopf, Richard C. Document Transcriptions of the War of 1812 in the Northwest, Vol. X, Pt. 1. Columbus: Ohio Historical Society, 1962, p. 191-2: One of Woodward's most implacable critics was Lewis Bond, who wrote, *"The other civil officers, such as remained in the country, declined serving, and no American citizen could be found abandoned enough to accept an office under Proctor, the execrable Mr. Woodward excepted…He is certainly an intriguing man…I*

Today the judge was meeting a representative sent by the inhabitants of the River Raisin settlement. They were to discuss how the citizens of the territory should behave towards the enemy and their legal status as parolees.

Judge Woodward received Lt. Col. François Navarre cordially, and the two quickly got down to business. Navarre carried with him a letter dated the previous day, which deputized him to speak for all the *habitants* of the River Raisin. It was signed by Jacques, François, and Jean-Baptiste Lasselle, as well as Duncan Reid, Jean-Baptiste Jerome, and Jean-Baptiste Beaugrand.

After Hull's surrender last August, the River Raisin militiamen had been placed on parole, which they understood to mean that they could no longer legally fight for either side. This was, at best, an awkward position for them, especially now that the Indians were pressing them to shift their loyalties towards the British.

This was nothing new. Ever since Pontiac's siege of Detroit, Native warriors had urged French *habitants* to take up the hatchet alongside them in their wars against the British, the Americans, or enemy tribesmen. At times, the Lasselles and others had joined them in such battles as Fallen Timbers.

This time, however, Native recruiting efforts along the River Raisin had not produced any major results, except among a few fur traders and some of the mixed-blood population, such as Poulain, a *métis* with dark, fiery eyes. With his father long dead, and only his Native mother to guide him, the youth was easily prevailed upon to join some of the Indian raiding parties that were lurking along the American frontier.[193]

As proof of the pressure they were under, Navarre handed Woodward a document that had been sent to him by the Hurons (Wyandots) and other

---

did not know of any service he had been to the people and could only consider him as a traitor to his country....The constitution says treason shall consist of levying war against the U.S., adhering to their enemies, giving aid, etc. Did not Mr. Woodward adhere to them by taking an appointment and aid them by means of that appointment?"

193 Interview with Mrs. Peter Ankenbrandt of Ash Township: Speaking of Indians, she stated that the last ones living nearby were Ojibwas and Odawas. She could also remember hearing Katie the Huron's powwow some half mile away, which lasted 3 or 4 days, and during which the Indians begged food from the nearby settlers. Regarding Poulain, she said: *"My mother remembered seeing a half-breed Indian Frenchman with eyes like coals of fire, whose name was Pollan, or a French name that means colt (a male colt.) His father died when he was quite young and he went with the Indians to kill white settlers. The story was sickening, and he regretted his part in it, for all his friends and his children, and their children, were white and Catholic. The descendants are called Colt, Colton, Pollain, Polland, Pullaw, Pullo, and similar names..."*

tribes assembled at the Maumee Rapids. It was undated, but addressed to the inhabitants of the River Raisin, and read as follows:

"Friends! Listen! You have always told us you would give us any assistance in your power. We, therefore, as the enemy is approaching us within 25 miles, call upon you all to rise up and come here to the Rapids immediately, bringing your arms along with you.

"Should you fail at this time, we will not consider you in future as friends, and the consequences may be very unpleasant. We are well convinced you have no writings forbidding you to assist us. We are your friends, at present."

Looking at the bottom of the letter, the judge recognized the horse emblem of Roundhead and the turtle sign of Walk-in-the-Water. There was no doubt these chiefs were sincere and fully capable of carrying out any threat against the *habitants.*

The Indians argued that there was no document expressly prohibiting the *habitants* from switching sides or assisting them or the British. However, the judge knew that the surrender of the Territory did not release the *habitants* from their duties as American citizens.

As technical prisoners of war, the River Raisin militiamen could not break their parole and take up arms for the Americans, nor could they join the British or their Indian allies. To do so would make them illegal combatants under the generally accepted rules of war, at least until officially included in a prisoner exchange between the two warring countries.

The status of the Michigan militia was not very high on the list of American priorities, so it was unlikely any of them could be released from their parole until the Territory was liberated from British occupation.

Woodward therefore informed Navarre that the *habitants* had to remain neutral, at least until such time as they were officially "exchanged." The enemy had no right to coerce them into fighting for them. Any American citizen who chose to fight alongside the Indians would be considered a renegade and a traitor. Such a person could be shot on the spot if discovered with arms in hand or be liable to arrest and prosecution once the war was over.

Navarre considered Judge Woodward's opinion as legally binding, even under the British occupation. The *habitants* had now obtained the official ruling by which they could refuse the demands of Roundhead and Walk-in-the-Water, if they dared.[194]

Two miles above the Maumee Rapids, Saturday Evening, Nov. 14, 1812:

The wrinkles in Colonel Elliott's aged brow deepened considerably as he listened to the reports from his scouts. Supply problems had impeded the advance of the enemy through the month of October, but now there was news that General Winchester had crossed the Maumee and was once again on the march. Furthermore, there was word that General Tupper had left Fort McArthur with a large force supported by a cannon on November 10.

The colonel hoped to hold the Maumee Rapids with his Indians, but not all of the Wyandots had yet arrived. So, Elliott sent a courier to Colonel Procter, urging him to support him with regular troops and artillery. Perhaps some men could even be drafted from the River Raisin settlement.

The rumor of Tupper's advance was true. The general had left at 11 a.m. on the 10th of November with 604 men, exclusive of officers, and one light 6-pounder. Unfortunately, the field piece was slowing them down so much, they abandoned it at a blockhouse after hauling it for only 15 miles.[195]

On the 14th, Tupper's army marched through wet prairies and woodlands studded with clumps of strawberry bushes until 9 p.m., when they reached the south bank of the Maumee River, about a mile above their intended crossing point. Here, they waited silently for several hours.

Meanwhile, scouts reported that the Indians were encamped near Beaugrand's house, and that the British had carelessly moored their boats some distance downriver. The Indians were drinking, singing, and dancing and seemed unaware of their presence.[196]

---

194 Letters # 28 and 29 in Barbarities of the Enemy, exposed in a Report of the Committee of the House of Representatives, and the Documents accompanying said Report. Troy: Francis Adancourt, 1813. pp. 132-3.

195 Letter from Tupper to Harrison, Nov. 16, 1812, in Knopf, Richard C. Document Transcriptions of the War of 1812 in the Northwest, Vol. V. Columbus: Ohio Historical Society, 1958, p. 278. Troop estimates range from 604 to 690 men. Tupper's was not the only American force to take the field at this time. Further west, General Samuel Hopkins began his march against Prophet's Town with a force numbering some 1,250 men from Barbour's, Miller's, and Wilcox's Kentucky militia regiments plus Zachary Taylor's regulars. Marching up the east bank of the Wabash, they would capture Prophet's Town on November 19th, and destroy several deserted Indian villages along their way.

196 Cruikshank, Lt. Col. E. A. Harrison & Procter; The River Raisin, from Transactions of the Royal Society

Encouraged, General Tupper led his men downstream and into the river, which was swollen by recent rains, and now had a very fast current. The water was extremely cold, but it didn't feel half as bad as the frigid night wind, which was blowing out of the northwest at almost gale strength.

Each company was divided into two platoons, with each platoon to ford the river in a line abreast. The first section got across on foot, but the next section was swept away into deeper water. Mounted officers went splashing after them and succeeded in saving every man.[197]

After several disorderly attempts, the crossing had to be abandoned. Few men had gained the opposite bank, and ten had lost their rifles on the way. Many more had their powder and cartridges soaked in the waist-high water.

The horses were too weak carry the entire army across, so those already on the far side had to ford the river again, in the opposite direction. It was now going on 3 in the morning, so Tupper and his men made camp in the woods, where they could build fires and dry their clothes. A messenger was sent to inform Winchester of the setback, asking for reinforcements and food.

The men were hungry, their provisions having run out the day before. The troops dried out their wet muskets, and the men who had not been in the river shared their dry cartridges with those who had.[198]

A new strategy now had to be devised. Tupper could continue upriver to find a better fording place, but it would require an effort that his men seemed too fatigued to accomplish. Tupper decided to try to tempt the Indians to

---

of Canada, Vol. IV, Section II. Ottawa: Royal Society of Canada, 1911, pp. 138-9.

197 Patrick, Jeff L., edit., "We Lay There Doing Nothing: John Jackson's Recollection of the War of 1812", Indiana Magazine of History, LXXXVIII, June, 1992, published by the Trustees of Indiana University: *"We were formed and started to cross over. The night was pretty dark, when the foremost had got partly over, and those that were behind had swaged downstream to where the water was deeper. Some men had begun to lose their feet, and an alarm was raised that some men were drowning, which throwed the line all into confusion. Those that were in front of the confusion marched on, and those in the rear turned back. The field officers rode in and rescued those that was likely to drown, and there we were, part on one side of the river and part on the other side. Some few lost their guns that were never found. Gen. Tupper ordered those that had got over to re-cross back, so that we were all where we started from. We then went a short distance from the river, built fires to dry our clothes, and bivouacked on the ground until morning."*

198 Knopf, Richard C. Document Transcriptions of the War of 1812 in the Northwest, Vol. V. Columbus: Ohio Historical Society, 1958, p. 279. See also: "Journal of Mathew Newsom," as transcribed by James Ohde, Ohio State Museum, Columbus: Anthony Wayne Parkway Board, 1957, p. 9: *"...some men stayed on the Indian side of the river that night without kindling any fire, for fear the Indians would discover them. On the next morning early, they were assisted with horses to cross the river, when they joined the army again."*

British Musicians on the March
Photo by Bill Saul
Note the metal fife case slung under the arm of the man in the foreground.

cross over to his side. He stationed a few scouts as a decoy across the river from the Indian camp and drew up his troops in columns a mile behind them.

At dawn, the scouts observed a canoe full of Indians coming across the river. They fired on them as they landed, killing one and wounding another who crawled behind a fence. The scouts then fell back while Tupper brought his troops forward towards a clearing.

The Native warriors followed the scouts to within a hundred yards of their supports, but did not take the bait. Instead, they retreated rapidly back to their own camp, where others were already seeing to the safety of their non-combatants. The Native women sought shelter in the woods, while some of the British headed downstream toward their boats, with the evident intention of securing the *Queen Charlotte* from attack.

From there they would rally reinforcements and advance once again, probing the enemy to discover his numbers and weaknesses.

Tupper's men advanced and formed their battle lines on the river bank, drawing an irregular fire from the opposite side, which increased in intensity as the numbers of Native warriors grew.

To the Americans, the river began to seem less of a barrier, as shots from a British cannon mounted on a gunboat began landing nearby. It appeared to be a 4-pounder. Soon, some British infantry came into view, marching to the cadence of fife and drum.[199]

Downriver, more Indians could be seen swarming around their canoes, while hundreds of warriors were discharging their muskets in the direction of Tupper's men. They made a great show of this long-distance shooting in an effort to fix the attention of the Americans and keep them from maneuvering.

At this point, in a display worthy of a medieval warlord, Colonel Elliott galloped onto the field, followed by mounted Wyandot warriors. Most prominent among them was the Wyandot chief, Split Log, sitting astride a fine, white horse. Of medium build, and considered less gifted than Roundhead, Split Log nevertheless displayed a noble bearing and great stamina.

The mounted Wyandots headed upriver to the ford where Tupper's men had failed to cross the night before. Fearing his position would be turned, Tupper immediately countered by ordering a withdrawal upstream.

A number of the Indians made it to the ford and began crossing to block Tupper's retreat, but Major Bentley's battalion arrived on the run and drove them off with only a few wounded.[200] Several warriors fell into the river, their bodies bathed in the golden light of the sun as they floated downstream a short distance in front of their horses.[201]

---

199 "We Lay There Doing Nothing: John Jackson's Recollection of the War of 1812," edited by Jeff L. Patrick, appearing in the Indiana Magazine of History, LXXXVIII, June, 1992, published by the Trustees of Indiana University: *"The Queen Charlotte had brought up the troops from the lake, and was now lying at the foot of the rapids. She fired two guns, and started down the river, while the British paraded with drum and fife, and the Indians yelled all round.*

200 Lossing, Benson J. The Pictorial Field Book of the War of 1812, Glendale, New York: Benchmark Publishing Corp., 1970, Reprint. pp. 344-5.

201 "We Lay There Doing Nothing: John Jackson's Recollection of the War of 1812," edited by Jeff L. Patrick, appearing in the Indiana Magazine of History, LXXXVIII, June, 1992, published by the Trustees of Indiana University: *"As our rations were nearly gone, and we had no way of crossing the river, Gen. Tupper concluded to return back to camp McArthur; so we proceeded up the river probably two miles, when one of the spies came running back and told the General that the Indians were crossing the river just above us as thick as black-birds. We went with a quick march, or rather ran, until we got opposite to where they were crossing, and formed a line on the bank, which was probably about one hundred yards from the river. Some few Indians had got over, and the river was filled with them, and the woods on the other side also perfectly alive with them. We commenced firing on them, and they commenced retreating, every one fired off his gun, before starting back through the water. In the midst of the flurry, it was discovered that a number of mounted red-coats had crossed the river somewhere and was about to attack our rear. A regiment was immediately ordered to meet them,*

Meanwhile, Tupper's men had to fight off more of the enemy who had crossed the river at another point and were coming up behind him. Gaining a bit of a respite after a 20-minute firefight, Tupper resumed the retreat in two columns, dogged by Split Log and a number of mounted warriors.[202]

As he harried the retreating Americans, Split Log sometimes fired from the back of his impressive white horse. Other times he leapt off and fired from behind a tree. Later, another warrior was seen riding that same horse until it was wounded. Many of the pursuing Wyandots rode on spirited horses and were well-armed with pistols and holsters.[203]

Split Log and the Wyandots chased the retreating Americans for several miles in the fading light, wounding a number of them. Too few to overrun the soldiers, they tried to harass them into a panic and cut off any stragglers.

Colonel Elliott was able to keep up with the Indians, but he remained at a respectable distance, riding about 300 yards behind the rear right column.

Before and during the retreat, some of Tupper's hungry men slipped away, contrary to orders. One group at the rear of his right column spotted a herd of hogs. They shot at them and chased them for half a mile.

Eight or ten equally hungry soldiers on the left flank wandered into a nearby field to pull some corn. They were surprised by a group of mounted warriors, and four of them were killed.

Out of food and seeing no support from Winchester's army, Tucker led his starving, exhausted, and demoralized troops back 15 miles to the Portage River. The column took on a ghostly pallor in the Sunday morning

---

and fired at them, when they retreated in quick time..."

202 Knopf, Richard C., Document Transcriptions of the War of 1812 in the Northwest, Vol. V. Columbus: Ohio Historical Society, 1958, p. 279: Tupper says, "...The Indians which had made the attack upon our rear crossed at a ford below the rear of our columns..."

203 Knopf, Richard C., Document Transcriptions of the War of 1812 in the Northwest, Vol. V. Columbus: Ohio Historical Society, 1958, pp. 279-280. Tupper says, "A number of the Indians were shot from their horses. They with great dexterity threw them on again and carried them off the field; from the information of a number of men on whom I can rely, as well as from what I was witness to, from 15 to 20 Indians were carried off, either killed or wounded."
According to Lewis Bond's account, About 500 Americans appeared on the opposite side of the river. Some shots were fired across the river and the Americans retired. The Indians crossed over and a few miles on the road discovered 3 or 4 wounded men that appear to have been left behind, whom they killed and scalped. See: Knopf, Richard C. Document Transcriptions of the War of 1812 in the Northwest, Vol. X pt 1. Columbus: Ohio Historical Society, 1958, p. 194.

mist as they straggled on towards Fort Findlay. They would not stop until they regained the safety of Fort McArthur on November 20th.[204]

Meanwhile, at Camp Number 3, General Winchester detailed Colonel Lewis with 410 picked men to reinforce Tupper's advance. Unaware Tupper was already retreating, Lewis marched his detachment till 9 p.m. and made camp in the dark. Forbidden to start fires, the men huddled together for warmth.

Having received a courier with news that Tupper had been unable to ford the Maumee River, Lewis sent Ensign Todd ahead with an escort to suggest that they join forces at Roche de Boeuf.[205]

When the messengers returned, they reported finding Tupper's deserted camp with the bodies of two of his men who had been scalped and stripped.[206]

---

204 "Journal of Mathew Newsom," as transcribed by James Ohde, Ohio State Museum, Columbus: Anthony Wayne Parkway Board, 1957, p. 11.

205 William Atherton claimed Lewis *"...thought if it were necessary for Tupper, with 650 men, to retreat, and the river too between him and the enemy, he could not be justified in meeting it on the same side with 380."* Atherton, William, Narrative of the Suffering & Defeat of the North-Western Army under General Winchester, Frankfort, KY, A. G. Hodges, 1842. p. 20.

206 "We Lay There Doing Nothing: John Jackson's Recollection of the War of 1812," edited by Jeff L. Patrick, appearing in the Indiana Magazine of History, LXXXVIII, June, 1992, published by the Trustees of Indiana University: These men had been left behind by General Tupper where they *"...had bivouacked during the night...one was sick, and the other was not right well, who stayed to take care of the sick man. We did not go back to where they were but angled to the left so as to strike the road that we came on, some miles in advance. I did not know there was any persons left there until there was inquiries made along the lines that evening for two volunteers to go back and ascertain what had become of the two men. I think ten dollars to each was offered. One of our boys volunteered with another man to go, and they went back that night, and found them killed and scalped. They covered them over with logs and brush, and it then being near morning, they went a short distance, got into a thicket, and stayed all day. At night they followed on, but did not overtake us until we got in camp..."*

ROCHE DE BOUT (Roche de Boeuf)
An important landmark island in the Maumee River[207]

Upon hearing this, Lewis ordered a hasty retreat back to Winchester's camp. His leading elements straggled into camp in the middle of the night, but many were unable to make it that far. The men speculated that double their number of Indians were following them, and would probably attack that night.

William Atherton was among those whose strength gave out. He spent a fearful night about 5 miles from the main army. Morning dawned peacefully, however, and Atherton soon reached the safety of Camp Number 3.[208]

Enemy spies were spotted in the area for the next couple of days, but

---

207 This ancient limestone outcropping in the Maumee River was used as a meeting place by Native Americans long before the French arrived. Some controversy exists about the original French name, but the rock island was known as both *Roche de Bout* (End Rock) and *Roche de Boeuf* (Buffalo Rock). The name could even have been derived from *Roche Debout* (Standing Rock). A third of the island was destroyed by the construction of an interurban railway bridge in 1907, which was abandoned 30 years later. The rock formation is located at Waterville, Ohio.

208 Darnell, Elias, <u>Journal</u>. Philadelphia: Lippincott, Grambo, and Co., 1854, pp. 33-4. LTC Lewis' detachment had set out on November 15. Although there are some discrepancies among the various accounts, Darnell carefully states the expedition consisted of 6 captains, 6 subalterns, 6 sergeants, 6 corporals, and 386 privates, with provisions for 6 days. See also: (Harrison & Procter, pp. 139-140 and Draper, 11u.) Also: Atherton, William, <u>Narrative of the Suffering & Defeat of the North-Western Army under General Winchester</u>. Frankfort, KY, A. G. Hodges, 1842. p. 20.

made no attempt to kill any guards or steal any horses, leading the officers to think the enemy was near and would attack if any weaknesses were spotted.

The men were put to work strengthening the breastworks, and the 40-acre camp was placed on heightened alert.[209]

Inspections revealed several soldiers had just three or even fewer cartridges in their *cartouche* boxes, and one man had no ammunition box at all.

Orders of the day called for each officer and private to have 10 prepared cartridges on hand. Company commanders were made responsible for taking a daily count of every man's cartridge supply and to confine any offenders under Provost Guard. If the missing cartridges could not be accounted for, the men would be charged 6¼ cents apiece.[210]

The soldiers built huts to ward off the cold, but they could do nothing to speed up the transportation of warm clothing and food across the Black Swamp. Weakened by deprivation and fatigue, many succumbed to sickness and died. Private Elias Darnell of Lewis' Regiment soon began referring to Camp no. 3 as "Fort Starvation."[211]

Tupper's raid had at least accomplished one thing. The British and Indians at the Maumee Rapids felt they were too exposed. Soon they would pull back to French Town. Thereafter, the River Raisin would become Colonel Procter's forward defense line.

Strife between civilians and the military, Nov. 5-23, 1812:

On November 5th, Joel Leftwich's 700-man Virginia Brigade reached the Delaware, 150 miles north of the Ohio. The town was bulging with settlers from New England and refugees from Michigan and northwest Ohio. The influx created a rise in prices that fell especially hard on the Virginia militiamen.[212]

---

209 The orders for the day on November 18 required the troops to lay on their arms all night, in readiness to defend the lines at the sound of the drum. The next day, piquet guards were set out around the camp. A captain, subaltern, sergeant, corporal and 50 privates were posted on each flank and in front; and a smaller force to the rear.

210 After Orders, Camp No. 3, Nov. 18, 1812, and General Orders, Camp No. 3, Nov. 19, 1812. <u>Michigan Pioneer and Historical Collections,</u> Vol. 35, pp. 291-2.

211 In 1845, canal diggers exposed a nearby burial ground containing thousands of bones thought to be the remains of 300 Kentucky soldiers who died at the camp. Source: historical markers at Independence Dam State Park, near Defiance,

212 Expecting to be quickly supplied from Cincinnati merchants, the Virginia Brigade would spend a couple months waiting for needed shoes, wool blankets, socks, and coats. At Delaware, they had

Similarly, the people of Franklinton, Ohio, woke up to find their town was now an important headquarters and depot for the Northwestern Army. They soon tired of the inconveniences, delays and setbacks caused by the military.

In the recent presidential election, Madison had received 7,000 of the 10,000 votes cast in the state. Although most Ohioans wanted to continue the war, not everyone was happy. Both pro- and anti-government protests occurred.

A couple of prominent leaders were burned in effigy, including Thomas Worthington.[213] Rumors were rife, indicating that Harrison might be suspended from command unless he resigned as Governor of Indiana Territory.[214]

Captain William Garrard's company of dragoons arrived at Franklinton on November 5th. They were quartered in the local courthouse due to a lack of tents, which had been left behind with Winchester's army because there were no wagons to transport them. It was here that the dragoons were finally able to exchange their muskets for sabers, pistols, and short (jaeger) rifles.

Their quarters were unexpectedly warm and spacious, but they had to guard their horses picketed outside against angry protesters who feared the military's presence would make their town a target for Indian raiders.[215]

Meanwhile, General Harrison had arrived in Franklinton with 800

their first encounter with Indians. Fortunately, these Delawares and Wyandots were friendly to the American cause. See: Butler, Stuart L., Real Patriots and Heroic Soldiers; General Joel Leftwich and the Virginia Brigade in the War of 1812, Westminster, Md.: Heritage Books, 2008, pp. 62-65.

213 Harrison to Meigs, Nov. 21, 1812; Harrison to Piatt Nov. 30, 1812; in Harrison Papers, Indiana Historical Society. Worthington was an Ohio Senator, surveyor, land developer, farmer, investor, bank director, anti-slavery advocate, supporter of public schools and libraries, and Ohio militia officer. Although a Democratic-Republican, he was initially against the war, for which he felt the country was unprepared. In 1814, he became the 6th Governor of Ohio, replacing Governor Meigs.

214 Letter John Kerr to Worthington, Nov. 23, 1812, in Knopf, Richard C. Document Transcriptions of the War of 1812 in the Northwest, Vol. III. Columbus: Ohio Historical Society, 1957, p. 122. One Franklinton resident, John Kerr, thanked his good fortune that he had been unable to accept the military commission that offered General Worthington. Otherwise, he would have been captured with Hull's army at Detroit. "To take the cursed, petty fort of Malden would require an escort costing as much as all Canada is worth. However, it is not my place to complain of this. Our state will be benefited by the expense, and in proportion to its amount...War is a very pretty thing in theory. How it may terminate in practice is altogether a different consideration. If the people of the United States are to be heavily taxed for the support of the war...The fever of war would be greatly reduced..."

215 CLIFT, G. GLENN. "WAR OF 1812 DIARY OF WILLIAM B. NORTHCUTT, PART II." The Register of the Kentucky Historical Society, vol. 56, no. 3, 1958, pp. 253–269. JSTOR, www.jstor.org/stable/23374306. Accessed 21 Apr. 2021.

horsemen and 300 regular infantrymen. He quickly got busy with the details of supplying his armies in the field.[216]

Mouth of Turkey Foot Creek, Nov. 22-25, 1812:[217]

Logan,[218] Captain Johnny, and Lightfoot[219] were riding together along the north bank of the Maumee, 12 miles from Defiance, on a scout towards the rapids. Although they were Shawnees, they disliked Tecumseh and the British.

However, despite their faithful service to the U.S. Army, they were still distrusted just because they were Native Americans. Having failed on their last mission, they were determined to bring in a prisoner or at least a scalp.[220]

While climbing their horses up the bank of a stream, they suddenly came face to face with a party of 7 Indians, led by a British Indian Department officer. Seeing they were outnumbered two to one, with no time to retreat, Logan made a sign of friendship. Approaching the officer, he explained they had just deserted the Americans at Camp Number 3, and wanted to join the British.

---

216 Letter John Miller to Worthington, Nov. 24, 1812, in Knopf, Richard C. Document Transcriptions of the War of 1812 in the Northwest, Vol. III. Columbus: Ohio Historical Society, 1957, pp. 123-4. On November 21st, he wrote Governor Meigs that there were too few drivers for the army's wagons and pack horses. In an effort to recruit more civilian teamsters, the letter authorized the governor to treat their service the same as duty in the army or militia, with the same benefits. In a November 30th letter to John Piatt, Deputy Commissary General, Harrison complained that he was no longer willing to allow contractors to "trifle" with the army, and he ordered Piatt to arrange for supplies to be delivered to Fort Jennings immediately, regardless of cost.

217 The South Turkeyfoot Creek fishing access is on OH-10, between County Roads 5A and 6B at mile 38 of the Maumee River, just downstream from the mouth of Turkeyfoot Creek, near Liberty Center, Ohio, but on the south bank of the river. North Turkeyfoot Park is on the northern bank.

218 McAfee, Robert, History of the Late War in the Western Country, Bowling Green, Ohio: Historical Publications Company, 1919 (reprint of 1816 original edition.) pp. 194-5. Also known as Spemica-Lawba, or High Horn, Logan had seen much service as a guide and spy for the Americans. He had gone with General Hull to Detroit and was with the Kentucky army on its expedition to relieve Fort Wayne. As a youth in 1786, he had been captured by General Logan of Kentucky, from whom he acquired his name. He had married a fellow captive and wanted to have his children brought up and educated *in the manner of the white people.* See also: "Deeds / Nations, Directory of First Nations Individuals in South-Western Ontario, 1750-1850," by Greg Curnoe, at www.adamsheritage.com.

219 Also known as Bright Horn. See: McAfee, Robert, History of the Late War in the Western Country, Bowling Green, Ohio: Historical Publications Company, 1919, (reprint of 1816 edition.) pp. 192-3.

220 McAfee, Robert. History of the Late War in the Western Country. Bowling Green, Ohio: Historical Publications Company, 1919 (reprint of 1816 original edition).

The officer replied courteously, but cautiously. He allowed Logan and his comrades to keep their weapons, but had them dismount and walk in front. They freely answered questions about the American army.

Potawatomi Chief Winnemac knew of Logan, and didn't really believe he would change sides so readily. After traveling about 8 miles, he suggested to the British officer that they should seize Logan and his friends and tie them up.

The officer replied, however, that Logan and his 2 companions were completely in their power. The odds were too much against them to chance a fight, and if they tried to run, they could be shot or easily ridden down. Logan overheard these remarks, and cautioned his friends to be ready.

When the others relaxed their guard somewhat, Logan gave the signal, and all three turned their weapons into the nearest enemy. Logan's shot struck Winnemac, knocking him from his horse. The British officer and a young Odawa warrior also went down. Startled by the sudden attack, the remaining British-allied Indians pulled their mounts back a short distance, wheeled, and opened fire as well.

Logan and his friends picked up the rifles from those they had shot, took cover behind trees, and returned fire, but with little effect. Logan called for his companions to retreat. Seizing one of the enemy's horses, he leaped upon its back, but slumped as he felt the searing pain of a bullet pass through his breast and down into the small of his back.

Lightfoot was also wounded slightly in the thigh. Together, he and Logan galloped off. Their opponents did the same, leaving behind the officer and 2 warriors.

Seeing his chance to take some scalps, Captain Johnny let his comrades ride off without him. He went over to one of the bodies and lifted his head. He saw he was an Odawa, but didn't know the warrior's name. With his knife, Captain Johnny made a circular incision around the scalp. In his excitement, however, he cut too deep, wedging the blade into the skull and snapping it in two. He was barely able to get the scalp off.

His knife broken, Captain Johnny gave up and fled. He didn't know if the other two were dead or still alive, but he did recognize them. One was the Potawatomi chief Wynemac; the other was Alexander Elliott, the son of the British Indian Department Superintendent, Colonel Matthew Elliott.[221]

Notwithstanding the seriousness of his wound, Logan rode the 20 or 30 miles back to the American camp in about 5 hours, with the help of his friend, Lightfoot. The next morning Captain Johnny joined them, displaying the scalp he had stayed behind to take at the risk of his own life.[222]

The army surgeons tried to save Logan's life, but their care was inadequate for the task. He survived only a couple of days, dying on November 24. On his deathbed, Logan asked that his family be protected and taken safely to Kentucky. His dying words were, *"I suppose this will be taken as evidence of my bravery, and I shall be no longer suspected as a traitor."*

Logan's body was transported to his family at Wapakoneta and buried in a mixed Native/military ceremony. The scalp of the slain Odawa was carried on a pole in the funeral procession and displayed at the council house.

The British, too, reclaimed their casualties. Colonel Elliott's Métis son died of his wounds, and his body was placed on a British vessel at the rapids. The season being late, the ship was blown down the coast towards Sandusky, where it became mired in slushy floes of ice. Not until December was the ice strong enough for a sleigh from Malden to retrieve Alexander Elliott's body.[223]

---

221 Darnell, Elias, <u>Journal</u>. Philadelphia: Lippincott, Grambo, and Co., 1854, p. 36. Darnell actually says Winemac was the Indian who was scalped. See also: Cruikshank, Lt. Col. E. A., <u>Harrison & Proctor: The River Raisin</u>, from the <u>Transactions of the Royal Society of Canada</u>, Vol. IV, Section II, Ottawa: Royal Society of Canada, 1911, p. 140. Cruikshank says Elliot was mortally wounded, but lived a day or two. Before the war, he had been practicing law in Amherstburg. Alexander Elliott was the son of Col. Matthew Elliott and Marie-Louise Sanschagrin (aka: No Worries Rising Sun.)

222 In the mid-19th century, it was estimated that an army horse could walk at a rate of 4 miles an hour; slow trot at 6 mph; full trot at 8 mph; and gallop at over 12 mph. It could travel 35 miles in a good 8-hour day's ride on about 10 pounds of grain. See: Alexander, Steve, <u>Believe in the Bold: Custer and the Gettysburg Campaign</u>, Madrid: Andrea Press, 2013, p. 22.

223 Knopf, Richard C. <u>Document Transcriptions of the War of 1812 in the Northwest, Vol. X pt 1</u>. Columbus: Ohio Historical Society, 1958, p. 194. Bond was in Detroit when news came of the death of 2 Indians along the Maumee: *"A Mr. Clark of the Indian Department was taken near there and a son of Colonel Elliott's, a half Indian, being up the Miami River with a party of Indians, met with some of the American Indians, by whom he was killed. The Colonel had his body brought down to the foot of the Rapids where a vessel had also been left, and the body was put on board... Colonel Elliott, having loaded the vessel, sailed from the Miami, but the season being late and the weather bad, was driven down to the Sandusky Coast, where the vessel froze up, and he was obliged to remain on board until the ice was strong enough to cross the lake, which he effected in December. Sleighs were sent and much of the property was brought from the vessel, and the body of young Elliot was*

Mississinewa River, December 17 and 18, 1812:

A 600-man expedition led by Lieutenant Colonel John B. Campbell[224] left Dayton in mid-December, carrying 12-days' rations per man and a bushel of corn for each horse.[225]

The troops would be heading into an unknown country, where, at times, they would have to follow a trail marked only with broken branches laid out by a passing fur trader.[226]

Their goal was to secure the western branches of Winchester's supply lines by destroying the Miami villages near the Wabash River, about 80 miles away. The villages were thought to contain major food stores, permitting the Miamies to concentrate their forces in this area.

The soldiers were to spare certain pro-American individuals, as well as the women and children, who were to be taken away as captives.[227]

---

conveyed to the seat of his father near Malden, and there interred. Having evacuated the Miami, a party of militia with one piece of cannon and a body of Indians were posted at River Raisin..." See: Atherton, William, Narrative of the Suffering & Defeat of the North-Western Army under General Winchester. Frankfort, KY, A. G. Hodges, 1842, pp. 21-23. See also: Lossing, Benson J., The Pictorial Field Book of the War of 1812, Glendale, New York: Benchmark Publishing Corp., 1970, Reprint, pp. 345-6.

224 Holliday, Murray, The Battle of the Mississinewa, 1812, Marion, Indiana: Grant County Historical Society, 1964, p. 10: General Harrison intended to give the command to Duncan McArthur, but this general was still on parole from Hull's surrender. Harrison therefore settled on Lt. Col. Campbell. Campbell was a relatively inexperienced Virginia officer in the 19th U.S. Infantry. He would later die of wounds suffered in the 1814 Battle of Chippewa.

225 McAfee, Robert, History of the Late War in the Western Country, Bowling Green, Ohio: Historical Publications Co., 1919, (reprint of 1816 original edition,) p. 309: General Harrison would later write, "The Indian towns cannot be surprised in succession, as they give the alarm from one to the other with more rapidity than our troops can move...The horses that are now to be found, are not like those of the early settlers, such as the Indians and traders now have. They have been accustomed to corn, and must have it..." The Indians "invariably take their families with them on their hunting excursions, and...their provisions are always buried in small parcels, each family hiding its own."

226 CLIFT, G. GLENN. "WAR OF 1812 DIARY OF WILLIAM B. NORTHCUTT, PART II." The Register of the Kentucky Historical Society, vol. 56, no. 3, 1958, pp. 253–269. JSTOR, www.jstor.org/stable/23374306.

227 Letter Harrison to Campbell, Nov. 25, 1812, Knopf, Richard C., Document Transcriptions of the War of 1812 in the Northwest, Vol. VI, Part 4, Columbus: Ohio Historical Society, 1959, p. 118: "There are, however, some of the chiefs who have undeviatingly exerted themselves to keep their warriors quiet and to preserve their friendly relations with us. This has been the case with respect to Richardville (a half French man, the 2nd Chief of the Miamies), Silver Heels, the White Loon, certainly, and perhaps Pecan, the principal chief of the Eel River Tribe. It is not my wish that you should run any risk in saving those people, but... it would be extremely gratifying to me, and no doubt to the President, the same remark will also apply to the sons and brothers of the Little Turtle, who continued to his last moment the warm friend of the U. States...Your own character as a soldier and that of the troops you command is a sure guarantee of the safety of the women and children. They will be taken, however, and conducted to the settlement. ...There are probably some white men at Mississiniway, but I am

The expedition included an ad-hoc mix of mounted dragoons, riflemen, and infantrymen. To provide extra mobility, the foot soldiers were mounted on packhorses taken from the baggage trains.[228]

In Ball's Battalion was a 22-man contingent from the River Raisin. They were led by Cornet Isaac Lee, a 33-year-old former lawyer and teacher educated at Brown University. Completing the force was a small company of spies, which included James Knaggs from the River Raisin.[229]

The infantrymen made an awkward sight as they sat upon the uncomfortable pack saddles, encumbered as they were with camp axes and other tools. The light dragoons were armed with pistols, sabers, and short rifles without slings, which they balanced with the rest of their gear.

The men carried their own rations of pork and biscuits. With no cooking equipment, the pork had to be roasted on sticks over the occasional campfire, or laid directly on the coals.[230] In the evening, they made camp in the form of a hollow square and slept on brush and grasses piled next to their fires, with nothing but their blankets to cover them.[231]

The first casualty occurred the second night out of Greenville, when Private Roger West of William Garrard's company was trying to rekindle a fire with gunpowder. As he unstopped his powder horn and began to pour

uncertain whether they are citizens…The safe way will be not to kill them if it can be prevented. An old Canadian by the name of Godfroy has lived there several years and has a squaw for his wife. He is and always has been a friend to the U. States. There will be no difficulty in saving him, as his house is apart from the rest."

228 Raynor, Keith, "The Battle of the Mississinewa, 1812," on the web site of The Discriminating General. Raynor gives a detailed organization for Campbell's force, which numbered 787 men. The order of battle can be found in Appendix B at the end of this book. See also: Glenn, Elizabeth J., B.K. Swartz, Jr., and Russell E. Lewis, "Ethnohistorical and Archaeological Descriptive Accounts of the War of 1812, Mississinewa Campaign and Aftermath: Project Report," Archaeological Reports, No. 14, Ball State University, 1977.

229 Isaac Lee migrated to the River Raisin area in 1809. His was the only active Michigan territorial militia unit to avoid the surrender of Hull's army in August of 1812. Lee would become a militia colonel, and would die in Monroe, Michigan, June 9, 1824. See Draper, 17s.

230 Little thought was given to the effect the cold weather might have on the men and horses. Rather, it was considered a blessing. The ice would make the streams and swamps easier to navigate, while the snow would reveal the tracks of any Indians lurking about. See: Pittsburg Gazette Account by a Pittsburg Blue, Appendix II-G, Glenn, Elizabeth J., B.K. Swartz, Jr., and Russell E. Lewis. See also: Ethnohistorical and Archaeological Descriptive Accounts of the War of 1812, Mississinewa Campaign and Aftermath: Project Report, Archaeological Reports, No. 14, Ball State University, 1977.

231 Egli, Bruce, "Major Alexander's Battalion: U. States Volunteers in the Northwest Army," 2012.

out its contents, the fire flashed up, exploding the horn and blinding him. He was evacuated the next morning.[232]

At sundown on the 3rd day, they halted in the snow 20 miles from their goal. After taking some refreshment, a council of officers decided to continue the march all through the night, and attack the Native villages located on the Mississinewa River early on Thursday morning, December 17.[233]

The march through the chill night air was something of a nightmare. The guides got lost. Men tried to get warm by dismounting and walking, but the effort produced sweat, which froze against their bodies.[234] Closing to within 3 miles of the first village, they halted an hour to wait for daylight, and then resumed the advance in total silence.[235]

As they cleared a swamp at about 8 a.m., they were spotted by four Indians on ponies, who galloped off to warn their village, Munceytown, half a mile away. The troops pursued, and in minutes, they reached and surrounded what was thought to be Silver Heel's village of Delawares and Miamies.

James Knaggs was the first trooper to enter the village, where he killed two of his adversaries and took another prisoner.[236] The dragoons lost all

---

232 Clift, G. Glenn. "WAR OF 1812 DIARY OF WILLIAM B. NORTHCUTT, PART II." *The Register of the Kentucky Historical Society*, vol. 56, no. 3, 1958, pp. 253–269. *JSTOR*, www.jstor.org/stable/23374306. Accessed 21 Apr. 2021.

233 McAfee, Robert, History of the Late War in the Western Country, Bowling Green, Ohio: Historical Publications Company, 1919 (reprint of 1816 original edition.) p. 197. This was in accordance with Harrison's instructions: "*Your marches should be so arranged as to get near the Town and ascertain the situation of the enemy at night, and the greater the distance you encamp the night before you reach the town, the less will be the probability of your being discovered. In other words, the last day's march must be a forced one.*" (See: Letter Harrison to Campbell, Nov. 25, 1812, Knopf, Richard C., Document Transcriptions of the War of 1812 in the Northwest, Vol. VI, Part 4, Columbus: Ohio Historical Society, 1959, pp. 118-120.

234 The troops advanced single-file, in several parallel columns: the staff and baggage columns in the trail, paralleled by a column of infantry and riflemen on either side, Ball's squadron in 4 columns on the right, and Simrall's Regiment in 4 columns on the left. See: Raynor, Keith, "The Battle of the Mississinewa, 1812," on the website of The Discriminating General. See also: Letter Campbell to Harrison, Official Letters of the Military and Naval Officers of the United States during the War with Great Britain in the Years 1812, 13, 14, and 15, Edit. by John Brannan, Washington: Wax & Gideon, 1823.

235 A Lexington newspaper carried a letter from Lt. Payne of Simrall's Regiment which stated the men suffered a 3-hour delay and were thoroughly drenched while attempting to cross a stream. Consequently, they didn't arrive within striking distance of the village until 4 a.m. The Reporter, January 9, 1813, p. 3, col. 1-2, Courtesy John Trowbridge.

236 "The Historical Society of Northwestern Ohio, biographical field notes on Frenchtown," note 166. James Bentley, however, said Knaggs' claim and many others were untrue. See Draper 17s.

semblance of a military formation in the mad dash forward, but the infantry and riflemen managed to dismount and form a ragged, half-mile-wide line along the edge of the village. Most of the Indians retreated over the river and fired back across the water for a short time, before finally disappearing.[237]

A dozen cabins were put to the torch and the cattle shot. Seven Munsie-Delaware men were killed and eight more captured, along with over 30 women and children. The troops left 2 cabins intact to hold the prisoners.[238]

Moving 3 miles farther, Simrall's and Ball's dragoons destroyed a couple Native villages, including Metocinyah's village at the mouth of Jocinah Creek.[239] The villages had recently been deserted, so the dragoons had to be content with killing the Indian dogs and cattle and capturing about 40 horses.[240]

That night, the exhausted army camped on the bank of the river near the first village. Half the men were kept on guard, while the other half worked.

---

237 Knopf, Richard C. Document Transcriptions of the War of 1812 in the Northwest, Vol. 5, Part 2, Columbus: Ohio Historical Society, 1958, p. 3: *"Some Indians fled over the river, on the bank of which the town was; some made a slight resistance, and others surrendered. The resistance made by those in the town was very slight, perhaps not more than two or three guns fired. Those who fled over the river kept up a fire for some minutes...After the skirmish was over, a sergeant in Capt. Hopkins' troop went out to get some provisions he had lost in the charge, and was killed..."*

238 One of the dead Indians was discovered to be a large, muscular black man. Another was an elderly man who was shot and scalped when he tried to surrender. Letter Campbell to Harrison, in Official Letters of the Military and Naval Officers of the United States during the War with Great Britain in the Years 1812, 13, 14, and 15. Edited by John Brannan. Washington City: Wax & Gideon, 1823, p. 104. Murray Holliday states that one sergeant was killed by friendly fire in the mad rush on the first village, while a second sergeant was shot and mortally wounded by an Indian while strolling too far from camp. Holliday, Murray, The Battle of the Mississinewa, 1812, Marion, Indiana: Grant County Historical Society, 1964. See also: Brown, Samuel, Views of the Campaigns of the North-Western Army, Troy, NY: Francis Adancourt, 1814, p. 34; *"The prisoners were treated with humanity, even the warriors who ceased to resist were spared, which was not the usual custom in expeditions against the Indians."*

239 Metocinyah, and thus his village, was not technically at war with the United States.

240 Knopf, Richard C. Document Transcriptions of the War of 1812 in the Northwest, Vol. 5, Part 2. Columbus: Ohio Historical Society, 1958, p. 3: Little corn was found; it had been eaten or buried underground. One sick, gray-haired woman was captured, but left behind in her house. *"...The infantry and riflemen being left as a guard over the prisoners, the cavalry marched down the river about 2 or 3 miles to Silver Heels' and two other villages, which we found evacuated by all but one squaw, whom we found and left in a cabin; the other houses, amounting in all, perhaps 40, were reduced to ashes, and property of every description we could find destroyed. The towns had been very suddenly abandoned, leaving their victuals over the fire. In the evening we returned and encamped on the ground where stood the first town attacked."* A Miami man later told John Hunt that one of the soldiers returned to kill and scalp the old woman who had been left behind. See: George Hunt's "Narrative of Escape from the Indians," MPHC, Vol. 12, pp. 452-5.

Although battle casualties had been light, 50 men were incapacitated with frostbite, and the 50 axes they had brought along were defective.[241]

They were hungry, as many of the men had discarded their provision sacks during their mile-long charge on the Indian village earlier that day.[242]

When completed, their new camp measured 200 yards square, a larger space than needed to enclose the horses. Suspecting an attack, a line of fires, corner redoubts, and picket guards were positioned 60 yards outside the camp, and a chain of sentinels placed another 60 yards beyond them.[243]

Every third man kept watch through the night. The rest slept till 4 in the morning and then stood under arms 2 hours before the sky began to lighten on a frigid Friday, the 18th of December.

Meanwhile, Lt. Col. Campbell met with his officers to decide his next course of action. They could attack another Native village a dozen miles down the river, but Campbell wondered if they shouldn't just declare their mission accomplished and go back to Fort McArthur.

About half an hour before daylight, as the assembled troops were being dismissed for breakfast, a sentry stationed 120 yards in front of the camp heard someone approaching and challenged the intruder to identify himself. The answer was a bullet and a cry in English, *"Potawatomi, God damn you!"*[244]

---

241 Egli, Bruce, "Major Alexander's Battalion: United States Volunteers in the Northwest Army," 2012. See also: "The Report of the Detachment Adjutant," Knopf, Richard C. Document Transcriptions of the War of 1812 in the Northwest, Vol. 5, Part 2, Columbus: Ohio Historical Society, 1958, p. 4: Only 10 of the axes resisted more than a few hours of hard service without breaking. They had also lost two crates of reserve ammunition when a packhorse bolted and ran away. The pack slipped under the horse's belly, trampling and breaking open the crates and scattering paper cartridges for over a quarter mile in the snow.

242 Raynor, Keith, The Battle of the Mississinewa, 1812, web site of The Discriminating General: A few, however, had thought to cut some fresh meat from the animals they had slaughtered while destroying the villages. For the morning, they could look forward to a little meat, perhaps with some coffee and hard biscuit.

243 The infantry and riflemen formed the center of the front line, facing the river, with Elliott's 19th U.S. Infantry on the right, Butler's Pittsburgh Blues in the center, and Alexander's Pennsylvania riflemen on the left. Major Ball's force formed the right side of the square, also taking up half of the rear line. In order from the river, Ball's force was made up of Markle's Pennsylvania Dragoons, Pierce's Ohio Dragoons, Garrard's Kentucky Dragoons, and Hopkins' U.S. Dragoons. Simrall's men covered the left side and the other half of the rear line of this rectangular formation. From the river stretched the dragoons of Trotter, Elmore, Johnston, and Young. A slight gap existed in the rear separating Ball's and Simrall's dragoons. Captain Bennoni Pierce and his men occupied an isolated redoubt beyond the right rear corner of the square.

244 The Potawatomi was Sa-ce-miah, also known as Francis Lafountain. See: John Hunt's "Narrative of Escape from the Indians," MPHC, Vol. 12, pp. 452-5.

Several hundred Potawatomies, Miamies and Delawares, led by François Godfroy, Joseph Richardville, and Little Thunder attacked the camp, driving the army's pickets and redoubt guards back to their respective companies.[245]

Concentrating against Major Ball's squadron on the right and rear of the American camp, some Miami warriors captured the northwest redoubt, killing Captain Pierce, who was hit by two balls in his back and finished off with a tomahawk as he made a tardy retreat after covering the withdrawal of

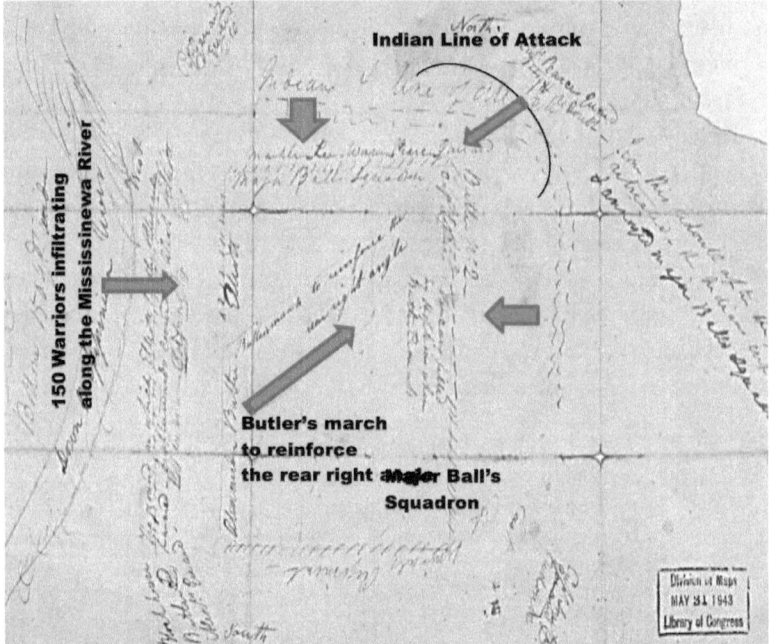

Map of Lt. Col. John R. Campbell's camp on the Mississinewa River, with details of attack by Indians. 1812. Map. Retrieved from the Library of Congress, <www.loc.gov/item/2012591022/>.
Arrows and bold captions by author.

his men. From the redoubt, the warriors poured in a heavy fire.[246]

---

245 Raynor, Keith, "The Battle of the Mississinewa, 1812," on the web site of The Discriminating General: Keith Raynor suggests there were at least 3 main leaders of the Indians. Francis Godfroy was the son of Jacques Godfroy, the Indian trader. Joseph Richardville was the son of Chief Richardville of the Miamies. Little Thunder was the nephew of Little Turtle of the Miamies.

246 Many of these assaults may have been launched by a group of Miamies, who were creating a diversion so that the Indian prisoners could escape in the confusion. See: George Hunt's "Narrative

The dragoons fell back, dousing their campfires and continuing to shoot, using their horses as breastworks. Despite the confusion and the fiendish yells of the Indians, they retained control of the prisoners.[247]

Michigan Volunteers at near side of the firing line
Mississinewa 1812 Reenactment

Looking for a reserve force to throw in to relieve Ball's hard-pressed troops, Campbell spotted ten of the guides under Captain Bain and ordered them forward into the fray. Seven of them complied, including some Michigan men. They were James Audrain, William Conner, Silas McCullogh, James Thomson, James Knaggs, John Ruland and Joseph G. McClelland.

Other Raisin volunteers also fought bravely, and a couple of them were

---

of Escape from the Indians," MPHC, Vol. 12, pp. 452-5: *"It was a very cold night. This small party of Miamies, commanded by two boys not twenty years old, attacked at a point where our mounted men had formed, and having no breastworks save their horses, seventy of which were killed that night, this small party could charge up to the line, hallowing, "Fight on you d.-r.; the day is ours" when in fact they had no idea of doing so. Their object was to give the Muncie Indians an opportunity to make their escape from Col. Campbell, but did not succeed. When daylight came, the Indians scattered and took off their dead and wounded, if they had any. I never heard they had a single man killed. It put a stop to the advance of the Americans, nearly all mounted men. Such a crippled set of men who came into Dayton was a sight to look upon."*

247 "Mississinewa Battle Restored Nation's Faith in Army," by Martin Lake, Journal of the War of 1812 and the Era 1800 to 1840, Winter, 1995/6, p. 5.

wounded. Attached to Major Ball, Cornet Lee's men *"... behaved with great firmness and used their pistols and carabines to the best advantage."*[248]

In a further attempt to relieve Major Ball's squadron, whose ranks were becoming dangerously thin, Lt. Col. Campbell ordered Captain James Butler to withdraw his 52-man company of the Pittsburg Blues from their position in the line and plug the gap in the northwest corner left by the retreat of the dragoons.

Armed with muskets and bayonets, the Blues formed three 16-man sections and fired several concentrated volleys at close range. After a while, the smoke became so thick that the enemy could only be targeted by the tongues of flame that issued from the muzzles of their guns.

The southwest corner, defended by Markle's dragoons and the 19th U.S. also came under heavy pressure, but the lines held.[249] The Native force lost its enthusiasm and began to disperse.[250]

At this time, most of Simrall's men had not yet been engaged. As the light increased, the troops opened their ranks to allow the dragoons to pass through. Captains Trotter on the left and Johnston on the right led their mounted men on ragged charges through and behind the wavering Indians. The sun was far above the horizon, when the warriors disappeared in all directions.

The battle had lasted for an hour. Out of 590 or more men engaged, American losses amounted to at least 8 soldiers and 107 horses killed, and 48 men wounded, some fatally. The dead were buried inside the prison huts,

---

248 James Bentley may have played an important part in the battle as well. Afterwards, General Harrison called the River Raisin men "the best soldiers the world ever furnished." See: Wing, Talcott E., "History of Monroe County, Michigan," in Michigan Pioneer & Historical Collections, Vol. IV, 1881. Lansing: W. S. George & Co., 1883, p. 323. See also: Letter Campbell to Harrison, dated Fort Greenville, Dec. 25, 1812, in Official Letters of the military and Naval Officers of the United States during the War with Great Britain in the Years 1812, 13, 14, and 15, Edited by John Brannan, Washington City: Wax & Gideon, 1823, pp. 110-117. See: Glenn, Elizabeth J., B.K. Swartz, Jr., and Russell E. Lewis, "Ethnohistorical and Archaeological Descriptive Accounts of the War of 1812, Mississinewa Campaign and Aftermath: Project Report," Archaeological Reports, No.14, Ball State University, 1977.

249 "The Report of the Detachment Adjutant," Knopf, Richard C., Document Transcriptions of the War of 1812 in the Northwest, Vol. 5, Part 2, Columbus: Ohio Historical Society, 1958, pp. 4-5: "After the action, our guide, Mr. Wm. Conner, described to the prisoners...the length of line attacked, and requested to know what number they though had attacked us. They answered about 300."

250 Holliday, Murray, The Battle of the Mississinewa, 1812, Marion, IN: Grant County Historical Society, 1964, pp. 20-22.

which were then burned to hide the graves. Fifteen Native American bodies were found on the field, but their wounded had all been taken off.[251]

Campbell ordered a retreat to Greenville, which they reached in less than a week, many without horses to ride, and all of them suffering from hunger, exhaustion, or frostbite. Fortunately, they were not pursued, as the Indians feared injuring the Muncies who were still being held captive by the soldiers.

Christmas Day at the River Raisin, December 25, 1812:

At the River Raisin, Shawenaba, Wassagan, and Ponette were making one of their frequent visits to the farm of Joseph Bissonette.

Bissonette's late father had been in the fur trade, and Joseph was himself well known as a man of his word by the Indians. He had purchased his farm from the Potawatomies for a pony and a yoke of oxen.

Bissonette had then brought his widowed mother and his two younger brothers, Étienne and Gabriel, down to the River Raisin, where he married Eunice Robert and built a fine 20' × 30' cabin of hewn timbers, with whitewood siding and a large fireplace on one end.

The Bissonette family was active in the church and often welcomed the traveling priest, Gabriel Richard, into their home. They were respected by everyone and consistently left the latch string on the outside of their door so all could enter freely.

The three Potawatomies frequently visited their friend Joseph, as well as his wife Eunice, and their young children. They particularly enjoyed the antics of Joseph's 2½-year-old son, Gabriel. One or another of the chiefs would grab the little one's hands while he tried to dance a jig for them. Pretty soon they would all be laughing and tumbling about.

On this visit, however, as they entered the single downstairs room, their mood was a little more restrained. The Potawatomies glanced about as though they were inspecting the premises for defense. They noted the heavy oak batten door on the north side of the house, between two small windows.

---

251 An article in the December 29th issue of The Kentucky Gazette claimed Campbell's losses were 10 killed and 40 wounded; two of them fatally. Thirty Native warriors were said to have been killed and scalped. Forty-one prisoners were captured, including 9 warriors. The adjutant's official report listed army casualties as 8 killed in action, 2 died of wounds, 48 wounded, and 303 disabled by frostbite. Information courtesy of John Trowbridge.

Two more windows pierced the south side, between which hung a large mirror, a crucifix, and a chaplet, above a bureau of cherry wood.[252]

A large bed enclosed by a curtain sat in the southeast corner. To its left was a voluminous black walnut commode with paneled doors, which held the family's linens and underwear.

A large cupboard occupied the northeast corner, while a big, square, black walnut table occupied the center of the room. The rest of the furniture consisted basically of splint bottom chairs and rocking chairs.[253]

The chiefs told Bissonette that a week before Christmas, a war party of 31 Indians had stopped at the home of Ambrose Charland.[254] With them was a prisoner they had captured along the Maumee River.

There was tension throughout the settlement as Indian scouts reported the advance of Winchester's army. The chiefs said they had come to warn Bissonette that trouble was brewing, and he had better take measures to protect his family. Joseph responded that he would remain to look after his farm, but he was sending his family to Detroit for safety.

The Indians nodded their approval, and Shawenaba added that he would adopt little Gabriel and consider him as if he were his own son, which would protect him from harm.[255]

The Bissonettes were devout Catholics. Although Christmas did not bring the heavy round of parties, family visits, and gift giving that occurred at New Year's, it did call for special religious services and a midnight meal, or *réveillon*. Perhaps they would burn a Yule log, and it might be wise to save a bit of that blessed log to burn later in the year, just for some extra luck.

Those River Raisin *habitants* who were able traveled to Detroit where they could spend the holiday visiting with friends and attending Mass at Ste-Anne's Church. Afterwards, they would spend the night with relatives and enjoy *tourtière* meat pies and other holiday treats at the midnight *réveillon*.[256]

---

252 A Chaplet consists of a set of beads for personal devotion. A Dominican Rosary is a Chaplet, but there are a variety of other forms which may use fewer beads and different prayers.

253 Genealogical Sketch and History, *Michigan Pioneer Collections*, Vol. 38, pp. 502-9. The upstairs was also a single room, partitioned in half to separate male and female occupants for sleeping.

254 Affidavit of Ambrose C. Charland, taken July 15, 1853, in Monroe County, Michigan, original in G. Godfroy papers, Burton Historical Collection, Detroit Public Library.

255 *A History of Monroe County, Michigan*, p. 21, "Joseph Bissonette," Bios of Early Settlers.

256 Henderson, Robert. "A Soldier's Christmas; Christmas in the British Army during the War of 1812," posted on the web site of Militaryheritage.com. Even the English troops over at Amherstburg, who had a tradition of celebrating Christmas, usually did little more than throw a few pieces of

Christmas Day at Detroit, December 25, 1812:

Off to the north, the people of Detroit were having their own worries this Christmas Day. Elizabeth Ann Godfroy felt she and her family were too exposed to the whims of the Indians who daily passed by their Detroit store.

She had heard that a close family friend, Judge Woodward, was moving across the river into Canada. He owned a large, comfortable home in town that would make a perfect retreat. Hoping the judge would look kindly on her request, she sat down to write him a note. Although she was the daughter of Judge James May and spoke colloquial English quite well, she struggled with the spelling — trying to sound out the letters as she wrote. Regardless of the spelling, her language was clear and direct. She thanked Woodward in advance for speaking to Procter to authorize the relocation and setting a rental price on his house for her.[257]

In the meantime, and barring any progress in finding a new home in Detroit, the Godfroys could always do what they had done right after the fall of that city to the British last summer. That is, they could remove themselves to the Godfroy farm at French Town on the River Raisin.

Christmas Day in the field, Friday, December 25, 1812:

Limited as it was, the Christmas season at the River Raisin contrasted sharply with what was happening far to the south, where the hungry, frost-bitten remnants of Lieutenant Colonel John B. Campbell's expedition were staggering into Greenville on their retreat from the Mississinewa. A number of Campbell's men bore recent wounds, and 17 were in such bad shape they had to be carried on litters between two horses.[258]

---

greenery about the buildings of the garrison. Duties might be lighter, the workday shortened, and perhaps a collection taken up to provide better fare than the usual daily rations.

Several residents of *le Détroit* were of Scottish extraction. Their heartiest reveling was at New Year's or "Hogmanay," when bonfires and torch parades could drive the old year out. In contrast to the British soldiery, the more sober, Anglo-American Protestants considered any frivolous celebrations, parties, or dances during this Holy Season to be a mockery of Christ's birth.

257 Letter Eliza Godfroy to Judge Woodward, dated Detroit, Dec. 25, 1812, in Michigan Pioneer and Historical Society Collections, Vol. VIII, 1907, p. 637: *"Sir: I am sorry to trouble you so often, but, has I have herd that you was agoing over the river, if you will let me have your house as our family is large, and I do not find myself safe where we are — if you will be so good has to speak to Gouvenier Proctor, and let me have an answer, if it is not too much trouble, and the price, you will do me a great favor..."*

258 Raynor, Keith, "The Battle of the Mississinewa, 1812," on the web site of The Discriminating General: The litters were made of two 12'-long poles, with canvas sewed in between. They were carried between two horses; one in front, the other in back. Each horse was led by a man on foot. The

Cold and lack of food on the journey home had conspired to put about 300 of his men out of service for any further duties, at least until they had a chance to recuperate.[259] [260]

By contrast, Winchester's Army celebrated Christmas with some extra rations and by firing a few muskets on Christmas Eve, which caused an alarm.

An hour before daylight, the entire army was paraded and given strict orders that there should be no more shooting. At sunrise, the troops were told to round up any loose horses and prepare for their march to the Rapids.[261]

The celebration was more orderly at General Tupper's camp, "...*on New Year as well as Christmas morning, two rounds were fired in succession all around the lines, preceded by a discharge from a cannon.*"[262]

December 25th was post day at the town of Franklinton, where Lt. Joseph Larwill was able to enjoy a Christmas dinner of wild turkey with his friends.

Here, too, the old year was ushered out with rolling musket fire in a "*feu de joie,*" on an unseasonably warm New Year's Eve that would soon turn cold.

The troops would leave Franklinton by noon the next day, to the sound of 7 shots from Lieutenant Larwill's cannon.[263]

---

ride was often jolting, especially since the rear horse could not see where it was stepping.

259 Lossing, Benson J. The Pictorial Field-Book of the War of 1812. Glendale, New York: Benchmark Publishing Corporation, 1970, pp. 345-9. If nothing else, the raids on the Mississinewa villages drove a wedge between the tribes. The destruction forced those who favored the British to depend more wholly on their ally for food and basic survival. To avoid further destruction, tribes who favored the Americans moved into zones of American control and even offered to supply scouts for campaigns against their cousins fighting for Tecumseh. There was little room left for neutrality. The White River Delawares sued for peace and moved behind the American lines, but the event pushed the neutral-leaning Miamies into the British camp. After the Battle of Mississinewa, Silver Heels surrendered with 30 of his tribe, but Chief *"Richardville mounted his horse and said he was going to Malden, and all who could, followed him."* See: George Hunt's "Narrative of Escape from the Indians," Michigan Pioneer and Historical Collections, Vol. 12, pp. 452-5.

260 "Mississinewa Battle Restored Nation's Faith in Army," by Martin Lake, Journal of the War of 1812 and the Era 1800 to 1840, Winter, 1995/6, p. 5. The troops were praised by General Harrison, and also by President James Madison, grateful to have some sort of victory to announce. Campbell was brevetted to the rank of full Colonel and Major Ball to Lt. Colonel.

261 Darnell, Elias, Journal, Philadelphia: Lippincott, Grambo, and Co., 1854, pp. 40-42.

262 "Journal of Mathew Newsom," as transcribed by James Ohde, Ohio State Museum, Columbus: Anthony Wayne Parkway Board, 1957, p. 14. Also, on January 1st, two men were buried, having died of sickness. On New Year's Eve, the weather turned cold and it snowed for the next 48 hours.

263 "Journal of Joseph Larwill," Burton Historical Collection, Detroit Public Library, pp. 22-24. *"We... had considerable difficulty to get Need, a private, along — he being very drunk."* Meanwhile, General Harrison had the men at Upper Sandusky hard at work building a blockhouse.

WINCHESTER'S MARCH TO THE RAPIDS
LA MARCHE du GÉNÉRAL au SAULT DES MIAMIS

Winchester's Camp Number 3, December, 1813:[264]

In December, an expedition was organized to take advantage of high-water levels in the St. Marys River to float supplies down to Winchester's army on the Maumee. Nearly 200 barrels of flour were loaded onto 15 pirogues escorted by Captain Jordan and some 20 men. Their progress was slowed, however, by log jams and overhanging trees.

On December 5, some clothing arrived at Winchester's camp, but the joy was dimmed as the troops were placed on half rations of alcohol. As for food, hickory roots and poor beef had become staple items. The company butchers would periodically attack one of the weakened cattle when it was lying down and couldn't escape. At other times the troops contented themselves with freshly killed pork, which they deemed less nourishing than the salted kind.

To save ammunition, salutes were no longer fired at burials after December 8. The men were permitted to hunt for extra food, but by now there was not much left to shoot at, not even a squirrel.[265]

General Harrison was often in the dark about the exact situation of Winchester's army. On December 14th, he wrote the Secretary of War that he had received information that four or five hundred Indians were at Swan

---

264 General Winchester remained near Defiance with the Left Wing of the army, while General Leftwich's Virginians were stationed at Delaware; General Crooks' Pennsylvanians were at Mansfield; and General Perkins' Ohioans were at the Huron of Lake Erie. See: Lorrain, Alfred, The Helm, the Sword, and the Cross: A Life Narrative, Cincinnati: Poe & Hitchcock, 1862, pp. 108 -116. As he marched north with other reinforcements, Alfred Lorrain, a private in the Petersburg Volunteers, described the area between Franklinton, Delaware, and Upper Sandusky, where they would arrive on January 10th: "Through most intolerable roads, and severe weather, we reached the town of Delaware, which was even then a handsome village. Before reaching this desirable spot, we were frequently stalled and our baggage wagons broken down. Delaware was the ultima thule of American civilization... We passed only one cabin between it and Sandusky."

265 "Fort Winchester," by Charles Slocum. Ohio Archaeological and Historical Publications, Vol. ix. Columbus: Heer Publishing Co., Ohio State Archaeological Society, 1901, pp. 253-277: "...I have not heard from the general for 18 or 20 days. I shall go forward and send an express through the woods directing him if he has not reached the Rapids to make a detachment to his left towards the head of Swan Creek, whilst his main body shall advance to the Rapids. The position occupied by the Indians is a complete cul-de-sac, unless Swan Creek, which is 15 feet deep for many miles, is frozen over..."

Creek of the Maumee.[266] He sent orders to Winchester to *"...March for the Rapids as soon as 10 days' provisions could be provided."* Assurances were given that a cooperating force from the center column would meet them there.

The orders from General Harrison were delivered to Winchester by Ensign C.S. Todd, who was guided by 3 Wyandots and 2 men from the Michigan Territory. Harrison hoped that a swift advance would trap hundreds of Native warriors between the rapids and Swan Creek of the Maumee.

At the rapids, Winchester's men were to fortify their camp and build winter huts to make the enemy think they were going into winter quarters, but they were also to build sleds in secret, to make it possible to stage a winter attack on Detroit or Malden.

Over several days, detachments of the army moved out of Camp Number 3. Some of Wells' regulars left December 26. Cold weather froze the Maumee River, preventing canoe transport, so they hauled their equipment on the sleds.

The rest of the 17th Infantry broke camp December 29th and marched for 6 miles. The militia followed the next day, leaving General Winchester, his headquarters staff, and the sick behind in Camp Number 3, protected by a company from each regiment.[267]

A thaw set in a day later, melting the snow, so the army managed only a couple miles through the slush and mud. Winchester tried to take advantage of the sudden break-up of the river ice by using pirogues, but they barely made a few hundred yards before getting wedged in the ice, and had to be off-loaded.

Ten days rations had been assembled and placed on those boats, but the Maumee remained choked with icy flows. Two days of efforts to push their way through came to naught. The army's tents and enough kettles to establish a kitchen were then shifted onto the backs of the pack horses.[268]

---

266 McAfee, Robert. History of the Late War in the Western Country, Bowling Green, Ohio: Historical Publications Company, 1919 (reprint of 1816 original edition.) p. 210. See also: Winchester, James. Historic Details Having Relation to the Campaign of the North-Western Army under Generals Harrison and Winchester. Lexington: Worsley & Smith, 1818, p. 21.

267 Orderly book of Captain Bland Ballard, Winchester Papers, Burton Historical Collection, Detroit Public Library: Ballard lists Kerley's company as being the company from the 1st Rifle Regiment that was designated to stay behind. Further orders were issued to suppress any form of gunfire.

268 Letter Response of General Leslie Combs, Verhoeven Collection, Monroe County Museum Archives. See: Winchester, James, Historic Details Having Relation to the Campaign of the North-Western Army under Generals Harrison and Winchester, Lexington: Worsley & Smith, 1818, p. 21.

On Dec. 30, Winchester sent Leslie Combs and Abraham Riddle to Harrison and Tupper, reminding them to reinforce him at the rapids.

Winchester's message to General Tupper at Fort McArthur stated that he intended to be at the Maumee Rapids in 7 or 8 days and to send flour, salt, and whisky there, as he expected to be out of those items.

In response, Tupper put 50 of his men to work making light sleds to be drawn by 2 horses. He also began assembling more supplies at Fort Findlay.[269]

Winchester finally left "Camp Starvation" on December 31st, the last day of the year. He left his wagons behind, using the army's weary and underfed pack horses to carry his tents and kettles through a blinding snow storm.[270] The weather turned cold once again on Friday, January 2, bringing a heavy snowfall that continued for two days and two nights. Three days out of camp, General Winchester received Harrison's message countermanding his previous order to advance, unless the army had already departed.

Tecumseh was reported to be gathering Native warriors on the Wabash, and Harrison believed it prudent to pull his left wing back to a more consolidated position at Fort Jennings. However, Winchester was already on his way to the rapids, so he decided not to return to Camp Number 3.

The weather broke two days later, and Winchester resumed his march through 2-foot drifts of fallen snow. By the 7th they were encamped at Prairie Demaske,[271] where they drew two days' provisions in double rations of pork and salt, still without flour, and prepared to continue the next day.[272]

The troops looked like impoverished vagabonds as they plodded along in dirty, threadbare clothes and blankets. The army's sleds were too lightly constructed to carry all the supplies placed upon them, and too low to safely

---

269 Winchester, James, Historic Details Having Relation to the Campaign of the North-Western Army under Generals Harrison and Winchester, Lexington: Worsley & Smith, 1818, p. 23.

270 Speech of General Leslie Combs at the 1872 Veterans Reunion in Monroe.

271 Prairie de Masque (also known as Prairie des Mascoutins or Damascus Prairie) was the site of a Mascoutin village. In 1742, the Kickapoos moved there at the behest of the Governor of Montréal. The 1807 Treaty of Detroit allowed white settlers to claim land in the area. A town grew there during the canal era, but died with the coming of the railroads. An historical marker is on the Maumee River at or near 7461 Old US24, Liberty Center, OH 43532.

272 Meanwhile, General Harrison was still concerned about the availability of supplies for Winchester's troops. He ordered Deputy Commissary Piatt to deliver supplies to Fort Defiance, Fort Winchester, and Fort Wayne, and for 20,000 rations of bacon and biscuits to be discretely assembled at Greenville, but it would take weeks for the supplies to reach those places. See: Letters Harrison at Franklinton to Piatt, Jan. 1,6, and 7, 1813, Harrison Papers, Indiana Historical Society.

ford the streams that, although icy, were not completely frozen in the center. Consequently, much of the army's gear got wet.

Each company had 3 sleds to haul their baggage, but the packhorses were not used to pulling sleds with harnesses made of green hides. Having subsisted on brush for the last two weeks, the horses became so weak that they often gave out, especially in deep snow. Each incapacitated horse was replaced by 5 or 6 Kentuckians, and the march was painfully continued.[273]

French Town on the Raisin, the First Week of January, 1813:

At the River Raisin, the young men had spent their New Year's Eve in an outlandish procession gathering clothing and provisions for the poor. Driving their carts from house to house, singing songs, they wore masks and dressed in the most peculiar garments they could scrape together.

On New Year's Day the children of every family performed their annual duty of entering their parents' room and asking for the blessing of their elders. The *habitants'* modest prayer this holiday season, as in many years to come, was basically, "*Lord, if you can't give us any more happiness than you did last year, please don't give us any less.*"[274]

January 8-10, 1813:

Winchester's army stopped early every afternoon to set up camp for the night. The men were forced to stand in snowy ranks as the camp was laid out. It took quite a bit of effort for the tired soldiers to rake the snow away,

---

273 Darnell, Elias, <u>Journal</u>. Philadelphia: Lippincott, Grambo, and Co., 1854, p. 43 + Atherton, William, <u>Narrative of the Suffering & Defeat of the North-Western Army under General Winchester</u>, Frankfort, KY, A. G. Hodges, 1842, pp. 25-27. *"The reader may ask how such a number of sleds could be drawn, seeing there was not a supply of horses. Some of them were drawn by the men themselves — five men were hitched to a sleigh, and, through snow and water, dragged them on at the rate of about ten miles a day…Some time was required to arrange the encampment, during which time the men were compelled to keep their places in the lines, and thus become so chilled as to be almost unfit for the necessary exertion of preparing a resting place for themselves. The snow, which was about knee deep, had first to be cleared away, then fire to be struck with flint and steel, and when no lynn bark could be had, brush was substituted in its place, which formed our bed…"*

274 Austerberry, John. "Christmas on the River Raisin, 200 Years Ago," <u>Monroe Evening News</u>, Dec. 24, 1984. Based largely on an interview with Dennis Au, Assistant Director, Monroe County Historical Museum. Since it was an annual custom, I have assumed it may have continued in some fashion during the war, at least until the destruction of the community after January 22, 1813.

make fires with flint and steel, pitch tents, and search for lynn bark or bushes to lie on. Darkness came early. At least, the exhausted men slept soundly.[275]

U.S. soldiers as portrayed in the "Battles of the River Raisin" Documentary produced by the Friends of the River Raisin Battlefield
Bill Saul

As the soldiers slept, Leslie Combs and his guide, Abraham Riddle rode their tired horses in to Fort McArthur in the dead of night on Friday, January 8. The two men, bearing news of Winchester's advance, were hungry and exhausted, having been delayed several days by a snowstorm, which dumped 2 feet of snow across their path.

General Tupper quickly sent another horseman on with Winchester's

---

275 Atherton, William, <u>Narrative of the Suffering & Defeat of the North-Western Army under General Winchester.</u> Frankfort, KY, A. G. Hodges, 1842, p. 27. The going was slow, averaging about 10 miles per day. The army would rise at 5 a.m., with reveille at 6. The 6:30 "troop" was followed by the "general" at 7:00, "assembly" at 7:15, and the "march" at 7:30. The procession to the Rapids was terribly fatiguing for Winchester's men, but they encountered little sign of Indian resistance. The soldiers all complained of being cold and wet. Their clothing was worn out and covered in grime and soot, although a timely supply of clothing arrived from Kentucky on Dec. 27th. Some were still without proper footwear. Many felt sick from eating the meat of freshly killed wild boars, without bread or salt. They much preferred their normal diet of salt pork.

message to General Harrison. After a good rest and some food, Combs took an open sleigh and returned to General Winchester.[276]

Winchester continued to advance, even in the face of bad weather.[277] No one was permitted to ride any harnessed horses. Sleds that broke down were pushed off the trail, repaired, and returned to the rear of the passing column. The army marched through "Wolftown," and established Camp *Roche de Bout* on the 8th or 9th, only 4 miles from where Hull's Road struck the Maumee.[278]

The next morning was one of the coldest on record, but Winchester sent

276 Letter, General Leslie Combs, Verhoeven Collection, Monroe County Museum Archives. See also: "Journal of Mathew Newsom," as transcribed by James Ohde, Ohio State Museum, Columbus: Anthony Wayne Parkway Board, 1957, p. 15: "*From the 7th to the 10th, it snowed almost continual, the weather continued excessive cold. On the 11th and 12th, many hundred hogs were started to the Rapids of the Maumee for the use of the army. On the 14th, about 100 packhorses arrived at McArthur's Block-house with store-goods and provision. They were principally from Kentucky. These horses were mostly taken and hitched to about 38 sleds made by the artificers in a very bungling shackling way. Three barrels of flour were put on a sled, and each man who undertook to drive one of the sleds received six bushels of corn as forage to feed the two horses for 11 days...On the 15th, these sleds all started. The most of the men were taken from the lines who drove those sleds. The remainder were Kentuckians, who had brought the packhorses....*"

277 Harrison was trying to build up sufficient forces and supplies to attack Detroit during February. A frozen Detroit River might enable him feint towards Detroit, cross the river on the ice, and invest Fort Amherstburg. He was not, however, totally committed to this plan of action, as he stated in his letter of January 4, 1813, to Secretary of War James Monroe. Much depended on the weather and the difficulty of getting supplies to the troops as they moved into Michigan Territory.

   Above all, he didn't want to proceed directly to Detroit without first taking strategically placed Malden. "*The latter in the hands of the enemy, with a disposable force of half the size of that with which we should advance to the former, would place us completely in a cul-de-sac.*" In other words, they could be trapped and cut off in Detroit just like General Hull had been.

   As early as mid-December, Harrison had suggested to the War Department that if the capture of Detroit were not politically urgent, the increased cost and effort of supplying an army on the Northwest Frontier might be more efficiently diverted to building a fleet on Lake Erie. At the beginning of the war, General Hull had insisted that Detroit would not be secure without naval control of the lakes, but the War Department had made only token efforts to construct a naval force. Harrison believed that Hull had been right in his strategic assessment of the situation, after all.

   There had also been a change in the War Department. William Eustis had resigned as Secretary of War in December and was temporarily replaced by James Monroe until John Armstrong was confirmed and able to assume those duties on Feb. 13, 1813. See: Lossing, Benson J., The Pictorial Field-Book of the War of 1812, Glendale, NY: Benchmark Publishing Corporation, 1970, p. 348.

278 General Orders, Jan. 7 and 8, 1812, Winchester Papers, Michigan Pioneer & Historical Collections, Vol. 35, p. 311. Companies from the 17th and 19th U.S. and 1st Rifle Regiments were posted on the right flank; the 1st and 5th Kentucky on the left; the regimental baggage in the center. Wolftown probably refers to Wolf Rapids, the location of Odawa villages in the Providence area, near Grand Rapids, Ohio.

ahead a detachment of 676 men to make sure there were no Indians entrenched below the rapids. The army finally arrived at Hull's Road at the Rapids in the early afternoon on January 10, some 50 miles from Fort Defiance.[279]

Here, they halted to scrape away the drifts, pitch their tents, gather brush and bark on which to make their beds. Their camp was on Presque Isle Hill, an oval-shaped rise of ground studded with trees, but clear of underbrush. It was a good defensive position, surrounded by open prairie, overlooking the river just opposite Hull's old 1812 campground.[280]

Many of the inhabitants of the rapids had disappeared, leaving only the isolated chimneys of their burned-out homes as silent witnesses of a once-thriving settlement. About 300 acres of corn still stood in the fields.

The men could hardly restrain themselves. They rushed out and picked the frozen ears, boiled the corn, and ate it on the cob without salt. Many gorged themselves to the point they could barely walk.[281]

From the rapids, Winchester sent a column of pack horses to pick up supplies from General Tupper.[282] Uncertain of Harrison's location at this time,

---

279 Winchester, James. Historic Details Having Relation to the Campaign of the North-Western Army under Generals Harrison and Winchester. Lexington: Worsley & Smith, 1818, p. 22. By now, he was down to 1,100 effectives, not counting the garrisons left in the rear. The number of able-bodied men under Winchester's command varied due to sickness, desertion, expired enlistments, detachments, reinforcement, etc. Nearly every report cited a different number of troops.

280 They also received some warm clothing to augment their lightweight garments of linen and cotton. It was a common saying that, while the sons of Kentucky had provided volunteers to meet the British, it was the daughters of Kentucky who enabled them to *"meet the blasts of a northern winter."* See: Atherton, William, Narrative of the Suffering & Defeat of the North-Western Army under General Winchester. Frankfort, KY, A. G. Hodges, 1842. p. 30: *"...I hope it is not still too late...to express my unfeigned gratitude to the daughters of my native state for the blessings bestowed on me as an individual...Help, in real need, is not forgotten."* The women of Dayton, Ohio, had previously made 1800 heavy shirts (out of cloth originally destined for Indian annuities), but only a portion of them had reached Fort Winchester before the men had left Defiance. See also: Gilpin, Alec R., The War of 1812 in the Old Northwest, East Lansing: MSU Press, 1958, p. 156, and Lossing, Benson J. The Pictorial Field-Book of the War of 1812. Glendale, New York: Benchmark Publishing Corporation, 1970, p. 350.

281 Atherton, William, Narrative of the Suffering & Defeat of the North-Western Army under General Winchester, Frankfort, KY: A. G. Hodges, 1842, p. 31. For pounding, hardwood stumps were drilled with holes about 2 feet wide and a foot deep. After parching the corn in pots over the campfire, it was placed into the hollow stumps and pounded with hickory stakes into a course corn meal. Mixed with pork fat or tallow, it made a substantial food.

282 Dissertation of Rex LeRoy Spencer, Ph.D., "The Gibraltar of the Maumee: Fort Meigs in the War of 1812." Muncie, Indiana: Ball State University, 1989. While *en route*, Winchester had received a message from Harrison canceling his advance to the Maumee Rapids, for fear that Tecumseh's warriors were preparing to raid along the Wabash. This rumor resulted from Campbell's raid on

Winchester along a message addressed to him, along with the excuse that his horses had been too winded to make the delivery during their march.[283]

Once the spring thaw arrived, army transport would be immobilized as the dirt trails, frozen puddles, and hard ground turned to mush.[284] It was too risky to move men and supplies by boat as long as the British fleet controlled the waters of Lake Erie.[285]

With no entrenching tools and no artillery, Winchester felt vulnerable. He delayed the release of two militia regiments whose enlistments had expired and set them to work felling trees to build a breast work and some store houses.[286]

Each corps was responsible for cutting trees in front of their lines, while

---

the Mississinewa. Winchester, however, had decided to push on. He sent messages to Generals Tupper and Harrison asking them to forward men and supplies to the Rapids.

283 Winchester, James, <u>Historic Details Having Relation to the Campaign of the North-Western Army under Generals Harrison and Winchester</u>, Lexington: Worsley & Smith, 1818, p. 25: The next day, Winchester wrote to Gen. Tupper, hoping he was on his way to the rapids with supplies.

284 On Dec. 26, 1812, Acting Secretary of War James Monroe wrote to General Harrison that the delay and expense of his campaign against Detroit was causing the president much concern. *"...It is expected that you will forthwith form a clear and distinct plan as to the objects which you may deem attainable, the time within which they may be attained, and the force necessary for the purpose, and that you communicate the same with precision to the Department. As soon as you have formed this plan, you will proceed to execute it, without waiting for an answer..."* Secretary Eustis resigned in December and John Armstrong was appointed to that office on January 13. James Monroe took over temporarily on September 27 of the following year, while still serving as Secretary of State. In 1947, the *"Secretary of War"* became the *"Secretary of Defense."*

285 Knopf, Richard C. <u>Document Transcriptions of the War of 1812 in the Northwest, Vol. VII, pt 1</u>. Columbus: Ohio Historical Society, 1961, p. 35: Mr. Greeley left Detroit to report British naval strength on the Great Lakes. He listed 4 warships; the *Queen Charlotte, Lady Prevoste, Governor Hunter*, and the schooner *Chippewa*. There were also 3 gunboats, each carrying two 12-pdr. carronades and crewed by 25 men. Several merchant vessels were also under British control; the *Nancy, Ellen, Mary, Salina, Erie*, and *Friends Goodwill*, which, except for the *Nancy*, had been seized from their American owners. Also, he mentioned Peter Cott's sloop of 30 tons, taken near Buffalo, and the schooner of 25 tons burthen belonging to Chapin of Buffalo, which the British had seized on her passage from the Maumee to Detroit with the baggage belonging to the officers of General Hull.

286 Winchester estimated his current number of effectives at a little over 900 men fit for duty. See: Statement of General Winchester, Notices Vol. 1, Apdx 7, Memorandum of statements made by General Winchester and Major Madison to the Secretary of War on their return from captivity. Typed copy in Bidlack's Notes, Monroe County Historical Museum Archives. *"... my effective force on my arrival at the Rapids would not have exceeded 400 effectives, left to defend themselves and the magazines with muskets and rifles only against the attacks of a British and Indian force which General Harrison did not estimate at less than 4,000 combatants...Of our arrival and situation, the General was informed, by the best means I had — a party returning to McArthur's blockhouse; by whom I also requested a fulfillment of his promise of reinforcement..."*

intervals between units were fortified by a general detail. The retention of the men, however, weakened the supply situation. They consumed a lot of rations, and the army's regular troops were still without their winter clothing.[287]

Provisions were issued every day between 2 and 4 p.m. Extra cartridges which had been drawn by the detachment from General Payne's force were returned to the brigade quartermaster, leaving each man ten rounds.[288]

On the 11th, there was a sharp fight between Captain Williams' 24-man mounted patrol and a small force of Indians.[289] Williams retreated a half mile back to camp with a couple of wounded, having taken two horses and a brass kettle from the enemy's camp.[290] The warriors withdrew to the River Raisin, claiming to have killed two Americans, wounded several, and captured 3 horses.[291]

La Rivière au Loutre, 2:30 p.m., January 12, 1813:

---

287 Letter Harrison to Secretary of War Monroe, Jan. 6, 1813: Writing from Franklinton, Harrison complained, *"In my letter of yesterday, I mentioned the nakedness of the regular troops under Colonel Samuel Wells* [serving with Winchester's army]*...A part of the clothing has arrived here; the balance of it is, I fear, arrested by the ice on the Ohio. There has certainly been great negligence upon the part of some person in relation to this clothing. The troops marched from Kentucky in August to relieve General Hull, and the clothing for them left Philadelphia in late November. I beg leave also to mention to you that by the unpardonable negligence of the officer who examined and received them from the manufactory, the axes which have been sent on to this army are so worthless, that not above one in a dozen will stand the cutting of a stick six inches in diameter without breaking...Nothing can be more distressing than to see soldiers naked at this season, and nothing can certainly be more hurtful to the public service..."*

288 General Orders, Camp Miami Rapids, Jan. 11, 1813, MPHC, Vol.35, p. 312. The standard cartouche box contained a wooden block with holes for a couple dozen cartridges, below which was a tray with two tin compartments capable of holding 6 spare cartridges on each end of the box, with a middle section for extra flints, an oily rag, and cleaning attachments.

289 Probably Capt. Samuel Luttrell Williams, 5th Kentucky Volunteer Regiment.

290 Darnell, Elias, Journal. Philadelphia: Lippincott, Grambo, and Co., 1854, pp. 43-45: One man was wounded in the arm and another received a ball through his hat. Captain Edmiston's gun was shot through the breech. Native Americans traveled light, but it was not unusual for them to carry kettles as part of their camping gear. Brass or tin was easier to transport than cast iron. In addition, their usual utensils included a spoon, looking glass, awl, flint and steel for making fire, paint, pipe, and tobacco pouch. Their weapons usually included a trade musket or rifle, powder horn, shot pouch, tomahawk, and a knife, often suspended from a cord around their neck.

291 Cruikshank, Harrison & Procter, p. 153. See also: Atherton, William, Narrative of the Suffering & Defeat of the North-Western Army under General Winchester. Frankfort, KY, A. G. Hodges, 1842, p. 32. *"On the evening of the 13th, two Frenchmen arrived from the River Raisin with information that the Indians routed by Capt. Williams had passed that place on their way to Malden, carrying with them intelligence of our advance."*

It was the middle of the afternoon, and Isaac Day was just putting the finishing touches on his letter to Generals Winchester and Harrison from his hiding place in the woods along Otter Creek, 5 miles south of the River Raisin. His hand shook as he wrote, both from cold and from fear, for he dared not even light a fire. It might give away his position to the British and Indians.

Some American sympathizers at Detroit and the River Raisin had already been arrested and taken to Malden. Spies were everywhere. People feared that there would be nobody left at the Raisin, except for Indians and fur traders.

The British were hiring sleighs to transport all the flour and grain to their base at Fort Amherstburg. Native Americans were gathering along the River Raisin to oppose any American advance northward from the Maumee.

Earlier that day, a war party had stopped by on their way to Malden. They had been in a skirmish with Winchester's army just the day before, and had lost a couple horses, a brass kettle, and some other plunder, which they were hoping the British would replace. It was from talking to these warriors that the local French *habitants* learned of the location of Winchester's army.[292]

These Indians then left and reported to Colonel Procter at Malden on the 13th. Realizing French Town was in range of Winchester's army, Procter sent more Canadian militia and Native warriors to control or dismantle it.[293]

Isaac Day was aware of the situation and also knew that Winchester's army must be in great need of supplies. The *habitants* had managed to secrete some 50 barrels of flour and 200 bushels of wheat, but there were still 3,000 barrels of flour and a lot more wheat and corn at the River Raisin, which was occupied by only 40 or 50 Canadian militiamen and maybe 100 Indians.

In his letter, Day asked Winchester to send some cavalry and riflemen to the River Raisin. If arms and ammunition could be delivered to the 30 *habitants* he had with him, they could secure all the supplies at the River Raisin.

Day estimated that the *"English, French, and Savages"* assembled at

---

292 McAfee, Robert. History of the Late War in the Western Country, Bowling Green, Ohio: Historical Publications Company, 1919 (reprint of 1816 original edition). p. 223.

293 Fearing his forces would be too weak to hold the line at the River Raisin and protect the valuable supplies and resources located there, Colonel Procter ordered Major Ebenezer Reynolds to break up the River Raisin settlement and remove its inhabitants. Reynold's force at the Raisin would consist of two flank companies of Essex militia and a band of Potawatomies. A sled-mounted 3-pdr cannon commanded by Bombardier Kitson of the Royal Artillery and crewed by a 3-man detachment of trained militia volunteers would be his artillery support. Cruikshank, Harrison and Proctor, p. 153.

the nearby British base of Malden numbered under a thousand. Thus, he assured Winchester, *"Five hundred true and brave Americans can secure the District of Erie. A timely approach of our armies will secure us from being forced to prison, and the whole place from being burned by Savage fury."*[294]

The next day, two local River Raisin Frenchmen galloped off, carrying Day's letter. They reached Winchester's camp on the evening of the 13th, telling him the Indians were threatening to kill the inhabitants and burn the settlement.

The River Raisin *habitants* refused to abandon their settlement and bitterly resented the destruction of property and seizure of cattle by some Potawatomies, who appeared helter-skelter in groups of 20 to 100 warriors.

On the 14th, Winchester received further confirmation of problems at the River Raisin.[295] By January 15th, he was convinced of the urgency for taking action. To make sure he had enough troops, he sent a letter to General Perkins, at Lower Sandusky, asking for reinforcements.[296] A couple more *habitants* arrived from the Raisin late on the night of Saturday, January 16.[297]

---

294 Letter Day to Harrison, Otter Creek, Jan. 12, 1813. Typed copy in Bidlack's Notes, Monroe County Historical Museum Archives: *"I have taken the liberty to send per express to inform you that the enemy are apprised of your being at the Rapids and have removed all the friends of our Government to Malden Prison, and at present, we are beset with spies. I expect the Guard to search for me every moment....If you do not come tomorrow or the next day, you will not find a man at this place. The English are collecting all the savages to rally at the River Raisin for the purpose of giving battle. They are engaging sleighs to transport the flour and grain to their Pandora's Box, Malden..."* Isaac Day was a resident of Detroit as early as 1806.

Readers may note the liberal use of "savage" in quotations from the period. Depending on the context, the term did not necessarily have as bad a connotation as it does in modern English. The word *"sauvage"* in old French denoted a person living in a state of wildness or nature, free of the vices and constraints of European civilization. In English, a stereotypical savage would be some-one who acted savagely, but there was also the countervailing concept of the "Noble Savage." Of course, most Euro-Americans still considered their culture as superior and destined to dominate.

295 Atherton, W., Narrative of the Suffering & Defeat of the North-Western Army under General Winchester, Frankfort, KY: A. G. Hodges, 1842, p. 32. *"On the evening of the 13th, two Frenchmen arrived from the River Raisin with information that the Indians routed by Capt. Williams had passed that place on their way to Malden, carrying intelligence of our advance. They said the Indians threat-ened to kill their inhabitants and burn their town, and they begged for protection..."*

296 Gen. Harrison was at Upper Sandusky, where he sent a letter to Sec. of War James Monroe requesting $40,000 in gold or silver to buy supplies for his army when it reached Detroit. See: Letter Harrison to Monroe, Jan. 15, 1813, Harrison Papers, Indiana Historical Society.

297 Winchester, James. Historic Details Having Relation to the Campaign of the North-Western Army under Generals Harrison and Winchester. Lexington: Worsley & Smith, 1818, pp. 25-26. They said the enemy had hundreds of men at the Raisin, including two companies of Canadians, and the numbers were growing. They promised the *habitants* would supply Winchester's men. It was

The messengers informed the General that Isaac Day had been arrested. They also confirmed that 2 companies of Canadian militia were there, along with more Indians. Rumor had it that the British and Indians were planning to burn people out of their homes on the upcoming Wednesday, January 20.[298]

Winchester called a council of his officers and told them the enemy was at the Raisin *"...with orders to seize and send to Malden all inhabitants attached to the United States government, or suspected of being so attached, and with them all the horses and cattle, sleds, carioles, and provisions of every kind, and condemning at once the whole settlement to starvation, imprisonment, or slaughter, in case of refusal or resistance."*[299]

Colonel Samuel Wells at first opposed dispatching any of the command to the River Raisin. However, Colonel John Allen reasoned that taking French Town would restore the troops' confidence and that a few days in the comfort of an established settlement would improve their morale.

Waxing oratorical, Allen asked, *"Can we turn a deaf ear to the cries of men, women, and children about to perish under the scalping knife and tomahawk of the savage?*

...Can it be possible that the wisdom of defeating an enemy in detail can either escape our notice or require arguments to obtain our approbation?

For what purpose are we here but to seek, to find, and to fight this very enemy?"[300]

---

imperative to disperse this body before they could threaten Winchester's base camp on the Maumee. Winchester claimed his officers unanimously supported his decision to take French Town.

298 Information gleaned from interviews with veterans was published in the Pittsburgh Gazette and Mercury, and partially reprinted with comments in the Monroe Commercial of Thursday, March 23, 1871, contents posted at http://monroe.lib.mi.us/bygonesofmonroe/bomwarof1812.htm.

299 Statement of General Winchester, Notices Vol. 1, Apdx 7, Memorandum of statements made by General Winchester and Major Madison to the Secretary of War on their return from captivity. Typed copy in Bidlack's Notes, Monroe County Historical Museum Archives.

300 Armstrong, John. Notices of the War of 1812, Vol. I. New York: George Dearborn, 1836: Allen continued, *"And shall we permit his advanced guard to perpetrate all the mischief it meditates, and return in safety to its main body? Is it by such conduct we shall wipe out the disgrace of Hull's surrender or fulfill the promises made to our friends when, leaving our own firesides, we took upon us the temporary profession of arms? ...will it be said that the force of the hostile detachment is too great to be successfully combated, or in other words, that a thousand freemen are unequal to contend with 300 savages and slaves? ...will it be said that so near an approach to the den of the Lion would be imprudent? To this I reply that danger is inseparable from war, and that the soldier who goes upon a plan of running no risk is necessarily self-condemned to inaction and disgrace. ...this was the fault of Hull, and cannot be thought worthy of our imitation. If the Lion, as he has been called, moves at all, he will do so in one of 2 ways; he will either send a 2nd detachment to support the 1st, in which case*

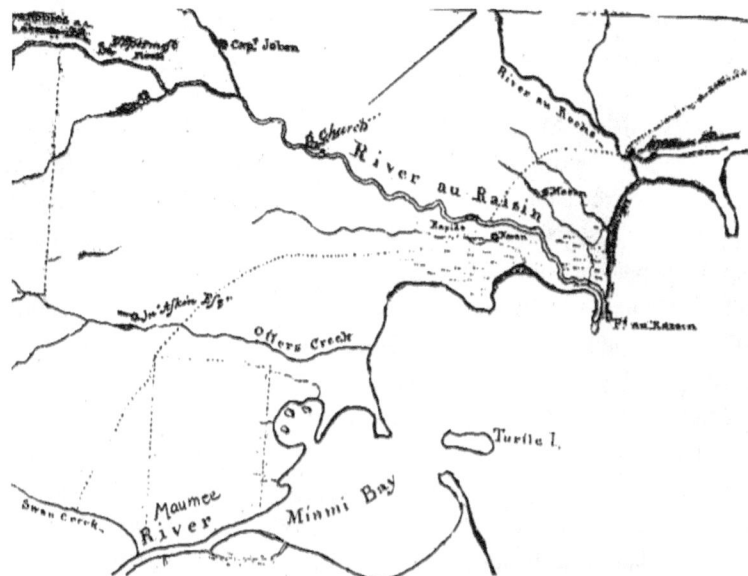

River Raisin Country, McNiff Map, J. S. Gray Collection
Monroe County Historical Museum, ca. 1790s

Indeed, Winchester's men almost unanimously supported an advance to the Raisin to protect American citizens and seize the supplies at French Town. Winchester dispatched a relief force early the next morning. He also wrote a letter to General Harrison, asking for additional reinforcements.[301]

Winchester's relief detachment initially totaled 550 volunteers. They

---

both may be separately beaten, or he will put his whole force in motion, and thus furnish us with a sufficient excuse for falling back upon our own army, which cannot now be far in the rear. ...I am led to conclude that we should hasten our march to Frenchtown; attack, and if possible, destroy the advanced corps of the enemy; give protection to a meritorious and suffering people, and obtain the control of resources, of which we are much in want and which otherwise will go to sustain the war against us."

301 Letter Winchester to Harrison, Jan. 17, 1813, typed copy in Bidlack's Notes, Monroe County Historical Society Archives. "...Isaac Day, the writer of the enclosed note, has been taken and sent to prison. I am also informed that the enemy is engaging all the sleighs he can procure for the purpose of carrying off the flour and grain. In this latter purpose, I have determined to disappoint him, or oblige him to pay a dear price for it; for which purpose I have this morning detached Colonel William Lewis and John Allen with a command suitable to effect the object intended. I am informed they will have to contend with two companies of Canadians and about 200 Indians. If we get possession, it is my intention to retain it; therefore, a cooperating force from the right wing may be acceptable. Nothing will reconcile an extension of the period of service of the volunteers, but progressive operations..."

were organized in nine companies and commanded by Lieutenant Colonel Lewis, seconded by Majors Madison and Graves.[302]

Presque Isle of the Maumee, 7 p.m., January 17, 1812:

Lt. Col. Lewis' force left Winchester's camp early that morning with orders to attack the enemy, beat them, take possession of French Town, and hold it.[303] Lewis had 550 men, but the *habitants* from the River Raisin said it would not be nearly enough. The Indians and redcoats would eat them up.

So, at noon, Winchester ordered out a second reinforcement under Lt. Colonel Allen consisting of 110 more Kentuckians from Hickman's, Bledsoe's, and McCracken's companies of the 1st Rifle Regiment, with a few volunteers from the 1st and 5th Kentucky who had stayed behind when Lewis departed.

In the meantime, the troops under Lt. Colonel Lewis had proceeded down the Maumee River to the small French village of *Presqu'Île*.

Established near the mouth of the Maumee River about the year 1807, the village contained a mixture of Odawa and French families, largely from

---

302 Ballard, Bland. Orderly Book, Jan. 17, 1813, in Winchester's Orderly Books, Burton Collection, Detroit Public Library. Captains Gray, Pugh, Redding, and Morris stayed behind with General Winchester, but some of their men volunteered to go. Some men of other companies remained behind when their officers left, so Capt. Simpson took over Ballard's company; Capt. Langhorne, Matson's; Lt. Brooks, Hickman's; Lt. Keller, Bledsoe's.

    Note: It was common for companies to be "equalized" for the march. As an example of how it was done in the French army of the period; the adjutant and sergeant majors made sure each company or firing platoon had roughly equal numbers of men, in order to facilitate large-scale maneuvers and to spread the number of muskets equally along the firing line. Each morning, the companies were formed and adjusted by transferring men from large units to smaller ones. The men were marched by files from the left of their company to the rear and center of the battalion, and then reformed on the left of their new unit. It is believed that they returned to their parent companies at the end of the day, if possible. The process might take only 5 minutes for trained regulars, but Winchester was taking volunteers. See: Crowdy, T.E., Napoleon's Infantry Handbook, South Yorkshire, U.K.: Pen & Sword, 2015.

303 McAfee, Robert. History of the Late War in the Western Country. Bowling Green, Ohio: Historical Publications Company, 1919 (reprint of the 1816 original edition.) pp. 224-5: That same morning, Winchester wrote a dispatch to General Harrison explaining the main purpose of Lewis' expedition was to prevent French Town's flour and grain from being carried off by the enemy. If he took the settlement, he suggested, reinforcement from Harrison's right wing might be needed. Before sending the dispatch, however, Winchester included a last-minute report that some 400 Indians were already gathered at the Raisin. See also: Au, Dennis. War on the Raisin. Monroe: Monroe County Historical Commission, 1981, p. 26, based on orderly books in the Burton Collection of the Detroit Public Library.

the River Raisin. Hutreau Navarre moved there at that time with his family. His son, Peter Navarre would become a famous scout for General Harrison during the War of 1812.[304]

The people of *Presqu'Île* were somewhat worried at the sight of hundreds of ragged, heavily-armed Kentuckians approaching their homes, so they sent out a white flag with a delegation to express their friendship and support for the American cause.

For their part, the Kentuckians were overjoyed to see a friendly settlement. They had started out early that morning hauling 3 days' provisions on sleds. Muskets had been inspected, and every man was ordered to take along 18 rounds of prepared ammunition, an extra gun flint, and a lock cover to keep his gun lock and flash pan dry.

The men had marched some 20 miles down the river and onto the ice of Maumee Bay before reaching this village on the south bank of the Maumee. After 5 months of campaigning in the wilderness, the double row of 60 white-washed, squared-log cabins made this small, isolated *métis* settlement seem like an oasis of civilization.

At *Presqu'Île*, the local *habitants* informed Lt. Colonel Lewis that, the last they heard, the British had withdrawn from the River Raisin and were currently at Brownstown. Lewis immediately sent word back to General Winchester at the rapids, while he waited for Lt. Colonel Allen to catch up.

Like the troops of Lt. Colonel Lewis, Allen's men were equipped with three days' worth of rations. However, they also had been assigned four packhorses to carry their tents and camp gear.

After marching for seven hours, they arrived at the village in the evening darkness, a little past 7 p.m.[305]

---

304 The Métis village of *Presqu'Île* (Presque Isle) was located near what is now East Toledo and the city of Oregon, Ohio. It was composed of French and Odawa families formerly living along the River Raisin. The village was largely abandoned after the U.S. government moved the Odawas to Kansas in 1836. Some of the Odawas fled to Walpole Island in Canada after the War of 1812. See: Tucker, Patrick M., "The French Colony at Fort Stephenson During the War of 1812," posted by Kathy Warnes, April 7, 2017.

305 U.S. Naval Observatory, astronomical applications Department, Sun and Moon Data for Monday, January 18, 1813, Eastern Standard time: Morning twilight = 7:27am, Sunrise = 7:58am, Sunset = 5:31pm, End twilight = 6:02pm. No estimate is available for cloud conditions. The volunteer companies were somewhat ad-hoc compositions.

THE FIRST BATTLE OF THE RIVER RAISIN
LA PREMIÈRE BATAILLE DE LA RIVIÈRE AUX RAISINS

Winchester's camp on the Maumee, morning of January 18, 1813:

General Winchester had the sad duty to inform the troops that Lt. Col. Scott, commander of the 1st Kentucky, had died on Dec. 20.

However, for Captain James Price there was relief that his arrest and trial had been suspended for two days, and his sword returned to him. He was supposed to turn himself back in at 9 a.m. on Wednesday, but coming events would postpone that action, indefinitely.[306]

After a comfortable night at *Presqu'île*, LTC Lewis marched his men out of camp at an early hour, sliding along on the ice of the frozen Maumee River. Their route was to take them across Maumee Bay and along the edge of Lake Erie to the River Raisin, about 18 miles away.[307] Guiding them were Antoine and Medard Couture, who currently resided at French Town, along with Hutreau Navarre's sons, Peter, Jacques, and Robert Navarre, from *Presqu'île*.[308]

It was not difficult going, though the ice was covered by a crust of snow that crunched beneath their feet. In spots where the snow was blown away, or where a crack descended into the depths, they could see that the ice was comfortingly thick.

They were traversing a wide, open expanse, across which they could hear the echoing of their voices and the tinkling of their equipment. On their right, the flat, sparkling whiteness stretched eastward to meet the horizon.

---

306 Orderly Book of Captain Bland Ballard, Winchester Papers, Burton Historical Collection, Detroit Public Library. During the night, an express courier arrived from the River Raisin with news that 400 Indians and 2 companies of Canadian militiamen were occupying the settlement, and reinforcements under Col. Elliott were expected from Malden. The Kentuckians would have to leave early the next morning in order to beat the enemy reinforcements to the River Raisin.

307 Darnell, Elias, <u>Journal</u>. Philadelphia: Lippincott, Grambo, and Co., 1854, pp. 46-48. In Reverend Thomas P. Dudley's account, however, the troops only got as far as the mouth of Swan Creek, which flows into the Maumee in what is today, downtown Toledo, Ohio. Their starting point was Winchester's camp, on the north side of the Maumee, in present-day Maumee, Ohio, just opposite the later site of Fort Meigs.

308 "Soldiers, your ancient enemy is before you," Chapter 4 of an unpublished manuscript written by Prof. Bidlack and edited by Dennis Au, typed copy in the Monroe County Historical Museum Archives. These Navarres were the sons of François Navarre dit Utreau, not to be confused with the son, brother, or father of Utreau's nephew, Col. François Navarre dit Tchigoy, who bore the same names.

The only visible change came from the dark shadows cast by the clouds as they moved across the sky. Close by on their left, bare trees lined a bleak shoreline that seemed to bow endlessly in and out.[309]

The troops were dressed largely in linen or linsey-woolsey hunting shirts colored blue from indigo dye, pale yellow from hickory bark, or dull brown from black walnut. Their pants were of Kentucky "jean" material, while their feet were covered with shoes or homemade moccasins.[310]

The men in Hickman's Company of Allen's rifle regiment carried either their own flintlock rifles from home or were issued smoothbore muskets.[311] Their hunting frocks were bound about the waist with leather belts and sheaths to hold tomahawks and large knives. Most carried fixed rounds in cartouche boxes on their belts, while extra powder was stored in horns and lead shot in pouches slung across the shoulder. Tin cups dangled from knapsacks in which they kept their spare clothing and personal supplies.[312]

To William Bratton of Frankfort, this trek must have seemed quite easy. Almost a decade earlier, he had been one of 9 young Kentuckians who joined the Corps of Discovery. Led by Meriwether Lewis and William

---

309 This scenic description is interpolated from the author's personal experience. Quite often, I used to walk out on the frozen lake to visit the ice fishermen in their shanties on Brest Bay.

310 The terms *Jean* and *fustian* are often confused. *Fustian* was a stout, relatively cheap fabric of cotton and flax or a strong twilled fabric of cotton and wool, with a short nap or pile. The word *"jeans"* stems from *Gênes*, the French word for Genoa, Italy, one of the first places it was manufactured. *Jean*, at the bottom of the scale for fustians, seems already to have gained an association with working dress by the 1600s. In America, before the advent of Levi Strauss in the 1870s, the term *jean* referred to a sturdy cloth commonly made with a cotton warp and wool weft. It also could be called "Virginia Cloth," and was probably what was used to make "Kentucky jeans." However, jean cloth could also be made just of cotton, similar to modern denim. The name, *denim*, apparently comes from the town of Nîmes, France, where weavers produced a twilled fabric called *serge de Nîmes*. This product was originally a blend of silk and wool, but the silk was eventually replaced by cheaper cotton.

311 Way back when the expedition was being organized, LTC Allen had informed them just before they reached Newport, Kentucky, that they would not be issued rifles from the public supply. If they truly wanted to be a rifle regiment, they would have to use their own weapons.

312 Information gleaned from interviews with veterans was published in the Pittsburgh Gazette and Mercury, and partially reprinted with comments in the Monroe Commercial of Thursday, March 23, 1871, at http://monroe.lib.mi.us/bygonesofmonroe/bomwarof1812.html: *"The commencement of the war of 1812 is an event entirely within our personal memory, although we were too young to do much besides making a part of a very attentive set of listeners to those who were on the eve of their departure for the Canadian frontier. Soldiering was not then what it is now...The Government did not equip the Kentucky volunteer in the rifle regiments. He furnished his own gun and his own clothes, and was paid 8 dollars a month..."*

Clark, he had journeyed across the continent from St. Louis to the Pacific Ocean and back.[313]

As Lewis and his men trudged along, they met a number of French Town refugees fleeing towards the safety of the American army. The Kentucky troops eagerly plied them with questions about the British and Indians at River Raisin. They were especially worried that the enemy might be well supplied with artillery, of which the Kentuckians had none.[314]

Not all the people on their route were helpful refugees. The British had their Native scouts out to give advance warning of the enemy. As the long column of Kentucky troops neared the mouth of Otter Creek, about 5 or 6 miles from French Town, they were spotted by a party of Indians, who hastened away to warn Major Reynolds that the American Long Knives were coming.[315]

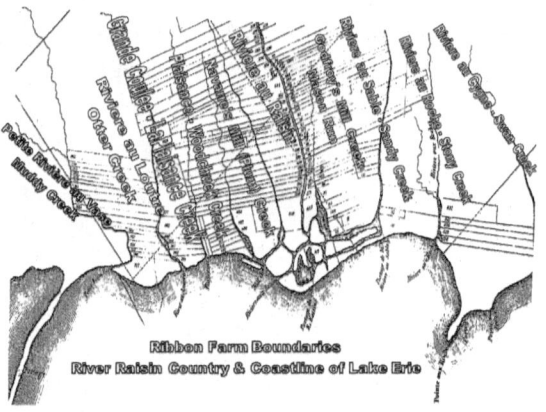

Streams and Ribbon Farms[316]

---

313 Communication from John Trowbridge, Kentucky Historical Society, April 27, 2006. Another connection to the Lewis and Clark expedition was George Drouillard, actually from Windsor, but related to the Drouillards of Otter Creek, who served as the corps' official hunter. He died in 1811.

314 Dudley, Rev. Thomas P. "The Battle and Massacre at Frenchtown, Michigan, January, 1813." Historical and Archaeological Tracts, No. 1. Cleveland: The Western Reserve Historical Society, August, 1870. An account related by one of the Kentucky survivors of the battle. It's difficult to pinpoint the exact spot or spots where the refugees were encountered, whether on Lake Erie, Maumee Bay, or the Maumee River.

315 McAfee, Robert. History of the Late War in the Western Country. Bowling Green, Ohio: Historical Publications Company, 1919 (reprint of 1816 original edition.) p. 225.

316 Note the ribbon farms (long lots) fronting on all the streams. Some of the streams are hard to

Medard Labadie's home, LaPlaisance Creek, Monday, Jan. 18, 1813:

The Labadie house sat upon private claim number 356, near where LaPlaisance Creek emptied into the shallow, broadening waters of the Grande Coulée, about 3 miles south of the River Raisin.

It was early afternoon, and 27-year-old Medard Labadie was working up a sweat, chopping wood in his yard to keep his wife and six children warm. Looking up, he saw Antoine Couture coming towards him.[317]

"Bonsway,"[318] said Antoine, as he came into the yard, *"Colonel Lewis has been asking for you. He has come to liberate French Town, and he needs trustworthy local men to guide him."*

"Avec plaisir — It will be my pleasure, and I'll tell him that myself," said Labadie, hoping the colonel could understand his French.

Sticking his ax in the end of a log, Labadie went inside his house to get his rifle and shot pouch, and then went with Couture to join Lt. Col. Lewis.

It was about noon when they reached Lewis and his men, still out on the snow-covered ice of LaPlaisance Bay. They were sitting down on their blankets, partaking of a cold lunch. The soldiers had spent a very long morning walking across the ice from *Presqu'île*, a distance of about a dozen miles. They were still a few miles from their final destination at French Town, and were anxious to learn as much as they could about the intentions and disposition of the enemy.[319]

A number of Otter Creek *habitants* were with them, including Antoine Momini and Dominique Drouillard.[320]

Lt. Colonel Lewis asked Labadie if the British force was still occupying

---

find nowadays, but Plum Creek flows into Plum Creek Bay; LaPlaisance/ Woodchuck Creek into LaPlaisance Bay at Avalon Beach; Otter Creek into Lake Erie at North Shores, Muddy Creek into the lake south of Toledo Beach. Not shown on the map is Mortar Creek / Sulphur Creek, located between Woodchuck Creek and Otter Creek. Also, Bay Creek and Halfway Creek that flow into North Maumee Bay. Based on Aaron Greely's French Claims Map, 1810, Monroe County Historical Museum.

317 Grant, Linda, "History of the Labadie Family," Spiral Bound Manuscript, p. 163. Monroe County Historical Commission Archives.

318 Local pronunciation of *Bonsoir*, which normally means *good evening* and is generally said after 5 p.m., but could be used earlier in the day. Source: Carl J. Cousino (1916-2006), who learned the native French dialect as a child. His is the only example I have of such a usage.

319 Darnell, Elias, <u>Journal</u>. Philadelphia: Lippincott, Grambo, and Co., 1854, pp. 47-48.

320 Affidavit of Antoine Mominie, August 19, 1852. Mominie was a private in Hubert Lacroix's company, which he stated was part of John Anderson's second regiment of Michigan volunteers. On parole since the surrender at the River Raisin as part of the capitulation of General Hull at Detroit, he joined Lewis' detachment of Winchester's army during its advance to Frenchtown.

the town and was supported by artillery. Labadie, struggling to make sense of Lewis' English, answered in the affirmative, but added there was little to fear from the British cannon, which was only "*...about large enough to kill a mouse.*"

Lewis then ordered the men to fall in, and Labadie led them off the ice. Passing through the woods, the troops found themselves in an open prairie, about 3 miles from the enemy position at French Town, where they were reformed into 3 columns and an advance guard.[321]

At this time, Lewis' general orders were read to the troops by each of the battalion commanders; Allen, Madison, and Graves: "*Soldiers! Your ancient enemy is before you. The wrongs that he has inflicted upon your country are fresh in your memory. That country calls upon you this day to vindicate her honor and her interests by inflicting upon him condign punishment. In the hour of battle, remember what the Patriot Orator said to you at Georgetown. You have the double character of Americans and Kentuckians to sustain! Do so, as I feel assured you will, and all will be well.*"[322]

French Town, River Raisin, 3 p.m., Monday, January 18, 1813:

Some 22 families inhabited the immediate area on the north bank of the River Raisin where Hull's Road crossed at a rocky ford, while half as many lived on the south bank. The gardens, close by the houses, were surrounded by high fences constructed of split saplings driven into a trench in the ground.[323]

---

321 Atherton, William, <u>Suffering and Defeat of the North-Western Army</u>. Frankfort, KY: A. G. Hodges, 1842, p. 34. See also: Dudley account. Recollections printed in the <u>Michigan Sentinel</u>, 2 Aug., 1834, and the Labadie deposition in the Lyon Papers. In Dudley's account, it was a Raisin refugee who stated, "*They have two pieces about large enough to kill a mouse.*" Describing the smaller-sized cannons used in the battles of January 18 and 22, Dudley called them swivel guns. He was probably referring to the 3-pounder (2.91") howitzers the British had captured at Detroit and French Town after Hull's surrender in August of 1812. Other accounts mention only a single artillery piece. Some experts suggest it was an American King Howitzer taken from the Wayne Stockade after Hull's surrender. It could also have been a light 5.5-inch howitzer, although that could not have been considered a 3-pounder. A 3-pdr gun would probably look too big to be called a "mouse cannon."

322 Au, Dennis. <u>War on the Raisin</u>. Monroe: Monroe County Historical Commission, 1981, p. 27. See also Clift, G. Glenn. <u>Remember the Raisin</u>. Frankfort: Kentucky Historical Society, 1961, pp. 50-53. Lewis wrote out his orders of the day and gave copies to his battalion commanders, with instructions to read them to the troops just before they went into battle. See also: <u>Michigan Sentinel</u>, Monroe, Aug. 2, 1834.

323 Lossing, Benson J. <u>The Pictorial Field-Book of the War of 1812</u>. Glendale, New York: Benchmark Publishing Corporation, 1970, p. 352.

During the fall and winter, French Town had been occupied by groups of Indians, Canadians, and British. Most recently, Major Ebenezer Reynolds had arrived with 50 or 60 Canadian militiamen from Elliott's and Maisonville's flank companies of the 1st and 2nd Essex Militia Regiments[324], a small howitzer commanded by Royal Artillery Bomardier Kitson, and a couple hundred Native warriors, mostly Potawatomies, with perhaps a few Wyandots.[325]

These militiamen had no uniforms, but they were nonetheless well-clothed in white, hooded blanket coats (*capotes*) with black stripes along the edges. Knee-length, oiled, winter moccasins (*shoepacs*) protected their feet. Woolen stocking caps (*tuques*) covered most of their heads, although the few anglophones among them seemed to prefer fur caps.

The mostly French-speaking Essex militiamen were well-acquainted with the River Raisin settlement, having been sent there frequently through the fall and winter. They knew many of the local families and had even received medical care at times from the resident physician, Dr. Joseph Dazet.[326]

Eight men of Maisonville's company had already deserted, disliking occupation duties over their French Town cousins, and dismayed at being kept on active duty for a month beyond their six-month term of service. Captain Maisonville had appealed for his company to be relieved, but without effect. Procter had simply decided no other available units could be spared.[327]

Since it was Monday, January 18th, the British forces, plus some of

---

324 The most able, active and motivated men were placed in the flank companies of the Canadian militia regiments. The 1st and 2nd Essex Militia Regiments each had two flank companies.

325 By the time Rev. Dudley wrote his journal the "mouse cannon" had "grown" into a 6-pounder. If it were a small howitzer, fitting the *habitants'* description, it would have been capable of firing shells and cannister, although the Kentucky accounts don't mention those types of ammunition.

326 Henderson, Robert, "The American Attack at Frenchtown on the River Raisin, January 18, 1813," posted on the War of 1812 Website, citing Chartrand, René, A Scarlet Coat: Uniforms, Flags, and Equipment of the British in the War of 1812, Ottawa: 2012, p. 20. *Shoepac* comes from a mid-18th century Delaware word for moccasins (*čipahkpo*). Shoepacs often had an extra sole and were worn over heavy stockings for insulation. In the same article, Henderson references Dr. Dazet's request for compensation from the British government (LAC RG 19 E5 (a) vol. 3728 file 5 War Losses Claim #58 Joseph Dazet of River Raisin.) Henderson also indicates that the Essex militia companies were organized somewhat along linguistic lines, as a result of their location and to aid in comprehension within the unit. Caldwell's company, for example, was mostly made up of Anglophones.

327 "Rally at the River Raisin for the Purpose of Giving Battle," Chapter 3 of an unpublished manuscript written by Dr. Bidlack and edited by Dennis Au, typed copy in the Monroe County Historical Museum Archives.

the local settlers, planned to hold a grand ball that night in honor of Queen Charlotte.

Most of the Raisin *habitants* were still in their homes around 3 p.m. when the alarm was sounded. American soldiers had been spotted south of the river, opposite Willow Island.[328]

In one house, an old Indian seemed unconcerned as he sat smoking by a Mushrat Frenchman's fireplace. When word came that the American army was nearby, he merely took another puff on his clay pipe and sighed, *"Ho, de Mericans come; I suppose Ohio men come. We give 'em anodder chase, jus' like we do at de Rapids."*

He then got up and walked nonchalantly to the door, from where he could see for himself the Americans forming up in the open fields on the south side of the river. His unconcerned manner seemed to change, however, when the British opened up with their cannon and the enemy began to move forward in a rush. As their shouts and battle cries began to rise in the distance, the Indian suddenly exclaimed, *"Kentuck, by God!"*

Picking up his musket, he ran out the door and bounded off into the woods as swiftly as a deer.[329]

Interior of the Navarre-Anderson trading post, ca. 1789

---

328 The Monroe Civic Reflector of 1904: Willow Island has long since disappeared, but was slightly downstream from the actual battleground.

329 Darnell, Elias, <u>Journal</u>. Philadelphia: Lippincott, Grambo, and Co., 1854, p. 47, footnote.

The best example of late 18th century French-Canadian and fur trade architecture still extant in Michigan's lower peninsula[330]

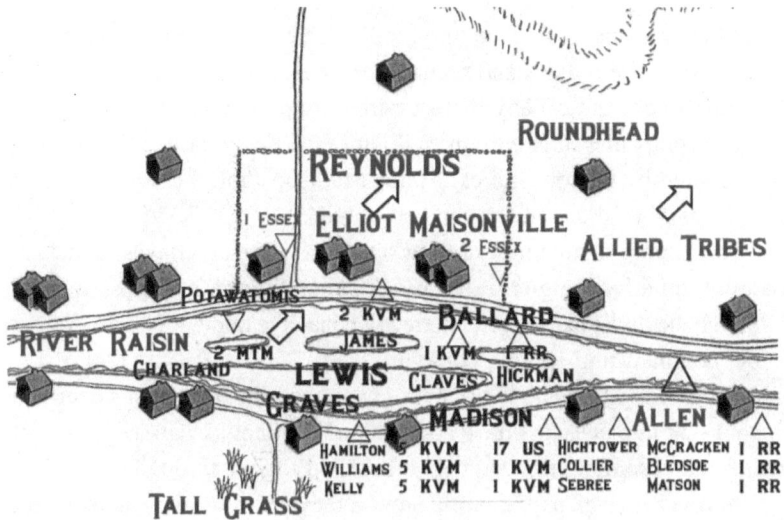

Approximate locations of units as the Kentuckians crossed the River Raisin.
(map not to scale)

The American Attack across the River Raisin, 3 p.m., January 18, 1813:

By 3 in the afternoon, the American army under Col. Lewis appeared on the open prairie, forming their battle line in the sedge grass, in full view of the enemy across the river, a quarter mile away.[331] It was an open invitation to the British to come out and attack them in a stand-up field battle.[332]

The troops were tired from their long march, but exhilarated at the prospect of finally going into action against their traditional enemies.

---

330 John Gibney and Ralph Naveaux, two former directors of the Monroe County Historical Museum, are shown wearing period garb in the trade room of the original *pièce-sur-pièce* building built around 1789. The building, which is one of the oldest still standing in the State of Michigan, housed Dr. Dazet in 1812 and bears the marks of bullets fired during the war. No longer on its original site, it is currently located on North Custer Road on the River Raisin, just west of the city of Monroe, and is maintained by the Monroe County Museums System.

331 See the order of battle for January 18 in Appendix C.

332 McAfee, Robert. History of the Late War in the Western Country. Bowling Green, Ohio: Historical Publications Company, 1919 (reprint of 1816 original edition). p. 225.

The right wing, under Col. Allen, was composed of 3 companies led by Captains McCracken, Bledsoe, and Matson.

Allen's objective, which he was urged to accomplish without fail, was to outflank the enemy and capture the British cannon while the rest of the line drove off the Indians and secured the houses on the riverbank. He was also supposed to cut off any British retreat from the village.

The companies of Hamilton, Williams, and Kelly formed the left wing, commanded by Major Graves. Major Madison took the center with the companies of Hightower, Collier, and Sebree.

Three more companies, under Captains Hickman, Glaves, and James made up an advance guard, led by Captain Ballard, acting as major.[333] Although the divisions were not perfectly equal, the number of men averaged 55 per company and 165 per column.

There was a foot and a half of snow on the ground, with a frozen crust so hard that in places an entire company of men could walk right over the top of it, and sometimes even the horses didn't break through.[334]

Across the river, a quarter mile away, they could see the enemy already in motion. A large number of warriors crossed the river and formed a thick, irregular skirmish line, but did not press the attack.[335]

---

333 Atherton, William, Suffering and Defeat of the North-Western Army, Frankfort, Kentucky: Hodges, 1842, pp. 35-40. Bland Ballard, the leader of the advance guard, perhaps epitomizes the image of the "Indian Fighter." Born in Virginia, he came to Kentucky in 1779 at the age of 18, just in time to participate in some of George Rogers Clark's expeditions against the Indian towns of Ohio and the Wabash. He suffered from a hip wound received in Clark's attack on Piqua in 1780. He later served with General Wayne at the Battle of Fallen Timbers. His father, stepmother, sister, and half-sister were all killed by Indians. In retaliation, he claimed to have killed 30 or 40 Indians in his lifetime. (See History of Shelby County, Kentucky, by Geo. L. Willis, Sr., Shelby County Genealogical-Historical Society's Committee on Printing, 1929, pp. 147-151).

334 Letter James C. Price to wife, in camp near River Raisin, Jan. 16, 1813, in History of Jessamine County, Kentucky, by Bennett H. Young, page 3, Algonquin Club, Detroit, Michigan, 1937.

335 Bond, Lewis, "Journal of Battle and Massacre of River Raisin, January 22 and 23, 1813, and of the War of 1812," Document Transcriptions of the War of 1812 in the Northwest, Vol. X, Part I, Western Reserve Historical Society War of 1812 Collection, transcribed by Richard C. Knopf. Columbus: Ohio Historical Society, 1962: "On the 18th of Jany., 1813, a party of Indians who had been out spying came in to French Town and gave the alarm of the Americans being near, and in a few minutes, they were seen at the distance of a mile or two on the ice. The Indians ran to meet them, and a sharp firing immediately commenced. The field piece also fired from the village a number of shot but did no execution. The Indians being pressed by our people gave way and were pursued; part towards the village of F. Town and part over the prairies towards the woods, but a continued fire was kept up. The snow was deep and in consequence the advance and the retreat were slow."

Instead, their main purpose seemed to be to delay the American advance. Earlier that morning, they had gone out to break up some of the hard-crusted snow to inhibit any American approach from the direction of Hull's road.[336]

Major Reynolds, the British commander, drew his militia and artillery up into line near the homes of Jean-Baptiste Jerome and Jean-Baptiste Couture.

Aware of the dangers of his situation, the major was determined to make the enemy pay a price for their assault, but not to allow his own force to be trapped and cut off by superior numbers.

While the American troops were still forming, the first shot from the enemy artillery sailed 20 feet over their heads.[337]

Lieutenant Colonel Lewis ordered Captain Bland Ballard's advance guard forward to screen the attack. Shielded by Ballard's men, the American army broke off by the right of companies and marched forward.

At this moment, the British opened up with their cannon positioned among the houses of French Town. Twice more, a shot passed harmlessly over the heads of the Kentuckians, as they advanced to the river. Although startled, the soldiers quickly regained their confidence after the second shot, and private Strode's voice rang out with a perfect imitation of the crowing sound made by a Kentucky game cock.[338]

As the American soldiers moved through the farm fields on the south bank, Hyacinth Tuot and several other local *habitants* emerged from their houses. Standing in their dooryards, the settlers cheered the Kentuckians, and then cheered even more upon seeing their friends and relatives from Otter Creek and La Plaisance within the ranks of the advancing soldiers.

Antoine Sargent, Laurent Durocher, and a considerable number of local *habitants* ran out ahead of the Kentuckians, ahead of even Ballard's advance

---

336 Letter William Caldwell, in camp near Newport, Ky., Feb. 20, 1813, in History of Jessamine County, Kentucky, by Bennett H. Young, page 5 of excerpt printed by the Algonquin Club, Detroit, Michigan, 1937. Also, from Captain Price's last letter to his wife, January 16, 1813: "*The snow is 2 feet deep, the crust is very hard and we walk over it and ride upon it on horseback. We often sleep under such deep snow; we cover up in our blankets and we sleep warm during the night.*" See: Clift, G. Glenn. Remember the Raisin. Frankfort: Kentucky Historical Society, 1961, p. 161.

337 The rate of fire was not terribly fast, for each time the British touched off their cannon, the recoil pushed it backwards several feet. The crew then had to push it back into position, search, sponge, and reload the piece before it could again be aimed and fired. The American army did not shoot back at first; the range was too great. See Appendix N for the effectiveness of musket fire.

338 A Stephen Strode is listed as a private in Martin's company of the 5th Kentucky. Captain Martin was not present at the battle, but volunteers from his company were.

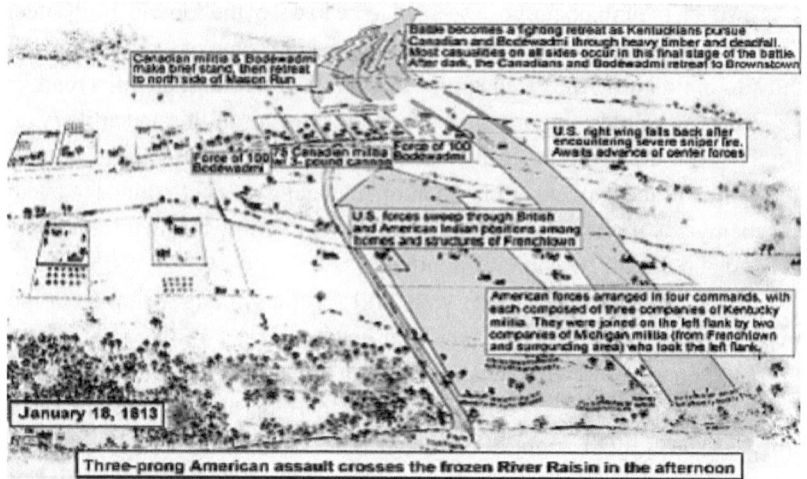

From: "Native Ground, Middle Ground, Battle Ground: The River Raisin, the War of 1812, and the Course of North American History, A Historic Resource Study of River Raisin National Battlefield Park," by Mark David Spence, Ph.D., 2019, p. 229, River Raisin National Battlefield Park

guard. Led by Lt. Ambrose Charland, they were the first of the American forces to shoot back at the enemy.[339]

Almost 70 yards wide at this point and studded with islands, the frozen River Raisin proved a minor, though slippery, obstacle, as Ballard's men slid down onto the ice and fired a ragged volley.

Captain Hickman, suffering from lameness, was riding a horse in front of his men in the advance guard, when the animal broke through the icy, reed-studded shallows along the northern riverbank. The captain fell as his horse floundered, but his men stopped to help him remount.[340]

---

339 Report of Dr. Gustavus Miller Bower, Surgeon's Mate, 5th Kentucky Volunteer Infantry Regiment, received at Monroe on Feb. 25, 1858, found in clipping files, Monroe County Historical Museum Archives. *"Here, let me state that the first guns that was fired was from some Canadian Frenchmen that joined us in the march. They ran ahead and behaved most gallant and were the only men that took an Indian prisoner after a dreadful struggle. The battle continued until dark, the British retreating and we in pursuit. About dusk, a party of Indians fell in on our rear that was coming to the village, and succeeded in doing us nearly all the damage that we sustained during the engagement."*

340 Clift, G. Glenn. Remember the Raisin. Frankfort: Kentucky Historical Society, 1961, p. 53.

As he rode up the bullet-creased bank, Captain Hickman went down once more, hit by a disabling ball that broke his ankle.

As the main body of Kentuckians neared the river, they reformed from columns into line of battle. During the crossing, the command was given to halt and drop packs.[341]

Lt. Col. Lewis then gave the order for Majors Graves and Madison to storm the village in support of the advance guard.[342]

The long roll was beaten by the drummers as a signal for a general charge, and the entire force swarmed up the opposite bank into a shower of enemy bullets.[343]

The troops continued their forward rush, raising a "Kentucky" yell. Some of them crowed like roosters, others barked like dogs, and yet others called out, *"Fire away with your mouse cannon again!"*

The British position in French Town collapsed, as more *habitants* poured out of their houses, guns in hand. Giving full vent to their pent-up frustrations, they picked off any Indians who failed to retreat fast enough.[344]

As the men scrambled over and around the picket fences, Major Graves led the left wing through the picketed area to secure the buildings. Meanwhile the center prepared to move out into the open fields in support of the right wing.

341 Knopf, Richard C. Document Transcriptions of the War of 1812 in the Northwest, Vol. V, pt. 2. Columbus: Ohio Historical Society, 1958. p. 36: Report in the Feb. 25, 1813, issue of the Pittsburgh Mercury: *"In the battle of the 18th, on the first onset, the savages raised their accustomed and horrid yell. But the noise was drowned in the returning shouts of the brave assailants. They advanced boldly to the charge and drove the enemy in all directions. On the first fire, sixteen of the savages were distinctly seen to fall."*

342 Letter Lewis to Winchester, Jan. 20, 1813, typed copy in Bidlack's Notes, Monroe County Historical Society Archives.

343 McAfee, Robert. History of the Late War in the Western Country. Bowling Green, Ohio: Historical Publications Company, 1919 (reprint of 1816 original edition.) p. 225: *"When they arrived within a quarter of a mile of the village, and discovered the enemy in motion, the line of battle was formed, in the expectation of receiving an attack; but it was soon evident that the enemy did not intend fighting in the open field. The detachment then broke off by the right of companies and marched under the fire of the enemy's cannon, till they arrived at the river, where the small arms began to play upon them. The line of battle was then formed again, on the bank of the river, and the long roll beat as the signal for a general charge, which was immediately executed with much firmness and intrepidity."*

344 Lewis' Orderly Book, Burton Collection, Detroit Public Library. LTC Lewis noted that the *habitants* sallied out of their houses, arms in hand, and attacked the straggling Indians. They willingly shared their provisions with the troops and behaved more valiantly than his own men.

Fighting on the North Bank, January 18, 1813:

The enemy retreated out of the village in a northeasterly direction, trying to gain the shelter of the woods, over half a mile away. Before they could reach it, twelve of the enemy warriors were killed and scalped by the Kentuckians. Despite the warm reception, the Kentuckians had lost only 3 wounded while crossing the river. Bland Ballard, leader of the advance guard, received a flesh wound.

Over on the right flank, half a mile to the east, Lt. Colonel Allen was moving into position to pursue and intercept the enemy as they exited the village and retreated towards the edge of the deep woods.[345]

However, the enemy was not routed. They halted their retreat and took shelter amongst some buildings and fenced lots. Their rear protected by the edge of the forest strewn with fallen trees, the Canadians and Indians made a stand with their howitzer and small arms, concentrating their fire on the hundred or so men of the American right wing who were out in the open field.

Kentucky Troops Prepare for Bayonet Charge
As portrayed by Rick Simmons & Gary Carpenter
Photo by Bill Saul

---

345 Casselman, Alexander Clark. <u>Richardson's War of 1812</u>. Toronto: Coles Publishing Co.: *"...efficient service was rendered by the three-pounder under Bombardier Kitson of the Royal Artillery, aided simply by a few militia acting as gunners, compelled them to retire across some intermediate open ground to a wood, distant nearly a mile from their original position. Here the enemy were kept in check not only by the fire from the three-pounder, but by a running fusillade from the Militia and Indians, chiefly of the Potawatomi tribe. After the conflict had continued at this point upwards of half an hour, Major Reynolds...gave up the contest..."*

MOVEMENT OF THE TROOPS

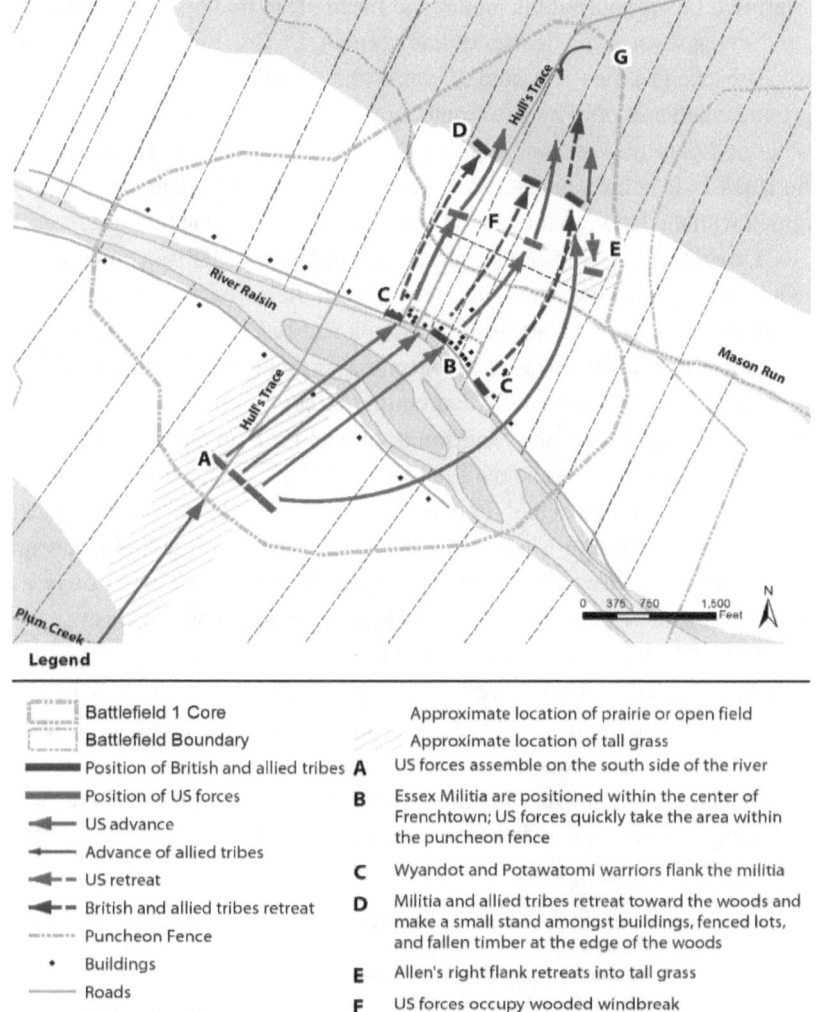

Legend

Battlefield 1 Core	Approximate location of prairie or open field
Battlefield Boundary	Approximate location of tall grass
Position of British and allied tribes **A**	US forces assemble on the south side of the river
Position of US forces **B**	Essex Militia are positioned within the center of Frenchtown; US forces quickly take the area within the puncheon fence
US advance	
Advance of allied tribes	
US retreat **C**	Wyandot and Potawatomi warriors flank the militia
British and allied tribes retreat **D**	Militia and allied tribes retreat toward the woods and make a small stand amongst buildings, fenced lots, and fallen timber at the edge of the woods
Puncheon Fence	
Buildings **E**	Allen's right flank retreats into tall grass
Roads **F**	US forces occupy wooded windbreak
Ribbon Farm Lots	
River **G**	The battle devolves into a series of running skirmishes in the woods, where most of the US casualties occur
Stream	
Approximate location of woods	

Battlefield Map Courtesy of River Raisin National Battlefield Park

From the back of his horse, Lt. Colonel Lewis was congratulating the conquerors of French Town, when he heard heavy firing off to the right. Alarmed, Lewis spurred his mount and raced off to find his subordinate.

Seeing several of Allen's men had been hit, Lt. Col. Lewis ordered them to fall back. The men retreated 50 yards and then threw themselves to the ground, sheltered only by snow and the tall sedge grass. Beyond the range of smoothbore muskets and hunting fowlers, they were still close enough for rifles to do some damage. Fortunately, Allen's men were predominantly armed with the latter, so they could dominate any firefight at that distance.[346]

Lewis then sent Major Garrard[347] with orders for Madison and Graves to advance against the enemy in the woods to their front. By pressing forward, they would be endangering the flank and rear of the main Canadian and Indian force, which was now concentrating against Lt. Colonel Allen.[348]

Lt. Col. Lewis believed Allen could thereby pin the enemy in place, thus permitting Graves and Madison to turn and roll up the British right.

Allen was ordered to hold his position until he heard general firing to his left. This would be the signal for Allen's battalion to go back onto the attack.

Meanwhile, Major Madison, at the head of the center column, saw an intervening fence row about 200 yards from the woods that could serve as a serious obstacle to his advance, should it be occupied by the enemy.

Ensign William O. Butler, attached to Hightower's company of the 17th U.S. Infantry, led a dozen men at a dead run to reach the fence shortly before the enemy. From there, they fired on the Indians, keeping them at bay until the rest of the center column could reach them.[349]

Hearing the gunfire, the right wing now attacked and pushed their wavering opponents away from the fences and deeper into the woods, where

---

346 Dudley, Rev. Thomas P. "The Battle and Massacre at Frenchtown, Michigan, January, 1813." Historical and Archaeological Tracts, No. 1. Cleveland: The Western Reserve Historical Society, August, 1870. See also: Michigan Sentinel, Monroe, Aug. 2, 1834.

347 According to John Trowbridge, in Kentucky, Major Garrard's name is pronounced *GAIR,id*.

348 Letter Lewis to Winchester, Jan. 20, 1813, typed copy in Bidlack's Notes, Monroe County Historical Society Archives. "...*they made a stand with their howitzer and small arms covered by a chain of enclosed lots and a group of houses. Having in their rear a thick bushy wood full of fallen timber, I directed Brigadier [Brigade major James] Garrard, one of my aides, to instruct Majors Graves and Madison to possess themselves of the wood on the left, and to move up towards the main body of the enemy as fast as practicable, to divert their attention from Colonel Allen.*" See also: Armstrong, John. Notices of the War of 1812, Vol. I, New York: George Dearborn, 1836.

349 Clift, G. Glenn. Remember the Raisin. Frankfort: Kentucky Historical Society, 1961, pp. 54-5.

a running fight began from tree to tree. The action and maneuvering around the edge of the woods had taken about half an hour.

In Allen's wing, several *habitant* volunteers from Otter Creek had fallen in with the men of McCracken's Company. They didn't understand all the shouts and commands, but the Kentuckians' movements were familiar enough, and they could watch and copy what the other men were doing.

Antoine Momini was in the act of climbing a fence, when he was hit in the right arm by a musket ball. The bullet lodged in the bone halfway between his elbow and shoulder, disabling him immediately.

Two other soldiers fell in the same volley, suffering wounds that would prove fatal before nightfall.[350]

Re-enactors at the Bicentennial of the Battle of the River Raisin
Photo courtesy of Dave & Sue Grassley
Floral City Images, Monroe, Michigan

Momini's comrade, Dominique Drouillard saw the shot had come from the direction of several Indian warriors. He went after them, but they retreated. Drouillard's parting shot went wide of its mark.

Meanwhile, back on the south bank, Hyacinth Tuot dit Duval was watching the battle's progress. His excitement turned to concern, however,

---

350 Affidavit of Antoine Mominie, August 19, 1852. Pension Application Files, War of 1812, Death or Disability, the national Archives "Old War" Invalid and Widow Rejected File No. 16545.

as he noticed a solitary figure crossing the river, holding his arm. It was Antoine Momini. As he got closer, Hyacinth could see he was bleeding.[351]

The Tuots took Momini inside their house, relieving him of his coat, accoutrements and musket. One of the regimental surgeons, Dr. McIlvain, had applied a quick plaster to his wound, but it had failed to stop the bleeding.

Madame Tuot undid the bandages and plaster, and examined the large gash made by a musket ball. She tore up some cloth and rebandaged his arm. It would have to do until Antoine could report to Dr. Bower, the surgeon, and have the ball extracted.[352]

The Raisin *habitants* continued to press forward in the forefront of the fighting, at last free to vent their frustrations against the uninvited occupiers of their settlement. Medard Labadie saw one Potawatomi fall and another taken prisoner and sent to the rear.[353]

The captor was Jacques Navarre, the brother of Peter Navarre. The Potawatomies had mistaken him for one of their own and allowed him to approach unmolested, only to be startled by his demand that they surrender.

They started to resist, but Jacques was too quick, ripping both their rifles and a tomahawk away from their grasp. As François Benac and Peter Navarre approached, one of the warriors made a run for it.

He didn't get very far before Benac raised his rifle and shot him down.

---

351 Affidavit of Hyacinth Tuitt, aged 53, August 23, 1833, Pension Application Files, War of 1812, Death or Disability, the national Archives "Old War" Invalid and Widow Rejected File No. 16545. The spelling of the family name varies in the old accounts: Thuot, Tuitt, etc. It is also sometimes completed by "dit Duval," or simply replaced by "Duval."

352 Surgeon's Affidavit of September 17, 1853, Pension Application Files, War of 1812, Death or Disability, the national Archives "Old War" Invalid and Widow Rejected File No. 16545: "...*he received a wound from a musket ball in his right arm, between the shoulder and elbow, causing the muscles to adhere to the bone, and...impeding and injuring the natural rotary motion of the arm, causing pain and numbness to that arm, when exercised or closely examined, from which there seems to have been extracted particles of bone, and he is thereby not only incapacitated for military duty, but...is one half disabled from obtaining his subsistence from manual labor.*

See also: Affidavit of Antoine Mominie, Age 67, August 23, 1852. Pension Application Files, War of 1812, Death or Disability, the national Archives "Old War" Invalid and Widow, Rejected File No. 16545. Copy in Monroe County Historical Museum Archives, courtesy of Chris and Steve Momany. Despite several sworn testimonies on his behalf, Mominie was never enrolled in McCracken's company. He was acting as a civilian volunteer when wounded at the River Raisin, and therefore his application for a disability pension was rejected. Furthermore, his participation in the fighting was illegal, being technically still a prisoner of war on parole from Hull's surrender of Detroit

353 Grant, Linda, History of the Labadie Family. Spiral Bound Manuscript, p. 163. Monroe County Historical Commission Archives.

The other Potawatomi was escorted back to French Town as a prisoner.[354] A couple of Canadian militiamen were also captured during the fighting.

Bombardier Kitson of the Royal Artillery was in charge of the British gun. His three crewmen were just militiamen, but he had trained them well. They stood by the gun and followed orders without hesitation.

Like a well-oiled machine, the militiamen fired, and then pulled the gun back, trying to follow the road to Detroit. Once they were safely behind the screen of Indian skirmishers, they would halt, reload their piece, and wait till the flow of battle brought the enemy once more into view.

Unfortunately, as the trees appeared to close in around them, their field of fire became severely restricted, and they were hard pressed by the advancing Americans. At this point, the officers on both sides began losing control of their men. As the fight continued through the woods, it began to take on a life of its own.[355]

The Native warriors fought in small groups. Hidden by trees and brush, they would fire, then retreat rapidly out of sight to pause and reload. When the Indians broke cover to retreat, the Kentuckians would get a fleeting shot. By the time they caught up to the fleeing enemy, however, the Indians would be prepared to pepper the Kentucky ranks with another burst of bullets.

The Potawatomies were also adept at making flanking movements and firing from unexpected directions. At one point, a group of warriors managed to get behind the advancing Americans. Had they been in greater numbers, they might well have cut the militiamen off and destroyed them in the woods.

Although inexperienced in this style of combat, the Kentuckians quickly took to the trees themselves. They kept up the pressure, slowly pushing the enemy back almost two miles over a period of 2 or 3 hours. Men dropped out as they grew tired. The wounded were left where they fell in hopes they could be picked up and cared for when the fight was over.[356]

---

354 The Historical Society of Northwestern Ohio, Biographical field notes on Frenchtown, note 155.

355 Letter Proctor to Sheaffe, January 25, 1813, Number 24 in James' Military Occurrences, Vol.1. "This party, with the gun, fell back 18 miles to Brownstown, the settlement of the brave Wyandots, where I directed my force to assemble."

356 Darnell, Elias, Journal. Philadelphia: Lippincott, Grambo, & Co., 1854, pp. 47-49. Darnell recognized the advantage the Indians had in the woods, noting that "It would have been better for us if we had been contented with the possession of the village, without pursuing them to the woods." Just as the sun was going down, William Atherton saw John Locke and Joseph Simpson advancing on his left, ahead of the main body. One was killed and the other wounded. Then Atherton was hit in the right shoulder.

The Americans continued their advance, but more slowly now. Many were exhausted. A number of the officers had been wounded or fell behind, leaving the men to fight without much higher direction. At dusk, Col. Lewis sent Major Graves to stop the pursuit and collect the battalions. The troops returned in good order and established camp at French Town for the night.[357]

The British force was left to retreat, unhindered, towards Brownstown, about 17 miles to the northeast, where they arrived after 1 a.m. In their haste, they were forced to abandon some of their dead on the battlefield.[358]

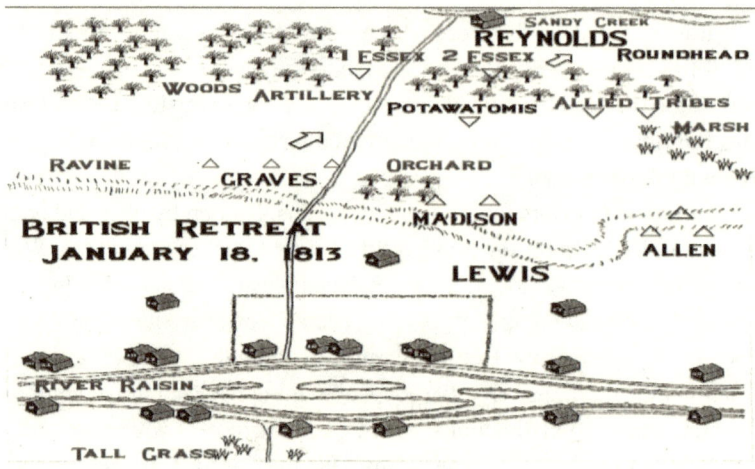

French Town on the Raisin, night of January 18, 1813:

Darkness was falling as a solitary sleigh drawn by a single pony crunched through the snow atop the Lake Erie ice. A clear sky announced a cold night for Perish Manor and his son. Suddenly, they heard the distant sound of gunfire.

---

357 Letter William Caldwell to Mrs. Mary Price, February 20, 1813, in History of Jessamine County Kentucky, by Bennett H. Young. At 10 p.m., Captain James Price was ordered to take his Jessamine County Blues, round up as many sleds as possible, and bring in any wounded he could find, lest they fall victim to lurking Indians. This is a confusing letter; however, so this may have happened at 10 a.m. on January 22. The bodies of a dozen Native warriors were scalped and mutilated by the Kentuckians. This unfortunate act would come back to haunt them on January 23rd.

358 At Detroit, sunset occurs at about 5:30 p.m. on January 18th. Dusk, or astronomical twilight, arrives around 7 p.m. If they left at dusk, the retreating Canadians and Indians could have covered the 17 miles on foot in roughly 6 hours, averaging in the neighborhood of 3 miles an hour. At 2 miles an hour, it would take close to 9 hours.

Leaving his son, Manor grabbed his rifle and continued on foot until he encountered the American troops bringing their wounded back to French Town, having left the dead on the field.

He also met Medard Couture and Peter Navarre who gave him the details about their skirmish. Realizing the fight was over, Manor gathered his son and some female friends, and sent them to the safety of the Navarre house.[359]

The *habitants* rejoiced. None of their women or children had been hurt, although the battle raged right through their farm lots. Several of their men may have been wounded or killed, but their homes and property had been saved.[360]

Lieutenant Ambrose Charland of Lacroix's company came to see Lt. Colonel Lewis. His Michigan militiamen were wondering if they should remain with the army in case the British returned, but Lewis replied, *"We thank you exceedingly. But it would be best for you to return to your homes in case the Indians try to seek vengeance on your families."*[361]

Many of the Raisin families began preparing for the worst.[362]

---

359 Hosmer, Hezekiah Lord, Early History of the Maumee Valley, Toledo: Hosmer & Harris, 1858, p. 35. There were Navarres at the River Raisin and at *Presqu'île* on the Maumee. I suspect Manor sent his sons and female friends to the Maumee.

360 A dozen warriors were found dead on the field and the Indians probably carried away several more, either killed outright or dying of wounds. One Indian and 2 Canadians were taken prisoner. A settler from Sandy Creek came in with a wild report that the enemy had lost 54 killed and 140 wounded, some of whom had been left at his house. The British reported only 4 killed. American casualties amounted to 12 dead and 55 wounded, of whom one died shortly after the battle. John McCalla, acting as adjutant, produced a detailed report on the American casualties, stating that 1 sergeant and 11 privates had been killed, while 3 captains, 1 lieutenant, 1 ensign, 3 sergeants, 1 corporal, and 46 privates had been wounded. The report named the individual casualties and was enclosed in a letter from Col. Lewis to Gen. Winchester on January 20, 1813. I've tabulated it and found that the numbers are not quite in agreement. Two names are apparently missing from his report. He also confuses the companies of Captain Langham (19th US) and Captain Langhorne (1st Rifle Regt.) — which I corrected in the table in Appendix D. There was no attempt to tally casualties among the local *habitants*. See Appendix D for a list of the numbers of dead and wounded by company.

361 Lt. Charland also wanted reassurance that the army would not abandon French Town. Charland feared the enemy might take reprisals against the *habitants* and their families for taking up arms against them. Charland was shocked to see Lewis pull 3 scalps from his pocket and hold them up, exclaiming, *"I'd give 40,000 Louis d'or, Halifax, if they'll come back!"* The colonel then dismissed Charland and sat down to write a report to General Winchester. He would send a courier to deliver it that night, along with the Indian who had been taken prisoner and two French guides. Charland File, Monroe County Historical Museum Archives.

362 Peckham, Miss Harriet L., Local History by the Class of '96, Monroe High School. Monroe: Monroe Commercial Print, 1896, p. 15. They were old hands at this. At the home of Jean-Baptiste Lasselle,

However, some of the men, including Antoine Sargent, chose to remain attached to Lewis' force. He would participate in the battle he felt was sure to come.[363]

Lt. Colonel Lewis ordered his acting quartermaster, Brigade Major James Garrard, to secure the town and find accommodations for the men and especially the wounded. By 9 p.m. he had finished posting all the guards and sentinels and had given them their instructions for the night.[364]

Most of the Kentucky camp in French Town was squeezed into the yard and orchard of Jean-Baptiste Jerome, which was surrounded by a tall fence, thick enough to offer some protection against small arms fire.

The *habitants* opened up their homes for the surgeons to work on the wounded. No doctor would rest until every casualty was attended to.[365]

The wounded were divided among 3 buildings, including one belonging to Gabriel Godfroy, about a hundred yards away from the main encampment.[366]

Lewis sent Dr. McIlvain and a sergeant to procure extra medicine for the wounded from a local doctor.

Besides the hospital buildings, six others were occupied for army use. Though dispersed in neighboring lots and separated by fences, the majority of companies were within about 30 paces of one another.[367]

---

the family was already preparing their secret hiding place. The thick, log walls were covered with wainscoting which hid several secret cupboards and closets. On more than one occasion, family members had hidden from marauding Indians in these cubbyholes, and the Indians had never discovered them. The site was later occupied by the Ives house on Elm Avenue next to or in the front lawn of the IHM sister house. The location is currently marked with a memorial stone.

363 Affidavit of Antoine Sargent, February 21, 1853, National Archives. See also: Charland File, Monroe County Historical Museum Archives.

364 After this, Garrard attended the wounded and then sought out LTC Lewis at the home of Jean-Baptiste Couture to make his report and take up quarters there with other officers, including LTC Allen and Major Madison. Lewis' orders were entirely verbal and all passed through Major Garrard. See the Dec. 11, 1828, affidavit of James Garrard of the County of Bourbon and State of Kentucky, taken at the request of Col. Godfroy, Hubert Lacroix, and others of French Town in the Territory of Michigan, in relation to the occupation of said town by the American army and its subsequent destruction by the British and Indians in 1813.

365 Atherton, W., Suffering & Defeat of the North-Western Army, Frankfort: A.G. Hodges, 1842, p. 39. Among the wounded was John Davenport, enrolled in Williams' company of the 5th Kentucky. He had received a ball in the right leg that cracked his bone, but not shatter it. He would still be "in hospital" when combat resumed on January 22, and would find himself a prisoner of the Indians on January 23. See: Narrative of Mr. John Davenport at the end of Elias Darnell's Journal.

366 Journal of Lewis Bond, in Knopf, Richard C., Document Transcriptions of the War of 1812 in the Northwest, Vol. X, pt. 1. Columbus: Ohio Historical Society, 1962. p. 195.

367 Knopf, Richard C. Document Transcriptions of the War of 1812 in the Northwest, Vol. V, The National

The Kentuckians were jubilant, despite their losses, and happy to spend the night in a friendly and well-supplied settlement.[368]

Intelligencer Reports, pt. 2. Columbus: The Ohio Historical Society, 1958. Interview with Capt. Matson, "Battle of Miami," Paris, Kentucky, Feb. 13. Matson was hit by a ball through the thick of his right thigh.

368 Letter McCalla to parents, French Town, River Raisin, January 21, 1813, original in Monroe County Historical Museum Archives: Yet, he could not contain his excitement at hearing the balls whistling as thick as hail as he galloped from one column to another to deliver orders and messages. Flushed with victory, he had never felt better in his life. "…I can only say of the engagement, that our movements were continually advancing, generally in a run. Once the right wing halted for a movement of the left, but only a short time. Our situation…is an enviable one, compared to our past. Plenty of apples, cider, butter etc., etc., provisions in abundance. The Inhabitants are numerous and very friendly. They are almost to a man in our favour. Several took arms and fought valiantly at our sides…The French ladies are very pretty and sociable."

INTERLUDE
ENTR'ACTE

Malden, before dawn, Tuesday, January 19, 1813:

The Queen's Ball had begun on a clear Monday evening. The moon had risen about 8 p.m. and was almost full, just slightly starting to wane. At the grand council house, people expected to be dancing and celebrating well into the wee hours of the following morning.

**Belles & Bachelors of Detroit
at the Monroe County Community College Meijer Theater
Benefit Performance in support of the Bicentennial of the War of 1812
by Harriet Berg and the Madame Cadillac Dance Theater**
photo courtesy of John Patterson

Shortly after midnight, Captain Elliott arrived with news of the battle that had taken place at the River Raisin. The mood instantly changed from gaiety to melancholy as people worried about the local militiamen who had been stationed on the Raisin.[369]

---

369 Journal of Lewis Bond, in Knopf, Richard C., Document Transcriptions of the War of 1812 in the Northwest, Vol. X, pt. 1, Columbus: Ohio Historical Society, 1962, p. 195. Bond claims the Canadian militiamen were the first to retreat from the battle, as he writes: *"The militia doing duty at River Raisin was commanded by Major Reynolds and were mostly from the Town of Malden. They however*

146

At 2 a.m., Colonel Procter was roused and told that French Town had been lost. If left unchallenged, this would deprive the British of a source of supply and provide Harrison a forward base. Procter decided to attack before Winchester's detachment could be reinforced.

Procter turned to the ailing Captain (brevet major) Muir to take charge of the Detroit garrison with Captain Askin's company of the 2nd Essex. Lt. Col. Baby would command Fort Amherstburg with some Royal Artillerymen, some invalids, and the least effective militiamen. Every other able-bodied man was called out for the expedition against the River Raisin.

Over at Draper's Tavern, a ball was still in full swing as the young men of the coast toasted old Queen Charlotte. Suddenly the door burst open, and there stood Lt. Colonel Thomas Bligh St. George, Inspecting Officer of the Militia, kitted out for a campaign.

In a commanding voice, he shouted, *"My boys, you must prepare to dance to a different tune; the enemy is upon us, and we are going to surprise them. We shall take the route about 4 in the morning, so get ready at once."*[370]

The *jeunes gens de la côte* were excited by the news and claimed they liked the thought of fighting as much as dancing. The ball broke up, and almost every man reported for duty at the proper time.[371]

In all, some 578 regulars and militiamen were assembled for the march, supported by 3 three-pounder cannons and 3 small howitzers mounted on sleds (although one of the guns may have been a 6-pdr). It was feared that heavier guns might break through the ice while crossing the Detroit River.

The artillery, manned by Royal Artillerymen, militia volunteers, and Provincial Marine seamen off the *Queen Charlotte*, was escorted by 60

---

took care to provide for their safety in time, leaving the Indian allies to fight the battle, made the best of their way home. It was supposed that this was the advanced guard of General Harrison's army, and that the main body was not far behind, and the ice being very good, an attack on Malden was apprehended, and created much alarm. On the other hand, the spirits of the inhabitants of Detroit were much heightened; expecting speedy relief, but their joy was of short duration..."

370 Au, Dennis. <u>War on the Raisin</u>. Monroe: Monroe County Historical Commission, 1981, p. 33.

371 Reynolds Narrative in Coffin, William F. <u>1812: The War and its Moral; A Canadian Chronicle</u>. Montreal: John Lovell, 1864. *Jeunes gens de la côte* = "Young men of the Coast." French Canadians often used the word for coast to indicate a settled area. The direct word for a "settlement" would be a *colonie*, which can also be translated as "colony." As far as can be determined at this time, the River Raisin *habitants* didn't use either word to describe their *zone de peuplement*. Rather, they were simply the inhabitants of the River Raisin. (Les habitants de la Rivière au Raisin / aux Raisins.)

men from the Royal Newfoundland Regiment.[372] A battalion of the 41st Regiment of Foot made up the bulk of the infantry, led by Procter himself, and Captain Joseph Tallon. Auxiliaries included a couple hundred men of the 1st and 2nd Essex Militia under Lt. Col. Thomas Bligh St. George and Major Ebenezer Reynolds.[373]

On January 19th, Captain Tallon took his company across the river and marched the 4 miles to Brownstown, along with the artillery and some sailors and militia. They were to be joined by the rest of the army within 24 hours.[374]

The troops made a less colorful sight than they had during the summer campaign against Detroit. Marching in open order, the regulars still wore the pre-1811 uniform of black, stove-pipe cap, brick-red coatee with distinctive bastion lace around the buttons, collars, and shoulder straps, white woolen breeches and black, knee-length gaiters, but their red tunics would have been hidden under a warm, gray overcoat with an attached cape that descended over the shoulders. Trousers of grey wool may have been worn instead of (or over) the gaiters, and heavy scarves were wound around the head and ears.

To complete the equipment, white shoulder straps crossed over the body to support a bayonet on the left hip and a black cartridge box on the right. Underneath the black, leather bayonet scabbard hung a linen haversack and over it was a blue, wooden canteen marked with the regimental number or the British "broad arrow" symbol, painted in white, or possibly the initials

---

372 Cruikshank, Lt. Col. E. A., <u>Harrison and Proctor</u>, Ottawa: The Royal Society of Canada, 1911, p. 158. Cruikshank asserts that the artillery pieces used in both the battles on the 18th and 22nd were all mounted on sleds. Other authors and witnesses are less clear. Some Canadian authors claim the 3-pdrs were sled drawn or "sleigh" drawn. Yet others believe it was the smaller howitzers that were placed on sleds. Some American accounts insist at least one of the guns was a 6-pdr. Even the exact number of cannons is in dispute. The Royal Artillerymen probably manned the howitzers, while the Provincial Marine crewed the 3-pdr guns, with which they may have been more familiar. See: "Remarks on the Evolution of the Sea Service 3-pounder Swivel Howitzer into the U.S. Army's King Howitzer, 1775-1820," by William E. Davidson. See also: Appendix P at the end of this book.

373 The numbers given in "The Incredible War of 1812" for Procter's force were 273 regulars, 61 fencibles, 212 militia, 28 Provincial Mariners, and about 600 Indians. Four of the regulars were from the 10th Royal Veterans Battalion.

374 The Wyandot village of Brownstown was located near the present-day site of Carlson High School in Gibraltar, Wayne County, Michigan. A monument for the Battle of Brownstown was erected in 2006 by the Brownstown Historical Society. The Memorial is on South Gibraltar Road 0.1 miles east of West Jefferson Avenue, on the right when traveling east.

"BO" for the British Ordinance Department. Other essentials were carried in a backpack.

It was very cold, although no snow was falling, and the troops marched in extended order.[375] Gentleman Volunteer John Richardson found it quite inspiring as he noted the rumbling of the artillery echoing off mounds of ice, sunbeams glittering off polished muskets, and the cries of the Indians.

Upon reaching Brownstown, Tallon's command received an alarm. The sailors unlimbered the guns and prepared for action, but no attack came.[376]

Colonel Elliott directed Captains William Elliot and William Caldwell to assemble the Indian Department and the Native allies at Brownstown as well. In the absence of Tecumseh, leadership fell to Roundhead and Walk-in-the-Water of the Wyandots, the Wyandots being the senior tribe in the region.[377]

Between five and eight hundred Native warriors turned out, including 70 Wyandots and an equal number of Delawares, plus a couple dozen Mingoes from Canada.

Many Potawatomies also joined the assembly, along with their relatives of the 3 Fires; the Ojibwas and Odawas.

The rest of the warriors were a mix of Miamies, along with some Winnebagoes, Sauks and Fox who had recently arrived from the West and some Creeks from the South.[378] They were well-supplied with muskets, rifles, and horses.

By the following evening, the British force at Brownstown would number well over a thousand fighting men. They would soon be on the march to the River Raisin.

Rivière au Sable et Rivière aux Raisins, Monday, January 19, 1813:

Early on the morning of January 19th, 14-year-old Geneviève Lebeau and her 8-year-old brother, Alexis, hobbled into the settlement, their bare feet

---

375 Reynolds Narrative in Coffin, William F., 1812: The War and its Moral; A Canadian Chronicle, Montreal: John Lovell, 1864. The weather at Detroit is often different from that of Ohio. The River Raisin sometimes finds itself on the dividing line and can go either way.

376 Letter John Richardson to Charles Askin, his uncle, dated Feb. 4, 1813, printed in "The Battle of Frenchtown," issued by the Algonquin Club, Detroit, April, 1937. See Appendix F for order of battle.

377 The addition of officers and interpreters from the British Indian Department brought the total of British and Canadian military to 597 men of all branches.

378 Excerpt from The Journal of Major John Norton, pp. 313-15, see: www.windsorpubliclibrary.com as posted on Sept. 28, 2003.

bleeding from having run 2½ miles from their home on Sandy Creek. The panicked children were joined shortly after by their older brother Étienne.[379]

They were taken into a nearby home where, fighting back their tears, they reported the horrible news. They had just witnessed the murders of their widowed father, René LeBeau[380] and his son-in-law, Jean-Baptiste Solo.

Apparently during their retreat after the battle on the 18th, a band of Native warriors passed through the Sandy Creek settlement, which was home to about 16 families. There they encountered Solo, who was returning from the house of François Gandon. Hallooing to the Indians, 29-year-old Solo asked if they were running away from the Big Knives.

A bullet came in response, and Solo staggered off towards his father-in-law's house. Reaching the door, he called out for help.

Inside were René LeBeau, his adult son Étienne, and his two youngest children, Geneviève and Alexis.[381] Yelling for the children to go upstairs, René moved to the door. As he opened it, his son-in-law collapsed into his arms.

At 6'9", weighing 280 lbs., the 58-year-old LeBeau had no difficulty carrying his son-in-law over to the bed, but Solo was already dead.

Hearing another commotion at his door, LeBeau left his son-in-law's body, and moved to the window. Looking outside, he thought he recognized

---

379 Hosmer, Hezekiah Lord. Early History of the Maumee Valley. Toledo: Hosmer & Harris, 1858, p. 42: "On the retreat of the Indians from the engagement of the 18th January, with Capt. Lewis, some of them entered the cabin of Achan Leboo, an old Frenchman, living upon Sandy Creek. They killed Leboo and his son-in-law John Solo. Two children, Alexis and Genevieve, the eldest only fourteen, crept between the beds, where they remained all night without discovery, and by running barefoot, the next day, a mile or more over frozen ground, escaped with their lives."

380 Like the Navarres, the LeBeau family claimed association with the nobility. In this case, it was with the lords of Les Baux, France, who controlled sizeable estates until the French Revolution. The progenitor of this Sandy Creek family left France a bit earlier, however. With 19 other Frenchmen, he came to America about the same time as Lafayette and fought for Washington in the Revolutionary War. Jean-Baptiste Lebeau's son, Alexis, would survive the war and operate an inn, stagecoach stop, and stables near the old family farm, about 3 miles south of Oldport. Alexis would marry Angelique Lenfant, said to be a relative of Colonel Charles L'Enfant, who laid out the design for the city of Washington, D.C. See: Carlson, Oscar A. It Happened at Rockwood. 1951.

381 Obituary of Alexis Labo, Monroe Democrat, July 15, 1886, front page: "He saw much of the war of 1812, although he did not enter the army. He saw his father shot beside him in their house on the north side of the river by an Indian after opening the door to speak with several of them. The deceased, his sister, and an uncle were obliged to fly for their lives and were pursued by the savages. After hiding and wandering about...several days, they succeeded in escaping."

some of the local Potawatomies. Having no fear of them, he reached for the still partly opened door.

As the door swung wide open, however, another shot was fired, hitting LeBeau in the chest and killing him instantly.[382]

Étienne rushed to the door and slammed it shut. As the Potawatomi pulled his arm back in pain, Étienne latched and barred the door. The Indians made no further attempt to break in, and drifted away, out of sight.

While this was happening, the children rushed upstairs and hid under their beds. As soon as it appeared safe, Étienne called them down, and they made a break for it. Silhouetted against the white snow, they were quickly spotted and some shots rang out, but they kept on running, reaching the River Raisin settlement in the early light of dawn.

After hearing this horrifying tale, the local citizens sent a delegation to Lt. Colonel Lewis, asking for his assistance. Lewis, however, told them it was beyond his power to protect the isolated settlers at Sandy Creek. All he could do was order them to come in to French Town for safety.[383]

The *habitants* then formed their own patrol to recover the bodies. Their leader was Jean-Baptiste Sanscrainte, an old hand at dealing with the native tribes. Joseph Navarre served as scout. Étienne LeBeau went along, as did many of his neighbors: Jean-Baptiste Latour, the Nadeau brothers, Joseph Menard, Medard Labadie, and the church cantor, Alexis Loranger.[384]

After a short skirmish with a small band of Indians, they rescued Marie Solo, but were unable to locate her two missing children. They took the

---

382 Deposition of Joseph Robert, Feb. 4, 1813, in Barbarities of the Enemy, exposed in a Report of the Committee of the House of Representatives, and the Documents accompanying said Report. Troy: Francis Adancourt, 1813, pp. 125-6: *"The deponent says further, that after the first action on the river Raisin, the Indians fired on one named Solo, son-in-law to Stephen Lebeau, an inhabitant on the river aux Sables, when returning from the house of Gandon to his father-in-law; on his arrival, he hallowed to his father-in-law to open the door, saying that he was mortally wounded; Stephen Lebeau opened the door, and told his son-in-law to throw himself on his bed, but that in trying to move, he fell dead. An Indian knocked at the door, and Lebeau, having opened it, received a ball in his breast and fell dead. The son of Lebeau made his escape; the Indian shot several shots at him, which did not reach him."* Some details from a LeBeau family story, as told by Dr. Laboe, indicate René was 6'9" tall, weighed 280 lbs., and probably knew his assailants by name (Personal Interview 7-21-1999).

383 Deposition of Laurent Durocher, Knopf, Richard C. Document Transcriptions of the War of 1812 in the Northwest, Vol. X, pt 1. Columbus: The Ohio Historical Society, 1962, pp. 39-41.

384 Family story told by Charles F. Sanscrainte in letter to Dennis Au, typed copy in Small Collections, Monroe County Historical Society Archives.

bodies of LeBeau and Solo by sleigh to St. Antoine's rectory to prepare them for burial.

Meanwhile, Lt. Colonel Lewis had become concerned that his men might suffer from the cold, so he ordered Major Garrard to get as many of the troops indoors as possible and to take a survey of the available supplies. Garrard then took possession of every building in the immediate area, trying not to disturb the *habitants*. With some difficulty, they found enough firewood to keep the men from getting frostbitten in their camps.

That morning, Lewis ordered the occupation of the Lacroix house. Hubert Lacroix, the owner, objected that his home was as yet unfinished and he feared it would be damaged if the soldiers tried to light a fire inside. Major Garrard assured him it would not happen, so Lacroix reluctantly complied.[385]

Some of the wounded men were temporarily placed in Lacroix's unfinished house, and his bedding and furniture requisitioned for their use.[386]

Lacroix's landlord and father-in-law, Jean-Baptiste Jerome, similarly furnished a number of barrels of flour, pork, whisky and lard (or bacon), and offered his house, barn, stable, store, and outbuildings for the army's use.[387]

Joseph Loranger had a store stocked with flour and other provisions worth about $10,000. Knowing the Kentuckians' need for supplies, Loranger turned his entire stock of supplies over to the army.[388]

Some of the *habitants*, such as the tenants living in McDougall's house, were less than enthusiastic upon being ejected from part of their living quarters to make room for the troops.[389] Nonetheless, when several officers showed up

---

385 Dec. 11, 1828, affidavit of James Garrard of the County of Bourbon and State of Kentucky, taken at the request of Col. Godfroy, Hubert Lacroix, J.-B. Jerome, George McDougall and others of French Town in the Territory of Michigan, in relation to the occupation of said town by the American army and its subsequent destruction by the British and Indians in 1813. (See also: Dennison, pp. 1146, 709, 710), (Civilians, by Au), (Gandon dep.), (War on the Raisin, D. Au), (Darnell's Journal), (Labadie dep., Lyon Papers)

386 Petition of Hubert Lacroix, Frenchtown, Dec. 12, 1819. Lacroix also supplied butter, flour, lard (bacon?), and other necessities for them. His oats, hay, and corn were requisitioned to feed the army horses, with Winchester's assurances that Lacroix would be properly compensated.

387 Report of the House Committee of Claims on the petition of Jean — B. Jerome and others, Jan. 25, 1822. Statement of J-B. Jerome, taken at Frenchtown, Dec. 12, 1819.

388 "Monroe Town Plan Drafted by Fur Trader."

389 Deposition of George McDougall, County of Wayne, Territory of Michigan, August 6, 1825: "*The United States Troops, they having forcibly dispossessed my tenants as a measure of necessity for their immediate shelter and protection, on or about the 18th of January, 1813...*"

to direct their men to take possession of the building, Pierre Jacob's mother was able to negotiate a payment to cook for them.[390]

Later in the afternoon, Elias Darnell stared blankly at the bodies of his comrades who had been killed the evening before. All but one had been stripped and scalped, and they looked like they had been tortured to death.

The 12 bodies had lain out all night, until daylight made it safe to venture out. A hundred men had combed the woods looking for them. They placed the bodies temporarily in Jean-Baptiste Jerome's barn and Lacroix's unfinished house, while a dozen mutilated Indian bodies were left in the fields.

Darnell contrasted this scene with his otherwise peaceful surroundings. The settlement was substantial, as well supplied as any place in Kentucky. There were plenty of apples, cider, sugar, and butter, and even some whisky.

The cluster of 20 or so clapboarded log cabins looked like frame houses to him, and he was impressed with the 5-foot-tall fencing which protected their yards and gardens. The officers took most of the buildings, and the men were left to camp in and around the out buildings, in no particular order.

To the Kentuckians, the River Raisin was a pleasant stream, even in winter. Some 70 yards wide, Elias Darnel noted that it flowed "*through a level country, interspersed with well-improved farms.*"[391]

Towards evening some *habitants* came riding into the settlement to say that they had followed the retreating enemy north as far as Brownstown. Hanging on the rear of the Canadian militia, they had seen the British gathering more troops and Indians. The enemy was definitely regrouping.[392]

En route for the Raisin, morning of January 19, 1813:

Major McClenahan watched his general race by in a *cariole*, unwilling to follow the slow pace of the relief force led by Colonel Wells. About 2 hours before daylight that morning, General Winchester had received a delegation informing him of the victory at the River Raisin. They brought along

---

390 Deposition of Pierre Jacob, County of Monroe, Territory of Michigan, Sept. 30, 1825.

391 Darnell, Elias, Journal. Philadelphia: Lippincott, Grambo, and Co., 1854, p. 50.

392 Monroe Civic Reflector, 1904. Over the next few days, rumors of a British counterattack flew through the settlement, persisting in the face of reassurances by confidant American officers.

the captured Potawatomi. After interrogating him, Winchester assembled reinforcements and sent a message to General Harrison asking for more.[393]

Winchester thought he could reinforce French Town before the British could mount a counter offensive.[394] So, Wells left the Maumee somewhere between 10 a.m. and noon that morning with about 300 troops bound for the Raisin, including regulars from the 17th and 19th U.S. Infantry, and volunteers from three of the militia companies that had been left at the Maumee.

They took 4 pack horses per company to transport their equipment and 2 days-worth of rations, and were followed by a herd of 200 hogs. One of the companies fell behind, however, because it was detailed to drive the hogs and bring on additional baggage.[395] Their departure left General Payne with only 300 men to hold Winchester's camp on the Maumee.[396]

Judging by the speed at which Winchester was traveling, McClenahan estimated the general would reach his advanced force at French Town sometime during the night. Too bad his infantry couldn't move that quickly.[397]

Meanwhile, back at the Maumee Rapids, Leslie Combs came sliding into Winchester's old camp on a horse-drawn sleigh. He was surprised to find only General Payne, commanding a mere remnant of Winchester's army.

Instead of the well-fortified stronghold he had expected, Combs saw a still largely open camp on the north side of the river, a location exposed to

---

393 Letter Winchester to Harrison, Camp Miami Rapids, Jan. 19, 1813, in Knopf, Richard C. Document Transcriptions of the War of 1812 in the Northwest, Vol. VIII. Columbus: Ohio Historical Society, 1961: *"Sir, in my last, I informed you I had sent out a detachment under the command of Lt. Col. William Lewis. I have the honour now to communicate the result. The village of River Raisin is ours with all the public store …The action commenced yesterday at 3 o'clock in the evening near the village and continued until dark. The enemy was driven at the point of the bayonet from his strongholds and pursued two miles, notwithstanding he was covered by his artillery. Twelve warriors were left on the field of battle. One Potawatomi made prisoner, who is now at this camp. My express left the scene of action as soon as it closed, therefore has not a list of the killed and wounded…The latter I fear is considerable, tho not a commissioned officer was killed and only one wounded, Capt. Hickman slightly in the ankle. The troops, to a man, behaved in this action in a manner that would do credit to the oldest veterans."*

394 Winchester, James. Historic Details Having Relation to the Campaign of the North-Western Army under Generals Harrison and Winchester. Lexington: Worsley & Smith, 1818, p. 30.

395 Letter Wells to Cushing, Feb. 9, 1813, in MPHC, Vol. 40, p. 503.

396 Au, Dennis. War on the Raisin. Monroe: Monroe County Historical Commission, 1981, pp. 29-30.

397 Letter McClenahan to Harrison, Knopf, Richard C. Document Transcriptions of the War of 1812 in the Northwest, Vol. VIII. Columbus: Ohio Historical Society, 1961, p. 61.

British assault and not at all what Winchester had planned and indicated in the letter Combs had carried to General Tupper.[398]

French Town on the Raisin, Wednesday, January 20, 1813:

General Winchester and his aide, Capt. Woolfolk, arrived at the River Raisin by *cariole*, along with some of his staff and an escort. Over the course of the day, the General visited the militia camp and discussed the situation with Lt. Colonel Lewis at the home of Jean-Baptiste Couture.[399]

Securely ensconced within the garden pickets, and with plenty to eat, Lewis' men showed no desire to return to their forlorn base on the Maumee. Furthermore, Lewis had over 50 wounded men who would be difficult to

---

398 Letter Response of General Leslie Combs, Verhoeven Collection, Monroe County Historical Museum Archives. At this point, Winchester no longer seemed to be the cautious general who had carefully fortified his camps during his advance along the Maumee River the previous fall. Was it fatigue? Overconfidence? The weather?

399 Hosmer, Hezekiah Lord, Early History of the Maumee Valley, Toledo: Hosmer & Harris, 1858, p. 36, has Wells arriving on the 19th of January and Winchester following on the 20th. Elias Darnell's Journal indicates that Winchester, Wells and 230 reinforcements arrived the day after this, on the afternoon of January 21st. Lossing says Winchester arrived at 3pm on the 20th, along with the reinforcements. Atherton puts his arrival on the night of the 20th. Clift says Winchester arrived on the morning of the 20th; and the reinforcements, at 3pm. Dennis Au places Winchester's arrival at 2 a.m. on the 20th, and the reinforcements 12 hours later. This would have been the day that French Town was to have been looted and burned by the British and Indians. In his 1818 deposition, François Navarre states Winchester arrived at his house at 2 a.m. on the 21st and 150 reinforcements arrived about the same time. John Baptist Jerome also mentions the morning of the 21st as when Winchester approached him to ask if he could stay at his house. Possibly, a variety of officers and troops were seen to arrive at different times, confusing the locals, who often were interviewed years after the event. I think Winchester arrived on the 20th, but did not immediately secure his quarters and settle in at the Navarre house until the early morning hours of the 21st.

See also: Statement of General Winchester, Notices Vol. 1, Apdx 7, Memorandum of statements made by General Winchester and Major Madison to the Secretary of War on their return from captivity. Typed copy in Bidlack's Notes, Monroe County Historical Museum Archives.

As far as the main body of reinforcements under Colonel Wells is concerned, if the troops left the rapids between 10 a.m. and noon on January 19, as Winchester and McClenahan reported, and they traveled 3 miles an hour through the snow, with about 6 hours of daylight remaining, they could have covered about 18 miles the first day, over half way to the Raisin along Hull's Road. Leaving by 9 a.m. the next day, and traveling at the same rate, they could have reached the Raisin by 3 p.m. on the 20th. However, on their earlier march down the Maumee, encumbered with more baggage, they must have averaged much less. Lewis' detachment had reached the Raisin in only two days, but they were not accompanied by a lot of baggage, nor followed by a drove of hogs.

transport. There was also the question of what to do with the 30 barrels of flour and the 2,000 pounds of beef that had been captured.

Not the least enticement for the young soldiers was the presence of a variety of eligible, young females, an exceedingly rare sight for the past 5 months.[400]

Tall fences stretched along 3 sides of the small cluster of adjacent farmsteads and store houses that gave that spot the appearance of a sort of village, but they were meant to shelter the gardens and prevent animals from wandering. They were not sufficiently solid to protect the troops if attacked by even light artillery.[401]

Between 2 and 3 p.m., Wells arrived with Major McClenahan, Surgeons Irvine and Montgomery, the reinforcements, and some civilian sutlers and camp followers. They were eager to partake of the local apples and cider, and were impressed by the grape vines and fruit trees lining the River Raisin.

Finding Lewis' militiamen in possession of the houses, Wells' regular infantrymen made a temporary bivouac in an open field on the Reaume farm a couple hundred yards down river, as directed by the Brigade Major.[402]

Lewis suggested there was enough room for Wells' men to camp to the left of the militia on Godfroy's property inside the pickets, but the colonel did not want his regulars in close contact with the militiamen, whose discipline had become rather lax.[403]

Instead, Wells placed his 250 men in their customary position of honor,

---

400 Letter Winchester to Harrison, Jan. 21, 1813, typed copy in Bidlack's Notes, Monroe County Historical Museum Archives. *"There was taken in the public stores of the enemy 30 barrels of flour, 2,000 pounds of beef and 12 blankets; but no arms or ammunition. All accounts from Brownstown and Malden agree in stating that the enemy is preparing to retake this place; if he effects his purpose, he will pay dear for it. A few pieces of artillery, however, would add to our strength and give confidence to our friends in this quarter."*

401 Still, with the addition of the reinforcements brought up by Colonel Wells, there seemed little danger the defeated British could muster sufficient force to overwhelm the Kentuckians, especially if they constructed a new, fortified camp. But they would need proper entrenching tools, a good supply of wood, favorable weather, and time.

402 Wells arrived with Meade's and Edwards' companies of the 17th and Langham's of the 19th, as well as some militiamen, but some questions remain. Some of Hightower's company of the 17th were involved in the retreat of the right wing, but others were within the fences. Were Wells' militia reinforcements integrated into Lewis' camp, Wells' camp, or lodged in the vicinity of Winchester's headquarters at the Navarre house? Did Morris' company ever catch up and join them?

403 Lossing, Benson J. The Pictorial Field-Book of the War of 1812. Glendale, New York: Benchmark Publishing Corporation, 1970, p. 353.

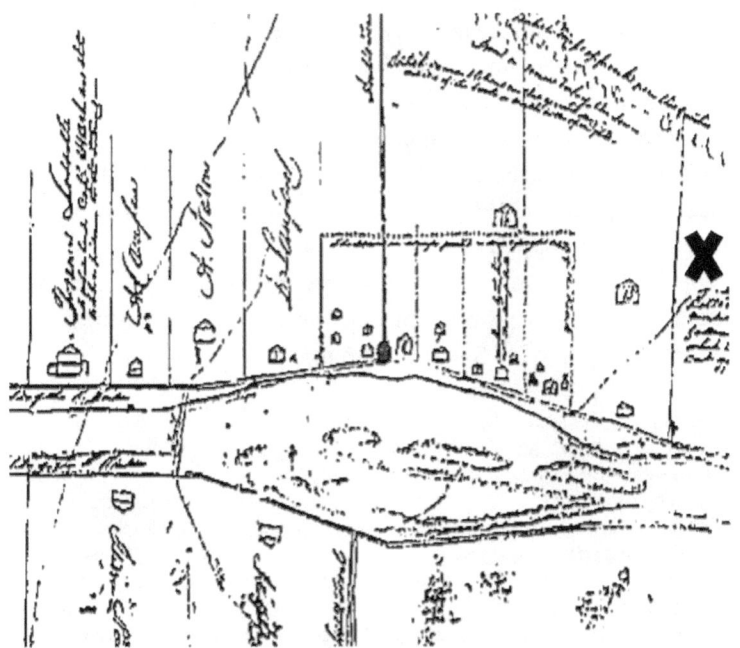

**Location of Buildings Inside Garden Pickets of French
Town & the Neighboring Farmsteads
From Original Map Drawn by Col. John Anderson,
2nd Michigan Territorial Militia Regiment
Reaume's ribbon farm is marked with an X.**
(Map is not to scale)

on open ground to the right of the militia. Three companies set their tents in a line going north from the river, with the 4th at a right angle trailing downriver.[404]

Winchester advised, but did not order, Wells to fortify his position for the

---

404 McClenahan to Harrison, Jan. 26, 1813, <u>Official Letters of the military and Naval Officers of the United States during the War with Great Britain in the Years 1812, 13, 14, and 15.</u> Edit. by John Brannan. Washington City: Wax & Gideon, 1823, p. 131: Straw from Godfroy's barn was used to line their tents.

night, but the colonel did not follow through, thinking they would move to a more permanent camp the next day.[405] Besides, little daylight remained.[406]

Jerome's house had originally been designated as Winchester's head-quarters, but when asked to provide a room for the general, Jerome replied his house was full of wounded men from the battle of the 18th.[407]

Not wanting to displace the wounded, the general turned to Jocko (Coco) Lasselle, who had already helped arrange boarding for Lewis and his officers in the homes of the *habitants*.[408]

Winchester, his son, and his staff were invited to stay at the house of the settlement's leading citizen, François Navarre, where Winchester would retire for the night around 2 in the morning.[409]

---

405 Atherton, W., Suffering & Defeat of the North-Western Army, Frankfort: A.G. Hodges, 1842, p. 41. Au, Dennis, War on the Raisin, Monroe: Monroe County Historical Commission, 1981, p. 30. There are varying estimates of the distance between Wells' camp and the rest of the army. Dennis Au proposes the near end of Wells' camp was about 150 yards to the east and stretched 280 yards further downstream from that point. Morris' company was not with them, having fallen behind to bring up the baggage. I believe Well's camp was located roughly 200 yards from the militia camp and 200 yards north of the river. Each company would have needed only about 15 tents, capable of housing 2 to 6 men. (Capt. Ballard's company, for example, had 1 wall tent and 14 common tents.) With each tent averaging about 3-4 yards of frontage, a company's tents would have covered only a single line of about 45-60 yards. If arranged in an L-pattern, with 3 companies stretching away from the river and only one parallel to the stream, the camp could have stretched about 180 yards south to north and 60 yards west to east. The wall tents were not normally placed in the same row with the common tents. In his Journal, Elias Darnell states materials were at hand to fortify the right wing, but it was not thought worthwhile, since they planned to move the camp to a better position early the next morning.

406 Letter Samuel Wells to Thomas Cushing, February 9, 1813, Michigan Pioneer and Historical Collections, Vol. XL. Lansing: Michigan Historical Commission, 1929, pp. 503-7. Peter Manor and a couple of Navarre brothers from the Maumee were anxious to go out and locate the enemy who, according to St. Bernard, were within striking distance. Wells asked Winchester to send scouts out as far as Brownstown. The General agreed to do so the next morning, January 22.

407 Deposition of John Baptist Jerome of Monroe County, Aug. 22, 1818: "*The deponent further states that in the morning of the 21st, Gen. Winchester called upon deponent and inquired if he could have a room at deponent's house, it being near the encampment. Deponent replied that his house was full of wounded, but if he (the Gen.) would have them removed, he could have a room. Gen. Winchester afterwards sent to deponent to inquire if he could have a room at his, deponent's house — deponent replied as before. ...deponent further states he did not see Winchester again that day.*"

408 "A Nonogenarian," The Detroit Free Press, May 3, 1891, p. 43, col. 1-4. From an interview with James Knaggs, nephew of the famous scout by the same name: "*LaSalle was an English subject in heart. He had a daughter who was a half-breed Shawnee. She married an English officer by the name of Caldwell. LaSalle showed marked hospitality to General Winchester, showed him where to camp his men, and then quartered the officers at the different neighbors'. ...Some were quartered at Navarre's, some at LaSalle's, and some at Col. Anderson's, an uncle of mine.*"

409 Deposition of Francis Navarre, Aug. 22, 1818, William Henry Harrison Papers, on microfilm at

François Navarre had built his first log cabin along the River Raisin in 1784, on land he received from the Potawatomies. His house was about ¾ of a mile upriver from the Kentucky camps, and on the opposite side of the stream.

With Whitmore Knaggs interpreting, Lieutenant Colonel François Navarre, the ranking local militia officer, freely expressed his misgivings about the defenses of the American army, especially the suitability of the garden fences as a fortification. Moreover, the distance between his home and the main body of the army naturally exposed his new houseguest to some danger of being cut off if the enemy attacked.[410]

While the fussy, heavy-set general was distancing himself from Lewis' horde of unkempt militia, Jocko Lasselle was quietly observing their numbers and disposition. Upon returning to his own home, Lasselle found his Shawnee brothers-in-law, George and Jim Blue Jacket, were waiting for him.[411]

Lasselle quickly dictated a letter to his daughter Nannette, which she wrote out in the careful script she had learned at school in Québec. Soon, Young George Blue Jacket would race off across the ice to find Colonel Procter and deliver Lasselle's letter.[412]

Central Michigan University.

410 Statement of General Winchester, Notices Vol. 1, Apdx 7, Memorandum of statements made by General Winchester and Major Madison to the Secretary of War on their return from captivity. Typed copy in Bidlack's Notes, Monroe County Historical Museum Archives. See also: Winchester, James. Historic Details Having Relation to the Campaign of the North-Western Army under Generals Harrison and Winchester. Lexington: Worsley & Smith, 1818, p. 43.

411 The Historical Society of Northwestern Ohio, biographical field notes 84, 135, 137, 153: There is some confusion between a number of Shawnees bearing the name of the famous Chief Wayapiersenwa, or Blue Jacket. His daughter, Marie Louise, became the wife of Jacques Lasselle, and Nanette was their daughter. Bluejacket's son, George, was an Indian interpreter for the British at Fort Malden. Another son was Jim Bluejacket. A Jim Bluejacket was reportedly killed at Brownstown on August 5, 1812, but there was also a Jim Bluejacket who fought at the Raisin and the Thames. See: "Deeds / Nations, Directory of First Nations Individuals in South-Western Ontario, 1750-1850," by Greg Curnoe, available online at www.adamsheritage.com.

412 Journal of Lewis Bond, in Knopf, Richard C., Document Transcriptions of the War of 1812 in the Northwest, Vol. X, pt. 1, Columbus: Ohio Historical Society, 1962, p. 195. According to Lewis Bond: *"Some traitors at River Raisin, having got all the information they could, sent privately to Malden, giving a full account of the number of the Americans, how they were camped, and the very spot where the General quartered, that they had no cannon, etc. On the receipt of this intelligence, Proctor collected the militia and Indians, manning the forts of Detroit and Malden with militia, taking all or nearly all his regulars and sailors…determined to attack the American camp at French Town. He accordingly left Malden on the 21st, crossed on the ice with his cannon, and that night encamped about 4 miles from R. Raisin…"* Marie-Antoinette "Nannette" Lasselle was born in 1792. It is thought her mother

Harrison's Relief Force, January 16-22, 1813:

After receiving Winchester's letter of December 30, informing him of his move to the Maumee Rapids, General Harrison sent forward a large drove of hogs and readied his artillery. On January 16, Harrison received a note from General Perkins with Winchester's request for reinforcements, so Harrison ordered the artillery sent via the Portage River and Hull's Road.[413]

He also detached Major Robert Orr's 200 men from General Joel Leftwich's Brigade to serve as escorts for the artillery. Major Orr was to travel a newly cut path connecting Upper Sandusky with Hull's Road and the Portage River. He took with him 7 companies of Virginia and Pennsylvania militia, Captain Cushing's company of artillery, and a large baggage train.[414]

On Sunday, January 17th, troops at Upper Sandusky were assembled in a hollow square to listen to Rev. Hensey, Chaplin of the Pennsylvania Brigade. Standing atop a stump, the Reverend invited those who wished to sing to come to the center. After several hymns, Hensey gave a rousing sermon, pointing towards Crawford's old battlefield, and urging the militiamen to advance even into Canada to uphold the honor of the old heroes of the Revolutionary War.[415]

The same day, Harrison left headquarters to rouse the troops at Lower Sandusky, riding in such haste that one of his aide's horses dropped dead upon arrival. Knowing Winchester was expecting a reinforcement of at least 500 men, he ordered Major W. W. Cotgreave to depart the next morning.[416]

On the 18th, Major Cotgreave's battalion took up the march. Three hundred men from Virginia and Ohio shouldered their muskets and stepped

---

was Mary Bluejacket, daughter of the famous Shawnee war leader. Her mother married Jacques Lasselle in 1801, but died in 1806. After the war, Nannette would marry Thomas Caldwell of Amherstburg. Caldwell, the son of William Caldwell and Suzanne Baby, was an ensign in the 1st Essex Militia Regiment and fought on the British side at the Battle of the River Raisin.

413 Winchester, James, Historic Details Having Relation to the Campaign of the North-Western Army under Generals Harrison and Winchester. Lexington: Worsley & Smith, 1818, p. 34.

414 Major Orr's men were supposed to leave Jan. 18, but their departure was delayed until the 21st.

415 Journal of Joseph Larwill, Burton Historical Collection, Detroit Public Library, p. 30. Washington, Montgomery, and Crawford were heroes of the American Revolution: "...*cross the Canadian line, telling them that the great Washington from the banks of the Potomac cries aloud to go forward, Montgomery from the walls of Quebec, Crawford and his heroes that fell in yonder grave.*"

416 Notices Vol. 1, Apdx 9, Extracts from affidavits in relation to the affair at Frenchtown, of the 22 of January, 1813, made by the late Governor Madison of Kentucky, Colonel William Lewis, and Major S. Garrard. Typescript copy in Bidlack's Notes, Monroe County Historical Museum Archives.

off onto a partly-built road leading into the Black Swamp. Along with them, they hauled one of Lieutenant Levi Huikill's precious cannons.

General Harrison was awakened from his slumber at 2 in the morning on Tuesday, January 19th, when a message came in that Winchester, was sending troops to French Town. Harrison sprang from his bed at the news he had been expecting since leaving Upper Sandusky on the 17th.[417]

Immediately, he ordered Colonel John Andrews and his 300 men from the 2nd Regiment of Brigadier General Simon Perkins' Brigade of Ohio militia to march for the Maumee Rapids. He then set out for the same destination in a sleigh, along with 41-year-old General Perkins and an aide.

Realizing that Winchester's column was in an exposed position, he sent an express to Upper Sandusky ordering more troops to be sent to the Maumee. Unfortunately, it would take time to concentrate enough troops in time to support General Winchester.[418]

Lower Sandusky was 35 miles from the rapids, which was another 30 miles from the River Raisin. Conversely, French Town was only 18 or so miles across the ice of Lake Erie from the British base at Malden; a distance that could be covered by the enemy's mounted warriors in less than a day.

Harrison found the going too slow with General Perkins and his troops, so, he took his servant's horse and rode on alone through the night, following in the wake of Major Cotgreave's detachment.

The swamp was so poorly frozen that the horse kept breaking through and falling up to its belly in the icy water. Compelled to dismount and lead his horse, Harrison jumped from one piece of solid ground to the next.

He had reached the point of exhaustion, when one of Cotgreave's men came straggling back on the trail, looking for his lost bayonet, which would have cost him a dollar stoppage in his pay.

The general offered to cover his loss and get him a brand-new bayonet in exchange for his assistance in pulling his horse through this miserable swamp. With the straggler's help, Harrison managed to reach the Maumee Rapids in the early morning hours.

At Winchester's camp, Harrison found out that General Winchester had

---

417 Cruikshank, Lt. Col. E. A., Harrison and Proctor. Ottawa: The Royal Society of Canada, 1911, p. 155. See also: Dissertation of Rex LeRoy Spencer, Ph.D., "The Gibraltar of the Maumee: Fort Meigs in the War of 1812." Muncie, Indiana: Ball State University, 1989.

418 Letter from General Harrison, Portage River, Jan. 26, 1813, in Document Transcriptions of the War of 1812 in the Northwest. Columbus: The Ohio Historical Society, 1957, Vol. I, pp. 81-83. At the Rapids, he could coordinate his efforts to reinforce Winchester's advance to the River Raisin.

already left with reinforcements for the River Raisin, leaving behind only a 300-man rear guard under the direction of General Payne.

Harrison was not surprised, however, for on the way, he had received General Winchester's message of the 19th, which detailed the successful capture of French Town on the 18th.

On the 21st, he found two more letters waiting for him at the rapids, with more of the details of Lewis' victory and the current disposition of Winchester's forces at the River Raisin.

In his letter, Winchester requested that his force be increased from a thousand to twelve hundred men. Harrison sent the Inspector General, Captain Nathaniel G. S. Hart, with orders for Winchester to maintain his position, while he hurried up the reinforcements.[419]

The 2nd Regiment of Perkins' brigade was expected to arrive with 350 men during the night or early the next day, while Cotgreave's force was also still slogging its way through the partially frozen swamps.

In the meantime, Harrison directed General Paine to march his remaining 300 Kentuckians to Winchester's relief at daybreak on the 22nd.[420]

Harrison also sent word for Cotgreave to cross the ice of Maumee Bay and head directly for French Town. Given a couple weeks, Harrison figured he could assemble a force of 4,500 men at the Rapids. He then sat down to draft a letter to the Secretary of War, explaining the present situation.[421]

---

419 McAfee, Robert, <u>History of the Late War in the Western Country</u>, Bowling Green, Ohio: Historical Publications, 1919 (reprint of 1816 original edition.) p. 250. McAffee concluded Harrison had done everything in his power to support Winchester's advance, both to the Rapids and to the Raisin, as soon as he had sufficient information. *"If it should be asked why detachments from the center and right wing were not sent sooner to the Rapids…the answer is obvious. The object of the advance to that place was to guard the provisions…to be accumulated there for the main expedition…and it was important that a force unnecessarily large should not be sent there, to consume the accumulating provisions before the main expedition was ready to move."*

420 Dissertation of Rex LeRoy Spencer, Ph.D., "The Gibraltar of the Maumee: Fort Meigs in the War of 1812." Muncie, Indiana: Ball State University, 1989. Winchester had requested enough reinforcements to raise his force to about 1200 men, sufficient to hold off any attack the enemy could mount against him. These reinforcements were on the way, but they would arrive too late to help Winchester in the coming battle.

421 Although General Harrison realized that Winchester's force was now in a dangerously exposed position, he could see why the general had chosen to reinforce his position at French Town. The local French *habitants* had armed themselves and sallied out of their homes in support of LTC Lewis, and had shown the utmost bravery in combating the enemy. In all good conscience, they could not be abandoned to reprisals by the Indians or arrest by the British. They had opened

Meanwhile, Major Orr's detachment was finally getting under way. The troops paraded at 8 a.m. on Thursday, January 21st, and marched off 2 hours later, in sections of 4 files, on a trail heading northwest towards Hull's Road.

Captain Cushing's company of artillery consisted of a dozen artillery pieces of various calibers and two caissons full of cartridges, powder, and fuses. Only one of the guns was mounted on a field carriage, the rest being transported on sleds.

About $3\frac{1}{2}$ miles into their trip, they passed the grove of timber where Col. Crawford was defeated by the Indians nearly 40 years earlier. Towards sunset that night, full of foreboding, they made camp in the snow near the creek where the Colonel had been burned at the stake. Later, they were joined by a company of volunteers from Petersburg, Virginia.[422]

Lower end of Grosse Isle, early morning, Thursday, January 21, 1813:

The four sons of Eutreau Navarre peered out across the icy Detroit River at the solitary individual running towards them. It turned out to be Joseph Bordeaux, escaping from Fort Amherstburg.[423]

When he came up to the Navarre brothers, he halted and gasped, *"The Americans will be attacked by the whole British army tonight. I know it... They were ready to march when I left Malden."*[424] The *habitants* all then took off to warn General Winchester.

---

their homes to the troops, and the supplies gathered there were quite substantial. Even their *carioles* could be used to ease the army's transportation problems. See: Letter Harrison to Monroe, Miami Rapids, Jan.20, 1813. Typed copy in Bidlack's Notes, Monroe County Historical Museum Archives: *"The detachment under Col. Lewis remains at the River Raisin and Gen. Winchester very properly marched yesterday with 250 men to reinforce him and take the command. The force at present there amounts to about one thousand effective men, and I am at this moment dispatching a fine battalion of Ohio Infantry from the Connecticut Reserve, with a small company of artillery and a field piece. It is absolutely necessary to maintain the position at the River Raisin, and I am assembling the troops as fast as possible for the purpose...I directed a part of the heavy artillery to set out from Upper Sandusky yesterday on sleds."*

422 Lorrain, Alfred, The Helm, the Sword, and the Cross: A Life Narrative, Cincinnati: Poe & Hitchcock, 1862, pp. 108-116. On page 80 of Real Patriots and Heroic Soldiers, author Stuart L. Butler claims the major's detachment would eventually be comprised of Orr's Pennsylvania Volunteers, the Petersburg Volunteer company from Virginia, hundreds of pack horses, and Captain Cushing of the artillery, with 20 cannons. Crawford's defeat occurred in 1782, at the end of the Revolutionary War.

423 Hosmer, Hezekiah Lord, Early History of the Maumee Valley, Toledo: Hosmer & Harris, 1858, p. 36. Joseph Bordeaux would later become Peter Navarre's father-in-law.

424 Bordeaux's estimate was *at least* double the actual size of the enemy's force, but his conclusion

At the River Raisin that morning, four *habitants* were playing a hotly contested game of cards at Loranger's storehouse.[425] On each hand of play, one player or another would yell and slam his card down with a loud thump of his knuckles. Having "taken the trick," he would sweep the cards into a pile near the edge of the table.

The room was abuzz with playful banter and filled with the sweet smell of pipe smoke when Louis Lafountain's Indian guide rode up to the building, dismounted, and flung the door wide open without knocking. Leaning in, the guide excitedly announced to the startled group that the redcoats were coming. He had seen them at Swan Creek.

The men dropped their cards with hardly a word. Lafountain wanted to join his family in Detroit. Loranger and Beaugrand thought of securing their property at French Town and joining their wives at Sandusky. Laurent Durocher, postmaster and clerk for Godfroy and Beaugrand, argued they should first warn Winchester, then lay low and weather the coming storm.[426]

---

that they were gathering for a counter-offensive was correct. Eutreau Navarre's sons were named Peter, Robert, Alexis, and Jacques. Formerly a River Raisin *habitant*, Eutreau had moved his family to Presqu'île near the mouth of the Maumee.

425 This location is uncertain. In his postwar claims for damages, Joseph Loranger stated he had a dwelling house, store, and other buildings on the Maumee in 1812, but these were destroyed by the Indians after the surrender of General Hull. Whereupon, he relocated his operations on a reduced scale to the River Raisin, converting his goods into staples, such as flour, wheat, corn, and oats.

These were safely stored in the settlement. He resisted several lucrative offers to sell the British his provisions, hoping to preserve them for Winchester's approaching army. After Winchester's defeat, Loranger fled to Upper Sandusky to offer his services to General Harrison. The goods left behind were pillaged or destroyed by the British and Indians. (His claims for his losses at the Maumee and River Raisin were subsequently denied by the U.S. Government.) See: S. Misc. Doc. No. 118, 35th Cong., 1st Sess. (1857). A digital copy is available via the University of Oklahoma College of Law Digital Commons as "J. Loranger vs the U.S.," 12-18-1857.

There were a number of Joseph Lorangers. The Loranger family was related to the Rivards, French *habitants* prominent in early Detroit history. The Loranger grist mill, which has been preserved in Henry Ford's Greenfield Village, was built by Edward Loranger along Stony Creek around 1828. Edward Loranger (1796-1887) migrated to the River Raisin from Three Rivers, Québec in 1816, and thus was not present at the battle. See: Item, folder, box, accession 92.188, Loranger Family papers, Benson Ford Research Center, The Henry Ford.

426 "The Observer," Monroe Evening News, Nov. 2, 1946. Traditionally, the card game was said to have been euchre. It is unknown when euchre was first played in this area. Historians have suggested the game of euchre originated from Americanized versions of similar French games called *piquet* and *écarté*. One theory is that it was introduced by French players in Louisiana and gradually spread northward in the 19th century. It is likely that its origins are Germanic, or possibly Alsatian. Some of the vocabulary of the game resembles German words; bower (*bauer* = farmer), euchre

Winchester's Headquarters, 11 a.m., January 21, 1813:

While the bodies of Solo and LeBeau were being buried in the churchyard of St. Antoine's, General Winchester was writing another letter to Harrison.[427]

The general was not entirely comfortable with the position of his army. It would be difficult to improve French Town's defenses because wood had to be hauled quite a distance and there was a shortage of axes. Winchester also was still waiting for reinforcements, enough to bring his effective force up to about 1,200 men, and some extra ammunition for "offensive operations."[428]

Wells' regulars paraded and called their morning role as usual, but the militia inside the pickets no longer bothered with morning formations.

(*junker* = joker), etc. The areas in the U.S. where the game has retained some of its 19th century popularity are those with the most German immigration — Pennsylvania, upstate New York, Michigan, Ohio, and much of the Midwest. It is also played in Britain, Canada, and Australia.

427 Winchester's estimate of his situation, which he would send to Harrison by express rider stated that the community could produce 3 or 4 hundred barrels of flour and some beef. In addition, forage and sleds to help transport the supplies could be purchased locally. Dr. McIlvain was even able to find local sources of medicines for the men.

Funeral expenses in those days were paid to the Church. An adult burial cost 24 French *livres*; a Requiem Mass, 9 *livres*; and an adult funeral, 6 *livres*. Six *livres* were worth about a dollar. In hardship cases, the *curé* could dispense with the charge. With no resident priest, Alexis Loranger probably took care of the arrangements in St. Antoine's Parish. As head singer and catechist, he was provided an annual salary of 225 *livres* ($37.50). Both he and the Beadle would be involved in a funeral, as it was the Beadle's job to dig the graves. In general, the Beadle acted as janitor and bell ringer, assisted at funerals and other services, prepared the altar for Mass, and distributed the Blessed Bread. See "The Organist and the Beadle," St. Antoine Parish Minutes, St. Mary's Church. Although it is very rare, there are still some old timers who know how to hand dig a grave in frozen ground. For some hints, see: "Digging Graves the Old-Fashioned Way," by Jennifer Mitchell, NPR's "All Things Considered." See also: "Meet the Wisconsin men who still dig graves by hand — even when the cemetery ground is frozen," an article by Rick Romell, Milwaukee Journal Sentinel, updated March 6, 2020. St. Antoine's graveyard was in generally sandy soil, but was often flooded.

428 Letter Winchester to Harrison, French Town, Jany 21, 1813, Typed copy in Bidlack's Notes, Monroe County Historical Museum Archives. See also: Knopf, Richard C. Document Transcriptions of the War of 1812 in the Northwest, Vol. VIII, Columbus: Ohio Historical Society, 1961, p. 49.: "*Your communication of yesterday by Capt. Hart, I have just had the honor of receiving. I am not yet able to give you any certain information as to the quantity of provisions which can be collected from the citizens of this place...perhaps three or four hundred barrels of flour and some beef. I would rather that my force was increased to 1,000 to 1200 effective men, sufficient to repel any force that could be brought against me. The ground I am compelled to occupy is not very favourable for defense and wood not convenient, but it is my only alternative, unless I abandon the protection of the village. No pains or reasonable expense shall be spared to acquire the necessary information concerning the enemy. A quarter master stationed at this place might render service by purchasing forage, as well as procuring the means of transportation of supplies from the Rapids, which could be done by sleds, put in requisition here, on good terms. Axes are much wanted, as well as fixed ammunition, the one for defensive; the other for offensive operations...*"

Many of the regulars still had only 10 cartridges apiece. A supply of fixed ammunition arrived from the rapids, but it was taken to Winchester's headquarters.[429]

Upon their return to the Raisin, Bordeaux and the Navarre brothers immediately sought out the general at his headquarters. They found him in the presence of Jocko Lasselle. When asked if they had personally observed the British troops, the Navarres had to admit they had not.[430]

Winchester then dismissed the scouts with a laugh, sure that it would take several more days for the British to organize a counter offensive.[431]

All doubts to the contrary, however, Procter's force of British, Canadians, and Indians was even then marching towards Swan Creek.[432]

Colonel Wells requested leave to return to the rapids for his baggage or to deliver a personal report, but Winchester told him that his place was with

---

429 McLenahan to Harrison, Jan. 26, 1813, in <u>Official Letters of the military and Naval Officers of the United States during the War with Great Britain in the Years 1812, 13, 14, and 15</u>, edited by John Brannan, Washington City: Wax & Gideon, 1823, p. 131: If true, this seemingly was a major mistake. McClenehan says the fixed ammunition delivered to Winchester's headquarters was never distributed. There was a reserve within the picketed area, but this would be largely used up by the end of the coming battle. The regulars on the right flank would quickly run out of ammunition, if their initial allotment were only 10 rounds. British troops would complain about being issued American-style buck and ball cartridges late in the battle. It's unlikely, but perhaps these could have been captured at Winchester's headquarters and redistributed to the enemy. The British Brown Bess was of a larger caliber than the American weapons and could fire the American cartridges, although the looser fit of the smaller balls diminished accuracy.

430 Statement of General Winchester, Notices Vol. 1, Apdx 7, Memorandum of statements made by General Winchester and Major Madison to the Secretary of War on their return from captivity. Typed copy in Bidlack's Notes, Monroe County Historical Museum Archives. Winchester claimed his patrol had seen nothing. Alexis Solo arrived at the Kentucky camp late that afternoon and reported to LTC Lewis that he had learned the British were at Brownstown, intending to march to the Raisin. Lewis ordered his men not to leave camp and had the camp sentries stationed further outside the perimeter than usual.

431 Lossing, Benson J. <u>The Pictorial Field-Book of the War of 1812</u>. Glendale, New York: Benchmark Publishing Corporation, 1970, p. 354. Lossing states the Kentuckians received at least 3 separate visits from *habitants* reporting the advance of the British. All were on the 21st; one in the morning, a second in the afternoon, and the third very late in the evening. After the battle, Winchester could recall only one. Rumors seem to have been circulating through the settlement for several days, but often the estimate of the number of British troops was exaggerated.

432 Letter Proctor to Sheaffe, Jan. 25, 1813, #24 in James' <u>Military Occurrences,</u> Vol.1. *"On the 21st instant, I advanced 12 miles (from Brownstown) to Swan Creek, from whence we marched to the enemy..."* (It is possible they spent the night at Swan Creek, although others say Stony Creek.)

his regiment.[433] At 11 a.m., Winchester agreed to Wells' demand to tour the camps and look for a more defensible site.

Riding through the encampment, Wells and Lewis got into a heated exchange, with Wells refusing to camp with the undisciplined militia, and boasting: *"My men's bayonets are their breastworks!"*[434]

Judging the garden fences to be inadequate, Winchester spent several hours with his officers locating a spot to erect a new camp with breastworks.

About 3 p.m., the officers returned to their respective headquarters to enjoy some apples and hard cider.[435]

Headquarters, Navarre House, an hour before sunset, Jan. 21, 1813:

On the evening of January 21, General Winchester invited his officers to dinner at his headquarters at the Navarre home. While eating, they were interrupted by the arrival of Captain Nathaniel Hart, bearing dispatches from General Harrison. His message was to *"hold fast the position at any rate."*[436]

Despite the warnings, Winchester remained confident and unruffled. He gave no specific orders that night, although he expected his officers would send out patrols and picket guards as a matter of routine. In fact, however, some of these measures would not be taken on that bitterly cold night.[437]

Major Madison noted that the losses on January 18 had reduced the effective strength of Lewis' battalion to 600 men, but Wells' troops had swelled that number to almost 900. It was thought the British could assemble at most a thousand fighting men, including only 300 regulars.

Colonel Wells knew that extra ammunition had arrived from the rapids,

433 Dudley, Rev. Thomas P. "The Battle and Massacre at Frenchtown, Michigan, January, 1813." Historical and Archaeological Tracts, No. 1. Cleveland: The Western Reserve Historical Society, August, 1870. An account related by one of the Kentucky survivors of the battle. Wells had been against sending any troops to the River Raisin in the first place. It was too far from their base of operations and too close to the enemy.

434 Au, Dennis. War on the Raisin. Monroe: Monroe County Historical Commission, 1981, p. 30.

435 Darnell, Elias, Journal. Philadelphia: Lippincott, Grambo, and Co., 1854, p. 50. As it was getting late, it was decided to put the work off till the next morning. It would take some time to gather the needed tools and teams of horses, which were rather scarce in the community.

436 Armstrong, John. Notices of the War of 1812, Vol. I. New York: George Dearborn, 1836. Lt. Col. Navarre had difficulty following the half-hour-long conversation in English, but it appeared that Hart got fed up and abruptly departed.

437 Statement of General Winchester, Notices Vol. 1, Apdx 7, Memorandum of statements made by General Winchester and Major Madison to the Secretary of War on their return from captivity. Typed copy in Bidlack's Notes, Monroe County Historical Museum Archives.

so he asked for the reserve cartridges to be immediately distributed and the camps to be fortified and rearranged to place the men in line of battle.

The officers soon left, except Col. Wells, who stayed to speak privately with the general. They were interrupted by Captain Thomas Smith, an *aide-de-camp* to General Payne. Winchester had a dispatch for Smith to take to General Harrison, but just as it was being sealed, Louis Lafountain arrived to report that Joseph St. Bernard had seen the British at Brownstown and thought they would be ready to attack by Saturday, January 23. [438]

General Winchester asked Lafountain if he could personally confirm that, but the *habitant* replied, "*I cannot say.*"[439]

Turning to François Navarre, he asked if he could take him to camp early in the morning. Navarre replied he could transport him by *cariole* at any hour he desired, no matter how early. There was no need to ask anyone else.

Colonel Wells wanted to know if the local population truly favored the American cause. Colonel Navarre assured him that "*You have our hearts.*"[440]

---

438 Atherton, William, Suffering & Defeat of the North-Western Army. Frankfort, Ky: Ag. G. Hodges, 1842, p. 41: "On the 21st, a place was selected for the whole detachment to encamp, in good order, with a determination to fortify the next day. About sunset, Colonel ---- solicited and obtained leave to return to the Rapids. On this day, certain information was obtained that the British were preparing for an attack, and that we might look for it in a very short time. A Frenchman came from Malden with information that a large force of British and Indians — which he supposed would number near three thousand — were about to march from that place shortly after he left it. But even this was not credited, or if believed, was little regarded by many of the troops!"

439 Deposition of Francis Navarre, Aug. 22, 1818, in William Henry Harrison Papers, on microfilm at Central Michigan University. It was the general opinion of the people he had spoken to that the enemy could indeed attack within a few days at most. Lafountain knew something was already astir, as he had seen some American sergeants out rounding up their men.

440 Au, Dennis, War on the Raisin, Monroe: Monroe County Historical Commission, 1981, p. 31. Winchester also asked how many men could be raised locally. Whitmore Knaggs repeated the question in French to make sure their host fully understood it's import. Although 200 to 250 men were theoretically available, a hundred of whom had participated in the fighting on January 18th, most of the *habitants* had followed LTC Lewis' advice to return to their homes, which were dispersed over a couple dozen miles of marshlands, streams and forests. Many were now occupied with securing their property and making plans to get their families away from the scene of conflict. When Navarre mentioned they were still currently prisoners of war on parole, as a result of Hull's capitulation of Detroit the preceding summer, Winchester was surprised and said, "I did not know that." The general then advised Navarre to evacuate his family to safety and suggested he should go with them. If any of the local *habitants* were caught under arms, they could be accused of violating their parole and punished.

With that, Wells brought up his earlier request to return to the rapids. Captain Hart had given him a report, which he offered to deliver in person.[441]

Winchester replied, "*If you are disposed to leave your command in the immediate vicinity of the enemy, when a battle is certain, you can go.*"[442]

A little after sundown, Colonel Wells and Captain Langham of the 19th Infantry set off in a French *cariole*, leaving the regulars under the command of Major McClenahan. They arrived at the rapids at 1 o'clock on the morning of January 22, a day that would prove fateful for their men at the Raisin.[443]

Wells declined to take Winchester's messenger along with him, leaving the disgruntled Captain Smith to make his own way with a guide unfamiliar with the route.

It took a while for Smith to find a more suitable replacement for his incompetent guide, so he would not reach the Maumee until a couple hours after the Colonel. Wells would use this head start to give Harrison his own views on the disorder prevailing in Winchester's ranks.[444]

Camp of Colonel Wells
From Ed Long's Diorama on display in the former Visitor Center
River Raisin Battlefield National Park

---

441 Atherton, W., Suffering & Defeat of the North-Western Army, Frankfort: A.G. Hodges, 1842, p. 41.

442 Dudley, Rev. Thomas P., "The Battle and Massacre at Frenchtown, Michigan, January, 1813." Historical and Archaeological Tracts, No. 1, Cleveland: The Western Reserve Historical Society, August, 1870. Dudley seemed to think the General had already received a report that the enemy was now just 5 miles away at Stoney Creek. I think he got this final intelligence around 9 p.m.

443 Letter Samuel Wells to Thomas Cushing, February 9, 1813, Michigan Pioneer and Historical Collections, Vol. XL. Lansing: Michigan Historical Commission, 1929, pp. 503-7.

444 Winchester, James, Historic Details Having Relation to the Campaign of the North-Western Army under Generals Harrison and Winchester, Lexington: Worsley & Smith, 1818, p. 33.

Back at the Raisin, Major McClenahan had caught some of Wells' anxiety after hearing wild rumors that an enemy force of up to 4,000 was on its way.

After waiting expectantly for a summons to a council of officers, the major began to issue his own orders. Considering the exposed position of the regulars, he told his company commanders they should immediately form up if attacked and move to close the gap between them and the militia.[445]

In the meantime, his men had erected a makeshift barricade out of materials found in and around Godfroy's barn.[446]

Detroit, after dark, January 21, 1813:

John Whipple and Joseph King advanced stealthily through the dark towards the fort which guarded the town of Detroit. Behind them, back in the streets of town, a group of citizens had formed as if on parade. Some of them were stamping their feet to stay warm, while others were coughing from the ill effects of a hard winter and an epidemic of whooping cough, which was still raging among the settlement's children.

With most of the British garrison gone to attack the River Raisin, it seemed now was the time to take back their city from the British. Unfortunately, they did not have many firearms at their disposal. The occupiers had seen to that. They had recently confiscated as many as they could from the local *habitants*. Nonetheless, a few muskets remained. If the plotters could seize the fort, they would no doubt find all the weapons and ammunition they would need.

It all depended on catching the Canadian militia garrison off their guard. If surprised, they might abandon the fort without a fight. Whipple and King were sent to find out, but when they arrived very near the outer works, there was a sudden commotion. Flickering lights appeared all around the palisades. A changing of the sentries by torchlight was underway.

---

445 McClenahan to Harrison, Jan. 26, 1813, in <u>Official Letters of the military and Naval Officers of the United States during the War with Great Britain in the Years 1812, 13, 14, and 15,</u> Edited by John Brannan, Washington City: Wax & Gideon, 1823, p. 1331. Although General Winchester did not call an official council of war on the evening of the 21st, there does seem to have been a general plan to form up and support the right wing, if necessary. Perhaps this was discussed at dinner at the Navarre house. See also: (Niles Weekly Reg., Feb. 13, 1813 and Au, p. 31)

446 While the Godfroys had a house, barn, stable, and storehouse near Hull's Road, there was another Godfroy barn downriver from where Lewis' militiamen were camped.

Whipple and King quietly retraced their steps and reported the enemy was prepared and vigilant. Liberation Day could wait for a better time.[447]

French Town on the Raisin, 9:15 p.m., January 21, 1813:

A number of Winchester's soldiers had found overnight lodging outside the pickets. The Brigade Adjutant (McCalla?) was staying at Joseph Ruland's home, some distance upstream, nearer to Winchester's headquarters.[448]

Medard Couture and Adjutant McCalla were just returning from a visit to Dr. Austin, surgeon of the 2nd Michigan, who was sick with consumption.[449] In the dim light, they noticed the shadowy figure of John LaBresh approaching.[450]

As he passed, Couture called out, *"What's the matter? T'es pressé?"*

"Oui," came the answer, *"It's time to be in a hurry."*

"Pourquoi? Why so?" asked Couture, as the shadow kept on without stopping.

All LaBresh could say, before disappearing into the darkness, was, *"The British and Indians, in full force, are at Stony Creek, only 4 miles distant."*[451]

Later, at the home of Jean-Baptiste Couture, Colonels Lewis and Allen were in the parlor with Majors Madison and Garrard and regaling themselves

---

447 Journal of Lewis Bond, in Knopf, Richard C., Document Transcriptions of the War of 1812 in the Northwest, Vol. X, pt. 1, Columbus: Ohio Historical Society, 1962, p. 198: *"Whipple was one that was ordered away and actually went as far as the river Thames, but apprehensive of being sent to Quebec, returned privately and kept himself hid until the approach of the American army under General Harrison. Several small parties of citizens at different times found means to effect their escape and got safe to the American army at the Miami Rapids, notwithstanding the enemy were continually on the alert and lookout parties of Indians continually watching the movements of the Americans and to get prisoners for information, which they frequently did, and generally accompanied by some scalps."*

448 Reminiscences of an Actor in the War of 1812," Typed text. Algonquin Club. Taken from the Canadian Emigrant, 1835. Author unidentified.

449 Dr. Peter J. Austin received a contract on June 7, 1812, to take care of the militia in the area from the River Raisin to the Maumee Rapids. He was paid $33.33 per month, but had to provide his own medical supplies. ANDERSON, FANNY J., "MEDICAL PRACTICES IN DETROIT DURING THE WAR OF 1812." Bulletin of the History of Medicine, vol. 16, no. 3, 1944, pp. 261–275. *JSTOR*, www.jstor.org/stable/44446086. Accessed 9 Oct. 2020.

450 Jean-Baptiste LaBresh was said to be a half-breed Yankee who had assimilated into the local population. He was also a chief of the Miami and nephew of Chief Richardville. See: "Journey to Discovery" by Dawn Evoe-Danowski, Michigan's Habitant Heritage, Vol.42, #4, Oct., 2021, pp. 194-195.

451 Hosmer, Hezekiah Lord. Early History of the Maumee Valley. Toledo: Hosmer & Harris, 1858, p. 36. See also: (Darnell, p. 51), (Jos. Robert bio, Wing, p. 115).

with loaf sugar, whisky, and cider, when Medard Couture came in with Adjutant McCalla.

As Medard leaned on Garrard's chair, the major asked him if he had any news. *"Very bad news, Major,"* replied Couture. *"The British and Indians, in full force, are within 4 miles of us."*

"Then we must prepare to meet them," shouted Garrard, as he and the other officers all leapt to their feet and several rushed out to inform their men. Garrard stationed a picket guard in a perimeter outside the fence line.[452]

Lewis doubled the guard on the fence and sent word to Winchester. Unfortunately, the night was too cold to establish a picquet post out on the road to Detroit to give timely warning of the approach of an enemy force.

On the contrary, many of the troops were so unconcerned about an attack that they were still wandering about the settlement, so Lewis sent Ensign Harrow with a detail to round up those outside the camp and send them back to their quarters.[453]

Ensign Harrow's mission eventually took him to a brick house a mile up the river.[454] Approaching the door, he knocked, but there was no response.

Finding the door was unlocked, the ensign entered. From above, he heard voices, so he walked upstairs, where he encountered three men. One was the landlord, but Harrow suspected the other two were British agents.

The landlord immediately took him back downstairs to the stove room and handed him a bottle of whisky. While he drank, the landlord assured him *"there was no danger, for the British had not a force sufficient to whip us."*

Harrow reported back to Col. Lewis' headquarters at about 1 in the morning, but Lewis warned him not to leap to conclusions. Those mysterious gentlemen were maybe just a few locals getting together for a late-night drink.[455]

Over at the Navarre house, General Winchester had finished an evening

---

452 Hosmer, Hezekiah Lord, Early History of the Maumee Valley, Toledo: Hosmer & Harris, 1858, p. 37.

453 In the battle of 18 January, Ensign Joseph Harrow served in Captain Williams' company in the left wing commanded by Major Graves. He would be taken prisoner on January 22. See: Clift, G. Glenn, Remember the Raisin! Frankfort: Kentucky Historical Society, 1961, pp. 51 and 198.

454 Antoine Lasselle, an Indian trader who settled on a farm on the north side of the River Raisin, was said to have built the first two story brick residence in the settlement. He died in 1811.

455 Darnell, Elias, Journal. Philadelphia: Lippincott, Grambo, and Co., 1854, pp. 51-52. After their initial flurry of activity, most of the officers were now retiring to bed, thinking that General Winchester was right after all, and that it was unlikely any attack was forthcoming.

of cards while enjoying a little hot whisky and loaf sugar with his aides, but he, too, had now retired for the evening.[456]

His host, François Navarre, also went to bed, but slept fitfully, especially after hearing Winchester get back out of bed and prime his pistols. If the Indians discovered he was harboring their enemy's leader, they might take it out on his family.[457]

Winchester's Headquarters on the River Raisin[458]

Beyond the Maumee, night of January 21, 1813:

Meanwhile, far to the south, the longed-for reinforcements had made camp near Swan Creek of the Maumee. It had been an exhausting trek through the "horrid" swamps separating the Sandusky and Maumee Rivers. After a

---

456 Affidavit of Ambrose C. Charland, taken July 15, 1853, in Monroe County, Michigan, original in the Godfroy papers in the Burton Historical Collection, Detroit Public Library.

457 Deposition of Francis Navarre, Aug. 22, 1818, in William Henry Harrison Papers, on microfilm at Central Michigan University.

458 John Barber, and Henry Howe, The Loyal West in the Times of the Rebellion; also, Before and Since: Being an Encyclopedia and Panorama of the Western States, Pacific States and Territories of the Union, Historical, Geographical, and Pictorial, Illustrated by more than two hundred Engravings, presenting views of all the Cities and Principal Towns Public Buildings and Monuments Battle-fields — Historic localities natural curiosities, and scenes, Illustrating the times of the Rebellion, etc., Principally from Drawings taken on the spot by the Authors; John Barber, and Henry Howe, Cincinnati, Ohio; P. A. Howe, Successor of Henry Howe, 1865, pg. 764. Sarah Noble's sketch in Lossing's Pictorial Field Book of the War of 1812, Vol. I, p. 354, shows picketing in front, but not the addition in the rear. The log home was altered by Navarre's son in 1830, who made additions and raised the roof to create a 2-story building. It was clap-boarded when Lossing saw it in 1860. Note the line of pear trees along the side of the house.

night's rest, and reinforced with some light artillery pieces, they planned to proceed on to the Raisin early the next morning.[459]

Major W.W. Cotgreave, 1st Battalion, 2nd Regiment, 2nd Brigade of the Ohio Militia, sat down to write a report. He had 200 men ready and anxious to go on to the River Raisin. They were only waiting to be re-supplied.[460]

The supplies had been transported with much difficulty, because Wagon-Master Beach had failed to obtain enough oxen. The ammunition and other baggage had been left behind on the trail. Using matross ropes from the artillery, the men attached themselves to one of the ox sleds and brought the ammunition and other supplies into camp that night by dint of hard work.[461]

Unfortunately, it would not be possible to follow the quickest route to the Raisin, which was that taken by Lt. Colonel Lewis across the ice on Maumee Bay. The oxen pulling the baggage could not negotiate the frozen surface. Those that were poorly shod slipped and fell, while even the best shod, were incapable of working in tandem on the slick surface. It would be necessary to take Hull's Road to the River Raisin.[462]

---

459 Letter Harrison to Monroe, Jan. 26, 1813, typed copy in Bidlack's Notes, Monroe County Historical Museum Archives. Cotgreave is sometimes spelled Cotgrove in historical accounts. See also: Speech of General Leslie Combs at the 1872 Veterans Reunion in Monroe. This Swan Creek is north of the Maumee and meanders through the city of Toledo, Ohio.

460 Letter from Cotgreave to Wadsworth, Jan. 21, 1813, Knopf, Richard C. Document Transcriptions of the War of 1812 in the Northwest, Vol. X, pt 2. Columbus: Ohio Historical Society, 1962, p. 53: *"The detachment agreeable to your first order are encamped, and will be in readiness to march to the River Reasin as soon as they are supplied with provisions, for the procurement of them the Qr. Master Sergt. is now engaged. The men are anxious to go on, as for poor me, you will readily guess, I trust, how I feel..."* (Hopefully, the Pennsylvania militiamen had become more disciplined since December 13th, when General Harrison wrote a letter to Secretary of War Eustis saying he would have dismissed them all, were it not for the fact that it would have wounded the reputation of their state.) See: Gilpin, Alec R., The War of 1812 in the Old Northwest, East Lansing, MSU Press, 2012 edition, p. 158.

461 Letter Cotgreave, Jan. 21, 1813, Knopf, Richard C. Document Transcriptions of the War of 1812 in the Northwest, Vol. X, pt 2. Columbus: Ohio Historical Society, 1962, p. 58: *"Our men, however, with cheerfulness, with the dragrosses of the piece of ordnance hitched themselves to one of the ox sleds and hauled on the ammunition and baggage which was left in the road."*

462 Letter from Cotgreave, dated Jan. 21, 1813, *"camp about 2 miles below old B. Fort,"* Knopf, Richard C. Document Transcriptions of the War of 1812 in the Northwest, Vol. X, pt 2, Columbus: Ohio Historical Society, 1962, p. 57: *"I find it impossible to go on with the baggage M. Stores and on the ice, as the best shod oxen in consequence of their pulling off from each other, slip and cork themselves, and those that are poorly shod, by the same means, throw themselves. I have taken what is called Hull's road and encamped, under the circumstances attending my case, I have thought advisable to send Mr. Beach the bearer of this, for all the remainder of unshod cattle, with directions for them to repair immediately to camp, as it would prevent them coming on possible if your order was waited*

BATTLE OF THE RIVER RAISIN
UN DÉBÂCLE POUR LE GÉNÉRAL

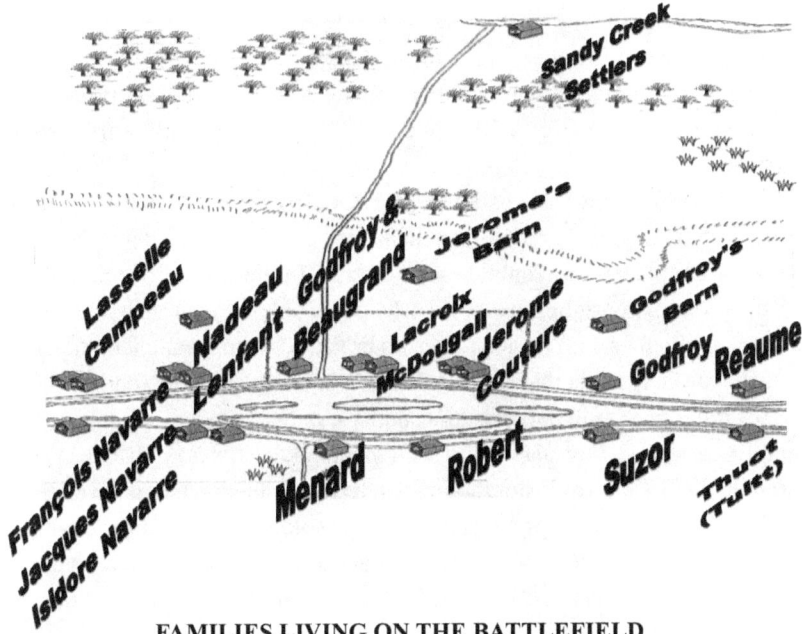

FAMILIES LIVING ON THE BATTLEFIELD
(Image not to scale)

French Town on the River Raisin, early morning, Friday, Jan. 22, 1813:

In the wee hours of the morning, General Winchester's sleep was interrupted by Laurent Durocher and several other *habitants*. They had come to warn him once more that the enemy was very near. The general, however, went back to bed, convinced that his army was not in imminent danger.[463]

While their commander tried to get some shut-eye, the soldiers of the American army dozed fitfully through the night. Although somewhat insulated by straw, the men who were lodged in tents outside the buildings shivered under their blankets.

---

for. We have not sufficient strength without them."

463 Deposition of Laurent Durocher, Knopf, Richard C. <u>Document Transcriptions of the War of 1812 in the Northwest, Vol. X, pt 1.</u> Columbus: The Ohio Historical Society, 1962, pp. 39-41.

At least the sentries were provided with warm, woolen watch coats, but they had to turn them in to their replacements when they finished their guard duty. Many returned to their quarters wearing only their light summer uniforms.

The fences of French Town formed a continuous line across the back of several adjoining lots near Hull's Road. Though not cannon-proof, they were between 5 and 7 feet high and could offer some protection from small arms fire.

Stretching along the western edge of Godfroy's property, the fence was constructed of pairs of split, 4-inch diameter posts set in the ground, between which were placed horizontal boards or rails. In the rear, or northern edge, of the property, upright poles were set side by side into a trench and lashed or nailed together with horizontal cross braces to form a puncheon fence.[464]

It was in this area that Captain James' company of spies, 2nd Kentucky, took shelter in a small barn, a stable, and a storehouse belonging to Godfroy and Beaugrand. It was planned to send them out to locate the British shortly after daylight. Godfroy's storehouse, where Laurent Durocher had worked as a clerk, held a large supply of salt which the soldiers procured for their use.

Godfroy's 1½-story, 60x30-foot residence stood ready to serve as a convenient hospital. Gabriel Godfroy, Jr., had left the River Raisin on business to Detroit some 6 weeks earlier, but his wife was still there.

Further downstream, troops took over Hubert Lacroix's unfinished home. It was a 2-story building, about 40-feet-square. They removed Lacroix's furniture, placed it in Jerome's house, and used his floorboards for fuel.[465]

George McDougall was an absentee landlord, but his house was occupied by Pierre Jacob and his mother, who charged some of the Kentuckians for room and board. In addition, this was where the army had kept François

---

464 Archaeological investigations by Michael Pratt, Ph.D., Heidelberg University, witnessed by Ralph Naveaux, Monroe County Historical Museum Assistant Director, in 2001-2002. The Godfroy property was in a strategic position, as the British army advanced along Hull's Road. One branch of the road angled directly into French Town along the eastern, downstream side of Godfroy's property (as Dixie Highway does today), while another branch swung around the western, upstream edge of the property to cross the River Raisin at a shallow ford. The main road then went south from the ford (following the present-day route of Kentucky Avenue and the railroad tracks alongside). The sections of Hull's Road were connected by the river roads on each bank.

465 Report of the House Committee of Claims on the petition of Jean — B. Jerome and others, Jan. 25, 1822. Statements of Francois Lasselle and John Anderson, Nov. 28, 1816. Lacroix's unfinished house was valued at $1100; his furniture and personal possessions at $3000.

Sanscrainte, who had been captured fighting for the British and Indians on January 18. McDougall's stable was used to shelter the army's horses.

Jean-Baptiste Jerome actually owned two houses. He and J. Fortier stayed in one, a nicely furnished and painted home, measuring 40 by 30 feet, with 2 main rooms, a central kitchen, and an addition, which was set up as sort of a combination guard house and hospital for some of the wounded of the 18th.

Hubert Lacroix's family and J.B. Bruneau, an illiterate trapper, occupied Jerome's other house, which was smaller, but equally well furnished and painted and also prepared for use as a hospital. Jerome's large, double stable contained some of the army's horses, as well as housing a few more of the soldiers who had been wounded on the 18th. Towards the back of his lot was a bake house, which the army used as an ammunition magazine.[466]

A hundred yards north of the picket fence sat Jerome's 70x40-foot barn. Attached to the barn was a threshing machine, or fanning mill, while inside were kept some of the bodies of those who had died on the 18th. Some of the wounded of January 18 had also been placed there temporarily. It contained 5,000 oversized French sheaves of wheat, worth about $500. The hay and oats inside were used to feed the Kentucky horses.[467]

The last property within the adjoining fence lines belonged to Jean-Baptiste Couture. He and his family reoccupied their home after the fighting on January 18, thinking they would be safe with the American army there. Just in case, however, the family made plans for the women and children to flee to François Navarre's house, if the settlement should again be attacked.[468]

Major Garrard located the officers' horses in Couture's stable, and the quartermaster's stores and baggage were kept in his storehouse, which was already full of lumber. McCracken's company took shelter in his bake house, which was also used as the family laundry.

The Couture family shared their home with many American officers,[469]

---

466 Deposition of Hubert Lacroix, County of Monroe, Territory of Michigan, Sept. 28, 1825.

467 Deposition of Jean-Baptiste Latour, Monroe on the River Raisin, July 13, 1813: The lumber for Jerome's barn came from a great distance and cost about $35 to $45 per thousand feet, which would seem to amount to more than the $25 Latour stated for the cost of the barn.

The threshing machine was invented in Great Britain in 1786. It was claimed that it could clean 10 times as much grain from the stalk in a day than could be done by a man with a flail, but the grain still had to be separated from the chaff by winnowing with a basket or by using a fanning mill.

468 Deposition of John McCalla, Fayette County, State of Kentucky, Sept. 12, 1818.

469 Petition of Catherine Couture, Report of the Committee of Claims on the Petition of Jean B. Jerome & Others, Jan. 25, 1822. Copy at William L. Clements Library, University of Michigan.

and it served as Lt. Colonel Lewis' headquarters. Antoine Nadeau also resided there, and the army payroll — some $2,500 — was secured within its walls.[470]

Of course, the River Raisin settlement was not a compact village. It stretched for miles beyond the picketed area nominally referred to as French Town. Upstream were the farmsteads of Lenfant, Campeau and Lasselle, including several houses, barns, and a horse mill. Just downstream was another property owned by the Godfroy family, containing a barn and stable.

The next property, a couple hundred yards below the picketing, was the Joseph Reaume farm on which the 17th U.S. Infantry made its L-shaped camp.

Godfroy's barn was near the camp and served to shelter some of the regulars. This barn was smaller than Jerome's barn and was framed and sided with vertical planking. Cedar shingles were nailed on the roof. Timber for building a distillery was stored around the building, and the troops had taken some of it to construct makeshift, temporary breastworks. The soldiers took straw from the barn for bedding inside their tents, while a few actually sheltered inside the building.

About 10 or 15 feet from the barn was an 18' x 20' stable, finished on the inside, and made like a blockhouse. P. Robidou took care of Godfroy's barn and stable, and had his own residence about 20 rods, or a bit over 100 yards, away. Joseph Reaume, who owned the adjoining farm, worked the farmland.

The 934 men of the American army were thus camped almost in battle order. On the extreme right flank was Major McClenahan commanding

---

470 It was on the Couture property that former Captain Edmiston noticed an empty 30-foot space between the companies of Bledsoe and McCracken. Although delegated to Captain McCracken, the area was unimproved, with little or no picketing. Bledsoe assigned some of his men to Edmiston, who promised to hold the position if they were attacked. See: Deposition of Richard Bledsoe, Fayette County, Kentucky, Sept. 29, 1818: Indeed, Edmiston (or Edmundson) would be killed defending that spot, on January 22, 1813. See also: Dec. 11, 1828, affidavit of James Garrard of the County of Bourbon and State of Kentucky, taken at the request of Col. Godfroy and others of French Town in the Territory of Michigan, in relation to the occupation of said town by the American army and its subsequent destruction by the British and Indians in 1813, as printed in the House Report No. 51 of the 20th Congress, 2nd Session, January 19, 1829. :*"The buildings of J. B. Couture were occupied as follows : No. 11, as marked on the map, was a stable, in which my horse and others were kept ; No. 12 was a store or lumber-house, in which we kept our baggage, saddles, andc.; No. 13, the dwelling where we quartered, and which was considered as headquarters ; No. 14 was, I believe, a bake-house, or, probably, a wash-house, which was occupied by Capt. McCracken and his company, it being on the right, as marked by the dotted line on the map. There was also another building, adjoining the dotted line on the map, which formed a small avenue between the back of that and the front of No. 13, about three or four feet in width, through which many shot of the enemy passed, and in which Capt. Hart was wounded."*

Re-enactors huddled in a farm field while filming a documentary on the battle for the Friends of the River Raisin Battlefield
2003

Wells' battalion of 150 to 250 men, the majority regulars of the 17th and 19th U.S. Infantry.

Across an open field were about 600 or 700 men of the militia regiments under Lt. Colonel Lewis, including over 50 who had been wounded on January 18. They were positioned in a loose sort of order within the French Town fences, with the 1st Rifle Regiment on the right, the 1st Kentucky Volunteer Regiment in the center, and the 5th Kentucky Volunteer Regiment on the left. Up to a hundred of the men may have been at Winchester's headquarters or had found billets in the scattered homesteads of the *habitants*.[471]

La Rivière au roche, Stony Creek, Friday, January 22, 1813:

It was about 5 o'clock in the morning when the British troops roused themselves from their resting spot on the banks of Stony Creek. After dusk the previous evening, they had moved forward from their temporary staging area at Swan Creek under the cover of darkness and spent the night in the open air, huddled in their great coats, with fires kindled by their feet. Sixteen-year-old John Richardson, gentleman volunteer with the 41st Regiment, rubbed his tired and sleepy eyes, and then set about gathering his gear.[472]

---

471 See Appendix E for an approximate order of battle for U.S. forces. (Troop estimates for Winchester's army range from 750 to 1020 including the 50-odd casualties left from the Jan. 18 battle.)

472 Ensign James Cochran of the 41st wrote in his reminiscence "The War in Canada 1812" that, owing to the depth of the snow, they halted a few hours at Swan Creek on the night of the 21st,

As he stood up, he stretched out his hand to pick up his musket. It was a typical Brown Bess, like all the other issued muskets, but he had taken very good care of it. He knew he would have to rely on it in the coming battle. It felt strange to the touch, but it was too dark to tell for sure if it were really his musket. Anyway, it was too late. They were now only 3 or 4 miles from the Raisin, where victory or death awaited them.[473]

The march warmed them considerably. The red tunics of the British regulars were well-concealed by comfortable, gray overcoats, while the wool capotes of the militia bore a black stripe across the hood to identify them to their Native allies.[474]

Nearing the settlement, the men tramped doggedly through the brush and marched a quarter to a half mile out onto the open, snow-covered farmland,

---

then proceeded to the River Raisin, where they arrived a little before daybreak on the 22nd. He makes no mention of stopping at Stony Creek.

473 Casselman, Alexander Clark. Richardson's War of 1812. Toronto: Coles Publishing Co., John Richardson's letter of Feb. 4, 1813, with an account of the action can be found on pages 301-4. Some accounts refer to "Swan Creek," while others say "Rocky River," which would presumably be Stony Creek. The distance from the River Raisin often mentioned in these accounts was 5 or 6 miles, which could correspond to Swan Creek. Swan Creek is about 7 miles north of the River Raisin, while Stony Creek is about 4. The question remains as to whether the British army would have gotten up 2 hours before daybreak, marched up to 7 miles through the snow, and still have had time to form up and launch an attack before daylight. There also seems to be some confusion in the accounts between Stony Creek and Sandy Creek, which are about 2 miles apart.
Richardson, with the British regulars, reported halting and bivouacking in the open air about 5 miles from French Town, but later says they camped at Rocky River 6 miles from the River Raisin. Lossing states in his Field book that the British halted at Swan Creek till dusk on January 21, when they resumed their march. The local French *habitants* reported them at Stony Creek during the night. Perhaps Procter halted at Swan Creek, but then moved into closer range during the night.

474 The evidence for this is lacking, but the addition of a black stripe was done for the Detroit campaign, and may have carried through to Winchester's. Although there were periods of shortages, the regular British troops seem to have been amply supplied with gray overcoats called greatcoats. (The 10th Royal Veteran Battalion's greatcoat was blue.) Starting in 1811, British troops in Canada received a new, single-breasted great coat every 2 years. The great coats of the 41st regiment were made by the regimental tailors, assisted by the women of the regiment. Unfortunately, some shortcuts had to be taken. The knee-length coats were lined with flannel or green baize, instead of more durable, white serge, and were not greased or chemically waterproofed. Coats for the 10th Royal Veterans and the Royal Newfoundland Fencibles were contracted out, to be made in 3 basic sizes, with standing collar and a cape falling somewhat short of the elbow. A fourth, or extra-large, grenadier size was added in 1812. When camping in the field, the greatcoat often served as bedding along with the infantryman's blanket. For a wonderful discussion of this topic, see: "British Army Greatcoats during the American War of 1812" by Robert Henderson, as posted on the War of 1812 Website, adapted from the original text published in the Spring, 1997, issue of the Journal of the Society for Army Historical Research.

towards a point approximately opposite the home of Jean-Baptiste Jerome. Silently, under low-voiced commands and with barely a clattering of equipment, they formed their lines for battle in two adjacent fields, while large parties of Indians headed off around both flanks of the American army.[475]

Sketch of Hull's Road leading from French Town towards Detroit
Artist's Conception by Ed Long
Formerly on display at the former River Raisin
Battlefield National Park Visitor Center[476]

Because of the cold, the Americans had not placed an advance picket guard on the road to Detroit, just some forward sentinels a couple hundred yards away, out in the fields. They were silhouetted by a series of fires set forward of the dark fence line. Seeing these fires, some of the British thought the American army was encamped in the open fields just outside the village.[477]

The Americans seemed much too close, so close that some of the Native

---

475 See Appendix O for a discussion of where the war bands of various Native Nations may have been during the battle, which may not correspond exactly to some of the following maps.

476 Note the unfinished Lacroix house and the McDougall house with the ravine and Jerome barn in distance. The barn should be between the fence line and the ravine (Mason's Run).

477 Atherton, William. Narrative of the Suffering and Defeat of the North-Western Army under General Winchester. Frankfort, KY.: A. G. Hodges, 1842, pp. 42-3. See also: Byfield, Shadrack, "A Common Soldiers Account," Recollections of the War of 1812. Toronto: Baxter Publishing Company, 1964 reprint of 1828 edition.

warriors wondered if the enemy soldiers might not easily catch a whiff of their *kennickanick* tobacco.

The advanced sentries appeared to take no notice, however. They seemed numbed by the cold, or perhaps distracted by the noise of morning drums within the picketed gardens. A number of them had already left their posts and retreated to the warmth of their fires.

The British continued to deploy to left and right in the open and prepared to fire.[478] Unsure of what he was facing, Procter hesitated to launch an all-out attack. It was hard to distinguish between the garden fences and a line of standing troops. He wanted to stall until there was more light.[479]

While Indians and militia formed on the flanks of the main British line, two of the cannons were sent off to the west of the American position, escorted by Indians and militiamen, to provide enfilade fire all along the enemy's front. One gun was kept in reserve, while the remaining 3 artillery pieces were positioned out in front, with a clear line of fire at both American camps.

The only obstructions in the way were Jerome's barn on the right, about a hundred yards in front of the village fences, and an orchard, about 150 yards out in the center. The orchard stretched alongside a 4½ foot deep swale, or hollow, which angled across Hull's road on the northwest towards the river just southeast of the American right wing.

Off on the British left flank, Godfroy's outlying barn appeared near the spot where the 17th Infantry was beginning to assemble.

---

478 Reynolds Narrative in "Chronicle of the War."

479 Armstrong, John, Notices of the War of 1812, Vol. I, New York: George Dearborn, 1836: Armstrong says that Procter deliberately waited for dawn to launch his attack. At any rate, it was light enough for one of the sentries to spot the oncoming British and shoot their leading grenadier. Ensign James Cochran of the 41st wrote in his reminiscence "The War in Canada 1812" that Col. Proctor did not sufficiently reconnoiter the American position before launching his attack, and that he mistook the fences for a line of enemy troops until the light of dawn revealed his error.

General Location of the 17th Infantry Camp Site
View of a barn-like pavilion and the rear of the former visitor center.

J-B. Couture's house before the attack, 6 a.m., January 22, 1813:

Eighteen American officers were staying in the house of Jean-Baptiste Couture, local militia captain in the 2nd Michigan Territorial Militia Regiment.

As he prepared to leave his father's house, Couture's son, Medard, noticed the reclining figures of three junior officers; McCalla, Baker, and Butler. They were sleeping crosswise, all on the same bed.[480]

How could they manage to sleep wondered Medard, after he had warned them that the British were coming near? Perhaps it was all that whiskey and loaf sugar they and the other officers had consumed the previous night.[481]

---

480 These may have been Ensigns William O. Butler and Isaac L. Baker of the 17th U.S. The McCalla in question may have been Capt. John McCalla of the 5th Kentucky or Lt. Joseph McCalla of the 1st Kentucky.

481 Darnell, Elias. A Journal Containing an Interesting and Accurate Account of the Hardships, Sufferings, Battles, Defeat, and Captivity of Those heroic Kentucky Volunteers and Regulars, Commanded by General Winchester, in the Year 1812-1813, Paris, Kentucky: 1813. (As reprinted under the title "Remember the Raisin" in Captured by the Indians, edited by Frederick Drimmer, Dover Publications, New York, pp. 256-267.)

Home of Captain Jean-Baptiste Couture
Painting by Darlene Belair
Provided Courtesy of the National Park Service,
River Raisin National Battlefield Park

Looking outside, Medard saw there was still not much activity in the Kentucky camp. There were some sentinels, standing half asleep, shivering from the morning cold, but they should have sent out a picket guard on the road north to give an early warning, and perhaps ambush any approaching enemy.

Major Graves had gotten up some hours earlier to rouse his men, but had by now returned to his quarters. The only other officer active that early was Captain Hart, who had already gone out, in the blackness of the night, to awaken the men of the Lexington Light Infantry.

Medard was glad to think at least some of the Kentuckians would be ready if they were attacked that morning.[482] Just to be sure, he then went

---

482 Dudley, Rev. Thomas P., "Battle and Massacre at Frenchtown, Michigan, by one of the Survivors," in Historical and Archaeological Tracts, Number 1. Cleveland: Western Reserve Historical Society, 1870.

over to the drummer, lying beside the fireplace. Nudging him with his foot, Medard told him he better wake up and beat the reveille.[483]

The drummer roused himself, then, still grumbling, grabbed his drum and went outside into the cold, early morning darkness. As the night was giving way to a dull, gray, pre-dawn daylight, he began to play "Three Camps."

For those who had feared a British and Indian attack during the night, the sound of reveille brought short relief. Within less than two minutes, however, and while the drummer was still playing, one of the forward sentries caught the noise of enemy cannons being pulled through the wintry morning mist.

The sentry turned and saw a dark mass approaching across the hard-crusted, moonlit snow. Raising his musket, he fired into the enemy column, striking the leading British soldier in the head.

Grenadier William Yates slumped down into the snow, the bullet passing completely through his cranium, in one ear and out the other. He was the first casualty of that day.[484]

Two more rifle shots rang out, as more sentries detected the movement across the field. Moments later, they heard the boom of British cannons.[485]

At the first cannon shot, Major Graves rushed back outside and ordered

---

483 Hosmer, Hezekiah L., Early History of the Maumee Valley, Toledo: Hosmer & Harris, 1858, p. 37.

484 Letter Winchester to Sec. of War, Feb.11, 1813, in Knopf, Richard C. Document Transcriptions of the War of 1812 in the Northwest, Vol. V, pt. 2. Columbus: Ohio Historical Society, 1958. p. 38. Laurent Durocher claims the time of the first attack was between 4 and 5 a.m. Others place it closer to 6 or even 7 a.m. Squire Reynolds says the British came out of the woods at dawn and the reveille was beating in the American camp. On the march, Winchester usually had reveille beaten at 6 a.m. Wake up was an hour earlier. (See: Deposition of Laurent Durocher, Knopf, Richard C. Document Transcriptions of the War of 1812 in the Northwest, Vol. X, pt 1. Columbus: The Ohio Historical Society, 1962, pp. 39-41, Reynolds Narrative in Coffin, William F. 1812: The War and its Moral; A Canadian Chronicle. Montreal: John Lovell, 1864, and Clift, G. Glenn. Remember the Raisin. Frankfort: Kentucky Historical Society, 1961, p. 29.) See also: Winchester, James, Historic Details Having Relation to the Campaign of the North-Western Army under Generals Harrison and Winchester, Lexington: Worsley & Smith, 1818, pp. 36 and 79: Winchester remembered the attack starting at reveille, with scarcely a minute between the firing of the alarm guns and the commencement of the battle. In a letter written at Fort George, Feb. 11, 1813, Winchester recalled the battle commenced at 6 a.m. and constant firing continued for 3 or 4 hours. John Hunt wrote he was informed the first British charge was made "in the gray of the morning."

485 Darnell, Elias, a Journal of the Hardships, Sufferings, Battles, Defeat, and Captivity of the Kentucky Volunteers & Regulars commanded by General Winchester. Philadelphia: Lippincott, Grambo, & Co., 1854, p. 52. According to the U.S. Naval observatory's Astronomical applications Department, moonrise occurred at 10:53 p.m. on the preceding day and set at 11:14 a.m. on January 22, 1813. It was waning gibbous with 67% of the moon's visible disk illuminated. This may have provided some night time visibility, but does not consider possible cloud cover.

his men to stand to arms, not knowing the strength or design of the sudden attack. The militia camp was thrown into immediate confusion. The officers shouted *"To Arms! To Arms!"* and the men scrambled in every direction.

**Scene from Documentary Produced by the Friends
of the River Raisin Battlefield**
*Photo by Bill Saul taken on location at the ca. 1789
Navarre-Anderson Trading Post*

Knots of soldiers soon began assembling among the various small camps scattered at intervals of about 30 paces between the adjoining lots and gardens. Responding to the shouts of their officers, the militiamen took up well-covered positions behind the garden fences.[486]

Benjamin Franklin Graves, Major of the 2nd Battalion of the 5th Kentucky, took charge of the American left flank, posted along the western wall, with 2 companies, or firing platoons, of the 5th Kentucky.

The 5th Kentucky was not under direct assault here, but the British rapidly established an artillery position with 2 guns upstream in the open field, protected by militia and Indians. Many warriors continued beyond the western flank, intending to cross the river and circle around and behind the Americans.

---

486 Knopf, Richard C. <u>Document Transcriptions of the War of 1812 in the Northwest, Vol. V, pt. 2</u>. Columbus: Ohio Historical Society, 1958. p. 27. (Captain Matson's description of the battle.)

The 2nd Brigade Inspector, Major James Garrard, and Major George Madison, 2nd Brigade major of the 1st Rifle Regiment, each took charge of 2 companies, mostly from the 1st Kentucky Regiment, but including some of the 5th Kentucky and 17th U.S. They manned the northern fence line.[487]

Lt. Colonel John Allen and his 1st Rifle Regiment held the eastern fence. Allen was essentially in command of the American center and was to ensure liaison with the regulars on the extreme right, under Major McClenahan.

The soldiers were no sooner in position than, looking up, they saw the fiery tails of the bomb shells fired from some British howitzers positioned just 300 yards away.

The first cannonball flew high overhead and landed across the river, hitting the house of Joseph Robert. The log home sat on a rise of ground and provided a commanding view of the British forces and their operations.

Besides the members of the Robert family, the house was crowded with civilian contractors, teamsters, and sutlers who had been following the army. They were sleeping on the floors and taking up every inch of space.

The projectile struck the log house with a deafening roar, damaging one end of the gable roof, and shaking everyone out of their sleep. Joseph rushed to close the heavy wooden shutters over the windows, while his family took refuge in the cellar.[488]

---

487 This is a conjecture based on the battalion organizations on the 18th, with Garrard replacing the wounded Ballard. By the time the fighting ended, Madison appears to have been in charge of all the troops within the picketed area, with Graves and Garrard acting as his seconds.

488 Wing's History of Monroe County, 1890, pp. 115-116. Note: This would have been an extremely long shot for a small howitzer. Marc Meyer estimated the distance of the British howitzers from the Robert home at the start of the battle at 950 yards. The range for a 2.9-inch (3-pdr) howitzer firing an exploding shell is about 660 yards (although a 1792 test with an elevation of 31° gave an unlikely range of 1,562 yards).

However, one or more of the field pieces could have been a 5.5-inch howitzer, which could fire a shell 1600 yards, was accurate out to 700 yards, and could fire cannister 500 yards.

Alternatively, the Robert house would have been just within the maximum range of one of the British light 3-pdr guns. According to the Royal Canadian Artillery Museum, the brass 3-pounder smoothbore gun, sometimes called a grasshopper, could fire a 3-pound projectile up to a distance of 1,000 yards (914 meters). The normal crew consisted of 7 men.

The British artillery may have been posted too close to the American lines to be effective. Their first shots were seen to sail harmlessly over the heads of the enemy. Other round shot and shells fell into the river, hit the upper stories of the houses, or burst 50 feet overhead.

In his letter to William Powel, written January 25, 1813, John Askin stated "...Col. Proctor with our regular forces began the attack at so little distance that our cannon was of little use, being so near that our men from the first were within musket shot of the enemy."

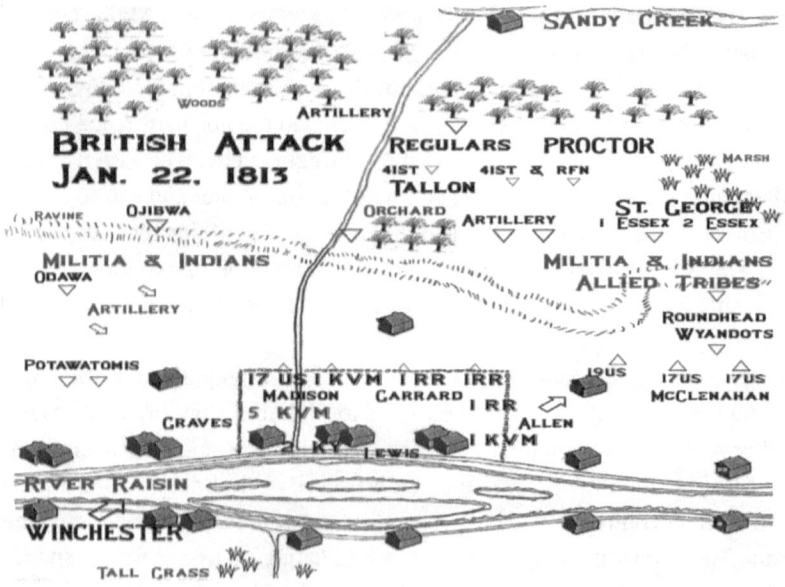

Nearby at the Tuot dit Duval farm, cannon balls began hitting the front of the house, causing people to jump out the back windows. The Tuots abandoned their property and fled 3 miles south to seek shelter at the home of a friend.[489]

Much of the artillery fire was concentrated in the direction of Jerome's dwellings and his bake house, where Lewis' reserve ammunition and some

---

For the howitzers, it was not simply a matter of elevating the muzzle to achieve various distances and trajectories. The powder charge might have to be adjusted, as well. Also, the length of the fuse in the shell had to be cut perfectly to time the explosion. This would have been difficult under heavy enemy fire.

See: "Remarks on the Evolution of the Sea Service 3-pounder Swivel Howitzer into the U.S. Army's King Howitzer, 1775-1820," by William E. Davidson. For a discussion on the brass 3-pdr. King Howitzer, see: Davidson, William E. "Summary Remarks on the Evolution of the Sea Service 3-pounder Swivel Howitzer into the U.S. Army's 2 ¾ inch King Howitzer: 1775-1820, Myths and Facts," Military Collector & Historian, Vol. 67, No. 1, Spring, 2015, pp. 48-75.

489 Affidavit of Hyacinth Tuott dit Duval, Age 53, Nov. 18, 1852. Pension Application Files, War of 1812, Death or Disability, The National Archives "Old War" Invalid and Widow Rejected File No. 16545. Copy in Monroe County Historical Museum Archives, courtesy of Chris and Steve Momany. Note: The balls that hit the Duval (Thuot/ Tuitt/ Tuot dit Duval) house may have come from the cannon posted on the far left of the British line, which could have been a 3-pdr. or even a 6-pdr., according to some accounts. It may also have happened a bit later in the battle, when the right flank of the American army retreated to the shelter of the river bank.

of the wounded from the battle of the 18th were kept. The upper part of Jerome's house was badly damaged, but there were few hits lower than a man's head. [490]

In the rear of the main British line, John Nettles of the 41st Regiment was in charge of a horse-drawn supply sled carrying square boxes of artillery ammunition and a quarter cask of ball cartridges. The only other ammunition sled present was one driven by a *Canadien*, who withdrew soon after his horse was wounded in the fore-foot.[491]

Nettles watched the battle from his position about 60 yards in the rear of the guns, which had begun their barrage about 250 yards from the enemy fence line. He could see that the British attack force would have to cross over 100 yards of open field to reach the shelter of an orchard and gently sloped ravine. Between this ravine and the fence was another 150 yards of open ground.

The British artillery was about 30 paces out in front of their main line, firing shot, shells, and grapeshot with great abandon. Their infantry, however, had to fire volleys past their own artillerymen, who had manfully dragged their guns through the snow after their initial barrage.[492]

---

490 Darnell, Elias, A Journal of the Hardships, Sufferings, Battles, Defeat, and Captivity of the Kentucky Volunteers & Regulars commanded by General Winchester, Philadelphia: Lippincott, Grambo, & Co., 1854, p. 55. Perhaps because of the snow-covered roofs, only one building was set ablaze by shell fire during the course of the battle. See: "Remarks on the Evolution of the Sea Service 3-pounder Swivel Howitzer into the U.S. Army's King Howitzer, 1775-1820," by William E. Davidson. For a countervailing impression, see: Brown, Samuel, Views of the Campaigns of the North-Western Army, Troy, N.Y.: Francis Adancourt, 1814: Brown visited the battlefield later on during the war and found fences completely shattered by the enemy's shot and human bones still bleaching on the ground.

491 The artillery ammunition probably consisted of British 3-pound solid round shot and 3-pounder tin caseshot. The caseshot, or cannister shot, would contain 32 iron balls, each weighing an ounce and a half, coming to a total weight of 3 pounds for the complete round. British tin caseshot could be modified to fit the bore of captured American 2.9-inch (3-pdr.) howitzers, but the explosive bomb shells used in the howitzers probably came from American supplies captured at Detroit the previous summer. See: "Remarks on the Evolution of the Sea Service 3-pounder Swivel Howitzer into the U.S. Army's King Howitzer, 1775-1820," by William E. Davidson.

492 Round shot could be used to batter down some obstacles. Against infantry in a thin line, a ball might only cause a few casualties as it passed through the ranks. Technically, the "grapeshot" referred to by chroniclers of the Battle of the River Raisin was actually canister.

The British had developed shrapnel shells, also called spherical case, which contained musket balls as well as gunpowder, but the howitzer shells fired at the River Raisin were probably just common shells filled with gunpowder.

They would have been captured at Detroit, along with the howitzers. The fuses were cut to

The Ravine (Mason Run) near the present-day Battlefield Education Center

Procter's troops advanced in that order, into the orchard at the edge of the ravine and halted. The fences of Frenchtown loomed before them in dark lines studded with tongues of fire and rifle smoke, giving them the appearance of ranks of enemy soldiers in the early morning gloom.[493]

---

explode the shells at a certain distance over the heads of the enemy, showering the area with iron shards or musket balls that could fly well beyond a hundred yards.

The terms grape shot, cannister, and case shot were often used interchangeably. Technically, grape consisted of 36 iron balls placed between 2 wooden disks, covered by cloth, and secured by a wire or cord, which resembled a bunch of grapes. The term could also apply to any odd collection of bullets or other objects fired loosely from a cannon. Canister, or case shot, employed a tin container to hold a number of musket balls. Case shot was used at River Raisin. See: Noseworthy, Brent, Battle Tactics of Napoleon and his Enemies, London: Constable & Co., 1995, p. 364 and pp. 373-375. See also: Caruana, Adrian B., "Tin Case-Shot or Cannister Shot in the 18th Century," Military Heritage, 2020.

493 Little is known about the location of Colonel Procter or Roundhead during this part of the battle. I assume Procter was occupied with the British center, which I further assume was composed of the left wing of the 41st Regiment, supported by Captain Mockler and his Royal Newfoundland Fencibles. Mockler was also tasked with providing security for the artillery.

Due to the terrain, in particular an orchard and a hollow that angled gently towards the southeast, the British attack was coming in obliquely from the northeast. Indians swept around both flanks, but a large force of Canadian militia under Colonel St. George headed for Godfroy's outlying barn, located on the eastern edge of the battlefield, near the 17th U.S. Infantry's campsite.

Sketch of Winchester's Headquarters at the Navarre House
From Benjamin Lossing's Pictorial Field Book of the War of 1812

The Navarre House, early morning hours, January 22, 1813:

Lt. Colonel François *Tchigoy* Navarre's log house stood quietly in the darkness, the front door facing north, with a view of the River Raisin. To the west was a line of stately pear trees, which had grown from saplings Navarre had brought from Detroit almost 30 years before.[494]

General Winchester was asleep in the large room to the left of the front door. It was the room where Navarre conducted his trading business, and where visiting Indians would often spend the night.[495]

---

494 Lossing, Benson J. The Pictorial Field-Book of the War of 1812. Glendale, New York: Benchmark Publishing Corporation, 1970, p. 353. Lossing visited Navarre's house in 1860, and credited Sarah Noble for a sketch of it as it probably appeared in 1812, with a steep, high peaked roof, with no dormers, but an attic window in the gable end. In 1830, Navarre's son raised the roof to make it a full 2 story building. Lossing claimed it was not clapboarded until about the time he saw it. By then, it was being used as an Episcopal Church rectory.

495 The John Hunt Memoirs, edited by Richard J. Wright, Bowling Green University. Maumee, Ohio: Maumee Valley Historical Society, p. 42: "*We reached that place* [now Monroe] *and put up for the night with colonel Navarre. He gave us the best he had for supper, which was a small piece of pork, corn bread, and a cup of tea…Col. Navarre showed us a place in the corner of the room which was very much stained by scalps, put there after the defeat of two companies of men that had encamped*

Sometime after 5 a.m., Navarre gave up on trying to sleep, rose, and went outside to check on his horses. As the day began to break, he heard the muffled beat of a distant drum playing reveille in the American camp.

Suddenly, he saw a light flash against the sky. It was a bomb flying out over the treetops near the American camp. Excited and visibly agitated, he rushed inside to the bottom of the central stairway and cried out, *"General Winchester, the enemy is upon us! Hurry, before we are cut off."*

Navarre then sent his son, Robert, into Winchester's room to rouse the general and his staff, while he went back outside to get their horses.

Robert found the General and Whitmore Knaggs near the great fireplace, struggling to wake up and shake off the effects of the wine they had drunk the evening before. Once they realized the danger, however, they got dressed quickly and began clamoring for their horses.

The house was so crowded with the general's aids and with Navarre's wife and 11 children who were preparing to flee in a French *"carabeau,"* that Winchester had difficulty reaching the door. In his haste, he ignored his uniform coat and began putting on his heavy overcoat.

Just then, Navarre came up to the window leading his fastest horse, which he had kept saddled overnight for the general's use. Winchester opened the window, climbed out, and dropped down onto the saddle.

He did not immediately gallop off, however. Instead, he dismounted, leaving his horse near the door. While waiting for his staff officers, the general walked back and forth in the yard, as if trying to assess the situation.

Indians appeared and then disappeared along the north bank of the river, before he finally rode off at a rather slow pace. Winchester was followed by François Navarre, Whitmore Knaggs, the two officers staying with him, and the rest of his staff and guards.[496]

---

near his house. It was at this house that General Winchester and Capt. Knaggs were sleeping when his army was attacked by the British and Indians under Genl. Procter..." Hunt was one of those who claimed Winchester was captured on the way to join his troops. He also got the date of the battle wrong, writing that it took place on January 28, 1813.

496 Hosmer, Hezekiah Lord. Early History of the Maumee Valley. Toledo: Hosmer & Harris, 1858, p. 37. I assume the two officers staying with Winchester were his secretary, Captain Woolfolk, and his aide, Dr. Overton. Various accounts of this incident differ in their details. In 1881, Talcott Wing interviewed Francois Navarre's son, Robert, then 90 years old, who remembered his father going upstairs to rouse the general and his staff, the general going to the barn to get his horse, both of them riding off on two of Navarre's horses, and the general leaving his coat behind. He also disputed the rumor that the American officers were under the influence of liquor. See: Wing,

Meanwhile, other outlying elements of Winchester's command also roused themselves and headed towards the sound of the guns. So did a number of French Town *habitants.*

Over at Joseph Ruland's house, the Brigade Adjutant rushed out of his bedroom, leaving his official papers lying on the table. Everywhere, there were scenes of confusion and excitement.[497]

Some people were heading in the opposite direction. At the first alarm, Madame Couture rousted her family from their beds. As planned, they raced towards the house of François Navarre. All arrived safely, but frightened. They had left home in distress, half-clothed, and some without shoes or stockings.[498]

Ceremonial Musket Volley at 2006 River Raisin Battle Commemoration
Photo by Bill Saul

Talcott E., "History of Monroe County, Michigan," in Michigan Pioneer & Historical Collections, Vol. IV, 1881. Lansing: W. S. George & Co., 1883, p. 321.

497 "Reminiscences of an Actor in the War of 1812," Typed text. Algonquin Club. Taken from the Canadian Emigrant, 1835. Author unidentified. See also: (Life Col. Francis Navarre by Miss Sawyer), (Navarre Genealogies, MCHM Archives.) The reference to the Brigade Adjutant could have been to Captain John McCalla, but he was the adjutant of the 5th Kentucky, and other reports put McCalla at Couture's house. Perhaps the man referred to was Major Garrard, the Inspector of the 2nd Brigade. Possibly also in the vicinity of the headquarters was a security force to protect General Winchester. The lodging for as much as 2 companies of Kentucky troops is uncertain.

498 Deposition of François Navarre, County of Monroe, Territory of Michigan, Nov. 29, 1822.

17th U.S. Infantry Camp, River Raisin, 6:30 a.m., January 22, 1813:

The attack on the U.S. regulars posted on the American right developed rather quickly into an ugly situation for the Americans. The day was just breaking when firing erupted to their front. The 150 regulars of the 17th and 19th U.S. Infantry and some accompanying militiamen began taking cannon and musket fire while Native warriors were circling around through the woods to their right and rear.[499]

Their main line was formed to the north and east of Godfroy's barn, but at a distance from it. The regulars tried to seek shelter behind a rail fence, 4 or 5 rails high, but several men were killed when the fence was knocked down by the British artillery.[500]

Major McClenahan, assisted by Captains Meade and Edwards, ordered the regulars to hold steady. Unfortunately, their line was drawn up basically in the open with no *point d'appui* on either flank. Indians and Canadian militia quickly moved forward towards Godfroy's barn and into the gap left between the regulars and the main militia force inside the picketed area of French Town.

The American regulars sustained the unequal contest for about 20 minutes. The brisk firing quickly expended their limited supply of ammunition. Some had barely fired half a dozen rounds before their cartridge boxes began to seem uncomfortably depleted.[501]

---

499 Many accounts mention the attack beginning at dawn. Morning twilight on January 22 doesn't begin till a bit before 7:30 a.m. Sunrise occurs at nearly 8 a.m. Lossing says the attack began between 4 and 5 a.m. However, those who state times generally agree on 6 a.m. as the start of the shooting. If observers were basing their estimates on the sun, these times should be adjusted by about an hour. High noon (solar noon or the point when the sun is highest in the sky) happens at 12:43 on January 22nd. If so, 7 a.m. (in terms of today's standard Eastern Daylight Time) might be a realistic estimate. On January 22, the moon would have already set by the time the battle began. In any case, Procter delayed the attack until there was enough light to navigate, but people and objects were still indistinct.

500 This may have been the British artillery's single most important contribution to the battle. To Rev. Dudley, British artillery fire seemed to be directed mainly against the regulars on the American right wing. See: Dudley, Rev. Thomas P., "Battle and Massacre at Frenchtown, Michigan, by one of the Survivors," in Historical and Archaeological Tracts, Number 1. Cleveland: Western Reserve Historical Society, 1870. Elijah McClenahan reported the regulars had only been issued 10 rounds apiece, and that their reserve ammunition had been delivered to Winchester's quarters at the Navarre house on the evening of the 21st, where it had remained, undistributed.

501 "The Weekly Register," No. 24 of Vol. III, Feb. 13, 1813, in: Price, Wilma. The Battle and Massacre of the River Raisin; Excerpts from the Niles Weekly Register of Baltimore. Monroe: Monroe County Historical Society and Library Commission, 1981: "*The Americans are said to have fought bravely*

Seeing the Americans waver, the whole of the Indians in this quarter and part of the Canadian militia redoubled their efforts, but they also suffered casualties. Adam Brown, for whom the Wyandot village was named, was shot through the body as he accompanied old Colonel Matthew Elliott into the fray.

So was eighteen-year-old Ensign Thomas Kerr, shot fatally through the lungs while leading the Royal Newfoundlanders in a charge against a barn occupied by Kentucky riflemen.[502]

Mounted on his horse, Lt. Col. St. George led the Canadian militia forward in attempt to capture the barn, since it was so *"favourably situated for annoying the enemy"*[503] The militiamen soon found themselves hotly engaged in the attack on both the American regulars' camp and the French Town fence line.

At one point, they ventured too near the French Town pickets. Captain Mills and Lt. Gordon of the 1st Essex Militia Regiment were both wounded in the struggle, the latter having his hip shattered by a bullet.[504]

As balls began battering about the militiamen's ears like hail, Lt. Col. St. George rushed forward on horseback to bring the Canadians back out of close range.

St. George's horse was shot and he, himself, was badly wounded in the effort, being hit 4 or 5 times by enemy bullets.[505]

---

until they had exhausted their ammunition, with which general Winchester had not taken the precaution of supplying the troops; and they were scarcely able to fire five rounds."

502 Cruickshank, Harrison & Procter, Royal Society of Canada, p. 160: The Newfoundlanders, under Captain Mockler, were probably formed on the left wing of the main line of British regulars. Ostensibly attacking the pickets, it is possible they were attacking Godfroy's barn or Jerome's. They evidently played an important role in pushing the American right and center off the open field. In the course of the fight, Procter apparently shifted his men to the left and concentrated against the failing American right flank. The lay of the land, particularly the angle formed by Mason Run, suggests the first and closest contact may have been between the British left and American right.

503 Letter Proctor to Sheaffe, January 25, 1813, #24 in James' Military Occurrences, Vol. 1. *"I cannot, however, refrain from mentioning lieutenant-colonel St. George, who received four wounds in a gallant attempt to; occupy a building which was favorably situated for annoying the enemy..."* I am assuming this was the Godfroy barn.

504 Couture, Paul Morgan. "War and Society on the Detroit Frontier, 1791-1815," manuscript report of Parks Canada, 1986. It is not clear exactly where or when Mills and Gordon were wounded.

505 Algonquin Club: "Reminiscences of an Actor in the War of 1812," From Canadian Emigrant, 1835. Author unknown. Typed copy in Bidlack's Notes, Monroe County Historical Museum Archives. St. George's wounds *"...of which he afterwards recovered, and for which he was dubbed a Knight*

When St. George fell, four soldiers rushed out to defend him. While three of them fired away at the enemy, the fourth picked him up and carried him to shelter. His wounds appeared so bad that he was not given much hope for seeing the end of the battle.[506]

Nonetheless, the British and Canadians continued to drive a wedge between McClenahan's regulars in the open field and Lewis' militiamen behind the garden fences. Capt. Wm Smith's Company of the 2nd Essex Militia Regiment was the first to enter the abandoned camp of the retreating 17th U.S. Infantry.

The Newfoundlanders and Essex militiamen laid down a heavy fire in front, while Indians fired from the cover of the captured barn and fence line as they began to work their way around the flanks of the 17th Infantry.

The American right wing was being squeezed into a box, fired on from three sides, with the River Raisin behind them. 41-year-old Captain Robert Edwards was killed, and the troops continued to give way until they reached the shelter offered by the north bank of the river. Here, the regulars rallied and returned fire for a short time.[507]

At the forefront of the 17th U.S. Infantry, Captain Meade tried to turn the tide. Pointing towards the oncoming enemy, he yelled, "*My brave fellows, charge upon them!*" His men had no time to obey, however, as Meade immediately fell to the ground, victim of a fatal bullet.[508]

There was no respite for the harried troops as a band of Native warriors

---

of the most honorable military order of the Bath.

And pray, what honors and rewards were conferred on the brave Canadian militia, whose gallantry occasioned it? Why, remuneration for the losses they sustained by the inroads of a rapacious enemy, while abroad fighting the battles of their king and country, was — most graciously withheld! — the voluntary assurances had and received from the legal representatives of said king and government to the contrary notwithstanding..."

506 Byfield, Shadrack, "A Common Soldiers Account," Recollections of the War of 1812. Toronto: Baxter Publishing Company, 1964 reprint of 1828 edition.

507 Battery Edwards at Fort Mott, New Jersey, was named in honor of Capt. Edwards in 1903. It consisted of two casemates for 3-inch rapid fire coastal defense guns.

508 McAfee, Robert. History of the Late War in the Western Country, Bowling Green, Ohio: Historical Publications Company, 1919 (reprint of 1816 original edition.) pp. 234 and 409. Another account says Meade gave the initial order to retreat. McAffee, who visited the scene with Johnson's regiment in September of 1813, adds to the confusion: "Captain Meade of the regular army...was killed where the action commenced. Finding that the situation of the corps was rendered desperate by the approach of the enemy, he gave order to his men, 'my brave fellows, charge upon them,' and a moment afterwards he was no more...The gallant Meade fell on the bank..."

gained their flank and poured in a galling fire from that direction. Meanwhile, another band was circling around far behind the American army in a wide maneuver that threatened to cut them off from their comrades.[509]

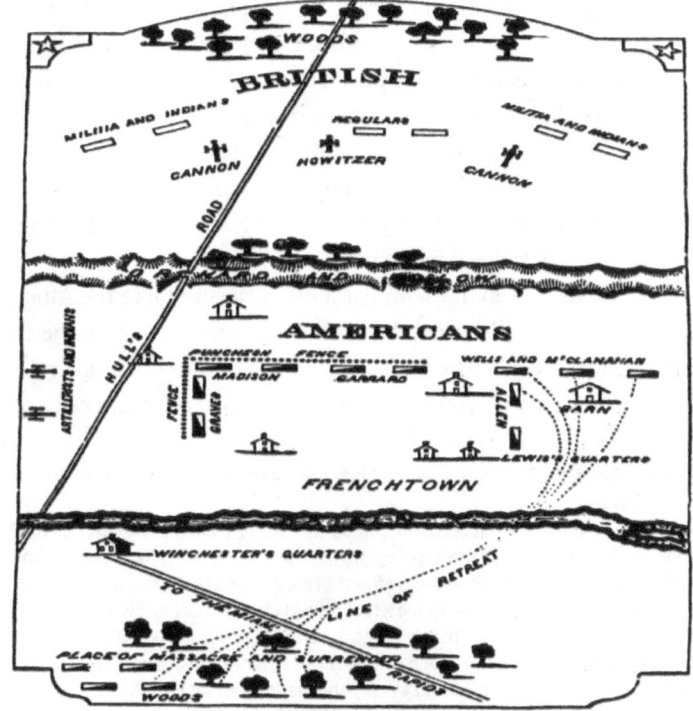

Early Sketch Map of Battleground
(Map not to scale)[510]

---

509 Letter Winchester to Sec. of War, Malden, Jan. 23, 1813, Typed copy in Bidlack Notes, Monroe County Historical Museum Archives: *"The action commenced at the dawn of day; the piquet guards were driven in; and a heavy fire opened on the whole line, by which a part thereof was thrown into disorder; and being ordered to retire a small distance, in order to form on more advantageous ground, I found the enemy doubling our left flank with force and rapidity."*
Deposition of Joseph Robert, County of Monroe, Aug. 22, 1818, in the William Henry Harrison Papers, on microfilm at Central Michigan University: *"The deponent further states that soon after the action had commenced, that part of the army which was exposed to the fire of the British ... took shelter under the bank of the river, where they remained for a considerable time."*
510 From Wing's History of Monroe County, Vol I, Chicago: Lewis Publishing, 1913, p. 56, originally published in Major Richardson's War of 1812 from papers accompanying Procter's battle report.

Tallon's attack, between 6 and 7 a.m., January 22, 1813:[511]

The right wing of the main British line was made up of two grand divisions of the 41st Regiment of Foot. Captain Tallon personally commanded the grenadiers of the 1st grand division.

On Tallon's left, and also under his command, was the 2nd grand division, made up of Capt. Muir's old company, which was now being led by Lt. Benoit Bender. Each division was formed of about 25 or 30 files, two ranks deep, plus their officers and covering sergeants.[512]

Cursed with a weak voice and a feeble constitution, Captain Tallon had nonetheless survived a night in the wintry open, and was now rasping out orders as best he could. Fortunately, he could rely on his sergeants to repeat his commands in their usual, bellowing tones.[513]

Seeing movement in the semi darkness, it seemed like the Americans were forming in the open ground and possibly seeking to turn the British right flank. Lt. Bender noticed some Americans filing off to his right and quickly shouted, *"Fire away 41st, you will soon make them all prisoners!"*[514]

---

511 If watches were set by the sun, the attack might have been between 7 and 8 a.m. in our current eastern daylight time.

512 Testimony of Capt. Tallon, Proceedings of a Court Martial, Holden at Quebec, for the Trial of Lieutenant Benoit Bender, of the 41st Regiment of Foot, in July, 1815. Montreal: J. Lane, 1817. Courtesy Jim Yaworsky. The remaining 3 officers of the 41st evidently were with the other half of the regiment, separate from and to the left of Tallon's divisions. Generally, in the 18th century, British regiments were divided into two wings, each divided into 2 grand divisions. Each grand division contained 2 companies. Each company had two platoons. Given the small size of the 41st Regiment at the River Raisin (224 men), the grand divisions were just a single company strong. See: MacNiven, Robbie, Battle Tactics of the American Revolution, Great Britain: Osprey, p. 7.

513 Confidential Reports of the 41st Regiment, Nov. 1, 1810 — May 24, 1811, copies in the Fort Malden Archives. Tallon was a 40-year-old Irishman with about 2 decades of military service under his belt. He had been an attentive, even zealous officer, who, despite certain physical frailties, had earned a temporary brevet as a Brigade Major during the Detroit Campaign.

514 Testimony of Cpl. William Denis, Proceedings of a Court Martial, Holden at Quebec, for the Trial of Lieutenant Benoit Bender, of the 41st Regiment of Foot, in July, 1815. Montreal: J. Lane, 1817. Courtesy Jim Yaworsky. This movement on the part of the Americans remains a mystery. A Potawatomi leader once claimed there was an attempt to outflank the British right, but American accounts don't mention it. There were sorties to burn a couple of barns, as well as capture an advanced British cannon, but these are generally thought to have occurred later in the battle and were conducted by individuals or small groups. A major reinforcement was sent out from the pickets early in the fight to rescue the retreating regulars, which may have headed west towards the ford and down Hull's Trace from there. Another possibility was a small force of 2 companies from the area near Winchester's headquarters that may have arrived to link up with the men inside the French Town pickets, which would have been pretty early in the battle.

As the battle lines solidified, the British found themselves in control of a ravine and orchard, while their opponents manned a series of adjoining garden fences. Although the French Town fences seemed inadequate protection to the Kentuckians, they loomed as a formidable obstacle to the British.

Much of the firing took place at a range of 150 to 200 yards, but three times over the course of the morning the British advanced within 80 yards of the fence. When they did so, Tallon's division would first march forward, then stop to fire and reload while Bender's division advanced.

As the divisions leap-frogged forward, they could see the enemy's muzzle flashes as they fired through holes in the picketing, which did not make for much of a target.[515]

Within the dark line of British regulars stood gentleman volunteer John Richardson. Exhausted and cold, He could barely suppress a yawn, even with the enemy's bullets whistling over his head. As they marched forward, he could not help wondering how the enemy had been so negligent as to allow them to get this close.

Richardson unfortunately had to deal not only with physical fatigue, but also with a serious technical problem. During the previous night, someone had taken his well-tended musket and replaced it with one that was badly fouled.

On the first volley, Richardson pulled the trigger and saw the powder flash in the priming pan, but he felt no recoil. Looking at his pan, he realized that the priming powder had ignited, but the main charge had not gone off. With a wire, he worked away at clearing the touch hole, but to no avail.

Frustrated and bitter, he stood helplessly in line, exposed to a veritable torrent of enemy bullets, without being able to fire a single shot in return.[516]

---

515 Testimony of Lt. McLean, Proceedings of a Court Martial, Holden at Quebec, for the Trial of Lieutenant Benoit Bender, of the 41st Regiment of Foot, in July, 1815. Montreal: J. Lane, 1817. Courtesy Jim Yaworsky. A more detailed description of this type of advance is given in Napoleon's Infantry Handbook, by T. E. Crowdy, Barnsley, South Yorkshire, U. K.: Pen & Sword Books, Ltd., 2015, p. 198: The process alternated between companies or battalions, with the first advancing at a quick pace, while the second continued to march at its regular pace. The first unit would stop and fire after about 30 paces. When the second came on line with the first, they would halt and fire (or take up the accelerated pace for another 30 steps, then halt and fire). The two units would continue to advance and fire alternately until ordered to halt. The procedure could be done in reverse, as well. By 1813, this *feu en avançant* technique was going out of style in the French army but was still used in the British.

516 Casselman, Alexander Clark. Richardson's War of 1812. Toronto: Coles Publishing Co., John Richardson's letter to his uncle, Feb. 4, 1813.

The firefight against the Kentuckians behind the fence was definitely an unequal contest. Under the current battle conditions, in limited light, firing at soldiers hunkered down behind a fence, barely an enemy was scratched. Even with a good musket, Richardson thought, he might as well shoot at the moon.[517]

After the fourth or fifth volley, John Richardson was called to assist his brother, fourteen-year-old Midshipman Robert Richardson, who was with the artillery. Young Robert had ignored an order to remain behind at the previous night's bivouac. Now, he found himself the target of a Kentucky marksman.

As he was applying the slow match to fire his artillery piece, a bullet crashed into his knee, toppling him to the ground. Screaming, he begged his companions not to take him to the rear, for there, among the surgeons, he would come face to face with his father, a doctor serving on Procter's staff. Instead, he requested to be taken to the surgeon of the 41st.[518]

---

517 "A Theoretical Examination of the Effectiveness of 18th Century Musketry, Pt. 2" by Norman Fuss, in The Brigade Dispatch: the Journal of the Brigade of the American Revolution, Vol. 34, No.1, Spring, 2004. Period firing trials for flintlock muskets produced an average between 20% and 40% hits on a solid 6' high target. Mr. Fuss used statistical analysis to conclude that musket men firing in a two-rank formation in ideal conditions could achieve 14.2% hits on an actual line of soldiers at a range of 150 yards. Of course, that's not counting the effect of the fence, which would probably stop 90% of the bullets at that distance. Under battle conditions, Mr. Fuss estimated a soldier would have to fire 40 times to cause a casualty at that range. Our 120 British regulars might then be lucky if they hit 2 or 3 Kentuckians in a single, massive volley.

  Meanwhile, the British were taking casualties from the constant fire of the Kentuckians behind the fence. Tallon's men were probably facing a couple hundred Kentuckians under Major Madison. In theory, if Madison's men fired off 10 rounds, they might have caused 50 casualties. Re-supplied with another 10 rounds, they could have accounted for all the British casualties in Tallon's force. They had a couple hours to inflict this damage, even though a competent musket man could have easily shot off those 20 rounds in 10 or 15 minutes. Of course, the British attacks were not continuous. The Kentuckians were told to conserve ammunition until the British were close, and only 3 times did the British come within 80 yards. Between advances, the British took shelter in the ravine, where, by crouching or lying down, they were completely protected.

518 Casselman, Alexander Clark, Richardson's War of 1812, Toronto: Coles Publishing Co.: Young Richardson was taken to a dressing station in a barn where he met the regimental surgeon. This would have been Assistant Surgeon William Faulkner of the 41st Regiment. While there, he was observed by Shadrack Byfield, also wounded in the fighting, who noted the boy was crying for his mother and saying he would surely die. After 6 months of intense suffering, Robert was well enough to move to Quebec, where he was commissioned a lieutenant. Unfortunately, his wound would eventually prove fatal. See also: Byfield, Shadrack, "A Common Soldiers Account," Recollections of the War of 1812, Toronto: Baxter Publishing Company, 1964 reprint of 1828 edition: *"While in the barn, I was much affected by seeing and hearing a lad, about 11 or 12 years of age, who was wounded in one of his knees. The little fellow's cries from the pain of his wound; his crying after his dear mother; and saying he should die, were so affecting that it was not soon forgotten*

**British Artilleryman with 3-Pounder and Infantryman
with Brown Bess Musket**
Exhibit created by Ken Osen, River Raisin Battlefield Visitor Center,
Monroe, Michigan

After their initial advance, the British line fell back to the shelter of the ravine, and the artillery crews again found themselves in the line of fire between the opposing forces.[519]

---

by me. He was a midshipman, belonging to one of the gun boats; I think his name was Dickenson."
519 The three British 3-pounders were usually serviced by crews of 7 or 8 men each, under the direction of a skilled artillerist. (In a pinch, the gun could still be operated by a crew of 4). Each gun was supplied with about 60 rounds of ammunition in boxes that were normally carried on the trail and axle of the field carriage. To load, a round, 3-pound ball was rammed down the 3-foot-long brass barrel on top of a 6 or 8-ounce charge of powder. A brass pick was jabbed into a touch hole at the breech of the gun to pierce the bag of powder, then withdrawn to insert a priming fuse, quill, or some loose powder, which, when touched off by a burning linstock, would send the projectile some 900 yards. For a massed infantry target within 400 yards, the gun crews could fire case-shot, containing dozens of smaller balls, which would spread out with devastating effect. The three small howitzers were possibly on garrison carriages mounted on sleds. Two of them had been captured at Detroit, and the third taken at French Town after General Hull's surrender

Lt. Felix Troughton of the Royal Artillery was in overall command of the guns at the River Raisin. He went down with a serious wound in the leg.[520]

Bombardier Kitson also received a wound that would prove mortal in a few days.

1st Lt. Frédéric Rolette of the Canadian Provincial Marine was in charge of the center gun. Luckily, the 29-year-old Royal Navy veteran from Québec had tied a heavy bandana around his head to help ease a bad headache that morning. Apparently, he also had a thick skull.

While directing his crew, he was suddenly struck in the back of the head by a British bullet that was fired from the support troops behind him. The ball tore through the folds of silk and flattened against his cranium, raising a huge, black, but not fatal, lump.

From the other direction, he was hit in the side by flying buckshot from a typical American musket load of buck and ball. Nonetheless, he refused to abandon the gun of which he was in charge.[521]

---

in the summer of 1812. The barrels were very short, but their bore size was close enough to fire the same case-shot as the British 3-pounders, with minor modifications, and they could elevate their muzzles to fire explosive shells in a high arc over the heads of their foes. See Appendix P.

520 Wright, Richard J. The John Hunt Memoirs; Early Years of the Maumee Basin, 1812-1835, Maumee Valley Historical Society, p. 43. See also: Irving, L. Humfray, Officers of the British Forces in Canada During the War of 1812, Welland Tribute Print., 1908, p. 21. Four companies of the Royal Artillery were in Canada when the war began. Lt. Troughton led a detachment at the capture of Detroit and also at the River Raisin. He died on the voyage home to England on June 26, 1815.

521 Reynolds Narrative in "Chronicle of the War:" Rolette entered the Royal Navy at a young age and was in the Battles of the Nile (where he was wounded) and Trafalgar. In April of 1812, he became 1st Lieutenant on board the *Hunter*. In July, he boarded the *Cuyahoga Packet* and captured General Hull's papers. During the War of 1812, Rolette was credited with capturing a dozen American boats. He participated in the actions at River Canard, Detroit, and French Town, but was severely wounded and taken prisoner at the Battle of Lake Erie in September of 1813. He was released at the end of the war. He returned to Québec, where the Canton of Rolette was named in his honor. Rolette never entirely recovered from his wounds. He died in 1831 at the age of 48. In 2015, a Canadian arctic patrol vessel was named after him. See also: Cruikshank, Harrison & Procter, pp. 159-60.

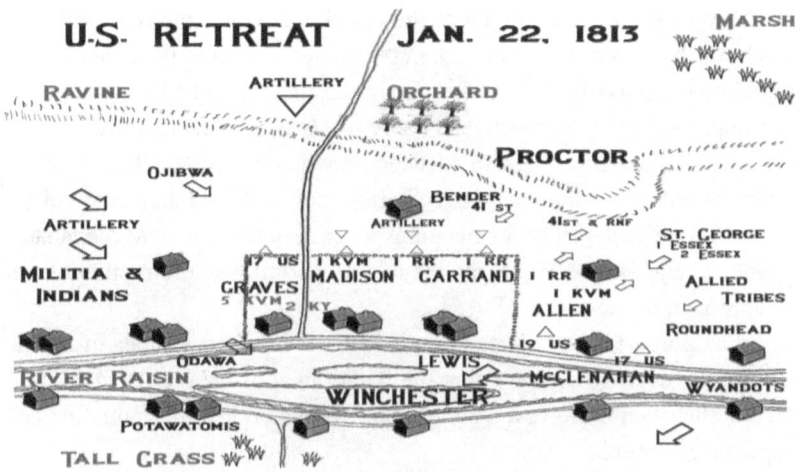

Note: locations of individual tribes and leaders are conjectural[522]
(Map not to scale)

Retreat across the River Raisin, 7:30 a.m., January 22, 1813:

Around 7:30 a.m., the early morning twilight reached its peak, followed by full sunrise just before 8 o'clock.[523] By this time, General Winchester had ridden along the Raisin's south bank to a point opposite the eastern edge of the picketed area. It had not taken him long to cover the distance from his headquarters at Navarre's House, but it was already becoming full daylight.[524]

---

522 Details about the exact disposition of Procter's forces can be partially deduced from anecdotal descriptions of the battle. Tallon and Bender's élite companies of the 41st Regiment formed the right wing of the main British line, with the rest of the regiment in the center and left. Mockler's Newfoundland Fencibles probably anchored the left wing or covered the advance of the artillery. The Canadian militia and Indians covered both flanks.

   It is possible that Lieutenant Colonel Thomas Bligh St. George may have led the battalion companies of the 1st and 2nd Essex to the left of the British line, while Major Ebenezer Reynolds may have taken the flank companies (under Maisonville, Caldwell, and Elliott) of those same regiments off to the right. See Appendix O for a discussion of some alternate locations of Native American forces.

523 U.S. Naval Observatory, Astronomical Applications Department, Sun and Moon Data for Friday, January 22, 1813, Eastern Standard Time: Morning twilight = 7:25am, Sunrise = 7:56am, Sunset = 5:36pm, End twilight = 6:06pm. However, time was not standardized in the United States until 1883.

524 Deposition of John Baptist Jerome of Monroe County, Aug. 22, 1818: Jean-Baptiste Jerome had remained with the wounded at his home when the fighting commenced that morning. About

As Winchester stood in a gate, he could plainly see the regulars' line, which was being severely handled. In pursuance of a tentative defense plan formulated previously, Winchester requested Lt. Colonel Allen to advance his troops to plug the gap between the regulars and the fence line.

From Allen's line, Captain Bledsoe turned and saw Winchester standing in the rear of his company, even before they had fired their first volley. Since Bledsoe's men had been manning the eastern fence line, McLenahan's retreating regulars were in their line of fire, partially shielding them from the approach of the enemy.[525]

In response to his orders, Allen led two 50-man companies of militia out into the open ground to cover the withdrawal of the regulars and their stand at the river.[526] However, some of the troops broke ranks and ran back along the riverbank.

Panic was in the air, as Allen's men also began heading for the river. The officers were unable to retain order as they shouted above the din of battle.[527]

Major McClenahan was relieved as he caught sight of the General riding

---

sunrise, he noticed General Winchester ride slowly past, accompanied by 2 other officers, coming downstream from his headquarters. The general shortly returned, riding fast in the direction he had come. About the same time, Jerome noticed the regulars streaming south across the river in every direction. The fighting was still hot and heavy.

525 Winchester, James., Historic Details Having Relation to the Campaign of the North-Western Army under Generals Harrison and Winchester, Lexington: Worsley & Smith, 1818, p. 82, citing a certificate of acting Captain Richard Bledsoe.

526 Information gleaned from interviews with veterans was published in the Pittsburgh Gazette and Mercury, and partially reprinted with comments in the Monroe Commercial of Thursday, March 23, 1871, and the contents posted at http://monroe.lib.mi.us/bygonesofmonroe/bomwarof1812. htm. See also: Knopf, Richard C., Document Transcriptions of the War of 1812 in the Northwest, Vol. V, pt. 2. Columbus: Ohio Historical Society, 1958. p. 34: The Pittsburgh Mercury of February 25, 1813, reported that *"Two companies of 50 men each from the pickets sallied out and unfortunately joined the retreating party."* According to G. Glenn Clift, these were probably McCracken's company of the 1st Rifle Regiment and Glaves' company of the 1st Kentucky Volunteer Militia. Clift does not list Glaves as commanding any of the companies within the pickets, but some of his company was attached to McCracken's command, and he does appear during Winchester's retreat, being one of the lucky ones to escape with Major McClenahan.

527 Atherton, William, Narrative of the Suffering and Defeat of the North-Western Army, Frankfort: Hodges, 1842, p. 44: Just at this time, General Winchester came up and ordered the retreating troops to rally and form behind the second bank of the river, inclining toward the center so as to move behind the picketing. These orders were probably not heard, and being hard pressed both by the British and Indians in front and on their right flank, the troops retreated in disorder over the river. Another detachment which was sent from the pickets to reinforce the right wing, and a few others, who supposed the whole army was ordered to retreat, joined in its flight.

Militiamen Firing Muskets and Rifles
200th Anniversary of the Battle of the River Raisin
Photo courtesy of Floral City Images

along the river bank with Lt. Colonels Lewis and Allen. In a subdued voice, Winchester issued new orders to reform on the south bank of the river.[528] From there, they could move upstream and cross back under cover of the pickets.[529]

Meanwhile, Joseph Robert was watching all this from his house across the river from Jerome's. A few minutes after sunrise, he had noticed three men appear on the south bank of the river, at the mouth of the lane heading south.

The men watched the battle for a time, as though expecting some movement from the troops huddled along the opposite bank. Soon, one of the men rode across to meet them.[530]

---

528 McClenahan to Harrison, Jan. 26, 1813, Official Letters of the military and Naval Officers of the United States during the War with Great Britain in the Years 1812, 13, 14, and 15, Edited by John Brannan, Washington City: Wax & Gideon, 1823, pp. 131-2.

529 Winchester, James. Historic Details Having Relation to the Campaign of the North-Western Army under Generals Harrison and Winchester. Lexington: Worsley & Smith, 1818, pp. 36-7: Winchester ordered them reformed in the shelter of the right bank, and followed them, along with LTC Lewis, in order to rally them. Parts of 2 companies followed them outside the pickets. They couldn't rally the troops. Indians from right and left overwhelmed them with numbers.

530 Deposition of Joseph Robert, Aug. 22, 1818, in the William Henry Harrison Papers, on microfilm

The officer soon re-crossed to the south bank, but the troops did not follow. Twice more he returned to reissue the order before the troops finally broke from their cover like a flock of startled ducks.

Crossing the river at an angle, the regulars and militiamen passed the Robert farm, heading for a lane that ran onto Hull's Road. The road could provide a path to rejoin their comrades barricaded withing the garden pickets. It could also serve as an escape path south towards Harrison's forces on the Maumee. If they took that route, there was no turning back, for the Indians were closing in behind them.

Musket balls began to strike the Robert house as the American officers tried to rally their men behind a fence and among the farm buildings that stretched in an irregular line about 60 yards from the south bank of the river. A considerable number of the troops rallied here and renewed their firing under the personal direction of Colonels Lewis and Allen. Unfortunately, the buildings and fences served to break up the retreat even more.

Meanwhile, General Winchester had gone ahead and was standing at a gate to direct the retreating troops back across the river. But when the van of the right wing arrived within a few paces of him, the men turned and fled.

Unable to sustain their defense, the Americans broke into small groups, retreating south onto Hull's Road, losing men at every turn.

Native warriors mounted on ponies were rushing ahead to cut them off. More Indians had circled around French Town and were infiltrating the wooded areas south of the river from the west, threatening to close any chance that the regulars could ever rejoin their comrades inside the village pickets.[531]

As the tide of battle receded, the civilian contractors at the Robert house

---

at Central Michigan University: *"The deponent further states that a few minutes after sunrise, he saw 3 men mounted on the opposite side of the river from the battleground, viewing the action; in a short time, one of the men advanced across the river and ordered the men who had sought shelter under the bank from the fire of the British to retreat, and immediately retreated himself; the order was not obeyed. He returned and repeated it, which was still disobeyed, he returned a third time, and with the most violent threats in the name of the General ordered them to retreat. At length they gave way and retreated across the river towards the place where the 3 men had stood, at the head of a lane heading to the Miami, up which lane the 2 men who had been left had retreated. The deponent further states that the men who had retreated were pursued by the Indians up the lane before referred to."*

531 "Battle of Frenchtown," <u>Kentucky Reporter,</u> March 13, 1813, typed copy in Bidlack's Notes, Monroe County Historical Museum Archives: *"...we, the undersigned officers engaged in the battle have deemed it proper to make the following statement, which represents, so far as it extends, a true picture of the transaction, as it transpired on the day of battle."*

thought of making their own escape. Joseph warned them to head east through the marshes and onto the ice of La Plaisance Bay.[532]

Among them was Thomas Shields of Canton, Ohio. He had been sent to the River Raisin to obtain 800 barrels of flour from the *habitants*. Unarmed, he had no thought of joining in the fighting. His only desire was to escape.[533]

Back across the river, Captain Matson had been wounded in the meaty portion of his right thigh on January 18 and was in a makeshift hospital some distance from the encampment. Grabbing a musket from his fellow patient, Edward McConnell, he headed for the door, but was stopped by Dr. Davis, who told him he was too badly wounded. Taking the musket, Davis went out instead.

Matson remained in the doorway, watching the battle. The artillery fire died away, but then bullets began to strike the house so rapidly, he decided it was time to go. Seeing men retreat across the river, he fell in with them.[534]

---

532 According to Joseph B. Nadeau, the retreat began at a little alley a few rods east of where the Detroit, Monroe, and Toledo Railroad crossed Front Street in 1871. See: "Historical Reminiscences, Anniversary of the River Raisin Massacre," Detroit Free Press, Jan. 22, 1871, p. 5, col.1. The Monroe Civic Reflector of 1904 says the retreating column struck Hull's Road near the old Lake Shore pumping station. The Library of Congress' 1899 Sanborn map shows the L.S. and M.S. pump house and hand cart yard on the north-east corner of East Front Street and Kentucky Avenue. See: Sanborn Fire Insurance Map from Monroe, Monroe County, Michigan. Sanborn Map Company, Jun, 1899. Map. Retrieved from the Library of Congress, <www.loc.gov/item/sanborn04115_003/>. This location could fit in with the route of Price's company, which followed the main retreat. Otherwise, it would appear that the right wing crossed the river and retreated westward, parallel to the river, before heading south on Hull's Road.

533 Letter Shields to Armstrong, March 8, 1813, in Knopf, Richard C. Document Transcriptions of the War of 1812 in the Northwest, Vol. VIII. Columbus: Ohio Historical Society, 1961, p. 160: Shields stated he had visited the Raisin while it was still occupied by the enemy, had returned to Sandusky to report on his successful dealings, and then been sent back to French Town, arriving the evening before the battle. When the army retreated, he fled, but was captured by the Indians. Turned over to the British, he was taken to Fort George, where he was finally released. Another man, named Henderson, was there with his children. At first, he refused to leave, but Joseph finally convinced him he would be putting all of them in danger if he stayed. Leaving his children in the care of the Roberts, Henderson reluctantly took off towards the lake. Wing, Talcott. "Biography of Joseph Robert," History of Monroe County, Michigan. New York: Munsell & Company, 1890, p. 116. In Remember the Raisin, G. Glenn Clift lists both a Samuel and a Thomas Henderson in West's company of the 1st Kentucky Volunteer Militia Regiment. Both seem to have survived the battle.

534 Knopf, Richard C., Document Transcriptions of the War of 1812 in the Northwest, Vol. V, pt. 2. Columbus: Ohio Historical Society, 1958, pp. 27-28: From Matson's description of the location of the hospital in which he was placed, it sounds more like Godfroy's barn near the 17th Infantry camp, or even the Robert house rather than the Jerome house, unless he was rushing to join Price's company. G. Glenn Clift says it was probably Hugh Newell of Captain Price's Company,

Captain Bland Ballard had been wounded slightly in the previous battle, and was hit once again. It was by a spent ball, but the wound would annoy him the rest of his life.[535]

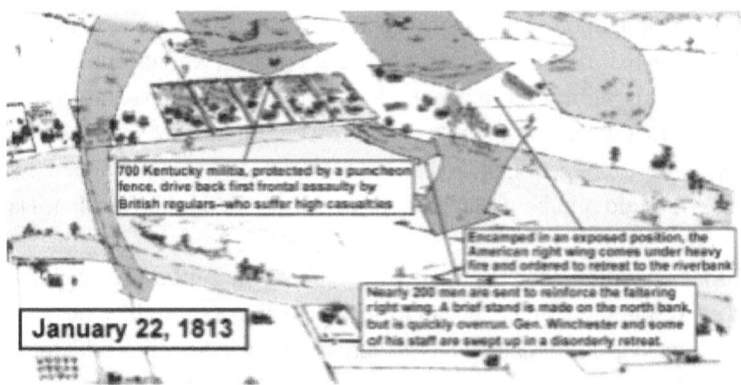

700 Kentucky militia, protected by a puncheon fence, drive back first frontal assault by British regulars—who suffer high casualties

Encamped in an exposed position, the American right wing comes under heavy fire and ordered to retreat to the riverbank

Nearly 200 men are sent to reinforce the faltering right wing. A brief stand is made on the north bank, but is quickly overrun. Gen. Winchester and some of his staff are swept up in a disorderly retreat.

January 22, 1813

From: "Native Ground, Middle Ground, Battle Ground: The River Raisin, the War of 1812, and the Course of North American History, A Historic Resource Study of River Raisin National Battlefield Park," prepared for the National Park Service by Mark David Spence, Ph.D., 2019, p. 231.
Provided Courtesy of the National Park Service, River Raisin National Battlefield Park

Some of the *habitants* also joined the retreat, including Capt. Jean-Baptiste Couture and his son Medard. As they neared the Robert house, they were caught in a crossfire. Jean-Baptiste went down. Medard was swept along in the retreat; his last view of his father was of him being scalped.[536]

As soon as he got clear of the retreating soldiers, Medard returned to pick

---

rather than Matson, who took a musket from his comrade Edward McConnell and tried to join the battle, but was stopped and the weapon taken by Dr. Thomas C. Davis of Frankfort. See: Clift, G. Glenn. Remember the Raisin. Frankfort: Kentucky Historical Society, 1961, p. 67. Clift lists an Edward M. McConnell as a sergeant in Langhorne's company of the 1st Rifle Regiment from Bourbon County, Kentucky, and says he was wounded on January 18th and taken prisoner on January 22.

535 Actually, Ballard survived the battle. Although debilitated by wounds and by a stint as a POW, he would live to the age of 92, and have a Kentucky county named after him.

536 Affidavit of Joseph Robert given at Detroit, Feb. 4, 1813: *"...He also says that that Baptiste Couture was killed near deponent's house, on the day of the second battle, a little after sunrise..."*

up his father's bloodstained corpse. Carrying it half a mile back home, he hid it in a straw stack, intending to bury the captain's body when night fell.[537]

Battle of Frenchtown
Provided Courtesy of the Monroe County Historical Commission
And the River Raisin National Battlefield Park
Panoramic Painting created and donated by Tim Kurtz

Main British charge, between 8 and 9 a.m., January 22, 1813:

It was now a full 2 hours since the first shots had been fired. It had now grown much lighter, and the British could better distinguish their targets behind the fence line. As their front narrowed on nearing the American

---

537 Michigan Pioneer & Historical Society, Annual Meeting, 1896, biography of Mrs. Alice Knaggs. Alice was born in Lewis County, New York, in 1808. The daughter of Peter Benson, she married Medard Couture in 1831. After Medard's death in 1859, she married James Knaggs, who died shortly thereafter, in 1860. Alice died in 1895, survived by 4 of her children. See: <u>Michigan Pioneer and Historical Collections</u>, Vol. I, 1896, 2nd edition. Lansing: Robert Smith, 1900, p. 153. See also (Robert, Wing's Hist., p. 116), (Atherton, p. 46), (Jos. Robert in Niles Weekly Register, 4-10-1813.) A few of the other Raisin *habitants* died during the fighting. Joseph Bissonette's two younger brothers, Étienne and Gabriel, were said to have been killed and scalped by Colonel Procter's Indians as they retreated alongside the Kentuckians. See: "Genealogical Sketch and History," <u>Michigan Pioneer Collections</u>, Vol. 38, 502-9.

line, they fell into a sort of crossfire that erupted all along the length of the oak pickets.[538]

During the first two advances into close range, a number of men had been hit in the head or upper chest as they marched up the long, gentle slope out of the ravine, which put a definite damper on the enthusiasm of their comrades.

Captain Tallon had been wounded, leaving Lt. Bender as the sole officer directly attached to the right wing.[539]

The lieutenant found that each time they fell back to the ravine, it was harder to get the troops to move forward again. Nonetheless, Bender was able to get his men to emerge from shelter once more, halting to fire 3 or 4 volleys by each grand division before the order to charge was given.[540]

Private Noonan was about 10 files away from his Lieutenant, when he was hit by a musket ball and fell down behind the firing line. Over the space of 15 minutes, he called out to his officer several times that he was severely

---

538 Knopf, Richard C. <u>Document Transcriptions of the War of 1812 in the Northwest, Vol. V, pt. 2</u>. Columbus: Ohio Historical Society, 1958. pp. 36-7. According to the <u>Pittsburgh Mercury</u> of Feb. 25, 1813, *"...the British advanced in platoons to charge the pickets, keeping up a street fire. The men within the pickets, with the most determined bravery and presence of mind, reserved their fire until the enemy advanced within point blank shot. They then opened a cross fire upon the enemy; their pieces well leveled; and thus, they mowed down his ranks in such a manner as rendered all his efforts vain, and compelled him to retire...Their loss of regulars of the 41st Regiment was estimated at 150, in making three unsuccessful charges..."* (Actually, this number would cover the recorded casualties of all the British regulars and artillerymen, suggesting a single battle line across the entire front.) Technically, point blank is the point in the trajectory of a musket ball where it descends below the horizontal point of aim. For a smoothbore musket, this is calculated at 70 yards. To me, "street firing" would involve a company in column in a street or on a bridge, with the front of the column firing, then breaking off to right and left and reforming at the rear of the column to reload. Subsequent ranks would do the same as the column advanced or retreated. Here, however, the term might simply refer to the leapfrogging of firing platoons, as in the descriptions given at Lt. Bender's court-martial.

539 Perhaps an hour or so into the battle, Captain Tallon was wounded, leaving the only other remaining officer, Lt. Bender, in charge of the right wing. See the testimonies of Lt. McLean and Private Thomas Neil at Bender's court-martial. Estimates vary as to the exact moment Tallon was shot. Tallon stated it was an hour and a half after the start of the battle, while Sgt. Dukes testified the news was passed down the ranks about half an hour to 45 minutes into the fighting.

540 Testimony of Sgt. Joseph Stagnell, <u>Proceedings of a Court Martial, Holden at Quebec, for the Trial of Lieutenant Benoit Bender, of the 41st Regiment of Foot, in July, 1815</u>, Montreal: J. Lane, 1817. Courtesy Jim Yaworsky. Stagnell, who was in the right wing, right division, grenadiers, puts the end of the final charge at 2 ½ hours after the start of the action. He was wounded in that charge and lay on the ground for 2 or 3 more hours, until the shooting stopped entirely. He estimated there were 80 or 90 killed on the right. Also, Ensign James Cochran of the 41st wrote in his reminiscence "The War in Canada 1812" that the British attacks lasted 2 hours.

wounded and asked permission to quit the field. Bender at first ignored him, and then told him he could go see the surgeon.[541]

On his way to the rear, Noonan saw Col. Procter and his aide-de-camp, Lt. McLean, coming forward to observe the charge. Procter stopped to tell Noonan to report to the field dressing station and motioned in its direction.

As he limped away, Noonan could hear the troops working up their courage. The word to charge was passed up and down the line, but the men didn't advance. They just stood there, 60 or 70 yards from the fence, firing as fast as they could without orders.

Lieutenant Bender tried to get them to return to firing massed volleys, but in vain. Seeing a man struggling with his musket, Bender stepped out to help him. It discharged, and he stepped back into the line.[542]

In a last effort to get his troops moving again, Lieutenant Bender waived his sword in the air and yelled, *"Come on my lads, charge them my boys, we shall soon have the place. Come on boys, come on. Follow me."*

The men went forward, but the momentum petered out about 20 yards from the fence. Without orders, the 41st began to fall back.[543]

In the thick of the action, all but one of the crewmen manning the three guns directly in front of the line were killed or wounded. The disabled survivors staggered back, unable to withdraw all of their guns.[544]

As they did so, 2nd Lieutenant Robert Irvine of the Provincial Marine saw several American soldiers leap over the fence to take possession of

---

541 Testimony of Private Noonan, <u>Proceedings of a Court Martial, Holden at Quebec, for the Trial of Lieutenant Benoit Bender, of the 41st Regiment of Foot, in July, 1815</u>. Montreal: J. Lane, 1817. Courtesy Jim Yaworsky.

542 Testimonies of Lt. McLean and Private Thomas Neil at Bender's court martial. This incident bears some similarity to Richardson's complaint of trying to fire a fouled musket. Flintlock firearms were notoriously unreliable if not properly cared for. Some historians estimate a misfire rate of up to 15% of the weapons fired in a typical volley.

543 Testimony of Capt. Tallon, <u>Proceedings of a Court Martial, Holden at Quebec, for the Trial of Lieutenant Benoit Bender, of the 41st Regiment of Foot, in July, 1815</u>, Montreal: J. Lane, 1817. Courtesy Jim Yaworsky. This was in line with one of the major tactics of the British, which was to silently hold their fire until in close range, then let loose with a crushing volley (to throw the enemy into confusion) followed by a loud cheer and a swift charge with the bayonet. Unfortunately, this could not effectively be done to the American troops who were sheltered behind the tall fence.

544 Byfield, Shadrack, "A Common Soldiers Account," Recollections of the War of 1812, Toronto: Baxter Publishing Company, 1964 reprint of 1828 edition.

a canon that had been abandoned barely 20 yards from them, but British musket fire drove them back.[545]

Taking advantage of the covering fire, Lt. Irvine rushed forward to grab the drag rope of the abandoned cannon. As he pulled away, a ball tore into the center of his heel, saturating his boot with blood. Ignoring the pain, the young lieutenant succeeded in dragging the gun out of immediate danger.[546]

As musket balls flew back and forth, one of the British soldiers, twenty-three-year-old Shadrack Byfield, spotted a likely target. He turned to his comrade and exclaimed, *"There is a man; I'll have a shot at him."*

As Byfield pulled the trigger, he felt the searing pain of a musket ball passing just under his left ear. It traveled down his neck and lodged near his shoulder blade. He fell, dropping his musket. The attached bayonet neatly sliced his neighbor's leg, causing him to shout, *"Byfield is dead!"*[547]

Shadrack replied, *"I believe I be,"* wondering if this is what death felt like. Raising his head, he crawled towards his covering sergeant posted behind the line. The sergeant asked, *"Byfield, shall I take you to the doctor?"* Shadrack gamely answered, *"Never mind me, but go and help the men."*[548]

By this time, there were only 40 men left standing in the right wing. A few broke and ran for the aid station far in the rear. The rest retreated to the ravine, where they crouched down, out of the line of fire.[549]

---

545 It has been suggested that this was one of the howitzers, which would have been easier for one man to pull, rather than the heavier 3-pdr gun. A contemporary sketch map shows a howitzer in the middle of the advanced line of guns. However, another assumption is that the Provincial Marine was probably manning the guns, while the Royal Artillery crewed the howitzers.

546 Casselman, Alexander Clark, Richardson's War of 1812, Toronto: Coles Publishing Co.: *"Mr. Irvine received a wound immediately in the centre of his heel, the ball entering and saturating his boot, which was with some difficulty removed, with blood; and from the effect of this, he suffered for some time. The ball was never found."*

547 Note: From Byfield's description, we see that the British regulars were loading and firing with bayonets fixed.

548 Byfield, Shadrack, "A Common Soldiers Account," Recollections of the War of 1812. Toronto: Baxter Publishing Company, 1964 reprint of 1828 edition: Byfield made it to the doctor, who dressed his wound with a plaster and ordered him off to join other wounded men in a barn. *"...As I was going, the blood flowed so freely as to force off the plaster. I now saw a man between the woods and asked him what he did there. He told me he was wounded in his leg. I observed to him that if I had not been wounded worse than he was, I should be back, helping the men. I then asked him to give me a pocket handkerchief to tie around my neck, to stop the blood. He replied, 'I have not got one.' I said, 'If I do not get something, I shall bleed to death.' He immediately tore off the tail of his shirt, and wound it round my neck. I then got to the barn and laid down with my fellow sufferers..."*

549 Testimony of Sgt. Dukes, Proceedings of a Court Martial, Holden at Quebec, for the Trial of

Some of the wounded redcoats were bowled over by enemy bullets as they tried to drag themselves through the snow to safety. Rifle-armed marksmen showed them no mercy, dispatching the helpless men as though they were slaughtering hogs.[550]

Grenadier Sergeant Joseph Stagnell had been hit during the final 15-minute charge. He fell about 30 yards from the fence. From the position where he lay, Stagnell could see the rest of the 41st retreating.

It looked like about 80 men were lying dead or wounded on the field, along with a couple abandoned cannons, their crews having been shot down. At least the cannons had been spiked, so they could not be of immediate use to the enemy, who was, in any case, no longer venturing out to capture them.

Not desiring to make himself a target by moving, Stagnell would lay there in the snow, as still as possible, for the rest of the battle.[551]

As his men sheltered in the ravine, Lt. Bender was joined by one of Procter's aides, Lt. Hector McLean.

McLean had watched their final charge and retreat. He had seen many of the troops straggling towards the rear without orders, so he gave instructions for Bender to go after them and bring up the extra ammunition. In the meantime, the 41st could head down the ravine towards the reassembly point, which he estimated was about 400 yards away.[552]

Lieutenant Benoit Bender, of the 41st Regiment of Foot, in July, 1815. Montreal: J. Lane, 1817. Courtesy Jim Yaworsky. The Americans were probably firing individually from loopholes made in the fence, which allowed for a steadier aim, but did not deliver the psychological effect of a tremendous volley fired at very short range. For better or worse, this might have helped the well-disciplined British regulars to sustain such a high rate of casualties before breaking. For deeper insight into the psychology of such tactics, see: Noseworthy, Brent, Battle Tactics of Napoleon and his Enemies, London: Constable & Co., 1995, pp. 37-47.

550 Casselman, Alexander Clark. Richardson's War of 1812. Toronto: Coles Publishing Co., John Richardson's letter to his uncle, Feb. 4, 1813.

551 Testimony of Sgt. Stagnell, Proceedings of a Court Martial, Holden at Quebec, for the Trial of Lieutenant Benoit Bender, of the 41st Regiment of Foot, in July, 1815, Montreal: J. Lane, 1817. Courtesy Jim Yaworsky. See also the following: (Niles Weekly Register, Feb. 13, 1813), (History of the Maumee Valley, p. 37), (Joseph Robert biography in Wing's History of Monroe County, p. 116)

552 Testimony of Lt. M'Lean, Proceedings of a Court Martial, Holden at Quebec, for the Trial of Lieutenant Benoit Bender, of the 41st Regiment of Foot, in July, 1815, Montreal: J. Lane, 1817. Courtesy Jim Yaworsky. Procter's 25-year-old aide-de-camp was a foreigner who had seen only a few years of service, but that had already given him cause to dislike many of his fellow officers in the Amherstburg garrison. In particular, he had an abiding hatred for Colonel Elliott of the Indian Department.

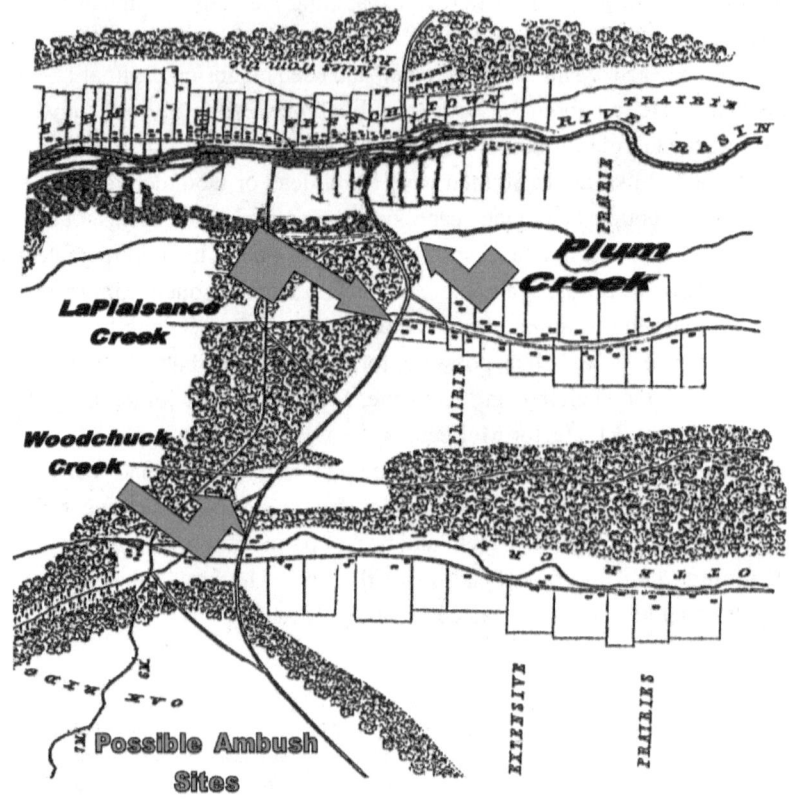

Retreat and Ambush of the American Right Wing
Image based on the Post War Map of the Michigan Road from Otter Creek
to River Raisin
by Col. Anderson, annotated by author
Courtesy Monroe County Historical Museum Archives

8:30 a.m., Hull's Road, in the direction of Plum Creek, Jan. 22, 1813:
It may have been an hour or two since General Winchester had left his headquarters, but Lt. Col. Navarre had already witnessed the confusion in the American camp and had observed the retreat of a considerable portion of Winchester's army. Judging that he could be of no further use to the

Kentuckians, he turned his horse's head back towards home, thinking he should look to the welfare of his family and neighbors.[553]

Meanwhile, Waindawgay was leading his Potawatomies across the river and into the rear of the American position. While on their way, they encountered soldiers who were trying to follow their general and join up with Lewis' command. Unaware of their purpose, Waindawgay assumed the Kentuckians were attempting to outflank the British. He and his comrades obligingly chased them into the picketed area of French Town.[554]

200th Anniversary Commemoration of the Battle of the River Raisin
Photo Courtesy of Dave and Sue Grassley, Floral City Images

---

553 Deposition of Francis Navarre, Aug. 22, 1818, in the William Henry Harrison Papers, on microfilm at Central Michigan University: Accounts differ as to whether or not Navarre accompanied General Winchester when the latter left his house that morning.

554 Monroe Civic Reflector, 1904: *"The troops north of the river were divided into 3 camps...An attempt was made to concentrate the 3 camps, the soldiers of the most easterly camp coming down under the bank of the river and marching to the west. But they were discovered by the Indians and driven... Meanwhile the other two detachments north of the river had succeeded in uniting and were bravely holding their ground..."* This would seem to indicate there was a substantial force upriver, perhaps having sought accommodations in *habitant* homes, or maybe serving as security for General Winchester.

They then quickly took up ambush positions in the timber near the River Raisin to block any sorties from the village or movement along Hull's Road. Here they would encounter the retreating American right wing and those units sent to support them.[555]

The American right wing reached Hull's Road and turned away from the river, streaming south towards the reinforcements who were supposed to be coming from the Maumee. On either side of the road, tall grass protruded high above the snow, concealing Native warriors lying in ambush.[556]

The Kentuckians pressed as rapidly as they could down the lane, trying to run the 100-yard-long gauntlet of fire. At every step, Indians popped up to fire and then disappeared back into the tall grass. There was no let up, since enemy warriors pursued them for a full mile on both sides of the road.[557]

John Simpson, the towering captain of the 1st Rifle Regiment was felled and tomahawked at the edge of the woods near the mouth of the lane. From here the bodies fell thickly; about a hundred men went down in the space of a hundred yards.[558]

Meanwhile, on the other side of the Raisin, Captain Price and his Jessamine County Blues had been doing quite a bit of damage to the enemy

---

555 "Minutes of an Indian Council," <u>Michigan Pioneer & Historical Collections</u>, Vol. XXIII. Lansing: Robert Smith & Co., 1889, p. 453: *"At the River au Raisin, the Potewatemys composed the Right Wing of the Army under the command of Genl. Procter, and when 300 of the Enemy under Genl. Winchester made an attempt to out flank our English Father, the Potewatemys rushed upon them and cut those 300 into pieces, in consequence of which, our English Father gained a signal victory, for the remainder of the Enemy's Army surrendered."* Ensign James Cochran of the 41st wrote in his reminiscence "The War in Canada 1812" that $^2/_3$rds of the Indians had formed on the British right and attacked the American left that was sheltered by a wood. The Americans were finally dislodged when 200 mounted warriors detoured around and behind them. The British troops *"moved to the left."* Without the protection of the picketing and fences, the Americans fled in all directions. *"The Indians with infernal yells followed closely on the heels of the fugitives, very few of whom received quarter, and such as escaped on foot were certain of falling by the tomahawks of the mounted Indians who, with a single blow, felled the affrighted victim, galloping on and left him to be scalped by the foot warrior."*

556 Dudley, Rev. Thomas P., "Battle and Massacre at Frenchtown, Michigan, by one of the Survivors," in <u>Historical and Archaeological Tracts</u>, No. 1, Cleveland: Western Reserve Historical Society, 1870.

557 Atherton, William, <u>Narrative of the Suffering & Defeat of the North-Western Army under General Winchester,</u> Frankfort, Kentucky: A. G. Hodges, 1842, p. 45. This lane could have been a farm lane, but was probably Hull's Road, which led them directly to a crossing of Plum Creek, presumably by means of a small bridge . An article Written by H.M. Noble in the <u>Monroe Monitor</u> of April 24, 1872, claimed a hundred bodies were later found within a hundred yards of that crossing.

558 McAfee, Robert. <u>History of the Late War in the Western Country.</u> Bowling Green, Ohio: Historical Publications Company, 1919 (reprint of 1816 original edition.) p. 233. Simpson was 6' 7" tall.

with their rifles from within the garden fences of French Town when they received orders to follow Winchester's trail for the purpose of bringing in the wounded and keeping them out of the hands of the Indians.[559]

The balding, 33-year-old captain, dressed in his unit's distinctive blue uniform with light facings, led 50 men out from behind the protective fences. They crossed near the upriver ford, directly across from Hull's main road, intending to follow it until they struck Winchester's trail. As they floundered through the roughly trampled snow, they were fired on by Indians concealed in the timber near the riverbank. Many were killed and scalped before they could extricate themselves from the 2-foot drifts and join the retreating regulars.[560]

All through the retreat down Hull's Road, the regulars and militiamen returned an occasional, but undisciplined fire.[561] Eventually, the Indians began to fall behind as they finished off the wounded or rounded up stragglers.

Near Plum Creek, about a mile from the River Raisin, the Kentuckians at last seemed to be outdistancing their pursuers. Captain Matson urged Lt. Colonel Lewis to stop the retreat. Both were worried about the wounded and exhausted men who were having difficulty keeping up. Their attempted stand at Plum Creek failed, many of the men having thrown away their firearms.[562]

---

559 Bulkley's History of Monroe County, vol. 1, p. 79. There is some confusion whether Price's company was one of the two companies mentioned earlier as being sent out from French Town. There is also some disagreement in the accounts regarding the timing and location of their intended link-up with Winchester. Bulkley places "Pierce's" company in the eastern end of the picketing and has them joining the retreat just as it started. In Caldwell's report, he mentions Price's company being sent out to pick up the wounded later, at 10 o'clock, but he could be referring to the night after the first battle, on January 18.

560 Not all the scalping was done by the Indians. A family history records that a man named Banta had killed an Indian and was scalping him, when he was overpowered, thrown over a log, and pinned to it with his own bayonet. See "Some Recollections of John M. Shively," compiled by Ralph E. Pinnick and printed in Orange Peelings, July, Aug., Sept., 1997, Vol. XV, Issue 3. G. Glenn Clift's notes on veterans of the War of 1812 lists a Peter Banta, but does not state he was killed at the Raisin, or that he was even there. Anyway, this Banta died in 1875.

561 McClenahan to Harrison, Jan. 26, 1813, in Official Letters of the military and Naval Officers of the United States during the War with Great Britain in the Years 1812, 13, 14, and 15. Edited by John Brannan. Washington City: Wax & Gideon, 1823, p. 132.

562 Matson's statement, Feb. 13, as reported in the National Intelligencer, Feb. 26, 1813, transcribed by Richard C. Knopf in Document Transcriptions Vol. V., Columbus: Ohio Historical Society, 1958, p. 27: "After crossing, they attempted to form and give battle; but, owing to the houses being in the way, they were frustrated in the attempt. They then pursued their retreat through a lane for 100 yards, on the side of which was placed a number of Indians, who injured them very much. Capt. Matson, though wounded, joined in the retreat, and says the Indians pursued on each side for about a mile,

Lieutenant Francis Chinn of Matson's Company, 1st Rifle Regiment and 2nd Lieutenant Ashton Garrett of Hightower's Company, 17th U.S. Infantry, managed to form another group of about 20 men into a line. As they faced about, they saw 60 Native warriors running towards them, in front and on both sides, their arms at the trail.

Recognizing that they were being cut off with little chance of repelling the enemy, Garrett ordered his men to ground their arms. Captain Billy Caldwell of the British Indian Department took command of the prisoners. As they moved the Kentuckians off, each of the warriors took one or two and walked along beside them.[563]

Suddenly, one of the captured American officers walking behind Caldwell produced a scalping knife he had hidden up his sleeve. In one swift move, he thrust it through the captain's neck. As Caldwell went down, the Kentuckian fell upon him.

Before he could stab Caldwell a second time, a chief of the Fox[564] tribe ran up from behind and shot the Kentuckian with a holster pistol. Dragging him off, the chief pulled the knife from Caldwell's neck. At the same instant, the other Indians jumped upon their own prisoners, tomahawking them to the ground, scalping them and mangling them where they lay.[565]

---

they then fell back in the rear. He then saw Col. Lewis and insisted on him to form the men and make a stand, as some of them were wounded, and very much exhausted. The attempt was made without success, owing to the men's not having arms…"

563 Billy Caldwell, or Sauganash, fought at the Raisin, Ft. Meigs, and Ft. Stephenson. Tall and lithe, at 6' tall and 155 pounds, Caldwell had started out as a clerk in the Indian trade at Chicago. His father was a British colonel, and his mother, a Mohawk. Although rusty in Mohawk, Caldwell was at home speaking English, French, and Potawatomi, making him invaluable as an interpreter and a war leader for the Chicago area Potawatomies. Some say his mother was a Shawnee, a sister of Blue Jacket. Others say his mother was a Potawatomi. He would become Assistant Deputy Superintendent for the Western District of Canada in 1814, but would return to the Chicago area after the War of 1812. After becoming a Justice of the Peace and aiding the Americans in the Black Hawk War, he would negotiate the removal of his people to Iowa, where he would die in 1841. See also: "Deeds / Nations, Directory of First Nations Individuals in South-Western Ontario, 1750-1850," by Greg Curnoe, available on the internet at www.adamsheritage.com.

564 Draper 17s: The prisoner was killed by a Fox warrior. Could the alleged chief have been Black Hawk? Billy Caldwell was born in 1781. The first of his three wives was a Potawatomi; the second, a Chippewa; the third, a French woman.

565 Wright, Richard J., The John Hunt Memoirs: Early Years of the Maumee Basin, 1812-1835, Maumee Valley Historical Society, p. 44. Friend Palmer, on page 332 of his History of Detroit, places this incident near Plum Creek, about a mile and a half due south of the River Raisin. However, Henry Hunt says he found a battle location in early January of 1814, 4 miles south of the Raisin at Otter Creek. Otter Creek is actually more like 5 or 6 miles: "The morning we left the house of Col. Navarre

Seeing the knife had missed Caldwell's windpipe and artery, the Indians expressed relief that his wound was not mortal. They couldn't resist lecturing him, however, pointing out it was all his own fault, "...*for if you had allowed us to deal with our prisoners our own way, this would not have happened to you. You know as well as us that the Big Knives are a faithless and treacherous kind of people and not fit to be trusted in a case like this.*"[566]

Lt. Garrett was the only man saved. The Indians delivered him to the British Indian Department Superintendent, Lt. Colonel Matthew Elliott.[567]

Other Kentuckians continued their flight. By this time, Captain Price was worn out, but he and his remaining men managed to catch up to the van of the retreating soldiers. He immediately demanded a halt to the retreat.[568]

About half a mile beyond Plum Creek, Lewis and McClenahan made a third stand in some woods, but could not rally most of the fleeing troops.

Quite a few men gained the shelter of the woods off to the west, but the

---

was a very cold, windy day, the rain and hail beating in our faces. When we reached Otter Creek, about 4 miles from the River Raisin, we saw twenty skeletons of our soldiers laying within a space of 2 rods square. Before they commenced crossing the Creek, an Indian who could talk English hallowed to them and told them if they would surrender, they should not be killed, they concluded to do so, but soon as the Indians came up, they killed every one of them..."

566 Algonquin Club: "Reminiscences of an Actor in the War of 1812," From <u>Canadian Emigrant</u>, 1835. Author unknown. Typed copy in Bidlack's Notes, Monroe County Historical Museum Archives: I have combined two anecdotes here, that of the Caldwell wounding and that of Garrett's surrender. They were most likely separate incidents. Garrett, himself, gave no reason for the killing of his men after they surrendered.

     An alternative version of this incident comes from John Richardson's account, claiming that Caldwell had saved an officer from being tomahawked. On conducting him back towards the main scene of action, the American officer drew a knife and cut him almost from ear to ear, though not deeply. Caldwell caught his assailant's arm, pulled his own dagger, and thrust it repeatedly into his enemy's body until the American lay dead.

567 Deposition of Lt. Ashton Garrett, April 13, 1813, in <u>Barbarities of the Enemy, exposed in a Report of the Committee of the House of Representatives, and the Documents accompanying said Report.</u> Troy: Francis Adancourt, 1813. p. 150. Ashton Garrett was a 2nd lieutenant in Hightower's company of the 17th U.S. Infantry. See pp. 66-67 of G. Glenn Clift's <u>Remember the Raisin</u> for his account of the fates of Lieutenant Garret and Lieutenant Chinn.

568 Clift, G. Glenn. <u>Remember the Raisin</u>. Frankfort: Kentucky Historical Society, 1961, p. 65. See also: Knopf, Richard C. <u>Document Transcriptions of the War of 1812 in the Northwest, Vol. 5, Part 2.</u> Columbus: Ohio Historical Society, 1958. p. 22: According to <u>The National Intelligencer</u>, Feb. 13, 1813, quoting an article in <u>The Liberty Hall</u>, a Cincinnati newspaper, Captain Price actually reached Winchester, for he "...*was seen retreating 3 or 4 miles, apparently exhausted, and was heard to say to Colonel Lewis, 'I can go no farther. Let's form and fight.' The col. answered, 'the men cannot be rallied; we must do the best we can.'..."* This, of course, would mean Price was ordered out much earlier than 10 a.m. This description sounds similar to Matson's account of how he pleaded with Lewis and Winchester to make a stand.

Indians hunted them down. Unable to form an effective perimeter, the woods soon became a trap as more and more Native warriors arrived within range.

SCENE FROM "BATTLES ON THE RAISIN"
A Video Documentary Produced by the Friends of the River Raisin Battlefield
Photo by Bill Saul

Lt. Colonel Allen was another of those who had reached the end of the line. Having earlier attempted to rally the retreating troops for a stand, he had been hit in the thigh and gradually fell behind. Finding himself alone after struggling along the trail for a couple miles, he sat down on a log to catch his breath.

Mentally and physically exhausted, the colonel had given up on life and was ready to meet his fate when a small group of 3 or 4 Hurons (Wyandots) came upon him.[569]

Their leader saw that Allen was a man of distinction, so he told his warriors to back off. Sitting down in front of the colonel, the Huron laid his gun across his lap and told him that if he surrendered, he would be spared.

Tragically, Lt. Colonel Allen did not understand the Indian's language.

---

569 Knopf, Richard C. Document Transcriptions of the War of 1812 in the Northwest, Vol. 5, Part 2. Columbus: Ohio Historical Society, 1958. p. 22: *"Col. Allen was discovered on foot two miles on the retreat, nearly exhausted, and opposing with his sword 3 or 4 Indians..."*

As he puzzled the strange chief's gesture, one of the Indians made a hostile move towards him. Allen rose and laid him low with one blow of his sword.[570]

Seeing the commotion, another warrior raised his rifle and fired as Allen's blow struck home. The colonel fell together with his enemy.[571]

The retreat continued beyond Plum Creek and the woods, but the chance for any effective resistance was long past. The Kentuckians left about 40 bodies of their comrades behind within 10 or 20 yards of the stream.

Among those who scattered through the woods was Private John Hamilton of Brasfield's company. Heading south, he saw an Odawa warrior about 60 yards behind him. Hamilton jumped behind a tree and trained his still-loaded musket on his pursuer.

The warrior quickly found his own tree, but then reappeared, waiving his hand and calling out in broken English for Hamilton to give up. Shouting back a definite refusal, Hamilton took aim once again.

As the Odawa ducked back behind his tree, Hamilton bolted for the next piece of cover, and his pursuer followed suit. From tree to tree they went; neither daring to empty their weapon with an uncertain shot.

But then a Potawatomi appeared off to Hamilton's west and fired at him. Fearing he could not hold off both of his pursuers, Hamilton leaned his rifle against a tree, motioned to the Odawa, and surrendered.[572]

The Potawatomi, however, wanted to claim his share of the capture. He ran up to the prisoner and flourished his knife over Hamilton's head as though to scalp him. Eventually, he settled for the private's long knife and overcoat, leaving Hamilton behind as the prisoner of the less-menacing Odawa.[573]

---

570 McAfee, Robert. History of the Late War in the Western Country. Bowling Green, Ohio: Historical Publications Company, 1919 (reprint of 1816 original edition) p. 234.

571 "Death of Col. Allen," Document Transcriptions of the War of 1812 in the Northwest, Vol. V, Pt. II, Columbus: Ohio Historical Society, 1957, p. 121. *Capt. Bledsoe, while at Malden and Sandwich, became acquainted with a Huron Indian, whom he took to be a chief, and who spoke English. Capt. Bledsoe one day asked him if he could tell him anything of Col. Allen. The warrior replied, "Yes, he is killed; yonder is his sword," pointing to an Indian some distance off. At the request of Captain Bledsoe, he called up the Indian; the Captain knew the sword well…The chief attributed his death to the conduct of the warrior who advanced on him, and spoke of it with regret…."*

572 Antrim, Joshua, History of Champaign and Logan Counties, Bellefontaine, Ohio: Press Printing Co., 1872.

573 There were 3 men named John Hamilton in Winchester's army: a captain in charge of a company of the 5th Kentucky, a private in Brasfield's company of the 5th Kentucky, and a corporal in Morris' company of the 1st Kentucky Rifle Regiment. Private Hamilton was listed as missing and presumed dead until the Indians delivered him up at Detroit, very much alive, a year after the battle.

Securing the flanks, 8-10 a.m., January 22, 1813:

Within the French Town pickets, the bulk of the American soldiers had long-since recovered from their initial confusion. Crunched down behind and along the fences, they had fashioned holes through which they could fire with the greatest security. At the battle's height, the small arms fire had blended into one continuous roar, although a careful listener could soon learn to distinguish between the sounds of the American and British weapons.[574]

About an hour after the commencement of the fight, and with General Winchester and Colonels Lewis and Allen being occupied with stemming the retreat of the right wing, Major Madison found himself in command of the remaining troops. Seeing the enemy taking shelter around Godfroy's barn, he ordered Major James Garrard, Brigade Quartermaster, to destroy it.

Garrard found a brave volunteer, James Higgins, from Hart's Company of the 5th Kentucky, who was willing to take on the almost suicidal task.

Under a heavy covering fire, Higgins sprung over the pickets with a firebrand in hand and quickly raced to the barn. Pushing the torch into a pile of straw, it caught fire, and the barn, along with its contents, was destroyed.[575]

Inside the barn may have been the body of Paschal Reaume, a wounded Canadian volunteer who had sought shelter there, only to expire.[576] After the battle, the British found his body in such a charred state that they could only identify him by his pistols and other personal effects.[577]

---

574 Atherton, William, <u>Narrative of the Suffering & Defeat of the North-Western Army under General Winchester,</u> Frankfort, Ky: A. G. Hodges, 1842, p. 42-43. Probably between muskets and rifles.

575 Affidavit of John McCalla, dated Sept. 12, 1828, attesting to the destruction of Godfroy's barn, #15 on Anderson's map. See also: Dec. 11, 1828, affidavit of James Garrard of the County of Bourbon and State of Kentucky, taken at the request of Col. Godfroy and others of French Town in the Territory of Michigan, in relation to the occupation of said town by the American army and its subsequent destruction by the British and Indians in 1813.

576 Clarke, Peter Dooyentate. <u>Origin and Traditional History of the Wyandots.</u> Toronto: Hunter, Rose, 1870. Early Canadiana Online. It is merely a guess that this building was Godfroy's barn.

577 Excerpt from Colonel Henry Procter's Papers, National Archives of the United States, courtesy of Robert Burke: *"In these houses, burnt by the Americans, one of our men, Paschal Reaume, was burnt. He was missing after the engagement. The last time he had been seen was near these houses wounded. When search was made among the rubbish of the house, his body was found so disfigured that it could not be recognized, but was known by his pistols and other items. When he found himself wounded, he had crept into the house out of the way and had probably expired before the house was set on fire."*
Another possibility was offered by Barb Sandre, a descendent of Pascal Reaume, who posted on the French-Canadian Heritage Society of Michigan's Facebook page that he was shot on his uncle's (Jean-Baptiste Reaume's) property and crawled into his uncle's barn, which was then

Later, as the firing began to die down, the Kentuckians noticed a party of the enemy approaching the rear of Jerome's large, double barn, located a hundred yards north of the French Town pickets, near the road to Detroit.

Major Madison asked Major Garrard to find another volunteer to put Jerome's barn to the torch. It was within easy rifle shot of the American lines and could offer shelter to the British attackers.

It would not be easy to reach the barn, which was covered on the east by Indians firing from an orchard and fence. Canadians posted to the west, commanded the open ground between the barn and the Kentucky lines.[578]

Nonetheless, a man soon came running out from the American lines. Carrying a firebrand, he headed directly towards the barn across a hundred yards of open space. Native warriors and Canadian militiamen shot him down. Two other intrepid volunteers met the same fate.

The deadly challenge was then taken up by Ensign William Orlando Butler, from Hightower's company of the 17th U.S. Infantry. Grabbing some blazing faggots from a nearby fire, he passed within pistol range of the Canadian militia, protected only by a furious covering fire delivered by his comrades.

The Canadians were so astonished by the man's speed and audacity, however, that not one of them fired a shot as he calmly threw his torch into a pile of straw to set the barn on fire.

Retreating to the American lines, Butler looked over his shoulder and saw the fire was dying down. He turned around and ran back to the barn to fan the flames back to life and add more fuel to the fire. As he turned once again and raced towards the American lines, the Canadian militiamen

---

burned by the Americans. This would put him on the Reaume property at the far end of the line, near Godfroy's barn. According to military records, he was a corporal in Elliott's company of the 1st Essex Militia Regiment, so that unit may have participated in the fight that resulted in the retreat of the American right wing (contrary to my expectations). Rusty Davis has kindly pointed out that J.-B. Reaume, Sr., did indeed own P.C. 81, but had died in 1807, leaving his son, Joseph, in charge of his estate.

578 I am guessing that Major Reynolds took the 3 Essex flank companies to the far right of the British position while Lt. Col. St. George retained the hat companies on the left. The flank companies were led by Captains Caldwell and Elliott of the 1st Essex and Maisonville of the 2nd. The hat companies were under Mills and Buchanan of the 1st and Smith and Labute of the 2nd. It was not unusual for flank companies from different regiments to be combined together into an élite battalion. Of course, the companies could have been divided strictly by regiment, instead. At least, we know that Smith's company of the 2nd Essex was the first to enter the 17th infantry camp.

suddenly sprang into action, sending a hundred bullets flying in his direction. The valiant Kentuckian nevertheless managed to make it to safety. Only his clothes were riddled with bullets.

Ensign Butler, now securely back inside the fence, was enjoying the congratulations of his comrades when a musket ball flew over the pickets and hit him full in the chest. Falling backward, he pressed his hand over the painful spot and called out to Captain John McCalla, saying *"I fear this shot is mortal, but while I am able to move, I will do my duty."*

Butler's friends quickly rushed to his aid and were surprised when he greeted them with a smile. Opening his vest, he showed them where the spent bullet had been stopped by the thick wadding of his coat.

Although not a mortal wound, his breastbone had taken such a beating from the force of the ball, he would be in severe pain for several weeks.[579]

Jerome's barn was where a number of American casualties from the fight on the 18th had originally been placed, and where some of the dead had been left. Several Canadians and Indians ran towards the burning barn to see if they could put out the flames, but it was no use. By the time they had reached the rear of the building, fire was already engulfing the front.[580]

To the west of the American line, local *habitants* Benjamin Lenfant, John Paxton, Antoine Sargent, François Durgate, and François Cousino

---

579 "General Wm. Orlando Butler," from the History of Jessamine County, Kentucky, by Bennett H. Young: Corporal William O. Butler was a volunteer in Nathaniel G. Hart's Company of the Lexington Light Infantry, part of the 5th Kentucky. He was promoted to ensign and attached to Hightower's company, which took part in the fighting at French Town on January 18th and 22nd. Having survived his wound and subsequent captivity, Butler served as a captain at the Battle of New Orleans, where he was brevetted Major for his gallantry, and was an aide to General Andrew Jackson. After the war, he studied law, was elected to Congress, and ran unsuccessfully for governor of Kentucky. In 1846, President Polk appointed him a major general of volunteers, in which capacity he fought in the Mexican War. At the end of that war, he was Cass's vice-presidential running mate in the latter's unsuccessful bid for the presidency against Taylor and Fillmore. Butler died in 1880 at age 89.

580 "Reminiscences of an Actor in the War of 1812," Typed text. Algonquin Club. Taken from the Canadian Emigrant, 1835. Author unidentified. This account adds one other odd detail that is not found in any other: *"Some of the Canadian militia and Indians, who were not very far distant, perceiving the barn on fire, ran towards it. When they arrived a number of the wounded men were crawling out by the barn door; but when they saw the sanguinary savages standing before them, brandishing their war clubs, they crept in again, and were all consumed with the barn."* Some authors have suggested that the bodies of the Americans who died on the 18th were placed in the barn, and that the charred cadavers were found after the barn burned, thus giving rise to this story. Solo and Lebeau were buried on the 21st, but the frozen ground may have deterred other burials.

were sniping at the enemy from covered positions in and around Lenfant's old horse mill. Armed with rifles, and being good shots, they did considerable execution among the British and Indians as they surged around the American-held fence line.[581]

In particular, they singled out the gunners manning the British artillery in that sector. The artillerymen got some revenge, however, when an exploding howitzer shell caught the roof of the mill on fire, causing the occupants to tumble out of the upper floor of the building.[582]

The British took over Benjamin L'Enfant's barn, which then became the next target for an American firebrand. This time, British defenders managed to wound the Kentucky volunteer in three places and extinguish the flames before much damage was done.[583]

---

581 McAfee, Robert. History of the Late War in the Western Country. Bowling Green, Ohio: Historical Publications Company, 1919 (reprint of 1816 original edition.) pp. 254-3: The local settlers "... proved their fidelity again, by engaging in the battle of the 22nd. Whatever firing was done from the windows on that day, according to Procter, must have been done by the inhabitants..." Unfortunately, they may have contributed to British complaints that some of their wounded were inhumanely shot as they tried to crawl to safety.

582 Report of the House Committee of Claims on the petition of Jean–B. Jerome and others, Jan. 25, 1822: Benjamin Lenfant lost his dwelling house, furniture, grain, flour, and mill, located on the western edge of the battlefield. Lenfant, John Paxton, and Francois Dungate were at the mill on January 22, 1813, when part of Lewis' detachment was fighting from Lenfant's horse mill, which was on the battle ground, against the British and Indians, in consequence of which, the mill was burnt on the same day by the enemy. L'Enfant's house was burned a few days after the battle, obviously in retaliation, since the houses on the side next to him were spared. See also: Navarre clipping files, Monroe County Historical Museum Archives), (Peter Navarre dep., small coll., Monroe County Historical Museum Archives.)

583 Au, Dennis. War on the Raisin. Monroe: Monroe County Historical Commission, 1981, p. 41. Also: Deposition of John M. McCalla, Fayette County, State of Kentucky, Sept. 12, 1828. The Boerstler battle map shows a burned barn on L'Enfant's property, but that may have been his horse mill. Lenfant never claimed the loss of a barn.
There is one factor that may spread doubt about the roof of Lenfant's mill being destroyed by a shell burst (unless it was made of thatch). The British land service hand grenade, which was about the same size as the 3-pdr Howitzer shell, weighed less than 2 pounds and had a 1½ ounce bursting charge. Note that the 3-pdr howitzer was classed as such by reason of its muzzle diameter of 2.91 inches, not by the weight of its shell. See: "Remarks on the Evolution of the Sea Service 3-pounder Swivel Howitzer into the U.S. Army's King Howitzer, 1775-1820," by William E. Davidson.

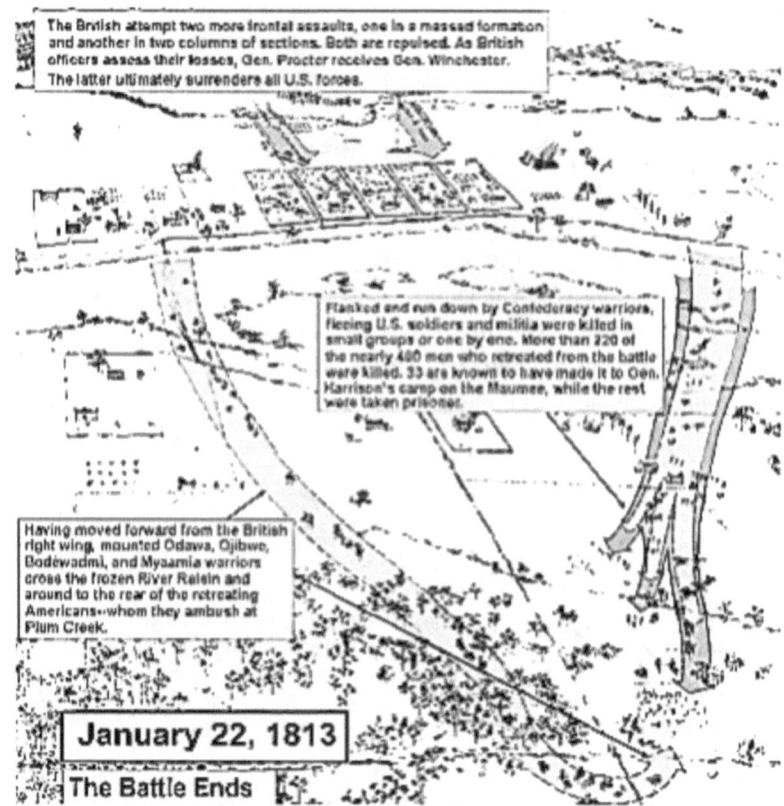

The British attempt two more frontal assaults, one in a massed formation and another in two columns of sections. Both are repulsed. As British officers assess their losses, Gen. Procter receives Gen. Winchester. The latter ultimately surrenders all U.S. forces.

Flanked and run down by Confederacy warriors, fleeing U.S. soldiers and militia were killed in small groups or one by one. More than 220 of the nearly 400 men who retreated from the battle were killed. 33 are known to have made it to Gen. Harrison's camp on the Maumee, while the rest were taken prisoner.

Having moved forward from the British right wing, mounted Odawa, Ojibwe, Bodéwadmi, and Myaamia warriors cross the frozen River Raisin and around to the rear of the retreating Americans--whom they ambush at Plum Creek.

January 22, 1813
The Battle Ends

From: "Native Ground, Middle Ground, Battle Ground: The River Raisin, the War of 1812, and the Course of North American History, A Historic Resource Study of River Raisin National Battlefield Park," prepared for the National Park Service by Mark David Spence, Ph.D., 2019, p. 233.

Provided Courtesy of the National Park Service
River Raisin National Battlefield Park

Winchester's Capture, 9 a.m., Between Plum (Mill) Creek and Otter Creek:

Having passed Plum Creek, also known as Navarre's Mill Creek, as it flowed along the rear of Navarre's old French claim, General Winchester, accompanied by his 16-year-old son, several officers, and about 40 or 50 men, appeared to have outrun the encircling Indians, but they were exhausted.[584]

Lieutenant Colonel Lewis reflected on the apparent coolness and calmness Winchester had exhibited throughout the action. Major McClenahan, on the other hand, had become impatient.

He estimated they were now 3 miles from the river. It seemed to him that both Winchester and Lewis were riding so slowly at the head of their infantrymen, that they could yet be caught.[585]

Lifting the wounded Capt. Glaves up behind him on his horse and taking his son, John, by the hand, McClenahan decided to make his escape.

He might have taken Capt. Price, as well, but was afraid his horse was too weak to carry them all. Abandoning the others, they left the road and struck out cross-country.[586]

Falling behind on the trail, the exhausted Captain Price was soon overtaken. His right arm rendered useless by a wound to the shoulder, the captain still gamely attempted to fend off the assault of 3 warriors with his sword. One of the warriors fell, as Price thrust his sword through his heart, but the other two grappled with him, killing and scalping him.[587]

---

584 Harrison to Secretary of War James Monroe, Official Letters of the Military and Naval Officers of the United States during the War with Great Britain in the Years 1812, 13, 14, and 15. Edited by John Brannan. Washington City: Wax & Gideon, 1823, p. 124.

585 Statement of LTC Lewis, Notices Vol. 1, Apdx 9, Extracts from affidavits in relation to the affair at Frenchtown, of the 22 of January, 1813, made by the late Governor Madison of Kentucky, Colonel William Lewis, and Major S. Garrard. Typed copy in Bidlack's Notes, Monroe County Historical Museum Archives. Glaves was wounded in both the hand and the upper jaw, from which he lost several teeth. He later received a disability pension of $10 a month and died in 1822.

586 McClenahan to Harrison, Jan. 26, 1813, in Official Letters of the military and Naval Officers of the United States during the War with Great Britain in the Years 1812, 13, 14, and 15. Edited by John Brannan. Washington City: Wax & Gideon, 1823, p. 132: McClenahan gives the wounded officer's name as Captain Graves, which could refer to Lt. Thomas Coleman Graves, serving in Hightower's company of the 17th U.S. Infantry. He was the younger brother of Major Graves. However, McClenahan says he took this officer to the safety of Harrison's camp. Unfortunately, Lt. Graves was killed in the battle. G. Glenn Clift has identified this officer as Captain Michael Glaves, who was listed as one of the fortunates who did escape. His company was in the 1st Kentucky Regiment, McClenahan's parent unit, and he may, like Matson, have been wounded in the fighting on the 18th. 18-year-old John McClenahan, was a private in Glaves' company.

587 Clift, G. Glenn. Remember the Raisin. Frankfort: Kentucky Historical Society, 1961, p. 65. Caldwell

Meanwhile, Captain Matson continued to struggle through the snow. He again caught up to General Winchester near LaPlaisance Creek, and asked him, for the love of God, to order a halt, but the worn-out general could only reply that the Indians were still in pursuit, and the men could not be rallied.[588]

The wounded captain last saw General Winchester, Lt. Colonel Lewis, Dr. Irvine, and Dr. Patrick going on, their horses much fatigued after retreating 3 miles, with the Indians still in pursuit.

They had been separated from their men upon encountering a fenced field. The men on foot went straight across, but the horsemen were forced to go around. It didn't look like they would be able to get away from the Indians who were approaching on fresh horses.[589]

---

was captured later that morning. Price's body was never found. One Indian showed a scalp to Caldwell, claiming it was Price's, but Caldwell "...*knew he was lying, for Captain Price was very baldheaded on the top of his head.*" See also: Letter Caldwell to Mrs. Price, Feb. 20, 1813, in History of Jessamine County, Kentucky, by Bennett H. Young: "...*the death of your brave and gallant son, Capt. James C. Price, who was killed and scalped by the Indians on the morning of January 22nd. He had been engaged in a severe skirmish early on the morning of the 17th. At 10 o'clock, he was ordered...to bring in all the wounded men and carry them in all the sleds beyond the reach of the Indians. In the discharge of his duty, Captain Price and myself, at the head of 50 men of our company, were attacked by a large body of Indians, who had concealed themselves in the timber, on the river bank...The Indians had succeeded in breaking the crust of the snow a mile above our camp, on the river, which was the only road through which we could reach the command of General Winchester, who had retreated about 3 miles and was awaiting the arrival of General Harrison. As soon as the Indians opened a heavy fire on us, we returned their fire and continued a rapid retreat to the main army under General Winchester over the only road on which the Indians...had early on the morning of the 18th succeeded in breaking the thick crust of the snow, which was 2 feet deep. In this trap we were caught. In getting away from the river, many of our men were killed and scalped before we got out of the deep snow. Captain Price was shot in the right shoulder by a musket ball, which disabled his right arm; he was attacked by 3 Indians; he ran his sword through the heart of one of them, but was soon overpowered, killed and scalped. Eight of our company, besides Captain Price, were brutally massacred; more than 30 got away...I had 5 bullet holes in my hat and clothing...*" Lt. Caldwell and most of Price's company were taken prisoner, thus surviving the retreat on January 22, 1813.

588 Atherton, William, Narrative of the Suffering & Defeat of the North-Western Army under General Winchester. Frankfort, Kentucky: A. G. Hodges, 1842, p. 46.

589 Knopf, Richard C. Document Transcriptions of the War of 1812 in the Northwest, Vol. V, pt. 2. Columbus: Ohio Historical Society, 1958. p. 27. This is Captain Matson's description. By contrast, Lossing places Winchester's capture at a bridge only ¾ of a mile from the village. Plum Creek is about a mile, as the crow flies, while Woodchuck Creek is about 4 miles. The farthest estimate of Winchester's capture puts him 8 or 9 miles from the camp. Some authors have Winchester being taken on his way from Navarre's house to the battlefield, but these ignore statements of his officers describing his presence during the retreat. The likeliest place to encounter fenced farms along Hull's Road would have been along LaPlaisance Creek, about 3 miles south of the Raisin, corresponding exactly to Matson's estimate of the distance.

When Matson saw the Indians were within a hundred yards of him, he took the opportunity of slipping through a nearby fence. Taking off his shoes, he ran along the fence for about 60 yards in a stooping position, and then hid himself in a bunch of tall grass. From there, he watched as the Indians raced by, stopping only long enough to tomahawk or scalp a straggler. By now, he guessed there were only about 50 soldiers continuing on ahead of him.[590]

About this time, Whitmore Knaggs found himself on foot, desperately trying to keep up with General Winchester and the others on horseback. Looking back, the general called out to him, *"Knaggs, jump behind me. Quick, get onto my horse behind me!"*[591]

Knaggs needed no second invitation; he jumped up behind Winchester. Two mounted officers followed behind. They went about 3 miles until they reached the frozen waters of Woodchuck Creek.[592]

As their horses slowly straggled onto the ice, they saw 7 horsemen approaching at a rapid pace.

Turning towards his passenger, Winchester asked, *"Knaggs, see those men? What shall we do?"*

"Well," Knaggs answered, *"What can we do? There are seven of them, and we are almost helpless here."*

Their pursuers numbered almost 20 by the time they caught up to them. Whitmore Knaggs threw up his hands and called out to them in several native dialects, offering to surrender. It turned out they were a band led by Jack Brandy, Lumpey, and George Blue Jacket.[593]

---

590 Knopf, Richard C. Document Transcriptions of the War of 1812 in the Northwest, Vol. V, pt. 2. Columbus: Ohio Historical Society, 1958. p. 27: *"...After the Indians had passed by, the captain then moved to a prairie, where he concealed himself till dark, and then pushed on to the Rapids, keeping a road a distance to the right. When he got there, the place was evacuated, and the houses and provisions on fire. He then went on to Defiance."*

591 Oct. 14, 1866 Peter Navarre Interview, Historical Society of Northwestern Ohio biographical field note 85. Navarre locates Winchester's capture near Plum Creek. Estimates of the road mileage from the River Raisin to Plum Creek range up to 2 miles. Official mileage on the 1818 military road map from the Raisin to Plum Creek is just 1 mile; LaPlaisance Creek, 2 miles; Woodchuck Creek, 3½ miles; and Otter Creek, 4½ miles. The road mileage published in the Weekly Register shows LaPlaisance Creek (Pleasant Town) at 3 miles from the Raisin and Otter (Beaver) Creek another 3 miles beyond that.

592 Wing, Talcott E., "History of Monroe County, Michigan," in Michigan Pioneer & Historical Collections, Vol. IV, 1881. Lansing: W. S. George & Co., 1883, p. 321.

593 "A Nonogenarian," The Detroit Free Press, May 3, 1891, p. 43, col. 1-4. This is an interview with James Knaggs, son of Whitmore Knaggs and nephew of the War of 1812 scout by the same

Lumpey, a Wyandot from Brownstown, was the first to catch up, followed by Blue Jacket and Brandy.[594]

George Blue Jacket had refrained from taking any scalps during the battle, though his brother James had taken several.[595]

Knaggs feared for his life, as he remembered having taken a whip to Jack Brandy during an argument some years before. As he rode up, however, Brandy called out with an oath, *"My friend Knaggs, you are my prisoner."*

In a forlorn gesture, General Winchester pointed his pistol at Jack and pulled the trigger. The weapon misfired with a loud click.

It could have been the general's last act, but Brandy just laughed and yelled, *"No good!"*

The general then addressed Blue Jacket, *"You must not take my sword from me; I will make you a present of it."* He also handed over his pistols.[596]

The offer Indians made prisoners of the entire group, including Winchester, his son Marcus, Col. Lewis, and Whitmore Knaggs.[597]

They stripped Winchester of his cocked hat and overcoat, which Brandy put on. His face painted in vermilion; Jack took on an odd air of authority.

The Indians gave Winchester a blanket in exchange, daubed some paint on him, and then led their captives away.

Shortly afterward, several Potawatomies and Ojibwas came up. Seeing Whitmore, they drew their tomahawks and rushed at him, screaming that he was responsible for killing one of their friends.[598]

---

name. *"...while he was an officer of the government the Indians still regarded him as their friend. He could speak nine languages. He was a fine linguist. He could speak the French, English, German, and he could speak the Shawnee, Delaware, Potawatomi, Ottawa, and Chippewa."*

Jack Brandy was also known as Samuel Rankin, according to the Draper Manuscripts. He was about 30 years old at the time of the battle, became a drunk in later years, and died in 1852. His Indian name was Te-Zau-Taah.

Lumpey, age 22, died in 1841. He was of the Deer Clan. Sometimes called Lump-On-The-Head, his name referred to the new sprouting of horns, which appeared as lumps on a deer's head.

594 Draper, 11-u.

595 Draper manuscript 17s.

596 Ross, Robert B., Edit., <u>History of the Knaggs Family of Ohio and Michigan</u>. Detroit: Clarence M. Burton, 1902: The full-stocked pistols were made in London. Blue Jacket later gave them to Capt. William Caldwell of Amherstburg.

597 Winchester fathered 14 children. Marcus was between 16 and 19 years old when he survived the battle. He later became a lawyer and the first mayor of Memphis, Tennessee. He was socially stigmatized for marrying a beautiful mixed-race French quadroon from New Orleans. See: Clift, G. Glenn, <u>Remember the Raisin</u>, Frankfort: Kentucky Historical Society, 1961, p. 209.

598 Draper interview with James, son of Whitmore, in 1863.

Whitmore pleaded for help, and Brandy bravely got between the warriors and their intended victim, saying they would have to kill him first.[599]

George Blue Jacket also joined in. He grasped Whitmore around the waist and swung him back and forth to ward off any tomahawk blows.

Brandy and George tried to cover Whitmore with their horses, but the Potawatomies tried to strike between the horses' legs.[600]

Eventually, the attackers tired of this, but one rather surly looking fellow stepped back, raised his musket towards Whitmore and pulled the trigger.

The shot went high, so he rushed forward with his tomahawk and flailed away at Knaggs over the backs of the horses.[601] Instead of hitting his intended victim, the Potawatomi managed to put a dent in the stock of George Blue Jacket's rifle.

Enraged, Blue Jacket turned and shot the offending warrior. The rest of the Potawatomies backed down.[602]

Later, Brandy and Blue Jacket would turn Winchester over to Roundhead, who took the general's waistcoat and sword and wore them.[603]

---

599 "A Nonogenarian," The Detroit Free Press, May 3, 1891, p. 43, col. 1-4. This is an interview with James Knaggs, son of Whitmore Knaggs and nephew of the War of 1812 scout by the same name: *"They were then taken to the Raisin and delivered to Gen. Proctor. They took my father and put him on board of a little sleigh and took him to Malden. My father was put in jail there, and as soon as Mr. Baubie heard my father was in jail, he applied to the commanding officer to let him out, and let him come to his house. He was a friend of my father, and said he would become responsible for any emergency. The request was granted. He was taken to Mr. Baubie's house, and staid there 3 days. Judge Woodbridge, of Detroit, took my mother and us boys in a sleigh to Malden (Amherstburg) to see my father before he left. It was a pretty sad meeting. My father stayed there 3 days, and then he was sent as a prisoner of war to Quebec. He remained there some ten or twelve months."* See also: Michigan Pioneer and Historical Collections, Vol. I, 1896, 2nd edition. Lansing: Robert Smith, 1900, p. 362.

600 Michigan Pioneer and Historical Collections, Vol. I, 1896, 2nd edition. Lansing: Robert Smith, 1900, p. 362. See also: Ross, Robert B., Edit., History of the Knaggs Family of Ohio and Michigan. Detroit: Clarence M. Burton, 1902: François Navarre, also taken prisoner, had admitted to Colonel Procter that Whitmore Knaggs had broken his parole and fought against the British during the battle. Whitmore replied he had merely been staying at his brother James' house upriver on his way to visit his family in Detroit. His presence at the River Raisin was merely a coincidence. Procter mistrusted Whitmore Knaggs and had him taken to Amherstburg in chains. François Baby, however, used his influence to have Whitmore released into his custody. Although he had once been assaulted by Whitmore, Judge Woodward also tried to procure his release, and the captured General Winchester provided an affidavit attesting that Knaggs was never a member of his army. Procter remained unconvinced. In July, Whitmore was sent off to prison in Québec and remained in custody until 1814, when he was included in a prisoner exchange.

601 James Knaggs Interview, Historical Society of Northwestern Ohio biographical field note 134-5.

602 Hosmer, Hezekiah, Early History of the Maumee Valley, Toledo: Hosmer & Harris, 1858, p. 40.

603 Historical Society of Northwestern Ohio biographical field note 148. I am interpreting this to be

It would be Roundhead who would have the honor of delivering the captured officers to Colonel Procter.

U.S. Regular Infantry crossing the Winchester Street Bridge during the 2013 Commemoration
Photo Courtesy of the Pontious Family.[604]

Hull's Road, 9-10 a.m., January 22, 1813:

Meanwhile, Ensign Isaac L. Baker, attached to Edwards' Company, 17th U.S. Infantry, estimated he had covered a good 3 miles in their retreat. He

---

the case, assuming Winchester had only one uniform coat at the Raisin, which he left behind in the confusion of leaving his headquarters that morning.

604 This photo was taken on the 200th anniversary of the Battle of the River Raisin. Oddly, there was no ice or snow on this particular January morning, but there was a cold winter wind that greeted the 300 participants, all clad in the uniforms and clothing of the period.

The bridge is located approximately at the point that General Winchester crossed over the icy river while trying to rejoin his command. In the absence of solid ice, the bridge came in handy.

and another officer led the last group of 40 soldiers towards a creek where they were cut off by mounted warriors. Behind them, they could see Indians tomahawking soldiers on the road.[605]

Baker ordered his men to take cover for a final stand, knowing their resistance would be short. Exhausted from running through the deep snow, those who still retained their weapons had barely five rounds left apiece.[606]

Ahead of them, from across the stream, chief Otussa stepped forward and called out to them in English, offering them quarter if they surrendered, which they agreed to do, handing over their remaining muskets.[607]

As soon as the pursuing Indians came up, however, they killed half the prisoners, disregarding all of Otussa's pleas to have mercy on their captives.[608]

The disastrous retreat of the right wing had cost the American army their highest-ranking leaders and a good 40% of their manpower. As many as 400 men were involved in the retreat, including Wells' battalion of up to

---

605 It's tempting to think the second officer was Lt. William Caldwell of Price's company of the Jessamine County Blues, who stated *"We were completely routed and all of our army taken prisoners. General Procter, the British commander, suffered the savages to kill and scalp more than twenty of our soldiers after we had surrendered."*

606 Draper notes of interviews, YY-6. See also: Au, Dennis. War on the Raisin. Monroe: Monroe County Historical Commission, 1981, p. 37.

607 Oct. 14, 1866 Peter Navarre Interview, Historical Society of Northwestern Ohio biographical field note 83: *"Otussown captured Capt. Baker at Plum Creek, south side of the Raisin, about a mile and a half, where were 300 Americans, mostly killed."* As the crow flies, however, Plum Creek is only a mile south of the River Raisin. I have combined several accounts to come up with this description of Baker's capture. It is possible this took place as far south as Otter Creek, where John Hunt claimed to have found 20 bodies a year after the battle. Otter Creek is well beyond the 1½ mile distance in Navarre's statement, and even beyond Baker's, who claimed to have retreated about 3 miles from French Town, which would put his surrender on La Grande Coulee, or LaPlaisance Creek. Baker put the time of his capture at 9 a.m., leaving only about an hour to cover the 5 miles from the River Raisin to Otter Creek through deep snow. He says they were running, not walking, however, and does not mention making any stops or participating in any attempted stands, since they were trying to escape from the Indians, who were tomahawking the hindmost.

608 Knopf, Richard C. Document Transcriptions of the War of 1812 in the Northwest, Vol. V, pt. 2. Columbus: Ohio Historical Society, 1958. p. 64: In his narrative, Baker says *"On the morning of the 22nd January, I was captured by the Indians, about 9 o'clock, with another officer and about 40 men. Closely pursued by an overwhelming force of Indians, we were endeavoring to effect our escape, and had obtained a distance of about 3 miles from Frenchtown... withal the men being very much wearied with running through the deep snow, we concluded it best to accept the chief's proposition. Accordingly, we assembled around him and gave up the few remaining arms that were still retained in the flight... I was led back towards the river along the road we had retreated in. The dead bodies of my fellow comrades, scalped, tomahawked, and stript, presented a most horrid spectacle to my view. I was at length taken to a fire near Col. Proctor..."*

250 regulars and militia, along with as many as 150 militiamen and volunteers who had left the French Town pickets. Of these, roughly 220 had been killed, 150 taken prisoner, and 33 escaped, including only 3 of the officers.[609]

British positions, between 10 and 11 a.m., January 22, 1813:

It was after 10 a.m. at the field dressing station, and Captain Tallon was limping over to Dr. Faulkner's *cariole* to find a place to sit down, when he noticed Lt. Bender come in. Tallon asked him if he were wounded, and Bender replied that he wasn't, but that he had been sent to collect stragglers. The captain told him to take a look around, and he wouldn't see anyone who was not bleeding or disabled. So, the lieutenant moved on and was able to gather 7 or 8 men who were not too badly wounded and send them back to the firing line.

On his way to the aid station, about 600 yards from the ravine, he had met Private John Nettles. Nettles was in charge of a king's horse and sleigh, with spare ammunition for each of the guns.[610] One of the guns had been pulled back about 200 yards behind the ravine, and one was still back near the surgeon. This was the only sled in sight, so Bender had ordered Nettles to find some musket ammunition, and take it forward to the ravine.

On his return, some time before noon, Lt. Bender caught up with Nettles, who was having trouble getting to the troops. Bender stepped out in front of the horse and set off at a brisk pace, telling Nettles to come along.

It was no easy task to move the ammunition sled. The horse was very skittish and the open fields were intersected by fences. Bender and Nettles

---

609 Au, Dennis, War on the Raisin, Monroe: Monroe County Historical Commission, 1981, p. 39. Piecing together various reports, we find some, but not all, of the members of the following companies and regiments were involved in the retreat: McCracken's, Matson's, Bledsoe's, Brasfield's (Kelley's) and Simpson's companies of the 1st Rifle Regiment; Glaves' company of the 1st Kentucky Volunteer Regiment; Meade's, Edwards', and Hightower's companies of the 17th U.S.; Langham's company of the 19th U.S.; and Price's company of the 5th Kentucky. Captain Wiley Brasfield had resigned and Lt. Joseph H. Kelley was promoted to captain in his place. I'm assuming that both Captain Richard Hightower and Ensign William O. Butler remained with Hightower's volunteer company inside the pickets after the battle on the 18th, while 1st Lt. Thomas Graves and 2nd Lt. Ashton Garret led the regulars of Hightower's original company in the retreat of the right wing on the 22nd.

610 Testimony of Lt. Bender, Proceedings of a Court Martial, Holden at Quebec, for the Trial of Lieutenant Benoit Bender, of the 41st Regiment of Foot, in July, 1815, Montreal: J. Lane, 1817. Courtesy Jim Yaworsky.

had to make a hole in each of the fences in order to get the sled through to his men, who were behind a barn and some out-buildings half a mile away.

As they moved along behind the ravine, they were exposed to sniper fire from the fenced area, about 200 yards away. Four or five Kentuckians rose up, took careful aim, and fired all together at the ammunition sled. A nearby militiaman fell with a mortal wound. Bender helped Nettles remove a railing, and then they drove down onto a small bridge that crossed the ravine where it angled back northward, away from the river.

About this same time, Bender was spotted by Captain Robert Mockler, who had been checking on the status of the right wing after the 41st had made its last charge. His detachment of Royal Newfoundlanders was now resting under cover of a barn several hundred yards further off.

Mockler had counted about 50 infantrymen left out of the original 121 in the right wing. About 20 dead and several wounded were visible in the open field. The others had been taken to the dressing station far in the rear.[611]

As he surveyed the dispirited soldiers of the 41st, he could see no officers among them. Glancing off to his left, however, in the open area beyond the ravine, the captain noticed Lt. Bender.

Mockler saw that the lieutenant had taken cover behind a small sled, about 40 yards from his men and 80 yards from the French Town picketing, from which the Kentuckians were still taking pot shots at him. On the sled was a field magazine, providing a 3-foot-high shelter against enemy fire. A number of wounded lay nearby, but Lt. Bender's face was to the ground, so it was hard to tell if he had been hit.

Mockler called his name and asked if he were wounded. Without moving, Bender yelled back that he was all right, but his horse was wounded and his men were about out of ammunition.

Upon hearing this, Mockler demanded to know what he was doing out there, when he should be standing with his men.[612]

---

611 Brown, Samuel, Views of the Campaigns of the North-Western Army, Troy, N.Y.: Francis Adancourt, 1814: Brown stated the British regulars made 3 charges, advancing by platoons. He also stated the attack started at reveille, with the American army composed of 800 effective soldiers; 600 in the picketed areas and 200 in the open. Some of those retreating from the right flank made it 3 miles before being overtaken and wiped out. (Samuel R. Brown was a veteran of the Siege of Fort Meigs, as well as a newspaper publisher.)

612 Testimony of Capt. Robert Mockler, Proceedings of a Court Martial, Holden at Quebec, for the Trial of Lieutenant Benoit Bender, of the 41st Regiment of Foot, in July, 1815, Montreal: J. Lane,

Bender answered that he had not been there for very long. Captain Mockler then yelled at the lieutenant, ordering him to get up immediately and rejoin his command. Turning to Bender's men, he told them to head down the ravine towards a barn occupied by Mockler's own detachment.

With bullets still landing around him, Lt. Bender stood up and called to Noonan to continue on with the ammunition. He then ran quickly back to the ravine, while Mockler moved off to the right. After collecting his men, Bender led them along the ravine to about a hundred or so yards from the barn.[613]

Madison holds out, between 10 and 11 a.m., January 22, 1813:
Within the pickets, the Kentucky sharpshooters were still rejoicing as they thought they had eliminated the ammunition sled's horse and its driver. Many estimated the distance at between 300 and 400 yards.

For some time, they had also been annoyed by a howitzer firing from a small house east of their camp, about 40 rods (220 yards) from the river, on the road to Detroit. At 200 yards, the Kentuckians were able to pick off 13

1817. Courtesy Jim Yaworsky. In dispute at the trial was whether Lt. Bender was hiding behind an object, and if there was a horse present, either wounded or dead. Mockler was the only person who testified to have seen both the sled and the horse. If true, it is more likely that Mockler noticed him while he was guiding the ammunition forward, rather than when he was actually leading his troops.

In the British army, it was considered un-soldier-like for an officer to flinch or duck when he heard the bullets whizzing past his head. Rather, he should inspire courage in his men by his erect and confident bearing. However, it was common to station most of the unit's officers behind an advancing line to give them some protection and to enable them to prevent men from straggling or running away. See: Noseworthy, Brent, <u>Battle Tactics of Napoleon and his Enemies</u>, London: Constable & Co., 1995, pp. 41, 238.

613 It is hard to pinpoint exactly where Lt. Bender, the sled, and Bender's men were in relation to each other at this moment. The ravine (also described as a swale) was not exactly parallel to the French Town fence line, but angled towards it, and then curved away, before finally turning to empty into the marsh or into the River Raisin. In the 20th century, Mason Run was channeled during the construction of the paper companies, so that its present-day course no longer precisely follows the original ravine. It is difficult, when comparing different accounts, to tell if Bender's men retreated to their left, down the ravine, or to their right.

Nor is it clear which barn Mockler's Newfoundlanders were sheltered behind. My guess is that the Newfoundlanders were behind the burned out remains of Godfroy's barn, while Bender's men were in the ravine and behind Jerome's barn, which had also been destroyed. If we assumed the movement was in the opposite direction, however, then Mockler's men would be behind Lenfant's barn or horse mill. Similarly, there was some confusion as to Col. Procter's location at any given time, except when he came near to the 41st to observe their last charge. Did he station himself on the right, on the left, or keep continually on the move? Was he one of the British officers that appeared at the Robert house to check on the pursuit of the American right flank?

of the 16 men on the gun and force the British to pull it back. Well outside rifle range, the howitzer could still hit the fence, but did little damage. It and a second gun stationed to the right of the Kentuckians would eventually cease fire.[614]

The wounded men in one of the hospital buildings saw Indians taking shelter in the riverbed and in some houses on the south side of the river. From there, they could snipe at the Kentuckians. Several Kentuckians were shot, and others were inhibited from moving freely about inside the picketed area.

Captain Hart was rushing hatless from one danger point to the next, and yelling, *"Huzzah boys. Kentucky will be proud of us!"* He was hit as he entered an open four-foot-wide lane between the pickets and the front of Couture's house.[615] A detachment was quickly sent to dislodge the Native snipers.[616]

Ammunition was dwindling, so Majors Madison and Garrard took a supply of cartridges from Jerome's bake house, wrapped them in their pocket handkerchiefs, and laid a handful on the ground at the foot of each man, urging everyone not to give up.

---

614 Darnell, Elias. A Journal Containing an Interesting and Accurate Account of the Hardships, Sufferings, Battles, Defeat, and Captivity of Those heroic Kentucky Volunteers and Regulars, Commanded by General Winchester, in the Year 1812-1813. Paris, Kentucky: 1813. (As reprinted under the title "Remember the Raisin" in Captured by the Indians, edited by Frederick Drimmer, Dover Publications, New York, pp. 256-267).: *"After a long and bloody contest, the enemy found they could not, either by stratagem or force, drive us from our fortification. They retired to the woods, leaving their dead on the ground, except a party that kept two cannons in play on our right. A sleigh was seen going towards the right, three or four hundred yards from our lines, and we supposed it was laden with ammunition to supply the cannon. Four or five men rose up and fired at once, and killed the driver and wounded the horse. Some Indians who were hid behind houses continued to annoy us with scattering balls."* Note: This description does not agree with the Boerstler map, which shows two cannons in play on the American left. It does agree with the statements from Bender's court-martial, except in regards to the distance at which the Kentucky sharpshooters fired. Also, if a house were located east of their camp, it wouldn't exactly be on the road to Detroit, although Hull's Road did curve to the northeast. It could be that at this moment, Procter was repositioning his artillery to enfilade both ends of the American line.

615 "Massacre of the River Raisin," by A. Burlingame, The New World, New York, June 17, 1843. Capt. Hart may have been attended by his black servant, Isham, but there is no mention of him till after the battle, when he is a prisoner of the Indians. His main duties during a battle would have been tending to his master's horse and personal property, but he also could be bringing water, food, or other items to the firing line. He could also serve as a nurse if his officer was wounded. Some, of course, could end up joining in the fight, especially if circumstances became dire.

616 Atherton, William. Narrative of the Suffering and Defeat of the North-Western Army under General Winchester. Frankfort, KY.: A. G. Hodges, 1842, p. 51. The riverside of French Town was not heavily picketed, but probably had some minor fencing.

While handing out the ammunition, Major Graves was wounded in the knee. Limping to a nearby tent, he sat down and began to bind his wound. As he did so, he shouted, *"Boys, I am wounded. Never mind me, but fight on!"*[617]

The firing then began to peter out. Still, the occasional shot from, or at, a prowling warrior kept everyone apprehensive and on the lookout. Now the men had time to think about what might have happened to the troops of the right wing. They had been seen to retreat, and heavy firing had been heard to the south. Captain Price and his men had been sent after them, and now, they too, had disappeared.

The anxious Kentuckians began to speculate, some saying that General Winchester was probably holed up somewhere, or even that his men had joined up with Harrison's reinforcements and were now marching up Hull's Road on their way back to rescue them. Others, however, cried out in panic, insisting they were all now cut off.[618]

As for the local *habitants*, many had joined the Kentuckians in the fight, but others had been intercepted by the Indians while on their way to the battle. Antoine Momini was among those who had advanced towards the sound of battle that morning. Despite liberal doses of whisky, his arm still ached with the pain of the wound he had suffered in the fighting 4 days earlier.

Still, he thought he could be of some help, but he soon changed his mind when he encountered some *habitants* fleeing down the road with their belongings piled on a sled. They told him the battle was already lost.[619]

Momini decided to join the refugees heading south towards the Maumee River. Perhaps there, he could hook up with the remnants of the Northwestern Army under General Harrison.[620]

---

617 Darnell, Elias, A Journal Containing an Interesting and Accurate Account of the Hardships, Sufferings, Battles, Defeat, and Captivity of Those heroic Kentucky Volunteers and Regulars, Commanded by General Winchester, in the Year 1812-1813, Paris, Kentucky: 1813. (As reprinted under the title "Remember the Raisin" in Captured by the Indians, edited by Frederick Drimmer, Dover Publications, New York, pp. 256-267.)

618 Atherton, William, Narrative of the Suffering and Defeat of the North-Western Army under General Winchester, Frankfort, KY: A. G. Hodges, 1842, p. 50.

619 Journal of Lewis Bond, in Knopf, Richard C., Document Transcriptions of the War of 1812 in the Northwest, Vol. X, pt. 1. Columbus: Ohio Historical Society, 1962. p. 195. Bond says, speaking of those local *habitants* who *"fought in this battle, two were killed, and some effected their escape with about 20 of the party who had retreated to the Miami Rapids…"*

620 Affidavit of Antoine Mominee, August 19, 1852. Pension Application Files, War of 1812, Death or Disability, The National Archives "Old War" Invalid and Widow Rejected File No. 16545, copies in Monroe County Historical Society Archives, courtesy Steve and Chris Momany. *Antoine Mommini*

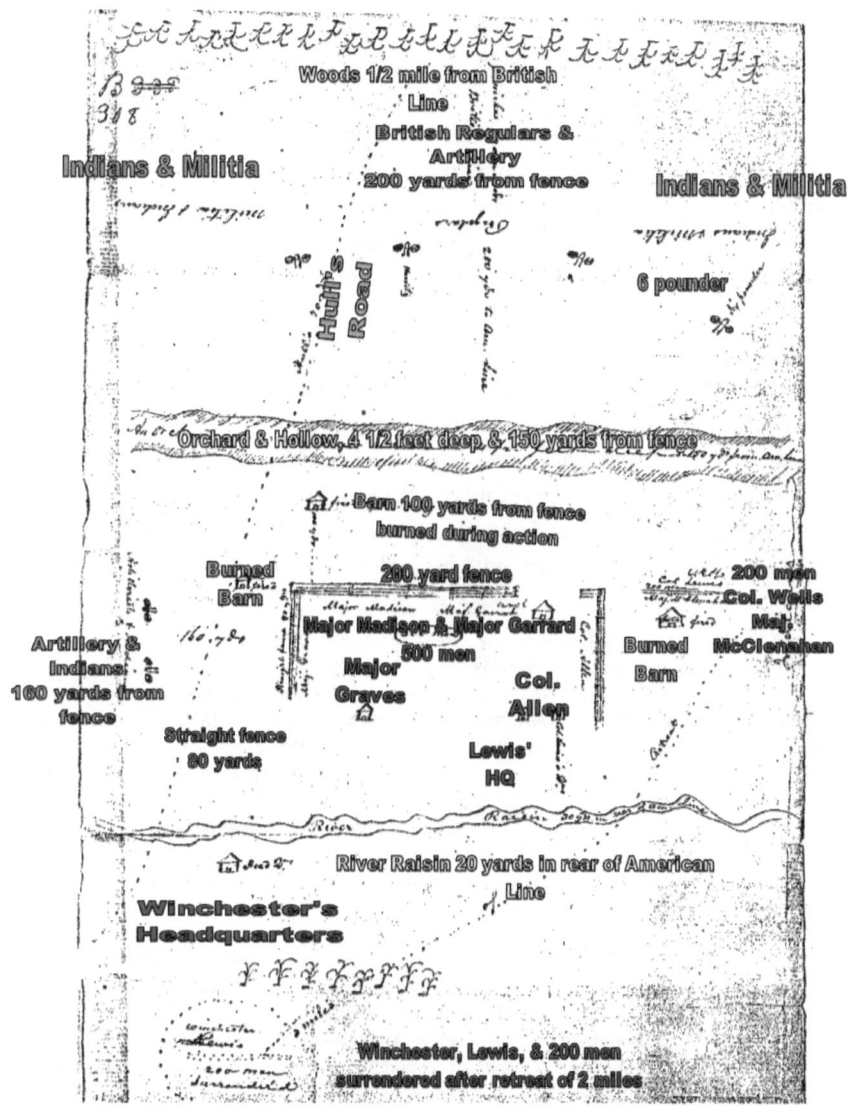

Reproduction of Boerstler's Sketch Map of Battleground
Based on interviews with American prisoners released by the British
Clarke Historical Library, Mount Pleasant, Michigan
Not to scale / Author's notations are based on the writings on the original map

***En route* to Colonel Procter, between 10 and 11 a.m.:**

Joseph Robert was relieved that the British officers were gone. Several of them had shown up after the American retreat to observe the situation in the rear of the American position. He had overheard them comment that if the Americans did not retreat, they would have to surrender, as they were probably nearly destitute of ammunition and provisions.

Between 10 and 11 o'clock, Robert saw a man resembling General Winchester being led past his house by the Indians. He was dressed in a white shirt and wore a handkerchief on his head.[621]

Outdoors, next to an open fire, Private John Hamilton also saw the captured Winchester pass by, along with other prisoners taken by the Indians, all "stripped of their honors and apparel."

He was wondering if he would ever see them again, when the Potawatomi who had earlier taken his knife and overcoat suddenly reappeared, deliberately cocked his weapon, and aimed it at Hamilton. He was only forestalled when Hamilton presented him with his remaining coat.[622]

---

and his comrade, Louis Drouillard would eventually go on to Urbana to join Colonel Johnson's Regiment of Mounted Rangers and participate in the Thames Campaign.

In the chapter, "Michigan Men in the War of 1812," Antoine Mominie is listed as a private in Lacroix's Company from May 18, 1812 to August 16, 1812. There is also an Antwain Momeni in Reading's Company of Kentucky Mounted Infantry from May 20, 1813 to November 19, 1813, and a Private Antoine Momine serving in Lee's Company from October 22, 1813 to April 21, 1814. The latter dates of service slightly overlap, but that does not preclude them from being the same man. If so, it would appear that Antoine was not as severely wounded at the River Raisin as reported. *Antwain* is probably the phonetic English spelling of how speakers of the local French dialect pronounced *Antoine*. See: Barnett, Le Roy and Roger Rosentreter, Michigan's Early Military Forces, Detroit: Wayne State University Press, 2003, p. 126.

621 Deposition of Joseph Robert, Aug. 22, 1818, in the William Henry Harrison Papers, on microfilm at Central Michigan University: Robert estimated it was about 3 hours after the Kentuckians retreated past his house. On the other hand, François Navarre noted it was about 2 hours after the retreat began when he recognized the horse that he had loaned General Winchester being led past his house by a crowd of Indians. He could just barely make out the figure riding upon the horse's back. The man was in his shirtsleeves and had only a handkerchief covering his head. Navarre could not help but exclaim aloud, *"Mon Dieu, My God, le général est prisonier."* This might mean the Indians did not immediately turn Winchester over to Procter. See: Deposition of Francis Navarre, Aug. 22, 1818, in the William Henry Harrison Papers, on microfilm at Central Michigan University.

622 Antrim, Joshua, History of Champaign and Logan Counties, Bellefontaine, OH: Press Printing Co., 1872. Hamilton was also cheated out of a small sum of money by a French-Canadian sutler who offered to safeguard it for him and return it once Hamilton was released at Detroit. Hamilton never saw him again, probably because his captors took him to a distant village, about 9-days' travel away, where he would remain until January 1, 1814.

Roundhead delivered General Winchester and Lt. Colonel Lewis to the British, clad only in their shirts, pants, and boots.[623] Winchester wrote a note to Procter, asking to see him, and Procter assented.[624]

To Winchester's relief, once they were properly introduced, Procter assured them of their safety and asked Roundhead to restore their clothing.[625] He then demanded that Winchester surrender his troops at discretion.[626]

General Winchester could not help but reflect on the harrowing experience he had just undergone.[627] The situation for those still holding out in French Town had to be desperate.

By this time, Colonel Procter had established a strong position on the American right flank, which had been vacated by the 17th U.S. Infantry.[628]

The British colonel asked Winchester if he were the commanding officer of the Americans. Winchester replied that honor had been his. Procter then said, *"Some of your troops, sir, are defending themselves from the fort in a state of desperation. Had you not better surrender them?"*

Winchester replied, *"I have no authority to do so. My command has devolved on the senior officer in the fort, as you are pleased to call it."*[629]

623 Peckham, Miss Harriet L., Local History by the Class of '96, Monroe High School. Monroe: Monroe Commercial Print, 1896. Navarre either escaped the retreat or was captured and released.

624 Winchester, James. Historic Details Having Relation to the Campaign of the North-Western Army under Generals Harrison and Winchester. Lexington: Worsley & Smith, 1818, p. 38.

625 Captain William Caldwell claimed that Roundhead protected Winchester and did not take his hat, coat, and waistcoat. See: Clarke, Peter Dooyentate. Origin and Traditional History of the Wyandots. Toronto: Hunter, Rose, 1870. Early Canadiana Online.

626 Hosmer, Hezekiah L. Early History of the Maumee Valley. Toledo: Hosmer & Harris, 1858, p. 38.

627 Among the officers killed in the retreat were Captains Price, Simpson, Edmiston, and Mead, as well as Doctors Irvine, Montgomery, Davis, McIlvain and Patrick. See: Dudley, Rev. Thomas P. "Battle and Massacre at Frenchtown, Michigan, by one of the Survivors," in Historical and Archaeological Tracts, Number 1, Cleveland: Western Reserve Historical Society, 1870. Some information on Dr. McIlvain was supplied by his family: He was born in Maryland in 1785. Years after his death at the River Raisin, some friendly Indians gave the doctor's horn drinking cup and a large powder horn to his father, which has been passed down through relatives in the Thomas Clarke family.

628 Bulckley, John M. History of Monroe County, Vol. 1, p. 59.

629 Winchester, James, Historic Details Having Relation to the Campaign of the North-Western Army under Generals Harrison and Winchester, Lexington: Worsley & Smith, 1818, p. 38. *"I have the means of setting fire to every house in the village, without risk to myself, and may thus soon and safely reduce the party which so unwisely attempts to defend it. But in this case, what will be the fate of the inhabitants, men, women and children, and of the American militia associated with them? Such as may escape the fire of our musketry and cannon will unavoidably fall to the tomahawks of our allies, whom it will be impossible to restrain in the heat of action…May I never witness such a spectacle. But, need I tell you, that private feelings cannot be indulged at the expense of public duty;*

Nevertheless, Procter continued to press the captured general, arguing that the fall of French Town was inevitable. But if Winchester surrendered the troops immediately, Procter would restrain the Indians and thereby guarantee the safety of the prisoners, their wounded, and the civilian population.[630]

Finally, Procter posed the question plainly: *"I have therefore to submit to you a single and short proposition containing the only remedy the case admits of, and that is that in your quality of commanding General, you will immediately surrender to me French Town and the garrison it contains."*[631]

Winchester replied, *"I have told you, sir, that I have no authority over them, but if you will send a flag, I will recommend to the commanding officer to surrender himself and his troops prisoners of war, on the additional conditions that the private property of the troops shall be protected, and the side arms of the officers returned. It was to make this proposition that I desired an interview with you."*[632]

Threatening the Flanks, between 10 a.m. and noon, January 22, 1813:

After almost an hour of effort, Private Nettles found the 41st scattered about behind some old log buildings. He saw Col. Procter, but nobody seemed to be in charge. The ammunition was off-loaded in the course of an hour.

The artillery ammunition was in square boxes, but the musket cartridges were packed in kegs. Nettles broke in the head of a banded quarter cask and poured its contents of ball cartridges onto a blanket.

Some soldiers helped themselves, but complained that the cartridges were American buck and ball. The smaller caliber balls and added buckshot made for less accurate, more barbaric projectiles.[633]

Once the ammunition was distributed, the men took occasional pot shots at the enemy, contrary to orders. Both sides remained under cover as much

---

and that, however agreeable it would be to me as a man to avoid the employment of means so terrible in themselves as those I have suggested, yet as an officer, I cannot be justified in omitting to do whatever may be necessary or useful to the king's service...."

630 Au, Dennis, <u>War on the Raisin</u>, Monroe, Mich.: Monroe County Historical Commission, 1981, p. 42.

631 Armstrong, John, <u>Notices of the War of 1812</u>, Vol. I, New York: George Dearborn, 1836:

632 Winchester, James, <u>Historic Details Having Relation to the Campaign of the North-Western Army under Generals Harrison and Winchester</u>, Lexington: Worsley & Smith, 1818, pp. 38-9.

633 Testimony of General Procter, <u>Proceedings of a Court Martial, Holden at Quebec, for the Trial of Lieutenant Benoit Bender, of the 41st Regiment of Foot, in July, 1815</u>, Montreal: J. Lane, 1817. Courtesy Jim Yaworsky.

British Troops Reloading at the 200th Anniversary of the Battle
Courtesy of Dave & Sue Grassley / Floral City Images

as possible. Lt. Bender would remain with his men until the battle ended, at which point he would be sent to count the British dead and wounded.

All through the battle, Colonel Proctor had been circulating behind his lines, observing the action and adjusting his plans accordingly. He had spent quite a bit of time near the right wing of the British regulars, which had been broken in attacks against the French Town fences.

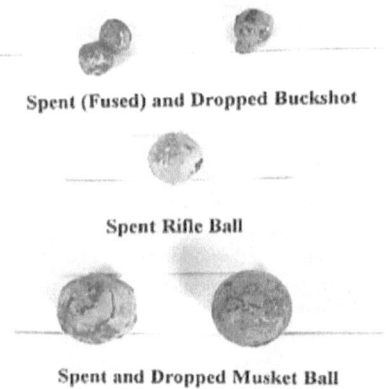

Spent (Fused) and Dropped Buckshot

Spent Rifle Ball

Spent and Dropped Musket Ball
Relics of the Battle of the River Raisin

Recognizing that the unproductive frontal assaults against the fence line were undermining his army's morale, Procter decided to shift the bulk of his remaining redcoats towards the American flanks.[634]

It would take time to reassemble all the Indians, who were still returning from hunting down the remnants of the American right wing, but he already had two artillery pieces positioned west of the village. These, he had covered by transferring more Canadian militia to his right.

The militiamen formed a line parallel with the road leading towards Detroit and tried to take possession of some farm buildings near enough to the western fences to serve as cover.

Procter planned to set up a new command post to the west of this line, near where Hull's Road crossed the ravine as it angled off to the northeast.

As for the rest of the artillery, two of the guns were out of action. They had been spiked and abandoned in front of the fence line.

That left the reserve cannon and the single gun that had been withdrawn by Lt. Irvine. One was positioned along Hull's Road, while the other was moved into the area vacated by the retreating U.S. 17th Infantry, about 200 yards east of the village and an equal distance north of the river.

No Man's Land, between 11 a.m. and 3 p.m., January 22:

After over 4 hours of mayhem, a relative quiet had descended on the battlefield, although a hidden *habitant* occasionally fired from high in the upper story of a house. The firing from the cannon that had been placed a couple hundred yards down river finally ceased. The men, who had fought the battle on empty stomachs, now began to look for food. Fresh bread was handed out from the commissary's house.[635]

---

634 There is some confusion in the testimony whether all of the British regulars withdrew to their left flank. Richardson, for instance, said they retired towards the American left (British right) under cover of some houses. Locations are unknown for several lieutenants of the 41st, including 25-year-old Lt. Clemow. Known as "Jemmy Jessamy," the delicate, foppish, almost effeminate Englishman was absolutely fearless under fire and was bearing up well, although covered with wounds. With him were two younger lieutenants, the handsome foreigner, Harris Hailes, and the dedicated punster, William Watson.

635 Darnell, Elias, A Journal Containing an Interesting and Accurate Account of the Hardships, Sufferings, Battles, Defeat, and Captivity of Those heroic Kentucky Volunteers and Regulars, Commanded by General Winchester, in the Year 1812-1813, Paris, Kentucky: 1813. (As reprinted under the title "Remember the Raisin" in Captured by the Indians, edited by Frederick Drimmer, New York: Dover Publications, pp. 256-267.)

In the distance, a party was seen approaching with a white flag. The sentry allowed them to advance within 30 yards from the fence, when he ordered them to halt or he would fire. They halted instantly.

Between two British officers, however, there stood a man who appeared to be a prisoner. The man bent over and wrote in pencil on a piece of paper supported on his knee. The sentry sent a soldier out to bring in the note.[636]

Twenty minutes passed before there was a reply. Major Graves had been wounded and taken to Jerome's house, so Majors Madison and Garrard went out to meet the flag bearer, accompanied by Captain McCalla.

They had expected the British to ask for a truce to take off their dead and wounded, many of who were still lying exposed on the open ground in front of the pickets. They were instead surprised when Dr. James Overton, Jr., Winchester's aide-de-camp, informed them that he was with the general until they were captured, and that Winchester was advising them to surrender.[637]

Madison and Garrard were somewhat taken aback at this news. They had hoped Winchester and his men had rallied and were waiting for reinforcements. Anyway, the remaining Kentucky militiamen and their leaders were still defending themselves very well within the pickets of French Town.

They had driven back every assault, inflicting heavy casualties on the British regulars, while losing only five men killed and less than 40 wounded. With 384 men still able to fight, not counting non-coms and officers, how could they think of surrendering? The instructions from their captured general, no doubt, had been extorted from him under pressure.[638]

---

636 Deposition of Joseph Robert, in the William Henry Harrison Papers, on microfilm at Central Michigan University: Robert states the prisoner could have been Winchester, himself, and that the British officers were invited inside the picketing. He claimed the negotiations lasted up to 3 hours.

637 Winchester to Sec. of War, Jan. 23, 1813, Typed copy in Bidlack's Notes, Monroe County Historical Museum Archives. "...I understood that our troops were defending themselves in a state of desperation, and...being desirous to preserve the lives of a number of our brave fellows who still held out, I sent a flag to them and agreed...with the commanding officer of the enemy that they should be surrendered prisoners of war on condition of being protected from the savages, allowed to retain their private property, and having their side arms returned to them."

638 "Battle of Frenchtown," Kentucky Reporter, March 13, 1813, typed copy in Bidlack's Notes, Monroe County Historical Museum Archives: "...384 of our men who remained behind the garden fence, exclusive of non-commissioned officers and those bearing commissions, were surrendered prisoners of war." See also: Hosmer, Hezekiah L., Early History of the Maumee Valley, Toledo: Hosmer & Harris, 1858, p. 38. The captured general's authority to surrender them was unclear, and his advice probably coerced and misrepresented by his captors.

Upon reflection, however, the officers were not all that sure of their ability to hold out indefinitely. They had no way to reply to the bombardment of the remaining enemy cannons, which, although not terribly effective, were now stationed in enfilading positions on both flanks.

The fence line had been much battered, and it appeared the British might even be able to use their howitzers to set French Town's buildings on fire. In addition to today's losses, there were another 50 or so wounded from the fight on the 18th who had to be cared for.[639]

Of even greater concern, their reserve ammunition supply had dwindled to a third of a keg of cartridges, while many of the men on the line had barely two or three cartridges left in their boxes. Their 3 highest ranking officers had all been killed or captured, and there was no sign that help was on its way.[640]

Most of the Indians had now returned from their pursuit of the American right wing and many joined their brothers who were infiltrating the wooded areas across the river. French Town was completely surrounded and cut off.

Upon communicating with the other officers left within the stockade, it was determined that their situation was now untenable. Captain Hart, in particular, insisted they must surrender to save both soldiers and citizens from a massacre by the Indians.

The troops were shocked by the decision to surrender. Some tearfully pleaded with their officers not to accept the humiliation, saying they preferred to die fighting.[641]

The officers decided that they would not ask for terms until they had spoken directly with their captured general. Returning to the open ground, they demanded to see him.[642]

---

639 Brown, Samuel, Views of the Campaigns of the North-Western Army, Troy, N.Y.: Francis Adancourt, 1814: Brown visited the battlefield later on during the war and found the fences completely shattered by the enemy's shot and human bones still bleaching on the ground.

640 McAfee, Robert. History of the Late War in the Western Country. Bowling Green, Ohio: Historical Publications Company, 1919 (reprint of 1816 original edition.) p. 236.

641 Darnell, Elias A Journal Containing an Interesting and Accurate Account of the Hardships, Sufferings, Battles, Defeat, and Captivity of Those heroic Kentucky Volunteers and Regulars, Commanded by General Winchester, in the Year 1812-1813. Paris, Kentucky: 1813. (As reprinted under the title "Remember the Raisin" in Captured by the Indians, edited by Frederick Drimmer, Dover Publications, New York, pp. 256-267.) *"We had only five killed and twenty-five or thirty wounded inside of the pickets. When the British came in, they asked what we had done with our dead, as they saw but few on the ground. A barn had been set on fire to drive the Indians from behind it, and they concluded that we had thrown our dead into these flames to conceal the number."*

642 "The Weekly Register," No. 24 of Vol. III, Feb. 13, 1813, in: Price, Wilma. The Battle and Massacre of

Winchester was brought forward, but kept at a distance, guarded by an Indian, and not allowed to communicate directly with his officers.

Madison was then escorted to Colonel Procter, where he made his final demand, *"We will not surrender without a guarantee for the safety of the wounded, and the return of side-arms to the officers. We do not intend to be dishonored."*[643]

Procter, somewhat ruffled by Madison's demeanor, then asked, *"Do you, Sir, claim the right to dictate what terms I am to offer?"*

Gritting his teeth, Madison said, *"No, but I intend to be understood as regards the only terms on which we will agree to surrender. We prefer selling our lives as dearly as possible rather than be massacred in cold blood."*[644]

Medard Labadie watched as the delegation carrying a white flag passed 3 times back and forth between the lines, over the course of more than an hour. Two Wyandots had surprised and taken him early that morning as he and a companion were rushing from their homes to the sound of the guns.[645]

Labadie couldn't understand much, but from what he overhead among the Indians, Colonel Procter was demanding an unconditional surrender, but the Kentuckians were holding out for better terms.[646]

---

the River Raisin; Excerpts from the Niles Weekly Register of Baltimore. Monroe: Monroe County Historical Society and Library Commission, 1981:"...*to the gallant captain Hart, the beloved of all who knew him, we are perhaps, indebted chiefly for the preservation of the lives of those taken prisoners, by the determined stand he took, forcing a capitulation.*" See also: Armstrong, John. Notices of the War of 1812, Vol. I. New York: George Dearborn, 1836. Madison swore to his men, *"We shall... perish, if such must be our fate, in a free and full use of our arms, unless the British commander will come under a solid engagement that private property shall in all cases be respected; that the side arms of officers shall be restored...at Amherstburg; that the wounded shall be promptly and securely transported to that fort; and that...a guard sufficient for their protection shall be assigned to them.*"

643 Lossing, Benson J., The Pictorial Field-Book of the War of 1812, Glendale, New York: Benchmark Publishing Corporation, 1970, p. 360.

644 Dudley, Rev. Thomas P., "The Battle and Massacre at Frenchtown, Michigan, January, 1813." Historical and Archaeological Tracts, No. 1, Cleveland: The Western Reserve Historical Society, August, 1870. This is an account related by one of the Kentucky survivors of the battle.

645 Medard Labadie put the start of negotiations at 11 a.m., and Dennis Au concludes they terminated about noon. John Nettles estimates 3 or 4 hours later. Lt. William Caldwell of the Jessamine Blues recalled being marched off at 12 o'clock. Jean-Baptiste Jerome estimates an hour between the receipt of Winchester's orders and the actual surrender. British time estimates seem consistently later in the day than do the American ones, sometimes up to a couple hours. Local *habitants* tend to be even earlier than the Americans, by perhaps an hour. A national standardized time with which to synchronize watches was not introduced into Britain until 1847 and the United States not until 1883, largely in order to coordinate railroad schedules.

646 Deposition of Medard Labadie, Extract of Letter from General Harrison to the Secretary of War,

Procter knew his force was too small to round up all his prisoners, care for the wounded of both sides, and still fend off Harrison's approaching army. He agreed in rather vague terms to Madison's conditions. Nothing was put in writing, but Madison accepted Procter's word as an officer and gentleman.[647]

The Horse Barn, January 22, 1813:

Towards the end of the battle, Peter Navarre and his brothers Jacques, Robert, Antoine, and François had taken refuge in a horse barn. It was Peter's birthday. He had just turned 28, but wondered if he would be getting any older.

Robert Navarre was the first to pose the awful question, *"Que faut-il faire? What should we do? If we surrender or get captured, they'll hang us."*

"Let's run," replied Peter, without hesitation. *"Better a bullet, than a rope."* But which way should they go? Their homes on the Maumee beckoned, but the way south was swarming with Indians. The Navarres decided to head east into the marshes and then out onto ice-covered Lake Erie.

Most of them were out of ammunition, so they reluctantly left their rifles behind as useless encumbrances. They would have to depend on their knives and tomahawks if they had to make a last-ditch defense.

Being dressed like the Indians, the Navarres hoped to slip away while the enemy was occupied with rounding up the Kentuckians. Unfortunately, they were spotted and ran off in a hail of whistling musket balls.

A large number of Indians chased after them, but the Navarres were all good runners and had a head start. With Peter yelling, *"Legs, now do your duty,"* they quickly out-distanced their pursuers.

Once in the grassy marshes, the Indians gave up the chase. The moccasin tracks of the Navarres blended in with earlier tracks made by Native American war parties, making it difficult to follow their trail.

The ice was beginning to break up at the mouth of the Raisin, leaving growing cracks covered by a watery film. It was frightening, but the fear of being captured was greater. The fleeing brothers managed to jump from one ice flow to another until they reached more solid ice.

---

dated Feb.11, 1813, #28 in <u>Barbarities of the Enemy, exposed in a Report of the Committee of the House of Representatives, and the Documents accompanying said Report,</u> Troy: Francis Adancourt, 1813, pp. 136-9. Labadie would eventually be released. His father would take his family to Detroit on the 24th of January.

647 Lossing, Benson J., <u>The Pictorial Field-Book of the War of 1812,</u> Glendale, New York: Benchmark Publishing Corporation, 1970, p. 357.

They then walked across the lake to Cedar Point, where they were able to rest a few minutes. From there, they took a circuitous route through the woods, back to their homes at Presqu'ile. That evening Robert would sneak back to the Raisin, to see what had become of the settlement.

Meanwhile, Peter and Jacques hitched some ponies to a sleigh and evacuated the family, heading eastward along the ice to Fort Stephenson off Sandusky Bay. The 36-mile journey took 30 hours through frightful weather.

Leaving their families there, the brothers turned westward by way of the Portage River and reported to General Harrison.[648]

The Surrender, between Noon and 3 p.m., January 22:

While the surrender negotiations were underway, Lieutenant-Colonel François Navarre was at his home, wondering what he should do next. Shortly after the firing had ceased, a British officer had called upon him with a request for the coat that General Winchester had left at headquarters that morning. Supposing a surrender was in the offing, Navarre requested an audience with Colonel Procter so that the civilian inhabitants of French Town could be included in the surrender terms and be placed under British military protection.

When Navarre met with the British commanders, Colonel Elliott of the British Indian Department asked him if the wounded Americans could be distributed among the inhabitants throughout the settlement. Navarre was suspicious of Elliott, so he replied only that "...he would see about it."[649]

---

648 Hosmer says this scene happened when the Navarres saw the Americans surrendering. Dennis Au places the scene of their escape at the Navarre Mill during the retreat of the right wing, rather than during the formal surrender, which was perhaps a more sensible time for the Navarres to have skedaddled. Hosmer, Hezekiah Lord, Early History of the Maumee Valley, Toledo: Hosmer & Harris, 1858, p. 38. See also: "Peter Navarre," by George W. Pearson, 1905, and "Recollections of a Pioneer," in the Family clipping files of the Monroe County Historical Museum Archives. Also housed there: "Statement of Peter Navarre," 1869, Small Collection 16.

649 Deposition of Francis Navarre, Aug. 22, 1818, in the William Henry Harrison Papers, on microfilm at Central Michigan University: *"The deponent further states that he was informed by a British Indian interpreter and some Indians, also by a man by the name of St. Germain, that a council was held among the British officers and it was concluded that as provisions were scarce and the prisoners numerous, it was best to abandon them to the Indians, and they accordingly were instructed to return to River Raisin and burn and destroy every house in which was an American. This the deponent in his own mind conceived to be the reason why the British wanted the prisoners distributed among the inhabitants one or two in each house."* The destruction of most of the settlement would thus be legitimized by reason of their being used to shelter the U.S. military.

Colonel Procter was rather evasive about protecting the *habitants*, but he did reiterate Elliott's proposal for the wounded to be accommodated in the homes of French Town. Navarre replied they could best be cared for if they remained in the four buildings that they currently occupied.[650]

In preparation for the surrender, the British officers collected their troops and reformed them on the open ground, then marched them across the front of the village. The Americans bitterly followed suit, marching out from behind the pickets to the place where they would ground their arms.[651]

The Indians immediately rushed in behind them to ransack and plunder the camp. Some harassed the wounded left in the buildings, insulting them and taking their belongings.

William Atherton stayed inside the pickets to take care of his comrades, John Locke and Jesse Fisher, both of whom had been badly wounded. Atherton was also hurt, but could walk, if not bear arms. Passing around the front of a house to watch the surrender, he noticed the Indians tearing up the army's tents and gathering everything left behind, whether clothing or knapsacks.

As the Kentucky troops marched onto the surrender field, Indians swarmed about them as well, grabbing at their belongings and menacing them with their tomahawks.

Major Madison, mounted on his horse, rode up to Procter and asked, "*Is this the way, sir, you observe the terms on which we surrendered?*" Procter answered that there wasn't much he could do, to which Madison retorted, "*Then, sir, I can. Boys, stand to your guns!*"[652]

At that moment, a warrior grabbed at the major's saddle, but Madison gave him a whack with the flat of his sword, and he quickly ran off. Colonel Procter then waived his sword and called on the warriors to back off. At this point, the Indians withdrew, leaving the Kentuckians unhindered. The effect, however, was to be short-lived.

---

650 Au, Dennis, War on the Raisin. Monroe: Monroe County Historical Commission, 1981, p. 45.

651 Accounts differ as to the exact location of the surrender. A sign currently marks the spot on the corner of Noble and North Dixie, just north of the location of the lot once owned by Godfroy and Beaugrand, along the old road to Detroit. At the 1872 veteran's reunion, however, it was said the surrender took place in the woods around Winchester's headquarters on the other side of the river. (It is assumed the veterans were recollecting where some of the troops were captured by the Indians.) Another description places the surrender about 20 rods (110 yards) from the house of François Lasselle.

652 "War of 1812," Monroe Commercial, March 23, 1871, citing the Pittsburgh Gazette.

Short, dark-complexioned Laurent Durocher was within hearing range of Major Madison as the latter addressed the troops, pointedly repeating the terms he thought had been agreed upon.

Colonel Procter said nothing, but made no objection. General Winchester then asked Procter to leave a guard for the wounded. The British colonel replied rather coolly that they would all be taken care of.[653]

As the Kentuckians surrendered their arms and rejoined the ranks, one soldier jumped up on a stile-block and said to the English: *"Well, you have taken the greatest set of game cocks that ever came from Kentuck."*[654]

Another soldier, Sergeant Simon Shover, would later claim such antics had saved him from being killed by the Indians when he was captured. The warriors would laugh and call him crazy whenever he jumped up on a stump or log, flapped his arms, and, in a clear, shrill voice, imitated a rooster crowing.[655]

---

653 Winchester, James. Historic Details Having Relation to the Campaign of the North-Western Army under Generals Harrison and Winchester. Lexington: Worsley & Smith, 1818, pp. 42-44. One youth who had been taken by the Indians managed to approach Procter and Winchester, imploring them for mercy, his arms bound behind him with a rope that extended into the hands of his captor. The young man, barely more than a boy, offered Procter anything he should ever possess in life, if only he would order him to be placed among the prisoners in British hands. He added that his widowed mother was dependent on him at home, and her heart would be broken if he never returned. Winchester insisted to Procter that it was his duty as an officer to intercede, appealing to his sense of mercy and justice, which caused the bemused British colonel to reply, *"Ah, do you acknowledge that there are such things in existence as British justice and magnanimity? I am glad to hear it. There is no danger for the young man. The Indians never hurt a prisoner. Moreover, the Indians took him, and we never force prisoners from them."*
See also: Lossing, Benson J., The Pictorial Field-Book of the War of 1812, Glendale, New York: Benchmark Publishing Corporation, 1970, pp. 357-360. Stung by certain criticisms the British made against the conduct of the United States during the Civil War, Lossing, in the course of finishing his book on the war of 1812, could not help but comment that the treatment which subsequently befell the wounded Americans *"...will always appear darkly in the history of nations as a crime against humanity, and a libel upon the character of the overwhelming majority of the English people. The employment of bloody savages to butcher their relatives in America...should forever close the lips of the English government when it attempts to lecture others on humanity..."*

654 Atherton, William, Narrative of the Suffering and Defeat of the North-Western Army under General Winchester, Frankfort, KY.: A. G. Hodges, 1842, p. 54. A stile block was used by people, especially women, as an aid in mounting or dismounting a horse or pony cart. A stile can also be defined as steps or ladders that allow people, but not animals, to cross a fence or obstruction.

655 Simon Shover also claimed that Col. Procter had allowed the Indians to abuse and insult General Winchester. Shover was an orderly sergeant in Langham's company of the 19th U.S. Infantry. After the war, he would tell entertaining stories to his neighbors at husking bees, barn raisings, log rolling, and militia musters. For the price of a dram of whisky, he would give a spine-tingling war whoop. Simon claimed he would live a hundred years, but he died at a community poor farm at

Although confidence had been somewhat restored, the prisoners still made a miserable sight. With unkempt hair and dirty faces, they shivered in their linen and cotton hunting frocks. Their slouch hats had lost any semblance of shape, and the only warm, wool garment they had was usually a dirty blanket wrapped around their waist and across their shoulders.

The officers didn't look much better. Often the only way to tell them apart from their men was by their fancy daggers and short rifles, and by their swords, which the privates didn't carry.[656]

Even the buff-colored Kentucky battle flag was torn and bedraggled, but still proudly proclaimed the state motto, "United We Stand."[657]

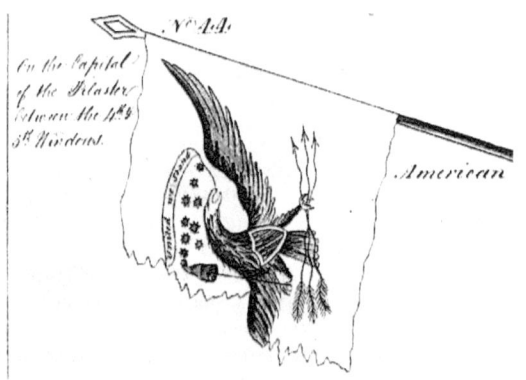

Sketch of an American flag said to have been captured at the River Raisin
Displayed as a trophy in the Royal Hospital, Chelsea England

---

age 79. See: The History of Union County, Ohio, containing a history of the county; its townships, towns ... military record; Chicago, W. H. Beers & co., 1883, pp. 430-431, available on-line at Hathi Trust, reference courtesy of Antoine Helou, River Raisin National Battlefield Park.

656 Casselman, Alexander Clark, Richardson's War of 1812, Toronto: Coles Publishing Co.: *"It has already been remarked that it was the depth of winter; but scarcely an individual was in possession of a great coat or cloak, and few of them wore garments of wool of any description..."* It should be noted that by the time Richardson saw the prisoners, many had been deprived of some of their garments. Some of the surrendered arms were of high quality; General Winchester gave up a very "handsomely-mounted" pair of pistols into the care of John Richardson, to prevent the Indians from taking them. Were these the same pistols supposedly taken by Blue Jacket?

657 The Kentucky flag captured at the Raisin was displayed in the Chelsea Hospital in England. It no longer exists, but a drawing was made. Courtesy: John M. Trowbridge, Kentucky Military History Museum. See also: Chartrand, René, Uniforms and Equipment of the United States Forces in the War of 1812, Youngstown, NY: Old Fort Niagara Association, 1992, p. 117.

Home of Rachel Knaggs, Jan. 22, 1813:

In her seventies, but still feisty, Rachel Knaggs stood off to the side as Indians swarmed through her house. She was shaking from cold and from fear of being punished for harboring a fugitive from Winchester's army.

Soon, the warriors found a soldier hiding in an empty, 63-gallon, hogshead barrel. After dragging the poor wretch away, the Indians plundered her house. They also seized her warm capote and hauled her off to see Colonel Procter.

Procter was not at all sympathetic to Rachel's plight, recognizing that she was the mother of several sons who were vehemently hostile to the British.

At least two of them were violating their parole under the terms of Hull's surrender. One of the latter, Whitmore, had been captured in arms during the morning battle. Procter peremptorily ordered Rachel to get out of town.[658]

He also ordered her son Thomas and her daughter Rebecca taken into custody.[659] Thirty-four years old and single, Rachel's large and athletic daughter Rebecca was normally a good-natured, fair-skinned blond, but she could also, at times, be just as stubborn and outspoken as her mother.

Another of Rachel's sons, James, was a scout in the American army, but fortunately, he had not been attached to Winchester's army and was safely out of harm's way. His wife, Polly Robert, however, was still in French Town. Prior to the battle, she took their 3 children and sought sanctuary in the Lasselle house. As an extra precaution, Antoine Lasselle cached James' first-born son, George, in the chimney above the fireplace.

Although lightly clad, Rachel Knaggs had no choice but to obey Procter's directive to leave the settlement. She would make the trip to her relative's house in Detroit in an open French *traineau*. When questioned about her ordeal, and how she endured the cold journey at her age, she answered, "*My spunk kept me warm.*"[660]

---

658 Rachel argued that Whitmore was not a combatant, and thus not violating his parole, but merely visiting his mother while on private business in French Town. She blamed Francis Navarre for blowing her son's cover. Despite the intervention of Judge Woodward and Colonel François Baby, Whitmore Knaggs was sent to Quebec, where he spent 10 months in captivity.

659 Knaggs, May, "Memoir of James Knaggs" in <u>Michigan Pioneer and Historical Collections</u>, Vol. XVII, 1890, 2nd edition, Lansing: Wynkoop, Hallenbeck, Crawford Co., 1910. Little is known of Thomas Knaggs, but he served in Jacques Martin's company in 1812 and was reportedly a guide for General Winchester. Born in 1782, it is uncertain at what date he married Catherine Pouget. Another son, William Knaggs, was also listed as a private in Martin's company in 1812.

660 Wing, Talcott E., "History of Monroe County, Michigan," in <u>Michigan Pioneer & Historical Collections</u>,

It was probably fortunate that it was Colonel Procter who was deciding the fate of the Knaggs family. Several Native warriors had grudges against them for past insults, and there was a definite feud going on with Colonel McKee, the British Indian agent at Malden, who had previously been beaten up by William Knaggs at Roche de Bout.

By this time, Procter had become thoroughly disgusted with the inhabitants of the River Raisin. This damnable Rachel was about the worst of the lot, but they all displayed a dangerous fondness for the American cause and an annoying nonchalance for following the terms of their parole. Besides the Knaggs family, he had also detained Captain Hubert Lacroix, Lt. Ambrose Charland, and Isaac Ruland. Within a few days, he would order all the families that remained to leave the Raisin. He would even consider asking the Indians to kill any people who stayed and to destroy anything they left behind.[661]

Vol. IV, 1881. Lansing: W. S. George & Co., 1883, p. 321. Polly's son, George, was about 7 years old, her son, James, was about 2, and her daughter, Jemima, barely 15 months.

Wing claims that Col. John Anderson was at his trading post at the time. When he heard of Winchester's capture, he broke open the liquor casks in his cellar and hid himself in a neighbor's barn, leaving his wife behind to protect their family and property from the Indians. I have found no independent, contemporary reference that he was in French Town at the time of the battle, however, and believe this incident happened after Hull's surrender of Detroit the previous summer. Anderson fled town in August of 1812 when vengeful warriors had threatened to cut off his hands.

Rachel's other daughter, Elizabeth, was the wife of John Anderson. In later years, the story was often told of how the Indians came into Elizabeth Anderson's home, as she sat on a chest containing the family fortune with her 3-year-old, Alexander, sitting on her lap. One of the invaders threatened her with his tomahawk, but she refused to budge, defiantly opening the top of her dress and daring him to strike her, if he dared. In admiration for her courage, the warriors left her alone. The only contemporary evidence that the Anderson home was invaded and ransacked, however, was in the summer of 1812. One of their properties was burned at that time, and the other became a British and Indian headquarters. The earliest mention I have found of this incident being connected to the battles in January 1813 is in Mrs. Anderson's obituary, which leads me to suspect the timing of the event was confused over the years.

See: Ross, Robert B., Edit., History of the Knaggs Family of Ohio and Michigan. Detroit: Clarence M. Burton, 1902: Her daughter Elizabeth also fled to Detroit with her 3 children, feeling it would be safer for them there. Rachel stayed with her relatives and gradually went back into the fur trading business, returning to the River Raisin, where she had a farm up river. Rachel dealt heavily in bears' oil, which was used for cooking, dressing a salad, and even grooming the hair. She is supposed to have died in 1815, on a trading expedition to Green Bay, where she also owned a store.

661 Lossing, Benson J. The Pictorial Field-Book of the War of 1812. Glendale, New York: Benchmark Publishing Corporation, 1970, pp. 361-2.

Rachel Knaggs and Family traveling by *traineau* to Detroit
From a Painting by Fran Maedel
Courtesy of the National Park Service, River Raisin National Battlefield Park

Maumee Rapids, 32 miles from the River Raisin, 3 p.m., January 22, 1813:

It had been about 3 hours since General Harrison had received his first word that Winchester's forces had been attacked at the River Raisin that morning and had been forced to retreat. A messenger had come in about noon with word from one of the columns marching to reinforce Winchester.[662]

Harrison immediately set out with his staff to overtake Payne's detachment of 300 Kentuckians who had set out that morning for the River Raisin. That detachment had originally attempted to reach French Town on the ice, but found the going too rough and had doubled back to take Hull's Road.[663]

---

662 Letter Harrison to Shelby, Jan. 24, 1813, typed copy in Bidlack's Notes, Monroe County Historical Museum Archives. Harrison wrote from his camp at the Carrying River, 15 miles from the Maumee Rapids that: *"As soon as I was informed of the attack upon General Winchester, about 12 o'clock on the 22nd instant, I set out, to overtake the detachment of Kentucky troops that I had sent that morning to reinforce him, and I directed the only regiment that I had with me to follow. I overtook Major Robb's detachment at the distance of 6 miles; but before the troops in the rear could get up, certain information was received of General Winchester's total defeat."*

663 Statement of Colonel Lewis, Notices Vol. 1, Apdx 9, Extracts from affidavits in relation to the affair at Frenchtown, of the 22 of January, 1813, made by the late Governor Madison of Kentucky, Colonel William Lewis, and Major S. Garrard. Typed copy in Bidlack's Notes, Monroe County

Now, more refugees were coming in, having escaped across the ice on their *carioles*. They all agreed that the army had been surrounded and cut off by 7 in the morning and was by now totally defeated.

The *habitants* reported seeing Winchester fleeing with a few exhausted officers. His men, having thrown down their weapons, had become easy prey as they were pursued by Indians on horseback and shot down as they ran.[664]

Soon, Colonel Andrews came marching up with Perkin's other regiment of 350 Ohioans. Their addition gave General Harrison a formidable relief force.

Furthermore, Cotgreave's Battalion was within a few miles of them. In total, the Americans had some 900 men relatively close at hand. Harrison debated whether he should take the fastest route along the ice, or head up Hull's Road, along which Winchester's men were last seen retreating.

Unfortunately, Colonel Cotgreave's men were nearly worn out. They had marched 12 miles towards the River Raisin, and were within 15 miles of the battlefield, but had turned back after learning of Winchester's defeat.

Besides, it was the unanimous opinion of Generals John Payne and Simon Perkins and the field officers that it was too late to save Winchester. If they advanced to the Raisin, they would risk losing their own force for no reason.[665]

Historical Museum Archives.

664 Letter Harrison to Monroe, Jan. 24, 1813. Typed copy in Bidlack's Notes, Monroe County Historical Museum Archives: *"About 12 o'clock on that day, I was informed at the Rapids by a messenger from an officer who was marching a detachment to reinforce Gen'l. Winchester that the General had been attacked that morning and that the Frenchman who brought this intelligence supposed that our troops were retreating. I had then with me a regiment of Ohio militia about 350 strong. Two detachments were on the way to join Gen. Winchester, but had taken different roads. One of 200 Ohio troops were marching on the edge of the lake, and the other, 300 strong, were pursuing Hull's road. Leaving directions for the regiment in camp to follow me, I proceeded on and overtook the detachment of Kentucky troops in about 5 miles.*

Additional information was now received that French citizens were flying in considerable numbers in carioles upon the ice, and about 3 o'clock, some of the fugitives began to arrive. All agreed that the defeat was total and complete; that the troops were nearly all surrounded and cut off or taken by 7 o'clock; that General Winchester was seen retiring a few miles from the river Raisin along Hull's trace with a few men and two or three officers, all of whom were entirely exhausted; that they were pursued by Indians on horseback who were constantly thinning their numbers by firing upon them and that our men were unable to resist as almost all of them had thrown away their arms.."

665 Letter Harrison to Monroe, Jan. 24, 1813. Typed copy in Bidlack's Notes, Monroe County Historical Museum Archives: *"...as there could be no doubt of the total defeat of Gen'l. Winchester, there was no motive that could authorize an immediate advance but that of attacking the enemy, who were*

Therefore, Harrison reluctantly ordered the main body of his army to turn back, but sent ahead a select force of 170 of the most active volunteers to assist any of Winchester's men who had gotten away.

Very few were found. Most of the survivors had escaped by heading towards the lake and following its margins south. From them, he learned that all resistance at the Raisin had ceased.[666]

Eventually, General Harrison began to wonder who would be held responsible for the disaster, so he began formulating a rationale for his actions. It was, after all, Winchester's decision to take French Town, made without Harrison's knowledge and consent.

Harrison could rightfully claim that once the ill-fated enterprise had been engaged, he had done all in his power to support Winchester. Surely Colonel Wells, who had managed to avoid the battle, altogether, would be eager to testify to Winchester's mistakes and to their efforts to save him.

Although Harrison felt his actions were justified, he knew that some of his military or political rivals might be tempted to point out that, despite his talk of a winter campaign against Detroit, he had taken no definite steps in that direction.

His hesitation had thus allowed one of his subordinates to exercise the initiative he might have shown, or so it would seem to those who discounted all the logistical problems that Harrison needed to overcome.

---

reported to be greatly superior in numbers and were certainly well provided with artillery; that after a forced march of 32 miles, the distance from our then position from the River Raisin, the troops would be too much exhausted to encounter the enemy..."

666 Letter Harrison to Meigs, Jan. 24, 1813. Typed copy in Bidlack's Notes, Monroe County Historical Museum Archives: "A detachment to the amount of 170 of the most active men was sent forward with directions to proceed as far as possible to assist those who were fortunate enough to escape; there were however but few, the snow was so deep that the fugitives were entirely exhausted in running a few miles; those that did get off effected it by turning down to the lake and secreting themselves. ...I know not what proportion the prisoners of General Winchester's late troops bear to the killed; some of the French who have come in report the latter at 500 and others at 800. The detachment amounted to near 1,000."

Le Fourche aux Cygnes, **Bay Creek Village, 3 p.m., January 22, 1813:**

A half-dozen narrow, ribbon farms stretched out from the edges of Bay Creek as it flowed on its southeasterly course towards North Maumee Bay. Above each of the bark-roofed log cabins, thin whisps of smoke rose from the exterior chimneys which were built of clay and sticks. The individual homesteads appeared like miniature fortresses, secured by heavy plank doors and shutters, and surrounded by six-foot-high palisades of split timbers.

Around 3 in the afternoon, Leslie Combs and a young soldier came riding down a track gouged out of the snow by *carioles* that had passed through the settlement a few days before. The two men had met at Major Cotgreave's camp the previous night when the soldier had borrowed a pack horse in an effort to rejoin his company at the River Raisin. They left camp by moonlight early that morning, and had just arrived.

Leslie Combs was greatly alarmed to find the whole population there in a state of bewildered consternation. The local *habitants* had received the news of the disaster that had befallen Winchester's army, and they were expecting bands of victorious warriors to descend upon them at any moment.

Combs also found a couple of Kentuckians who had escaped the carnage of the battlefield and were attempting to reach the safety of General Harrison's army. He decided to send them on ahead on a single pony, to inform Cotgreave, and then go on to General Harrison.

Most of the families who possessed horses or oxen loaded up their sleighs with a few belongings and headed out onto the frozen surface of Maumee Bay. But not the Tessier family, whose oxen were unshod. They hesitated to risk injuring their precious team on the slippery, jagged ice.

Combs told the Tessiers the road south was clear. The family gratefully accepted when the Kentuckian offered to escort them. Obviously, Combs and his companion could not continue to the Raisin, so they decided it would be best to fall back in the direction of Cotgreave's advancing troops.

Unfortunately, the oxen were so slow they only traveled 5 or 6 miles before the light began to fade. Although Combs feared they would soon be overtaken by the Indians, he realized they could make no further progress in the dark. Everyone was tired and cold. In the frosty twilight, they made camp and built a fire to keep Madame Tessier and her four children warm.

They remained there till after the moon rose, and then recommenced their plodding, southerly pace. Eventually they reached Cotgreave's camp, only to find it deserted. An abandoned wagon and a disabled cannon were all that remained to give silent testimony for what had been a very hasty retreat.[667]

Not all the *habitants* left the bay settlement at the same time. That morning, 19-year-old Angelique Martin Charland had been watching anxiously out her window, holding her baby Ambrose, Jr., perched on her knee. She was listening for sounds of battle at the River Raisin 7 miles to the north, and hoping for the return of her husband who had gone off to help the American army.

Eventually, in the distance, she discerned a lone figure, hobbling along as fast as he could. From the form, she could tell it was not her husband.

The stranger was breathing hard as he passed through the gate in the palisaded fence, and she saw he was a soldier, perhaps an officer of the American army. His leg was bandaged, and he had a musket ball in his foot. She immediately opened the door for him.

"The army has been destroyed," he gasped, *"and all the soldiers are being killed and scalped. There are dead men all over the trail behind me."*

Just then, over the officer's shoulder, Angelique noticed 3 Indians coming down the creek. Pulling the soldier inside, she had him squat down in a dark corner next to an empty flour barrel used for pickling pork.

The officer protested feebly, offering to make a run for it rather than risk her suffering at the hands of the Indians for giving him shelter.

"Don't be foolish," she replied, *"Our Indian neighbors would never harm a helpless white woman and her children."* Together, they tipped the large barrel over his head, hiding him completely.

---

667 Letter Response of General Leslie Combs, Verhoeven Collection, Monroe County Historical Museum Archives: *"We did not reach the foot of the Rapids, in sight of General Winchester's old camp, till late in the afternoon, and then only to find all the newly erected houses in flames and not a soldier to be seen. As soon as the commanding General heard of the defeat at Raisin, he fell back some 18 or 20 miles on Hull's trace, to Carrying River, to meet his expected reinforcements. Of course, we followed him, crossing the Maumee on the ice as he had done and overtook him the next morning, with our panic-stricken family, father, mother, and 3 or 4 children all safe, and then we felt happy. During our slow retreat, we were in constant fear of pursuing Indians, but, fortunately, while Harrison was falling back in one direction, the cowardly butcher Proctor was flying in the other direction. The father of this stricken family named, I think, Tessier, was killed at the Rapids a few days afterwards, while accompanying a flag of truce to the enemy to ascertain the fate of the prisoners taken at Raisin. His widow was sent into the interior of Ohio with her children. I hope they afterwards returned to their home at Bay Village, but have never heard of them since."*

When the Indians arrived, they walked right in the front door without a knock, and demanded to know if Angelique had any "*Maumee water.*"

She answered that she had no whisky in the house, but offered them a loaf of bread, instead. They took it and left without searching the building.[668]

It was late afternoon when Ambrose Charland finally returned home after being released on parole, with orders to report to Detroit.

The presence of the wounded Kentuckian presented Ambrose with a dilemma. Ambrose gave him his only horse, and the soldier left at dusk, heading for the safety of the American lines along the Maumee.

The next morning, Ambrose gathered a few belongings, Angelique picked up her 4-month-old baby, and the family headed out onto Lake Erie.[669]

French Town, Afternoon of January 22, 1813:

Meanwhile, back in French Town, Elias Darnell had stayed behind to care for his wounded brother, Allen. As soon as they had gotten the Indians out of the building, he proceeded to bolt the door. Unfortunately, the warriors returned. Finding the door shut, they battered it down with their tomahawks.

Darnell called to a British officer, who turned and shouted to another officer to send the guard.

The guard quickly restored order, but not before the invaders had

---

668 "Story of Angelique Charlan," family story passed down and recorded by George M. Smith of Monroe, Michigan, Sept. 27, 1984. Copy in Charland family file, Small Collections, Monroe County Historical Museum Archives. Although in his recollections, Ambrose Charland merely identified the man as a soldier, this story passed down in the family has General Winchester as the fugitive. It is tempting to think it may have been the General's secretary, Captain Woolfolk. Charland claimed the man was wounded in the foot. Woolfolk reportedly was wounded in the leg. Or perhaps it was one of the officers who actually escaped; Major McClenahan, Captain Matson, or Captain Glaves, who was wounded but placed on McClenahan's horse. Perhaps he was not an officer at all, but was one of the two men later sent south by Leslie Combs, on a pony, which could have been Charland's.

669 (Dennissen, Vol.1, p. 256) (LaVoy's Bay Settlement, pp. 88, 245) (Observer, 4-5-52) (Dep. Ambrose Charland, Godfroy papers, Burton): A few hours later, trudging on the ice, they looked back in the direction of their homestead. Sadly, they noted smoke rising above the treetops on the distant shoreline. The Indians were destroying all they had left behind. Tears in their eyes, they turned their backs on home and trekked onward towards Detroit, which lay almost 40 miles away. There they would live among strangers, with nothing to eat but what they could beg from others. The Charlands were survivors, but the strain proved too much for their baby. He would die on Sept. 11, 1813, one month shy of his first birthday. A child, Lucille, would be born the following year, and the Charlands would raise 7 more children over the next decade and a half.

plundered the commissary's house, piled rails against it, and set it afire. Darnell assisted the British officers in quelling the flames.[670]

Once the fire was out, Essex Militia Major Ebenezer Reynolds asked where the ammunition was kept. Darnell thought it might be upstairs. They went up to look, but found none.

Reynolds was sure the Indians would burn the settlement. There was no immediate way of transporting the wheat and other supplies, and it could not be left to fall into the hands of Harrison's advancing army.

There were many barrels of flour in the building, so Darnell asked the major if he could take some for the wounded. Reynolds told him to take as much as he wanted.

Encouraged, Darnell asked him if a British guard would be left to protect them. Reynolds replied that a guard would not be needed.

The Indians were already leaving for their camp, and a few interpreters would remain to walk from house to house to see that the American doctors and the wounded were not disturbed. All but 10 of the Indians soon departed for a rumored frolic sponsored by the British at Stony Creek that night.[671]

Nonetheless, Reynolds warned Darnell to stay inside the house that night. Any warriors still lurking about would just as soon shoot Darnell as not.[672]

Even the local *habitants* were worried. Jean-Baptiste Jerome sought out Colonel Elliott, of the Indian Department, to ask if a detail of soldiers could be left behind to guard the wounded left in his house.

Colonel Elliott told Jerome he would ask Jocko Lasselle and an Indian Department interpreter to watch over the wounded.[673]

---

670 Probably Couture's storehouse, where the quartermaster's stores and baggage were kept. It was also full of lumber. Another option was Jerome's bakehouse which was used to store extra ammunition. Bake houses were often used as laundry rooms and as summer kitchens during the warmer months.

671 Knopf, Richard C. Document Transcriptions of the War of 1812 in the Northwest, Vol. V, pt. 2. Columbus: Ohio Historical Society, 1958. p. 32, Deposition of Medard Labadie, Feb. 11, 1813.

672 Darnell, Elias. A Journal Containing an Interesting and Accurate Account of the Hardships, Sufferings, Battles, Defeat, and Captivity of Those heroic Kentucky Volunteers and Regulars, Commanded by General Winchester, in the Year 1812-1813. Paris, Kentucky: 1813. (As reprinted under the title "Remember the Raisin" in Captured by the Indians, edited by Frederick Drimmer, New York: Dover Publications, pp. 256-267.): "*As they did not leave the promised guard, I lost all confidence in them, and expected we would all be massacred before morning. Since I was the only person in this house not wounded, with the assistance of some of the wounded, I prepared something for about thirty to eat.*"

673 At age 47, Jocko Lasselle was one of those living bridges between the cultures that inhabited the

Most of the other *habitants* were busy looking after their families and evacuating them to Detroit, Malden, Sandusky, or Cleveland, but among those who remained to care for the wounded Kentuckians were Jean-Baptiste Beaugrand, Medard Couture, J.-B. Bruneau, and at least one of the Lasselles.[674]

Doctors Todd and Bower were the only remaining American medical personnel on site. As many as 30 other Americans had been allowed to stay behind and help them.[675]

Unfortunately, the Indian Department interpreters were anxious to get away, and some were leaving without orders. They feared the *habitants* might give the Indians whisky to render them incapable of resisting an advance by Harrison's relief troops. If that happened, all hell might break loose.[676]

Captain William Elliott of the Essex Militia went over to Jerome's house to find Major Graves, Rev. Dudley, and Captains Hart and Hickman, all wounded in the legs. Charles Bradford was there, too, wounded in the right hip.[677]

Elliott was acquainted with Captain Hart, who asked him what would be done with the wounded prisoners. Some of Hart's men had offered to carry him on their backs when they were marched off as prisoners, but Elliott

---

American west. His father was a fur trader, and Jocko had been born amongst the Indians, with whom he had solidly established both family and commercial ties. Lasselle's influence with the Indians was well known, and he had often obtained the release of prisoners from them. While most of his neighbors were happy that the American government had recognized their land claims through treaties with the Indians, he disapproved of the territorial administration's efforts to restrict the Native tribes to reservations and to lessen Michigan's economic dependence on the fur trade.

674 Deposition of John Baptist Jerome, County of Monroe, Aug. 22, 1818: *"Colonel Elliott then ordered a Mr. Bougrand, an American, together with a British Indian Interpreter, to remain and guard the prisoners who were wounded. Further, the deponent states that about 10 o'clock in the evening of the 22nd the Interpreter who had been ordered to remain, left the wounded, and went in pursuit of the British Army at Stoney Creek..."*

675 Drs. Montgomery, Davis, McIlvain, and Irvine, had all been killed during the fighting. Drs. Logan and Overton were with General Winchester and the prisoners being marched off to Fort Malden. Drs. Todd and Bower remained behind with the wounded. It is possible that Isham and other officers' servants were among the 30, but, if so, they would soon be seized by the Indians.

676 Antal, Sandy. A Wampum Denied. Canada: Carleton Library Series, Vol. 191, p. 194.

677 Affidavit of Charles Bradford, April 29, 1813, Lexington, Kentucky: *"This deponent further says that the British marched away; no guard was left to protect the wounded; and that Captain Elliott, when asked the reason, observed that some interpreters were left, whose influence among the Indians was greater, and that they were better able to protect us than a guard."*

promised that sleighs would be sent for the wounded men in the morning to take them to a British field hospital.[678]

The wounded Americans inside French Town could not be moved for lack of transport, but Hart insisted that he should be moved that very evening. So Elliott said he would see what could be done. He offered Hart the hospitality of his home in Malden, where he could stay until fully recovered from his wound.[679]

But Elliott would need a swift horse to round up the sleighs and carry him to Malden. Major Graves offered his own horse, saddle, and bridle, which were still in the stable. Elliott assured them the guards and 3 interpreters who remained would be more than enough protection.

Elliott repeated all this to Dr. Bower, who was reluctant to stay behind, despite the promises. He wouldn't feel at ease until the sleighs showed up.[680]

About this time, a small gang of young boys appeared and began jeering and cajoling the British. One soldier turned and dispersed them with a shot into their midst. The bullet grazed the face of 7-year-old François Deloeuil, leaving him blind in the right eye.[681]

---

678 Dudley, Rev. Thomas P., "The Battle and Massacre at Frenchtown, Michigan, January, 1813," Historical and Archaeological Tracts, Number One, Cleveland: Western Reserve Historical Society, August, 1870. Further information gleaned from interviews with veterans was published in the Pittsburgh Gazette and Mercury, and partially reprinted with comments in the Monroe Commercial of Thursday, March 23, 1871. See: http://monroe.lib.mi.us/bygonesofmonroe/bomwarof1812.htm: "...After the capitulation, a British officer, a Captain Elliot, who had been a classmate with him at Princeton College, waited on Captain Hart and, unsolicited, promised him his protection, declaring that the next morning he would have him taken to Malden, where he should remain until his recovery."

679 Deposition of Dr. John Todd, dated May 2, 1813, in Barbarities of the Enemy, exposed in a Report of the Committee of the House of Representatives, and the Documents accompanying said Report. Troy: Francis Adancourt, 1813. pp. 141-5. Dr. Todd was acting Surgeon General of Kentucky troops.

680 Deposition of John McDonnell, Feb. 4, 1813, Barbarities of the Enemy, exposed in a Report of the Committee of the House of Representatives, and the Documents accompanying said Report, Troy: Francis Adancourt, 1813. pp. 127-9.

681 Obituary of Francis Delye, 1903, Monroe County Museum Archives: "At the home of his son, Moses, Noble Avenue, Tuesday evening, occurred the death of Francis Delye, the oldest native-born citizen of Monroe County, and one of the oldest citizens of Michigan. The deceased was born at Monroe, Oct. 8, 1805...He recalled vividly the scenes in Monroe after the bloody massacre of 1813 and it was at this time that he lost the sight of his right eye. He with several other boys were laughing at the British soldiers when one of them shot into the crowd of boys and Mr. Delye's eye was rendered useless. In his early years, the deceased was a blacksmith, acted as an Indian interpreter, and as a guide. He could talk the language of the natives as fluently as English or French, and was a valuable guide since he knew all the Indian trails and short cuts...."

Within an hour after the surrender, Procter had the bulk of his army on the march.[682] As they herded their prisoners north along the road to Detroit, they passed some of their own wounded, as well as what appeared to be the bullet-riddled corpse of Lt. Colonel St. George, their highest-ranking casualty.

The British wounded would also have to wait until enough sleighs could be commandeered to take them to the commissary depot at Stony Creek. From there they would be moved to Brownstown, and then to Fort Amherstburg.[683]

However, several hours would pass before enough sleighs could be assembled to transport the more seriously wounded British, let alone the bodies of the dead.[684]

Meanwhile, Squire Reynolds, brother of Major Reynolds, had set up a supply depot at a French home at Stony Creek landing. When Procter's column came through, the Squire saw that the wounded were not with him.

Reynolds quickly ordered his men to off-loaded the supplies and led the empty sleighs to French Town to retrieve the British dead and wounded.[685]

---

682 Letter Procter to Sheaffe, Jan. 25, 1813, James' Military Occurrences, V. 1, No. 24: *"It is reported that a party, consisting of 100 men, bringing 500 hogs to general Winchester's force, has been completely cut off."* Other news indicated an American relief force was on the way. It has been suggested that some militia scouts reported Harrison's reinforcements advancing to French Town, when what they actually saw were some mounted Wyandots escorting a troop of hogs and cattle.

683 Lossing, Benson J., The Pictorial Field-Book of the War of 1812, Glendale, New York: Benchmark Publishing Corporation, 1970, p. 357. See also: Au, Dennis, War on the Raisin, Monroe, Michigan: Monroe County Historical Commission, 1981, pp. 44-45. Initial reports indicated 218 Americans killed and 495 captured, not counting those taken by the Indians. The numbers would grow over the next few weeks. See: Antal, Sandy. "Remember the Raisin! Anatomy of a Demon Myth," The War of 1812 Magazine, Issue 10, October, 2008. See also: "Return of Prisoners..." Michigan Pioneer & Historical Collections, Vol. 15, p. 229: Lt. Felix Troughten, R. A., listed 1 general, 1 colonel, 1 major, 9 captains, 6 lieutenants, 10 ensigns, 1 brigade major, 1 adjutant, 1 quartermaster, 2 surgeons, 27 sergeants, and 235 rank and file among the prisoners shortly after the battle, with more being brought in by the Indians each day.

684 Bulkley, John McClelland. History of Monroe County, Michigan, Vol. I. Chicago: Lewis Publishing Co., 1913, p. 136.

685 "Description of the Lands and Settlers in the Vicinity of Detroit," Feb. 17, 1804, American State Papers, Washington: Gales & Seaton, 1832: *"Rocky River discharges itself into Lake Erie, 3 miles north of the River Raisin, and 8 south of River Huron. It is a small, winding stream, too shallow to admit the passage of the smallest boats...It is timbered with elm, oak, hickory, and maple. At the mouth of this stream there is a safe harbor, formed by the projection into the lake of Point Raisin on the one side, and Rocky [Stony] Point on the other. The tenure by which these lands are held is derived from an Indian deed, executed by the chiefs in the year 1786, to Francis Pepin...Pepin sold his claim to George MacDougall, who, some years since, conveyed 2/3 of the tract to Meldrum and Park, a mercantile house in Detroit, and conjointly with them, has erected very valuable improvements. About half a mile above the mouth of the river, they have a dwelling house, a distillery, and a merchant mill, with*

They found Lt. Colonel Thomas Bligh St. George still hanging on to life, lying on the battlefield where he had fallen. Reynolds placed him in a sleigh full of straw, from which the seat had been removed, and brought him back to Stony Creek, along with 80 to 100 wounded comrades and 23 corpses. The wounded were placed on straw in the Frenchman's house.[686]

The British were also encumbered with a lot of captured weapons, including 10 swords with scabbards, 397 serviceable muskets with cartridge boxes and bayonets, and 1400 cartridges, although a third were in unserviceable condition. The Indians had made off with a considerable quantity as well.[687]

As the captured Americans marched off along Hull's Road, they passed a campfire near which Procter had stationed himself at one point during the fighting. Gathered around it were Lt. Baker, 2nd U.S. Infantry, and some men of the right wing, who had been captured by the Indians earlier in the battle.

Major Madison requested a temporary halt and asked the British guard to take Baker along with them. The guard replied, *"You have too many officers,"* and the column then continued its march. The Indians took Baker to Sandy Creek, where he would spend a tense night with 20 other prisoners.[688]

---

every necessary appendage for the convenient manufactory of wheat." McDougall's mill and house were burned soon after the fall of Detroit.

686 Reynolds Narrative in Coffin, William F. 1812: The War and its Moral: A Canadian Chronicle. Montreal: John Lovell, 1864: The bodies were eventually buried in a common pit in the churchyard at Amherstburg. St. George would recover, although he would be bedridden till July. See Appendix G for a list of British casualties at the Battle of the River Raisin. See also: Couture, Paul Morgan. "War and Society on the Detroit Frontier, 1791 to 1815," Manuscript Report for Parks Canada, 1986: Descriptions of the location of the hospital fit both Stony and Swan Creeks.

687 Report of arms taken at the River Raisin, dated Amherstburg, Jan. 25, 1813, signed by Felix Troughton and Samuel Wood, Michigan Pioneer & Historical Records, Vol. 15, p. 230. That would amount to 3 or 4 rounds for each of the 400 or so Americans still capable of fighting at the end of the battle. A third of them were spoiled, one might imagine, by exposure to moisture or snow. Many of the weapons taken were private arms belonging to the volunteers themselves. Research conducted by Dennis Au among the returns of private arms lost and surrendered at the River Raisin on January 22, 1813, indicates that regimental officers lost 2 swords, 3 pairs of pistols, and 1 surgical kit. Most of the privately-owned weapons were carried by the 1st Rifle Regiment, whose private losses, by company, were: Langhorne's: 1 sword, 27 rifles. Simpson's: 2 swords, 13 rifles, 13 powder horns, 13 shot pouches. McCracken's: 2 swords, 17 rifles. Bledsoe's: 8 rifles, 8 powder horns, 8 shot pouches.
Matson's: 2 swords, 14 rifles, 14 powder horns, 14 shot pouches.
Ballard's: 37 rifles, 37 powder horns and pouches, 42 tomahawks.
Hickman's: 1 sword, 23 rifles, 23 shot pouches and powder horns, 23 tomahawks.

688 Knopf, Richard C. Document Transcriptions of the War of 1812 in the Northwest, Vol. V, pt. 2. Columbus: Ohio Historical Society, 1958. pp. 64-5, Report of Lt. Baker. See also: Draper YY-6.

Medard Labadie and many other *habitants* were released when the line of march was formed. Lt. Colonel Navarre had also been taken into custody. He offered to send for his son Robert, who could bring a team and *traineau* back to at least carry the wounded men among them up to Sandy Creek.[689] The other Navarres had escaped, but a few citizens were less fortunate.[690]

Whitmore Knaggs, Hubert Lacroix and Antoine Lafountain were placed under arrest for violating their paroles. Isaac Ruland, accused of being a spy, refused to march when ordered, and received a bayonet in the thigh.[691]

---

689 Ford, H. A., Letter to the Editor, <u>Monroe Democrat</u>, July 31, 1884, P.1, Col.5: *"Two stories are told of his capture in the war, both of which may be true. One relates that Proctor marched him through Sandwich with the prisoners taken at the Raisin in the first action, January 18, 1813, but allowed him on parole to visit unattended, for one hour, his inamorata, Angelique (Couture of Sandwich). She besought him to flee, but the hero was true, and at the appointed time "wrenched himself from her detaining arms, and, with her despairing cries ringing in his ears, reached the camp as the sun was sinking below the horizon." His fidelity to the parole induced the Indians to leave him unbound. But he was to be burned with others at the stake the next day, and being now freed from his parole, he watched for the opportunity to escape, which came during the night. He bounded into the forest, found a canoe and paddled joyously homeward. The house of his Angelique was thoroughly raided by his savage pursuers, who even searched the chimneys and pierced the beds with bayonets. A fresh scalp was afterward shown her as that of François' and she faded rapidly, until the glad news of his safety reached her soon after."* This story may contain elements, such as the escape by canoe and being marched through Sandwich, which more properly fit the second of Navarre's alleged escapes, which took place in September of 1813, when Navarre went to Brownstown to parlay with the Wyandots in advance of Richard M. Johnson's column on its way to Detroit.
I have not been able to verify the identity of Angelique Couture, nor have I found any accounts of prisoners taken by the British on January 18. As a prominent citizen, Navarre could very well have been arrested just prior to or on the 18th, which would explain why I have found no references to him during the first battle for French Town. If so, he had to escape and get home by January 20, when General Winchester showed up as his house guest.
It seems more plausible that Navarre was arrested with other citizens after the battle on January 22 and given an hour to settle his affairs before being led off towards Malden. At this time, he could have sent word to his son, Robert, to get the family out of town. Somewhere on the way to Malden, he may have simply been let go by the Indians, as happened to a number of other Raisin *habitants.*

690 Wing, Talcott E., "History of Monroe County, Michigan," in <u>Michigan Pioneer & Historical Collections</u>, Vol. IV, 1881. Lansing: W. S. George & Co., 1883, p. 321. Robert and Platte Navarre, along with several others, were only later pressed into service.

691 Pension request of Isaac Ruland, dated March 25, 1836: *"That it appears from the petition of said Ruland that while in the service of the United States in the late war, he was taken prisoner at Winchester's defeat, and kept in close and rigorous confinement until the reduction of Fort George, Upper Canada; that while a prisoner he received a severe wound inflicted with a bayonet in the dead of winter, by order of a British officer, for refusing to march 18 miles through snow said to be 3 feet deep upon the level plain, which wound is now the cause of much suffering, having produced a diseased state of the thigh bone, and caused the loss in a great measure of the use of that limb."* Ruland did not state what day he was bayonetted. He also entered a claim for loss of property during his captivity, as

This was not the first time Captain Lacroix had faced a British prison term. The previous occasion had taken place after Hull's surrender, but he had been released on parole. This time, he would not be so lucky.[692]

Eventually, the British would take him to Malden, where he would be confined for several months before being transported by boat to Québec. There, he would be liberated by order of Col. Procter, and would finally return to the River Raisin, only to find himself practically destitute, with all his property destroyed.[693]

---

well as for other services rendered. Note: The distance from French Town to Brownstown is 18.9 miles. From Brownstown to Fort Amherstburg is 4 miles across the Detroit River. From French Town to Fort Amherstburg is 18-20 miles straight across Lake Erie.

692 After Hull's surrender in August of 1812, the British argued that, having been born in Montreal, Lacroix was a Canadian, not an American, and was thus guilty of treason. They kept him imprisoned aboard a ship at Malden, threatening to take him to Québec, where he would be tried and possibly hanged. Fortunately, Jean-Baptiste Beaugrand learned about Lacroix's predicament when visiting Detroit with his wife, and was able to influence Tecumseh to secure his release from the British.

After the Battle of January 22, Lacroix's unfinished house was burned, along with his father-in-law's house containing their furniture. Lacroix's damages amounted to $4,000. See: Petition of Hubert Lacroix, Frenchtown, Dec.12, 1819. Lacroix was "...taken to Malden, where he remained, confined, several months, and was conveyed from Malden, on board of a vessel, to be transported, with others, to Quebec, from which he was released, by the order of Gen. Procter, and returned to the River Raisin...Owing to the scene of carnage and conflagration which ensued, and the confined situation of your petitioner, he was unable to procure from General Winchester the necessary vouchers for the supplies furnished...the house of your petitioner, his furniture, notes, accounts, and some money, were burned and destroyed by the British and Indians."

693 LaCroix petition to Congress, Dec.12, 1819.

Damaged Portrait of Madame Lacroix
Mother of Capt. Hubert Lacroix,
Gift of MaryAnn Rees and Family to the Monroe County Historical Museum[694]

Godfroy House, French Town, January 22, 1813:

Madame Godfroy remained in her home with a number of wounded American soldiers after Winchester's surrender, thoroughly regretting her decision to leave the family store in Detroit.

Suddenly she heard an unusual noise, and she looked out the window to

---

694 Family tradition states that the damage above the shoulder was caused by an Indian tomahawk when their home was invaded during the War of 1812. Sue Rodich and other Monroe Museum staff interviewed Mrs. Rees, who revealed that: *"During the War of 1812, as my mother related to me, Indians came into this house and…took a tomahawk to this picture, and they made a slit, and they started to make another one, the little one at the top, and my grandmother or great grandmother Adeline said — No! No! That is a French lady! — And they were very apologetic…And I understand that they gave the family, that would be Hubert and his daughter and his wife, something to compensate for the picture. That's the truth…they gave them…the Indians gave them something…"* Although more likely to have happened after the initial occupation of French Town in the summer and fall of 1812, this story is sometimes related as happening at the time of the battle, when the Lacroix family was living in one of Jean-Baptiste Jerome's houses.

see an aged Métis, half-French, half-Indian, come running out of the woods. She noted his apprehensive glances as he headed straight for the house.[695]

Godfroy-Beaugrand Property:
House, Stable, Store, and Barn[696]
Painting by Darlene Belair
Provided Courtesy of the National Park Service
River Raisin National Battlefield Park

Opening the door, the old interpreter stammered that he had seen some of the Indians killing the prisoners they had taken in the woods. They were bringing some of their prisoners to one of her barns, and there was some talk of plundering and burning the place down.

Before she could ask any questions, the old man was off and running as fast as his tired old legs could carry him, and it was none too soon, as a group

---

695 Could this perchance have been Jean-Baptiste Sanscrainte?
696 Description: The Godfroys had a 60x30-foot dwelling house, a stable worth $20, a new barn built by Laurent Durocher for $800, and a store house built in 1811 worth $800-$1000. The store house was of a large size and finished off to include a bake house and kitchen. The lot also contained a number of smaller structures.

of Native warriors suddenly made their appearance. Seeing the disheveled appearance of their prisoners, Madame Godfroy felt sorry for them.

Nonetheless, she could afford to take no notice, for fear the Indians would become angry. Instead, she busied herself with some chores, but her charade was cut short when a warrior threw his tomahawk in her direction.

Madame Godfroy quickly changed her strategy and started bringing out small presents for her uninvited guests, in hopes such a gesture would pacify them. The warriors set about searching the house, entering every room, and descending into the basement, where they found a small quantity of liquor.

Soon, the Indians had ensconced their prisoners in her house and declared their intention of spending the night. As they started preparations for burning one of the prisoners out in the yard, the interpreter returned.

Calling to him, she asked what she could do to save the young man. After some negotiation, she was allowed to adopt him, in exchange for ten dollars, a fine black horse, two bundles of dry goods, and 5 gallons of whisky.

Fearing she would not soon be rid of these interlopers, Madame Godfroy bided her time. Once no one was taking any notice of her, she quietly gathered her family, left her house, and made her escape.[697]

At midnight, an Indian came to the Godfroy house to warn the wounded men sheltered there to take care through the night. He spoke English well, but was nervous, as though he thought some of his lurking comrades might be tempted to shoot into the house at any time. One Kentuckian spoke freely, but the rest were suspicious and guarded in their comments.

After a couple hours, the warrior left, saying, *"I fear some of the boys will do some mischief before morning."*[698]

As darkness came on, the fears of the Kentuckians increased. One large group of wounded Americans was housed at Godfroy's; an even larger group was at Jerome's. Smaller numbers were sheltered at 3 other houses.[699]

---

697 Letter George Ray to his son, written at Detroit, Jan. 20, 1841, containing an interview with Madame Godfroy. Original in the Clements Library, University of Michigan.

698 Atherton, William. Narrative of the Suffering and Defeat of the North-Western Army under General Winchester. Frankfort, KY.: A. G. Hodges, 1842, pp. 59-60.

699 Deposition of John Baptist Jerome, Aug. 22, 1818, William Henry Harrison Papers on microfilm at Central Michigan University: *"The deponent further states that about day break on the morning of the 23rd, the Indians who had retired the afternoon before, reappeared and came to the house of the deponent where were about 45 wounded; and commenced tomahawking the prisoners, and after plundering the house, set it on fire. Afterwards the Indians burnt 4 other houses, in which there were prisoners, but the number the deponent cannot determine."*

Navarre house, River Raisin, evening of January 22, 1813:

Catherine Lenfant Couture was the wife of Captain Jean-Baptiste Couture and the mother of Medard Couture. Her husband and son had stayed behind to fight while she took her younger children to François Navarre's house at the start of the battle. As the battle ended, Indian warriors invaded the Navarre house "like fierce lions." One wore a bloody, bullet-riddled coat, which Madame Couture immediately recognized as her husband's.

She had little time to mourn, however, as the Indians heaped scalps upon a table set in a corner against the wall. Blood dripped down from the fresh scalps, making a dark stain on the wooden floor.[700]

The Indians also rifled through the personal trunks and public property left behind by Winchester and his officers. At least Madame Navarre was able to save the general's watch, spectacles, and pen wiper.[701]

Jerome House, evening, January 22, 1813:

Jerome's house consisted of two large rooms separated by a central kitchen. About midnight, the local *habitants* who had been assisting Dr. Bower announced they had to leave. Thinking their presence might serve to protect the wounded from attack by wandering Indians, Bower tried to convince them to stay, but to no avail. At least one, however, did promise to return.[702]

---

700 Sawyer, Miss Jennie, "Life of Col. Francis Navarre," typed copy of manuscript in Monroe County Historical Museum Archives. See also: (Wright, R. J. ed. The John Hunt Memoirs, Maumee Valley Historical Society, p. 42.), (Au, p. 45) and (Catherine Couture, dep. to Congress, 12-12-1819): The Couture family's hogs, 4 cows, and 30 sheep had also been killed. The Indians would eventually burn the house, barn, stable, and bake house. In the process, a great quantity of wheat, corn, oats, and hay would be lost, along with all the family's personal possessions. Mrs. Couture and several small children would be left with little more than the clothing on their backs.

701 Letter Winchester to Navarre, Feb. 18, 1816, typed copy in Monroe County Historical Museum Archives: "*I feel myself very much obliged to Madame Navarre for preserving my watch, spectacles, and pen wiper from the general wreck and destruction of property on the morning of my defeat…*" Curiously, writing from Cairo, Tennessee, Winchester addressed the letter to "*Col. Francis Navarre, French Town, River Raisin, State of Ohio.*"

702 After they left, a man named Knaggs came to the door. He said he understood the Indians' language and had overheard some of them making plans to kill the wounded American prisoners. He advised any who could to slip away during the night and try to make it to General Harrison's forces at Winchester's old camp along the Maumee River. Knaggs then disappeared, leaving the wounded Kentuckians to pass a fitful night. See: Letter, Dr. Gustavus Miller Bower, Feb. 25, 1858, copy in clipping file, Monroe County Historical Museum Archives. Bower actually spelled the man's name as "Megs." He also states the three local *habitants* were "*Lasselle, Boiegraw, Cature.*"

In the cold, gray, pre-dawn light, Medard Couture trudged through the snow on his way back to Jerome's house. He had not heeded Colonel Elliott's order to leave the settlement, but had gone off, exhausted, to check on his father's remains and perhaps catch a short hour of sleep.

Medard Couture had once been destined for the priesthood and had received a better education than most of his neighbors. Perhaps that's what now made him turn his efforts to caring for the wounded men who had been left unprotected after the surrender of Winchester's army.[703]

River Huron, evening of January 22, 1813:

Friendship Medal
ca. 1766

Otussa fingered the small, silver medal which he wore for good luck. It was difficult to see in the evening darkness, but he could feel the design in relief on both sides; an image of King George III on one side and on the other, the outline of a church guarded by a British lion and a Native American wolf. The medal had belonged to his mother, the widow of Pontiac, but now it was his.[704]

Otussa and his son, Waseonquet, were on their way to Detroit with their prisoner, Captain Baker of the 17th U.S. Infantry. They had captured him in the ambush near Plum Creek, a mile or two south of the River Raisin.

On their way back north, they camped for the night on the bank of the River Huron. Otussa ordered his son to make a fire.[705]

Hosmer gives their names as Couture, Brineau, and Beaugrand.

703 Biography of Mrs. Alice Knaggs, Meeting of the Michigan Pioneer and Historical Society, 1896.

704 Oct. 4, 1866 Peter Navarre Interview, Historical Society of Northwestern Ohio, Biographical Field Notes 81-83, 89, and 139. Navarre placed this incident on the River Rouge instead of the Huron. The medallion supposedly was buried with Otussa, but resurfaced several decades later. I consider Otussa and Otussown to be the same person, given that they were both born about 1768 and have a son named Distant Cloud. Nonetheless, Navarre gives their mothers slightly different names; Kappeshkumoqua (Woman's Camp) and Kantuckeegun (Woman Canoe Paddler,) each of whom, he claims, was a widow of Chief Pontiac. Forthright and highly respected, Otussa was poisoned by another Indian and died at Presqu'ile about 1828, knowing, but refusing to disclose, the name of his killer. Kan-tuck-ee-gun was born around 1756 and died in 1822. The Maumee band of Odawa was descended from Pontiac and had villages on both sides of the Maumee at its mouth.

705 Otussa, the youngest son of Pontiac, had 4 sons by different mothers. Wassinoquet (A Cloud Far

"Why not make the Yankee dog build it?" responded Waseonquet, (Distant Cloud). *"He's our prisoner; we can make him do anything we want."*

His father answered sternly, *"My son, such language is wrong. This prisoner is a chief among his people. We must treat him as we would wish to be treated under like circumstances."*

The next day, they took Baker to Detroit, where they procured him some tea, butter, and sugar, and finally ransomed him off to be turned over to the British.[706]

La Crique au sable (Sandy Creek,) evening of January 22, 1813:

It was going on evening when Private Hamilton was herded past the Gandon house by his Indian captors. He, along with some other prisoners, arrived just in time to see one of their Kentucky comrades expiring. The poor soldier had been dreadfully tortured and burned, and an Indian was even now kicking the ashes off the dead man's back, saying *"damned son of a bitch."*[707]

Off) was born of a métis woman in 1779 and died in 1840. Other sons were Notano, Wasseon, and Ottokee. All four moved to Kansas in the 1830s. Pontiac's Odawa name was Obwandiyaq. He was born in 1714 near an Odawa Village on either the Detroit or Maumee River in what was then New France. Son of an Odawa father and an Ojibwa mother, he led a Native coalition that attempted to oust the British from the Great Lakes. Pontiac died at Cahokia, Illinois (then part of the Province of Québec), in 1769 and was buried at St. Louis. Pontiac married Kantuckeegun (Woman Canoe Paddler) and became the father of Marie Manon la Sauvagesse (or Sauteuse), Nevbankkum, Niiikwisena, Kasahda, Otussa, and 2 others. He was the brother of Louis Chevalier and Chenewabe.

706 Hosmer, Hezekiah, Early History of the Maumee Valley, Toledo: Hosmer & Harris, 1858, p. 42. The word Waseonquet used to refer to Baker was commonly used for prisoners of war. According to Bishop Frederic Baraga's Dictionary of the Ojibway Language, the term awakân was applied to prisoners of war, slaves, and domestic animals or birds.

707 Knopf, Richard C. Document Transcriptions of the War of 18112 in the Northwest, Vol. V, Pt. 2, Columbus: Ohio Historical Society, 1959, pp. 204-5. Affidavit of John McDonnell. He had purchased 4 prisoners from the Indians and related this statement by one of them, Private Hamilton. McDonnell also described the death of Searls, but then stated he had gotten Searls confused with Blythe. See also: Deposition of John McDonnell, Feb. 4, 1813, Barbarities of the Enemy, exposed in a Report of the Committee of the House of Representatives, and the Documents accompanying said Report. Troy: Francis Adancourt, 1813. pp. 127-9. *"...this deponent purchased 3 or 4 of the prisoners, amongst the number was one by the name of Hamilton, a private in the Kentucky volunteers, who declared to this deponent that on the 1st or 2nd day after the battle at the river Raisin (fought) on the 22nd day of January last, as he and some of his fellow prisoners were marching with the Indians between this place and the river Raisin, they came up to where one of the prisoners was burnt, the life just expiring, and an Indian kicking the ashes off his back, saying 'damned son of a bitch.'"*

A bit later, 37-year-old François Gandon finally arrived home. As he walked up to the front door, however, he saw a sight that made him recoil in horror. There, on his doorstep, were the burnt remains of a human being. One side of the body was charred completely black.[708]

Gandon's neighbor, Alex Gee, came by to tell him that after their victory at the River Raisin, the Indians had taken possession of his house, with a number of prisoners. They broke up his floor and made a fire inside with the boards, where they spent most of the afternoon roasting one of their captives alive. His cries could be heard for a mile, but he couldn't do anything, not even say a word, or try to communicate with the poor man, because the Indians would have killed him, too.

Gandon would consider staying over at Alex Gee's this night, as Indians were still wandering about his property with their prisoners. *Grace à Dieu*, he had been insightful enough to have already moved his family to Detroit. Tomorrow, he would go to join them.[709]

Gandon would be one more individual taking part in the mass exodus of families from the River Raisin and Sandy Creek. Many of his friends and neighbors were already heading north towards Detroit. The more fortunate ones rode in sleighs, snuggled beneath their blankets. Some galloped by on horseback. Those poor refugees whose conveyances had been requisitioned by the British had to travel on foot, carrying their children on their backs.

A number of them had seen their property destroyed. People who had

---

708 Affidavit of Francis Gandon, concerning Massacres, Etc., committed by Indians at Sandy Creek, sworn before J. J. Godfroy, Justice of the Peace, Nov. 25, 1834: "...And I, with the others, went to Detroit, and when the Indians left my house, they put fire to it, and it was consumed about two weeks after, as I was informed by Captain Joseph Jobin, who had seen it burning, and after the arrival of General Harrison at Detroit with the army, I returned to my farm and found the house and barn and fruit trees destroyed. And my wife would not agree to live there anymore on account of the dead bodies she seen there. Where the house stood, there were 3 or 4 skeletons which were burnt. As I had been informed, I was to exchange my house for a great loss for a piece up the creek. I am now 60 years of age."

709 Some of the murders I'm describing on the 23rd may have happened the day before. See: Affidavit of Francis Gandon, concerning Massacres, Etc., committed by Indians at Sandy Creek, sworn before J. J. Godfroy, Justice of the Peace, Nov. 25, 1834: "...on the 22nd they took possession of my house with a number of prisoners. One they roasted by the fire they made in the holes in the floor, and he was the whole day a-dying, as I was told by one of my neighbors, Alexis Gee, who had seen him often through the day and his cries could be heard a mile; but he dast say nothing, or even speak to him — would be certain death. When I came home in the evening to see my house, he was laying on the door step, one side black." Gee passed by several times through the day, and could see him inside.

become accustomed to a certain amount of economic independence were now reduced to begging.

A couple miles north of Sandy Creek, a small convoy of French *traineaux* passed swiftly over the icy tracks of Hull's Road. In charge were 21-year-old Robert Navarre and his cousin Platte. Robert's father, Lt. Col. Francois Navarre, had told him to take his mother and his 11 brothers and sisters to safety that night in Detroit.[710]

With them were many others, such as Medard Couture's mother and siblings, who had had fled to the Navarre house at the start of the battle. Afterwards, they had been placed on one of the heavy, sledge-like *traineaux* .

The sleighs were so crowded that Robert rode with his feet braced on the shafts. As they approached the British camp and temporary hospital at Stony Creek, they saw Indians near a large fire. They appeared drunk and were engaged in scalping a fatally wounded prisoner.

Although they sped by in haste, Robert noticed the flash of a large knife as it was passed in a circle around the crown of the prisoner's head. Looking back over his shoulder, he saw the Indian place his foot on the prisoner's neck and pull.

Turning his eyes away, he swore that could hear a "pop" as the scalp was peeled off the head of the unfortunate victim.

The next day, the Navarres and other former militia cavalrymen were pressed into service by the British at Stony Creek, for the purpose of transporting some of Procter's American prisoners to Malden in their pony-drawn sleighs.

Although only slightly wounded, these prisoners had been unable to keep up with Col. Procter's column on the march.[711]

Maumee Rapids, 9 p.m., January 22, 1813:

At about 10 a.m., General Harrison had learned that Winchester was under attack. The general ordered Perkin's Brigade to march immediately, and he would follow with General Payne and his men.

Major Cotgreave's battalion had left their camp on Maumee Bay earlier

---

710 Wing, Talcott E., "History of Monroe County, Michigan," in <u>Michigan Pioneer & Historical Collections</u>, Vol. IV, 1881. Lansing: W. S. George & Co., 1883, p. 321. Wing appears to place this incident, actually, on the night of the 22nd.

711 Navarre Genealogies, MCHM Archives. Also: Au, Dennis, <u>War on the Raisin</u>.

that morning and reached a point about 14 miles short of the River Raisin. They halted when they began to encounter refugees from the battle.[712]

Advancing by sleigh in front of Harrison's main column, Colonel Samuel Wells had gotten within a dozen miles of French Town when he received unequivocal news that Winchester had been completely defeated. Turning back, he met Harrison at the head of 700 reinforcements.

After learning of Winchester's fate, Harrison held a council with his field commanders and decided to retreat back to Winchester's camp at the rapids, but he ordered Wells to turn around once again and find out more about the situation on the Raisin.

At 9 p.m., Colonel Wells reported back with such discouraging news that General Harrison convened another council of officers. It was decided to abandon Winchester's camp and continue the retreat to Camp Deposit, where yet another council was held.[713]

Major McClenahan, having escaped from the Raisin, estimated the enemy had upwards of 2,000 British and Indians there. In all, only 33 of Winchester's men had managed to make it back to the American lines.[714]

The consensus of the officers was that their position at Camp Deposit was still too exposed to the enemy and they should retreat from the Maumee.

---

712 Letter Harrison to Meigs, Carrying River, Jan. 24, 1813, typed copy in Bidlack's Notes, Monroe County Historical Museum Archives.

713 *"Thus, both Harrison and Procter retreated from each other, as though they were in...terror of each other."* (See: Antal, Sandy, <u>A Wampum Denied: Procter's War of 1812</u>, Canada: Carleton University Press, 1997, p. 177.) Camp Deposit was near Roche de Boeuf, present-day Waterville.

714 Letter Harrison to Monroe, Jan. 24, 1813. Typed copy in Bidlack's Notes, Monroe County Historical Museum Archives: *"...I had dispatched Colonel Wells early in the evening in a cariole to procure intelligence. He progressed within 12 miles of the scene of action and returned about 9 o'clock. A council of war was then called, consisting of the general and field officers, and two questions were submitted to them, vis., whether it was probable that the enemy would attack us in our then situation, and if they did, could we resist them with effect? At the council, Major McClanahan of the Kentucky Volunteers, who escaped from the action, assisted. He was of opinion that there were from 1,600 to 2,000 British and Indians opposed to our troops and that they had six pieces of artillery, principally howitzers. It was the unanimous opinion of the council that under all circumstances it would be proper to return a short distance on this road, upon which the artillery and reinforcements were approaching, for should we be able to maintain our camp by getting in our rear, the enemy would defeat our troops in detail, and in spite of all the efforts we could make would take the all-important convoy of artillery and stores coming from Upper Sandusky. The march to this place was accordingly made yesterday, where I shall wait for the artillery and a detachment under Gen'l. Leftwich. I hope in a few days again to be at the Rapids."*

It was also imperative to protect the heavy artillery, which was still *en route* to the Maumee by way of Hull's Road and the Portage River.[715]

The general quickly ordered an immediate withdrawal. They would set fire to Winchester's old camp and destroy everything they could not transport, including a blockhouse and a storehouse full of pork and flour.[716]

By two in the morning, Harrison's 900 soldiers would be headed for the Portage River "Carrying Place," about 15 miles away.[717] The retreat of Harrison and the reinforcements that had been destined for Winchester would seem to go much faster than their advance.[718]

Initial reports were jumbled and confusing, but over the coming days and weeks, the Americans would slowly piece together the magnitude of the disaster. Over 300 Kentuckians were dead and another 50 or so severely

715 Letter Harrison to Shelby, Carrying River, Jan. 24, 1813, typed copy in Bidlack's Notes, Monroe County Historical Museum Archives. *"Having a large train of heavy artillery, and stores coming on this road from Upper Sandusky, under an escort of four companies, it was thought advisable to fall back to this place for the purpose of securing them. A part of it arrived last evening, and the rest is within 30 miles. As soon as it arrives, and a reinforcement of three regiments from the Virginia and Pennsylvania brigades, I shall again advance, and give the enemy an opportunity of measuring their strength with us once more."*

716 "Journal of Mathew Newsom," as transcribed by James Ohde, Ohio State Museum, Columbus: Anthony Wayne Parkway Board, 1957, p. 15: *"The goods there were free for everyone to carry off."*

717 In 1812, General Hull built a stockade near the site of an old French trading post to protect his supply lines between Fort Findlay and the Maumee Rapids. It was called Fort Portage, and a blockhouse was eventually built there. General Tupper used the small fort as a staging point for his abortive attack on the Maumee Rapids in November of 1812.

718 Letter Samuel Wells to Thomas Cushing, Feb. 9, 1813, Michigan Pioneer and Historical Collections. Lansing: Michigan Historical Commission, 1929, Vol. XL, pp. 503-7. The Carrying Place was another name for the Portage River, about 15 miles from the Maumee. See also: Dissertation of Rex LeRoy Spencer, Ph.D., "The Gibraltar of the Maumee: Fort Meigs in the War of 1812." Muncie, Indiana: Ball State University, 1989. Although General Harrison attempted to reassemble enough troops to continue his campaign against Detroit and Malden, his efforts were crippled when the Kentucky militia left for home after their 6-month enlistments expired in February. He was, however, able to build a large, fortified encampment (on the bluffs on the south side of the Maumee River near the Rapids) which he named Fort Meigs, in honor of the governor of Ohio. He would hold the line there, while a fleet was built to challenge British naval supremacy on Lake Erie.

wounded, not counting those from the battle of January 18th.[719] The British had taken around 500 ambulatory prisoners; the Indians, about 45.[720]

From the Portage River, General Harrison wrote to the Secretary of War, lamenting the collapse of his plan to concentrate his forces at the Maumee River: *"By the 5th of Febry., the whole force, four thousand and five hundred, which I contemplated assembling at the Rapids, would have been there; and provisions and Munitions of war in abundance."*[721]

---

719 Sandy Antal puts the final American losses at 397 killed and missing, 547 captured, and 33 escaped. No estimate was made of Indian casualties, but Procter lost 40% of his troops. The British regulars suffered the most, their 18 dead and 127 wounded amounting to almost half their number. Winchester reported Procter was wounded, but the British commander made no such claim in his official account of the battle. (See: Antal, Sandy. Wampum Denied: Procter's War of 1812. Canada: Carleton University Press, 1997.)

720 McAfee, Robert. History of the Late War in the Western Country. Bowling Green, Ohio: Historical Publications Company, 1919 (reprint of 1816 original edition.) p. 244. See Appendix H for a list of American casualties.

721 Letter Harrison to Monroe, January 26, 1813: *"When I left upper Sandusky—the Artillery was ordered to be sent on immediately to the Rapids, escorted by 300 Men. Detachments were also ordered for the Pack Horses, Wagons and Sleds, which were constantly progressing thither. Another Battalion could also have been drawn from Lower Sandusky so that the troops at the Rapids would have been almost daily increased. On this day they would have Amounted to Twenty-five hundred with two pieces of Artillery—and in four or five days more the Virginia Brigade and Pennsylvania Regt would have increased them to Thirty-Eight hundred, with a further supply of Artillery."*

RIVER RAISIN MASSACRE
LE CAUCHEMAR

Gathering of River Raisin Descendants of the War of 1812
Photo Courtesy of the Pontious Family.[722]

The Godfroy Home, French Town, early morning, January 23, 1813:

Over at Godfroy's house, Medard Labadie looked up at the sky and estimated it was between 9 and 10 in the morning. He had been captured during yesterday's battle, but was released and had gone home to care for his family.

He also wondered about his relatives over in Canada. One of them, Pierre Labadie dit Badichon, had been killed fighting for the British.[723]

Returning to help the wounded Kentuckians early that morning, he

---

722 This picture was taken at the 200th Anniversary Commemoration of the Battle of the River Raisin. All the people in the foreground and many of those watching from the porch have family ties to the French Town settlement and the surrounding area. Although a number of these descendants have since passed away, it is hoped their children will continue to honor the spirit and sacrifice of their forebearers. Many do so through membership in the Genealogical Society of Monroe County, the French Canadian Heritage Society of Michigan, and the Sons (or Daughters) of the War of 1812.

723 Denissen, Father Christian. Genealogy of the French Families of the Detroit River Region, Revision, 1701-1936, Vol. I., 1987.

279

had noticed a roving group of about 10 Native warriors who seemed to be looking for trouble.[724]

Not long after that, 50 more warriors returned looking for trophies after an evening of frolic at Stony Creek. These may have been members of Dickson's band from the Upper Lakes, many of whom had not even been in the battle.

Thinking these Indians must have gotten ahold of some whisky, Labadie was not surprised when a mob began to form in front of the Godfroy house.[725]

Inside, William Atherton readied himself to board the sleighs promised by the British, just as soon as they arrived. He was about to eat a morsel of the bread his comrades had left behind the day before, when he heard a noise in the passageway. Before he could think, a fierce-looking warrior forced open the door of his room and stood, tomahawk in hand, as if determined to commence some bloody work.[726]

The first warrior was soon followed by others. They quickly stripped the blankets and outer garments off the wounded men who were lying on the floor.

Atherton, at the far end of the room, was near a second door, leading into the front room of the house. Wasting no time, he quickly slipped out, only to find himself face to face with another frightening foe.

---

724 Deposition of Medard Labadie, Extract of Letter from General Harrison to the Secretary of War, dated Feb.11, 1813, in <u>Barbarities of the Enemy, exposed in a Report of the Committee of the House of Representatives, and the Documents accompanying said Report</u>, Troy: Francis Adancourt, 1813, pp. 136-9. Labadie would remain in area until the 5th of February.

725 Reynolds Narrative in "Chronicle of the War." It is difficult to identify individuals who participated in the burning of the houses. Draper claimed a Chippewa named Nor-Mee broke into a house for liquor and burned prisoners on January 23. See: Draper 17s. For a counter-story, see: Deposition of Dr. John Todd, April 24, 1813, in <u>Barbarities of the Enemy, exposed in a Report of the Committee of the House of Representatives, and the Documents accompanying said Report</u>, Troy: Francis Adancourt, 1813, pp. 141-5. *"It was asserted by Col. Proctor in a conversation at Amherstburg that the Indians had got some whiskey in the house we were stationed, and had become intoxicated. That the Indians may have had some whiskey, I shall not deny, but I think I can safely say, that they did not procure it there, and that was not the cause of the massacre, for on the preceding days and subsequent to the action of the 18th, I wanted some spirits, and made application to the housekeeper, who assured me there was none about the house, for it was all consumed by the British and Indians who had quartered in the house prior to the action of the 18th; besides the Indians showed no man-ifestation of drunkenness; their deliberate pilfering and their orderly conduct throughout, was not such as would be expected from drunken Indians."*

726 Atherton, William. Narrative of the Suffering and Defeat of the North-Western Army under General Winchester. Frankfort, KY: A. G. Hodges, 1842, p. 61.

This warrior's face was painted as black as charcoal, with a "half-bushel" of feathers knotted on his head, a large tomahawk in his right hand and a scalping knife fastened to his belt. He instantly grabbed Atherton by the collar and pushed him towards the front door.

Atherton tried to resist, passively, but the Indian insisted. Speaking harshly in a language Atherton didn't understand, the warrior forcibly dragged him away from what would soon be a scene of death.

At this same time, Elias Darnell came running outside in an attempt to reach an interpreter and get some help. As he passed through the door, an Indian seized his hat and put it on his own head.

Turning back, he was stopped by another warrior, who made signs for him to stand near the corner of the building. Darnell pleaded to be allowed to retrieve his hat, but what he really wanted was to check on his wounded brother.

The man refused, but sent in a boy to find the hat. The boy returned with one, and threw it down at Darnell's feet. Three other Indians then came up and pulled off Darnell's coat. All the while, Darnell was watching the Indians as they prepared to set fire to the building.

A group of warriors then stationed themselves near all the windows and doors of the Godfroy home, blocking off any chance for escape. Fearing the worst, some of the wounded tried to make a run for it, only to be chased down by their fleet-footed enemies. A number of the local dogs joined in the race, barking and yipping, and enjoying all the excitement.

The "Hunters of Kentucky," had now become the hunted, but few had the opportunity to grieve openly for these men, often as young as 18, who would never see their families again. Worse was still to come, as their tormentors began to burn the temporary hospital to the ground.[727]

Some of the wounded were still inside when the building finally caught fire. Many were too weak to move, and died in flaming misery. Others, also in very bad shape, were so terrified by the prospect that they rose from their beds and crawled or even walked naked into the yard. There, they cried for help or exclaimed in anguish, *"What shall we do?"*

They had not long to wait, however, as Indians rushed upon them,

---

727 Letter George Ray to James Ray, Jan. 20, 1841, written at Detroit. Contains interview with Mrs. Godfroy. Original in Clements Library, University of Michigan. The Godfroy home was a 1½ -story structure, 60 feet-wide across the front and 30 feet deep.

tomahawking and scalping the wounded prisoners. The ground was soon littered with splashes of blood and mangled flesh.[728]

Those the Indians did not already consider to be dead men were taken away as captives. They were made to carry the plunder taken from the buildings before they were set afire. Darnell was given a coat and led off towards Detroit with three wounded prisoners and half a dozen Indians.

Within a quarter mile, two of the wounded began to fall behind. Twenty yards ahead of them, a couple of the Indians turned around and fired. One wounded man fell dead, and an Indian rushed back to scalp him. The other wounded soldier, energized by the ball whistling past him, ran forward, begging the Indians not to shoot him. He promised he would keep up and even offered money to his captors if they spared him. Unmoved and showing no signs of pity, the Indians shot him down and scalped him.[729]

The House of Jean-Baptiste Jerome, early morning, January 23, 1813:
William Atherton was conducted downstream to Jerome's house, which

---

728 Darnell, Elias. Journal. Philadelphia: Lippincott, Grambo, & Co., 1854, pp. 60-61: *"...My feeble powers cannot describe the dismal scenes here exhibited. I saw my fellow soldiers naked and wounded, crawling out of the houses to avoid being consumed in the flames... The savages rushed on the wounded and, in their barbarous manner, shot and tomahawked and scalped them: and cruelly mangled their naked bodies while they lay agonizing and weltering in their blood."*

729 Darnell, Elias. Journal. Philadelphia: Lippincott, Grambo, & Co., 1854, pp. 61-3: *"...The road was, for miles, strewed with the mangled bodies, and all of them were left like those slain in battle on the 22nd for the birds and beasts to tear in pieces and devour. The Indians plundered the town of everything valuable and set the best houses on fire."*
Another victim was Elias Darnell's brother. He and his comrade, William Ficklin, had both been wounded in the fighting on the 18th. When the killing began, Ficklin tried to help the more seriously wounded brother escape, supporting him as best he could as they struggled along. When they came upon another knot of Indians with blood on their hands, however, Ficklin left Darnell behind and proceeded on his own. With difficulty, Darnell's brother tried to keep up, but only made it about 300 yards before he was murdered. See: Deposition of William Ficklin, County of Montgomery, State of Kentucky, November 5, 1821, as noted by Dennis Au in his research.
However, Ray Dushane kindly pointed out to me that there is some confusion in the accounts regarding the individual fates of Allen and Daniel Darnell. On page 198 of G. Glenn Clift's Remember the Raisin, they and Elias are listed on the roster for Captain Williams' company of the 5th Kentucky. Notations indicate Elias was taken prisoner, Allen was wounded January 18th and killed January 22nd, and Daniel was killed January 23rd. Ensign Isaac Baker's report also lists Daniel as the man killed on January 23rd somewhere between Sandy Creek and French Town. However, on page 85 of Clift's book, a quotation from Elias Darnell seems to imply that it was his brother Allen, who he had stayed behind to care for, who was killed on the 23rd. See Darnell's Journal, p. 54.

sheltered more of the wounded. There, Atherton was left alone, just inside the front gate. Helpless to intervene, he could only stand there and watch the horrible drama unfold, just as it had at Godfroy's.

There were 40 wounded Americans in Jerome's house, which had been turned into a hospital. Among them were many of the wounded officers, including Major Graves, Captain Hickman, and Captain Hart. The wounded were spread throughout the house; in the spacious loft and in the two main floor rooms separated by the kitchen.[730]

The pillaging of Jerome's house began an hour after daylight, when half a dozen warriors suddenly burst through the door. At first, they didn't molest anyone or take anything. They just wandered about as their numbers grew, but Medard Couture was immediately concerned by their demeanor.[731]

Entering a room occupied by Major Graves, and Captains Hickman and Hart, Couture blurted out, "*Capitaine Hart, nous sommes perdus — we are all lost. The Indians are coming instead of the sleds promised by the British.*"[732]

They could hear Indians breaking through the outside cellar door, looking for the stores of liquor they thought were hidden there. Rolling out some barrels, they broke open the heads, but grumbled at how little was left from the previous occupiers of the settlement.

Graves and Hart then took Couture into the adjoining room. "*What do the Indians intend to do with us?*" asked Captain Hart.

"*On a l'intention de vous tuer,*" came the reply, "*They intend to kill you.*"

"*Ask liberty of them for me to make a speech to them before they kill us,*" demanded the captain. But Couture explained, "*They can't understand. And if we undertook to interpret for you, they will as soon kill us as you.*"

As they talked, the Indians came into the first room the officers had

---

730 Algonquin Club: "Reminiscences of an Actor in the War of 1812," From <u>Canadian Emigrant</u>, 1835. Author unknown. Typed copy in Bidlack's Notes, Monroe County Museum Archives. Many of the wounded, like Charles Bradford, had hardly slept at all. Sometime between 2 and 3 a.m., Bradford had awakened to discover that the Indian Department interpreters had left, leaving the Americans defenseless. By the time the Indians arrived, Medard Couture had returned to help.

731 Deposition of Gustavus M. Bower, dated April 24, 1813, in <u>Barbarities of the Enemy, exposed in a Report of the Committee of the House of Representatives, and the Documents accompanying said Report.</u> Troy: Francis Adancourt, 1813, pp. 139-41. Bower said he was in Jerome's house with Major Graves, Captains Hart and Hickman, Doctor Todd, and 15 or 20 privates. He estimated the number of Indians grew to one or two hundred.

732 Hosmer, H. Lord. <u>Early History of the Maumee Valley.</u> Toledo: Hosmer & Harris, 1858, p. 39.

vacated and began taking clothes and blankets from the wounded. The room was furnished with two beds, a bureau, a small table and a couple of chairs. The Indians forced open the drawers of the bureau and tossed out towels, table cloths, shirts, and pillow slips.

The pillagers also attacked the bed, ripped open the mattress tick, threw out the feathers, and divided the sheeting between them. Several grabbed Reverend Dudley, taking his coat, overcoat, hat, and shoes.

Seeing what was happening, Sergeant John Dawson meekly got up. He had been shot early in the previous day's fighting, about 9 a.m., when a bullet passed under his right arm and lodged between his ribs.

Ignoring the pain, Dawson put on his coat and knapsack. As he glumly walked outside, a warrior seized his coat and another directed him to place his knapsack on a sled.[733]

His messmate, Albert Ammerman, followed Dawson outside, where an Indian demanded his knapsack, which he gave him. Shown to a nearby log, Ammerman nervously sat down to watch and wait.[734]

Private Ammerman had been hit by a ball in the fleshy part of his thigh on January 18th. He had watched the battle of the 22nd from the safety of the hospital and had begged to join the other prisoners after the surrender. Although his wound was slight, and he could walk, a British officer told him to stay behind, a decision that he feared would probably cost him his life.[735]

Meanwhile, Dr. Todd was helping Captain Hart find a place that had

---

733 Deposition of John Dawson, orderly sergeant, April 21, 1813, in <u>Barbarities of the Enemy, exposed in a Report of the Committee of the House of Representatives, and the Documents accompanying said Report,</u> Troy: Francis Adancourt, 1813, pp. 146-7. Dawson was an orderly sergeant in Capt. Glave's company of the 1st Kentucky Volunteer Infantry Regiment, but was attached to Captain Uriel Sebree's company, and was in both battles on the 18th and 22nd. About 9 a.m. on January 22, he was hit under the right arm, the ball lodging in his ribs. He couldn't understand why the interpreters were not there to talk the Indians out of what they were doing, but he thought he had heard one of them tell Captain Hart that he couldn't speak "Indian."

734 Deposition of Albert Ammerman, April 21, 1813, in <u>Barbarities of the Enemy, exposed in a Report of the Committee of the House of Representatives, and the Documents accompanying said Report,</u> Troy: Francis Adancourt, 1813, pp. 146-7. Ammerman was a private in Glave's company, 1st Kentucky Volunteer Infantry Regiment.

735 Deposition of Albert Ammerman, <u>Report of the Committee…as Relates to the Spirit & Manner in which the War has been Waged by the Enemy,</u> Washington: A & G. Way, 1813, pp. 160-161: Ammerman watched the burning of the houses occupied by the wounded. Many of them struggled to put their heads out of the windows while enveloped in the smoke and flames.

already been trashed and was unlikely to attract more Indians.[736] In relative quiet, he set about tending to Hart's wound, but they were soon interrupted by the arrival of a Native warrior.

Fortunately, the Potawatomi spoke English and knew Dr. Todd by name as well as rank. It was he who had, on the previous day, admonished the British to station interpreters in all the buildings where wounded prisoners were kept.

He asked Dr. Todd why the surgeons and the wounded were still there. Todd could only reply that he had promised to remain until the sleighs arrived.

The Indian shook his head and called the British "damned rascals" for not removing the wounded the previous day. The chiefs were still in council with each other, and maybe only the badly wounded would have to die.

Upon hearing this, Hart's countenance fell. In desperation, he offered the Potawatomi a hundred dollars to take him to Detroit. But the Indian refused, *"I cannot take you. You are too badly wounded. Boys, you are all to be killed."*[737]

Just then, a wounded man was murdered at the door of the house, causing an immediate panic.[738] The Potawatomi advised Hart and Todd to be quiet, and maybe they'd be spared. Then he left.

---

736 Lossing, Benson J. The Pictorial Field-Book of the War of 1812. Glendale, New York: Benchmark Publishing Corporation, 1970, p. 358. There has been much confusion of detail between the accounts of the deaths of Captains Hart and Woolfolk. The location to which Hart and Todd went is one of those points in question. Some of this was said to have happened at the house of Jacques Navarre, some distance from Jerome's. Other possibilities were that they went next door to Jerome's other dwelling house, or simply removed themselves to a room that had already been trashed.

737 Atherton, William, Narrative of the Suffering & Defeat of the North-Western Army under General Winchester. Frankfort, KY, A. G. Hodges, 1842. pp. 62-63.

738 The man murdered at the door may have been Captain Hickman, whose demise was witnessed by Reverend Dudley, William Atherton, and several others. As a warrior was pushing Dudley out onto the front steps, he passed within 6 feet of Captain Hickman, lying on a bed, clad only in a flannel shirt. Captain Hickman was a 6-foot tall, handsome, and popular ex-jailer from Franklin County, Kentucky, whose father was a noted Baptist preacher. See: Dudley, Rev. Thomas P., "The Battle and Massacre at Frenchtown, Michigan, January, 1813," Historical and Archaeological Tracts, Number One. Cleveland: Western Reserve Historical Society, August, 1870.

See also: Lee, Anne H., Franklin County GenWeb article, Sept. 24, 2003, www.rootsweb.com: *"…Captain Hickman was severely wounded and was carried from the battlefield, both of his legs were…so badly mangled that they were amputated the next morning, January 23, 1813…Captain Hickman was dragged to the door, his brains dashed out with a tomahawk, and his body thrown back into the house."* This account seems a bit sensational, but is not inconsistent with the result. Hickman's company, from Franklin County, Kentucky, was part of the 1st Kentucky Volunteer Rifle Regiment.

Soon, more Indians came swarming into the room, jostling Captain Hart's ankle enough to cause him a great deal of pain. Dr. Todd offered to help Captain Hart to a house upriver that had already been plundered by the Indians. Perhaps there, they would be undisturbed while Dr. Todd checked Hart's leg and ankle.[739]

Atherton could not bear to look, so he turned away and walked around the house towards the back yard. As he rounded the corner, he ran into an Indian who grabbed him and searched his pockets for money, then let him go.

Atherton continued to walk towards the back of the property, leaving the building behind on his right, walking very slowly. At this point, he noticed a small, dark, deserted log building nearby, which could provide a hiding place, and tried to make his way there without attracting attention.

Within a few paces of the gaping door, he was stopped by another Indian coming from the opposite direction, who demanded to know where he was wounded.

Atherton placed his hand on his shoulder, and the Indian examined the wound, feeling it with his own hand. Having decided it was not serious, the warrior took Atherton to another house, where he had stashed his plunder.[740]

There, he placed a blanket around Atherton, gave him a hat to wear, took him to the back door of the house where the wounded lay, and left him in charge of his musket. The surprised Atherton rejoiced that the warrior had not only spared him, but was apparently taking him on as some kind of servant.[741]

Atherton remained there a couple hours, watching several men from his company pass by, hobbling along with the use of some sticks.

Shortly thereafter, an Indian kindled a small fire inside the hallway near the back door, where he stood. Suddenly, a second Indian came downstairs,

---

They suffered one of the highest casualty rates of any unit in the battle. The author of this article counted 86 Franklin County volunteers at the River Raisin, but can account for only 13 who eventually made it back home.

739 Deposition of Dr. John Todd, April 24, 1813, in Barbarities of the Enemy, exposed in a Report of the Committee of the House of Representatives, and the Documents accompanying said Report. Troy: Francis Adancourt, 1813. pp. 141-5. Perhaps the intended house was that of Jacques Navarre.

740 Perhaps this house, or more likely the small log building, was Jerome's bake house.

741 Atherton, William, Narrative of the Suffering & Defeat of the North-Western Army under General Winchester. Frankfort, Ky: A. G. Hodges, 1842, pp. 60-65.

carrying an open keg of gunpowder. Slipping at the foot of the stairs, he nearly spilled the gunpowder onto the flames.

Gradually, the fire gained the roof, causing it to collapse. As he fled, Atherton could hear no cries from inside, which caused him to conclude that all the wounded had been killed or taken away before the house was burnt.

Prior to this, the Potawatomi had returned for Dr. Todd, claiming him as his prisoner. Leaving the distraught Captain Hart behind, they went outside, walking past the corpses of Captain Hickman and two others who had been tomahawked, stripped and scalped. The Indian tied Dr. Todd and took him to the British hospital camp at Stony Creek, some 4 miles away.

Soon another Indian came in, put his blanket over Major Graves, and led him outside, where they saw Reverend Dudley standing barefoot in snow up to his calf. Graves asked if he had been claimed by an Indian, and when Dudley replied that he hadn't, the major suggested he come along with them.

Dudley gamely replied, *"No, if you are safe, I am satisfied."* At this, Graves passed on by. Dudley was never to see him again.[742]

Several more Indians then arrived, giving Dudley the once over. Dudley made signs that he was wounded and the ball was still in his shoulder. The warriors shook their heads and went on.

Worn out with pain, fear, and suspense, Dudley reached his hand beneath his vest to feel the wound. It hurt to beat the Devil, despite the cold. Finally, a young warrior spied him and came over to inspect his wound.

By means of gestures, the warrior reassured Dudley that the bullet had passed safely through the shoulder, and he would be alright. The Indian took off a blanket *capote*, of which he had two, and placed it over Dudley's shoulders, tying it on by the sleeves. He also gave him a large red apple to eat.

As they headed off, the warrior noticed Dudley's feet were raw and bleeding. Since the Indian was wearing two pairs of moccasins, he slipped off the outer pair and placed them on Dudley's feet.[743]

In the meantime, Medard Couture and Dr. Bower had been stripped, tied,

---

742 The last sighting of Major Graves was by Sgt. John Dawson. On January 23, while in the custody of the Indians at Sandy Creek, Dawson saw the major in an Indian sleigh. Deposition of John Dawson, orderly sergeant, April 21, 1813, in <u>Barbarities of the Enemy, exposed in a Report of the Committee of the House of Representatives, and the Documents accompanying said Report,</u> Troy: Francis Adancourt, 1813. pp. 146-7.

743 Dudley, Rev. Thomas P., "The Battle and Massacre at Frenchtown, Michigan, January, 1813," <u>Historical and Archaeological Tracts, No. 1,</u> Cleveland: Western Reserve Historical Soc., Aug., 1870.

and left standing in the yard by some Chippewas. At that moment, Couture caught the eye of an old family friend, an Odawa chief named Waugon.[744]

Seeing the danger that Couture was in, the chief put his finger to his lips and gave a shrill whistle. Several warriors quickly came running to the spot.

"Take care of him," said Waugon, as he pointed to Couture. *"Give him his clothes. He is my son. His father lies dead in the yard, and I am now his father. Don't harm him. We shall call him Saguana — Be Brave."*[745]

Couture asked Waugon if he could protect Dr. Bower. Waugon agreed, took Bower to a horse standing about 20 paces from the house, and gestured for him to wait there. Left alone, Dr. Bower's fear subsided, and he became concerned for those left behind at Godfroy's house, about a hundred yards away.

He headed off in that direction, but stopped short when he saw the house was still surrounded by Indians.[746] At that moment, an Odawa-Ojibwa chief named McCarty came upon him. McCarty handed Bower his horse and blanket, motioning him to lead the horse back over to Jerome's house.

It did not take long for Waugon to notice Bower's absence and find him. Angry that Bower had tried to get away, he brandished his tomahawk as if to strike the frightened doctor. Fortunately, McCarty stopped him.[747]

Back at Jerome's house, Bower joined a small group of wounded prisoners standing around a *cariole* full of items taken from the *habitants'* homes. He immediately recognized Privates Bradford, Searls, and Turner.[748]

---

744 Hosmer, Hezekiah L. <u>Early History of the Maumee Valley</u>. Toledo: Hosmer & Harris, 1858, p. 39. This happened when warriors were still preparing to set the building on fire.

745 *Saguana* comes from local lore, but it is similar to *swangideed*, the word for *a brave person* in Frederic Baraga's <u>Dictionary of the Ojibway Language</u>. There are other words, however, that also seem close. None of them match the exact spelling.

746 Deposition of Gustavus M. Bower, dated April 24, 1813, in <u>Barbarities of the Enemy, exposed in a Report of the Committee of the House of Representatives, and the Documents accompanying said Report,</u> Troy: Francis Adancourt, 1813, pp. 139-41

747 Letter of Dr. Gustavus Miller Bower, Feb. 25, 1858, copy in clipping files, Monroe County Historical Museum Archives. Also, Deposition of Gustavus M. Bower, dated April 24, 1813, in <u>Barbarities of the Enemy, exposed in a Report of the Committee of the House of Representatives, and the Documents accompanying said Report,</u> Troy: Francis Adancourt, 1813, pp. 139-41.

748 Deposition of Gustavus M. Bower, dated April 24, 1813, in <u>Barbarities of the Enemy, exposed in a Report of the Committee of the House of Representatives, and the Documents accompanying said Report,</u> Troy: Francis Adancourt, 1813, pp. 139-41. Bradford had been among the first to leave the cabin, but was claimed by an Indian out in the yard. The warrior gave him some of his plunder to hold. A few minutes later, they were joined by James Ebenezer Blythe. He was limping badly from a wound he had received in the thigh about 8 o'clock on the previous day. Since none of

Not all the Kentuckians were wounded. Although uninjured, Thomas Pollard had stayed behind to care for his wounded messmates, Ammerman, Dawson, and Green. He and John Dawson witnessed Captain Hart, helped by Medard Couture, bargaining with Osamed, a Potawatomi warrior. After a while Osamed threw his blanket over Hart.

Since Captain Hart was wounded in the calf or ankle and couldn't walk very well, Osamed accepted Hart's offer of $100 to take him to Detroit.[749]

Pollard and Dawson watched as Osamed put a pair of socks on Hart's feet, helped him onto his horse, and led him off along the road to Detroit.[750]

The rest of the group was herded off as well. At the mouth of a lane, John Dawson was overtaken by a dozen Indians led by an aid to Roundhead dressed in a British officer's coat. A couple other warriors were busily scalping two of their victims, but got out of the way when the Native leader yelled at them.[751]

---

the Indians had taken him as a captive, Blythe felt more vulnerable and unprotected than the others. He begged a passing warrior to take him to Malden, offering him 40, then 50, dollars.

749 In a January 9, 1827, interview, Monroe County Justice of the Peace Peter P. Ferry recorded that Medard Couture "states there was in the house at that time two thousand five hundred dollars, placed there by Captain Hart, of the United States service: that this money was taken by the Indians, in his presence; this money, deponent understood, was money designed for the payment of the troops. In the storehouse, also, was a large quantity of provisions, belonging to the troops of the United States; and in the bake-house, which was occupied by Captain McCracken's company, there was a large quantity of military baggage; and in the stable a number of military saddles and sets of harness; and that these several buildings, with their contents, were all burned by the British and Indians, except the money aforesaid, which was in gold and silver, and distributed among the Indians. That all these several buildings were in the possession of the United States." See: House Report No. 51 of the 20th Congress, 2nd Session, January 19, 1829. See also: Hosmer, H. Lord, Early History of the Maumee Valley, Toledo: Hosmer & Harris, 1858, p. 42.

750 Deposition of Thomas Pollard, April 21, 1813, in Barbarities of the Enemy, exposed in a Report of the Committee of the House of Representatives, and the Documents accompanying said Report. Troy: Francis Adancourt, 1813, pp. 146-7. Major Garrard had this to say about the circumstances involved in Captain Hart's injury: "There was also another building, adjoining the dotted line on the map, which formed a small avenue between the back of that and the front of No. 13, about three or four feet in width, through which many shot of the enemy passed, and in which Capt. Hart was wounded."
See also: Dec. 11, 1828, affidavit of James Garrard of the County of Bourbon and State of Kentucky, taken at the request of Col. Godfroy and others of French Town in the Territory of Michigan, in relation to the occupation of said town by the American army and its subsequent destruction by the British and Indians in 1813, as printed in the House Report No. 51 of the 20th Congress, 2nd Session, January 19, 1829.

751 Deposition of John Dawson, April 21, 1813, Report of the Committee...as Relates to the Spirit & Manner in which the War has been waged by the Enemy, Washington: A & G. Way, 1813, pp. 158-160: Dawson was taken to Sandy Creek, where he was one of the last to see Major Graves

About half a mile further north on the road to Detroit, Albert Ammerman, was being prodded along by his Native captor. Stopping to rest, they were overtaken by two Indians leading Captain Hart on a horse. One was a Potawatomi; the other, a Wyandot.

The warriors were arguing loudly and motioning at Captain Hart. Unable to understand the language, Ammerman guessed it had something to do with whose prisoner he was. The dispute became so heated, both Indians raised their guns and aimed them at each other.[752]

As if by mutual consent, however, the muzzles were gradually lowered, and the Indians turned their attention to Captain Hart. Suddenly, the Wyandot raised his rifle and fired.

The bullet struck the captain in the left side, but he retained his balance on the horse's back.

The claimant then pulled Hart off his horse and one of the warriors knocked him down with a war club. The other then finished him off with a tomahawk and scalped him.

---

being transported in a sleigh by the Indians. On January 24, at Brownstown, he saw a man named Downey who was so crippled by rheumatism that he could no longer walk. The Indians tomahawked and stripped him on the spot. Dawson was taken to the River Rouge and remained with the Indians for 7 days before being ransomed by Captain Muir at Detroit, leaving John Davenport behind in the Indian camp. Muir sent him to Sandwich, from where he was taken to Fort George on Feb. 8 and finally released Feb. 19.

752 Lossing, Benson J., The Pictorial Field-Book of the War of 1812, Glendale, New York: Benchmark Publishing Corporation, 1970, p. 359. Lossing mentions another version of the story, in which Hart made a deal with a Potawatomi to take him to Detroit. At the house of Francois Lasselle, a Wyandot came out and demanded the prisoner be turned over to him. The Potawatomi attempted to defend Hart, but the Wyandot shot him and scalped him. Lossing, himself, did not completely accept this version, since the local *habitants* were not entirely familiar with all the officers in Winchester's army. Dennis Au has suggested the *habitants* were confused between Captain Wolfolk and Captain Hart. Since Albert Ammerman was at least in the same army with Captain Hart, his version, as given here, is considered the most reliable.

The location of Hart's death was estimated in various accounts at anywhere from a mile to 5 miles north of the River Raisin on the road to Detroit. That could put the incident as far north as Stony Creek, although Ammerman's narrative indicates a spot much closer to the Raisin. A historical marker for Hart's death was erected on North Dixie Highway, about a mile north of the river, at the entrance to Carter Lumber Company. See also: Brown, Samuel, Views of the Campaigns of the North-Western Army. Troy, N.Y.: Francis Adancourt, 1814, p. 37: "...*after traveling as far as the river Aux Sables, they were met by a fresh band of Indians, who shot the captain upon his horse, and tomahawked and scalped him.*" (Hull's Road crossed the river Aux Sables (Sandy Creek) about 2 miles north of the River Raisin.)

They looted the body and left it lying in the road.[753]

Captain Hart negotiating with Osamed
Diorama Created by Ken Osen for the Monroe County Historical Museum
Provided Courtesy of the National Park Service,
River Raisin National Battlefield Park

---

753 Deposition of Albert Ammerman, April 21, 1813, in Barbarities of the Enemy, exposed in a Report of the Committee of the House of Representatives, and the Documents accompanying said Report. Troy: Francis Adancourt, 1813, pp. 146-7: "...I was gratified in observing that, during the scene of trial, Captain Hart refrained from supplication or entreaty, but appeared perfectly calm and collected. He met his fate with that firmness which was his particular characteristic. No other prisoner of our army of the United States was present to witness this melancholy scene, the death of Captain Hart. During my captivity with the Indians, five days only, I was treated with more hospitality than I had any reason to expect, much more so than I experienced from the British after I was ransomed at Detroit by Mr. Benjamin Chittenden, who will ever be entitled to my utmost gratitude; by him I was humanely treated, and also by some of the French Canadians."
See also: "Narrative of Timothy Mallory," History of Monroe County, pp. 83-84. Mallory claimed to have been in a group of prisoners who witnessed the money being paid to the Indian. They were then marched off, and four of their number were tomahawked, including Captain Hart. Mallory had suffered 3 broken ribs when hit by a plank split off by a cannonball during the fighting on January 22. He would spend the night of the 23rd at a camp about 3 miles from Brownstown.

Private claim 98, ¼ mile upriver from the Jerome house, Jan. 23, 1813:

Several warriors with prisoners in tow were approaching his house, when Antoine Campeau caught sight of them. Knowing other Kentuckians were hiding on his property, Campeau thought it best to go out to meet them.

As the warriors came closer, Campeau noticed a young man and called to him, asking if he were hungry, and offering a basket of apples to the group.

Unfortunately, the prisoner, being closest, was the first to reach into the basket. He paid for his audacity with his life. The Indians then began searching the grounds around the Campeau house and barn.

A very young warrior, no more than a boy, caught site of a fugitive hiding under a haystack. He yelled to the warriors gathered around the body of their dead prisoner. With a whoop, they started after him.

Campeau, still dismayed and shocked by the death of the first Kentuckian, called out after their leader, saying, *"Chef, donne-moi ta parole! Sauve cet homme! Give me your word to save that man!"*[754]

Surprisingly, he did so. The Indians seized the unfortunate soldier and soon departed with their new prisoner. But not before warning Campeau that he might suffer a similar fate if he dared to bury their first victim.[755]

The next group to pass Campeau's house had one of Winchester's staff officers riding his own horse, on which he had been captured the previous day. Campeau motioned them to continue on to the home of François Lasselle, 40 rods further upstream.

Many of the local *habitants* thought the officer was Captain Hart, but he was probably Captain Woolfolk, Winchester's secretary. He had escaped the morning butchery, but was captured while hiding in a *habitant's* house.[756]

---

754 (Dennissen p. 199), (Palmer, p. 137)

755 The reason for the Indian insistence that the American dead be denied burial has been attributed to retaliation for similar actions on the part of the Americans. Blackbird would later complain that the Big Knives habitually cut up native casualties into "little pieces." Indeed, the Kentuckians had scalped and mutilated the bodies of Indian warriors, which had been left on the field after the fight on January 18th. Also, the threat to kill anyone found burying a dead American soldier could be seen as a sort of grisly loyalty test to be applied to the local *habitants*, most of whom had supported the American cause. (See: Antal, Sandy. A Wampum Denied: Procter's War of 1812. Canada: Carleton University Press, 1997.)

756 Report of Ensign Baker, Feb. 26, 1813 in Barbarities of the Enemy, exposed in a Report of the Committee of the House of Representatives, and the Documents accompanying said Report, Troy: Francis Adancourt, 1813, pp. 133-4. Baker named the following prisoners killed by the Indians: Captains Nathaniel Hart, Virgil McCracken, John Woolfolk, and Pascal Hickman, as well as Privates James E. Blythe, Charles Serles, Thomas S. Crow, Daniel Darnell, Thomas Ward, William

Woolfolk had become somewhat inured to the pain of the two wounds he had suffered, but he was desperate to be released. Nearing Lasselle's house, he offered a thousand dollars to anyone who would ransom him.

Although tempted, François Lasselle was already sheltering Polly Knaggs and her 6-year-old son George and didn't want to take the chance that the Indians would discover them. He had hidden the boy in the chimney above the fireplace. It was uncertain what these warriors might do if they found he was hiding the family of the notorious Indian fighter, James Knaggs.[757]

Lasselle knew it was out of his power to bargain with the Indians, but Jocko, his brother, had enough influence. Lasselle told the Indians to take the captain there.

In the meantime, Jocko's daughter, Nanette, had prevailed upon her father to rescue some of the American officers. Lasselle hitched up his pony cart, and together, they drove eastward along the north bank of the river.

About 15 rods upriver from François Lasselle's farm was a house belonging to Joseph Ruland. Antoine Boulard and Louis Bernard dit Lajoye also lived nearby. The main house was currently occupied by five Delawares who had come looking for plunder and found some whisky.

As Woolfolk was led by, they motioned his captor to join them. The warrior left Woolfolk on the horse, which he tied to a gate post, and went in.[758]

Butler, Henry Downy, and John Sidney. Of these, Downy and Butler were not scalped. In addition to those named above, Baker claimed to have personally seen two others tomahawked at Sandy Creek, and prisoner reports at Sandwich indicate possibly 15 to 18 more prisoners may have been similarly murdered. One reportedly had been burned to death. See appendices I and J.

757 Ross, Robert B., edit., History of the Knaggs Family of Ohio and Michigan. Detroit: Clarence M. Burton, 1902, p. 38. George was the first-born son of James Knaggs, the only child of his first wife, Jemima Griffin, who died shortly after he was born in 1806. He outlived all his siblings, dying in Monroe, Michigan, at the age of 94. François Lasselle had earlier been threatened by a band of Wyandots, who had occupied his backyard at the commencement of the battle. They had demanded to know if any Americans were within. François replied from an upper window that nobody but women and children were there. The Wyandots warned him to close up his doors and windows and not to allow any of the enemy to shelter in his house. If they found any, they would kill everyone inside and burn all his buildings.

758 Deposition of Antoine Boulard, Feb. 5, 1813, Report of the Committee...as Relates to the Spirit & Manner in which the War has been Waged by the Enemy, Washington: A and G. Way, 1813, pp129-132. Boulard said the officer's body lay in front of his door for 2 days. Another source says it was in front of Ruland's. I have tried to reconcile the accounts by placing Boulard in Ruland's house. According to the maps, the house in question would seem to be on land owned by Robert Navarre, private claim 58, or possibly even still on that of François Lasselle.

Just then Jocko and Nanette Lasselle pulled up in their *charrette*. Jocko jumped off the cart and offered a hefty ransom for the captive officer.

The Potawatomi agreed to give him up in exchange for some gold coins, a saddle, a bridle, and a few smaller articles.[759] But, when Jocko reached for the horse's bridle to lead the prisoner away, a shot rang out. The bullet passed right through Woolfolk's breast and back.[760]

The victim shrugged and leaned over, but did not fall from the saddle until an Indian ran up, drew out a saber, and struck him on the head several times.[761]

759 Lasselle and others who were on intimate terms with the Indians often found themselves in the potentially dangerous role of intermediary, as shown in this letter to Hyacinthe Lasselle at Vincennes, written after the first siege of Fort Meigs, May 26, 1813: "...concerning your Mom, she is, I believe, at Mr. Lafontaine's in Detroit...Mr. Lafontaine told me she was staying at his place in order to be closer to a church. As for your brothers, when General Winchester was defeated at the River Raisin, Chesne told me that he had seen and spoken to Jocko, but had seen neither Francois nor Antoine, and that the poor Jocko was in a state of great sadness still at the evening before of having all his goods reduced to ashes by the English and Indians, as they burned the houses of G. Godfroy and the old Jerome, with 100 prisoners who were in the 2 houses. A short while ago, Felix was at Urbana, where he saw a young Couture and Loranger, who told him that Colonel Proctor, the Englishman, had given permission to the soldiers and Indians to pillage and destroy all his goods. He unwisely confronted Proctor (you know how spirited he is) telling him those goods didn't belong to him at all, that he was in debt himself to the English, that if he were ruined, it would be a wrong done to his creditors. You know Tecumseh is a good friend of Jocko. And so, the blow was prevented and he is still residing at the River Raisin. However, I am very concerned for this area because of the defeat of the English at the foot of the Rapids. They are so mortified that I fear they will reduce the entire River Raisin country to ashes."

760 Hosmer, Hezekiah Lord. Early History of the Maumee Valley. Toledo: Hosmer and Harris, 1858, p. 42. See also: Burton untitled manuscript statement of the late Mrs. Thomas Caldwell and Judge Durocher's account of Captain Hart's Massacre, printed in MPHC, Miscellaneous Documents, pp. 644-5. These accounts all differ, and almost all refer to Captain Hart, rather than Woolfolk. I have tried to put them together in a logical sequence. The victim is almost always shot, whether in the back, head, or breast, and by either a Wyandot from a "waste house," one of the Delawares, or some unidentified Indian crossing the river. The killers always argue over the body. I'm crediting all these accounts as descriptions of the death of Captain Woolfolk, and accepting only that of one of the Kentuckians, Albert Ammerman, as the most accurate description of Hart's murder on January 23. Most accounts also place Woolfolk's death on January 23. Often, the victim is not identified by name, but rather by title, as the Secretary of Gen. Winchester. Woolfolk was the general's secretary.

761 Deposition of Antoine Boulard, Feb. 4, 1813, # 27 in Barbarities of the Enemy, exposed in a Report of the Committee of the House of Representatives, and the Documents accompanying said Report. Troy: Francis Adancourt, 1813. pp. 129-130. St. Cosme, however, informed Judge Bacon of Monroe that he was in the road and saw the captain, whom he identified as Hart, who *"fell from his horse instantly on being shot, and died without a groan."* Whether this was on the river road or on the road to Detroit is not mentioned.

No sooner had the prisoner hit the ground, than the Indians rushed forward to scalp and strip him.

Woolfolk's captor was enraged by the killing of his prisoner, but the Delawares restrained him till he calmed down. Then they led away the horse and left the body lying in the road to be eaten by hogs.[762]

"Residence of La Salle"[763]

Other local witnesses on January 23, 1813:

The Robert home was on private claim 161, just across the River Raisin from the Jerome property. Early in the morning, Joseph Robert was surveying the damage to his house, when he saw a commotion over at Jerome's house.

It was shortly after sunrise, and the wounded American prisoners were being taken outside. First, one was shot, then another, and finally a third. They were finished off with tomahawks.[764]

---

762 Deposition of Louis Lajoye, Feb. 5, 1813, #28 in <u>Barbarities of the Enemy, exposed in a Report of the Committee of the House of Representatives, and the Documents accompanying said Report.</u> Troy: Francis Adancourt, 1813. p. 130.

763 As sketched in the 1860s by Mrs. Sarah A. Noble to show what the house would have looked like in 1813, printed in Benson J. Lossing's <u>The Pictorial Field Book of the War of 1812,</u> Vol. I, p. 359.

764 Deposition of Joseph Robert, <u>Barbarities of the Enemy, exposed in a Report of the Committee of the House of Representatives, and the Documents accompanying said Report.</u> Troy: Francis Adancourt, 1813. pp. 125-6. *"...three were shot, the others were killed in the houses, and burnt with the houses...there were about 48 or 49 prisoners in the two houses. The deponent has seen dead*

Pretty soon the Roberts noticed flames rising up through the windows and onto the roof. Then another house upstream suddenly lit up like a torch.

"Isn't that where they set up the hospital for the wounded Kentuckians?" asked Madame Robert, *"What has happened to the ones who were inside?"* The answer was revealed when a dozen Indians crossed the river and came up to their house carrying a large number of scalps.

Entering the house, the warriors piled the scalps on the floor and made the women tear down the calico window curtains and the bed curtains. These they used to tie and wrap the scalps. While engaged in their project, several of them began to question Joseph Robert, demanding that he join them and fight against the Americans. Having finished, the Indians departed, and Joseph took his family to Detroit. They would not return until the following October.[765]

Another witness was Jean-Baptiste Bruneau, an illiterate hunter and trapper living in Jerome's boarding house. He remained unmolested during all this, and witnessed the Indians setting fire to Jerome's two dwelling houses, a barn, stable, storehouse, and hen house. Bruneau counted at least 10 prisoners taken away, but he estimated most of the 40 or so remaining prisoners were tomahawked and some of the wounded were left to perish in the flames.[766]

Meanwhile, Medard Couture tried to save as much of his family's property as he could. As he pulled items out of the burning buildings, he asked some of the nearby warriors why they were burning his home. They replied that they would not have done so if it had not been used to shelter the U.S. troops.[767]

---

bodies on the high-way, which the hogs were tearing and eating..."
It is hard to reconcile the various accounts in order to estimate the actual number of wounded and unwounded prisoners occupying each of the houses.

765 (Robert bio, Wing, p. 116.)

766 Deposition of J-B. Bruneau, Detroit, Oct. 26, 1816. Also: Testimony August 28, 1813, Report of the Committee of Claims on the Petition of Jean B. Jerome & Others, Jan. 25, 1822. Copy at William L. Clements Library, University of Michigan. See also: Hosmer's Early History of the Maumee Valley, p. 39. The numbers and types of buildings owned by Jerome vary according to different testimonies.

767 Report of the House Committee of Claims on the petition of Jean — B. Jerome and others, Jan. 25, 1822. Statement of Medard Couture, Oct. 29, 1816. Medard was eventually taken to Detroit, where he was released. He returned to the River Raisin and buried his father. Medard was fairly well educated. His family had intended him for the priesthood. He became a prominent citizen after the war, until his death in 1857. Two years later, his widow married James Knaggs, another well-known local veteran of the War of 1812.

Meanwhile, *Monsieur* Tuot (Tuott dit Duval) and several other citizens had returned to see what had become of the homes they had fled.

They were aghast when they arrived at their farmstead, located on private claim 346, across the river from the 17th Infantry's campsite. The house was littered with cannonballs and grapeshot. The beds and furniture were broken. Almost everything not plundered had been destroyed.

Across the river they could see houses burning and hear the screams of dying men. Horrified, but helpless to intervene, they gathered up a few items and returned to their families in hiding.[768]

The Tibbets farm, private claim 548, was located upstream, some distance away from the action. Little Benjamin Tibbetts was only eight years old, but he was happy to be helping his mother on one of her errands of mercy. They had gathered up some supplies for the wounded Kentuckians. On their way to deliver them, they were stopped by some rather stern-looking warriors.

Seeing Benjamin's light hair, a warrior grabbed him by his golden locks and pulled him right off the ground, demanding to know if he were French or a cursed Yankee. Fortunately, the whole family spoke the local French dialect convincingly. They were not allowed to proceed, but were close enough to see the houses burning and hear the shrieks of the doomed Kentuckians.[769]

---

768 Affidavit of Hyacinthe Tuott dit Duval, Nov. 18, 1852. Pension Application Files, War of 1812, Death or Disability, The National Archives "Old War" Invalid and Widow Rejected File No. 16545. Copy in Monroe County Historical Museum Archives, courtesy of Chris and Steve Momany. There were many different versions of the family name, several of which have appeared elsewhere in this book: Tuitt, Tuott, Duval, etc. The comment about solid shot and grape shot would indicate that the British artillery was supporting the assault on the American right wing and advancing with the attack, switching to grape (most likely in the form of case shot) as the range shortened.

769 Biography of Benjamin Tibbetts, History of Monroe County, Michigan, by Wing, p. 122: The Tibbets family moved to Detroit after the battle, where young Benjamin again ran afoul of a band of 50 Indians, who were encamped in a 6-acre field of oats opposite their house. This time, he was playing with a bow and arrow and managed to accidentally shoot a half-breed boy, the son of a British Indian Department officer named George Ironside. The blunted arrow struck the boy over the eye, creating a large black and blue colored bruise. The Indian boy's mother sought revenge, recruiting an older son with a heavy rope. Fortunately, Benjamin's grandmother saw her coming and hid him between two feather beads. Feeling Benjamin would continue to be in danger, Benjamin's mother went to see Detroit's commanding officer. Not wanting to offend the Indians, the British officer arranged a secret rendezvous. He would find an excuse to ride past the tall, board fence in front of their house and pick Benjamin up if he saw him there. So, Benjamin's mother went home and hid him behind some large currant bushes in the garden. As he waited, Benjamin could hear a number of Indians passing not more than 6 feet away. At his mother's signal, the boy quickly climbed the fence, just in time to hop onto the passing officer's horse. Benjamin stayed with the British officer in the fort until Detroit again changed hands in the fall of

Late that morning, James Knaggs arrived at François Lasselles' home looking for his family. Pleased to see them healthy and all in one piece, he resolved to move them to another hiding place.

However, George, his wide-eyed little boy, had witnessed such scenes of desolation and carnage that they would be burned into his memory and remain with him till the day he died, a white-haired old man.[770]

Enquiring into the fate of his other relatives, James was told that Whitmore, Thomas, and Rebecca Knaggs, along with their mother Rachel, had all been taken prisoner. It was presumed they would be sent to Québec.[771]

Alexis Labadie saw the houses burning as well, and was horrified at the thought that some of the wounded were still inside. He wanted to bury the many bodies that lay about, but the Indians had warned the *habitants* that anyone who dared to do so would be considered an enemy and a betrayer.

Alexis could only watch as the semi-wild hogs went positively mad, rooting among the bodies and gorging themselves on the flesh of those who had once been young, proud, Kentucky soldiers.[772]

It would not be until late evening the next day, January 24th, that Alexis Labadie and his son, Medard, would manage to evacuate their relatives to Detroit, traveling from the settlement through a countryside filled with packs of wild dogs and hogs, driven mad *"by the profusion of human flesh."*[773]

La Rivière au sable, January 23, 1813:

Sandy Creek was a rather swift flowing stream which terminated in vast beds of *folle avoine*, or wild rice, as it neared the margin of Lake Erie.[774]

1813. His trials were not completely over, however. During his stay at the fort, the soldiers made fun of him, trying to recruit him into their ranks. The boy indignantly rebuffed all such efforts.

770 Knaggs, May, "Memoir of James Knaggs" in Michigan Pioneer and Historical Collections, Vol. XVII, 1890, 2nd edition. Lansing: Wynkoop, Hallenbeck, Crawford Co., 1910.

771 "Memoir of James Knaggs," by May Stocking Knaggs, MPHC, 1890, p. 222.

772 Grant, Linda, History of the Labadie Family. Spiral Bound Manuscript, p. 162. Monroe County Historical Commission Archives.

773 Alexis was the father of Medard Labadie, a noted partisan and scout for the Americans. The British had placed a price on his head, and Alexis feared for his son's future, as well as that of his family. See: Grant, Linda, History of the Labadie Family, Nov. 24, 1834 affidavit of Medard Labadie p. 163, Monroe County Historical Commission Archives. See also: Deposition of Alexis Labadie, Feb.6, 1813, #29, Barbarities of the Enemy, Troy: Francis Adancourt, 1813, p. 130: *"The inhabitants have been threatened by the Indians, if they did not take up arms against the Americans."*

774 Wild rice is translated literally as *"riz sauvage,"* but the old fur trade term was *"folle avoine,"* (or *folle avoine d'Amérique*) which is the literal equivalent of "wild oats." The French name recalled the

Lt. Baker and about 20 other prisoners taken on January 22 had spent a fitful night there. Early this morning, Baker was left in the care of an old Indian, while his captor and other warriors headed back into French Town.

About 2 o'clock., the Indians returned with scalps and about 30 injured prisoners, although only one appeared to be seriously wounded.[775]

The warriors proceeded to dress the scalps by scraping off the remaining flesh and stretching each scalp over a hoop. After drying the hoops over a fire, they painted them red with vermillion. Some even decorated their scalps with feathers and tied them to small poles to carry around for show.[776]

The Head of a Pipe Tomahawk found along Stoney Creek
Monroe County Historical Museum and River Raisin Battlefield National Park

They also cooked some sweetened gruel, which they shared with their prisoners. Baker was able to mingle with the new prisoners and learn that

---

wild oat grass that was a common weed used for forage in Europe. Other names for wild rice include manoomin, Indian rice, Canadian rice, marsh oats, psin, fool's oats, and mad oats,

775 Draper YY-6.

776 Journal of Lewis Bond, in Knopf, Richard C., Document Transcriptions of the War of 1812 in the Northwest, Vol. X, pt. 1. Columbus: Ohio Historical Society, 1962. p. 197: "I have seen 5, 6, and 8 (scalps) on one pole. If the person killed has good hair, they take the scalp large accordingly, and often make 2 and sometimes 3 scalps from one head. I myself handled and examined 3 on one pole, which I am confident came off one and the same head. On what is commonly called the crown of the head is a curl, which will easily be seen if the scalp has not been divided; there were none on either of those which I examined."

Captain Hickman had been murdered, and some of the wounded had been scalped alive and burned in the houses of French Town.[777]

Around the same time, a party of Indians arrived with eight or ten more prisoners in tow. They made a large fire of fence rails and gave the famished prisoners some bread to eat. Among the prisoners were William Atherton, Jean-Baptiste Beaugrand, and a couple of Kentuckians named Jones and Blythe.

Ebenezer Blythe was a fine-looking young man, a Lexington doctor's son. Only slightly wounded, he sat trying to warm his bare, benumbed feet as he chewed on a crust of bread. Unnoticed, a warrior pulled out his tomahawk and walked around behind him.

Suddenly, the hawk blade flashed against the dull sky and came crashing down on the back of Blythe's head. The others stared in horror over the flaming fire as he fell and was struck twice more.[778]

As Blythe lay agonizing in the snow, the warrior stepped over to Jean-Baptiste Beaugrand, a local fur trader. The prisoners could not understand what was being said, but they could tell Beaugrand was protesting.

Their fear turned to shock when the Indian handed Beaugrand his tomahawk and then stepped back as Beaugrand moved over to the dying Kentuckian. Lifting his right hand, Beaugrand struck the hawk two inches

---

777 Knopf, Richard C., <u>Document Transcriptions of the War of 1812 in the Northwest, Vol. V, pt. 2</u>, Columbus: Ohio Historical Society, 1958, p. 64, Report of Lt. Baker.

778 Atherton, William, <u>Narrative of the Suffering & Defeat of the North-Western Army under General Winchester</u>. Frankfort, Ky: A. G. Hodges, 1842, pp. 67-71. This could have been James Ebenezer Blythe from Capt. Hart's Company of the 5th Kentucky Regiment, son of the president of Transylvania University, who was listed as killed on January 23 in G. Glenn Clift's <u>Remember the Raisin</u>, p. 192. However, Clift quotes Charles Bradford's claim to have seen Blythe killed and scalped by an Indian while standing in the snow next to Dr. Bower (p 84). Clift lists two other Blythes as present, but not killed, at the Raisin; Charles Blythe in Williams' company of the 5th Kentucky, and William Blythe in Hightower's company of the 17th U.S. Infantry. In a letter dated Feb. 25, 1858, Dr. Gustavus Miller Bower agrees with Bradford, saying he saw the "Indians kill young Blith of Capt. Hart's Company," although he's not really clear about the exact place and time. A photocopy of the original letter can be found in the clipping files of the Monroe County Historical Museum Archives. In the same letter, Bower identifies Beaugrand as a guard left by the British. Reverend Dudley, in his account, says they stopped to warm themselves by the fire at Stony Creek, where he saw a commotion among another group of Indians and their prisoners. One of the Indians tomahawked Ebenezer Blythe of Lexington. In one of the reports attributed to Ensign Baker, Jas. P. Blythe is listed as killed at French Town; while another report states he died at Sandy Creek.

into the skull of his unfortunate victim.[779] The warrior then took Beaugrand away.[780]

Atherton tried to ask the warrior who had claimed him as a prisoner if they were going to kill him and his comrades. Misunderstanding the question, which was posed in English, the Indian answered, *"Yes!"*

At this, the prisoners lost what appetite they had. They could feel the hair on the backs of their necks standing on end whenever a warrior passed behind the logs on which they were sitting.[781]

Finally, Jones could stand it no more. Moving to the far side of the fire, he began to cry and shake uncontrollably. His comrades urged him to be still, lest the Indians see this as a sign of weakness and kill him.

Atherton was relieved when his captor ordered him to get up and move along. As he was led away, he could not help but wonder what fate was in store for those who remained behind.[782]

---

779 Findings of the grand jury, Case 427: United States v. Jean-Baptiste Beaugrand, Oct. 19, 1814, Filed June 16, 1823, Typed copy courtesy Pat Tucker: *"…he, the said John Baptiste Beaugrand, with a certain tomahawk of the value of 4 shillings, which he, the said John Baptiste Beaugrand, in his right hand, then and there held and had, the certain person to the jurors unknown and of his malice aforethought did cut strike and thrust, giving to the said person then and there with the tomahawk aforesaid in and upon the head of the certain person aforesaid, an mortal wound of the breadth of two and a half inches of the depth of two inches of which said mortal wound the certain person aforesaid…died…"*

780 Note on Beaugrand, "Petition of Inhabitants of Miami against John Lee," Michigan Pioneer and Historical Collections, Vol. 37, p. 463: *"Capt. J. B. Beaugrand was in a company of militia in Col. John Anderson's regiment and resided at River Raisin. After the defeat of Gen. Winchester, he was taken prisoner and witnessed many cruel scenes. Every day the Indians would select a prisoner and kill him. Finally, one day they handed a tomahawk to Beaugrand and while one Indian stood behind him with an uplifted battle-axe, they ordered him to kill a soldier. He killed the prisoner, thus saving his own life…"*

781 These reports vary according the memory of the person relating them. Blythe was by various accounts killed at Godfroy's house on the Raisin, at Gandon's house on Sandy Creek, and at the British field hospital on Stony Creek. It is possible that Crow was killed at Stony Creek rather than at Sandy Creek. The actual location of the British field hospital is uncertain and some say it could have been on Swan Creek, or even Sandy Creek, instead of Stony Creek.

782 While several accounts say the name of this unfortunate victim was Blythe, Dr. Bower said he saw Blythe killed, along with McCracken, Darnell, and several others, when the Indians burned the hospital buildings at the River Raisin. Baker agrees Blythe was killed at French Town, but claims McCracken was killed the day before, on the 22nd. Bower reported other killings at Sandy Creek, but also said that was the site where the British had camped the night before the battle. He said a man named Surt was killed there, and another named Crow. The only other murder witnessed by Dr. Bower was that of Sidna, a man from Virginia, who was killed at Brownstown. Dr. Bower spent two weeks at River Canard until he was ransomed by Judge McDonald at Detroit. See: Report of Dr. Gustavus Miller Bower, Surgeon's Mate, 5th Kentucky Volunteer Infantry Regiment, received

Meanwhile, Thomas Crow, Charles Searls, Charles Bradford, Julius Turner, and Dr. Bower huddled together eating by the fire. Searls, Turner, and Bradford were wounded and had lost much of their clothing.[783]

Seeing Searls still wore his shoes and hat, a warrior made him hand them over. The Indian next asked Searls how many men were in Harrison's army, but Searls hesitated to answer. Calling him a "Madison," the warrior struck Searls a sharp blow on the shoulders, cutting deep into the cavity of his body. Out of reflex, Searls grabbed hold of the tomahawk.

In a voice of despair and resignation, Dr. Bower begged Searls to give up and submit to his fate. Otherwise, the enraged Indians might kill everyone. With a downcast look, Searls closed his eyes and released his grip.[784]

With that, the Indian tore the tomahawk away from Searles and struck him on the head, splattering blood and brains onto the edge of the blanket where Bower was sitting. Searles was then stripped and scalped.[785]

Fearing for his life, Dr. Bower ran off to seek the protection of the

at Monroe on Feb. 25, 1858. Copy in clipping files, Monroe County Historical Museum Archives.

783 Deposition of Charles Bradford, April 29, 1813, in Barbarities of the Enemy, exposed in a Report of the Committee of the House of Representatives, and the Documents accompanying said Report, Troy: Francis Adancourt, 1813, pp. 146-7. See also: Report of the Committee as Relates to the Spirit & Manner in which the War has been waged by the Enemy, Washington: A & G. Way, 1813, pp. 164-6.

784 Journal of Lewis Bond, in Knopf, Richard C., Document Transcriptions of the War of 1812 in the Northwest, Vol. X, pt. 1Columbus: Ohio Historical Society, 1962. p. 197: By conversation with Dr. Bower, Bond places this incident back at Godfroy's house. *"The Doctor observed that when the Indians entered the house and began the massacre, one man near him caught hold of the Indian's tomahawk and held it some short time, that he spoke and advised him to submit to his fate. He let go of the tomahawk, which was immediately sunk in his head. The brains flew in the Doctor's face, cruel fate, hard indeed to give such advice, but the Doctor saw no way of preventing it, and an act of resistance he feared might cause the whole to share a similar fate."*

785 Deposition of John McDonnell, Feb. 4, 1813, Barbarities of the Enemy, exposed in a Report of the Committee of the House of Representatives, and the Documents accompanying said Report, Troy: Francis Adancourt, 1813, pp. 127-9. Bower later said this description really applied to the death of Blythe. However, Dr. Bower told essentially the same story about Searls, adding other details, which can be found in the "Deposition of Gustavus M. Bower," dated April 24, 1813, in Barbarities of the Enemy, exposed in a Report of the Committee of the House of Representatives, and the Documents Accompanying said Report, Troy: Francis Adancourt, 1813. pp. 139-41

chief who had claimed him as his prisoner, but Thomas Crow was not so fortunate. He became the next victim.[786] Three others meet a similar fate.[787]

Charles Bradford was therefore somewhat relieved when his Native captor loaded him down with 50 pounds of goods and headed him off towards the River Rouge, where a number of Indians were encamped.[788]

After tearing out the smoking hearts of two of their victims, the Indians

---

786 The prisoners may have witnessed another murder mentioned by Dr. Gustavus Bower: *"They also butchered a man by the name of Crow in a most horrible manner; after tomahawking him, they sent some young Indian boys to scalp him. After cutting his hands until he could not use them, they finally got his scalp off. He was stripped naked and remained on the snow some 15 minutes or half an hour, when he rose to his feet and came right in the direction where I was. He was the most ghastly sight I ever witnessed, his scalp off, naked, and the blood running down his body, his eyes wide open with a wild frantic stare, which I still can see in fancy; but the poor man, his suffering did not continue long. The Indians smashed his head in with a squaw axe."* See: "Report of Dr. Gustavus Miller Bower, Surgeon's Mate, 5th Kentucky Volunteer Infantry Regiment," received at Monroe on Feb. 25, 1858. Copy in clipping files, Monroe County Historical Museum Archives.

787 Marc Meyer suggests that the three others were, perhaps, Daniel Darnell, Thomas Ward, and William Butler. Private William Butler of Langhorne's Company of the 1st Rifle Regiment was listed by the Niles Weekly Register, as one of those killed on January 22. Both Daniel Darnell and Thomas Ward were listed in the American State Papers, Military Affairs, Vol. I, as dying on the 23rd. See also: Knopf, Richard C., <u>Document Transcriptions of the War of 1812 in the Northwest, Vol. V, pt. 2</u>, Columbus: Ohio Historical Society, 1958, p. 64, Report of Lt. Baker: *"...Seven days afterwards, I was sold in Detroit to some American gentlemen, and the next day sent over to Sandwich, where I remained nearly three weeks. In this time, I had an opportunity of making inquiry about the massacres, and found that 60 had been massacred subsequent to the day of battle, and two officers the day on which the battle was fought, after they had surrendered. Of the first were Capt. N.G.S. Hart of Lexington, Capt. Pascal Hickman of Franklin, John H. Woolfolk, the general's secretary; and of the latter Capt. Virgil McCracken of Woodford, and Ensign Levi Wells, son of Col. Wells... Massacres were not only committed on the 22nd and 23rd, but also on the 24th, 25th, and 26th, and even three weeks afterwards fresh scalps were brought into Malden."*

788 Bradford was wounded in the right hip. After witnessing the killings at Sandy Creek, he was forced to carry a 50-lb. load of plunder to the Indian camp at River Rouge. See: Affidavit of Charles Bradford, April 29, 1813: *"...this deponent was then packed with forty- or fifty-pounds weight, and taken to the river Rouge, where the Indians had encamped; that whilst he was there, he inquired of an Indian whether he would take him to Malden, as he wished to be given to Captain Elliott. The Indian said, if Captain Elliott told him to do so he would, as they always did as he requested them. This deponent was six days with the Indians before they took him to Detroit, where he was purchased by Stephen Mack and Oliver Miller, for 80 dollars. That the British officer commanding at Detroit (Major Muir) again claimed him as a British prisoner, notwithstanding his having just been ransomed from their allies by his own countrymen, and sent him to Sandwich, where he remained until the 9th or 10th February, when he was sent to Fort George and there paroled. This deponent states that, while a prisoner at Sandwich, he was several times treated insultingly by the British officers, and by one John McGregor; that the citizens, generally, treated the prisoners with kindness and attention, as far as was in their power."*

threw the bodies into the house of François Gandon and set it on fire.[789] Antoine Cuillerie and Alexis Salliot of the River Ecorse were present at the scene, but unable to interfere.[790]

Elias Darnell and his guardian also passed along the road to Detroit, halting for just a few moments at a house occupied by two British officers. When Darnell asked the officers what was going to happen, they said he was being taken to Malden, where he would be reunited with the main body of Kentucky prisoners.[791]

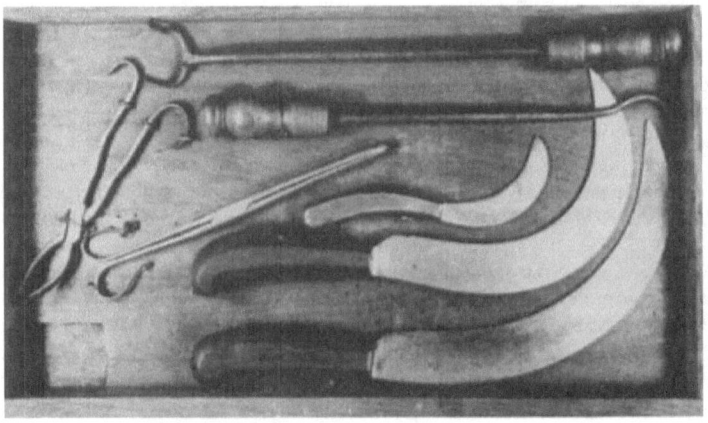

Surgeon's Field Case
U.S. Army Medical Dept. Office of Medical History: "The Army Medical Department, 1775-1818" by Mary C. Gillet, Army Historical Series, U.S. Govt. Printing Office, Washington, D.C., 1981.
This map is a work of a U.S. Army soldier or employee, taken or made as part of that person's official duties. As a work of the U.S. federal government, the text is in the public domain.

---

789 Deposition of Joseph Robert, <u>Barbarities of the Enemy, exposed in a Report of the Committee of the House of Representatives, and the Documents accompanying said Report,</u> Troy: Francis Adancourt, 1813, pp. 125-6.

790 Deposition, <u>Report of the Committee...as Relates to the Spirit & Manner in which the War has been Waged by the</u> Enemy, Washington: A & G. Way, 1813, pp. 124-129.

791 Darnell, Elias, Journal, Philadelphia: Lippincott, Grambo, & Co., 1854, p. 63. Darnell would later write, *"I judged these villains had instructed the Indians to do what they had done. A few miles farther, we came to the Indian encampment, where there were a great many hallowing and yelling in a hideous manner. I thought this my place of destiny. The Indian took off my pack, broiled a piece of meat, and gave me part; this I ate merely in obedience to him. Then we started and arrived at Amherstburg, 18 miles from Frenchtown."*

***La Crique aux roches*, (Stony Creek), early afternoon, on Jan. 23, 1813:**

The British troops and their prisoners had spent the night at Stony Creek and departed about noon for Fort Amherstburg. Setting an easy pace, they would not reach their destination till late that evening.[792]

The British had established a field hospital along the banks of Stony Creek. Here their wounded waited for sleighs to take them to Malden. It was here also, that Dr. John Todd was delivered by his Indian captor.

Todd was met by Captain Elliott and Dr. Faulkner, the surgeon of the 41st Regiment of Foot. Elliott recognized Todd immediately and asked him what he was doing and how he had gotten there. The American doctor explained the situation at the Raisin and requested him to send help immediately to save those who might still be alive, particularly his friend, Captain Hart.

But Elliott replied, *"It is now too late. You may rest assured that those who are once taken by the Indians are safe, and will be taken to Malden, and those who are badly wounded are killed by now."*

Undaunted, Todd answered, *"Many are unable to walk, and some will be killed after making an effort and walking several miles. Those are the ones who might be saved."*

"No," said Elliott, *"My own wounded are to be conveyed first, and if any sleighs remain, they shall be sent back for your wounded."*

Seeing he was getting nowhere, Todd turned to the surgeon and made him an offer he felt could not be refused. He told him the detachment's valuable surgical instruments were still in the room he had occupied. He could see the British had need of them for their own wounded.

Elliott sent an interpreter to get them, but he soon returned with news that the instruments had been destroyed in the fire.

By this time, many Indians were crossing Stony Creek with their prisoners. Dr. Todd recognized his brother and asked Captain Elliott to release the prisoners into his custody. Elliott told him it was impossible. Besides, he knew these Indians. He should have no fear. The prisoners would be safe.[793]

---

792 Armstrong, John, <u>Notices of the War of 1812</u>, Vol. I, New York: George Dearborn, 1836, p. 77: *"What remained of the day was assiduously employed by the enemy in preparing for an immediate retreat, and in actually retreating, as far as Stony Creek. At 12 o'clock, the prisoners (amounting to about six hundred) were put in motion, and in the evening of the 23d, arrived at Amherstburg; where they were penned up in a small and muddy wood-yard, and exposed throughout the night to a cold and constant rain, without tents or blankets, and with only fire enough to keep them from freezing."*

793 Dr. Todd had 2 brothers at the River Raisin; Robert and Samuel. Samuel was wounded, but all 3

Todd continued to press his case, reiterating all the details of the killings and destruction he had witnessed at the River Raisin. Exasperated, Elliott and the surgeon finally admitted the Indians could not be controlled. Once they had taken count of their own losses, and seen how many of the British had been wounded, they had gone off to French Town, with vengeance in their hearts.[794]

Ice of Lake Erie and Detroit River, January 23, 1813:

François Cicotte and his brother Jean-Baptiste left Detroit that morning, each driving a pony and *traineau* (large sledge). They had come to pick up the wounded, but now saw only dead bodies scattered around the settlement.

The Cicottes cut some thorn bushes to throw over the corpses and then agreed to transport some of the *habitants* who had been ordered to abandon their homes. On their way to Detroit, as they came near Blue Jacket's old home, they saw a young man, apparently hardy and robust, standing near a tree.

Suddenly, there was the crack of a rifle shot; then another. The man crumpled to the ground, blood flowing from his heart, as he breathed his last. Two Indians appeared, cut off his feet, and left the body lying on the ground.

The Cicottes dared not stop, but kept on to Detroit, surmising that the young man had been one of the Kentucky prisoners taken by the Indians. No doubt, he had run away, but had probably become confused and gotten lost.[795]

About this same time, two old friends were carefully negotiating frozen Lake Erie on horseback. They feared the weight of their horses might break through the ice even where a man could cross easily.

---

brothers would survive. Robert's daughter, Mary, would become the wife of Abraham Lincoln. Several other Todds were also at the battle.

794 Deposition of Dr. John Todd, April 24, 1813, in <u>Barbarities of the Enemy, exposed in a Report of the Committee of the House of Representatives, and the Documents accompanying said Report.</u> Troy: Francis Adancourt, 1813, pp. 141-5. *"I frequently, and on every occasion, urged the British officers to exert themselves and procure the release of the wounded from the Indians, urging the necessity of having their wounds dressed. In a conversation on this subject with Capt. Elliot…he replied, the Indians are excellent surgeons…Before I conclude, I must say that the terms of capitulation were violated in every particular by the enemy. The wounded were not protected; private property was not held sacred; and our side arms were not restored. With a few exceptions, I was treated respectfully by the British officers, save the abuse which was lavished on my government, and that was by no means sparingly bestowed."*

795 Palmer, Friend. <u>Early Days in Detroit,</u> p. 634.

The 43-year-old Macaunse, a respected Ojibwa leader from a village just west of Lake St. Clair, expressed his appreciation that Campeau had chosen to join him for the attack on the River Raisin. By being loyal to his Native friends, Campeau was risking a lot should the Americans catch him in the act.

As they picked their way slowly over the ice, they noticed a dark spot in the distance. It seemed to take forever, but as they approached, the spot got larger and larger, until they could make out the shape of a human form.

It was a dead American soldier, lying in a contorted position, with one leg sticking far out to the side.

Macaunse watched as Campeau dismounted and stared down at the man intently. He searched the man's clothing without finding anything and then pulled out his knife and tomahawk. Asking Macaunse if he needed a trophy, Campeau proceeded to swiftly sever the leg from the body.

Disgusted by the bloody stump, Macaunse refused to take the prize. So, Campeau stuffed the leg into his saddlebags and remounted his horse. Together, they rode on to their destination, the chief troubled, but Campeau saying it would make a great joke to spring on his relatives in Detroit.[796]

French Town, evening of January 23, 1813:

Louis Bernard dit Lajoye, Antoine Boulard, François Lasselle, Hubert Lacroix, and Charles Chovin gathered around the naked, mutilated corpse of the man they knew as the Secretary of General Winchester.[797]

---

796 Journal of Lewis Bond, in Knopf, Richard C., Document Transcriptions of the War of 1812 in the Northwest, Vol. X, Pt. 1. Columbus: Ohio Historical Society, 1962, p. 198: This incident may have taken place on the 23rd or the 22nd. Campeau does not appear in all versions of the story. Bond identifies this Campeau as a former major in the Michigan Militia, while Friend Palmer gives his name as Joseph Campau. Both agree he was a popular friend of the Indians. Bond was very jealous of the older residents of Michigan and had many personal, political, and business axes to grind, so it is possible this is an old example of "swift-boating" or destroying a rival with malicious gossip. Bond says, *"In the evening, he went to the house of a near relation of his, and asked for something to eat. The woman replied she had nothing. He told her he had the paw of a bear, if she would cook it, and threw the man's foot on the table. The poor woman, terrified at the horrid sight, gave a scream and nearly fainted, on which he went off leaving it on the table. It was afterwards buried. This worst of savages had been a major of militia in the Territory under Governor Hull and had made his election on the delivery of the western posts (agreeably to Mr. Jay's treaty) to be an American citizen. Some other citizens had been guilty of treason, either by taking arms with the British and Indians, or in aiding, abetting, etc."* See also: "Deeds / Nations, Directory of First Nations Individuals in South-Western Ontario, 1750-1850," by Greg Curnoe, www.adamsheritage.com.

797 This was probably Captain Woolfolk, but the stories of Captain Hart's burial are similar. I'm assuming Hart was buried by Chovin and Couture. Boulard's mention of Hubert Lacroix's presence makes

They had seen the hogs come by and root through the flesh of the fallen Kentuckians, and dogs with skulls, arms, and legs hanging from their mouths.[798] But they had done nothing, for fear of the Indians who had promised to kill anyone who tried to bury the dead Kentuckians.[799]

**Commemorative Speeches and Blessings
in front of the former Visitor Center, 2013.**
Photo Courtesy of the Pontious Family

Now, under the cover of dusk, they picked up the body and carried it into a field near the woods, where the hogs didn't go. Unfortunately, they did not have time to give the secretary a decent burial, for Indians were still prowling about the neighborhood. Instead, they covered the corpse with a few branches, and slipped hurriedly back to their homes, planning to return later.[800]

---

little sense in light of the latter's arrest after the battle. Perhaps his removal to captivity in Malden took place a few days later.

798 Letter Baker to Winchester, British Niagara, Feb. 25, 1813, typed copy in Bidlack's Notes, Monroe County Historical Museum Archives.

799 Deposition of Antoine Boulard, Feb. 4, 1813, # 27 in Barbarities of the Enemy, exposed in a Report of the Committee of the House of Representatives, and the Documents Accompanying said Report, Troy: Francis Adancourt, 1813, pp. 129-130. Boulard had witnessed some of the massacre: "I was near the house of Gabriel Godfroy, Jr. and the house of Jean Baptiste Jereaume, where a great number of prisoners were collected; and... I heard the screaming of the prisoners whom the Indians were tomahawking..."

800 Dep. of Louis Lajoye, Feb. 5, 1813, #28, Barbarities of the Enemy, Troy: F. Adancourt, 1813, 130.

The body of Henri Chovin was in the middle of the road, about a mile from where Captain Hart still lay.[801]

In the night, Chovin's father and Medard Couture covered Hart's body with some bark. They would later bury him secretly in a hollow formed by the roots of a tree.[802]

They also picked up Henri's body and hid it in his cellar, away from the prying eyes of the Indians.[803]

When Gabriel Godfroy arrived at his burned-out home, he was shocked to find so many dead bodies. He soon organized a crew of volunteers to remove the rubble and pull out the charred, blackened remains for burial.[804]

Not all the Kentuckians in French Town that day were dead. During the flight of the right wing, Private Newell had gotten separated from Matson's

801 Henri Chovin (Chauvin) served as a local guide for General Winchester. The circumstances of his death are unclear. Antal, Sandy. A Wampum Denied. Canada: Carleton Library Series, Vol. 191, p. 195. Antal, quoting from an undated draft document in Procter's handwriting, captured among his effects on Oct. 5, 1813, gives no name, but simply states a *Canadien* resident was killed by a warrior in a dispute over a pig. It is possible, but unlikely, that the statement could be a reference to the death of LeBeau or Solo on January 18.

802 Hosmer, Hezekiah L. Early History of the Maumee Valley. Toledo: Hosmer & Harris, 1858, p. 43.

803 The following July, the Ottawa Chief Blackbird explained the attitude of his people in a speech to British Indian agents at Mackinac: *"Last year at Chicago and St. Joseph's, the Long Knives destroyed all our corn. This was fair, but, my brother, they did not allow the dead to rest. They dug up their graves, and the bones of our ancestors were thrown away, and we never could find them to return them to the ground... If the Long Knives, after they kill our people of colour, leave them without hacking them to pieces, we will follow their example. They have themselves to blame. The way they treat our killed, and the remains of those that are in their graves in the west, makes our people mad when they meet the Long Knives. Whenever they get any of our people into their hands, they cut them like meat into small pieces. We thought white people were Christians. They ought to show us a better example..."* See also: Letter from John Strachan to Thomas Jefferson, January 30, 1815: The writer, who later became Bishop of Toronto, complained that the Americans frequently scalped Indians and the Kentuckians often burned them as a pastime. In his Journal, Major John Norton explained: *"While in the neighborhood of Detroit and Amherstburg, some of the Americans...fabricated many stories of the cruelties exercised by the Indians on the prisoners taken at French Town. That there may not have been some instances of the kind, it is difficult to say, but no such instances have been general ...It would be useless as well as endless to repeat the number of cruelties that had been asserted, and as bluntly contradicted, without proofs to substantiate either one side or the other, and as the Americans are fond of complaining of cruelty, without just cause, I should be more inclined to believe the contradiction than the assertion."*

804 Letter George Ray to James Ray, Detroit, Jan. 20, 1841, Clements Library, University of Michigan. The *habitants* gathered up the human remains, strewn about the yard, and respectfully assigned them to a mass grave in a trench dug along the bank of the River Raisin. This was made possible by the thaw on January 23 and the departure of most of the Indians.

company and hid in an old barn. From his hiding place, he saw mounted Indians passing by with scalps tied to their saddles.

When it got dark, he tried to escape to the Maumee, but became lost. After wandering in circles, he found himself back at the River Raisin, where the locals hid him. From them, he learned of the awful massacre.[805]

Many of the French Town residents were now refugees. They organized themselves into processions, or "trains," of horse-drawn sleighs laden down with whatever possessions had not been plundered or destroyed.

Joseph Momini, his family, and the Beaugrands wound their way over the melting ice of Maumee Bay to Cedar Point; the men pulling sleds and the women carrying babies in their arms.

All were tired and shivering from cold and fear. With numb faces and red eyes, they stumbled up the bank and found relief in the shelter of the trees. They knew the French-Métis community of Presqu'île was nearby, while the trails to the rapids or Sandusky were still open.[806]

Another French train was led by Pierre Meloche and included the Momini, Bissonette, Cavalier, Fontaine, Devoir, Minor, and Lapointe families.[807]

The first day was fairly easy, as the wooden runners of the sleighs slipped lightly over the snow and ice of Lake Erie.

The second day's journey from Locust Point to the Portage was more difficult, as they had to plow through deep drifts of snow. It was necessary to rotate the order of the sleighs so the horses could take turns breaking the trail.

On the third day, Meloche sped ahead to arrange for replacement horses

---

805 Knopf, Richard C. Document Transcriptions of the War of 1812 in the Northwest, Vol. V, pt. 2. Columbus: Ohio Historical Society, 1958. pp. 27-8. "...Mr. Nuvel, one of his company, came in. He informed Capt. Matson that he lay concealed in a barn, near where the Indians returned, and says they had a number of scalps tied to their saddles, and a number of our men tied, taking them back, and a quantity of red clothes. He says he left the barn on the 23rd, at night, lost his way, and went back to the Raisin in the night, and was there informed by an American woman, that those who stood their ground were all taken prisoners, and but few killed..." See: (Atherton, p. 47.)

806 Ketchum, W.A., "Cedar Point in the Light of Other Days," copy of typed manuscript, courtesy Sandra Bellehoffer.

807 Other sources regarding the exodus to Sandusky include the following family names: Navarre (Hutro), Dewar, Bourdeaux, Momenie, Fontaine, Bissonette, Gagnier, Jacquot, Rangeard, Jerome, Devoir, Odette, and Drouillard. The widow of Etienne Jacob went there also, along with her daughters Julie and Monique. See the Narrative of Albert Cavalier, Sept. 5, 1878, in the Rutherford B. Hayes Papers, Vol. I, Lower Sandusky (1810-1814), 1-4.

to meet the train at the mouth of Muskallonge Creek, allowing them to reach Sandusky, where they were lodged in government barracks for the winter.[808]

The *habitants* of the River Raisin settlement realized that their friendship and status with the Indians had been damaged by their support for the American cause. Those who left understood that they would probably lose their hard-worked-for property. Those who stayed might even lose their lives.[809]

Lewis Bond recorded that the Indians *"...set fire to and burnt all the village of French Town, plundered the inhabitants of the whole settlement because they had generally been friendly to the Americans, and some had fought for them. I speak of the French inhabitants, for the English settlers had all fled long before, and directly after the capitulation of Detroit."*[810]

However, that was not entirely the case. The local Potawatomies had not forgotten their former friends at the River Raisin. When the British proposed that the settlement be entirely destroyed, they once again took the side of the inhabitants and rejected the idea. In council, they declared, *"...it was they, the Potawatomies, who had given the lands to the first settlers, and had been*

---

808 History of Sandusky County, Ohio, p. 569: In the spring, they moved into cabins built near the fort. On August 1, 1813, the government ordered the French families to move to Upper Sandusky for security. As they left, they could hear Procter's bombardment of Fort Stephenson. They would return to the Lower Sandusky area only at the end of the war, where they founded a Catholic parish known as St. Pilomena's, or La Prairie.

While there is a dizzying array of statistics for the military's battle losses, that is not the case for the women and children, whether *habitants*, Native Americans, or army camp followers. The best we can do is to find an analogous situation. The 1885 Battle of Batoche in Saskatchewan comes to mind.

Many families fled the scene prior to the fighting, but others stayed to assist their menfolk by carrying messages, food or ammunition, loading guns, and helping the elderly and the wounded. At the Métis village of Batoche, for every 4 men who died of battle wounds, 3 women would die of exposure, influenza, tuberculosis, or miscarriage. Due to the degradation of their living conditions, infant mortality increased by 15% the year following the battle.

This sample is too small to be statistically valid, but it can suggest some ways that civilian families might have been affected by the Battle of the River Raisin. See: "Brave Women, Courageous Children; the Métis Resistance of 1885," by Lawrence Barkwell, posted on Academia.

809 Journal of Lewis Bond, in Knopf, Richard C., Document Transcriptions of the War of 1812 in the Northwest, Vol. X, pt. 1, Columbus: Ohio Historical Society, 1962, p. 196. Possibly half the population may have remained at the River Raisin. Many of the refugees returned in 1814, while others did not come back until after the war had ended.

810 Deposition of Laurent Durocher, Knopf, Richard C. Document Transcriptions of the War of 1812 in the Northwest, Vol. X, pt 1. Columbus: The Ohio Historical Society, 1962, pp. 39-41.

recompensed therefore, and had built on each piece so given, a fire thereon, and would not suffer the habitations to be destroyed."

British Indian Department Interpreters
2003 Commemoration Photo by Bill Saul

Malden, January 23, 1813:

On the way to Malden, the column of Kentucky prisoners was overtaken by the British wounded who were being transported from Stony Creek by sleigh. With them was Dr. John Todd. From him, they learned that the buildings they had occupied had been burned with the wounded who were unable to walk.[811]

---

811 Dec. 11, 1828, affidavit of James Garrard of the County of Bourbon and State of Kentucky, taken at the request of Col. Godfroy and others of French Town in the Territory of Michigan, in relation to the occupation of said town by the American army and its subsequent destruction by the British and Indians in 1813, printed in the House Report No. 51 of the 20th Congress, 2nd Session, January 19, 1829: *"After the battle of the 22d January, that is to say, on the 23rd January, when on our march to Malden, we were overtaken by Dr. John Todd, who had been left with our wounded at Frenchtown, who gave us the information of the massacre of our wounded, and the destruction, by the enemy, of the buildings which we had occupied, and within our lines; and it was then considered and believed, and I then and do now believe, that the burning of the buildings was in consequence of their occupation by us, joined to a belief on the part of the enemy that the inhabitants were friendly disposed towards us."* There is some confusion as to whether the Kentucky prisoners could have marched all the way to Malden on the 22nd, or stopped somewhere for the night and proceeded the next morning. Gilpin, in "The War of 1812 in the Old Northwest" states the British only marched as far as their camp on Stony Creek on the 22nd. Benson J. Lossing states

There was at least one female Kentuckian with the prisoners. She had hired on as a laundress in Lexington and followed the army all the way to the River Raisin with Colonel Wells.[812] The washerwoman had bundled up her belongings in a shawl across her back and joined the column as it marched off.

Jim Girty, an Indian interpreter and scout, noticed a Chippewa woman admiring the shawl and urged her to take it, saying, *"See. There's a damned Yankee woman among the prisoners with a fine shawl. Go, get it for yourself."*

Encouraged, she confronted the washerwoman, demanding the shawl, but the Kentuckian refused to hand it over. When the Indian woman reached out and grabbed the bundle, the laundress resisted, and the fight was on. The two women pounded each other with their fists and pulled each other's hair while a large crowd gathered to cheer them on.

Cadotte, a Métis interpreter, finally stepped in, wrenched the shawl away, and handed the shawl back to the original owner amid the huzzas of her comrades. The Indians also joined in, praising her courage and declaring she should not be disturbed again.[813]

---

they arrived at Malden on the morning of the 23rd, but if Dr. Todd met them on the way, they must have been still marching later in the day. Dr. Todd reported that he had been the first to inform the prisoners of the massacre, but failed to give the time or place. Armstrong says they left Stony Creek on the morning of the 23rd and arrived at Malden that evening. Todd was later paroled and returned to Kentucky, where he resumed his medical practice. In 1817 he moved to Edwardsville, Illinois; and in 1827, to Springfield, Illinois, where he died. He was noted for his kindness and support of charities for the poor.

812 Since 1802, U.S. Army regulations had allowed each company commander to employ 4 women to wash and mend clothes for the 65 men of each company. They laundered items on a "piece work" basis, and were paid by the individual soldiers. Debts were collected as prescribed for sutlers and other civilian suppliers of items for the troops. The laundresses received no government salary, but they did get a reduced food and liquor ration, and each group of 4 was allotted a common tent, bedding, a hatchet, a camp kettle, and a couple mess tins. They were also subject to army discipline. Back in the days of the American Revolution, washerwomen were required to be married to a soldier; but by the War of 1812, they simply had to be "of good moral character."

813 The women had been serious, but for the men, both captors and captives, the incident served to lighten the psychological burden of the battle they had so recently endured. This unnamed laundress stayed in Malden for about 6 months, long after the Kentucky prisoners were transferred and released. She ended up doing odd jobs to make a living, until she had earned enough to make her way back, on foot, to Kentucky. Most laundresses did marry soldiers, but it is not recorded if this was the case for her. It is said that she became a celebrity and lived for many years after returning to Lexington. The U.S. Army abolished the post of company laundress in 1878. See: History of Lexington, Draper Manuscript series 11-U, posted at www.cottonbalers.lynchburg.net/laundress, www.nps.gov/prsf/history/glossary, and www.fortatkinsononlinelorg/1strifles. I am uncertain if this Interpreter was Jean-Baptiste Cadotte, Jr., or Michel Cadotte. Both of them were listed as interpreters and were part French and Ojibwa. There were also other Cadottes in

It was evening by the time the British troops arrived in Amherstburg with their wounded and the prisoners. They were greeted by the soldiers' wives and families, anxious to know the fate of their love ones.[814] The hospital was soon filled to overflowing, so many of the wounded were sheltered in the barracks.[815]

Before confining the prisoners in an open wood yard, the British searched them for hidden weapons. Quite a few knives, tomahawks, and pistols were confiscated, along with powder flasks and other personal items. Within a short time, hundreds of thinly-clad prisoners were huddled together in the yard, where some bread was thrown to them as though they were hogs.

The British surrounded the yard with a string of militia guards to prevent an escape and to keep the Indians from disturbing the prisoners. Despite the lateness of the hour, Malden's inhabitants crowded around the enclosure, showing more sympathy than anger at their defeated foe.

Although beaten, not all the American prisoners were cowed. One in particular, a strapping six-foot-three specimen of Kentucky manhood, kicked up his heels and shouted, *"Hurrah, boys! We're the cocks of Kentuck!"* A British soldier quickly retorted, *"Why don't you crow, then?"*

A heavy wind started to blow about midnight. Driving rain turned to

---

the area, and the source for this story says he was half Potawatomi, rather than Ojibwa. For more on the Cadottes, see: Silbernagel, Robert, The Cadottes: A Fur Trade Family on Lake Superior, Madison: Wisconsin Historical Society Press, 2020. Also in the book is John P. Dulong's "Family Tree," Michigan's Habitant Heritage, French Canadian Heritage Society of Michigan, 2015.

814 At Fort Amherstburg, there was some controversy over the quality of care provided to the British wounded. See: Journal of Lewis Bond, in Knopf, Richard C., Document Transcriptions of the War of 1812 in the Northwest, Vol. X, pt. 1, Columbus: Ohio Historical Society, 1962, p. 196: *"Many if not most of those [British] wounded died after they were brought to Malden, and they circulated a report that the Americans poisoned their balls. The weather was very cold, and having been exposed for so long a time [it is 20 miles from French Town to Malden] in passing the lake, these wounded men were exposed to the extreme cold, which probably operated much against them, but the propagation of such a report would perhaps extenuate the horrid crimes they had suffered their allies to perpetuate, but a Scotch surgeon [Dr. Olgive] laughed at the idea of poisoning the balls, and laid some blame on the want of skill in the surgeons who had attended them."*

815 Byfield, Shadrack, "A Common Soldiers Account," Recollections of the War of 1812. Toronto: Baxter Publishing Company, 1964 reprint of 1828 edition. *"...I was among the latter. The next morning, I got my comrade to wash my neck and shoulder, and I told him there must be something the matter with my shoulder, as I could scarcely lift my hand to my head. On examining my shoulder, he thought he could feel a ball near the blade bone. I attended the doctor, and told him I had a job for him. On his examination, he found that the ball which had entered my neck was lodged in my shoulder; he went to work and extracted it, and in about three weeks the wounds were nearly well; and I was able to attend to my duty."*

hail, snow, and an intense frost, which covered the ground with a two-inch-thick sheet of ice.

By the time tents were sent for, the men were too benumbed with cold to set them up. Despite a supply of over 40 cords of wood, the fires did not last through the night. To ease the discomfort, two barrels of whisky were delivered to the sergeants to be distributed among their fellow prisoners.

Winchester and his officers were put up in local taverns. After the general appealed for better accommodations for the rank and file, they were moved to an empty warehouse, but fires could not be made inside. The men slept huddled together to keep from freezing. The next day, they would be parceled out to new quarters among the local inhabitants.[816]

One of the prisoners, although slightly wounded, managed to slip unnoticed out of the wood yard and mingle with the local population. Walking quietly through the mass of people, he headed down the road to the outskirts of the village. The cold was getting to him, as well as fatigue and hunger, so he took a chance. At the next house, he walked up to the door and knocked.

Young Olivier Belair opened the door and gaped at the dirty, ragged apparition standing before him. Soon his father arrived and quickly pulled the escapee inside. Half dead with hunger, the Kentuckian frankly explained his situation. To his relief, old Belair offered to do what he could to help.

Ignoring his own danger, Belair took the young man to a room where he could warm up and have something to eat. The fugitive remained hidden in Belair's house until he felt strong enough to go on. Belair then told him what direction to take, and described the house of a friend, with whom he could stay.

The escapee did as he was instructed. He found the house, and the owner hired him on as a laborer for several weeks.

Finally, fully recovered and provided with new clothes, the young man walked back into Malden, where he boldly hired a canoe to take him across the river. From there he made his way safely to join his friends in the States.[817]

816 Winchester, James. Historic Details Having Relation to the Campaign of the North-Western Army under Generals Harrison and Winchester. Lexington: Worsley & Smith, 1818, p. 45. See also: "Reminiscences of an Actor in the War of 1812," Typed text, Algonquin Club. Taken from the Canadian Emigrant, 1835. Author unidentified. The writer goes on to say "At the dawn of morning they were all marched out of the wood yard and distributed in small parties, by turns, amongst the private houses, the public houses being pre-occupied by their officers and wounded comrades."
817 It was not an easy thing for Belair to do, given the atmosphere of intimidation and terror that

"BARRACKS" FORT MALDEN, 1812. AMHERSTBURG, ONT. 9474

1908 Post Card of an old Barracks Building at Fort Malden
*Public Domain — Courtesy of Fort Malden National Historic Sites, Parcs
Canada, & Dan Boudreau*

reigned around Fort Amherstburg. In the days following the Battle of the River Raisin, the Indians brought large numbers of trophies to display on the streets. Great numbers of scalps were strung upon poles, twenty at a time. They were stretched on small hoops and painted red on the flesh side. These poles were carried about the town to music, dancing, and war whoops. Heads of fallen enemies were placed in rows on the sharp tops of picket fences. Whenever Belair went out, he would see their matted locks of hair, gory features frozen in death, eyes bulging like they were staring back. Some of the heads actually exhibited a pleased smile, while others bore expressions of pain, defiance, or hopelessness. See: Observer Column, Monroe Evening News, October 22. Also Judge Witherell's letters to the Detroit Free Press, written in the 1840s and edited by Lyman C. Draper in the Wisconsin Historical Society's 3rd annual Report in 1856. Typed copy in Bidlack Papers, Monroe County Museum Archives.

According to the archives of the Board of Claims and Losses, Canadiens helped the afflicted in many ways. Private Jean Baptiste St. Louis dit Villair of the 2nd Essex claimed his 3-point blanket was requisitioned for a wounded man of the 41st. Baptiste Reaume of Amherstburg spent three days transporting the wounded and dead with his horse and sleigh. John Troyer of Sandwich requested compensation for salts, castor oil, spirits of turpentine, scissors, and a syringe, used to care for the wounded and for performing three bleedings. See: "War of 1812 Canadian Stories," January, 1813, posted by Fred Blair, 2015-2021.

Indian council houses at Brownstown and Malden, January 23, 1813:

Reverend Dudley sat down next to the council house fire, fearing the worst. He currently had two bosses; the first warrior who captured him, and now the warrior's father. While still on the road, the two had stopped long enough to paint him before heading to the Indian council house at Brownstown, near the foot of Grosse Isle.

The Indians placed a small ear of corn in the fire to roast, and then shared it with Dudley. Afterward, they spread a blanket over some bark in front of the fire and motioned for him to lie down on it. Dudley's neck was so stiff he could not stretch out comfortably, so they placed some of their plunder under his head to serve as a pillow and covered him with a blanket.

Other Indians soon came in with their prisoners. They spent the night tying the scalps they had taken onto hoops and dressing them out as trophies.

A partial thaw had set in during the day, and about 9 o'clock a cold rain began to fall. That night, there was an unusually severe thunderstorm for the season. Water ran right into the council house and under Dudley's blanket, flooding the low area around the fire. Just after midnight, Dr. Bower was brought in, soaked to the bone.[818] Dudley was too tired to care, but in the morning, he awakened to find himself in 2 inches of water. He got up and dried himself as best he could.[819]

Many other soldiers remained captives of the Indians. Towards dusk, Elias Darnell found himself in Malden. His captor deposited him in Malden's large Indian Department council house, occupied by what seemed like hundreds of Native women, children, and dogs.

He could hear the British in Fort Amherstburg firing a salute as a large body of American prisoners was being marched in. Although he was just a prisoner, the women and children treated him much better than he expected. They gave him bread, meat, and hominy to eat.

As he was wolfing down the food, a warrior came up and asked if he were married. Answering in the negative, Darnell watched as the warrior went over to a group of women. It was soon apparent, by their chattering

---

818 Deposition of Gustavus M. Bower, dated April 24, 1813, in Barbarities of the Enemy, exposed in a Report of the Committee of the House of Representatives, and the Documents accompanying said Report, Troy: Francis Adancourt, 1813, pp. 139-41

819 Dudley, Rev. Thomas P., "The Battle and Massacre at Frenchtown, Michigan, January, 1813," Historical and Archaeological Tracts, Number One, Cleveland: Western Reserve Historical Society, August, 1870.

and grinning, that they were pleased. One in particular smiled broadly back at Darnell. Unfortunately, the lack of teeth betrayed her advanced age.

Darnell feared a forced marriage was in the offing, but he needn't have been so worried. In the morning, his captor took his family and Darnell off to their village, about 3 miles from Malden.[820]

Warrior with Prisoner by Ken Osen
Portion of Diorama on Display at Former River Raisin Battlefield Visitor Center
Photo by Author

Leftwich's Relief Force, Delaware and Upper Sandusky, Jan. 24, 1813:
On the evening of January 23rd, a steady rain began to pour. Within 3 hours, it put out the army's cook fires where bread was being baked. By 3 a.m., all the campfires were drowned and water was knee-deep inside their tents. The troops had to evacuate and rekindle their fires on higher ground.[821]

---

820 Darnell, Elias, Journal, Philadelphia: Lippincott, Grambo, & Co., 1854, pp. 64-70. As they passed Fort Amherstburg, Darnell *"...judged it to be 70 or 80 yards square; the wall appeared to be built of timber and clay. The side, from the river, was not walled, but had double pickets, and entrenched round, about 4 feet deep; and in the entrenchment was the second row of pickets."*

821 "Journal of Joseph Larwell," Detroit Historical Collections, Detroit Public Library, p. 9. Delaware, Ohio, is located less than 30 miles from Franklinton (Columbus) and 40 miles from Upper Sandusky. It was laid out in 1808 and incorporated in 1816. The town was established on the site of an

At 4 a.m., they received General Leftwich's note with news of the January 18th battle at the River Raisin and Harrison's orders to march to the Rapids.

At daylight, the men of the Virginia Brigade waded back to their tents to retrieve their soggy baggage. At 11 o'clock on January 24th, they splashed off through the flood towards their rendezvous with General Harrison.[822]

Meanwhile, many miles ahead of them, Major Robert Orr's Pennsylvania militiamen were struggling through the rain.[823] They, too, had received word of Winchester's victory, but then came the news of his defeat. Their new orders were to leave behind their heavy baggage, tents, and most of their artillery, with a small guard, and make a forced march to join Harrison at the Portage River.

Thunder and lightning made sleeping difficult that night. A cold, hard rain struck their camp at 9 in the evening, turning the winter slush into a sticky mass of mud a foot deep.[824] At 2 a.m., Major Orr set off with the infantry, Captain Cushing's 6-pdr, and a 450-horse pack train carrying salt

---

old Mingo village called Pluggy's Town. By 1813, it consisted of 40 or 50 houses, some of them brick, inhabited principally by settlers from New England. It was a good-looking village noted for a nearby sulphur spring and Noah Spaulding's Tavern. For a time, General Leftwich made his headquarters there. At age 52, General Joel Leftwich found himself in charge of a brigade attached to Harrison's Northwestern Army. The Virginia Brigade would see no serious fighting, but would still suffer casualties: 3% dead, 10% discharged for illness, and 7% deserted. See: Butler, Stuart L., Real Patriots and Heroic Soldiers, Westminster, Md: Heritage Books, 2008, p xxii. Leftwich's Virginia Brigade included the 1st Pennsylvania and the 1st and 2nd Virginia Regiments. They had been encamped on a level plain near Fort Ferree at Upper Sandusky since the beginning of January.

822 Lewis, Virgil A., Third Biennial Report of the Department of Archives and History of the State of West Virginia, Charleston: The News-Mail Company, 1911, Peter Davis' Journal, p. 165.

823 Robert Orr of Kittanning was elected battalion major of the First Regiment Pennsylvania militia, commanded by Col. Joel Ferree, which formed part of the Second Brigade, commanded by Brigadier General Richard Crooks. They were mustered into service at Pittsburgh.

824 Letter Alexander A. Meek to General John Sites Gano, Camp at Carrying River, January 25, 1813, Digital Journals, Cincinnati Historical Library and Archives, Cincinnati Museum Center. A participant would later write: "The country... was new and swampy, roads had to be opened as you passed along, and stopping at night... in swamps where you had to cut spice-wood brush and pile it up to lie down to keep from sinking into the mire, after traveling all day in mud and water from the ankles to the knees." See also: Davis, Aaron, History of Clarion County, Pennsylvania, Syracuse NY: D. Mason & Co., 1887, p. 89: "Do you recollect the afternoon when you were drawing a cannon on a log sled... the sled caught on a stump, and attempting to get it off it only went down deeper, and you continued to add more horses to the sled until you got 16 horses to 1 cannon...? The longer you worked the deeper it sunk into the mud; you lost your shoes in the swamp, and when you stepped on the cannon your feet froze to it."

and flour. They marched all day on the 24th. Each man was supplied with a musket, a blanket, and one day's ration.

For his part, Lt. Larwill grabbed a few biscuits, a piece of cheese, and a couple blankets and slung a hammock across his back. The artillerymen hitched up their cannon at 4 a.m., but found the going rough due to the passage of the pack train which churned up the road bed in front of them. After about 6 hours of struggling through ice and knee-deep mud and water, they finally got their artillery piece around the pack horses and began to make better time.

The head of Orr's column reached Hull's Road at sunrise, after a journey of 8½ miles. *"For most of the way the rails had been routed in disorder by the swales and scattered in every direction..."*[825] At noon, they halted at the main branch of the Portage (Carrying) River and waited for the rest to catch up.[826]

About an hour before sunset on January 24th, Major Orr's men began to straggle into Harrison's camp, located on a piece of low, wet ground on the south side of a small branch of the Portage River. Barely a third of them made it that night. They were thoroughly wet and without their tents, and the camp was covered in water high enough to come over the tops of the men's shoes.

As the men struggled to find a dry spot and light fires in the dampness, they shared their few cooking utensils. Fortunately, there was plenty of flour on the pack horses, which they used to make bread in the ashes. A hog was killed and butchered for them, and they broiled the pork over the coals.[827]

---

825 Lorrain, Alfred, The Helm, the Sword, and the Cross: A Life Narrative, Cincinnati: Poe & Hitchcock, 1862, pp. 108-116. *"It was midnight; the ground covered with snow, the heavens profusely flaking down additional supplies and our heavily laden tents were rocked to-and-fro by the howling winds when the troops were suddenly aroused by a call to arms. Orders were given to buckle on our knapsacks and blankets and to be ready to march at a moment's warning...It was a dark, dark night. An experienced pilot led the van and the whole detachment followed in Indian-file, every man taking care to keep in feeling relation to his predecessor. We plunged and floundered on through brush and brier, deep creeks and rising waters, mingled with drift and ragged fragments of ice...Those swales were often a quarter mile long...not more than half-leg deep; but sometimes ...when we were not expecting it, we sank down to our cartridge boxes. While fording such places our feet would get so benumbed that we seemed to be walking on bundles of rags; and it was a real luxury to come to a parenthesis of mud and mire, for then we could feel a returning glow of vitality."*

826 Journal of Joseph Larwill, Burton Historical Collection, Detroit Public Library, pp. 36-37.

827 Lewis, Virgil A., Third Biennial Report of the Department of Archives and History of the State of West Virginia, Charleston: The News-Mail Company, 1911, pp. 159-166: One volunteer reported:

The volunteers slept with their muskets in their hands and their cartridge boxes strapped on, ready for action. The rest of Orr's troops would stagger in during the course of the next day, and by Tuesday, the 26th, they had managed to build huts to live in. On Thursday, they were joined by General Leftwich, who arrived from Upper Sandusky with the rest of the Virginia Brigade.[828]

Detroit, January 24, 1813:

All of Detroit was abuzz with the news of the disaster at French Town. Two exhausted and panic-stricken female refugees from the River Raisin had arrived to spread the word of a defeat and massacre of Winchester's army.[829]

Upon Mrs. Godfroy's arrival in Detroit. she began to gather a number of the River Raisin refugees. Despite the impassibility of the roads, she rushed to personally plead their cause to Judge Woodward and Major Muir.[830]

Henry Hunt and his brother were standing on the dock near the town gate, when he saw Jack Brandy pull up in a *cariole*. In the *cariole* Hunt could see something covered over with a blanket.

"...In this swamp you lose sight of terra firma altogether; the water was about 6 inches deep on the ice, which was very rotten, often breaking through to the depth of 4 or 5 feet...It was with difficulty we could raise fires; we had no tents; our clothes were wet, no axes, nothing to cook in, and very little to eat. A brigade of packhorses being near us, we procured from them some flour; killed some hogs (there being plenty of them along the road.) Our bread we baked in the ashes and the pork we broiled on the coals — a sweeter morsel I never partook of; when we went to sleep it was on logs laid close to each other to keep our bodies from the damp ground..."

828 Journal of Joseph Larwill, Burton Historical Collection, Detroit Public Library, p. 38. See also: "The Petersburg Volunteers, 1812-1813," by Lee A. Wallace, Jr. A different timetable is given in Stuart L. Butler's Real Patriots and Heroic Soldiers, pp. 82-85: The Virginia Brigade followed Major Orr's route, leaving Upper Sandusky on January 24th, but were held up by rain and high water. They spent a couple days making canoes to ford a swollen river, but cold weather froze the stream before they could put them to use. Eventually, they met up with Captain Cushing and his men, who had been sent back to recover his sled-mounted cannons and build a blockhouse. They continued up Hull's Road on the 29th and arrived at the Portage camp on January 31st.

829 Antal, Sandy. A Wampum Denied. Canada: Carleton Library Series, Vol. 191, p. 195. Antal, quoting from an undated draft document in Procter's handwriting, captured among his effects on Oct. 5, 1813, gives no names, although one might suspect Rachel Knaggs and her daughter, or possibly Madame Godfroy.

830 Letter Mrs. Godfroy to Judge Woodward, dated Detroit, Jan. 24, 1813: *"Mrs. Godfroy's compliments to Judge Woodward...Mrs. Knags now be very happy if you will do her the honor to come and see her this evening. Mrs. G. begs that the Judge will excuse her if she did not go to Mrs. Mure's today, as the roads are very bad, and they is a number of pepol arrived here his morning from River Raisin. Mrs. G. would thank the Judge if he will be so good as to stop at her house wen he will return from Mrs. Knags, has she would wish to speak to him."* (Original spellings)

Unsure of where Brandy had been the last few days, Hunt asked, *"Well, have you brought us some venison today?"*

"Yes, Harry Hunt," replied the Wyandot, *"Good Yankee venison."* Throwing off the blanket, he revealed his prisoner, John Green.

The large, powerful Kentuckian had received a musket ball in the thigh and had been left behind at the River Raisin with the wounded. Jack Brandy had to break in the door of a burning house to save him.

They had spent the night in a Frenchman's house, and obtained a sleigh for the trip to Detroit in the morning.[831]

"Do you remember the promise I made you some days ago, that I would be kind to the Yankees, and bring any prisoners safely to Detroit? I told you Jack Brandy cannot lie."

After a bit of negotiation, Hunt was able to purchase Green's liberty. He took him to Dr. Henry, who dressed his wound, and Green remained with the Hunts, who eventually helped him to return to Kentucky.[832]

Detroit, 3 p.m., Sunday, January 24, 1813:

Dr. Bower was taken with some of the prisoners to an Indian village on the River Rouge, where he would remain for 6 days before being brought in to Detroit. Many of the prisoners were in sad shape. Sergeant John Dawson had been wounded at 9 a.m. on the 22nd, and still had a musket ball lodged between the ribs under his right arm.[833]

Private Downey was even less fortunate, his legs having given out with rheumatism as he struggled to walk that morning. The Indians put him down and stripped his corpse, but didn't take his scalp.[834]

On the other hand, Timothy Mallory had been stripped and re-clothed

---

831 The Historical Society of Northwestern Ohio, biographical field notes on Frenchtown, note 85: *"Navarre has repeatedly heard that Jack dragged Green out of the burning house and took him to Detroit, then reckoned 36 miles."*

832 Hosmer, Hezekiah Lord. Early History of the Maumee Valley. Toledo: Hosmer & Harris, 1858, pp. 40-1. See also: Wright, Richard J. The John Hunt Memoirs; Early Years of the Maumee Basin, 1812-1835, Maumee Valley Historical Society, pp. 43-4: *"...he remained with us until the arrival of the army of General Harrison, where he met 3 of his brothers, who had come out to avenge his death, as they had supposed him killed, and a more happy meeting I never witnessed."*

833 Deposition of John Dawson, orderly sergeant, April 21, 1813, in Barbarities of the Enemy, exposed in a Report of the Committee of the House of Representatives, and the Documents accompanying said Report, Troy: Francis Adancourt, 1813. p. 146-7.

834 See Appendix I for a list of prisoners known to have been executed by the Indians.

in Indian fashion. His head was shaved, except for a scalp lock, and his ears were pierced. Although he submitted to having his ears decked out with silver ornaments, he objected mightily to having his nose pierced, and the Indians didn't insist. They did paint his face black on one side, with red stripes, and red on the other, with black stripes.

He was then adopted by Asa Chipsaw, a Potawatomi, and offered a bride. But he refused, much to the dismay of his adoptive family. They dressed his wound and had him drink a strong tea of sassafras and cherry bark.[835]

While Bower's group slogged up the Rouge, Dudley's party headed straight for Detroit, arriving at 3 in the afternoon after walking since daybreak. As the Indians and their prisoners walked down the main street, some women came out to meet them, imploring the warriors not to harm the prisoners.

The Indians took no apparent notice and moved on, followed by the women. Encountering two British officers on horseback, they halted to chat.

The officers were lavish in praising the warriors on their great victory, but took no notice of the prisoners, not even after the women came up to renew their pleas for their release.

Reverend Dudley thought to himself, *"I'm of no more importance to these British officers than if I were a dog."*

That evening, Dudley and the Indians stayed at the house of a white woman, who gave the reverend a cup of tea and a loaf of bread with butter.

---

835 Narrative of Timothy Mallory, in Buckley's <u>History of Monroe County</u>, pp. 82-87. The village contained 2,000 women, children, and old men. Mallory remained with the Indians for several months, often pressed into service to carry provisions back to camp from Detroit. On these trips, he was not allowed to communicate with the residents who were offering to ransom him. The rations he carried were meant to last six days and usually consisted of 15 loaves of bread, weighing 3 pounds each, ten pounds of meat, such as pork or beef, and a peck of corn. All this would actually last only 3 days, and they would live off scraps of dog or horse meat the rest of the time. (Total weight would equal about 70 lbs. It is uncertain how many people this was meant to feed.)

According to Mallory, his captors *"...appeared indifferent whether they had killed the animal that day or whether it had died by some accidental cause 8 or 10 days prior to the meal. They appointed me cook, and as they did not appear to be fastidious in the least, it looked an easy job, but it wasn't; getting the necessary fuel and keeping up the everlasting stew was no sinecure."*

Mallory saw other prisoners in the camp, including Samuel Ganoe, John Davenport, and Major Graves. One evening, Mallory and Ganoe managed to escape, running 8 miles to Detroit, where they were hidden in a potato cellar for 4 days. Eventually, they were turned over to the British, and on May 16, 1813, taken across Lake Erie to be released in Cleveland.

Over the next few days, the citizens of Detroit saw dozens of prisoners herded into town like sheep.

Leading citizens and militia officers on parole offered generous ransoms, while Judge Woodward used his influence to improve their treatment. Gabriel Godfroy purchased six prisoners. John McDonnell, a Detroit merchant, bought another three or four, including Dr. Bower. Godfroy's neglected Detroit store served as a marketplace for ransoming captives.[836]

British Colonels Baby and Elliott did what they could for them, as did Major Muir, Detroit's British commandant, who bought Rev. Dudley's freedom in exchange for an old broken-down pack horse and a keg of whisky.[837]

According to Dudley, his Native captor took affectionate leave of him and *"...exhibited more the principle of the man and the soldier than all the British I had been in contact with up to the time I met Major Muir."*[838]

Detroit's young ladies also did their part. The *demoiselles* Lasselle and Labadie and the misses Scott and Hay begged their fathers for horses, which they gave to the Indians in exchange for prisoners.

Over 30 prisoners were ransomed at Detroit, for about 20 to 40 dollars a head, while a similar number were redeemed by the British Indian

---

836 Au, Dennis. War on the Raisin. Monroe: Monroe County Historical Commission, 1981, pp. 56-70. See also "John A. McDonnell and the Ransoming of American Captives after the River Raisin Massacre," by Vern L. Beal, in the September, 1951 issue of Michigan History, vol. 25, #3: He may have spent some 500 pounds in New York currency, which at the time was worth about half the corresponding amount in British pounds sterling. McDonnell continued his efforts even after Colonel Procter issued an order forbidding the practice *"on pain of being put in the Guardhouse and being sent to Quebec."* Procter's order was at least partly due to the inflated prices the civilian population was willing to pay the Indians for the release of their prisoners.

837 Letter Baker to Winchester, British Niagara, Feb. 25, 1813, Typed copy in Bidlack Notes, Monroe County Historical Museum Archives: *"...when they saw their countrymen driven through the streets like sheep to a market, lavished their wealth for their ransom; nor was the procuration of liberty all — we had been almost entirely stripped by the Indians; cloathes such as the exigence of the occasion permitted to be prepared were furnished to us."*

838 Dudley, Rev. Thomas P., "The Battle and Massacre at Frenchtown, Michigan, January, 1813," Historical and Archaeological Tracts, Number One. Cleveland: Western Reserve Historical Society, August, 1870. Rev. Dudley was well treated as a British prisoner until he was paroled and released at Niagara. Dudley eventually returned home, but late that year, when he heard that Major Muir had been captured at the Battle of the Thames and brought as a prisoner to Frankfort, he approached Governor Shelby, urging him to allow Muir the freedom of the town. Muir, however, declined the favor, fearing it would reflect badly on him when he returned to his own home.

Department at Malden.[839] Henry Disbrow estimated the Indians still had 40 or 50 prisoners, but were soon asking 50 to 100 dollars apiece in ransom.

The redeemed captives were usually taken into custody by the British, who removed them to Sandwich or Malden, out of sight of most American citizens.[840]

The ransomed prisoners were more than relieved at being handed over to the British. They rejoiced at meeting their comrades, and were eager to relate what happened to some of the others who hadn't been brought in. In particular, many asked after Captain Hart.

Not all the prisoners considered themselves ill-used by their captors. Charles Bradford of Lexington, wounded on the 18th, appreciated the way they had expertly dressed his wound, which appeared to be healing quite well.[841]

Soquet, a Saginaw elder, had adopted 16-year-old Henry Wilmarth to take the place of his son who had been killed in the fighting at the River Raisin. His attachment was such that he spurned any offers of ransom.

That is, until one woman came up and addressed Soquet in his own language, appealing to him as a father, and explaining that Henry was the only son of a widowed mother, who would not likely survive the knowledge of his loss. Touched, Soquet released the boy, but refused the liberal reward he was offered. He left with the blessings of the local citizens for his kindness.[842]

Detroiters also ransomed many civilians taken by Native war parties. On a beautiful Sunday morning, a war party landed by canoe and displayed a woman's scalp on a pole. They also had 9 captive children, dressed in tattered clothing, and ranging in age from 3-years-old to fully grow. Henry

---

839 Algonquin Club: "Reminiscences of an Actor in the War of 1812," Canadian Emigrant, 1835. Author unknown. Typed copy in Bidlack's Notes, Monroe County Historical Museum Archives.

840 Bulkley, John McClelland. History of Monroe, Michigan. Vol. I. Chicago: Lewis Publishing Co., 1913: Diary of Henry Disbrow, p. 519.

841 Sources for the above paragraphs are Barnett & Rosentreter, Michigan's Early Military Forces, Detroit: Wayne State University Press, 2003, p. 76. See also: Farmer, Silas, 1839-1902. The History of Detroit and Michigan. Detroit: S. Farmer & co., 1884, pp. 280-282. Also: "Journal of Lewis Bond," in Knopf, Richard C., Document Transcriptions of the War of 1812 in the Northwest, Vol. X, pt. 1. Columbus: Ohio Historical Society, 1962. p. 197.

842 "Massacre of the River Raisin," by A. Burlingame, The New World, New York, June 17, 1843. The woman who convinced Soquet to release Henry was only identified as Mrs. "A." I'm guessing it was Elizabeth Knaggs Anderson, although there are several other possibilities. Wilmarth does not appear on G. Glenn Clift's rosters of Kentuckians at the Battle of the River Raisin.

Hunt's sister invited the group into her house, fed them, and gave them some bread to take away. Later, Hunt ransomed the children for $500 and sent them home.

Although local civilians were anxious to redeem the captive Americans, they had problems of their own to deal with. Many Detroiters were depressed by the defeat. They were also very fearful, as most of their firearms had been taken away. There was little they could do to defend themselves if an emergency arose.

Native warriors constantly harangued the locals with a litany of their deeds. Exhibiting their scalps and other trophies, they filled the streets with their victorious cries, danced from door to door, and even barged into homes.

In order to avoid trouble, the citizens were obliged to watch in silence, sometimes expressing pleasure at the sight, and offering the Indians food and liquid refreshment.

The Indians plundered the outlying farmsteads indiscriminately, so, in hopes of being spared, the *habitants* began painting a red mark on their homes and livestock to show they were owned by *Canadiens* rather than the Yankee settlers.[843]

Beaugrand's House, Monday, January 25, 1813:

William Atherton trudged on through the snow, mud, and water, hardly caring if he lived or died. The last two days had been difficult. Always under threat of death or torture, he was separated from his companions and taken to Malden, where he was whipped and beaten by an angry Native woman.

Only at night did he find any respite. The first night, they camped deep in the woods. Scraping away a foot and a half of snow, the Indians laid down some bark on which they placed their blankets. A freezing rain was falling, so they rigged up a crude shelter with some poles and a blanket, to keep the rain and sleet out of their faces. Supper consisted of boiled hog with the hair still on, with neither salt for flavoring nor bread to round out the meal.

The prisoner slept under the same blanket as the man who claimed him, but he carefully tied a handkerchief over his head. Knowing the Indians were

___
843 Journal of Lewis Bond, in Knopf, Richard C., Document Transcriptions of the War of 1812 in the Northwest, Vol. X, pt. 1. Columbus: Ohio Historical Society, 1962. p. 197: *"Considerable sums of money were also among the spoil, and other articles of value. The citizens all sympathized with the unfortunate prisoners, and afforded them every comfort and relief in their power."*

careful not to waste any clothing, he figured they would attempt to remove it before tomahawking him. At least he would know it was coming.

Atherton was grateful to be alive. He just hoped he wasn't being spared only to suffer a more horrible fate. Looking at the campfire, he couldn't help but imagine himself being roasted there, in place of the hog. Every time a warrior touched his tomahawk, he immediately thought, *"Now I am gone."*[844]

At Malden, the Indians spent the day celebrating. At night, a French family took him in and treated him kindly. The next morning, they went back across the Detroit River to Brownstown, where his captor made his home.

On the way, the Indians made a stop. Atherton's eyes grew wide with surprise, and then narrowed with anger, when he recognized the apparent inhabitant of the house. It was Beaugrand, the man who had finished off poor Blythe with a tomahawk. He and the Indians seemed to have become friends!

Beaugrand showed no fear of the Indians, but appeared to be in a jovial mood, joking back and forth with them in their own language. Atherton wished he could understand what they were saying, but it seemed obvious they were in cahoots with each other. If not for his fear of the Indians, he would have run up and throttled him.[845]

---

844 Atherton, William, Narrative of the Suffering & Defeat of the North-Western Army under General Winchester. Frankfort, KY, A. G. Hodges, 1842. p. 72. Of his experience with the Indians, Atherton wrote, *"I have nothing to say against the Indian character...but much against their manner of life. They are a brave, generous, hospitable, kind, and among themselves, an honest people; and when they intend to save the life of a prisoner, they will do it, if it should be at the risk of their own. But after all this is said, no one can form any adequate idea of what a man must suffer, who spends a winter with them in the snows of Michigan."*

845 Atherton, William, Narrative of the Suffering & Defeat of the North-Western Army, Under General Winchester. Frankfort, Ky: A. G. Hodges, 1842, pp. 76-77: Atherton remained with the Indians till spring, when Cicotte secured his release by trading a horse for him. He then spent a summer in British captivity at Malden. After Perry's victory on Lake Erie, he was transferred to Québec and exchanged the following spring. Returning to Detroit with McArthur's army in 1814, Atherton accused Beaugrand of murdering Blythe, but he was tried and acquitted. Beaugrand would be the only person that ever tried the murders of any of the Kentucky prisoners. A jury of his peers acquitted him due to the extenuating circumstances. None of the Indians or British officers involved ever had to face a war crimes tribunal, although it is interesting to speculate on what would have happened to Col. Procter if he had been captured by the Americans. Atherton's complaints were generalized to condemn the local French population as traitors, causing a public outcry that led Laurent Durocher to write: *"...I further remark, in order to refute false statements against the French population here that no people could have been more loyal and more attached to the Government of the United States than were the inhabitants of the River Raisin, considering the loss of all their property, their sufferings, even to starvation, murdered friends, abandonment of their habitations, etc., their willingness to volunteer their services to defend the Country..."*

Milk River Point, Lake St. Clair, January 25, 1813:

Many of the Chippewas were passing by the house of 36-year-old Gagette Tremblé as they returned to their village just west of Lake St. Clair.[846]

One of them cut a very stately figure, dressed in a black coat bound with a wampum sash over a calico hunting shirt and gaudy vest. The flaps of his cloth leggings were decked with beads, porcupine quills, and tinkling cones that jingled as he walked. His moccasins were also decorated with dyed porcupine quills, and his fine physique was adorned with silver earbobs, head band, and nose ring. This was Macaunse, headman of the Chippewas.

Macaunse went up to Gagette's doorway, with a large bag in his hand, and said, *"My friend, I am hungry. I have brought you some venison. Have some of it cooked for me."*

Just then, a shot was heard in the yard. Gagette ran out to find that a warrior had shot a hog. Without a word, Gagette dragged it into the house to dress and salt it. The shooter followed, expecting to get a share, but Gagette ignored him until he asked for a piece.

"No, not a morsel," said Gagette, *"When did a hungry red man ever come to my wigwam and ask for food in vain? But you come to rob and steal, and maybe to kill me. Not a bite shall you have."*

"I'll burn your barn, then," said the shooter, grabbing a burning branch from Gagette's fire and heading towards the barn. The rest of the Indians watched as Gagette picked up his rifle and ran after him. Nearing the barn, Gagette stopped, cocked his rifle and aimed it at the Indian's head, warning him, *"Do it, do it, and you're a dead man."*

"Ty yaw," exclaimed the frustrated warrior, dropping his fire brand and walking off with an air of disgust. The others left also, although not without discretely lifting a few useful items from their brave, but foolhardy host.[847]

---

846 The 1.7-mile Milk River flows into Lake St. Clair at Pointe à Guignolet, named for a grape-like berry (possibly wild cherry) the French fermented into brandy. Thirty French families lived there by 1796. Later called Gaukler Point, the nearby settlement was incorporated into the village of St. Clair Shores in 1925, which became a city in 1961. Half of the Milk River was paved over in 1955.

847 Palmer, Friend. Early Days in Detroit, pp. 150-152. According to Friend Palmer, Macaunse actually dumped the bag on the floor, out of which spilled not venison, but a leg cut from a Kentuckian killed at the River Raisin. Gagette's horror quickly turned to anger.

Forgetting the other Indians in the band, he showered Macaunse with curses, shoving him into the road. Startled, Macaunse reached for his tomahawk, but Gagette angrily challenged him, *"If you are a brave man, as you say you are, strike now. You are armed; your young men are all around*

Black Hoof
From a lithograph published in <u>History of the Indian Tribes of North America</u>.
Printed in 1836. Original art by Charles Bird King. Image retrieved from
Wikipedia Commons — Public Domain

General Tupper's Headquarters at Camp McArthur, January 25, 1813:
The clock had already struck nine times, and General Tupper was sitting near the hearth in a cabin, deep in conversation with the friendly Shawnee chief Black Hoof. The old chief was a noted political opponent of Tecumseh and the Prophet. Tupper had always appreciated Black Hoof's attitude, and marveled at the old man's command of the English language.

At that moment, a noise was heard at the back of the fireplace, and both men instinctively turned toward the sound, squinting through the flames to ascertain its cause. Black Hoof's eyes widened, however, when he saw a pistol barrel pointing directly at him through the chinking behind the chimney.

Too late, the old chieftain tried to pull back as a shot rang out and smoke filled the room. The lead ball struck his cheek, breaking the bone near his left eye. Without a sound, he fell backward to the floor, and laid there as if he were dead. Tupper screamed for his guards and gave orders for the regimental surgeons to do what they could to save the wounded Shawnee.

After some time, Black Hoof sat up, the blood streaming down his face

---

you. *Kill me if you dare. Strike now, but you are a coward and no warrior. Puckachee — allez, go."*
Realizing he had offended his host, Macaunse backed off.
According to Lewis Bond, however, it was Joseph Campau, not Macaunse, who kept the severed leg and later displayed it to his relatives.

giving him a frightful appearance. The surgeons, however, assured everyone that the wound was not fatal and went about easing the victim's pain.

A search was made of the entire camp and everyone was questioned. Tupper put up a reward of $350, but the culprit could not be found. The investigators finally concluded that it must have been one of several itinerant wagon drivers that had left camp early in the morning. There was thus no identifiably guilty party to pay for Black Hoof's misery.[848]

---

848 "We Lay There Doing Nothing; John Jackson's Recollection of the War of 1812," edited by Jeff L. Patrick, Indiana Magazine of History, LXXXVIII, June, 1992, Trustees of Indian University. Born sometime between 1710 and 1740, Shawnee Civil Chief Black Hoof (Ca-Ta-He-Cas-Sa) was supposedly present at Braddock's defeat (1755) and the Battles of Point Pleasant (1774), Piqua (1780), Harmar's defeat (1790), St. Clair's defeat (1791) and Fallen Timbers (1794). After signing the Treaty of Greeneville (1795), he urged his people to adopt white ways and take up farming at Wapakoneta. He supported the United States in the War of 1812 and kept most of the Shawnees from joining Tecumseh. After the war, he was involved in the forced removal of the Shawnees to Kansas, but returned to his cabin in Wapakoneta, where he died in 1831, by which time he was probably over 100 years old.

THE LONG JOURNEY HOME
LE LONG TRAJET DE RETOUR

Malden, night of January 25, 1813:

The American prisoners in Malden were reposing more comfortably than they had the night before. Removed from the wood yard that morning, they had been dispersed among the warehouses of the town and cared for by the owners. The officers and wounded men were put up in the public houses.[849]

Elias Darnell had finally gotten away from his Native American wardens. For the past two nights, he had plotted his escape, but the Indians had taken his socks and shoes to prevent him from running off through the snow.

All day today, he had debated his escape. His captors had actually been treating him quite humanely. They had given him captured letters to read, and a book of Wesley's sermons. They always gave him plenty to eat, serving him before the rest of the family with more politeness than he expected.

There had been other little gifts of friendship and even affection, such as a razor, shaving box, and piece of mirror for him to shave with. They even had a sort of currency, which consisted of pieces of playing cards, with the monetary value in *livres* written on them.

But tonight, they had neglected to take his socks, and Darnell decided to make a go for it, even without his shoes. In the middle of the night, when all was quiet, he crept timidly towards the entrance of the lodge.

As he raised the blanket which served as a door, the Indian warrior coughed.

Darnell froze.

Hearing no further noise, he took the plunge and headed out into the snow in the direction of Fort Amherstburg.

Upon reaching the town of Malden, Darnell slowly worked his way

---

849 Deposition of Dr. John Todd, April 24, 1813, in <u>Barbarities of the Enemy, exposed in a Report of the Committee of the House of Representatives, and the Documents accompanying said Report,</u> Troy, NY: Francis Adancourt, 1813, pp. 141-5. *"Upon my arrival at Malden, I was again solicited to take charge of the wounded, the surgery was opened to me, and I had the use of the medicines and dressings necessary, and they had as comfortable rooms as could be procured...During our stay in Malden, some 8 or 10 of the wounded were brought in by the Indians; several made their escape, who were doomed to massacre, and found protection with the inhabitants of the territory, who brought them to Malden, and several made their escape, wandered in, and delivered themselves up at the fort...."*

through the streets, examining each yard and garden looking for a fire to warm himself. Turning down a street which stretched towards the Detroit River, he came to an old warehouse where other prisoners were being kept.

The guard did not seem too surprised to see him. Other prisoners who had escaped or been ransomed from the Indians were constantly turning themselves in.

Without much ceremony, he opened the door and let Darnell in.

The shivering Kentuckian quickly sought out a warm spot, squeezing himself in between two prisoners who were lying next to the door. It would be morning before he could regain the feeling and circulation in his feet.[850]

The next day, the first of two columns of Kentucky prisoners would be given cold rations and led off on a grueling 16-day, 280-mile journey by way of Lake St. Clair and the Thames River to Fort George on the Niagara Peninsula. At Niagara, 512 men would be paroled to return home. The British would retain Winchester, Lewis, Madison, and some of the other officers.[851]

Elias Darnell was part of that first group. For fear of being recognized and killed by the Indians from whom he had escaped, Darnell changed clothes and tied up his head. Although the Indians scrutinized the column of prisoners as they marched along, nobody recognized him.

After a trek of 17 miles, Darnell's band of prisoners arrived at Sandwich, where they were put up in the people's homes. At 1 o'clock on the 27th, they continued their journey after drawing a ration of bread and fresh beef. They traveled 10 miles that day, partly on Lake St. Clair, and were shut up for the night in some cold, unheated barns, with no means of cooking their meat.

January 28th dawned as cold as any day had been for a freezing walk of 24 miles on Lake St. Clair. The evening shelter consisted of another unheated

---

850 Darnell, Elias. Journal. Philadelphia: Lippincott, Grambo, & Co., 1854, pp. 66-7: *"The Indians came early in the morning to search for me, but they were not admitted into the house. The guard said it would be well for me to keep as much concealed as possible, for if the Indian I had left could get me, he would kill me. He came to the door, and made motions to show how he would scalp me. I disguised myself by changing my clothes and tying up my head, so that he did not know me."*

851 Au, Dennis. War on the Raisin. Monroe: Monroe County Historical Commission, 1981, p. 55. Some wounded prisoners did not accompany these two columns. Other prisoners were brought in after the departure of these two columns. Ensign Baker stayed behind and collected 52 Kentuckians, who were ordered on to Fort George on February 15. Modern road distance is about 243 miles between Amherstburg and Niagara-on-the-Lake, but it doesn't include a march along Lake St. Clair.

barn on the beach, although an unlucky few who could not get inside had to pass the night in the shelter of the woods.[852]

On the 29th of January, a 15-mile jaunt brought them to the mouth of the River *La Tranche*, or Thames, which they followed for 5 miles, running to warm themselves. After a brief rest stop, where the hungry POW's gobbled up a quantity of frozen potatoes and apple peelings that had been dumped in a yard, they trudged another 10 miles to Captain Dolsen's Landing and were lodged in a distillery. Some of the men slept in the still-tubs near the fire, while the rest went into the smoke-filled loft. During the night, they were served a bit of bread and meat.[853]

Dolsen's, January 31, 1813:

At Dolson's on the River LaTranche (Thames,) preparations were under way to send the captive Kentuckians further east to Fort George, well beyond the reach of any American raiding parties. On the 30th, the men in Elias Darnell's group of prisoners received two days' provisions and cooked them.

On the 31st, they marched off. Although it snowed all day, they made 24 miles before taking shelter for the night in a drafty, leaky old barn. Several had frostbitten feet, so they tried to keep their shoes from freezing by sleeping with them under their heads.

---

852 The mileage covered on January 28 and 29 seems excessive, but not out of line with the places mentioned. The overall daily average was 17½ miles per day. If they averaged 2 or 3 miles an hour, that would make for a 6- or 8- hour walk. For 30 miles, it would take an excessive 10 or 15 hours.

853 Darnell, Elias. Journal. Philadelphia: Lippincott, Grambo, & Co., 1854, p. 69. La Tranche is an alternate name for the Thames River, which flows for 170 miles through Ontario and empties into Lake St. Clair. Called *Askunesippi*, "Antlered River," by the Neutrals and Deshkan Ziibi, "Antler River," in Anishnaabemowin, as spoken by the Ojibwe, it was renamed *La Tranchée* (later *La Tranche*), "The Trench," by early French explorers and settlers. It was given its present-day name in 1792-3 by the lieutenant-governor of Upper Canada, Sir John Graves Simcoe after the Thames River in England, by many people continued to informally call it by its old French name. In his journal, Darnell calls it *La Tranche*: (January) 29th. *"We again resumed our march, and continued on the lake fifteen miles to the mouth of La Tranche river (called by some the river Thames). During this time, we had to run to keep ourselves from freezing. We continued up the river five miles, and stopped while the guards went in to warm and to get their dinner. Having drawn no provisions since we left Sandwich, some of the prisoners were driven to the necessity of picking up frozen potatoes and apple peelings that had been thrown out in the yard. One of the prisoners being unable to keep pace with the rest, was left on the lake, but was accidentally overtaken by a sleigh and brought on. After being in a stove-room some time, he was led out to march, trembling with cold. One of the guards observed, "he was a man of no spirit to freeze such a day as this."*

On February 1, they marched 22 miles, ate the last of their rations, and spent a cold night in the woods in the land of the Moravian Delawares.

The next day, the captives marched another 22 miles, suffering from both cold and hunger. In the evening, they arrived at the small settlement of Delaware on the River LaTranche, or Thames, where the locals allowed them to come into their homes and warm themselves by their fires.

On February 3, they drew rations for 3 more days and made an evening march of five miles in 2 feet of falling snow. Much to their relief, the guard was changed, and Captain Dolsen was replaced by a less demanding officer.[854]

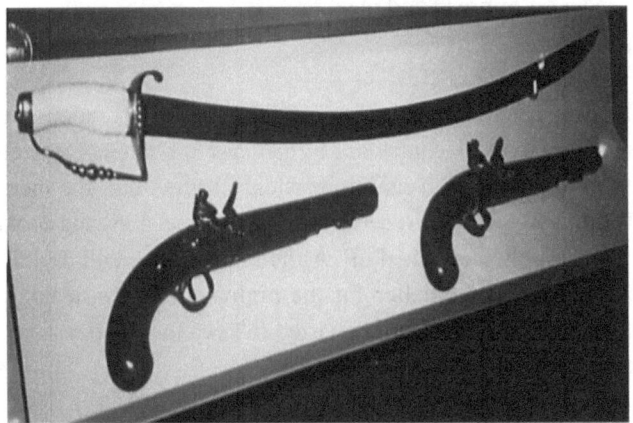

General Winchester's Sword and Pistols
Photographed by the author at the Maison Francois Baby
Windsor Community Museum

Harrison's Camp, Portage River, Saturday, January 29, 1813:

In late January, the American army began the process of evacuating the Portage River camp and reconcentrating their forces at the Maumee Rapids.[855]

---

854 Darnell, Elias. Journal. Philadelphia: Lippincott, Grambo, & Co., 1854, p. 70.

855 An Ohio historical marker for Harrison's camp is located in William Henry Harrison Park at Pemberville, Ohio. The marker reads: *"During the War of 1812, Northwestern Army Commander General William Henry Harrison led troops through northwest Ohio on the way to Detroit and Ft. Malden in Michigan. After the decimation of General James Winchester's division at Frenchtown (Monroe, Michigan) by British and Indian forces, Harrison retreated and led his troops southward to the Portage River. Near this site, now the William Henry Harrison Park, Harrison's men waited for supplies and reinforcements, which were delayed due to heavy rains and flooding in the Black Swamp. With the addition of General Leftwich's brigade at the end of January 1813, Harrison's forces reached approximately 1,700. The troops endured the harsh, wet weather and several soldiers died of exposure*

Worried about the fate of Winchester's men, Harrison assigned Dr. M'Keehan to take a light *cariole* sleigh with an officer of the 2nd Ohio Militia Regiment and a guide to ascertain the condition of the troops captured at the River Raisin and to ask permission for a detachment to bury the dead.

The officer was "Captain" Lemont, from the Connecticut Reserve. The guide was Tessier, whose family had fled the Bay Settlement to take refuge in the safety of Harrison's camp.[856]

General Harrison sent an advance party 7 miles ahead on Saturday, January 29th, while he remained at the Portage.[857] Actually, he had expected them all to be at the rapids by now, but heavy rains had broken up the roads and immobilized his sled-born artillery, which was stuck 25 miles away.

On January 31st, Harrison assembled his remaining troops at 4 a.m. with orders to prepare to march. By 8 o'clock, all was ready. A sleigh carrying tents for the artillery arrived just in time to join the column as it moved up Hull's Road. After covering only 8 or 9 miles, they made camp in 4½ inches of snow, unaware that a small drama was taking place some miles ahead.

On Monday, February 1st, Harrison's army arrived at the Maumee opposite Winchester's old encampment. Sliding down a steep, 40-foot embankment, the soldiers stepped onto the icy surface and followed the river several miles.

Although delayed by several days of rain, Harrison had scraped together 1,700 troops and enough artillery to re-establish an advance post on the Maumee. Having recovered from his initial panic, he now was determined to build a large, fortified camp on the bluffs along the right, or south, bank near the foot of the rapids. The post would soon be known as Fort Meigs, in honor of the governor of Ohio.[858]

The troops struck the Maumee Rapids about 8 miles from their camp

---

and were buried at the camp. Once the winter freeze set in, Harrison led the remaining troops to the rapids of the Maumee River where construction of Fort Meigs began."

856 Conflicting accounts render the dating uncertain. Dr. M'Keehan apparently left camp during the night, or very early in the morning, sometime between the 28th and the 31st of January. See: "Dr. M'Keehan's Narrative," Barbarities of the Enemy, Worcester: Isaac Sturtevant, 1814, pp. 67-71. M'Keehan's name is often spelled "McKeehan", while Lemont's name is also spelled "Lamont." Lemont was usually referred to as "Mr." Lemont, making his rank somewhat uncertain.

857 Lewis, Virgil A., Third Biennial Report of the Department of Archives and History of the State of West Virginia. Charleston: The News-Mail Company, 1911, Peter Davis' Journal, p. 166.

858 Lossing, Benson J. The Pictorial Field-Book of the War of 1812. Glendale, New York: Benchmark Publishing Corporation, 1970, p. 364.

and then marched 4 miles on the ice to make camp on the south side of the river. Work would begin the next day, February 2, 1813.[859]

One bit of luck would be the discovery of a supply of pork that had been saved by the local French *habitants*. It was part of the drove of hogs, which had been delivered to General Winchester, slaughtered, dressed, and salted down by the troops. They were stored with other provisions in sheds that were then set afire when Harrison retreated from the Rapids.[860]

Shortly afterward, the *habitants* moved in to salvage what they could from the blazing sheds. Quickly dousing the flames, they saved much of the meat. This would help feed the troops Harrison presently had on hand.

Luther Harvey would also show up, with 6 yokes of oxen pulling loads of flour. His contracted delivery to the Rapids had been interrupted in January when he met an express rider carrying Harrison's report of Winchester's defeat. Rather than turning loose the oxen and rejoining his military unit as directed, Harvey negotiated the storage of 60 barrels of flour with a farmer near the Huron River (in Ohio) and took the oxen back to Cleveland.[861]

The area around the Rapids was a scene of destruction, with burned-out cabins and miles of corn fields laid to waste. At one of the abandoned cabins, scouts noticed a white flag flying from the roof.

Upon investigation, they found an abandoned *cariole* and the scalped body of Lemont. There was a bullet wound an inch above and to the left of his left nipple and a large gash on the back of his head, made by a tomahawk.[862]

They could only try to imagine the scene, but on the evening of January 31st, a *cariole* sleigh carrying three men had pulled up to the darkened cabin near the Maumee River. Dr. Samuel M'Keehan, Surgeon's Mate of the 2nd Ohio Volunteer Regiment, was armed with a flag of truce and a letter describing his mission, which he was to show to any British officers he encountered.

---

859 Lewis, Virgil A., Third Biennial Report of the Department of Archives and History of the State of West Virginia. Charleston: The News-Mail Company, 1911, Peter Davis' Journal, p. 166.

860 The local *habitants* had never entirely abandoned their homes along the Maumee, but returned to occupy and rebuild them after each period of destruction. Their settlement was called Orleans.

861 Bulkley, John McClelland. History of Monroe County, Michigan, Vol. I. Chicago: Lewis Publishing Co., 1913: Narrative of Capt. Luther Harvey, p. 515. The Huron River mentioned here flows almost 15 miles through north-central Ohio and empties into Lake Erie, draining much of Erie and Huron Counties, which were part of the 1792 Firelands Grant to Connecticut residents whose homes were destroyed during the Revolutionary War.

862 Journal of Joseph Larwill, Burton Historical Collection, Detroit Public Library, pp. 38-40.

He also carried written instructions from General Harrison, and an open letter from Harrison to the captured General Winchester. These, too, he was to display to any British officer who might wish to see them.[863]

Dr. M'Keehan and his companions, Lemont and Tessier, had attached a white flag to their *cariole*. The doctor also possessed a hundred dollars in gold to purchase necessities to aid the American prisoners held at Malden.[864]

They had expected to meet a company of rangers to serve as an escort. Failing to find anyone, they left the *cariole* outside the cabin door, with the flag of truce still on it, and went into the cellar to catch a few hours rest.[865]

Shortly after midnight, the three men got up feeling refreshed and went out to load their belongings back into the *cariole*. Tessier thought something was odd, perhaps missing, but he couldn't quite put his finger on it.

As they began pulling away, Tessier suddenly noticed their white flag was gone. Within seconds, war whoops and shots rang out from the neighboring trees. Lemont went down, clutching his chest.[866]

Tessier and the doctor jumped off the *cariole* and tried to take cover. More shots spattered around them, and M'Keehan was hit in the ankle. Surrounded and unable to fire back, Tessier cried out, *"Cessez le feu! Don't shoot. Nous sommes français!"*

Uncertain whether his attackers had actually ceased fire or were just reloading, Tessier rose hesitantly, his hands in the air.

After a tense moment, an officer and nine Wyandot warriors emerged

---

863 Harrison to M'Keehan, Jan. 31, 1813, <u>Michigan Pioneer and Historical Collections</u>. Vol.15, p. 235: *"You will proceed with the two men who are to attend you to the River Raisin, bearing a flag of truce. The object of your trip is to ascertain the situation of the wounded which were left as it is said at that place. If a British officer should be there, you will deliver him the letter with which you are charged, and proceed to give such assistance to the sick as they may need, and you may be able to procure. You are furnished with 100 dollars in gold for the purpose. Should there be no British officer on the River Raisin, you will proceed toward Malden until you meet with one, unless there should be great danger from the Indians. Indeed, it is my wish that you should go on to Malden, if you are permitted to do so, to bring dispatches from General Winchester, or the senior officer remaining with our prisoners. If your professional services are wanted with the wounded you will remain with them, and send back the two men to bring me an account of your proceedings."* See also: McAfee, Robert. <u>History of the Late War in the Western Country.</u> Bowling Green, Ohio: Historical Publications Company, 1919 (reprint of 1816 original edition.) pp. 259-260.

864 Brown, Samuel, <u>Views of the Campaigns of the North-Western Army</u>, Troy, N.Y.: Francis Adancourt, 1814.

865 Dr. Samuel McKeehan's Narrative, H M&L Niles lv 224.

866 Letter Ensign Church to wife Jerusha, Feb. 11, 1813, Knopf, Richard C., <u>Document Transcriptions of the War of 1812 in the Northwest, Vol. X, pt. 2</u>. Columbus: Ohio Historical Society, 1962. p. 67.

from the trees and took them both captive. After putting Lemont out of his misery with a swift blow of the tomahawk, the Indians scalped and stripped him. They also seized the horse, harness, M'Keehan's great coat, blankets, some clothing, and the $100 in gold.

The prisoners tried to explain they had come under a flag of truce, but with no flag displayed, the officer was not convinced. The Indians called them liars and herded them 20 miles on foot to report to Captain William Elliott, who then sent them on into French Town to meet Colonel Mathew Elliott, Superintendent of the Indian Department.

Colonel Elliott received the doctor cordially, and packed him off to Colonel Procter at Malden. In the meantime, Tessier was allowed the liberty of the settlement.[867]

Left on his own at the River Raisin, Tessier waited dutifully for the return of Dr. M'Keehan. Over the next couple of days, he took the opportunity of telling the *habitants* what had happened. Eventually, Tessier was arrested as a spy and packed off to Malden.

Upon arriving there, he found M'Keehan at a tavern, guarded by a

---

867 McAfee, Robert. History of the Late War in the Western Country. Bowling Green, Ohio: Historical Publications Company, 1919 (reprint of 1816 original edition). p. 260. Procter suspected McKeehan was a spy, but finally *"he was recognized in his official character, and directed to attend the wounded. On the 2nd of March, he was arrested by Colonel Proctor, and accused of carrying on a secret correspondence."*
See also: Report of the Committee…as Relates to the Spirit & Manner in which the War has been waged by the Enemy. Washington: A & G. Way, 1813, pp. 78-85: M'Keehan wrote a letter to Procter on February 4, inquiring as to his official status. Procter replied the next day with a recognition of M'Keehan's official character. On the 12th came Procter's official determination to detain the doctor to care for the American wounded as per his original instructions from General Harrison. On March 2, however, he was arrested by McLean, Procter's aide-de-camp, and accused of carrying on an illicit private correspondence with the American forces. On the 8th, the British seized his property and sent him and a River Raisin settler named Ruland to Fort George. En route, they suffered such indignities as being forced to eat with the officers' servants. M'Keehan was then sent on to Montréal, where he arrived on March 28 and was thrown into solitary confinement. In M'Keehan's own narrative of May 24, 1813, he says *"…I was put in a dungeon, eight or ten feet below the surface of the ground, where I had neither bed nor bedding, chair, bench or stool — denied pen, ink, paper, or even the use of a book for two weeks. The only fresh current of air that passed through my apartment came through the bowels of the privy! Here I was kept 33 days, when I was to my great joy, put up with the American prisoners, and with them permitted to remain till last Monday, when I was liberated by the intercession of Lt. Dudley of the Navy. Colonel Baynes, aid to the governor, told me that the outrage which had been committed on my person was contrary to his orders."* M'Keehan was released on May 17, 1813.

French-Canadian. Procter had seized the doctor's documents, and was deciding what to do with him.

Meanwhile, one night between January 28 and February 5, a *habitant* appeared at Harrison's camp and was brought in to see the General. Through an interpreter, the man stated that his name was Peter Navarre and he had come from the River Raisin.

Harrison asked for news about French Town, and then suggested that if Navarre were willing to remain with the army, he would engage him as a scout or spy at the rate of one dollar per day.

Navarre accepted, and soon found himself employed in scouting expeditions to the Maumee and River Raisin, as well as carrying messages to Sandusky, Urbana, and other places.[868]

Harrison was also worried about the fate of two men he had sent to check on the American wounded. Navarre assured the general he had seen the two, and that he had left them both safe and sound at the River Raisin.[869]

Medard Labadie had also seen the prisoners the day they were captured, when Elliott and his party took them right past the Labadie home. He had recognized Tessier, but had not had a chance to talk with him.

At the Raisin, however, Elliott had talked a little too freely, bragging about the clever way in which the ambush had been planned.

It appeared that Captain Elliott and 15 Wyandot warriors had been out on a scouting mission when they spotted M'Keehan's sleigh about 4 miles away.

Fearing the Wyandots might not attack a party flying a flag of truce, Elliott hid his men and waited until M'Keehan stopped at a cabin for the night. He then sent one of the Wyandots to steal the flag.

With the flag secured, Elliott sent the other Wyandots to set up the ambush. Several warriors climbed onto the roof of the cabin. It was they who fired the shot that killed Lemont.

---

868 Deposition Pierre Navarre, 1830. Harrison's Frenchman was not identified, but Peter Navarre did state that he met up with General Harrison at the Carrying River about this time.

869 Extracts of letters, Knopf, Richard C., Document Transcriptions of the War of 1812 in the Northwest, Vol. V, pt. 2, Columbus: Ohio Historical Society, 1958, p. 24. Again, there are conflicting dates. Navarre also said the Kentuckians had fought desperately and might have won if part of their line had not given way and if they had been better supplied with ammunition. Unfortunately, extra ammunition was placed in a house some distance away from the fighting. He had personally counted 61 British dead on the field, but they were taken away in sleds. There were about 600 American prisoners.

After the ambushers departed with their two prisoners and the horses, Elliott had a Wyandot replace the flag at the cabin.

Now that some of the *habitants* had related the full story about what had happened to his friend, Labadie decided it was time to depart. He had received a warning that a British patrol was on its way to arrest him, and they were in no mood for taking prisoners. No doubt the price the British had placed on his head was for "dead or alive." Fortunately, he had several guns in the house, and they were all loaded by the time the British rode up, their pistols drawn.

His first shot brought the patrol to a halt. His second saw them scatter for cover. Taking advantage of the confusion, Labadie grabbed his remaining musket and bolted out the door. Mounting his horse, he galloped off towards Fort Meigs, determined to find General Harrison and volunteer as a scout.[870]

Labadie was not alone. Scouts sent out on February 7th returned to Harrison on the 9th to report that hundreds of Native warriors were camped near Maumee Bay. By the evening of the next day, 600 men were assembled and ready to march, supported by a 6-pdr with a crew of 14 artillerists commanded by Lt. Larwill. An hour later, they were followed by a second detachment that would increase their numbers to 1,100 men.

Other French Town refugees also joined the army about this time, forming an irregular company of spies under the nominal command of Antoine Couture.

Although these Franco-American inhabitants of Michigan were sometimes distrusted because of their intimacy with the Indians, as well as their former status as British subjects, and their connections with relatives and business partners in Canada, the American authorities often depended on their services as scouts and guides.[871]

---

870 Grant, Linda, History of the Labadie Family. Spiral Bound Manuscript, p. 163. Monroe County Historical Commission Archives. Medard Labadie would return to French Town in the fall with Colonel Johnson's Regiment. Journal of Joseph Larwill, Burton Historical Collection, Detroit Public Library. See also: Deposition of Medard Labadie, Extract of Letter from General Harrison to the Secretary of War, dated Feb.11, 1813, in Barbarities of the Enemy, exposed in a Report of the Committee of the House of Representatives, and the Documents accompanying said Report. Troy: Francis Adancourt, 1813, pp. 136-9. Labadie would remain in the area until the 5th of February. Labadie did not speak directly to General Harrison. Captain Gratiot, although an engineer officer, served as interpreter and signed as a witness to Labadie's testimony, sworn before Judge-Adjutant Todd and Aide-de-Camp Graham.

871 Familiar with the Detroit region and its culture, Bela Hubbard wrote in his 1888 work, Memorials

Criticisms of the commanders, Detroit, January 31, 1813:

Already the nation was buzzing with wild tales of the disaster at the River Raisin. Some claimed General Winchester had been killed, scalped, and horribly mangled. One letter printed in Baltimore's Weekly Register even asserted that Winchester's hand was cut off and shoved into a wound in his body.

After hearing from both victors and vanquished, Judge Woodward wrote a letter to Secretary of State James Monroe, detailing several major errors committed by General Winchester in the Battle of "La Rivière aux Raisins."

First of all, the troops were posted on the left (or north) bank of the river, with the stream at their back. Although the river was frozen, a position on the right bank would have presented an extra obstacle to the British, and the tree-lined banks and islands could have blocked the British artillery's line of sight.

Secondly, even on the left bank, the camp should not have been set up at so convenient a spot for the enemy — right at the end of the public road that any force equipped with artillery would certainly have taken. In fact, more thought should have been given to fences and woods which could have restricted the deployment of the British cannons.

Third, General Winchester set up headquarters too far away from his men. In permitting Wells and Langham to leave the day before the battle, he effectively removed officers who were badly needed to stem the rout of the right wing.

Fourth, the general did not credit the reports of scouts sent out to locate the enemy, even though some signals may have been conflicting.

Finally, if Winchester had indeed advanced without orders or permission of the commanding general, as some said, he was guilty of a greater military fault than any of the others.

Perhaps because he was still in British-controlled Detroit, Judge Woodward praised Colonel Procter for acting as brilliantly as General Brock

---

of a Half Century, "I cannot omit to mention a commendable trait in the French character, their early and sincere attachment to the United States and her republican institutions. To be known as a Frenchman was to be known as a patriot; and in the times which tried men's souls — and few parts of our country had more varied and bitter experience — the Frenchman was always our reliable and active ally; cool and unflinching in danger; shrewd and watchful when caution was most needed. If a man was wanted for a dangerous enterprise, it was a Frenchman who was chosen."

had in the Campaign against Detroit the previous summer. His laurels were only tarnished by the actions of some of his allies in killing the wounded.

In summary, Woodward wrote: *"Whatever credit is however given to the bravery of the men, the superiority of Generalship beyond all doubt or Question belongs to the British commanders."*[872]

Official British reports not only agreed with Woodward's assessment, but also defended Procter's handling of his Native American allies.[873]

Although rewarded for his victory by promotion to Brigadier General, and given votes of praise by the legislatures of both Upper and Lower Canada, Henry Procter came in for his own share of criticism, nonetheless.

Dr. Robert Richardson claimed the victory was due more to a lack of initiative on the part of their enemy than to any genius on the part of the British commander. Procter's main error was in not rushing the fence with a bayonet attack before the Americans could organize an effective defense.

The resulting losses to enemy fire left the British assault force so scattered and demoralized that they would have been swept from the field if the Americans had dared to sortie out from behind their protected positions.

Richardson also considered Procter responsible for breaking his promise to protect the wounded Americans left in French Town.[874]

---

872 Letter Woodward to Monroe, Jan. 31, 1813, in <u>MPHC, Vol. 15</u>, p. 234. The Americans *"fought like lions,"* from behind the fences. This was the first time in the war in the west that the British had tasted the type of tenacious defense that militiamen could put up from within a covered position.

873 British Official Account, as filed in the Adjutant-general's office, Quebec, Feb. 8, 1813, printed in <u>The Weekly Register</u>, Baltimore, Saturday, March 6, 1813. British praises included that *"...this occasion the gallantry of Colonel Procter was most nobly displayed, in his humane and unwearied exertions, which succeeded in rescuing the vanquished from the revenge of the Indian warriors."* Moreover, *"... the Indian chief Round Head, with his band of warriors, rendered essential service by their bravery and good conduct."*

874 Letter Richardson to Askin, Feb. 7, 1813, in "Battle of Frenchtown," manuscript issued by the Algonquin Club, Detroit, April, 1837. The original letter is in the Burton Historical Collection at the Detroit Public Library. Dr. Richardson's young son was seriously wounded in the knee during the battle. Dr. Richardson stated that *"...the loss has been very severe, indeed ten times more than was necessary. Our men ought either to have been brought up in contact with the enemy at once (which they might have been before half of them was fairly awake) or else kept at a sufficient distance for the guard to drive them out...If the Americans had been soldiers, they would have come out when our men were completely broke and nearly half of them kill'd and wounded, and would have taken or kill'd every man. I am sure two hundred men could not then have been got together...I suppose it would be considered high treason to speak out in this way."*

There is another circumstance which has hurt me more than I can express. That is with respect to some wounded men belonging to the Americans who were left without proper protection and some of whom I have been informed were the same evening murdered by the Indians. Had I been

To allay the effects of any criticism, Procter set in motion his own investigation, which would find that a few Indians behaved badly after obtaining liquor in the settlement.

He tried to lay the blame at the door of the local French *habitants*, surmising that they were trying to get the warriors drunk to make them easy prey for Harrison's troops, who were thought to be on the way.

The desertion of the interpreters, whether from fear of the Indians, fear of capture by the Americans, or because they also had gotten drunk, left the intoxicated warriors out of control.

According to Procter's findings, only six of the prisoners were actually murdered; two mortally wounded prisoners who could not be moved, two who couldn't keep up on the march, one who argued with his captors, and one local *habitant* in an unconnected dispute over a pig.

As for the destruction of the houses, they were set afire merely to keep them from being used by the enemy. An interrogation of widows revealed that all the living prisoners had been removed before the Indians burned the houses.

Stories to the contrary were thought to be exaggerations told by a couple of panic-stricken female refugees who arrived in Detroit shortly after the battle.

Finally, there were General Harrison and his subordinates. While not at the battle, they did not escape some criticism regarding the extent of their support of General Winchester's command.

Major George Madison expressed his frustration, testifying, *"I cannot say whether or not General Winchester had any right to expect reinforcements from Generals Tupper and Perkins, but it was generally believed we would receive troops from them. I am well persuaded that, could we have been reinforced with 500 additional men, a victory on the 22nd of January, 1813, would have been the result, instead of a defeat."*

Madison went on to say that Winchester's force, composing the left wing of the Northwestern Army, were *"...very badly supplied with provisions, and had no forage furnished...while the center and right wings, from the*

---

commanding officer, I should have considered myself responsible for the lives of every one of them, and within my hearing, protection was promised for those poor people. Be assured, we have not heard the last of this shameful transaction..."

report and information, were well supplied with both these articles, and not so much exposed to the enemy."[875]

Of course, General Harrison had his own view of the events, as he wrote in a letter to Governor Meigs on January 24: *"Never were the affairs of any army in a more prosperous situation than ours before the unfortunate step of marching the detachment to the River Raisin; it was made not only without any authority from me, but in opposition to my views.*

Everything in my power was, however, done to prevent any disaster, and reinforcements were pushed on with as much rapidity as possible; Major Cotgreave's battalion, the first in the army, was within 14 miles of the scene of action, when he heard of the defeat, and 300 regular troops were also on their way. I remained at the Rapids with one regiment only.

In justice to General Winchester, I must observe, that I have understood that the measure (marching the detachment to the River Raisin) was forced upon him by his officers; but whatever may have been the cause, and how-ever great the calamity, both as it regards the nation and individuals, it is certainly not irreparable. "[876]

Detroit, Candlemas, February 2, 1813:

It was the *Fête* of the *Chandeleur*, the Festival of Light, which occurred 40 days after Christmas; a time for lighting *chandelles*, or candles, at the church and tossing *crêpes* or buckwheat *galettes*. It was said that lighting a blessed candle offered protection from lightning strikes or other misfortunes, and that a deftly tossed crêpe could bring a year's worth of good luck.[877]

---

875 Winchester, James. Historic Details Having Relation to the Campaign of the North-Western Army under Generals Harrison and Winchester. Lexington: Worsley & Smith, 1818, pp. 65-7.

876 Letter Harrison to Meigs, Carrying River, Jan. 24, 1813, as printed in The Weekly Register, Baltimore, Saturday, February 13, 1813, No. 24 or Vol. III, Whole No. 76: *"I had but 360 men with me about 3 miles above the Rapids, where the news first reached me. I immediately ordered them to prepare to march and set out with my staff to overtake a detachment of 300 men that had set out that morning for the River Raisin. I overtook them at the distance of 6 miles, but before the other troops [Colonel Andrews' Ohio regiment] came up, it was ascertained that the defeat was complete, and it was the unanimous opinion of Generals Payne, Perkins, and the field officers, that we should return."* His decision to retreat created some criticism that followed Harrison right up through his 1840 Presidential campaign. Joseph Loranger, who witnessed Winchester's defeat and was at Fort Meigs with Harrison, felt compelled to write an article, "Testimony of an Old Soldier," in the June 30, 1840, issue of the Monroe Gazette, defending Harrison against charges of cowardice, and ending with *"Vive le Général Harrison!"* and *"Vive la Constitution!"*

877 D'Arpini, Brigitte, from an address made to the members of the Alliance Française de Detroit &

For George McDougall, such pious beliefs were not enough. Shortly after finding out that his River Raisin property had been destroyed, he felt compelled to write a letter to Judge Augustus B. Woodward.

His dwelling house, store, and outbuildings located next to Jerome's property had been burned by the Indians on the 23rd of January. But these were not the only losses he had incurred so far during the war.

Other holdings had been destroyed the previous fall, including a two-story house, farmhouse, barn and distillery. With his most recent losses, he was now pretty well wiped out financially. He was also ill and worn out.

Then, last Saturday, he got word that Colonel Procter was ordering all American citizens, with the exception of the French *habitants*, to leave Detroit.

He was being sent into a strange country with neither money nor friends.

Although in the past, he had railed against the British government, he now felt compelled to plead for clemency. On Sunday, he had gone to see William Jones to ask him to intercede with Colonel Procter.

"My God!" McDougall thought, *"What have I done to forfeit those rights for which the faith of the British government is plighted by the capitulation, with the proclamation of that great and generous hero, the deceased Major General Brock? What has become of that boasted faith which has been the prop to the prosperity of that government? I will call on my friend Judge Woodward, the champion of our rights."*

After all, since the surrender of Detroit last summer, he had honored his parole and remained steadfastly neutral. He had not taken up arms again in the recent battle at the River Raisin, nor had he even spied against the British.

Grosse Pointe, Feb. 6, 2005: Custom says this was the traditional day the Christ child was presented in the temple. Although established as a Christian festival by Pope Gelase I in 472 A.D., the festival's origins go back to the pagan Roman festival of Lupercalia, a day of debauchery and torch-lit parades. (Another descendant of Lupercalia is St. Valentine's Day.)

Crêpes and galettes or pancakes were a traditional food from Chandeleur through Lent. Their round shape reminded people of the sun, and by extension, of the Son of God, the Light of the World. European peasants believed their wheat would rot if they didn't make Crêpes at Chandeleur. For good luck, a Crêpe was tossed with the right hand while holding a gold coin in the left. Then the coin was rolled up in the Crêpe and carried in a family procession to the bedroom, where it was placed on top of an armoire. The old coin, still wrapped in the remains of last year's Crêpe, was recovered and given to the first needy person who came by.

In the new world, the Acadians of Prince Edward Island organized collections for the poor for the Chandeleur. It is not known to what extent these traditions were carried on in the Great Lakes, but pre-Lenten Crêpe making and tossing remained popular among the River Raisin French into the 21st century.

He knew that Judge Woodward, as well as his old comrade in arms, Colonel Hunt, had received assurances from Colonel Procter that they would not be deported. He wanted to obtain the same indulgence for himself.

Surely, with Woodward's support and his pledge of McDougall's good behavior, Colonel Procter would decide in his favor and allow him to remain in Detroit, at least until spring.[878]

Indeed, Woodward was at that very moment writing to Procter to ask for an investigation of the reports he was receiving from the River Raisin regarding the killing of prisoners, the burning of buildings, and the pillaging, harassment, and murder of citizens there.[879]

Procter believed Woodward's personal ambition was now leading him to court popularity with the citizenry and take actions designed to ingratiate himself with the U.S. authorities, should they return to Detroit. This led Procter to call for his dismissal.[880]

Meanwhile, from other inhabitants of Detroit, Colonel Procter had received a petition protesting his planned deportation of 29 citizens suspected of conspiring against the British occupation of their city, along with those refusing to take a loyalty oath.

He knew that a number of Detroiters had plotted to stage an uprising if he had been defeated at the Battle of the River Raisin on January 22. Since then, they had become increasingly insolent, holding meetings and passing resolutions in preparation for the day when General Harrison would arrive with an American army of liberation.

To combat this mounting challenge to British control, Procter had felt compelled to order 104 of the more suspicious and turbulent characters out of the territory. It also led Procter to increase pressure on anyone who was or had been a British subject to take an oath of allegiance to His Majesty. He might even arm and form them into a self-defense militia for the territory.

---

878 Letter McDougall to Woodward, Feb. 2, 1813, <u>Michigan Pioneer and Historical Society Collections.</u> Lansing: Wyncoop, Hallenbeck, Crawford Co., 1908. Vol. XXXVI, pp. 286-7.

879 Letter Woodward to Gen. Procter, Feb. 2, 1813, <u>Report of the Committee…as Relates to the Spirit & Manner in which the War has been waged by the Enemy.</u> Washington: A & G. Way, 1813, pp. 124-129.

880 Letter Procter to Sheaffe, Feb. 4, 1813, MPHC, Vol. XV. Lansing: Wynkoop, Hallenbeck, Crawford, 1909, pp. 242-3. See also: Antal, Sandy. <u>A Wampum Denied: Procter's War of 1812.</u> Canada: Carleton University Press, 1997, pp. 193-4.

Convinced an underground resistance movement had become operational, Procter declared martial law throughout the territory.

As for the French-speaking *habitants*, he would rely on their Indian friends to convince them that it would be in their own self-interest to support their cause if they intended to remain on good terms.

U.S. citizens with no British or Canadian ties would either be sent out of the territory or be forced to take an oath of neutrality.[881]

Upper Canada, February 5, 1813:

Another 26 miles was left underfoot as the prisoners reached the settlement of Oxford at the headwaters of the River Thames on February 4.[882]

The next day they plodded doggedly on. As the column stopped to take on more provisions, they met a detachment of the 41st Regiment heading towards Malden, where they would replace those killed at the River Raisin.

Most of the replacements appeared to be Irish, and one of their officers called out that in a few weeks they would drive back Harrison and all his army. According to Elias Darnell, a private in Williams' company of the 5th Kentucky by the name of James Allen replied, *"Yes, before that time your Irish hides will be riddled so that they would not hold hickory nuts!"*

Another of that party said, *"What nonsensical things those leather stocks were which we* [the Americans] *wore, with the sign of the eagle pecking out the eyes of the lion."* Allen again felt obliged to answer back, *"This is only the shadow, the substance will soon follow."* Due to the halt, the prisoners made only 5 miles that day, and were again housed with the locals.

On the 6th, the Kentuckians walked 24 miles through a wilderness of piney woodlands. That night they were taken in by the citizens of Burford.

Elias Darnell and his 5 messmates stopped at Major Boone's and asked if they could stay the night. Boone assented, and introduced them to his father, who had been a Tory major in New Jersey during the American Revolution. The conversation quickly turned unfriendly, as bitter memories were dredged up on both sides.

The old man claimed the Americans would never conquer Canada. He had heard that next spring the British would be reinforced by 70,000 Indians

---

881 Antal, Sandy. A Wampum Denied: Procter's War of 1812. Canada: Carleton University Press, 1997, p. 182.

882 Darnell, Elias. Journal. Philadelphia: Lippincott, Grambo, & Co., 1854, p. 71.

from the northwest, as many black troops from Santo Domingo, and 300,000 Turks. As if that weren't enough, he added that obviously, God himself was an Englishman.

Upon hearing this, the ever-fiery James Allen exclaimed, *"I suppose you will set the dogs on us next! If the Lord has joined with the British, Savages, and Negroes to massacre his own people, it is surprising, but I rather think it is only your Canadian lord that acts in this manner."*

A young woman of the house then boldly interrupted, saying the Americans were only coming to drive the Canadians off their lands.

To this, Allen answered they had come to set them free, so those lands might be their own and not belong to King George.

Unconvinced, the woman replied, *"The Americans killed at Queenstown had deeds in their pockets for all our best plantations."*

"I must believe it because you say so," said Allen, *"but if I had seen it myself, I would not."* For some reason, this semi-gallant response seemed to placate the old Tory, and he and Allen spent the rest of the evening in more congenial conversation.[883]

Maumee Bay, February 10-11, 1813:

On February 5, 1813, Major General John Armstrong assumed his new duties as Secretary of War. President Madison had appointed him in hopes he would bring a more professional approach to the war effort.

Initially in favor of a blow against the heart of the main British defenses at Montréal or Québec, Armstrong now found himself thinking of how he could best restore the strategic initiative in the west.

On the night of Wednesday, February 10th, General Harrison set off in pursuit of a band of Native Americans reported near the mouth of the Maumee River. His 1,100-man army marched in two separate detachments.[884]

Gen. Harrison and his staff led the way, with Gen. Perkins in charge of the detachment. About 100 yards behind came Lt. Joseph Larwill and 14 artillerymen with a horse-drawn 6-pdr cannon, using the frozen river as a

---

883 Darnell, Elias. Journal. Philadelphia: Lippincott, Grambo, & Co., 1854, pp. 71-74.

884 There is some confusion in the various accounts as to whether this happened on the night of February 9 or February 10. There were also discrepancies in the reported order and timing of events.

highway. He was followed by Major Todd and the companies of Langham and McCray.

Descending the Maumee, the troops spotted some fires on the north bank, and the column formed a battle line by simply facing to the left. The sound of Harrison's soldiers cocking their muskets could plainly be heard as they slipped quietly across the ice and up the bank, but they found the place deserted.[885]

After resting half an hour, those who felt too weak to go on were allowed to remain, while the rest of the column marched off down the river, headed for Maumee Bay. When they reached the river's mouth, however, they noticed something in the distance, moving on the dark, glassy surface of the bay, about half a mile from shore.

Harrison quickly ordered a pursuit. For a mile and a half across the ice, they chased the enigmatic figures. The mounted officers had difficulty at times, the thin ice breaking under the weight of their horses. The horse-drawn cannon, too, was nearly lost in the same fashion.

According to Lt. Larwill, the moon was just setting about a quarter past two in the morning, when the artillery horses started to break through the ice. Larwill unhitched the off-hind horse from the traces, then crossed around to release the other rear horse. The ice gave way, and he and two of his men fell into 5 feet of frigid water. Flailing about, all three managed to get out, but not without a great deal of effort.[886]

Harrison ordered the artillery crew and a company of militia to stay and extricate the cannon while the rest of the column continued another half a dozen miles onto Lake Erie, but then turned back.

They halted on an island out in Maumee Bay, where Larwill's artillery detachment joined them an hour after sunrise.[887]

---

885 One source puts the time at 4 a.m., but that would put this event later than the 2 a.m. estimate for the subsequent pursuit of the Indians on the ice of Lake Erie.

886 "Journal of Joseph H. Larwill," Burton Historical Collections, Detroit Public Library, pp. 43-45: Of his efforts to free the artillery piece, Larwill would write: "*I find it attended with great difficulty in getting the horses out, which I accomplished, then sent 4 or 5 hands to the shore to cut handspikes, and then took the canon off the carriage, then got all out. After it was out, I had the cannon mounted. We was much fatigued. Several of my men returned to the fires with Sergt. Kelly. The militia that was left, excepting 3 or 4, afforded no assistance.*"

887 I'm guessing this was Turtle Island, located 5 miles from the mouth of the Maumee. The British built a small blockhouse on the island but abandoned it before the War of 1812. The island was awarded to Michigan after the Toledo War, but Ohio owned the lighthouse on it. In 1973, the

While waiting, many of the recruits who had never seen Lake Erie expressed their amazement. One of them remarked that the endless, flat horizon looked like the "...*sky and the lake came so near together that there did not seem to be room for a fellow's hat between.*"[888]

Spies returning from the River Raisin also arrived on the island, bringing along a *habitant* who reported that the Indians had withdrawn from French Town, taking many cattle with them.[889]

Larwill's artillerymen had half an hour to rest and eat up the last of their rations before being ordered to move out. With no provisions and few of the enemy left at French Town, there was no point in proceeding on to the River Raisin, and their force was not strong enough to launch a raid against Malden.

Harrison decided to lead his army 5 miles back along the south side of the Bay to the village of Presqu'île, which they found abandoned. The troops gathered some frozen ears of corn and rested a short while before resuming their trek back to their base at Fort Meigs.

By the time the main body of the army returned to camp, they had been out for nearly 21 hours and had covered a round trip of almost 60 miles.[890]

Lt. Larwill, however, was not among them. After his dunking, his head had started to ache. Almost 2½ miles from Fort Meigs, he began vomiting and could go no farther. Larwill dropped out of line at the remains of old Fort Miamis. Many others had also fallen behind, and sleds were sent to pick them up.[891]

The lieutenant was brought in just as the evening gun was being fired. He revived a bit after drinking a few cups of coffee in his warm quarters, but the next day, he was still very weak, and suffering from severe pains in his

---

Supreme Court split the island with the northern half remaining in Michigan and the southern half, with the lighthouse, going to Ohio. Today, the island is privately owned and the lighthouse has fallen into ruins.

888 McAfee, Robert B. The Late War in the Western Country, Bowling Green, Ohio: Historical Publications Co., 1919 reprint of the 1816 edition. p. 261. See also: "We Lay There Doing Nothing: John Jackson's Recollection of the War of 1812," edited by Jeff L. Patrick, appearing in the Indiana Magazine of History, LXXXVIII, June, 1992, published by the Trustees of Indiana University.

889 Antal, Sandy, A Wampum Denied: Procter's War of 1812, Canada: Carleton Univ. Press, 1997.

890 Brown, Samuel, Views of the Campaigns of the North-Western Army, Troy, N.Y.: Francis Adancourt, 1814. The actual round-trip mileage would have been more in the range of 50 miles.

891 "Journal of Joseph H. Larwill," Burton Historical Collections, Detroit Public Library, pp. 45-46.

head and bones. On Monday, February 15th, feeling totally unfit for duty, Lt. Larwill wrote a letter of resignation, but Harrison refused to accept it.[892]

General Harrison had hoped to advance as far as Brownstown, but any attempt to liberate Detroit would expose his supply lines to attack from Malden, just as Hull had experienced the summer before. Harrison believed the militia would follow him across the border into Canada, but many enlistments were expiring in the next 4 days, and he was not sure if even 3,300 men would be enough to reduce Fort Amherstburg.

The last of Harrison's Ohio militiamen were discharged on February 24. Despite their refusal to stay even a month beyond their enlistment, Harrison was sure they would return if he announced he was invading Canada.[893]

Unseasonably warm weather had now returned, making the swampy roads impassable for wagons and sleds, and difficult for horses. Ammunition sleds that had left Upper Sandusky 18 days ago, were still 25 miles away.

To decrease the consumption of his carefully hoarded supplies and to save on expenses, Harrison told the Governor of Kentucky not to call out the latest levy of 1,500 men until they were needed.

The teams hired for public service would be discharged, and the small depots and blockhouses across Ohio would be garrisoned and stockpiled.[894]

---

892 "Journal of Joseph H. Larwill," Burton Historical Collections, Detroit Public Library, p. 47.

893 "We Lay There Doing Nothing; John Jackson's Recollection of the War of 1812," edited by Jeff L. Patrick, Indiana Magazine of History, LXXXVIII, June, 1992, Trustees of Indian University: Their trip home was uncomfortable: "We received our discharge papers on the 15th day of February, 1813, drawed and cooked 2 days rations, and started for home. The weather had become warm, and rain following for the past two days had melted the snow, and the ground was deluged with water. On arriving at the black swamp, it was discovered to be all flooded with water, so we built log heaps of fire and proposed to remain there all night.

"The weather in the evening had turned quite cold, and in the morning, there was ice on the water, more than a half inch thick, but would not bear a man's weight…so we formed in double file, and the ice broke through at every step, and the water underneath being from 6 inches to a foot in depth.

"When the 2 men in front were pretty well tired out breaking the ice, they would step aside and fall back to the rear and let the next file go ahead.

"In this way we continued on until we found some high ground where there was no ice, then we would halt and take the bits of ice out of our shoes…and after running and jumping around for a few minutes to warm and keep our blood in circulation, we would continue our wade for several miles, until we got through the swamp.

"We reached Fort Finley just at night, built large fires, changed our pants and socks, hung them up to dry, ate our rations, and prepared to remain there all night…Our feet had become very sore by the ice in our shoes."

894 Letter Harrison to Armstrong, Feb. 11, 1813.

Although his main effort was now aimed at turning Fort Meigs into a major bastion to block any British forays into Ohio, as well as an assembly point for a late spring or summer campaign against Detroit, General Harrison still retained some hope that he could at least mount a serious raid on the enemy's base.

After all, Michigan weather was changeable, and there was still time for a spell of cold weather to freeze the lake enough to support a swift, surprise raid on the British fleet laid up for the winter at Malden.[895]

Sandwich, February 10, 1813:

General Procter[896] received another letter from Judge Woodward, who was making himself increasingly troublesome, if not a complete bore. This time, the judge was complaining that the French *habitants* of the Territory were being intimidated by the Indians into taking an oath of loyalty to the British crown.

In addition, they were urging them to take up arms and join the Native war parties. In Woodward's view, this contravened the accepted practice of dealing with the inhabitants of a conquered territory, who still owed allegiance to the United States.[897]

An Indian brought in Captain McCracken's blood-spattered commission paper on the 10th of February. The Indian said he had captured McCracken, but while searching him, discovered he had hidden an Indian scalp under his shirt. Enraged at McCracken's audacity, he had killed him on the spot.

McCracken's commission was delivered to Ensign Isaac L. Baker of the 2nd U.S. Infantry Regiment, who had been ordered by Procter to make a return of all the prisoners killed by the Indians after the River Raisin battle.

Having himself been a prisoner of the Indians, Baker didn't believe the warrior's story. He doubted that Captain McCracken would have been so foolish as to carry a scalp with him after being captured. Nonetheless, Baker added McCracken to his list of 11 named victims. Witnesses related 18 other killings, but were unable to identify the soldiers by name.

---

895 Letters Harrison to Armstrong, March 12, 1813 and March 17, 1813.

896 As a result of his victory at the River Raisin, Colonel Procter was promoted to the rank of brigadier general on February 8, 1813. On June 4th of that year, he was named a major general.

897 Letter Woodward to Procter, Feb. 10, 1813, <u>Report of the Committee...as Relates to the Spirit & Manner in which the War has been waged by the Enemy.</u> Washington: A & G. Way, 1813, pp. 124-9.

Nor was there much he or anyone else could do about the 30 or 40 other Kentuckians believed to still be captives of the Indians. These included the black slaves and servants of Colonels Wells, Lewis, and Allen, who were now acting as valets for various Indian chiefs.[898] Hart's servant, Isham, was still alive also, although his exact whereabouts were being kept secret.[899]

General Procter ordered private individuals not to ransom any more captives. Although the British still paid Indians for bringing in live prisoners, the price was much less than what the civilians of Detroit and Sandwich had been offering.

Ensign Baker knew that he would soon be leaving for Fort George with several of the wounded prisoners who had recovered enough to travel. Regrettably, they would have to leave five more seriously injured men behind under the care of Dr. M'Keehan, who was himself wounded.[900]

Fort George, February 11, 1813:

In the heart of Upper Canada, the Kentucky prisoners captured at the Raisin were still on the march. On February 7th and 8th, the struggling column walked 30 miles towards a small village near the head of Lake Ontario, having passed through the Mohawk and Six Nations settlements on the Grand River.

Contrary to his expectations, Elias Darnell found these people to be incredibly light complexioned, although they did still dress in Native fashion. Even more astounding to this Kentuckian, they held a large portion of the best lands in the area.[901]

The next day they continued for 16 miles, descending the 200-foot Niagara escarpment onto the plain skirting Lake Ontario.

Over at Fort George in the Upper Canadian town of Newark (Niagara-on-the-Lake), the second group of Kentucky prisoners came marching into

---

898 Solomon, a servant of Col. Allen, survived the battle, only to be taken prisoner.
899 In September, 2020, Bruce C. Johnson, Jr., of Gibraltar, Michigan, shared his research on Isham (aka: Isaam): An article in the Cincinnati Enquirer of June 9, 1884, stated he was the slave of Henry Clay of Kentucky and had accompanied Captain Hart, the senator's brother-in-law, to the "River Resin," where he saw him taken away by two warriors. Other evidence indicates Isham was owned by Hart's mother. After the war, the Indians took Isham to St. Louis, where he was traded to a French merchant and eventually sold to a sugar plantation in Louisiana. In the 1820s, an effort was made to give Isham his freedom, but his location was no longer known.
900 See Appendix J for Baker's list of prisoners killed by the Indians.
901 Darnell, Elias. Journal. Philadelphia: Lippincott, Grambo, & Co., 1854, pp. 73-74.

town. The first group, with Elias Darnell, had arrived the day before, after making an 18-mile trek on the 9th and covering the final 16 miles on the 10th.[902]

There were now 512 prisoners in this town of handsome brick and stone buildings, doubling its population. Arrangements were made to exchange and parole the Kentuckians. Their names were recorded, with the companies and regiments to which they belonged. They all swore not to take up arms against Great Britain or her allies until legally exchanged.

Once the formalities were taken care of, they were sent to American-held Fort Niagara, just across the Niagara River, less than a mile away from where they were now being held. From there, they would head homeward via Black Rock, Buffalo, Erie, Waterford, Meadville, and Pittsburgh. At Pittsburgh, they would find water transport to take them to Kentucky.

While John McCalla was enjoying the free air of Fort Niagara, he wrote to his parents, assuring them he had made it safely through all the trials of warfare and captivity, and was now on his way home. Unfortunately, he would have to break the news that Ebenezer Blythe and Samuel Elder were dead. He had learned that Elder was killed during the retreat of the right wing, while Blythe was carried off or murdered in one of the houses on the 23rd.[903]

McCalla felt somewhat guilty. A ball had passed through his coat, and another had actually struck him on the ankle, yet he remained unhurt. Not only that, but he was still in good health, and had even gained weight since leaving home so many months ago.[904]

Erie, Pennsylvania, February 20, 1813:

The recently repatriated survivors of the Battle of the River Raisin joined

---

902 Town names were still somewhat fluid in this era. Technically, the town was named Newark by Lt.-Gov. John Graves Simcoe in 1792, but became simply Niagara in 1798. Niagara-on-the-Lake came into use in 1880, but the town did not officially adopt the name until 1970.

903 Clift lists both James Ebenezer Blyth and Samuel Elder as privates in Hart's company of the 5th Kentucky. There is also a William Blythe listed in Hightower's company of the 17th U.S.

904 Letter to parents from John McCalla, written at Fort Niagara, Feb. 10, 1813, typescript copy in 1812 Military Collections, Monroe County Historical Museum Archives: Writing of the killings on the 23rd, *"...Between 20 and 40 fell victims to this unheard of cruelty...Ebenezer Blythe was within the picketing and was wounded about 8 o'clock, through the thigh. I saw him lying with some wounded in one of the houses....I am told by Dr. Todd that Blythe's wound was of such a nature as to prevent his walking."*

in a meeting to protest their treatment at the hands of the British and Indians after their surrender at the River Raisin, hardly a month before.

A large number of the ex-prisoners attended, including Captains Sebree, Williams, Collier, and Bledsoe.

Captain Samuel L. Williams was elected chairman, and volunteer John Beckley was appointed secretary.

They met without three of their highest-ranking officers, for General Winchester, Lt. Col. Lewis, and Major Madison remained in British hands after the bulk of their troops were paroled and released at Fort George.[905]

Oddly, the Kentuckians directed their wrath more towards the actions of the British, rather than the alleged atrocities of the Native Americans.[906]

In the end, the assembly resolved to wear black bands on their hats and left arms for 90 days, in remembrance of their comrades who had been killed in battle, or murdered with the acquiescence, if not the connivance, of Brigadier General Henry Procter and his officers.[907]

---

905 General Winchester was not a stranger to captivity, for he had been captured and exchanged twice during the Revolutionary War. While detained at Québec, he worked tirelessly to better the condition of the American POW's. He was finally exchanged in the spring of 1814. Winchester requested an official inquiry into his conduct at the Raisin, but official proceedings were never held. In October, he was reassigned to duty on the Gulf Coast. After the war, he was instrumental in the founding of the city of Memphis, Tennessee.

Lt. Col. William Lewis was imprisoned in Québec for a year before being exchanged. Returning to Kentucky, he commanded Jessamine County's 9th Regiment of Militia until retiring as its colonel in 1815. He moved his family to Arkansas in 1819, and died at home, at age 58, in 1825.

Madison was freed from prison a year after his capture, as part of a prisoner exchange. He returned to Kentucky following his release and was honored at a public dinner on September 6, 1814. In 1816, he resigned as auditor of public accounts due to failing health, but he became a candidate for governor and was elected without opposition in August of that year. He died of tuberculosis on October 14, 1816, the first governor of Kentucky to die in office, and is buried in Frankfort Cemetery.

906 See: Atherton, William, Narrative of the Suffering and Defeat of the North-western Army, under General Winchester, Frankfort: A.G. Hodges, 1842, p. 4: *"It may be thought that I have been a little too severe in what I have said of British officers. Should any think so, all I have to say is, had they seen and felt what we did, there would have been no difference of opinion. By some it will be thought strange to find the savages, in point of feeling and humanity, placed above the British — but the truth ought always to be told."*

907 Massacre of French Town, Meadville, Pennsylvania, February 20, 1813, in Brannan, Official Letters, pp. 135-6. Typed copy in Bidlack's Notes, Monroe County Historical Museum Archives. They adopted an anti-British resolution, condemning His Majesty's officers for breaking their promises to provide protection for the wounded: *"…At break of day next morning, the savages were suffered to commit every depredation upon our wounded which they pleased. An indiscriminate slaughter took place, of all who were unable to walk, many were tomahawked, and many were burned alive*

CONCLUSION
EN FIN DE COMPTE

The Battle of the River Raisin was a major defeat for the American cause. The left wing of Harrison's Army of the Northwest, under the command of General Winchester, had been utterly destroyed.

Strategically, the defeat delayed the build-up of American forces in the campaign to retake Detroit. Worse yet, it opened up the Ohio frontier to British and Native American attacks by land and sea.

The Kentuckians who died or went missing were mourned throughout the state. The Lexington Gazette proclaimed, *"Never have the people of this town and its neighborhood met with a stroke so afflicting as that produced by the late battle of the Raisin... We all have lost a relative or friend."*

The survivors of the defeat were treated as heroes when they returned home. Perhaps none were more honored among their peers than Major Madison's African American servant, Peter Williams. Not only was he hailed as a veteran Indian fighter, but he became a well-known hotel cook and *"... got so fat upon the smell of the kitchen that he could scarcely waddle along, but he talked about the River Raisin to the last."*[908]

Those who did not survive were thought of as martyrs to the cause of freedom. Thus, although the battle was a discouraging defeat, it was also a challenge. The frontier settlers were united in fear, but also in a spirit of revenge for the massacre that occurred on January 23. Broadsides depicted the atrocities described by the survivors, and the new Kentucky battle cry in the northwest became *"Remember the Raisin!"*

Much of the River Raisin settlement was destroyed and a little over half the *habitants* became refugees. Some fled to British-controlled Detroit, while

---

in the houses. Among the unfortunate thus murdered, it is with regret and sorrow we have to name Captains Hart and Hickman...The arms of the officers, as promised, were never returned. Every species of private property remaining in the tents, belonging to both officers and soldiers, were plundered... ...In consideration of the high respect we hold the memories of both officers and soldiers who were thus cruelly murdered, by permission of the British commander, Proctor, and his subalterns, and those who gloriously fell in the field, defending the only free government on earth, that each of us wear black crape on our hats and left arm for the space of ninety days."

908 Clift, G. Glenn, Remember the Raisin, Frankfort: Kentucky Historical Society, 1961, p. 125, citing Colonel Orlando Brown's Governors of Kentucky, 1792-1824.

356

others sought safety at Fort Meigs or Sandusky. Those who stayed in French Town struggled to find food and shelter to survive the winter.

Over subsequent decades, *habitants* who were militia veterans, or their widows, applied for pensions or land patents for their service during the war. Since there was little official documentation, the government decided they should be compensated for their service during Hull's campaign and their subsequent "captivity" until the Battle of the River Raisin. This entitled each of them to about 80 acres of land, although a few received more, others settled for less, and many were denied or never applied.[909]

Over at Malden, the British were overjoyed when the Light Company of the 41st arrived to reinforce the Amherstburg garrison on February 7th. They had been sent after General Procter wrote to General Sheaffe that he was in urgent need of replacements after the Battle of the River Raisin.[910]

Procter had inflicted on Winchester the "condign punishment" which Kentuckians had once tried to bestow upon the British and Indians. Procter's personal reward was a promotion to the rank of Brigadier General.

The destruction of the American army at French Town did not, however, provide permanent security for the British position in the West. Although discouraged, the Americans could replace their losses from the burgeoning populations of the Ohio Valley and Western Pennsylvania and Virginia

Discounting the Canadian militia, which Procter considered unreliable, the defense of Detroit and Malden would have to rest on the shoulders of his British regulars and the tiny British fleet on Lake Erie...and on the Indians.[911]

Although the Indians frightened the Americans, they also enraged them. Tecumseh could assemble his warriors, but they had to be supplied and kept busy, or they would drift away, and their families had to be fed and protected.

Urged on by Tecumseh, General Procter led several offensive expeditions into Ohio in the spring and summer of 1813, but failed to capture the American strongholds at Fort Meigs and tiny Fort Stephenson.

The British fleet patrolled the waters of Lake Erie, making it difficult

---

909 See Appendix Q for the application of Susan Navarre, widow of Robert Utreau Navarre.
910 Cruikshank, Lt. Col. E. A. Harrison and Procter, Ottawa: The Royal Society of Canada, 1911, p. 165.
911 This was attested to in a letter from John Askin to William Powell, January 25, 1813: *"You may rely on it that without the Indians we never could keep this country...in the woods where the Americans must pass, one Indian is worth three white men..."* See: Cruikshank, Lt. Col. E., Documentary History of the Campaign upon the Niagara Frontier in 1813, pt. 5, Jan.-June, 1813, Welland: Tribune Office, 1901, pp. 49-51.

for the Americans to move their troops and supplies until they built their own small fleet of ships at Erie, Pennsylvania.

Thanks to that new fleet, the strategic situation was stunningly reversed when the entire British Lake Erie squadron was defeated and captured at the Battle of Lake Erie on September 10, 1813. After the battle, Commodore Perry, the American commander, issued his famous victory report, *"We have met the enemy, and they are ours."*

The Americans expected that an attack against the British base at Malden would run into heavy resistance. However, Procter concluded that the loss of the British fleet made his position completely untenable. Against the wishes of Tecumseh, he abandoned Malden and retreated back into the interior of Canada, pursued by a much larger army led by William Henry Harrison.[912]

On October 5, Harrison caught up with the British and Indians at the Thames River, where his men attacked with the cry, *"Remember the Raisin!"*

Tecumseh was killed, but most of his warriors escaped. General Procter got away, but the bulk of his regulars of the 41st Foot were captured and sent to Kentucky, where they became the objects of both curiosity and calls for vengeance.[913]

The loss of Tecumseh was a serious blow to the Native cause. Soon, various groups of Odawas, Chippewas, Potawatomies, Miamies, and Kickapoos came to Detroit to ask for an armistice. The people of Detroit and the River Raisin wanted to re-establish friendly relations with these tribes and asked the American authorities to allow them to return to their homes in peace.

The American authorities agreed, provided the Indians surrender some of their women and children as hostages, deliver up any white prisoners they had, and help track down any Indians still cooperating with the British.[914]

---

912 Knopf, Richard C. Document Transcriptions of the War of 1812 in the Northwest, Vol. V, pt. 2. Columbus: Ohio Historical Society, 1958. pp. 36-7. According to the Pittsburgh Mercury of Feb. 25, 1813, "...Great preparations are making at Malden for Harrison's reception. Every male from 16 to 60 is drafted, and many were on their march to Malden. Indians are collecting from every quarter..."

913 Obviously, not all of the credit for the American victory goes to the inspirational cry of "Remember the Raisin!" It also helped that Harrison had an overwhelming army of 3700 troops to throw against Procter's force of 1450 tired and dispirited combatants. American casualties were about 30 KIA and 50 WIA, while the British had 12 KIA, 30 WIA, and 566-579 POW. The Native Americans may have lost about 30 killed.

914 Antrim, Joshua, History of Champaign and Logan Counties, Bellefontaine, OH: Press Printing Co., 1872. One of the beneficiaries of this policy was Private John Hamilton, who was released by the Odawas. After the battle of the River Raisin on January 22, he had been taken to a distant Odawa

But the war was far from over. The northern tribes continued their resistance. In 1814, an American attempt to retake Fort Mackinac failed when U.S. ships were unable to elevate their guns high enough to bombard the fort at the top of the cliffs dominating the harbor. An infantry force was then landed at the far side of the island, but was defeated and forced to retreat, leaving Mackinac Island in British hands.

Fighting continued across Upper Canada and along the St. Lawrence and Lake Champlain invasion routes. Forts and towns were captured, burned, or surrendered as the tide of war ebbed and flowed, until the British, having finally defeated Napoleon in Europe, were at last able to send a sizeable army to invade the United States. British troops captured Washington, D.C., and burned the White House. They were unable to destroy the defenses of Fort McHenry at Baltimore, however, which inspired Francis Scott Key to write the words for the "Star-Spangled Banner."

On Christmas Eve, 1814, a peace treaty was finally signed in Ghent, Belgium. This was not in time to avoid one last major battle, however, at New Orleans, where General Andrew Jackson inflicted a crushing defeat on an invading British army on January 8, 1815.[915]

News of the cessation of hostilities did not reach the River Raisin until February. The inhabitants of French Town had already begun to rebuild their settlement, but they were so destitute that Judge Woodward wrote President Madison a letter asking for assistance from the government.

An emergency appropriation of $1,500 was approved to be used to buy flour. Father Gabriel Richard was put in charge of distributing this flour to the River Raisin *habitants* at their parish church of St. Antoine.

---

village, where he was presented as a gift to the father of the warrior who had captured him. Hamilton liked his "adopted" father, whom he came to regard as an honest, fair, and generous man whose moral character would have been praised in the "best civilized and Christianized communities." Nonetheless, he found his life with the Odawas to be very hard and rejoiced when the commanding officers at Detroit sent a delegation to his village offering terms of peace if they returned all the prisoners and horses they had taken. A council was held and the terms agreed to. By the 1st day of January, 1814, he joined other released prisoners in Detroit where they were cared for. Still, Hamilton found himself 300 miles from his home, thinly clad, and penniless in the depth of winter. Fortunately, he was furnished with enough rations to take him to Urbana. From there, he made it home on his own, arriving in Kentucky in the middle of February.

915 Actually, although the Treaty of Ghent was signed on December 24, 1814, before it could come into effect, it had to be communicated to and ratified by the respective governments of the United Kingdom of Great Britain and the United States of America.

At the end of the war, there was an exchange of captured territory. The British returned Fort Mackinac, which they had captured in 1812. The United States returned Fort Amherstburg, which they had renamed Fort Malden. Prisoners were released and allowed to go home. Both sides claimed victory.

Ironically, Great Britain, the richest and most powerful nation in the world at that time, had failed to beat the infant United States into submission. For the British, the war in North America was somewhat of an expensive sideshow compared to events in Europe, anyway.

Canadians experienced a growth of nationalistic spirit. Native people, French and British Canadians, loyalists and immigrants had united, at least to some extent, in opposition to the American invasions.

The United States had failed to conquer Canada, a British colony much weaker and smaller in population than itself. However, it did forcibly annex parts of West Florida from Spain, a country with which it was not at war.

Most of the causes for the war were ignored in the final treaty, which called for a *status quo ante bellum*. Impressment was not mentioned.

The state of Kentucky suffered a large part of the casualties, as the bones of its young men were left on battlefields from Canada to Louisiana. Nine counties would eventually be named after Kentuckians who fought at the River Raisin, all but one having died there.[916]

The war had strained American unity. The middle and Atlantic states had prospered from fat military contracts, while the south and northeast suffered the loss of their trade to the British blockade.

The country was divided along sectional lines, with the New England states represented at the Hartford Convention almost reaching the point of calling for secession.[917]

---

916 See Appendix L for the Table of Kentucky State Historic Markers dedicated to the counties named after River Raisin battle participants.

917 The Hartford Convention was actually a series of meetings from December 15, 1814, to January 5, 1815, in Hartford, Connecticut, in which the New England Federalist Party met to discuss their criticisms of the War of 1812 and the federal government's increasing power. They discussed removing the three-fifths compromise, which gave slave states disproportionate power in Congress, and requiring a two-thirds majority in Congress for the admission of new states, declarations of war, and creating laws restricting trade.

Nonetheless, the Democratic-Republicans proclaimed the international respect gained by standing up to Great Britain was well worth the 2½ years of effort at a cost of $158,000,000 and a tripling of the national debt. Wikipedia lists official American combat deaths at 2,260 and wounded at 4,505. Another 205 or so were executed. Non-combat deaths totaled 17,000 and

Reputations gained during the war helped catapult several leaders into the Presidency of the United States. They were James Monroe, John Quincy Adams, Andrew Jackson, and William Henry Harrison. Three others achieved the vice-presidency: Daniel Tompkins, John C. Calhoun, and Richard M. Johnson. After the War of 1812, General Winfield Scott earned further fame in the Mexican War and rose to the highest rank in Lincoln's military at the start of the Civil War.[918]

The French-speaking settlers of the River Raisin country were completely impoverished by the effects of the war, but they rebuilt their homes and were able to live in relative peace and security.

After the opening of the Erie Canal in the 1820s, however, large numbers of English-speaking immigrants arrived and soon outnumbered them. The *habitants* eventually became a minority in their own communities.

Still, the *habitants* persevered and remained on the land they had pioneered, except for a few who got caught up in the removal of the Native American tribes from southern Michigan and northwest Ohio. Within the next 100 years, their descendants would lose their ancestral language and most of their original culture through a century-long process of assimilation.[919]

Michigan was wide open for Yankee settlers. The Native alliance had been broken. The British peace negotiators had dropped their proposal to create an Indian buffer state north of the Maumee River.

---

there were over 500 civilian deaths. British and Canadian troops suffered about 5,000 killed or wounded. Indigenous people, like Native Americans, Métis and French *habitants* were not counted.

Federalist criticism of the motivations for the war and the way it was being waged had brought them some support, but this seemed to dissipate as the fighting ended and the public basked in a feeling of victory and pride. The Democratic-Republicans were able to get much of the credit for American successes, while shifting the blame for their failures onto the shoulders of the "defeatist," Anglophile Federalists. See: Hickey, Donald R. The War of 1812. Urbana & Chicago: University of Illinois Press, 1989, pp. 132-133.

918 Hickey, Donald R. The War of 1812. Urbana & Chicago: University of Illinois Press, 1989.

919 The submergence of this French-métis culture caused a great deal of regret and even some bitterness, as expressed by the Civil War general, Orlando B. Willcox in "A Boy of Old Detroit":

"...I began to muse over the times, faintly remembered at first, when the simple French people held undisputed and gentle sway along this whole frontier. Standing between the red-man and the white-man, mingling with both, disturbing neither, with little to defend, and no desire to aggrandize, their ephemeral existence was as glowing with the pleasure of light-hearted enjoyment, as the insects that sport away their hour of sunshine, and like them passing away unnoticed and soon forgotten... The Frenchman who left his cherries to the birds, his sheep to the dogs, and his fish seine to le diable, for the purpose of shouldering his musket at the call of General Hull, would have been astonished to have been branded as a foreigner..."

The Potawatomies and Odawas of the River Raisin were gradually forced to give up even their small reservations. By the 1840s, most had found themselves on a "Trail of Tears" across the Mississippi to new lands in Kansas and Oklahoma. Some, particularly among the Catholic Wyandots, managed to assimilate or "disappear" among the French and other Euro-American settlers.

Many of their more northern and western brethren, however, were able to retain reservations in Michigan. Other Indians relocated to Canada, where they received lands from the British. Generally, Native Americans could expect the same or similar treatment, regardless of which side they had supported during the war.[920]

---

920 Wikipedia gives the result of the War of 1812 as a return to the status quo ante bellum but mentions a number of effects on the combatants. The United States earned international respect and increased its military and industrial capability. Britain, already reeling from the Napoleonic Wars, felt little additional impact, but Canada emerged more unified.

SACRED GROUND
TERRE SACRÉE

According to Jeffrey L. Green, the *"... issues surrounding the settlement and battlefield — ownership, freedom, control, protection — are much the same as they were two centuries prior, with the exception that today we have added into the mix the concepts of public good and property rights. Rather than countries and armies and military leaders deciding the fate of a piece of land, today we find attorneys, corporations, and CEO's."*[921]

The fighting around the picketed homes of French Town took place on the north, or left, bank of the River Raisin on Private Claims 214, 64, 236, 96 and 81. Most of the incidents of the battle happened within a 2-mile radius of this area, which became known as the battlefield proper. Many of the houses and other improvements fronting on the Raisin were destroyed in the conflict and their residents forced to flee.[922]

Aerial View of the Registered River Raisin Battlefield Site, ca. 1984
Monroe County Historical Museum Photo

The French Town refugees eventually rebuilt their homes. Hubert Lacroix built a large brick mansion on the ruins of his former property. The majority

---

921 Green, Jeffrey L., "Historic and Contextual Significance," A Profile of the River Raisin Paper Company Site, Monroe, Michigan, Report of the Historic Preservation Program, Eastern Michigan University, September, 1998. Jeff Green is the Historic Preservation Officer for the City of Monroe.

922 Radzinski, Robin, "Land Ownership, 1812-Present," A Profile of the River Raisin Paper Company Site, Monroe, Michigan, Report of the Historic Preservation Program, Eastern Michigan University, September, 1998.

of the postwar growth, however, occurred in the new "Yankee" town of Monroe, south of the river and west of the battlefield site.[923]

A government canal eventually straightened out the mouth of the meandering River Raisin as it flowed through the marshes, which allowed larger vessels to reach the city docks, also on the south bank.

The central core of the battlefield was mildly affected by development during the 19th century. Nursery companies grew plants and seed stock and shipped them to western Michigan. There was also an active dairy farm.

In 1871, Joseph Guyor invited War of 1812 veterans to his home on Guyor's Island. The event was such a success that a committee of leading citizens was appointed to organize a grand reunion the following year.

The July 4, 1872, reunion attracted 150 elderly veterans, the majority coming from Kentucky, who brought with them a quantity of old relics, including a faded and tattered battle flag carried at the Battle of the River Raisin. They visited the scene of that battle, the retreat route, and the site in the woods near Winchester's headquarters at the Navarre house, where it was said the surrender had taken place by order of General Winchester.[924]

The Navarre house was then being dismantled to make room for the Sawyer mansion, and the discarded boards and beams were used to make a

---

923 The settlement was greatly disturbed by the War of 1812. Even the bodies of those killed in the 1813 Battle of the River Raisin were not allowed to rest. Some remains were buried along the riverbank or in secluded areas. Most of the corpses remained exposed to the elements for some time. Five months after the battle, Col. Richard M. Johnson arrived with a contingent of mounted infantry and buried 12 or 14 bodies in a mass grave. They may have been massacre victims or the bodies of the troops killed on January 18. The corpses were dug up by the Indians, and then buried once again by Johnson's troops in September. In October of 1813, Governor Shelby of Kentucky led a force through French Town, stopping long enough to bury 65 of their fallen comrades in a mass grave. In the years following the war, bones scavenged from the woods and fields were buried in the old protestant cemetery, which was eventually paved over and is now underneath Monroe Street in downtown Monroe.

In the 1830s, many bodies were disinterred for reburial in military cemeteries in Detroit. Some of them may have been taken to Kentucky in 1834, or to Memorial Place in Monroe. In 1848, these or other bones were exposed when a new street were being laid. The remains were placed in a box, sent to Covington, Kentucky, and eventually interred in a cemetery at Frankfort in 1851.

More skeletons and battle artifacts were found during the construction of the River Raisin Paper Company. The disposition of these remains is unrecorded, although at least two skeletons were reportedly buried near the battlefield's obelisk marker in 1910.

924 Bulkley, John McClelland. History of Monroe County, Vol. 1. Chicago: Lewis Publishing Company, 1913, p. 128.

stand from which General George Armstrong Custer and other dignitaries spoke to the assembled veterans and citizens.[925]

As the 19th century turned into the 20th, Monroe County's marshes and lakeshore attracted hunting clubs and resorts. Electric railway tracks were laid to bring city dwellers from Toledo, Detroit, and Chicago to the Monroe Piers, where they could enjoy these natural and man-made environments.

The rise of the automobile led to the demise of the interurban trains that fed these recreational areas, while the growth of manufacturing and the housing market turned the lakeshore and marshes into prime areas for urban and industrial development. Sterling State Park was established to preserve public access to a small portion of the Lake Erie beachfront.

History was not entirely overlooked. In 1904, a stone cairn was erected at the site of the battle and a large monument to Kentucky was dedicated at Memorial Place, where it was said that some of the bodies had been laid to rest.

Kentucky Monument at Memorial Place
Kentucky National Guard historian John Trowbridge and Adjutant General of Kentucky Maj. Gen. Edward W. Tonini pose with Kentucky Militia reenactors in front of the Kentucky Monument in Monroe, Michigan, on the occasion of the 200th anniversary of the Battle of the River Raisin.

---

925 No one then could have predicted that General Custer, who grew up in Monroe and was acquainted with many of the survivors of the Battle of the River Raisin, would lead the 7th U.S. Cavalry into a similar fate at the hands of the Sioux in 1876.

In 1910, G. Harley Wood bought 200 acres on the north bank of the Raisin and built the River Raisin Paper Company on the battleground. By 1915, he had completed a plant on Godfroy's old homestead. Hubert Lacroix's postwar brick mansion was torn down as more brick industrial buildings and workers' housing spread eastward across the site of old French Town. Vacant areas of the battlefield were covered by parking lots or deposits of construction debris, paper, cinders, ash, and other industrial waste.[926]

The 1913 Centennial Commemoration of the Battle of the River Raisin was marked by the placement of an old British cannon on Loranger Square in front of the Monroe County Courthouse.

Local legend has it that one of the British cannons, being badly damaged and its crew dead or wounded, was left behind, along with the bodies of 5 of the artillerists who manned it. Due to the press of events, the British never recovered the gun, which may have been hidden in a barn or shoved through the ice into the River Raisin.

Years later, it was rediscovered and put into service for ceremonies, ending up on a granite pedestal on the courthouse lawn, where it was labeled a "Relic of the Battle of the River Raisin, January 18-22, 1813."

Monroe County's Courthouse Cannon

---

926 Goldstein, Michelle, & Julie Dirkse, "Architectural History, 1785 — Present," A Profile of the River Raisin Paper Company Site, Monroe, Michigan, Report of the Historic Preservation Program, Eastern Michigan University, September, 1998. (Lacroix's house came to be referred to as the "blockhouse" and the "LaFountaine" house after a subsequent owner).

In the 1930s, labor unrest was occurring across the nation and affected the industrial centers of Monroe County. There were strikes and walkouts on or near the historic battlefield in 1937 and 1938.[927]

A World War II tanker ship was named the S.S. River Raisin as part of a series of ships commemorating famous American battles.[928]

During the ensuing years, a succession of companies ran the area's industries. In 1957, Union Bag-Camp bought the River Raisin Paper Company, making it one of their divisions in 1960. By 1966, they simplified their name to Union Camp Corporation.

During the 1960s, interest in creating a commemorative battlefield park in Monroe began to grow. Following the July, 1962, Sesquicentennial Observance of the War of 1812, the Monroe County Historical Society appointed a River Raisin Memorial Park Committee, with noted Custer author, Dr. Lawrence Frost, as chairman. This committee soon merged with the society's highly successful Historic Trails Committee, headed by Mrs. Edmund R. Childs.

In 1973, it was suggested that a panoramic observation post be erected on a knoll in Rauch Park, a small city-owned plot across the river from the western portion of old French Town.

However, the plan was shelved when an undeveloped 10-acre tract along Detroit Avenue owned by the Union Camp Corporation was identified as suitable for an actual, on-site battlefield park.[929]

Professionally-directed archaeological surveys were undertaken in the fall of 1976 and the spring of 1977, with the permission of the land owner. The digs were coordinated by the Monroe County Historical Commission, whose director, Matthew Switlik, obtained a Federal Matching Fund Grant sponsored by the Michigan History Division.

The 17th Infantry campsite was investigated in 1980 by Assistant Director Dennis Au, assisted by other Monroe County Historical Museum staff and volunteers from the River Raisin Chapter of the Michigan Archaeological Society, under the direction of archaeologist Steve Demeter and consultants from Commonwealth Associates, funded by an appropriation from the State

---

927 See Appendix M for more information on the strike.
928 See Appendix R for more information on the S.S. River Raisin.
929 "River Raisin Battlefield Among Historic Sites," Monroe Evening News, March 10, 1973.

of Michigan. Empty lots alongside and behind then current Battlefield Visitor Center were tested in an unsuccessful effort to find traces of Godfroy's barn.

In 1981, the corrugated plant was shut down and a feasibility study was conducted to determine the costs and benefits of converting part of the grounds covering the historic battlefield into a park.

Thanks to a decade of efforts by the Monroe County Historical Museum, 80 acres of the River Raisin Battlefield was placed on the National Register of Historic Places in December of 1984.

In 1986, Jefferson Smurfit and Monroe Paper Plant bought the paperboard mill from Union Camp. The mill went by the Monroe Paper Plant name until 1993, when it came to be called Jefferson Smurfit.

The previous year, Richard Sieb had purchased an early 20th century home on E. Elm Avenue near the southeast corner of the Paper Company's property, along with an easement that stretched over to Detroit Avenue. This would eventually become the museum's River Raisin Battlefield Visitor Center.

Also, in 1986, the County of Monroe paid $22,000 for a house on the property that had been built about 1915 for the plant's chief electrician.

A $40,000 state grant and a $60,000 donation from La-Z-Boy were acquired to turn the property into a battlefield park and museum. About a third of the funds would go to building a government-mandated access ramp.

The River Raisin Battlefield Visitor Center opened in the summer of 1990 on a 3½-acre parcel on the eastern edge of the battlefield site, on grounds owned by the Monroe County Historical Society and the County of Monroe.

A commemoration ceremony was held there January 20, 1991, and was repeated annually on the weekend closest to the date of the actual battle. Matt Switlik, Larry See, and Rick Manion organized the Friends of the River Raisin Battlefield to support programs at the site.[930]

With changing times and changing economic fortunes, the paper and cardboard plant had lost its competitive edge. In 1990, it was proposed to build a giant incinerator that would burn waste to produce energy. Public opposition was too great, however, and Jefferson Smurfit closed the plant in 1995.

---

930 Matt Switlik was the Director of the Monroe County Historical Museum, Larry See was a local newspaperman and chairman of a Civil War Reenactment Society, and Rick Manion was the Coordinator of the River Raisin Battlefield Visitor Center.

RECONCILIATION CEREMONY BETWEEN ENEMIES
RIVER RAISIN BATTLE COMMEMORATION
1812 Reenactors and Jefferson High School ROTC Students

Already in 1991, mills 1 and 2, west of N. Dixie Highway, were being torn down, and more archaeological surveys were subsequently conducted by Steve Demeter of Commonwealth Cultural Resources Group.

Shovel tests revealed prehistoric stone artifacts on what was once the Godfroy and Beaugrand property, along with some historic brick, glass, nails, ceramics, and other materials. However, nothing could definitely be connected to the Battle of the River Raisin.

In 1991 and 1992, with city and Historical Society support, Dr. Ted Ligibel's Historic Preservation class from Eastern Michigan University completed a battlefield profile in preparation for Phase II archaeological work directed by Bill Rutter of Midwest Environmental Consultants and Dr. G. Michael Pratt of Heidelberg University. Further research was done by Jennifer Jaworski.

In the 1980s and 90s, during the terms of Monroe Mayors Mignano and Cappuccilli, the city began to take an interest in acquiring and restoring portions of the property as a battlefield park, in cooperation with the Monroe County Historical Society and the Monroe County Historical Museum.

John Iacoangeli and Jim Tischler, working in the city planning and development agencies, organized studies and talks with a host of local, state, and federal agencies and preservation groups.

The most promising strategy for restoring the battlefield seemed to be attaching it to a Greenways Initiative to join the proposed battlefield park with city and regional recreational trails and with Sterling State Park.

It took a lot of negotiation to finally convince state officials that a Clean Michigan Initiative Grant could be used to establish a public park rather than reclaiming brownfields for private industrial redevelopment. It was expected to take 2 years to clean and restore the property.

The 2-year negotiation was stalled in 1997 as plant owners found a better deal by selling their property to Homrich, Inc., a demolition company that purchased almost 300 acres of industrial property, buildings, and marshland east of North Dixie Highway for $500,000.

Initially unaware of the city's plans to rezone the area from heavy industrial to planned unit development, Homrich intended to reactivate the site as a landfill for dumping 25 million cubic feet of debris from the demolition of the 24-story J.L. Hudson Department Store in Detroit.[931]

This move was unpopular with the community and did not fit in with changes in the regional master plan. The city opposed the permit process, and the company agreed to a compromise that would allow cleanup and development of the area north of the main battlefield site in exchange for transferring 30 acres to the city or other public agency.

Also, in 1997, as part of its development plan, the City of Monroe built a 6½ million-dollar ice arena on several battlefield acres west of Dixie Highway on former paper company land that had been obtained and cleared by the city.

Archaeological testing found no battle debris in this area, although it would have been close to the British lines.

The rest of the property west of North Dixie Highway was dedicated as Rivière aux Raisins Park. It serves as the location for the 1904 obelisk battle monument.

---

931 Monroe Evening News, 12-11-97 and 10-28-98.

Early Post Card View of 1904 Battlefield Obelisk
Monroe County Historical Museum Archives

In 2000, the city of Monroe obtained a $20,000 state grant for conducting archaeology at Rivière aux Raisins Park.

Despite the disturbance caused by the paper mill, the imprint of the northern and western portions of French Town's fence line was discovered 3 feet below ground. A few 1813-era artifacts were also found; such as a shoe buckle fragment, forged nails, and Pearlware sherds.[932]

In 2002 and 2003, the National Park Service gave the city $30,000 to conduct archaeology on the Homrich property east of North Dixie Highway.

---

932 "A Phase II Archaeological Investigation of the River Raisin Battlefield and Massacre Site, City of Monroe, Monroe, County Michigan," by Pratt & Rutter, March 24, 1999.

Metal Detectors revealed the presence of musket balls and other battle debris in the farm field north of the visitor center, while trenches were dug to locate the remains of the northern fence line as it came out from under the still-standing fiber plant building. The point at which the northern wall stopped and turned back towards the river remained elusive, however.

Archaeological Survey directed by Dr. G. Michael Pratt of Heidelberg and by volunteers from the Toledo Area Aboriginal Research Society and the River Raisin Chapter of the Michigan Archaeological Society

Cadaver Dog and Trainer at River Raisin Battlefield
Photos by Laurel Heymann and Bill Saul

The crawl space under the fiber plant building was sampled by contract archeologist Bill Rutter. Surveys were also done by teams of cadaver dogs trained to find traces of human remains that could still be underground.[933]

This was followed by renewed efforts on the part of U.S. Congressman John Dingell, Bill Anderson of the Michigan Department of History, Arts, and

---

933 On May 10, 2002, Lt. Governor Dick Posthumus ceremoniously presented the city of Monroe with a check for a further $1.4 million dollars to develop Homrich's parcel as a battlefield park. Unfortunately, the gesture turned out to be just a campaign promise. Mr. Posthumus was not elected governor and no state money was actually allocated for the project. Monroe Evening News, 5-11-2002.

Libraries, the Monroe County Historical Society, the Mayor of Monroe, and State Representative Richardville, who had been supporting the battlefield project since its inception.[934]

In August of 2003, the owner of Homrich, Inc., agreed to swap 104 acres of former paper company swampland between the battlefield site and Sterling State Park for a 26-acre public access site at Otter Creek, near his home overlooking Lake Erie. The following month, the Monroe Evening News announced that Homrich would include 30 acres of battlefield plus 215 acres of marsh in the trade for Otter Creek beach and two small lots.

The inclusion of the battlefield acreage induced the County of Monroe to give up its option to take over the public access site from the DNR, which would have blocked the deal with Homrich. The marshland would be incorporated into the state park, while the city would get the battlefield.[935]

In April, 2004, a mysterious fire broke out, which gutted the abandoned paperboard plant building east of North Dixie Highway.

In August, the Michigan Department of Environmental Quality announced $1.8 million dollars had been secured in state grant and loan funding for the city of Monroe to transform the Jefferson Smurfit paper plant at N. Dixie and E. Elm Avenue into a park in partnership with the Monroe County Historical Society. The loan portion, some $800,000, would go to clean up the area west of the main battlefield for a 500-home subdivision centered on Mason Run.

On September first, the newspaper announced that the state grant had been approved. Site work was expected to start in 4 weeks, with demolition of the factory buildings to be finished by the spring of 2005, even though the property east of Dixie Highway was technically still owned by Homrich.[936]

In June of 2004, the Historical Commission requested $30,000 from the museum's restricted funds held by the Historical Society to secure a

---

934 Around the same time, the Monroe County Historical Museum completed the terms of a Michigan DNR recreation grant to install interpretive signs and a period-themed outdoor learning shelter at the River Raisin Battlefield Visitor Center. This grant was worked on by the County of Monroe and shepherded by State Representative Randy Richardville.

935 Monroe Evening News, 10-11-2003, 11-2-2003, 9-9-2003, and 8-13-2003: At first, residents objected that the Otter Creek site was the only public access point in LaSalle Township. The County Board of Commissioners considered buying it so as to block its passage into private ownership. A deed restriction would preserve the natural environment, but close the area to public access.

936 Monroe Evening News, Sept. 1, 2004.

30-foot-wide strip of land along the Battlefield Visitor Center's driveway to ensure space for the installation of extra parking.

Negotiations and delays continued through 2005, although the Friends of the River Raisin Battlefield completed a video documentary on the battle, an unbudgeted project that had taken several years and involved hundreds of volunteers. It was later shown on local PBS stations.

In his last official act on Dec. 27, 2005, outgoing Mayor John Iacoangeli signed the 7-page contract, closing 8 years of meetings and negotiations over the future of this brownfield site. A deed restriction would guarantee the land would be developed for historical purposes only. On New Year's Day, January 1, 2006, the Monroe Sunday News was finally able to report that an agreement for the historic transfer of 35.5 acres of the River Raisin Battlefield site to the City of Monroe had been accepted.

Mayor C. D. Cappuccilli, and the Monroe Port Commission would administer a million-dollar Clean Michigan Grant to demolish the remains of the abandoned paper plant, while a master plan was being drawn up by the City of Monroe and the Monroe County Historical Society. It was expected that environmental testing would be done in the spring, and demolition could start by summer. Fencing and planting of prairie grass would be done by the city.

Jean Guyor, outgoing Monroe City councilwoman and president of the Monroe County Historical Society, announced the society would provide up to $100,000 for a million-dollar insurance policy for the site and would purchase an old office and pump house on E. Elm Avenue from Homrich and remodel it into a new museum and interpretive center.[937]

A foundation would also be set up to coordinate activities and promote development of the site, which it was hoped would become a tourist attraction.

By April of 2006, U.S. Representative John D. Dingell had introduced two pieces of federal legislation, the River Raisin National Battlefield Study Act and the River Raisin Battlefield Acquisition act, permitting the National Park Service to someday take over the 35-acre site. The April 19th deadline for delivery of a letter of "non-interest" by the Environmental Protection Agency was not met, however, and the city had to ask for an extension.[938]

---

937 The building was eventually torn down, and this aspect of the project was abandoned.

938 See the following Monroe Evening News Articles: "River Raisin Battlefield: A Federal Connection," April 16, 2006, and "Dingell Pushes for Battlefield, April 8, 2006.

The city, the historical society, and Mr. Homrich finally closed the deal on May 17th. The next two years would see much demolition, including the implosion of the large factory chimney and removal of the factory's water tower.

On November 19, 2007, the River Raisin Battlefield Visitor Center became the venue for Congressman Dingell to announce the next phase of cleanup for 30 acres of battlefield land. Efforts to reclaim a battlefield from an industrial site were unique in the annals of brownfield redevelopment.[939]

Former River Raisin Battlefield Visitor Center (as it appeared in 2008)
Photo by Bill Saul

About 45 people crowded into the visitor center's map room and another dozen or more stood just outside the door to hear Congressman Dingell applaud our community for its enthusiasm and unity in helping him push the project towards federal recognition and National Park Service status.

Funding through loans from the Clean Michigan Initiative, EPA, DABC, and Monroe Brownfield Development Authority enabled the project to continue.

Port of Monroe Attorney Tom Russow ended the program with an overview of current progress, including the destruction and removal of most of

---

939 Hosting were the Downriver Community Conference, the Downriver Area Brownfield Consortium, the City of Monroe, and the Port of Monroe. (Not to mention the staff of the Monroe County Historical Museum who readied the building for the expected representatives of federal, state, county, and municipal governments and agencies, as well as members of the Monroe County Historical Society, Friends of the River Raisin Battlefield, War of 1812 Bicentennial Steering Committee, members of the press, and other interested groups or individuals.)

the buildings, the water tower, and the tall smoke stack. He ended with the promise, *"By the end of next summer, we'll have grass growing."*

Future plans included the demolition of the fiber building on the north side of Elm Ave., removal of the parking lot and remaining rubble, backfilling and grading, removal of water pipes, cleanup of waste disposal trenches, removal of underground fuel tanks, mothballing of the office/lab/pump house on the river, and further archaeological investigation of the site. These plans were accomplished, with the last industrial building coming down in 2008.

On July 10, 2008, U.S. Representative John Dingell and Senator Carl Levin introduced legislation to formally establish the River Raisin National Battlefield Park. The legislation finally became law when it was attached to New Mexico Senator Jeff Bingaman's Omnibus Public Lands Management Act of 2009, which was signed by President Barack Obama on March 30th.

More archaeological surveys were conducted in 2009 by Drs. Pratt and Rutter, along with Richard Green at nearby sites north of Mason Run, on the south bank of the River Raisin, and at Plum Creek (formerly Navarre's Mill Creek). But not much was found.

Plum Creek, as it appeared at the turn of the 21st Century

The cleanup and capping of the industrial brownfield that covered most of the battlefield core area was essentially completed the following year.

Those mill properties, which had been held temporarily by Monroe's Port Commission, were transferred to the National Park Service in 2011.[940]

In 2014, the Battlefield Park established a satellite unit on the Huron River in Brownstown Township in Wayne County. Hull's Trace Unit preserves an original portion of General Hull's corduroy military road built in 1812. The old Macon Reserve, and to a lesser extent, the Old Mill Museum in Dundee, became associated with the Battlefield Park.

Since then, the River Raisin Battlefield Foundation, in cooperation with the city of Monroe, has been assisting in generating grants and other revenue for the purchase and removal of private buildings in the battlefield area.

Meanwhile, plans were being made to renovate the former ice arena building into a new visitor center and education center, and to reconstruct part of the River Raisin settlement. As a consequence, the old visitor center was decommissioned, its contents emptied and moved to the education center.

While this was being accomplished, Superintendent Scott Bentley and Wyandot Chief Ted Roll were already engaged in widening the scope of the park to tell the larger story of Native American resistance and removal.

With the cooperation of Oklahoma Wyandot Chief Billy Friend, they devised a series of "Journeys of Understanding" for Native tribal members, teachers, and community leaders. In addition, the Wyandots of Anderdon obtained property near Gibraltar for the development of the Six-Points cultural center near the site of the original Wyandot village of Brownstown.

Unfortunately, progress on improving the park was frequently obstructed by contractual, environmental, budgetary, and research issues, and by the sudden appearance of the coronavirus COVID-19 pandemic in 2020.

Nonetheless, 2020 saw great strides in recreating Native American structures inside the Battlefield Education Center. These included a large longhouse, a lodge, and several Native American-made canoes, along with partial facades of a settler's cabin and trading post. A small theatre was also installed for the viewing of educational videos produced by the battlefield.

In conjunction with the City of Monroe, houses have been purchased and removed along the north bank of the River Raisin to open up the view from park property, where plans have been made to reconstruct a portion of the River Raisin settlement.

---

940 The NPS officially accepted the park in October of 2010, and River Raisin National Battlefield Park opened for visitors in May of 2011.

The future story of the development of the park and other properties in the vicinity of the historic River Raisin Battlefield has not yet been told. It is up to the people of Monroe and southeastern Michigan, through their leaders and elected representatives, to make what they will of their past.

To quote the 3rd Biennial Report of the Department of Archives and History of the State of West Virginia: *"A people who have not the pride to record their History will not long have the virtues to make History worth recording; and no people who are indifferent to their Past need hope to make their Future great."*[941]

**First Nations military veterans from U.S. and Canada at
a River Raisin Commemoration**
Photo by Bill Saul

---

941 Lewis, Virgil A., Third Biennial Report of the Department of Archives and History of the State of West Virginia. Charleston: The News-Mail Company, 1911, title page.

ABOUT THE AUTHOR

Ralph Naveaux has earned degrees in history and institutional administration from Michigan State University, and in French from Eastern Michigan University. He is also a graduate of the Seminar in Historic Administration at Historic Williamsburg, Virginia, and the Michigan Police Reserve Training Council Basic Law Enforcement Course at Schoolcraft College.

From 1975 to 1990, he was employed as a teacher of history and French in the Monroe Public School System. In 1990, Mr. Naveaux was hired as Assistant Director at the Monroe County Historical Museum, retiring as Director in January of 2007.[942]

For 20 years, he served as co-chair of the Old French Town Days festival in Monroe, and then as chairman of Monroe's War of 1812 Bicentennial Steering Committee, a group facilitated by the Community Foundation of Monroe County.[943]

Of French and German ancestry, the author can trace his family line to an actual participant in the events of which he writes. That would be a great grandfather 5 generations back by the name of Joseph Neveu dit Francoeur, who served in Mack's artillery company of the Michigan Legionary Corps in 1812.

As in many of the old French families of southeastern Michigan, there may even be a Native American ancestor hiding somewhere in plain sight.[944]

---

942 During this time, he further developed and ran the evening Lantern Tour program at the Navarre-Anderson Trading Post and assisted in the creation the River Raisin Battlefield Visitor Center under the leadership of Museum Director Matt Switlik. Among other projects, he helped establish the Vietnam Veterans Museum at Heck Park and acted as historical consultant for the documentary "War of 1812: Battles on the Raisin," produced by the Friends of the River Raisin Battlefield.

943 An avid student of local history, Ralph Naveaux also is past president of the River Raisin Chapter of the Michigan Archaeological Society, past commander of both Campeau's company of the Detroit Militia and Lacroix's Company of Michigan Volunteers, former resident agent for the Monroe County Historical Society, former vice-president of the Center for French Colonial Studies, and officer for the Friends of the River Raisin Battlefield. In 2004, he was appointed an Honorary Kentucky Colonel by the Commonwealth of Kentucky. He also was on the board of the River Raisin Battlefield Foundation. Previous publications include Escape to Frenchtown, co-authored with Rachel Wilke, Women on the Raisin, co-authored with Mary Ellen VanWasshenova, "The Floral City," co-authored with Shana Gruber, and the "River Raisin Battlefield Driving Tour."

944 Note the spelling change in the family name that can be found in a single document — in this case, the 1871 pension declaration of Joseph's widow Marie-Louise: "...she is the widow of Joseph Neveu who served the full period of 60 days in the military services of the United States in the War of 1812...enlisted in Captain Mack's Company [in] General Hull's Division at Detroit, Michigan, on or

379

Mary Waumga, widow of Joseph Naveau
1812-era ancestors of the author
(The government used the date of the surrender of Detroit for the discharge date.)

about the 1st Day of May, 1812, and was taken prisoner and paroled by the British at Detroit, Michigan, on the 16th day of August, 1812, that she was married under the name of Mary Waumga [Boesmier] to said Joseph Naveau on the 29th day of November, A.D. 1810, at Monroe, Mich…" Marie Naveau claimed she was adopted by the Boesmiers (Bomias?). Curiously, the name she gave appears similar to *Wangoma*, the Ojibwa phrase for "I adopt her," as listed in Father Baraga's Dictionary of the Ojibway Language. It is also similar to White Loon's Miami name, Wapamongwa.

APPENDIX A

BACKGROUND ON THE FIVE MAIN GROUPS OF PROTAGONISTS

THE KENTUCKIANS:

The bulk of the army defending Detroit at the beginning of the war was composed of Ohio militiamen. After General Hull surrendered them to the British, the U.S. military turned towards the more populous state of Kentucky.

The American army that would fight at the River Raisin was therefore largely composed of Kentuckians. Most were militia volunteers with a patriotic lust for adventure, but a distaste for regular army discipline. Their senator, Henry Clay was a leading War Hawk and had pushed for the declaration of war. About 5% of Kentucky's population of 324,000 officially enlisted in the war, amounting to roughly two-thirds of the 25,000 males of prime military age.

Kentucky was now well-settled, so the volunteers were no longer the rugged frontiersmen that their fathers and grandfathers had been. They were townsmen and farmers, but many of them could still handle a rifle or musket with deadly accuracy and could survive in the wilderness if need be.

Kentuckians fought in most of the western battles from Canada to the Gulf of Mexico, and Kentucky would suffer more battle casualties than any other state. Over 1,200 would die in the 2½ years of war, and another 3,740 would suffer wounds, resulting in a casualty rate of roughly 30%. About a third of Kentucky's losses occurred in just two battles; the River Raisin in January of 1813 and the first siege of Fort Meigs the following May.[945]

The Kentucky militia officers were usually older and of a higher station than the average volunteer. Many were politicians, lawyers or landed gentry who had moved to Kentucky from Virginia or Maryland. A number had Indian fighting experience. Some had seen action at Tippecanoe, Fallen Timbers, or even as far back as the Revolutionary War.

There were still a few of the old-style Indian fighters like Bland Ballard. He was

---

945 Kentucky contributed slightly less than 5% of the total number of American soldiers who fought during the War of 1812, but officially suffered 64% of the total U.S. battle deaths. (See: Scott County Kentucky; A History, by Apple, Johnston, & Bevins, printed by the Scott County Historical Society, Inc.)

In February of 1813, Fort Meigs was built on the south side of the Maumee River, on the opposite side of the river and about 3½ miles upstream from the old, abandoned British Fort Miamis.

the least educated of the officer class, a bit of a throwback to an earlier Kentucky. Late in life, Ballard would boast he had killed six Indians one morning before breakfast, and it had not been a good morning for the business, either.

Kentuckians had been killing and getting killed by Indians for generations. It comes as no surprise, then, that these War Hawks of Kentucky looked forward to proving themselves as worthy as their ancestors in a renewed contest with their ancient Native American enemies. This was indeed a blood feud that frequently led members of both groups to neither give nor expect any mercy from the other.

THE NATIVE AMERICANS:

Native Americans did not present a totally united front in handling the pressures of frontier settlement. They were presented with the same three basic choices previous generations had faced in response to the oncoming tide of white settlers. As with any group reacting to cultural and economic changes being imposed from without, they could move away and avoid the changes, they could accept and try to profit from the changes, or they could resist.

The outbreak of the War of 1812 deepened the rift between the war and peace factions that could be found in every tribe. Those wanting to maintain peace with the Americans often asked for missionaries to teach them to live and farm in the white man's manner. They moved closer to army posts, where they felt safer from attack by Ohio or Kentucky militiamen, who frequently failed to discriminate between friendly and hostile Indians.

The peace factions were not necessarily pacifist. Most opted for a policy of neutrality during the War of 1812, but some Native groups supplied scouts for the U.S. Army and, to prove their loyalty, even helped track down and kill their British-allied brethren.

In the 1809 Treaty of Fort Wayne, the peace chiefs gave up their peoples' claims to some 3 million acres of land. Tecumseh denounced this sort of thing as a betrayal. The following year, while negotiating with William Henry Harrison at Vincennes, Tecumseh was quoted as saying: *"Sell a country! Why not sell the air, the clouds, and the great sea, as well as the earth? Did not the Great Spirit make them all for the use of his children?"*[946]

Tecumseh and his brother the prophet ranged far and wide as they tried to

---

946 Mobley, Doreen, "The Native American and French Influence Leading to the War of 1812," <u>A Profile of the River Raisin Paper Company Site, Monroe, Michigan</u>, Report of the Historic Preservation Program, Eastern Michigan University, September, 1998.

unite the various Indian nations in resistance to the encroachments of the white settlers and the federal government. They promoted traditional culture and argued that no single tribe or set of leaders could sign away the birthright held in common by all Native Americans. This "foreign" concept of private property rights could not be allowed to supersede tribal rights, nor conflict with the good of the people.

By the time war was officially declared in 1812, a large force had gathered together under the leadership of Tecumseh at the British base at Fort Amherstburg. The fort was at the settlement of Malden, situated along the lower Detroit River in what was then called the Province of Upper Canada. Here could be found a mix of Shawnees, Delawares, Mingoes and Senecas, Sauk and Fox, Winnebagoes, Miamies and related tribes.

Little Warrior of the Creeks would even lead 30 of his people north from Alabama in time to fight in the Battle of the River Raisin.[947]

At times, British Indian Department officers and Canadian fur traders brought in free-ranging warriors from the lands north and west of Lake Superior, including some of the fierce Sioux. From the opposite direction, in the neighborhood of the Grand River which flows into eastern Lake Erie, came yet more fighters from the Iroquois bands that had fled their homes in New York and settled there after the American Revolution.

The Nations of the Three Fires also declared for the British. The Odawas and Ojibwas of Michigan and the Maumee Valley, along with the Potawatomies of western Michigan and the River Raisin, were all prepared to fight.

Everyone waited to see which way the Wyandots would jump. They were the senior tribe in the Detroit area. In 1812, they offered their services to General Hull, the Governor of Michigan Territory, but they were rebuffed and ordered to remain neutral or suffer the consequences. Although the Sandusky Wyandots did adopt a neutral attitude, Tecumseh and Warrow finally pressured and cajoled Walk-in-the-Water, Roundhead, and other leaders into bringing the Brownstown Wyandots across the Detroit River to join him.[948]

---

947 Little Warrior's band was accused of murdering settlers at Duck River, Tennessee, on their trip north to join Tecumseh in the spring of 1812, and killing others at Mound City, Illinois, upon their return homeward in February of 1813. His execution by Creeks allied with the United States served as a *cause célèbre* for the Red Stick faction during the Creek Civil War and Andrew Jackson's subsequent campaign to subjugate the Creeks in 1814. See: Borneman, Walter R., 1812: The War that forged a Nation, New York: Harper Collins, 2004, p. 144.

948 The Wyandots had signed treaties in 1785, 1795, and 1807, giving up most of their lands in Michigan Territory, but they had retained the rights to their villages at Brownstown and Monguagon. The

Allied with the British, Tecumseh's followers would make one more fight to preserve their independence and their homeland. From here, they could not afford to retreat.[949]

Unfortunately, the Anglo-Indian alliance would prove to be unsuccessful. In the aftermath of the War of 1812, it would be the peace chiefs who managed to preserve some of their people's lands and hunting rights in the Territory (and State) of Michigan, through political and nonviolent negotiations.

THE BRITISH REGULARS:

The main responsibility for defending Upper Canada rested on the shoulders of the British regulars, particularly the 41st Regiment of Foot, which had been guarding the province since 1799. The 41st, however, was at the end of a very long supply line which stretched to Québec, and from there, to England. It was also feared that the 41st, having been split up into small garrisons since its arrival in Canada in 1799, was not as sharp as its European counterparts.

Prewar reports indicated, however, that the regiment was actually well disciplined, skilled in marching and field maneuvers, and particularly accurate in musketry. Most criticism fell upon the higher-ranking officers. Brevet Major Fuller, for example, was too fat and out of shape to march very far or to even ride a horse. Brevet Major Short was often absent and displayed little zeal or professional ability

---

sympathies of their leading chiefs differed. Walk-in-the-Water lived in Brownstown (now part of the city of Gibraltar) and favored neutrality. Roundhead lived near Monguagon (now part of the city of Wyandot), and preferred the British and Tecumseh. He was supported by his brothers; Splitlog and John Battise. Roundhead and his brothers were ¾ Wyandot and ¼ Delaware. A third village chief, Warrow, lived on the Canadian side of the Detroit River and supported the British. Tarhe and Between-the-Logs were pro-American leaders of the Wyandots at Sandusky. Tarhe (aka: Monsieur Grue, the Crane) was born at Detroit in 1792 and died at Cranetown, near Upper Sandusky, in 1818. The half-French Shetoon (Isadore Chesne) vied for overall leadership, but was edged out by Tarhe. Nicholas Vincent was chief of the Hurons at Lorette, in Lower Canada. Period documents use the tribal names *Wyandot* and *Huron* interchangeably. Although descended from the founding tribe of the Hurons, the Wyandots of Detroit were from independent tribes that were not technically members of the Huron Confederacy. Their immediate tribal ancestors were Tionontati, Attignawantan, and Wenro. See: "Our Great Chiefs" by Charles Aubrey Buser, 1989, posted on Wyandot-nation.org.

949 This Native alliance was almost as important for the British as it had been for the French before them. The psychological effect of employing Indians against the western settlements was incalculable. Memories and exaggerated tales of Native atrocities were so widespread, that news of just a handful of vengeful Indians being on the warpath could terrorize the entire frontier. The trick would be to ensure that no serious atrocities actually did occur, which could unite the settlers and provoke a violent backlash.

prior to the outbreak of hostilities. Captain Tallon had such a weak constitution he was thought incapable of actively performing the duties required for service in the field.[950]

The men of the 41st ranged in age from the low 20s for the bulk of the privates and many of the lower officers, to the mid 30s and 40s for captains. Their Colonel, Henry Procter, was in his mid-40s and had over 30 years of service. The 1811 rolls showed 8 drummers and 3 privates under the age of 18, and 15 privates aged 55 or older.

Ethnically, the vast majority of the 41st rank and file was of English stock, but about 15% were Irish, 5% were Scotsmen, and a smattering of soldiers were listed as foreigners. A disproportionate number of the officers were Irish. Physically, most of the soldiers were between 5'4" and 5'8" in height.

In addition to the 41st, there were small numbers of the 10th Royal Veterans Battalion available. These over-aged, sometimes alcoholic, men had prior military experience and were especially useful as garrison troops. As members of the royal establishment, their red coats were faced with blue, and they still wore the old-style white breeches, tall gaiters, and stove-pipe shako.

In 1812, England was too busy fighting Napoleon in Europe to worry much about what was happening in the wilds of western Canada. At best, it was hoped that a mobile force of Indians, backed by regular British troops, would so alarm the American frontier settlers, that large numbers of U.S. soldiers would be tied down protecting their frontiers from possible raids.

At least, a British threat in the Detroit area would divert forces away from more strategically vital targets at Montréal or Québec. Any delay would allow the British time to deal with Napoleon, after which they could release troops to reinforce or retake Canada. In the eyes of the high command, the western reaches of Upper Canada were temporarily expendable, which put them somewhat at odds with the aims of their Native allies.

THE LOYALISTS and *LES CANADIENS*:

Lieutenant General Sir George Prévost, Britain's Governor-General and Commander-in-Chief in North America, along with Major General Isaac Brock, President of the civil administration of Upper Canada, set British strategy in the

---

950 General Returns of the 41st Regiment of Foot, Courtesy Fort Malden Archives. Originally organized in the 18th century from the Independent Companies of Invalids, the 41st would eventually become known as the Welsh Regiment.

West. The empire's strength rested on the Indians and the regular army. These were supplemented by Canadian fencible and veteran battalions, provincial naval units, and local militia.

The Canadian Provincial Marine was conceived as a sort of naval reserve for the Great Lakes. It suffered from a lack of good warships, trained gun crews, and officers experienced in fleet maneuvers. Nonetheless, in the first months of the war, the Americans had little or nothing comparable to oppose the Provincial Marine's control of the waters of Lake Erie.[951]

Among the best-trained units raised by the British in North America was the Royal Newfoundland Regiment of Fencible Infantry. Some elements of the regiment participated in the Detroit Campaign, while others were scattered between Québec and various posts in Upper Canada. At Malden, two companies served as marines onboard the ships of the Lake Erie squadron. In discipline, pay, and uniform, the regiment was considered on a par with the regular British army.

The Canadian militia was organized into regiments. In addition to the normal battalion companies, each regiment would include two flank companies of 60 men each, chosen from among the younger, more active men, who would spend 6 days a month in drill.

Not much reliance was placed on the Upper Canadian militia in the western portions of that province, however, where there was a dearth of those stalwart British loyalists who had fled the United States at the close of the American Revolution.

Many English-Canadians had family and business ties south of the border and were thought to be susceptible to the radical republican ideas emanating from the United States. They often were, in fact, recent immigrants from the United States. Meanwhile, French-Canadians living there were suspected of having little loyalty to the British Empire.

Nonetheless, certain segments of the population could still be counted on; the old loyalist members of the Indian Department could recall the days when their war parties ranged far and wide.

The names of Mathew Elliott, Alexander McKee, William Caldwell, and especially Simon Girty, still spread fear along the American frontier. Then there

---

951 The Provincial Marine sailors were generally civilian seamen serving under contract. A prewar report showed the ethnic composition was <u>roughly</u> 40% English-Canadian, 20% Irish, 20% French-Canadian, 15% foreign, and 10% Scots. For more details, see "The Provincial Marine at Amherstburg, 1796-1813," by Bob Garcia, Parcs Canada, as posted on the War of 1812 Website.

were the fur trading companies that exercised great influence over their Native American trading partners. The North West Company had formerly operated freely in American territory and made their voyageur brigades available for transportation and other duties.

The American invasions of Canada forced the various groups within the provinces to come together if they wished to defend their independence from their neighbor to the south.

In the Essex Militia, the flank company men were all volunteers, although men under 40 could be drafted if not enough volunteers could be found. Drummers were called for, but none were actually obtained.[952]

Militia officers were outranked by their corresponding numbers in the regulars and fencibles. The officers in charge of the Detroit Region (the Upper Canadian counties of Essex and Kent[953]) were an odd assortment. Thomas McKee was an alcoholic. Capt. William Elliott had been in the U.S. military before the war.

Captain William Caldwell at first refused to serve in the 1st Essex because he disliked its commander, Colonel Matthew Elliott. Fortunately, Elliott was preoccupied with his duties as head of the Indian Department, so field command of the regiment often fell upon the shoulders of Major Ebenezer Reynolds or Lt. Colonel Thomas Bligh St. George.[954]

Poorly equipped, the militia did creditable service as soldiers, boatmen, and workmen, considering their situation. Their first priority, however, was not to the Empire, but to their communities. When General Hull invaded Canada in July of 1812, about 80% of the Essex militia deserted to look after their threatened homes and families.[955]

---

952 The 1st Essex was a mixed outfit, slightly more English than French. Of the 1st's two flank companies, Caldwell's, from the New Settlement area along the north shore of Lake Erie, was overwhelmingly English, while Elliott's, from the area around Amherstburg, were ¾ French. There were also a few free Black soldiers in the ranks. The 2nd Essex was largely composed of French-Canadians living north of Sandwich and around Lake St. Clair.

953 Essex County fronted on Michigan Territory to its west, while Kent County was adjacent to its east. In 1998, Kent County was merged into the Municipality of Chatham-Kent. (Information courtesy of Marc Meyer.)

954 The New Settlement stretched along the shore between Fort Amherstburg and present-day Kingsville, Ontario. The town of Sandwich was incorporated into Windsor, Ontario in 1935. (Information courtesy of Marc Meyer.)

955 Couture, Paul Morgan. "War and Society on the Detroit Frontier, 1791-1815," Manuscript Report for Parks Canada, 1986: The Canadian militia in the Detroit River region in 1812 was not terribly well trained or equipped. The Militia Act required militiamen to wear a short coat of dark colored cloth made to button well around the body, pants suited to the season, and a round hat. The Essex

THE PEOPLE OF THE RIVER RAISIN:

For the British, the most vulnerable target for a western campaign was the Territory of Michigan. Its small, scattered population was outnumbered 20-to-1 by that of Upper Canada, and at least 2-to-1 by Native Americans residing within the territory. Moreover, it was cut off from the rest of the United States by almost impenetrable swamps and wilderness. Heavy supplies were transported by water. Posts at Detroit and Mackinac controlled strategic trade routes into the Great Lakes.

But there was another Michigan settlement that would be seriously affected by all these plans for war; the farming and trading community on the River Raisin. It would become the scene of incredible carnage and destruction in January of 1813.

Prior to the 1780s, the *Numassipp*i, or River of Sturgeon, was home for two Native villages, one for the Odawas; the other, for the Potawatomies.

In the 1780s, French-Canadian families from both sides of the Detroit River began migrating down to the River Raisin, where they purchased land directly from the Potawatomies and Odawas who claimed the area. By 1785, the stream and settlement was widely known as the *Rivière au Raisin*.

Such land exchanges were not recognized by the British government, but that did not stop these *habitants* (free-holding inhabitants) from establishing narrow, ribbon-shaped farms on nearly every stream that emptied into Lake Erie.

Foremost among them was François Navarre, who obtained a claim on the south side of the River Raisin and urged many of his friends and relatives to join him. Soon, Detroit companies, like Meldrum and Park, were involved, large orchards were planted, and the settlement was producing surplus cider, corn and wheat, both for the Indian trade and to supply British garrisons.

Farming methods and equipment were outdated, but the natural fertility of the soil permitted much to be grown. The real wealth was in the Indian trade, and many of the *habitants* engaged in it.

While intermarriage with the Natives was not exactly the norm, most families

---

flank companies were promised a red jacket, gray great coat, gray trousers, shoes, and flannel shirt in 1812, but eastern units absorbed all the supplies. During Hull's invasion in the summer of 1812, the militiamen at Malden were described as dressed in fragments of hats and torn shirts. At Monguagon, some of them appeared dressed and painted like the Indians. At Detroit, some may have been loaned cast-off red coats from the 41st Regiment, but by that fall, they were wearing blanket coats, or capotes, edged in black. Each man was to provide his own musket, trade gun, rifle, or shotgun with at least 6 rounds of powder and ball. In July of 1812, Colonel St. George issued them arms from supplies destined for the Indians, although they preferred the French guns which were on hand from old stocks or those seized from the Americans.

could boast some sort of kinship or trading ties with the Potawatomies and other tribes.

Eventually, this alarmed the British authorities in Detroit. They began to see the River Raisin country as a haven for smugglers, rum-runners, political dissidents, and cultural malcontents who had left Detroit to get away from the supervision of the British garrison.

Edmund Burke, the first resident priest at St. Antoine's Church on the River Raisin, was an Irish loyalist, and a British agent, who rather uncharitably described his parishioners as a debauched gang of *"scoundrels, bred amongst the Indians, masters of the Indian customs and prejudices, speaking their language and all its different dialects, keeping their daughters as wives..."*

British suspicions were not entirely unjustified. Although some Raisin *habitants* fought alongside the Indians at Fallen Timbers, the aftermath of that battle saw the Navarres, the Lasselles, and many others scurrying off to convince Native leaders to sign the Treaty of Greenville in 1795. This helped open the door for the Americans to take over Detroit in 1796.

The Treaty of Greenville guaranteed the old French and British claims up to 6 miles inland from the shores of Lake Erie and 12 miles up the River Raisin. After 1796, the new American administration superimposed the square section and township designs provided in the Land Ordinance of 1785 and the Northwest Ordinance of 1787, but the traces of the old French land claims are still visible in the city of Monroe and its environs today.[956]

The key to gaining the loyalty of these "Mushrat Frenchmen" was the legal recognition of their land claims by the American government, as specified in the Greenville Treaty. This was further ratified during and after the government survey in 1810.

Lands along the River Raisin were divided according to the Roture, or Long Lot, system, and are known locally as ribbon farms. Culturally identified with Québec, this pattern of narrow riverfront properties was widely reproduced across North America, wherever French settlements grew up.

Ribbon farms were well suited to an environment in which stream frontage was important, not only as a source of water, but also to give access to a liquid "highway" for transporting heavy goods. Narrow river frontages allowed farmers

---

956 The French claims were surveyed in 1810, despite some opposition from local landowners who foresaw that they would not only be charged for the survey, but would also become subject to increased property taxes.

to live close enough together to foster social interaction and to assist one another in time of need. It was said information could be passed for miles down the River Raisin by yelling from one farm to the next.

As one proceeded away from the river, the land decreased in value, so that some farmers did not take all the land to which they might have been entitled. According to local legend, the uneven nature of the rear lot lines was due to the habit of the farmer going out with the surveyor and a jug of whisky. Wherever the jug was finished, the surveyor would plot the end of the farm.

Aaron Greeley was responsible for completing the survey and mapping 150 claims in the River Raisin settlement. Only 25 were for non-French claimants. The farms were generally of similar shape, narrow and rectangular, but somewhat variable in size, amounting to 80, 120, 160, or 200 *arpents*, or French acres. A very few farmers claimed 400 arpents. Most, however, fell into the 120-arpent category, with a river frontage of about 3 or 4 arpents, and a depth of 40 to 50 arpents.[957]

---

957 Fuller, George Newman. <u>Economic and Social Beginnings of Michigan</u>. Lansing: Wynkoop, Halenbeck, Crawford Co., 1916, p. 105: An arpent was used as both a linear and area measurement. As a linear measure, an arpent equaled approximately 192 feet. Sometimes called a French acre, a "square" arpent covered about .84 of one American acre. Old records were not always clear about which system of measurement was being used. According to Marc Meyer, a semi-retired engineer whose math is much better than mine, a 3x50-arpent farm would contain about 127 American acres.

This map is based on postwar maps
Drawn by Lt. Col. Anderson (1818) and Bela Hubbard (1838).
Copies of the original maps can be found in the Monroe County Historical
Museum Archives.[958]

---

958 Courtesy Ray Dushane, March 1, 2021. Note that on the map, *French Town* is listed as two words. Other period documents frequently list it as one word, *Frenchtown*. In this book, I have tried to stick with *French Town* in order to distinguish the historic settlement from modern-day *Frenchtown Township*. *French Town* was often used by English-speakers, but the French inhabitants preferred to go by *River Raisin*. The claims surveyed in 1810 were numbered in the order they were registered at Detroit. Records dated between 1805 and 1810 indicate that gristmills were built on claims, 56, 232, 471, 476, 498, 519, and 684. There were saw-mills built on claims 56 and 539, and two more on 476. A seat-mill was located on claim 425, and a horse-mill on claim 486. A trading post appeared on claim 53, and a store on claim 516. There was a blacksmith shop on claim 468, and distilleries on claims 414 and 486. The non-French claimants along the river were a mixture of old-time British families, who had often married in with the French and were themselves a product of the fur trading system. There were also some Yankee immigrants coming from the northeastern states. The Yankees distrusted their Indian neighbors and were not altogether sure of the French, who formed 80% of the white population of Michigan, a percentage that rose to 90% at the River Raisin. The reference to a seat-mill may be just a mill seat (mill site) on the property of Louis Gaillard, a baker.

The farms formed a contiguous double band a mile or so deep, fronting both banks of the River Raisin. They began a couple miles upstream from where the river's swampy mouth meandered through the marshes and into Lake Erie, and stretched for well over a dozen miles up the winding river. Beyond that point was the Macon Reserve, set up in 1807 for the Potawatomies.

A traveler going downriver from the Macon Reserve would eventually arrive at the Church of St-Antoine and a blacksmith shop, which formed a community focal point on the north bank. Several miles further downstream, and still on the north bank, were the Wayne Stockade and the home office of Dr. Dazet, the community's first resident physician.

At another point on the north bank, half a mile downriver from the Wayne stockade, a small group of farm and trade buildings were clustered close together, near the place where Hull's Trace crossed a rocky ford over the river.

Here, the farms were smaller, just a couple of arpents wide, and some of the river frontage had been subdivided into even smaller parcels, which gave this area the appearance of a compact village.

The settlement, as a whole, was rather dispersed, although it was said that the farmsteads were close enough for families to communicate with each other simply by yelling from one farm to the next, all along the river.

The majority of the farms were located on the north bank of the Raisin. All these points were connected by the river, accessible by shallow boats or canoes, and by a primitive riverside road that could be traversed on horseback or in a two-wheeled pony cart.

By 1811, the River Raisin had become the largest settlement in Michigan Territory outside of Detroit. The only other settlements of any size were scattered along the rivers Maumee, the Huron of Lake Erie, the Ecorse, the Rouge, the Huron River of Lake St. Clair (later renamed the Clinton River), and the St. Clair River, (sometimes, mistakenly, referred to as the Sinclair.)[959]

Mackinac Island hosted a significant trading settlement, whose population ballooned when the voyageur brigades arrived. There was also a remnant of a

---

959 The river has always been known as the St. Clair, or the Rivière Ste Claire, but old chroniclers sometimes confused it with Sinclair, which mimics how the masculine form of it sounds in French. Patrick Sinclair built Fort Sinclair there at the junction of the Pine and St. Clair Rivers around 1764. The British fort was abandoned by 1782, but remained a fur trading station. The fort's name also occasionally appears as Fort St. Clair. The Nottawassippi (rattlesnake River) or Huron of St. Clair was renamed in 1824 in honor of DeWitt Clinton, governor of New York from 1817 to 1823.

traders' settlement at old Fort Joseph (Niles). The wilderness began at the edge of everyone's backyard.

The white population of the territory was only 4,762, and the land-owning inhabitants, or *habitants*, were so scattered along over 300 miles of waterways as to make Michigan militarily indefensible, if left to its own devices. Outside of Detroit and without advance warning, it would be difficult to muster more than a couple hundred militiamen in any given spot.[960]

The loyalties of the old French and formerly British families remained suspect. With the organization of Michigan Territory came new laws that ran contrary to traditional ways.[961]

The disastrous fire of 1805 had burned down most of Detroit, destroying the life work of many of its residents. Government supported attempts to abandon the fur trade as the basis of Michigan's economy and replace it with a more diversified commercial agriculture had impoverished many others. Militiamen disliked the New England style militia laws, which required them to make their own uniforms out of cloth purchased from Governor William Hull. Many spoke of migrating to Canada.

Needless to say, the outbreak of the War of 1812 left many *habitant* families in a quandary. Their association with the fur trade, the Indians, and their cousins still living in Canada pulled them in one direction. Their duties as U.S. citizens and recognition of their land claims pulled them in another. Above all, the territorial

---

960 The 1811 Census of Michigan Territory signed by Secretary Reuben Atwater lists 2,227 non-Native people in the District of Detroit; 580 in the Huron District around Lake St. Clair; 615 at Michilimackinac; and 1,340 in the District of Erie, which covered the River Raisin area from the River Huron to the Maumee. The bulk of people living in the District of Erie, probably over a thousand, resided along the banks of the River Raisin. In some contexts, "River Raisin" refers to the entire settlement area from Swan Creek down to the Maumee River. In other contexts, it includes just the people living along the Raisin. Another name, "French Town," came to be used during and after the War of 1812. It, too, can refer to the settlers all along the river, but sometimes it is confined to just the cluster of buildings and farmsteads where Hull's Road crossed the River Raisin.

961 It was rumored locally that 45-year-old François Navarre was of royal blood, a descendant of Antoine de Bourbon, Duc de Vendome. Antoine de Bourbon was the father of King Henry of Navarre, who, in the 1500s, had become Henry IV of France, founder of the Bourbon dynasty. François Navarre's grandfather, Robert the Scrivener, had come to America in the 18th century to serve as a royal notary in Detroit. There was nothing royal about François Navarre's politics, however. He and 36 of his clan chose to fight for the United States during the War of 1812. Their rivalry with the Lasselles and their allies for influence within the River Raisin community had on more than one occasion approached the level of a feud.

militiamen had to provide for the welfare and protection of their families, who were living in a war zone.

In the event, the majority chose to do their duty. Some 80% of the eligible male population served in the Michigan militia during the war. And they would suffer the consequences; for they would risk death and disability, cultural and economic loss, and the complete, if temporary, dissolution of their community.

APPENDIX B
CAMPBELL'S FORCE AT THE MISSISSINEWA

SOURCE: Raynor, Keith, "The Battle of the Mississinewa, 1812," on the website of The Discriminating General. Raynor gives a detailed order of battle for Campbell's force, which numbered 787 men.

1. General Staff (1 commander, 2 adjutants, 2 surgeons, 1 secretary.)
2. Lt. Col. James Simrall's Regiment of Kentucky Light Dragoons (270 men total):
    a. Staff of 5 men.
    b. Capt. George Trotter's Troop of 12-month volunteers (72).
    c. Capt. Robert Smith's Troop of 6-month volunteers (34).
    d. Capt. Thomas Johnston's Troop of 12-month volunteers (62).
    e. Capt. William Young's Company of 12-month volunteers (53).
    f. Capt. Warner Elmore's Company of 12-month volunteers (44).
3. Major James Ball's Squadron, 2nd Dragoon Regt. (345 men total):
    a. Staff of 4 men.
    b. Capt. Samuel Hopkins' Troop, 2nd U.S. Light Dragoons (89).
    c. Capt. William Garrard's Troop, Bourbon Blues, Kentucky Vol. Light Dragoons (69).
    d. Cornet Isaac Lee's River Raisin Detachment, Michigan Terr. Vol. Lt. Dragoons (22).[962]

---

962 In the National Archives can be found the Dec. 31, 1812, payroll of Cornet Isaac Lee's detachment of 12-months Michigan Territory Volunteer Light Dragoons, listing 22 men, mostly from Anglo-American families who had fled the River Raisin in the summer and fall of 1812. Included are Cornet Isaac Lee, Sgt James Bentley, Cpl John Ruland, James Knaggs, Louis Drouillard, John Cramer, Orin Rhodes, John Murphy, Francis Moffit, Michael McDermott, William Hunter, Scott and Thomas Robb, Samuel Dibble, Robert Glass, Cyrus Hunter, James Robb, Silas Lewis, Samuel Young, David Hull, John Riddle, and Arthur Lapointe.

      e. Capt. Joseph Markle's Troop, Penn. Vol. Lt. Dragoons, Westmoreland County (57).

      f. Capt. James McClelland's Company, Pennsylvania Vol. Cavalry (47).

      g. Lt. Thomas Warren's Co., Pennsylvania Light Dragoons (30).

      h. Capt. Benoni Pierce's Detachment, 6-months Ohio Vol. Light Dragoons (27).

4. Corps of Infantry and Riflemen (158 men total):

      a. Capt. Wilson Elliott's Company, 19th U.S. Infantry Regiment (66).

      b. Capt. John Alexander's Company, Pennsylvania Vol. Riflemen (40).

      c. Capt. James Butler's Company, Pittsburgh Blues, Penn. Vol. Light Infantry (52).

      d. Guides: Seven men under Captain Patterson Bain.

APPENDIX C
ORDER OF BATTLE
FIRST BATTLE OF THE RIVER RAISIN, JAN. 18, 1813:

AMERICAN FORCES

Approximately 667 men, plus up to a hundred local volunteers

Commanded by Lt. Col. William Lewis, 5th Regiment Kentucky Volunteer Infantry

DIVISION	BATTALION COMMANDERS	COMPANY COMMANDERS	COMPANY SUBALTERNS
Advanced Guard	Capt. Bland Ballard (Acting Major) 1st Rifle Regt., Shelby County	Capt. Paschal Hickman 1st Rifle Regiment, Franklin County	Lt. John T. Chinn
		Capt. Michael Glaves 1st Kentucky Regiment, Pendleton County	Lt. Comstock (5th Ky) Ens. James King?
		Capt. Henry James Co. of Spies 2nd Kentucky Pulaski County	Lt. James Kennedy? Ens. David Farr?
Right Wing	Lt. Col. John Allen 1st Rifle Regiment Shelby County	Capt. Virgil McCracken 1st Rifle Regiment, Woodford County	Lt. William? Ens. McClary
		Capt. Richard Bledsoe 1st Rifle Regiment, Fayette County	Ens. Morrison (Act. Lt.) Ens. Thomas Chinn
		Capt. Richard Matson 1st Rifle Regiment Bourbon & Harrison Co.	Ens.Wm Nash, 5th Ky, (Act. Lt.) Ens. Caldwell
Center Column	Maj. George Madison 2nd Battalion, 1st Rifle Regiment Franklin County	Cpt. Richard Hightower 17th US Infantry Regt. Jessamine County	Lt. Caleb Holder Ens. Wm O. Butler (detached service)
		Capt. Coleman Collier 1st Kentucky Regt. Nicholas County	Lt. Story Ens. William Fleet
		Capt. Uriel Sebree 1st Kentucky Regt., Boone County	Lt. Bryan Rule (Morris') Ens. Bowles (Morris')
Left Wing	Maj. Benjamin Graves 2nd Battalion, 5th Kentucky Regiment Fayette County	Capt. John Hamilton 5th Kentucky Regiment, Fayette County	Lt. William Moore Ens. James Heron

		Capt. Samuel Williams 5th Kentucky Regiment, Montgomery County	Lt. John Higgins Ens. Joseph Harrow
		Capt. Joseph Kelly 5th Kentucky Regt. Clark County	Lt. William McGuire (Martin's Co., 5th Ky) Ens. John W. Nash (Ballard's Co., 1st Rifle)
Michigan Volunteers	Lt. Col. François Navarre (commander 2nd Regt.)	Lt. Ambrose Charland	With advance guard or in Kentucky units

BRITISH FORCES
+/- 300 Combatants

Up to a hundred Canadian militiamen, mostly *Canadiens* from the *Petite Côte*, Plus a couple hundred Indians

Commanded by Major Ebenezer Reynolds, Essex County Militia

DIVISION	UNIT COMMANDERS	SUBALTERNS
Artillery: 1 small howitzer (or a 3-lber)	Bombardier Kitson, R. A.	
2nd Flank Company, 1st Essex Militia Regiment	Captain William Elliott	Lt. T. Caldwell Ensign Thomas Girty
2nd Flank Company, 2nd Essex Militia Regiment	Capt. Alexis Maisonville	Lt. Joseph Parent Ens. Joseph Eberts
Native Allies Wyandots and Potawatomies	Roundhead	Walk-in-the-Water

The cap badge of the Essex and Kent Scottish
The modern-day Primary Reserve Regiment of the Canadian Forces based in
Windsor, Ontario.

The regiment carries on the tradition of the 1st and 2nd Regiments of the Essex
Militia, the 1st Regiment of the Kent Militia, the Loyal Kent Volunteers, the Loyal
Essex Volunteers (Essex Rangers) and the Western Rangers (Caldwell's Rangers).

APPENDIX D
List of American Casualties at the River Raisin
January 18, 1813

BATTALION and COMPANY COMMANDERS	COMPANY and REGIMENT (best guess at cross attachments)	KILLED	WOUNDED	TOTAL
Col. John Allen — Right Wing				
Capt. McCracken	McCracken's and Hickman's companies (1st Rifle Regt.)	1	1	2
Capt. Matson	Ellis' and Langhhorne's companies (1st Rifle Regt.)	3	7	10
Capt. Bledsoe	Bledsoe's and Simpson's companies (1st Rifle Regt.)	1	7	8
TOTALS FOR RIGHT WING		*5*	*15*	*20*
Major George Madison — Center Battalion				
Captain Hightower	Hightower's, Edwards' and other companies (17th US and militia)	0	1	1
Captain Collier	Collier's and West's companies (1st Kentucky)	1	4	5
Captain Sebree	Sebree's and Morris' companies (1st KVM)	1	4	5
TOTALS FOR CENTER		*2*	*9*	*11*
Major Benjamin Graves — Left Wing				
Captain Hamilton	Hamilton's and Hart's companies (5th KVM)	2	10	12
Captain Williams	Williams' company (5th KVM)	0	7	7
Captain Kelly	Brasfield's, Price's, and Martin's companies (5th KVM)	0	7	7
TOTALS FOR LEFT WING		*2*	*24*	*26*
Captain Bland Ballard– Advance Guard				
Captain Glaves	Glaves's and Wirt's (West's) companies (KVM)	0	2	2
Captain Hickman	Hickman's and Watson's companies	0	6	6
Captain James	James' company of spies (2nd KVM)	0	0	0
TOTAL ADVANCE GUARD		*0*	*8*	*8*

APPENDIX E
APPROXIMATE ORDER OF BATTLE FOR U.S. FORCES,
Jan. 22, 1813

Brigadier General James Winchester
Commander of the Left Wing of the Army of the Northwest
Approximately 934 fighting men

Staff:

Lt. Col. François Navarre, 2nd Mich. Terr. Militia Regt.

Capt. John H. Woolfolk, Sec. to Gen. Winchester

Capt. Whitmore Knaggs, 1st Mich. Terr. Militia Regt.

Dr. James Overton, Jr., aide-de-camp

Senior Surgeon, Dr. John Irvine

Headquarters guard or men camped or dispersed outside picketed area:

Capt. John Simpson, his co. and parts of Ballard's (WIA), 1st Rifle Regiment of Kentucky (if not assigned to Allen or Wells — probably arrived with Wells' regulars).

Capt. James Price, 5th Kentucky Volunteer Regiment (if not assigned to Graves or Wells — possibly arrived with Wells' regulars — within the pickets at one point, but also in retreat).

Capt. Ambrose Charland — local Michigan volunteers

Left Wing Commander: Lt. Col. William Lewis, 5th Ky Vol. Militia Infantry Regt.

Staff: Capt. John McCalla, Adj., 1st KVMI

Capt. Nathaniel Gray Smith Hart (Deputy Inspector Left Wing, NW Army, 5th KVMI)

Quartermaster Pollard Keene and Surgeon John Todd

Battalion Commanders:

Lt. Col. John Allen, 1st Kentucky Rifle Regiment.

Capt. Virgil McCracken: his co. and parts of Hickman's (WIA), 1st KRR

Capt. Richard Bledsoe: his co. and parts of Ballard's (WIA), 1st KRR

Ensign William Nash, 5th KVMI, replacing Matson (WIA), Matson's co. and Langhorne's, 1st KRR

401

Major James Garrard, Brigade Inspector, 2nd Btln, 1st Ky Vol. Militia Infantry Regt. (replacing Ballard, WIA)

Capt. Henry James' co. of Spies, 2nd Ky Vol. Militia Regt.

Capt. Michael Glaves, 1st Kentucky Volunteer Militia Infantry Regiment

Lt. John T. Chinn: replacing Hickman (WIA) 1st KRR (if Chinn was not also among the wounded.)

Major George Madison, 2nd Btln, 1st Kentucky Rifle Regt.

Capt. Richard Hightower, his co. and Edwards' 17th U.S. and Militia Volunteers from 1st KVMI, etc.

Capt. Uriel Sebree, 1st KVMI: his co. and part of Morris'.

Capt. Coleman Collier, 1st KVMI: his co. and parts of West's.

Major Benjamin Franklin Graves, 2nd Btln, 5th Ky Vol. Militia Inf. Regt.

Capt. Jos. Kelly: Brasfield's co. and part of Martin's, 5th KVMI

Capt. John Hamilton: his co. and part of Hart's and Price's, 5th KVMI

Capt. Sam Williams: 5th KVMI

Right Wing Commander:Major Elijah McClenahan, in absence of Lt. Col. Wells

Staff: Surgeon Alexander Montgomery

Regulars: Capt. Robt. Edwards' Co., 17th U.S. Infantry Regiment

Capt. James Meade's Company, 17th U.S. Infantry Regt.

Elements of Langham's Co., 19th U.S. Infantry Regt. (Langham absent with Wells)

Lt. Thomas C. Graves, Hightower's Co., 17th U.S. (Hightower retained inside the pickets.)

Support Elements: Artificers and sutlers (scattered on both sides of river)

Possibly parts of Morris' company, 1st Kentucky, still convoying baggage and hogs south of the river.

APPENDIX F

Approximate Order of Battle for the BRITISH FORCES, Jan. 22, 1813:
Colonel Henry Procter, 41st Regiment of Foot
597 soldiers plus as many warriors

STAFF:	004	Lt. Col. Thomas Bligh St. George
		Lt. A. H. McLean, A.D.C. to Col. Procter
		Robt. Reynolds, Esq. Dy. Adjt. Commg
		General
		Dr. R. Richardson, Esq., Garrison Mate
COMMISSARIAT:	001	Lt. Col. Francis Baby, Dep. QM-General Militia
FIELD TRAIN:	001	Samuel Wood, Esq., Field Train Dept.
ROYAL ENGINEERS:	001	Capt. Dickson
ROYAL ARTILLERY:	023	Lt. Felix Trouten
10TH ROYAL VETERAN BATTALION:	004	(4 privates)
41ST REGIMENT OF FOOT:	244	Capt. Jos. Tallon
		Lts. Jno. Clemow, Benoit Bender, Harris
		Hailes, Wm Watson
ROYAL NEWFOUNDLAND		
REGIMENT:	061	Capt. Robert Mockler
		Lt. John Gordon, Ens. Thomas Kerr
MARINE DEPARTMENT:	028	Lts. Frederic Rolette and Robt. Irvine
1ST ESSEX MILITIA:	116	Major Reynolds,
		Captains Caldwell, Elliott, Mills, and Buchanan
2ND ESSEX MILITIA:	096	Captains Maisonville, Smith, and Labute
INDIAN DEPARTMENT:	019	Lt. Col. Matthew Elliott, Indian Dept. Super.
		Capt. Billie Caldwell
		William Jones, Ind. Dept. storekeeper
TOTAL BRITISH and CANADIANS:	598	
WYANDOTS:	070	Roundhead, Walk-in-the-Water,
		Adam Brown, Jack Brandy, Split Log, Lumpey
DELAWARES:	070	?
MINGOES:	???	?
SHAWNEES:	???	George Bluejacket, Jim Bluejacket
SAUK and FOX:	???	Black Hawk?
WINNEBAGOES:	???	?
MIAMIS:	???	?

POTAWATOMIES:	???	Shavehead, Waindawgay, Chamblee, Otussa, Osamed
OTTAWAS:	???	Tontogany, McCarty, Squaganaba, Waugon
OJIBWAS:	???	MaCaunse, Normee
CREEKS:	030	Little Warrior

TOTAL NATIVE AMERICANS: 400-800[963]

TOTAL OF BRITISH FORCES: 997-1397

---

963 Known Métis participants = Cadotte, Jean-Baptiste Askin, George and Jim Bluejacket, Capt. William Elliott, Alexandre Saunders, Billy Caldwell, John Frederick Richardson, and Samuel Rankin (Jack Brandy). For information, see: Barkwell, Lawrence, "Métis Soldiers in the War of 1812," Winnipeg: Louis Riel Institute, 2012.

APPENDIX G

BRITISH CASUALTIES
at the
BATTLE OF THE RIVER RAISIN
Jan. 18-23, 1813

24 Dead, 158 wounded, not counting Native American losses, on January 22.

Staff: 1 wounded: Colonel St. George, Inspecting Officer of Militia.

41st Regiment of Foot:

15 dead:	Pvts. Sam Johnston the 1st, Wm Yeats (Gates), John Walker, Chas. Cogan, Wm Armstrong, Jos. Barber, Henry Clarke, David Higgins, John McCoy, Geo. Weston, Geo. Poole, John Horton, Robt Forsyth, Aaron Blakeman, John Tolly.
97 wounded:	Capt. Tallon, Lt Clemow.
	Sgts. Richard Tomstal (Fornstale), Wm Lane, Wm Dukes.
	Cpls. Wm Mathews, John Walters.
	Pvts. Sam Johnston 2nd, Thos. Colohan, Isaac Pomroy, James Mead 2nd, Sam Bancroft, Sam Brice, Henry Cass (died on Jan. 27), Jas. Minty, Peter Mansfield, Wm Carpmail, Wm Puy, John Morrison, Michael McMurray, John Scarlet, John Andrews, Henry Torrent, Wm Vincent, James Hobbs, Joseph Wilson, Henry Webb, Henry Yeates, Dennis Noonan, Wm Pearce, Danl Roberts, John Short, Ralph Smith, Wm Teague, Giles Smith, Wm Rooke, Thos. Kirby, Wm Ball, Jas. Webb, Wm Pierie, John Strickland, Robt Shekleton, James Plane, Robt Philimore, John Stevenson 2nd, Robt Ball, Jos. Stagnell, Jos. Wilson, Jas. Meade 1st, Geo. Holding, Shadrack Byfield, John Lucas, Thos. James, Wm Rowe, Geo. Hudson, John Dear, John Game, Wm Garrett, Christ Garret, Thos. Harris, Ewd. Billing, Thos. Humphries, John Spackman, Levi Stuart, James Tuckett, Timy

Javins, Jas. Humphries, John Gana, Thos. Neal,
Thos. Church, John Legg, Pholomen, McLachlane,
Owen Mognahan, Sam Bonkett, Waters, Bartin,
Jos. Chadwick, James Clarke, John Cokeley, Thos.
Downes, Wm Dunn, Fry, Jas. Higgins, Jas. Hopkins,
Wm Jackson, Henry Malhot, John McGrath, Wm
Fletcher, Wm Rawlins, James Watson, Richard
Watts, Thos. Young, John Cain, Beal, Geo.Bromley,
Wm Billington, John Whitely, Thos. Cummins,
John Lockett, John McCreary, Ben Goodger, James
Haleston, Thos. Harris, Chas. Lorain.

10th Royal Veterans Btln.:

2 wounded: Pvts. Patrick O'Conners and John McDougal.

Royal Newfoundland Fencible Regiment:

2 Dead: Ens. Thomas Kerr (died of wounds), Sgt. Shanahan (DoW)

17 wounded: Cpls. Mahoney, Duryer, and Osdell
                 Pvts. Bryan, Butler and Hore, plus 10 others

Royal Artillery:

2 dead: Sgt. Wm Mills, Volunteer Gunner Wm Dutson

8 wounded: Lt. Felix Troughton, Cpl. (acting sgt.) John Gibbs,
                 Bombardier Kitson (died later),
                 Gentlemen Volunteer Gunners: Thomas Cooper,
                 Hugh Williams, Henry Ramage, James Nichol, Adam
                 Waters.

Provincial Marine Dept.:

1 dead: Seaman Alex LeGrace.

16 wounded: 1st Lt. Fredric Rolette, Acting Lt. Robt Irvine,
                 Midshipmen: Robt. Richardson and Thomas Barwis,
                 Gunner: William Cooper,
                 Seamen: Louis Langlois, Alex Garrand, Peter Fouchae,
                 Augustin Pourier, John Plaisant, Joseph Fournier,

Ant'y Jounker, Henry Bourassau, Francis Friday, Alex'r Harrow, Michel Chamberlain.

1st Essex Militia Regiment:

4 Killed: Capt. William Mills (died of wounds), Corporal Paschal Reaume
             Private Louis Durham, Private James Stewart

11 wounded: Lts. McCormick and Gordon, 2 sergeants, and 7 privates.

2nd Essex Militia Régiment :

3 Killed :   Privates Jean-Baptiste Clément, B. Langlois,[964] and Pierre Badichon

4 wounded: Ensign Claud Gouin and 3 privates.

Native-American Allies:

Dead: Unknown number from among the nations of the Wyandots, Potawatomies, Odawas, Chippewas, Shawnees, Miamies, Delawares, Sauks, Winnebagoes, and Creeks. (At least 12 warriors died in the fight on Jan. 18, and at least 5 on January 22.)

Wounded: Adam Brown, Sr., Wyandot chief. (It is not unreasonable to estimate total wounded around 50.)

Sources:
1. "Woodbridge Papers," Historical Collections of the Michigan Pioneer and Historical Society, Vol.32, printed in Lansing, 1903, pp. 539-540.
2. "Return of the whole of the Troops; Regulars, Militia, Marine and Indian Dept. who were engaged in the action at French Town on the river Raisin on the 22nd January, 1813, with the number of killed and wounded," Michigan Pioneer & Historical Collections, Vol. 25, Lansing: 1903, p. 420.
3. "A Common Soldier's Account" by Private Shadrach Byfield, 41st Foot, in Recollections of the War of 1812, Toronto: Baxter Publishing Co., reprint, 1964, p. 16.
4. "War & Society on the Detroit Frontier, 1791-1815," by Paul Morgan Couture, Parks Canada Ontario Manuscript Report, March, 1986, (unpublished.)

---

964 According to GENI.com, Jean-Baptiste Langlois was in Labute's company and is buried in Tecumseh, Ontario.

APPENDIX H

AMERICAN CASUALTIES AT THE RIVER RAISIN
(incomplete)

There are many conflicting estimates of the AMERICAN CASUALTIES AT THE RIVER RAISIN, but this is what I've put together: Of Winchester's force of approximately 975 men, counting the casualties from January 18, 22, and 23, there were roughly between 322 to 397 dead or missing in action, 131 of whom are named below.

Nine counties in the State of Kentucky were named after participants in the Battle of the River Raisin. Eight were killed in that battle, including Allen, Edmonson, Graves, Hart, Hickman, McCracken, Meade, and Simpson. The ninth, Bland Ballard, survived, but was wounded twice.

Staff of General Winchester
Surgeons: Thomas McIlvain
Captains: John Woolfolk

17th U.S. Infantry

   (1 surgeon, 2 captains, 3 lieutenants, 2 ensigns, 112 non-coms and privates)

Surgeon: Alexander Montgomery
Capts.   Robert Edwards, James Meade
Lts.:   Robert Logan, Thomas Graves, Thomas Overton
Ensigns: Philip Sharer, Levi Wells
Privates: Braxton Blake, John Gardner, William Redding, Thomas Wells,
              Henry Downey, Beverly Blake, Robert Reed

19th U.S. Infantry Regiment

(Not known)

1st Kentucky Volunteer Militia Regiment

   (1 major, 1 captain, 1 surgeon's mate, 1 ensign, 36 enlisted men)

Ensign: Joseph Bowles
Privates: Thomas Ward, Cyrus Short, Thomas Crow, John Vincent

5th Kentucky Volunteer Militia Regiment

(1 major, 1 captain, 1 lieutenant, 73 enlisted)

Majors: Benjamin Franklin Graves
Captains: Nathaniel G. S. Hart, James Price
Sergeant: John Snyder
Privates: James Blythe, Alexander Crawford, William Davis, Samuel Elder,
Thomas Fant, Thomas King, Peter Mesmer, James Reiley,
George Shindlebower, Stephen Smith, Armstrong Stewart,
Allen Darnell, Daniel Darnell, William Frame, John McDonald,
Alfred Chinn, Luke Fields, Ezekiel Suddeth (former Lt.)

1st Kentucky Volunteer Rifle Regiment

(1 lt.-colonel, 1 surgeon, 4 captains, 1 ensign, 154 enlisted)

Lieut. Col.: John Allen
Surgeon: Thomas Davis
Captains: John Simpson, Paschal Hickman, Virgil McCracken, John
Edmiston
Lieutenants: John Williamson
Ensigns: Francis Chinn (WIA Jan 18, MIA Jan. 22)
Sergeants: Thomas Benson, David Quinn, John Nailor, George McClary,
(MIA: William Boswell, William Chinn.)
Corporals: Richard Chism, (MIA: Jeremiah Morgan, John Chinn)
Drummer: Jesse Cock
Bugler: (MIA: James Foxworthy)
Privates: Moses Morgan (KIA Jan. 18), Joseph Simpson, Robert Harrison,
Jesse Humble, Arnold Berrisford, James Biscoe, Isaac Boone,
Philip Clark, John Cox, Simon Kenton, John Lane, Lapsley
McBride, Francis Mayhall, Joshua Moore, James Parker, John
Phillips, Joseph Pitts, Meriweather Poindexter, William Prewitt,
Alexander Robertson, George Robinson, Samuel Smith, John
Smith, William Stevens, John Tate, Samuel Throckmorton,
James Wilson, Moses Morgan, (MIA's: Joseph Becket, William

Butler, Abraham Byrd, William Crawford, Thomas Ellis, Andrew Hamilton, William Johnston, John McCormick, William McDowell, William Shingleton, William Thomas, John Adams, James Adams, William Adams, Irvin Brown, James Craig, John Herring, Sam Herring, Dan Hailey, Isaac Jones, Erin Lewis, Joseph Milner, John McKinsey, John Morrell, John Ritter, William Scott, Spencer Shoemaker, John Sellers, Robert Sidner) Hugh Newell escaped January 22, but went missing and was presumed dead.

Captain William Garrard's Volunteer Light Dragoons

(Not at the Raisin - detached to another command a month prior to the battle)

Militia and Residents of the River Raisin and Sandy Creek

(4 known + 2 possible)

Capitaine :	Jean-Baptiste Couture
Habitants :	Henri Shovin, René LeBeau, Jean-Baptiste Soleau, Etienne Bissonette?, Gabriel Bissonette?

In addition to the dead and missing, U.S. casualties included at least 589 prisoners taken by, or eventually turned over to the British; of whom there were some 60 men from the 17th U.S., 108 from the 1st Kentucky, 193 from the 5th Kentucky, 140 from the 1st Kentucky Rifle Regiment, 21 from the 2nd Kentucky, plus one general and his staff. Between 40 and 70 escaped from, or were released from, Indian captivity. 33 escaped captivity altogether.

Sources:
1. Clift, G. Glenn. Remember the Raisin! Kentucky Historical Society, Frankfort, Kentucky, 1961.
2. Au, Dennis M. War on the Raisin. Monroe County Historical Commission, Monroe, MI., 1981.
3. Cruikshank. Harrison & Procter, Royal Society of Canada.
4. Antal, Sandy. "Remember the Raisin! Anatomy of a Demon Myth," The War of 1812 Magazine, Issue 10, October, 2008.

APPENDIX I

PRISONERS KILLED BY THE INDIANS

Knopf, Richard C. <u>Document Transcriptions of the War of 1812 in the Northwest, Vol. VIII</u>. Columbus: Ohio Historical Society, 1961: Ensign Isaac L. Baker of the 2nd United States Infantry produced the following list of men tomahawked by the Indians after the Battle of the River Raisin. He also reported he had himself seen two others tomahawked at Sandy Creek, and that others reported 15 or 18 more treated in the same manner. Two witnesses reported seeing a body that appeared to have been burned. Henry Downy and William Butler were killed but not scalped.

1. Paschal Hickman, captain, Hickman's company, 1st Ky. Vol. Rifle, Jan. 23, in Frenchtown.
2. Jas. P. Blythe, private, Hart's co., 5th Ky. Vol. Inf., Jan. 23, in Frenchtown.
3. Ch. Serles, private, Hart's co., 5th Ky. Vol. Inf., Jan. 23, at Sandy Creek.
4. Th. S. Crow, private, Seabree's co., 1st Ky. Vol. Inf., Jan. 23, Sandy Creek.
5. Dan. Darnell, private, Williams' co., 5th Ky. Vol. Inf., Jan. 23, between Sandy Creek and Frenchtown.
6. Thos. Ward, private, Redding's co., 1st Ky. Vol. Inf., Jan. 23, between Sandy Creek and Frenchtown.
7. William Butler, pvt, Langhorne's co., 1st Ky. Rifles, Jan. 23, between Sandy Creek and Frenchtown.
8. Henry Dacony (Downy), private, Edwards' co., 17th U.S. Infantry, Jan. 24, near Brownstown.
9. John P. Sidney, sergeant, Martin's co., 5th Ky. Vol. Inf., Jan. 26, River Rouge. (There could be some confusion between private John Sidney and Sergeant John D. Snyder, who was in the same company and was listed as killed January 22 or 23.)

Colonel Procter's investigation into the massacre of the wounded at French Town revealed only 6 murders; two mortally wounded prisoners who were killed outright, and two more who couldn't keep up with the march, plus a 5th American

411

who argued with his captors. The 6th murder was of a civilian in a dispute over a pig. He admitted the houses were burned on the 23rd, to deny their use to Harrison's army, but flatly denied any prisoners were inside at the time. However, the Americans had burned some buildings during the battle, including one containing the corpse of Paschal Reaume, a Canadian militiaman who had been severely wounded and had crawled into one of the buildings to die. See: Antal, Sandy. <u>A Wampum Denied</u>. Canada: Carleton Library Series, Vol. 191, p. 195. Antal, quotes from an undated draft document in Procter's handwriting, captured among his effects on Oct. 5, 1813.

APPENDIX J

BAKER'S EXPANDED LIST OF PRISONERS KILLED BY INDIANS AT THE RIVER RAISIN

Letter Baker to Winchester, British Niagara, Feb. 25, 1813, Typed copy in Bidlack's Notes, Monroe County Historical Museum Archives:

NAMES OF SOME PRISONERS KILLED BY THE INDIANS

NAME	RANK	COMPANY	`REGIMENT	DATE	REMARKS
Paschal Hickman	Captain	Hickman's	1st Ky Rifle	Jan. 23	Killed in French Town
Jas. P. Blythe	Private	Hart's	5th Ky Infantry	"	Sandy Creek (3 mi. n. Raisin)
Ch. Serles	"	"	"	"	Sandy Creek
Th. S. Crow	"	"	1st Ky Vol. Inf.	"	Sandy Creek
Danl. Darnel	"	Williams'	5th Ky Infantry	"	Between Sandy Creek and French Town
Thos. Ward	"	Redding's	1st Ky Inf.	"	"
William Butler	"	Langhorne's	"	"	"
Henry Downy?	"	Edwards'	17th US Inf.	Jan. 24	Near Brownstown
John P. Sidney	"	Martin's	5th Ky Inf.	Jan. 26	River Rouge
John H. Woolfolk	Captain	Secretary	General's staff	Jan. 23	French Town
Levi Wells	Ensign	Wells' staff?	7th U.S. Inf.	Jan. 22?	French Town
Nathaniel Hart	Captain	D. Insp.Gen.	5th Ky Infantry	Jan. 23	French Town

413

APPENDIX K

REMEMBER THE RAISIN[965]

How dread was the conflict, how bloody the fray,
Told the banks of the Raisin at the dawn of day;
While the gush from the wounds of the dying and dead
Had thaw'd for the warrior a snow-sheeted bed.

But where is the pride that a soldier can feel,
To temper with mercy the wrath of the steel,
While Procter, victorious, denies to the brave
Who had fallen in battle, the gift of a grave?

---

965 This poem, of unknown origin, was located by Joseph Johnstun, former Director of the Nauvoo Tourism Office in Nauvoo, Illinois, which was forwarded it to the Monroe County Historical Museum by Peggy Tyniw of the Monroe County IS Dept.

BATTLE OF THE RIVER RAISIN[966]

On Raisin darkness reigned around,
And silent was the tented ground,
Where weary soldiers slept profound,
Far in the wintry wilderness.

No danger did the sentry fear
No wakeful watch at midnight drear;
But Ah! The foe approaches near
Through forests frowning darkly.

And ere the sun had 'risen bright
Fast flashing mid the stormy fight
The thundering cannon's livid light
Glared on the sight most frightfully.

Then deadly flew the balls of lead!
Then many of the foemen bled
And thrice their branded legion fled
Before Kentucky's chivalry.

And long our heroes' swords prevail;
But hist! That deep and doleful wail-
Ah! Freedom's sons begin to fail
Oppressed by numbers battling.

But rise! Ye volunteers, arise!
Behold! Your right-hand column flies!
And hark! Your shouts which rend the skies!
When Indians yell tumultuously.

Rush o'er the bloody field of fame,
Drive back the savage whence he came!
For glory waits the victor's name
Returning home exultingly.

'Tis done. The dreadful fight is o'er
Thick clouds of smoke are seen no more,
The snowy plain is red with gore
Where fell the friends of liberty.

---

966 "Battle of the River Raisin," Bulkley, John McClelland. History of Monroe County, Michigan, Vol. I.
Chicago: Lewis Publishing Co., 1913, p. 86: A poem of the battle was left behind in a house where
Kentucky prisoners were confined in Amherstburg.

APPENDIX L

KENTUCKY HISTORICAL MARKERS REFERING TO PARTICIPANTS OF THE BATTLE OF THE RIVER RAISIN

TITLE	LOCATION	MESSAGE
Remember the Raisin	Georgetown, Courthouse lawn.	Rendezvous of Kentucky Volunteers, Aug. 15, 1812...of 1050 men, not half reached home... counties named for officers: Allen, Ballard, Graves, Hart, Hickman, Edmonson, McCracken, Meade, and Simpson.
Allen County Named 1815	Scottsville, Courthouse lawn.	For Lt. Col. John Allen...State Representative, 1801-07, State Senate, 1807-13. KIA River Raisin...
Hart County, 1819	Munfordville	For Capt. Nathaniel G. T. Hart...severely wounded at Battle of Raisin...brutally murdered...
Simpson County Named, 1819	Franklin, Courthouse lawn.	For Capt. John Simpson...killed at Battle of River Raisin...Fought under "Mad Anthony Wayne"], Battle of Fallen Timbers, 1794...Speaker of Ky. House, 1811. U.S. Congressman...
Hickman County Named, 1821	Clinton, Courthouse lawn.	For Capt. Paschal Hickman...River Raisin battle... one of nine Ky. Officers killed in that action for whom counties named...Resided Franklin county, extensive landowner.
Graves County Named, 1823	Mayfield, Courthouse lawn.	For Maj. Ben Franklin Graves...Presumed killed by Indians after being wounded and captured, battle of River Raisin...
Meade County Named, 1823	Brandenburg	For Capt. James Meade, recognized for bravery and daring at Battle of Tippecanoe, 1811...Killed at River Raisin.
McCracken County, 1824		For Capt. Virgil McCracken of Woodford County, Ky., who was killed in Battle of River Raisin.
Edmonson County Named, 1825	Brownsville	For Capt. John Edmonson...in War of Revolution a private in company led by father...Battle of King's Mountain, 1782. Killed at battle of River Raisin.
Ballard County Named, 1842	Wickliffe, Courthouse lawn.	For Capt. Bland Ballard, Scout for George Rogers Clark...in the Battles of Fallen Timbers, Tippecanoe, River Raisin...5 terms in Ky. Legislature.

Kentucky also has a county named after James Madison, 4th President of the United States, who led the country into the War of 1812. Jackson County was named for President Andrew Jackson, the "Hero of New Orleans." Monroe County, Kentucky, honors President James Monroe, who served as Secretary of State and as a temporary Secretary of War during the conflict.

APPENDIX M

THE 1937 "BATTLE" OF THE RIVER RAISIN:

On June 10, 1937, armed combatants came face to face once more on the River Raisin Battlefield, not far from the old site of the unfortunate 17th Infantry's camp.

This time, CIO strikers were pitted against Monroe's city police, special deputies, town vigilantes, and non-striking workers from the Newton Steel Plant, located at the mouth of the River Raisin.

The CIO had declared a strike against Newton Steel on May 28 and formed a picket line facing west across Elm Avenue at the Detroit Avenue intersection to prevent workers from entering the plant.

The road was barricaded with a flat boat and 4 cars turned sideways. Reinforcements were concealed in a line of automobiles that stretched from the riverbank northward along Detroit Avenue. Armed with bricks, stones, and clubs, they were determined not to let anyone through.

About 6 p.m. on June 10, Police Chief Jesse Fisher received a phone call from Mayor Daniel Knaggs, ordering him to disperse the picketers. He quickly launched a gas attack on the picket line, followed by an advance of 150 police, special deputies, and vigilantes wearing gauze armbands on both arms to identify themselves.

The attack soon ran into trouble as the reserve group of strikers emerged from their vehicles on Detroit Avenue. They took the police in flank and pelted them with a shower of bricks from the shelter of a news truck.

The news truck quickly took off, depriving the CIO brick throwers of cover. At this same time, a hundred gun and club toting company men from the steel mill appeared from their hiding place around a downstream bend of the river and assaulted the rear of the picket line.

The strikers lost heart, scattered up Detroit Avenue and fled across the fields and marshes, chased by the victorious vigilantes.

It was all over in 15 minutes. The strikers' camp was pillaged and their cook tent set afire. 16 cars were damaged, including 8 that were pushed into the river. 12 people were injured, of whom 7 men and 1 woman were sent to the hospital. Five men and two women were arrested for throwing bricks.

The mayor applauded the police and townspeople for uniting against a group of outside agitators, but he was in turn criticized for escalating the situation into an armed confrontation.

Unwilling to accept defeat, the CIO established a new strike camp at Sterling State Park, while the governor sent in the Michigan National Guard to keep the peace in Monroe.

Eventually, the workers returned to their jobs at the plant, but by Christmas, Newton Steel had gone out of business.

APPENDIX N
The Soldier and the Common Musket

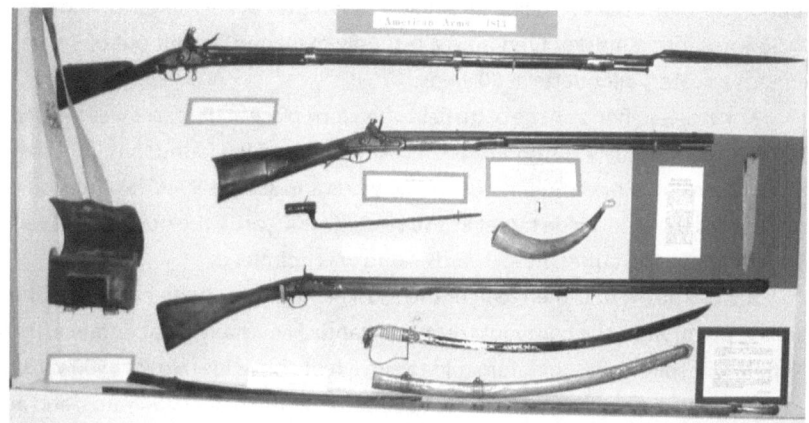

Weapons on Display at the former River Raisin Battlefield Visitor Center
American military flintlock musket with bayonet (top)
Harper's Ferry rifle (middle)
Civilian rifle converted from flintlock to percussion (lower)
Photo by Author, Courtesy National Park Service

Although the standard American smoothbore musket, patterned after the French Charleville, could throw a lead ball weighing 4/5ths of an ounce about 1000 yards, effectiveness against even a massed target, was negligible beyond 250 yards. Any farther, a ball would sometimes not even penetrate, although one American calculation showed a ball should be able to go through a one-inch-thick pine board at 500 yards.

For firing at an individual soldier, a good marksman with a carefully loaded flintlock rifle could hit a person at 100 yards and had a decent chance at up to 300 yards, if the individual remained stationary and in the open.

However, a man armed with a common musket might as well shoot at the moon as try to hit a man standing beyond a hundred yards away, especially if the battlefield became obscured by the thick smoke of exploding gunpowder.

It was when the range narrowed to 75 yards or less that the smoothbore musket became especially deadly, due to its faster rate of fire over that of the rifle. At 40 yards or less, a marksman could be reasonably sure of hitting a man-sized target.

The staff at Fort Niagara tested volley firing with reproduction muskets and found 30% of the balls hit a line of "soldier" silhouettes at 75-100 yards, and 66% at 50 yards, but a musket fired from a rest only managed one hit out of 3 shots against a solitary silhouette at 50 yards.

Nonetheless, firing on the battlefield often took place at distances well beyond 100 yards. British trials of smoothbore muskets in the 1840's found the .75-caliber Brown Bess had a maximum range of 700 yards and scored 50-75% of hits on a six-foot-tall by 4-foot-wide target at 150 yards. At 200 yards, the point of aim was 5½ feet above the target. At 250 yards, firing was pointless.

It was known that the recoil of the musket would send the ball above the aiming point, while the ball would drop substantially over any great distance. The Napoleonic soldier was therefore told to aim 3 feet above his target at 500 yards; 1 foot above at 400 yards; at the hat at 300 yards; at the belt at 200 yards; and at the knee at 100 yards or less.

In his tactical guide of 1808, William Duane recommended aiming at the hat at 200-300 yards, at the middle of the body at 100-200 yards, and at the knees at less than 100 yards. This was to compensate for the natural trajectory of the bullet, as well as for the tendency of the soldier to flinch when pulling the trigger. For volley fire, correct elevation was more important than windage. Some experts even suggested aiming at the feet for distances as close as 60-80 yards.

Even at short range, loading was cumbersome. The soldier had to put his lock on half-cock, pull a cartridge from his cartouche box, bite off the end of the paper cartridge, open his priming pan, pour some of the powder into the priming pan, shut the pan, draw his rammer, ram the rest of the cartridge and ball down the barrel, return the ramrod, go to full cock, take aim, and fire. All this was done in unison and at high speed to create the maximum firepower effect.

The best trained musket-armed troops could perform this procedure in about 15-20 seconds, at least on the parade ground. In the field, twice a minute would be more likely. A rifle, on the other hand, could take a minute to reload. Rifles also fouled much more quickly than smoothbore muskets.

Thanks to intensive training, British troops could often get off 3 shots for every 2 fired by the soldiers of France or other European countries. After 25 shots in fairly quick succession, the barrel would be hot enough to make loading difficult. After about 50 shots, the course, black gunpowder could cause enough fowling in the barrel to require a good cleaning before another ball could be rammed down. Flints often wore out after a few dozen shots and had to be replaced. If the powder got wet, the firearm would no longer function.

A volley-firing platoon or company of 50 men in two ranks, would cover a frontage of about 15-20 yards and could theoretically lay a wall of bullets across that space, amounting to 6 to 10 shots put into each yard of frontage during a period of one minute. However, they would be lucky to get off two volleys against a line of troops charging across 100 yards of open ground.[967]

---

967 Chandler, David G. The Campaigns of Napoleon. New York, Macmillan Publishing Co., 1966, pp. 341-351. See also: Hughes, Major-General B. P., Firepower: Weapons Effectiveness on the Battlefield, 1630-1850, Staplehurst, Kent, U.K.: Spellmount Ltd., 1997, Crowdy, T. E., Napoleon's Infantry Handbook, Barnsley, U.K.: Pen & Sword Books, Ltd., 2015, and Noseworthy, Brent, Battle Tactics of Napoleon and his Enemies, London: Constable & Co., 1995, pp. 195-196. The Brown Bess was a smoothbore, muzzle-loading, flintlock musket. The barrel was bored to .75 caliber ($^3/_4$"), which was arrived at by the weight of its ammunition. A pound of lead produced twelve .729-inch balls suitable for firing in a traditional 12-bore (12-gauge) musket. It was sometimes thought that the large bore gave the Brown Bess a deadlier punch than that of the .69 caliber French and American-made military muskets.

Based on period range trials, a smoothbore musket was theoretically capable of producing hits on a stationary man-sized target more than 50% of the time at 100 yards, and as much as 30% of the time at 200 yards, but its actual battlefield performance was much lower. In the field, an infantryman would be lucky to get 15% hits at 100 yards.

Studies of after-action reports indicate that only about half of 1% of the bullets fired during a typical battle would actually cause a casualty. See: Hughes, Major-General B. P., Firepower; Weapons Effectiveness on the Battlefield, 1630-1850, Staplehurst, Kent, U.K.: Spellmount Ltd., 1997.

APPENDIX O

ALTERNATE LOCATIONS FOR THE VARIOUS NATIVE NATIONS DURING THE BATTLE OF THE RIVER RAISIN

Roundhead's Wyandots are generally credited with a strategic movement around the American flank, but it is uncertain whether they were stationed on the left or right. Chief Norton, who was not an eye-witness, but spoke to Wyandot and Mingo veterans of the battle, says: *"In the evening, General Procter came up with several hundred of the 41st Regiment and Newfoundland and about 500 warriors, principally Potawatomies, Chippewas, and Odawas — excepting about 70 Wyandots, the same number of Delawares, the party of Mingoes... In forming for the attack, the regular troops took the centre, the Wyandots, Mingoes, and Delawares were on the right, and the Potawatomies and Chippewas composed the left wing... the warriors of the right wing advancing rapidly, attacked a body of 5 or 6 hundred men, principally regulars, who had formed on the plain. The Wyandots were mostly mounted..."*

If the Wyandots were posted on the British right, they would not have encountered the American right wing until they had swept behind the American position and caught the Americans already on their retreat. The statement about attacking the regulars formed up on the plain seems to contradict this. Furthermore, Wayndawgay, a Potawatomi, places his people on the British right.

It is not always clear if the speaker is referring to the British or American right. For example, Ensign James Cochran of the 41st wrote in his reminiscence "The War in Canada 1812" that the American army occupied the *"village and the wood to its left"* and that 2/3rds of the Indians penetrated the woods on the right but could not dislodge the Kentuckians on the American left until 200 mounted Indians appeared in their rear.

The number 200 would seem to coincide with the number of Wyandots, Delawares, and Mingoes, but does this suggest that they may actually have been on the right flank and conducted the deep penetration that cut off the retreat of Winchester's men? However, I have always placed them on the British left (American right) where the retreat of Winchester's right wing commenced.

APPENDIX P

BRITISH ARTILLERY AT THE RIVER RAISIN

The basic tactical field unit for the British was the battery which usually consisted of 6 to 8 pieces, most of which were 6- or 9-pounders, plus a 5.5-inch howitzer. However, since the artillery used at the River Raisin would have to be transported through ice and snow, lighter guns were taken.

No official list has been found, so we have to depend on eye-witness descriptions, most of which are contradictory.

Shadrack Byfield recalled that they had 6 field pieces which were placed in the front of the line.

Describing the River Raisin battle in his book, A Canadian Campaign, John Richardson mentioned 2 howitzers and several 4- or 6-pounders. However, in a letter to his uncle Charles Askin, dated Feb. 4, 1813, he says there were three 3-pdrs and three small howitzers.

From the opposing side, Rev. Dudley noted that the River Raisin habitants reported that the British had "…two pieces about large enough to kill a mouse" on the 18th, and described the two smallest British cannons as "swivel guns."

In a Letter from General Harrison to James Monroe, dated Jan. 24, 1813, he wrote: "…At the council, Major McClanahan of the Kentucky Volunteers, who escaped from the action, assisted. He was of opinion that there were from 1,600 to 2,000 British and Indians opposed to our troops and that they had six pieces of artillery, principally howitzers."

The Boerstler map, drawn from statements made by American prisoners, shows the locations of 6 pieces of artillery, but identifies only 2 as to type: a 6-pdr on the British left and a howitzer in the center of their line.

Secondary Sources are equally confusing: Quimby states the British had one howitzer on the 18th and there were three 3-pounders and 3 howitzers on the 22nd. Sandy Antal gives on 3-pdr howitzer on the 18th and three 3-pdrs + 3 small howitzers on the 22nd. Gilpin claims a 3-pdr on the 18th and three 3-pdrs + three howitzers on the 22nd. Cruikshank adds that the artillery pieces used in both the battles on the 18th and 22nd were all mounted on sleds.

One intriguing theory comes from William Davidson, who traced the path of the 2¾-inch (2.9-inch) howitzers captured at Detroit and the River Raisin from there to Queenston Heights and back. "The three captured 3-pdr howitzers eventually appeared officially as *"three brass 2 and 9/10 — inch howitzers on the Royal Artillery Establishment when a comprehensive Return of all of the ordnance at posts west of Fort George...was recorded on 31 March 1813."* Then on 1 April 1813 Lt. Troughton filed his third and final Return for the Ordnance captured at Detroit, and he listed *"three brass howitzers 2 and 9/10-inch."*

Effective ranges are open to question, but the Napoleonic Guide to Artillery Ranges indicates the a British 3-pdr could fire a solid shot a maximum of distance of 1000 meters, but had an effective range of only about 400 yards. Canister range was estimated at 275 meters.

If one or more 6-pdrs were on the field, they could have sent a projectile a maximum of 1350 meters, with an effective range up to 640 meters. Cannister range was 360 meters.

The Napoleonic Guide to Artillery Ranges fives the maximum range for a British 3-pdr as 1000 meters, an effective range with round shot as 400 meters, and the cannister range as 275 meters.

There is little statistical evidence for the effectiveness of 3-pounders firing case shot, but a couple of 6-pounders were tested in Hampshire England in 1780. According to an article by Donald E. Graves, in the War of 1812 Magazine (Issue 12: November 2009), a 6-pdr shot could penetrate 7 feet of compacted earth at 600 yards.

The test recorded the number of hits against a target resembling the size of the French Town fences, with about half the balls hitting the target at 200 yards and about 13% at 500 yards.

Less than half of the hits actually penetrated the target at 300 yards, and less than 20% at 500 yards. Nonetheless, using case shot (or canister) a battery of six 6-pdrs could deliver a salvo equal to a volley from an infantry battalion.

The 3-pdrs, of course, would have been much less effective.

The gun crews depended on highly trained gunners supported by less qualified artillerymen or militiamen. Officers commanded the battery or sections of 2 or 3 guns. Non-commissioned officers generally commanded each gun. Most pieces required a couple of trained gunners and 6 to 10 crewmen. Untrained men could be drafted for use in moving or supplying the pieces.

The British light 5.5-inch howitzer had a barrel twice as long as the captured King howitzers, but half as long as the 3-pdr gun. It could fire a shell 1550 meters, was effective out to 640 meters, and could fire cannister 460 meters.

Like the 3-pdr guns, howitzers needed to have a direct line of sight to their targets. However, they did have an advantage in being able to fire in a higher trajectory that would allow them to clear intervening obstacles.

Howitzer shells were hollow iron balls filled with gunpowder and equipped with a timed fuse that automatically lit by the flash when the cannon was fired. When the shell burst, it scattered small shards of iron that could fly about 80 yards in all directions, which lessened its effect.

British shrapnel, technically called spherical case, contained musket balls in addition to the gunpowder, which could prove even more deadly to enemy soldiers if they burst in the air over their target.

The author was present at a test of live, explosive shells from a Civil War era cannon several decades ago. Unfortunately, defective powder caused the shell to fall short. The explosion seemed distant enough, but then we could see spurts of dust being kicked up by fragments heading in our direction.

Everyone ran for cover as other pieces whistled overhead, cracking tree limbs as they started to come down through the leaves. Nobody was hurt, but one of the vehicles behind the firing line was slightly damaged.

APPENDIX Q

The National Archives
Act of 50-80 w.t. 55-560
Veteran: Robert H. Navarre, War: 1812, Grade: Pvt., Service: Mich Mil Capt.
Jobin
Can No. 908 Bundle No. 71

In the case of Susan Navarre, Widow of Robert Hutro Navarre, deceased.

The Declaration in this case is precisely similar, in all material aspects, to those of Francis Cousineau, Dom: Suzor, Peter Navarre and James H. Navarre, as to the commencement and duration of the soldier's service — his captivity after and surrender by Genl. Hull — his escape, and subsequent service in a spy compy. &c.

On 23d. Septr. 1853 and on 23d. Novr. 1853, the Auditor made reports confirming his 1st report of May 5, 1853, that "Robert Hutro Navarre served in Capt. Jobson's Jobean Co. Michigan Militia from 4th. August 1812 to 18th. August 1812, when surrendered by Genl. Hull--Engaged to serve till 4th. January 1813. — Claimant's ^husband was actually detained in captivity till 23d. January 1813 — when he escaped from his captivity, and again attached himself to the American Army.

Warrant, No. 92.673 for 40 acres appears to have been inadvertently issued on 26th. August 1853, there being no endorsement on the papers to show for what the claim was allowed. Party is entitled for 80 acres, of which claimant was advised on 5th. Decr. last, when the warrant for 40 acres was recalled. Not yet heard from.

The testimony offered is support of the claim for the alleged service from January 1813 to October 1813, are the depositions of Antoine Sargent and Laurent Durocher, the former of whom is reported upon unfavorably by the auditor, and the claims of both are supported by Claimants, who swear for each other as to the spy service, which is not found on any rolls in the auditor's office.

For any greater allowance than 80 acres, this case stands upon the same ground as the applications of Consineau, Suzor and Peter Navarre, among the cases referred to me by the Com. which are not believed to be entitled to more than 80 acres which they have severally received. The cases of Durocher, Fortier, James H. Navarre, Jms. Paston and Antoine Sargant and many others of the same class of cases in which warrants for 160 acres have been issued, are believed to be improperly issued for a larger quantity of land that their services properly entitled to.

The service in these cases is proved from 4th. August 1812 to 16th. August 1812, when they^parties were surrendered as prisoners of war and, according to the declarations made by them all, remained in captivity until January 1813, when they escaped--joined the American forces and remained with them in active service until September or October 1813. But they would seem to have been entitled only from the 4th. to 16th. August 1812, and in actual detention by the enemy from the 16th. Augt. to January 1813, making a period of about five months.

In most of the cases referred to, the auditor reported that they engaged to serve for six months; and this fact, taken in connecion connection with the service and detention in captivity for about five months, would seem to warrant the refusal to allow more than 80 acres in any of that class of cases; and especially as the auditor reports that his rolls afford no evidence in relation to the service as spies, claimed by the long list of applicants whose claims are prepared and advocated by Alex. D. Anderson, who is both Judge and Executioner, or Magistrate and Agent.

**Susan Navarre, Widow
of Robert H. Navarre dec[d.]
War of 1812.**

APPENDIX R
THE S.S. RIVER RAISIN

During World War II, the Battle of the River Raisin was remembered by the U.S. Maritime Commission when a series of tankers, type T2-SE-A1, were being named after famous battles. The *S.S. River Raisin* was launched into the Columbia River at the Kaiser Swan Island Shipyard near Portland, Oregon on May 25, 1943, some 130 years after the battle.

According to William Rau of the Steamship Historical Society of America, Inc., the T2 series was the prime mover of petroleum products for nearly two decades, with 481 ships of that design completed. The SE stood for "steam-electric," and the A-1 showed it was the first of 3 or 4 variations.

It took about 3 months to build the 500-foot, 10,000-ton, steam-powered, steel-hulled tanker for the Coastal Oil Company of New Jersey. It was capable of transporting 6 million gallons of oil at a top speed of 14 knots.

The *S.S. River Raisin* saw no important action, other than an unconfirmed report of a submarine attack on December 23, 1943, a day after leaving the Port of Bahrein. It is doubtful that the reported attack actually happened. It was not unusual for nervous sailors to see phantom periscopes in those hazardous days and log "an apparent submarine attack" just in case.

Harry Cooper of Sharkhunters International checked their extensive records and could find only two Axis submarine attacks in any ocean for that date; a Japanese sub that damaged the American Ship *Cache* in the Pacific, and a U-boat that missed a French destroyer in the Mediterranean. There were no attacks reported in the Indian Ocean, and none against the *River Raisin*.

The *River Raisin* was sold after the war and placed under Liberian registry, being renamed several times: *Rosina Marron* in 1948, *Aeolus* in 1954, *Andros Sparrow* in 1957, *Valiant Warhead* in 1959, and *Transarctic* in 1960. She was sold and reduced to scrap at Kaohsiung in 1963.

Thanks also for the research done by Matt Switlik and Jim Ryland of the Monroe County Historical Museum, Pat Vincent of the Monroe County Historical Society, Dorothy Harrington of the Oregon Historical Society, Irene Stachura of the National Park Service, T. Lane Moore of the National Archives, Elisa Tomaszewski of the Monroe Evening News, and Carolyn Covell, whose ancestor served on the ship

INDEX

Caldwell, William 'Billie' (Capt. GB) 37, 48, 149, 218-219,

Camp Deposit (OH) 276

Camp McArthur 101, 111, 113, 329

Camp Number 3/Fort Starvation 77-78, 90-91, 94, 110-111

Camp *Roche de Bout* 114, 254

Campbell (Major US) 5

Campbell, John B. (Lt. Col. US) 97, 101, 103-105, 107

Campeau, 178, 307

Campeau, Antoine 292

Canadiens 11, 67-68, 189, 326, 385,

Candlemas (Feb.2) 344

Cannon (British relic) 366

Capote (coat) 129, 287

Captain Johnny (Shawnee) 94-96

Carabeau 192

Cariole 153, 155, 168-169, 234, 256, 258, 288, 321, 335-336-337

Cass, Lewis (Col. US) 17

Cattle 17, 37-38, 47, 52-53, 59, 66-68, 76, 81, 100, 109, 119-120, 350

Cavalier, - 310

Cedar Point (OH) 249, 310,

Centennial Celebration 366

Chambers, - (Major GB) 74

Charland, Ambrose 106, 134, 143, 254, 259-260

Charland, Angelique Martin 259-260

Charette 294

Chief Moran (Potawatomie) 7

Chinn, Francis (Lt. US) 218

Chipsaw, Asa (Potawatomie) 323

Chovin, Charles 307

Chovin, Henri 309

Christmas 105-108, 344, 359

Cicotte, Francois 306

Cicotte, Jean-Baptiste 306

Clark, Thomas (Captain) 80

Collier, - 132, 355

Combs, Leslie 111, 113-114, 154-155, 258

Conner, William 103

Corn 35, 63, 66-68, 80, 89, 97, 115, 118, 317, 336, 350

Cotgreave, W. W. (Major) 160-162, 174, 256, 258, 275, 344

Cousino, Francois 224

Couture, - (Madame) 193, 275

Couture, Antoine 124, 127, 340

Couture, Catherine Lenfant 271

Couture, Jean-Baptiste 133, 155, 171, 177, 183, 208-209, 237, 271

Couture, Medard 124, 143, 171-172, 183-184, 208-209, 262, 271-272, 283, 287-289, 296, 309

Craig, Thomas E. (Capt.) 81-82

Crawford, - (Col.) 160, 163

Creeks 149

Crow, Thomas (Pvt. US) 302-303

Cuilliere, Antoine 304

Cushing, Thomas (Capt.) 160, 163, 319

Custer, George Armstrong (Gen.) 365

Cuyahoga Packet 13

Darnell, Allen 260

Darnell, Elias (Pvt. US) 33, 69, 92, 153, 260-261, 281-282, 304, 317-318, 331-333, 347, 353-354

Davis, - (Dr.) 207

Dawson, John (Sgt. US) 284, 289, 322

Day, Isaac 118-120

Dayton (OH) 20, 97

Dazet, Joseph (Dr.) 129

Defiance (OH) 43-44, 46-51, 53, 73-75, 94

De la Mothe- Cadillac, Antoine 3

Delawares 38, 65, 68, 75, 92, 99-101, 149, 293, 295, 334

Deloeil, Francois 263

Devoir 310

Dewar, Edward (Lt. GB) 65-68

Dickson's Band 280

Dingell, John (Congressman) 372, 374-376

Disbrow, Henry 325

Dolsen, - (Capt.) 333-334

Downey, Henry (Pvt.) 322

Dragoons 35-36, 51-52, 57, 70, 93, 98-100, 103-104

Drouillard, Dominique 127, 139

Dudley, Thomas (Rev.) 262, 284, 287, 317, 323-324

Durgate, Francois 224

Durocher, Laurent 133, 164, 175-176, 251

Edwards, Robert (Capt.) 194, 196, 232

Edwards, Tinian (Governor, IL) 81-82

Elder, Samuel 354

Elliott, Alexander 95-96